International Conflict

International Conflict

Michael Haas

THE BOBBS-MERRILL COMPANY, INC.
Indianapolis · New York

Library of Congress Cataloging in Publication Data
Haas, Michael, 1938–
International conflict.

Includes bibliographical references.
1. International relations—Research.   I. Title.
JX1291.H32   327'.1   73–8943
ISBN 0–672–60737–9 (pbk.)

For my parents

Preface

The urgent need for a great creative effort has become apparent in the affairs of mankind. It is manifest that unless some unity of purpose can be achieved in the world, unless the ever more violent and disastrous incidence of war can be averted, unless some control can be imposed on the headlong waste of man's limited inheritance of coal, oil and moral energy that is now going on, the history of humanity must presently culminate in some sort of disaster, repeating and exaggerating the disaster of the Great War, producing chaotic social conditions and going on thereafter in a degenerative process towards extinction.

H. G. Wells

This book was conceived to supply answers to raison d'être questions, rather than to take its place as just another of the proliferating attempts to employ multivariate analysis in the field of international relations. Originally I began some research on a subject close to my dissertation, focusing on the impact of social change upon the foreign policymaking process. But as I proceeded to assemble data, it became increasingly clear to me that the results of such a study would be interesting to some, baffling to others, but would by and large be filed tidily into a box within a box, with very little impact on the development of international relations into the status of a theoretical science. And it occurred to me that the reason for such a reception would have nothing to do with the intrinsic merit or sophistication of the research but to the state of the study of international relations itself, especially the failure of scholars in the field to make substantial contributions toward the normative goals of peace research.

The behavioral revolution in international relations gained impetus with the publication of a number of volumes that supplied theoretical vistas so broad that they promised to serve as sourcebooks for inspiration and challenges for the operationalization and testing of hypotheses. Due to the pioneering efforts of Karl Deutsch, Johan Galtung, Robert North, Richard Snyder, and many others, a generation of younger, methodologically up-to-date scholars has been trained, starting in the early 1960s at the graduate schools of such institutions as Northwestern, Oslo, Stanford, and Yale. The products of these institutions have brought the vision of a science of international relations to several dozen institutions located at far-flung points on the map. Systematic research on international relations has increased from a trickle to a flood. But amid such progress it seemed to me that something was lacking. Sheer volume in output seems to have beguiled many into neglecting the relevance of the research for advancing theory or policy payoffs. Many of the publications of the younger generation might stand in danger of being overlooked because the problem selected was itself vapid or narrow in scope. And, inasmuch as selecting problems is fundamentally a theoretical choice, I could only draw the conclusion that theory has been receiving less and less emphasis. Indeed, in some circles a "theory versus research" debate has ensued, rather than a conscientious discussion of how best to reunite the two sides of the same coin. A perspicacious methodologist, as Paul Lazarsfeld has said, "is a scholar who is above all analytical in his approach to his subject matter." The chasm between schools of thought devoted to "theory for theory's sake" and "method for method's sake" would, in short, retard science in the field of international relations.

It is the purpose of this volume to demonstrate how best to bring together theory and research in studying a particular problem area—namely, the subject of international conflict, which has hitherto needed a theoretical structuring perhaps more than any other topic in the field of international relations. In Part I a series of alternative approaches is outlined to demonstrate the multifaceted character of writings on international conflict and the merits of each effort to come to grips with the subject. By the time that Chapter 1 closes, however, a narrowing process selects out three main levels of analysis—the interpersonal, societal, and systemic. J. David Singer and Kenneth Waltz have urged scholars to tackle problems in the field from these three main perspectives, which comprise the foci of Parts II–IV. But in attempting to marry research and theory at three levels of analysis, I soon discovered that only the most miniscule efforts had appeared so far. The decisionmaking approach, which has been urged as a strategy for studying interpersonal factors, has remained essentially untried except in a few case studies. Societal approaches using communication theory have been artfully employed to investigate regional linkages between states but, at the time that this book was conceived, seemed less appropriate for the study of international conflict without some conceptual reworking. And some studies that employ societal variables have proceeded to select variables without an explicit theoretical justification or rationale. The third level of analysis, that of the international system as a whole, still remained encapsulated in its primordial theoretical stage because major efforts to operationalize variables had not received encouragement.

In other words, the main task in approaching international conflict with all of the present methodological armor is to build more specific conceptual apparatuses that will insure a solid growth in future research. Others might prefer to gain recognition for the use of quantitative methods in international relations by carefully studying very specific problems, which in an article form might be able to ignore the larger questions of theoretical and policy relevance. However, I elected to cease some quantitative processing for a year or so of reflection on how to develop metatheory, conceptual frameworks, and the like. My main interest in the early stages lay in sketching out the kinds of data needed to obtain a broader view of international relations, rather than utilizing existing data as if it were by some coincidence sufficient for multiple theoretical purposes.

When the conceptualization phase was over, I next attempted to locate existing data that would be required in mapping the three main levels of analysis. To my chagrin, the harvest in data collection was lean. Few of the variables that I wished to study could be traced with direct and valid statistical indicators. In sorting out the dimensions of the data by factor analysis (one of the most frequently used techniques for such a preliminary exercise), the incompleteness in the findings came to haunt my confidence in the conclusions drawn in Part V. As with studies in the natural and social sciences, replication is one test of the generality of results from research of a finite scope. However, the need to transcend existing data to obtain more information for the cells in various conceptual frameworks remains the paramount task for the future. It is in this respect that the volume should be viewed as an attempt to demonstrate the vastness of many of the problems in conducting research in international relations—as well as a modest suggestion toward bridging the gap between present efforts and future imperatives.

Parts of the volume were originally published in another form and are revised herein, with permission from the following publishers: The Free Press for "Sources of International Conflict" in *The Analysis of International Politics,* edited by James N. Rosenau, Vincent Davis, and Maurice A. East; "Communication Factors in Decision-Making" from *Peace Research Society (International), Papers;* "Three Approaches to the Study of War," *International Journal of Comparative Sociology;* "Societal Approaches to the Study of War" from the *Journal of Peace Research;* "Types of Asymmetry in Social and Political Systems," *General Systems Yearbook;* "Dimensional Analysis in Cross-National Research," *Comparative Political Studies,* published by Sage Publications; "Societal Asymmetries and World Peace" from the *Proceedings of the International Peace Research Association, Second Conference;* "International Subsystems: Stability and Polarity," *American Political Science Review.* In presenting the material at conferences over the past few years, I am also indebted to the constructive suggestions of my colleagues in the fields of international relations and peace research. For the complexities, difficulties, and proteanness of the volume I have only myself, my penchant for conceptual order, and the cantankerousness of international realities themselves to blame for writing three or four books instead of one in my effort to account for the origins of international violence at several levels of analysis.

The book is the culmination of four years of reflection and research. I am indebted to many persons for their helpful and generous assistance in preparing the manuscript. Frank Ahern and Guy Cutrufo, as programmer and research assistant, respectively, are responsible for making it possible for data manipulation and data collection to proceed smoothly. The scaling talents of C. M. Douglass, J. Fitzsimmons, C. S. Long, R. L. Smith, L. A. Wiegle, and D. L. Williamson are gratefully acknowledged so that judgmental variables could be checked for reliability in coding. The typing was impeccably performed by Rita Albright, Deirdre Copeland, Linda Finale, Marcia Madsen, and Peter Po Ressurection. The research support came from the Hawaiian Electric Company, as administered through the University of Hawaii Foundation, and the Social Science Research Institute of the University of Hawaii, as well as the International Relations Program at Northwestern University. Computer time was provided by computing centers at the University of Hawaii, Northwestern University, and Purdue University.

M. H.

Analytical
Table of Contents

xi

Detailed
Table of Contents

Tables

Figures

PART I
Introduction

PART 1
Introduction

chapter 1
Approaches to the Study
of International Conflict

1.1 INTRODUCTION

Blockades, movements of troops toward a country's borders, impressment of seamen on the high seas, sporadic firing upon airplanes that intrude into foreign airspace, clandestine supplying of volunteers and munitions in order to aid parties to an international dispute, and assassinations of foreign leaders constitute several distinct forms of international conflict behavior. The most dramatic and perplexing type of international conflict situation, however, is war, in which soldiers representing separate actors of the international arena engage in armed clashes to resolve mutually incompatible claims. International aggression, once conceived of as a noble spectacle in which such virtues as courage and valor gain fullest expression, has achieved a much uglier reputation in the twentieth century. Some 25 million persons were killed on the battlefield in World Wars I and II alone. Many soldiers have died in hospitals or have been stricken by disabling injuries and diseases. Doomsday bombs are now possible, and research continues on methods of chemical and bacteriological warfare.

A reconstruction of physical facilities and communication patterns has been accomplished after each war, but various indirect consequences have been eroding the very fabric of civilized society. As a result of war casualties, the most energetic age group of a country has often been decimated. Total war has promoted the growth of entrenched industrial-military elites. Psychologically, a penchant to settle disputes by force rather than by negotiation has gained a certain reinforcement within states that prove victorious in wartime, with revenge looming as a motive for the vanquished. History does not record how many potential Einsteins died at Verdun,

3

Shakespeares at El Alamein, Tschaikovskys at Stalingrad, or Edisons on Pork Chop Hill. Instead, military strategists and weapons-systems analysts have emerged as important figures in the arsenal of thermonuclear super-powers. In contrast, peace researchers seldom enjoy contemporary notoriety.

Speculative thinkers from the time of Plato to the present day have sought to assess the causes of war, the conditions necessary for the mainte-nance of peace, and the arrangements that might reduce the probability of war or at least lessen the barbarities of warfare. Centuries of expostulations on the futility and horrors of war have culminated in the establishment of international organizations as forums within which to air disputes before the eyes of nearly all governments of the world. The existence of such structures as the League of Nations, United Nations, and various regional bodies has en-couraged a more amicable settlement of many minor disputes; but such notable exceptions as the Sino-Japanese, Italo-Abyssinian, Arab-Israeli, and Sino-Indian wars, plus the cataclysmic world wars of the present cen-tury serve to remind mankind that few restraints can be imposed upon major or even middle powers by merely consultative organs. The ever-present possibility of World War III haunts us all.

Recent advances in social science theory and methodology seem to offer a more sanguine promise. For if the outbreak of international aggres-sion has been consistently associated with certain antecedent patterns, syste-matic inquiry may turn up common factors of which decisionmakers have been hitherto unaware. Because an increase in knowledge assists in modify-ing behavior, the discovery of processes that inexorably lead to war may contribute to the reduction of thoughtless or accidental wars in some modest way. Increasing attention directed toward the conceptual and theoretical side of social science, and the familiarity of today's social scientist with statistical and mathematical methods, mean that research on war and peace is on the threshold of assembling a definitive body of knowledge about in-ternational conflict that has proved elusive for centuries. The speed and versatility of modern computers permit more penetrating, exhaustive, and immediate investigations of underlying behavior patterns.

Despite the methodological sophistication of many conflict researchers, there is a paucity of theoretically relevant data for studying international conflict. Theoretical guides are employed very seldom, and conceptual slop-piness often prevents meaningful communication of the results from empiri-cal inquiries. It is the disparity between theoretical and methodological prowess that this volume is designed to remedy. Why is theory on interna-tional conflict at such a primitive level? One of the main reasons is that most empirical researchers have been bulldozing exhibitionistically without attempting to put the subject in order analytically.

If we elect to undertake research on war and peace, one analytical problem is which theoretical framework may be most profitable. The multifaceted manifestations of international conflict can be analyzed from a variety of theoretical perspectives; each may seem equally sound and fruitful for acquiring a full comprehension of critical parameters and variables. There is no a priori or empirical guide at present for selecting any one best approach to the subject. Accordingly, an overview of the various ways of studying international conflict would be a reasonable point from which to depart in this volume, which attempts to survey findings so far accumulated and to propose some new directions for future research on international conflict. However, an even more elementary task should come at the very beginning: namely, a definition of basic terms and a delimiting of the scope of the inquiry within the vast terrain of international affairs.

1.2 "INTERNATIONAL CONFLICT" DEFINED

A *definition* strives to establish a correspondence between verbal symbols and a phenomenon conceived to exist in the "real world." As terms are defined more and more carefully, one eventually reaches a point where a word is defined in terms of primitive symbols, which are themselves undefined. Since one cannot escape from primitive terms, either in the social or in the natural sciences, the most efficient way to avoid semantic traps is to foster a consensus among scholars on the meaning to be attached to a very few basic notions. Pedagogically, the best method for achieving such an agreement on fundamentals is to provide copious examples and to distinguish each concept being defined from other members of the same genus or class.

The word "international" refers to a level of analysis. Rather than treating conflict among members of the family, peer group, voluntary membership group, or even within a large political unit, such as the nation-state, we shall focus upon the international arena. We may define *international,* then, as a level of analysis the basic actor units of which are relatively autonomous political units that control mutually separate territories or populations. The internal autonomy and coercive control of international actors varies from a low to a high degree, but it must be above some minimal threshold.[1] More succinctly, the international arena is simply one level above the national or societal level; actors within an international system consist of various national, extranational, transnational, supranational, and intergovernmental entities.

---

[1] A high degree of autonomy implies *sovereignty;* a moderate degree, *penetration* by a foreign power. See Andrew Scott, *The Revolution in Statecraft* (New York: Random House, 1965). Further complexities in determining membership in international systems are treated in detail in Section 9.5.1.

One distinction central to most definitions of "conflict" at the international level is whether active means are employed. Purely verbal and diplomatic moves may contain elements displeasing to international actors, but "conflict" generally is regarded as a phenomenon manifest in active behavior. Verbal disagreement is merely *contention*.[2] Talcott Parsons's typology of deviant behavior[3] may be instructive on this point (Table 1–1). "Conflict" and "combat" are distinguished from "neutralism" and "self-abnegation" along an *activity-passivity* continuum. A state may appear to engage in neutral or self-abnegating behavior by sitting on its hands, as it were, but conflict and combat take place only when agents of a state overtly do something.[4] The *attention focus* dichotomy is somewhat more subtle, for behavior of one state directed at international norms, rules, and law is sometimes difficult to distinguish from activity targeted at the physical attributes of a particular state, such as the latter's military installations, supply depots, and soldiers of a country's armed forces.

Conflict seems more properly to be associated with norm-oriented activity. A declaration of war is implicitly or explicitly coupled with certain grievances that warfare promises to resolve. Lewis Coser refers to social conflict as "a struggle over values and claims to scarce status, power and resources in which the aims of the opponents are to neutralize, injure or eliminate their rivals."[5] *Combat* occurs when nationals of two or more states engage in some sort of physically destructive activity, such as piercing soldiers with bayonets, dropping napalm on villages, pushing the buttons that release intercontinental ballistic missiles, or assassinating foreign potentates. *Neutralism,* used in a very broad sense, characterizes states that disagree with international norms, rules, or arrangements and assert their disapproval by refusing to support states that uphold the rules.[6] Neutralism

---

[2] Cf. Section 7.5.3 for an elaboration of my acceptance of a conflict-as-behavior instead of a conflict-as-attitude conception.

[3] Talcott Parsons, *The Social System* (New York: The Free Press, 1951), Chapter 7. The idea that the four types of behavior are called "deviant" is irrelevant for our purposes. The two conceptual axes interest us primarily as means for determining conceptual boundaries.

[4] The *personification fallacy,* in which a state is treated as a person rather than an abstract entity composed of individuals, is avoided in this formulation. Inevitably the need for smooth prose leads to sentences in which the state is described as something that acts, feels, or possesses attributes; once the nature of the fallacy is grasped, literary shortcuts may be followed without producing confusion.

[5] Lewis A. Coser, *The Functions of Social Conflict* (New York: The Free Press, 1956), p. 8.

[6] "Neutralism" differs from both *neutrality,* which is a legal term referring to non-participation in war, and *neutralization,* a legal agreement providing that a territory cannot be occupied by, or aligned militarily with, an outside power.

TABLE 1–1
A Typology of International Behavior[a]

	Personality Types	
Attention Focus	Active	Passive
Norms	Conflict	Neutralism
Persons/States	Combat	Self-abnegation

[a] Adapted from Talcott Parsons, *The Social System* (New York: The Free Press, 1951), Chapter 7.

in its narrower contemporary meaning implies a reluctance to side with competing sets of norms put forward by international rivals. *Self-abnegation,* a concept adapted from Arnold Wolfers,[7] indicates withdrawal from the assertion of self-interest in international affairs. A self-abnegating state is willing either to withdraw from world politics or to allow its sovereignty to erode.

One might prefer a more concrete guide to the fourfold distinction. Conflict may be indexed by such countable events as decisions to go to war, expulsions of ambassadors, and the imposition of economic sanctions; combat, by battles, border clashes, and piratical raids; neutralism, by nonalignment with power blocs; self-abnegation, by instances of voluntary annexation.

Another exercise for sorting out types of international conflict would be to intercorrelate indicators of all sorts of interstate activity and, through a procedure known as *factor analysis,*[8] to delineate empirically separable clusters of variables that suggest the existence of an underlying concept called "conflict." Rudolph Rummel, using 94 assorted international behavior variables, has chosen the latter procedure, and his factor analysis yields 16 such basic dimensions (variable clusters) of international behavior (Table 1–2).[9] What is most significant for the student of international conflict is that a factor labelled Conflict emerges as a distinct cluster. The 12 indicators loading highest on the conflict dimension in the analysis, correlate higher with each other than they do with variables correlated with other factors (Table 1–3). The only variable that does not intuitively

[7] Arnold Wolfers, "The Pole of Power and the Pole of Indifference," *World Politics,* IV (October 1951), 39–63.

[8] Factor analysis is discussed briefly in Section 2.4.2. The aim of this chapter is to provide the reader with an intuitive feel for behavioral forms of analysis, which will fall into place in the more formal discussion to follow in Chapter 2.

[9] Rudolph J. Rummel, "Some Dimensions in the Foreign Behavior of Nations," *Journal of Peace Research,* III, No. 3 (1966), 201–24. Rummel makes no effort to sample from the fourfold classification presented in Table 1–1; self-abnegation and neutralism are underrepresented and, thus, have little opportunity to emerge as separate factors.

TABLE 1–2
Dimensions of International Behavior[a]

Name of Factor[b]	Highest Three Variables Loading on Factor
1. Participation	Much trade High United Nations budget assessment Many embassies and legations abroad
2. Ideology	Many pro–United States votes in UN Few pro–Soviet votes in UN Acceptance of International Court of Justice jurisdiction
3. Conflict	Many threats Many accusations Many foreign killed
4. Popularity	Many foreign visitors/home population Many foreign college students/all college students Much foreign mail/population
5. South American	Short air distance from United States Low ratio of air distance from US/air distance from US and USSR Expulsion and recall of many ambassadors
7. Aid	Many training and research fellowships received High ratio of IFC and IBRD aid/gross national product Much aid received from United States
9. Migration	Many immigrants/population Many immigrants Many emigrants/population

[a] Adapted from R. J. Rummel, "Some Dimensions in the Foreign Behavior of Nations," *Journal of Peace Research*, III, No. 3 (1966), 201–24.
[b] Labels for dimensions 6, 8, 10–16 are not specified by Rummel.

involve a behavioral clashing is the static characteristic "prominent in bloc politics." But, if common sense rejects this variable as a form of international conflict, the fact that bloc leadership is related so intimately to a high frequency of conflict behavior supports the view that most international conflict is undertaken by major powers who have the resources to play the power politics game for keeps.

The multivariable approach to empirical aspects of international conflict may seem incomplete in at least one respect. Surely there are additional categories for differentiating subtypes of foreign conflict behavior. Conceptually, we may distinguish between at least three varieties of international conflict on the basis of the channels in which conflict is articulated. First of all, conflict could be expressed within existing procedural channels, such as through conventional diplomacy or at the United Nations. A second type of international conflict could be outside of, but not antagonistic to, cus-

TABLE 1–3
Foreign Conflict Factor[a]

Variable	Loading[b]
Many threats	.87
Many accusations	.85
Many foreign killed	.84
Many military actions	.82
Many protests	.67
Many troop movements	.67
Many wars	.66
Many mobilizations	.64
Prominent in bloc politics	.58
Many negative sanctions	.52
Many antiforeign demonstrations	.44
Many severances of diplomatic relations	.44
Many expulsions or recalls of minor diplomats	.41

[a] Adapted from R. J. Rummel, "Some Dimensions in the Foreign Behavior of Nations" (1966), 207.

[b] *Factor loading* represents the correlation between a variable and an underlying factor.

tomary channels. A third kind would be conflict that destroys existing channels in order to replace them with new procedures and mechanisms. Before giving a name to each of the three types, it is interesting to note that in separate factor analyses of foreign conflict variables, two investigators have been able to derive these three categories empirically (Table 1–4).[10] *Diplomatic* conflict involves the use of formal methods by means of which states traditionally have dramatized differences of opinion nonviolently, such as by lodging protests, by declaring diplomatic officials to be personae non gratae, and by withdrawing ambassadors or officials of lower rank. Belligerent or *noninstitutionalized* conflict is nonviolent yet takes place outside polite channels for articulating demands and displeasure; examples of noninstitutionalized international conflict behavior include severances of diplomatic relations and impositions of sanctions. *Military* conflict is manifest in the decisions to embark upon wars or limited military actions short of war; military conflict includes all of the overt steps taken by decisionmakers from the decision to go to war up to the actual outbreak of large-scale combat between armed forces. According to the logic of factor analysis, when we encounter separate clusters of variables, each is noncorrelated with

[10] Rummel, "Some Dimensions of Conflict Behavior Within and Between Nations," *General Systems Yearbook*, VIII (1963), 1–50; Rummel, "Dimensions of Conflict Behavior Within Nations, 1946–59," *Journal of Conflict Resolution*, X (March 1966), 65–73; Raymond Tanter, "Dimensions of Conflict Behavior Within and Between Nations, 1958–60," *ibid.*, 41–64. Some of the original labels for factors have been altered herein to accord with theoretical perspectives of this volume.

TABLE 1-4
Subdimensions of Foreign Conflict

Name of Factor	Years	Highest Three Variables Loading on Factor
Diplomatic	1955–57[a]	Expulsions and recalls of ambassadors Expulsions and recalls of diplomatic officials ranking lower than ambassador Troop movements
	1958–60[b]	Protests Threats Expulsions and recalls of ambassadors
Belligerency	1955–57[a]	Severances of diplomatic relations Negative sanctions Antiforeign demonstrations
	1958–60[b]	Severances of diplomatic relations Antiforeign demonstrations Negative sanctions
War	1955–57[a]	Foreign killed Wars Accusations
	1958–60[b]	Wars Foreign killed Military action

[a] From Rudolph J. Rummel, "Some Dimensions of Conflict Behavior Within and Between Nations," *General Systems Yearbook*, VIII (1963), 13.
[b] From Raymond Tanter, "Dimensions of Conflict Behavior Within and Between Nations, 1958–60," *Journal of Conflict Resolution*, X (March 1966), 49.

all others; so conditions that account for the appearance of any one subtype of international conflict might fail to apply to the other two forms.

Within the present volume the emphasis will be on military conflict, in order to treat a subject that is both manageable in scope and theoretically significant. The other two forms of international conflict will have to be examined in a subsequent study.

1.3   TYPES OF APPROACHES

International conflict has been glorified, condemned, described, and analyzed by creative minds for several millenia. Fortunately, there is a wide variety of approaches, for a full grasp of the subject requires familiarity with many ways of looking at how man has engaged in war—and why. One may divide the various types of approaches into three groups. The first group deals with what might be called the *domain,* under which we list the motive for study, main variables, and levels of analysis. A second set consists of *theoretical* choices. The third group consists of *empirical* alternatives that might be pursued in a study on international conflict. Questions concerning the nature of the raw data, sampling and time elements, and ways of manipulating data fall under this final category. The existence of so many alternatives should underscore the necessity of avoiding the arrogant view that there are "approaches and *Approaches.*" A conscientious student of international conflict will find it worthwhile to explore all possibilities.

1.4 DOMAIN APPROACHES

Studies of international conflict diverge most sharply in accordance with the choice of domains and areas for inquiry. Deciding upon the motive for studying conflict behavior, sorting of dependent from independent variables, and selecting levels of analysis are basic preliminaries in embarking upon an examination of the subject.

1.4.1 Motives

Four equally legitimate aims may account for the variety and richness in writings on the subject of international conflict. Diversion, description, exhortation, and explanation are sometimes pursued in combination, though attempts by an artist or a scientist to intrude into one another's bailiwick have proved embarrassing at times. Each approach has its own particular merits and shortcomings.

The *entertainment* approach seeks to divert or to shock an audience by representing war in a stylized manner. Warriors have been a favorite subject for sculptors since the time of the Greeks; Michelangelo's *David* portrays one of the most famous of all military heroes. Memorable battles appear in the paintings of Delacroix and in the murals of Rivera and Orozco. In concert music the martial strains of John Philip Sousa are as familiar to us as Tschaikovsky's *Overture 1812* and Beethoven's *Wellington's Victory.* Today, rock music has its *Universal Soldier* and *Snoopy Versus the Red Baron,* the latter based on comic strip characters created by Charles Schulz. Aristophanes' *Lysistrata* and the historical plays of Shakespeare, notably *Richard the Third,* are perhaps the most celebrated dramas dealing with war and peace. Eisenstein's *Alexander Nevsky* is one of the most stirring dramatic films depicting international conflict, with a musical score by Prokofiev. Novels and short stories abound on the subject, from Tolstoi's *War and Peace* to Remarque's *All Quiet on the Western Front.* In verse, Homer's *The Iliad* and *The Charge of the Light Brigade* by Tennyson are among the most vivid poetic descriptions of battle.

In contrast with the artist's desire to distort reality in order to beautify or to highlight tragic and comic elements, the *historical* approach attempts to capture reality in full accuracy and with considerable detail. Craftsmanlike descriptions of background and foreground factors prior to war come down to us from the writings of Thucydides and the chroniclers of ancient China to the present day. To know exactly what has happened may secondarily serve to entertain, to stimulate moral observation, or to invite us to seek for regularities in phenomena, but the historical approach nevertheless remains as a distinct contribution to the study of international conflict.

The *normative* approach is employed by those who exhort us to do good and avoid evil by such injunctions as "Thou Shalt Not Kill." What constitutes a "just" or "unjust" war has been debated for centuries. The Hebrews were more inclined toward a moralistic outlook on war than any of the peoples of the ancient and classical civilizations, and the Judaeo-Christian tradition is often linked to the growth of international law on warfare. But in today's world the crucial policy question seems to revolve around what constitutes an unjust or miscalculated escalation in an international conflict, because the advanced character of military weapons systems makes it theoretically and technically possible to limit war at several levels. The strategy for waging peace, in contrast, is quite underdeveloped.

War technology has advanced far beyond peace technology, in large part because of the former's use of the *empirical* approach. In contrast with the historian's desire for elaborate detail, the scientist's task is to explain phenomena on the basis of a parsimonious set of determining conditions. Physicists and engineers know much about their empirical worlds, so instruments for mass destruction can be constructed with considerable precision. The paucity of empirical knowledge concerning international conflict accounts for the occasional lapse of dedicated but frustrated peace researchers into pure normative phantasy. If we wish to reduce the number of unnecessary international conflicts, research on a scale never before envisaged will unlock a comprehensive body of knowledge. Empirical research is useful in supplying estimates of relative feasibility and costs of alternate routes to peace. Just which route to take, the weighing together of human as well as material costs, and the image of the kind of peace at the end of each rainbow are all moral questions that science does not pretend to answer. Neither militarist nor pacifist ideological views can be verified scientifically. Empirical research may tell us the probability with which certain situations will occur and may specify conditions that give rise to such situations. It is thus the empirical approach that offers hope for a technology of peace.

The aim of the present volume is to prepare groundwork for an outpouring of empirical research on war and peace. Within the next decade the number of empirical studies may reach such a quantity that separate academic departments of "paxology" might seem convenient devices for housing together the interdisciplinary community of scholars engaging in peace research.[11] The following chapters undertake more than a simple eulogy on the utility of research, or a codification of extant findings, however. It is the aim of this volume to unveil vistas that have been as yet unperceived due to the protean character of peace research. Virtually all of the remaining choices in approaches follow from the commitment to stimulate empirical efforts that may bring about a more peaceful world for future generations.

1.4.2 Main Variables

A *variable* is a measure of a phenomenon that one may observe in different states. A crucial difference in approach is whether international conflict is considered to be a dependent or independent variable for purposes of analysis. In Figure 1–1 one can locate the nature of this distinction. *Antecedents* are independent variables that nurture the onset of conflict. *Consequences* are changes produced as a result of conflict. Consequences of one war, however, often become antecedents for new wars, and the cycle may recur. One of the aims of peace research is to eliminate such feedback loops. In Figure 1–1 conflict is a dependent variable with respect to "antecedents" but an independent determinant of "consequences."

If international conflict is established as one's *independent variable,* one studies the impact that war and other such variables have on a country, a world power distribution, regional resource allocations, and so forth. Emile Durkheim, for example, has found that suicides taper off during wartime.[12]

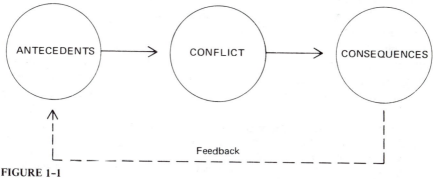

FIGURE 1-1
A Causal Chain

[11] See Theodore Lentz, "Towards a Technological Orientation for Peace Research," *Proceedings of the International Peace Research Association, Second Conference* (Assen: Van Gorcum, 1968), I, 62–72; John W. Burton, *Peace Theory* (New York: Knopf, 1962), Chapter 10.

[12] Emile Durkheim, *Suicide,* trans. John A. Spaulding and George Simpson (New York: The Free Press, 1951).

Lenin regarded World War I as redounding to the benefit of the bourgeoisie, who could overcome the class struggle by stressing superordinate national identifications.[13] The "war does not pay" theme is sounded most stridently by Norman Angell in *The Great Illusion* (1910).[14] According to Georg Simmel, however, conflict may have beneficial consequences insofar as it raises disagreements to such a level of visibility that they may be more capable of resolution.[15]

As a *dependent* variable, international conflict is viewed as the outcome of various antecedent conditions. Empirically, there is no observable phenomenon that one can bottle up and label as a "cause" of conflict. Causation is a logical or analytical concept, to be inferred cautiously at best. Furthermore, in assessing various antecedents of international conflict one must be aware that there are likely to be multiple determining conditions for explaining dependent variables.

Despite the overwhelming interest in ascertaining causes, to date no systematic research has moved very far in the direction of explaining international conflict as a dependent variable. Sidney Fay's classic *The Origin of the World War* (1930),[16] instead, discusses a number of possible trends that may have led to the onset of war in 1914, but its discussion is more historically descriptive than scientifically rigorous. Lionel Robbins's *The Economic Causes of War* (1940),[17] makes a similar foray into the realm of thoughtful speculation without presenting findings based upon rigorous scientific procedures.

The aim of the present volume is to study international conflict as a dependent variable. The present lack of tested theory dictates a survey of all available variables that may be postulated as independent variables bringing about foreign conflict. When more research is conducted it will be possible to test causal theories by using various statistical procedures and by moving our analytical frameworks into the setting of small-group laboratory experiments, where a fuller control over variables is obtainable. With an adjustment for differences between the laboratory, computer, and ex-

---

[13] Vladimir I. Lenin, "The War and Russian Social-Democracy," *Selected Works,* ed. J. Fineberg (New York: International Publishers, 1935), V, 123–30; Lenin, "The Tasks of Revolutionary Social-Democracy in the European War: Resolution of a Group of Social Democrats," *Collected Works* (New York: International Publishers, 1930), XVIII, 1–64.

[14] Norman Angell, *The Great Illusion* (New York: Putnam, 1910).

[15] Georg Simmel, *Conflict and the Web of Group-Affiliations,* trans. Kurt H. Wolff (New York: The Free Press, 1955). Cf. Robert C. North, Howard E. Koch, Jr., and Dina A. Zinnes, "The Integrative Functions of Conflict," *Journal of Conflict Resolution,* IV (September 1960), 355–74.

[16] Sidney B. Fay, *The Origins of the World War,* 2d ed. (New York: Macmillan, 1930).

[17] Lionel Robbins, *The Economic Causes of War* (London: Cape, 1940).

periential "real" worlds, our level of confidence in a body of knowledge concerning conflict among nations will continue to rise.

1.4.3 Levels of Analysis

Within academic disciplines, broad orientations tend from time to time to develop into orthodox ways for defining boundaries and variables within domains of inquiry. It is therefore possible to speak of an approach followed by sociologists, psychologists, or political scientists. At times the lines become blurred; therefore a characterization of approaches on the basis of disciplines will necessarily be somewhat shallow, informing one only of some of the units and levels of analysis, rather than of the substantive theories or methods chosen.[18] Economists, for example, are regarded as investigators of exchanges in goods and services; sociologists, of roles and status within collectivities; anthropologists, of habits prevalent among preliterate as well as literate peoples. No brief definition can do justice to the fullest range of phenomena studied by members of academic professions. Some scholars even identify with two or more academic homes. An inventory of approaches to international conflict within various academic disciplines will shed light on the variety of levels of analysis that one must be prepared to pursue in a truly interdisciplinary study.

For a *psychologist,* an investigation of international conflict would most likely be located within a large body of theory on the nature of aggressive behavior. Psychologists often divide their domain of inquiry into three basic problem areas—perception, learning, and motivation. War has been studied as a function of misperception, selective perception, and selective recall on the basis of the principle that social reality can be perceived quite differently by persons with differing cognitive styles; once reality is grasped in a distorted manner, cognitive processes within adversaries are postulated to lead up to irreconcilable disputes and violent means of resolving differences in objectives.[19] Learning theory deals with how disparate images of reality are attained in the first place, and many social psychologists have focused on the way in which nationalistic and aggressive attitudes are adopted by persons hoping to establish self-identity as a member of an in-group.[20] Atti-

[18] See Elton B. McNeil, ed., *The Nature of Human Conflict* (Englewood Cliffs, N. J.: Prentice-Hall, 1965); Quincy Wright, "Approaches to the Study of War," *A Study of War,* 2d ed. (Chicago: University of Chicago Press, 1965), pp. 423–37.

[19] Ross Stagner, *Psychological Aspects of International Conflict* (Belmont, Calif.: Brooks/Cole, 1967); Joseph H. de Rivera, *The Psychological Dimension of Foreign Policy* (Columbus, Ohio: Merrill, 1968). See also the useful codification by Stagner, "The Psychology of Human Conflict," *The Nature of Human Conflict,* ed. McNeil, pp. 45–63.

[20] Stephen Withey and Daniel Katz, "The Social Psychology of Human Conflict," *ibid.,* pp. 64–90.

tudes, after all, are strategies for coping with an otherwise unpredictable universe,[21] and aggression is a complicated form of activity that must be learned and reinforced in order to recur. If social learning suffices to make resort to aggression seem natural, then specific targets for aggression are discovered through the functioning or malfunctioning of perceptual processes. The trigger is motivation. As Ross Stagner observes, "If we can perceive the opponent as less than human, superego controls do not operate and no guilt is felt over a resort to violence."[22] Though Freud argued that the motivation to engage in destructive acts is rooted in basic instincts, John Dollard and his associates have presented the theory that aggression is a means of coping with intense frustration.[23] Both of these preliminary views are transcended in Leonard Berkowitz's *Aggression* (1962), which conceives the aggression-prone individual as one whose ability to control destructive impulses breaks down when certain combinations of cues are present in a particular situation, and when punishment or satisfaction of affiliative and dependency needs is not anticipated as imminent.[24] Since aggression-proneness varies from a low to a high degree throughout a culture, Berkowitz sees the incidence of violence to be more closely related to situational than to cultural elements.

Anthropologists tend to study war as more of a cultural characteristic. Societies do differ in the frequency with which they attack their neighbors, so there must be some skewing within a culture on aggressive personalities. For some anthropologists the question of aggressive cultures has led to national culture analysis; but, because a systematic comparative analysis has been lacking, individual national culture studies have only suggested that differential conditions account, for instance, for the presence of militaristic Junkers or Apaches alongside peaceful Bavarians or Navajos.[25] An important exception is a study by Raoul Naroll in which 22 traits relevant

[21] Daniel Katz, "The Functional Approach to the Study of Attitudes," *Public Opinion Quarterly,* XXIV (Summer 1960), 163–204; Elton B. McNeil, "The Nature of Aggression," *The Nature of Human Conflict,* ed. McNeil, pp. 14–41; Arnold H. Buss, *The Psychology of Aggression* (New York: Wiley, 1961).

[22] Stagner, "The Psychology of Human Conflict," *The Nature of Human Conflict,* ed. McNeil, p. 51. The phrase is illustrative of the model of a "fight," as opposed to a "game" or a "debate"; Anatol Rapoport, *Fights, Games, and Debates* (Ann Arbor: University of Michigan Press, 1961).

[23] John Dollard et al., *Frustration and Aggression* (New Haven: Yale University Press, 1939).

[24] Leonard Berkowitz, *Aggression* (New York: McGraw-Hill, 1962).

[25] Cf. Alex Inkeles and Daniel J. Levinson, "National Character: The Study of Modal Personality and Sociocultural Systems," *Handbook of Social Psychology,* eds. Gardner Lindzey and Elliot Aronson, 2d ed. (Cambridge: Addison-Wesley, 1968), IV, 418–506.

to the problem of war and peace are coded for primitive cultures. Nearly all of the variables, however, prove to be unrelated to foreign conflict. Correlations with war participation above the .20 level include only military preparations (.55), territorial instability (.28), and the tendency of a people to suppress the desire for overt expression of hostility (.21), the latter correlation being consistent with a hypothesis of Ruth Benedict in *Patterns of Culture* (1934).[26]

Sociologists search for elements in social structures that might recurrently give rise to what Berkowitz has called "aggression-evoking" situations. Social position, such as one's religion, socioeconomic status, or residential location, may be related to propensities to espouse attitudes favorable to war, international conflict, and aggressive solutions to human problems. Status differences between persons and nations have been hypothesized to breed insecurity, envy, and many other motives that may seem to justify entry into wars.[27] Muzafer Sherif has attempted field experiments in which the presence of a superordinate goal among previously noncommunicating groups has led to a mitigation in intergroup conflict.[28] Robert Angell and others stress transnational linkages between countries as a factor for peace: if representatives of states participate with one another in many different governmental and nongovernmental international organizations, the network of communications established thereby might tend to break down cognitive barriers and irrational suspicions between peoples.[29] Many aggregate characteristics of societies might also be related to international conflict. Erich Fromm has advanced a theory of the "sane society" as a condition necessary in order to keep war to a minimum.[30]

[26] Raoul Naroll, "Does Military Deterrence Deter," *Trans-Action*, III (January–February 1966), 14–20; Ruth Benedict, *Patterns of Culture* (Boston: Houghton Mifflin, 1934). See also Tom Broch and Johan Galtung, "Belligerence Among the Primitives," *Journal of Peach Research*, III, No. 1 (1966), 33–45.

[27] Robert C. Angell, "The Sociology of Human Conflict," *The Nature of Human Conflict*, ed. McNeil, pp. 91–115; Johan Galtung, "A Structural Theory of Aggression," *Journal of Peace Research*, I, No. 2 (1964), 95–119.

[28] Muzafer Sherif and Carolyn W. Sherif, *Groups in Harmony and Tension* (New York: Harper, 1953); Muzafer Sherif et al., *Intergroup Conflict and Cooperation* (Norman, Okla.: University Book Exchange, 1961).

[29] Robert C. Angell, "Discovering Paths to Peace," *The Nature of Conflict*, ed. International Sociological Association (Paris: UNESCO, 1958), pp. 204–23; Angell, *Peace on the March* (Princeton: Van Nostrand, 1969). See the many references cited in Angell, "The Sociology of International Relations: A Trend Report and Bibliography," *Current Sociology*, XIV, No. 1 (1966), esp. pp. 16–18, 47–55. See also Paul Smoker, "A Preliminary Analysis of an International Subsystem," *International Associations*, XVIII (November 1965), 638–46.

[30] Erich Fromm, *The Sane Society* (New York: Holt, Rinehart and Winston, 1965).

Economists studying international conflict tend to center on calculation and maximization.[31] War is regarded as one of a number of alternative courses of action for a state. Each alternative is regarded as having a particular payoff, either in strictly monetary or in social values. Within a state, war may be a response to unemployment crises, demands for relief from starving masses, or longings to achieve glory or prestige. Externally, war is a tool of statecraft that a state could employ for redressing an unfavorable distribution of scarce resources in the world. Economic competition, autarky, and tariff wars between states illustrate the ways in which conflict can become manifest in the international economic arena. Because it conceives of war as a proximate means to achieving various goals, economics has been the parent discipline of much deterrence theory, which is now studied on an interdisciplinary basis. Thomas Schelling has applied game theory to the problem of controlling moves of an opponent in a situation where the stakes could be thermonuclear war and planetary extinction.[32] Deterrence, of course, has been studied by noneconomists in small-group laboratories and by others who examine historical cases systematically, but their findings on deterrence are usually fed back into the policy question of alternatives and payoffs, as handled in terms of a model of a rational economic man.[33]

Political scientists have analyzed international conflict within the framework of two characteristic disciplinary orientations.[34] Decisionmaking theory focuses on pressures surrounding a governmental leader empowered to com-

[31] This somewhat unconventional formulation of the scope of economics is in keeping with Kenneth E. Boulding, "The Economics of Human Conflict," *The Nature of Human Conflict,* ed. McNeil, pp. 172–91.

[32] Thomas C. Schelling, *The Strategy of Conflict* (New York: Oxford University Press, 1963).

[33] See John R. Raser, "Deterrence Research," *Journal of Peace Research,* III, No. 4 (1966), 297–327.

[34] The scope of political science has expanded even more than economics in recent decades. Max Weber's classical view of *politics* as the sphere of life dealing with coercion and power has been echoed by such writers as Morgenthau. Easton, however, has stimulated political scientists to look at "authoritative allocations of values," and Riggs regards politics quite broadly as dealing with regulations affecting a wide range of individuals. Max Weber, "Politics as a Vocation," *From Max Weber,* eds. Hans H. Gerth and C. Wright Mills (New York: Oxford University Press, 1946), pp. 77–78; Hans J. Morgenthau, *Politics Among Nations,* 4th ed. (New York: Knopf, 1967); David Easton, *The Political Systems* (New York: Knopf, 1953), Chapter 5; Fred W. Riggs, "The Ecological Basis for a Dialectical Theory of Development," paper presented to the Development Administration Seminar, East-West Center, Honolulu, June 1966. See also Karl W. Deutsch, "On the Concepts of Politics and Power," *Journal of International Affairs,* XXI, No. 2 (1967), 215–31; Michael Haas and Henry S. Kariel, eds., *Approaches to the Study of Political Science* (San Francisco: Chandler, 1970).

mit the resources of his state in the international arena. As developed particularly by Richard Snyder, the decisionmaking approach looks at spheres of competence, communication patterns, and motivational elements, any of which might be responsible for decisions to engage in various forms of international behavior.[35] The system-theory approach, secondly, regards international politics as a coherent system, with actors, members, boundaries, and a particular type of power stratification arrangement. One of the perennial concerns of such systems analysts as Morton Kaplan, Richard Rosecrance, and J. David Singer is whether a world divided into two antagonistic blocs can long endure; a more equalitarian distribution of power among states is hypothesized by many to guarantee peace.[36]

Many other disciplines investigate aspects of international conflict, but they seldom do so from a scientific point of view. The arts are more interested in representing war than in studying antecedents of conflict. The natural sciences are concerned largely with technological preparations for, or consequences of, combat between nations. Historians and geographers describe the course of international events, a useful but insufficient step in assembling data to test theories of conflict. Moral philosophers and legalists judge the justifiability of wars between nations and often prescribe measures for avoiding inhuman practices in conducting war and for overcoming the anarchical state of affairs which gives rise to international aggression as a way to resolve disputes.[37]

The preceding enumeration of disciplinary approaches may be almost anachronistic in contrast with the interdisciplinary character of much contemporary peace research. The existence of many units of analysis and conceptual foci underscores the fact that any choice of concepts and variables presupposes a preference for one of about three analytical levels of analysis (Figure 1–2).[38]

---

[35] Richard C. Snyder, H. W. Bruck, and Burton Sapin, eds., *Foreign Policy Decision Making* (New York: The Free Press, 1963).

[36] Morton A. Kaplan, *System and Process in International Politics* (New York: Wiley, 1955); Richard N. Rosecrance, *Action and Reaction in World Politics* (Boston: Little, Brown, 1963); J. David Singer, "The Political Science of Human Conflict," *The Nature of Human Conflict*, ed. McNeil, pp. 139–54.

[37] Students of international law are now moving more in the direction of a social scientific orientation. See Richard A. Falk, "World Law and Human Conflict," *The Nature of Human Conflict*, ed. McNeil, pp. 227–49; Roger Fisher, ed., *International Conflict and Behavioral Science* (New York: Basic Books, 1964), Part II.

[38] Kenneth N. Waltz, *Man, the State and War* (New York: Columbia University Press, 1959); J. David Singer, "International Conflict: Three Levels of Analysis," *World Politics*, XII (April 1960), 453–61; Singer, "The Level-of-Analysis Problem in International Relations," *ibid.*, XIV (October 1961), 77–92. The threefold formulation presented herein is designed to incorporate North's six levels, Rosenau's five levels, and Singer's revised four-level schematization: Robert C. North et al., *Content Analy-*

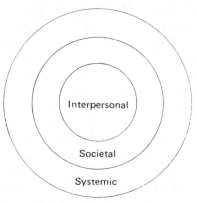

FIGURE 1-2
Levels of Analysis

The *interpersonal* level consists of individuals in decisionmaking settings. Idiosyncratic, predispositional, and immediate situational factors that impinge upon decisionmakers are studied at this level of analysis. Relevant disciplines include psychology and social psychology, and decision theory in economics and political science. At the psychological level, war is seen as beginning in the minds of men, to use UNESCO's epigram. Part II of this volume treats the interpersonal level in greater detail. Some of the propositions that are tested at this level are as follows:

1. A decision to go to war is made by small, rather than large, decisionmaking bodies.

2. A decision to go to war is made when decisionmakers stereotype the world, instead of searching for accurate images.

3. Decisionmakers are more likely to decide on a violent course of action when they are dealing with a group whose cultural background is dissimilar to their own.

4. The younger a decisionmaker, the more peace-loving.

5. Authoritarian personalities are more prone toward violence than nonauthoritarians.

The *societal* level is composed of the aggregate of individuals within political and social systems, together with various governmental structures and private associational groups. The usual independent variables consist

sis (Evanston, Ill.: Northwestern University Press, 1963), pp. 5–7; James N. Rosenau, "Pre-theories and Theories of Foreign Policy," *Approaches to Comparative and International Politics,* ed. R. Barry Farrell (Evanston, Ill.: Northwestern University Press, 1966), p. 43; Singer, "The Political Science of Human Conflict," *The Nature of Human Conflict,* ed. McNeil, p. 140.

of types of economic and political arrangements. Relevant disciplines are anthropology and sociology. The stable society is viewed by many as the key to peace, and will be analyzed in Part III below. The following propositions pertain to societal factors:

1. Democracies are more peaceful than autocracies.
2. As a country becomes more developed economically, it becomes more peaceful.
3. Trade imbalances are precursors to war.
4. Countries with heterogeneity in religious groups are more likely to go to war than homogeneous countries.
5. As a country devotes more of its governmental budget to military defense, the likelihood of its entry into war increases.

The level of analysis containing all societal units, plus public and private trans-, supra-, and interstate organizations, is labelled *international*. Most international systems lack legitimate governments and accepted legal principles, so it has often been argued that all international systems are inherently warlike.[39] Nevertheless, in the analysis of an exhaustive compilation of deadly quarrels by Lewis F. Richardson for the years 1820–1949, we find that more conflicts are actually internal, rather than international.[40] It is the principal task in Part IV of this book to explore factors that account for differing rates of military international conflict in different times periods and regions of the globe. Sample propositions are the following:

1. The more alliances within an international region, the more wars.
2. As power is distributed more evenly across the countries in an international region, war is more likely.
3. War has declined with the growth of international organizations.
4. Eras of domestic strife coincide with eras of intense international warfare.
5. The more independent countries within an international region, the more wars.

International conflict is regarded by many scholars to be best approached on just one of the three levels. The *interpersonal* level is characterized by Sidney Verba as less important because "foreign policy elites are

---

[39] Wright, *A Study of War*, p. 733; John F. Dulles, "The Institutionalizing of Peace," *Department of State Bulletin*, XXXIV (May 7, 1956), 739–46.

[40] Lewis F. Richardson, *Statistics of Deadly Quarrels* (Chicago: Quadrangle, 1960). The assertion of the greater prevalence of internal wars is found in Bruce M. Russett, *Trends in World Politics* (New York: Macmillan, 1965), p. 56.

subject to more of the conditions that tend to inhibit the impact of personality-oriented pressures," while Werner Levi urges "an investigation of the conditions under which emotional support of a peaceful international society can be obtained." With respect to the *societal* level, similar a priori preferences and prejudices abound: Sigmund Neumann has asserted that without knowledge of societal pressures in foreign policy "international politics becomes an abstract game," while Rudolph Rummel concludes on the basis of a 3-year, 22-variable study that "foreign conflict behavior is generally completely unrelated to domestic conflict behavior." J. David Singer believes that "the *international* system itself is the key element in explaining why and how nations attempt to influence the behavior of one another," but Charles Kindleberger argues that "the total system is infinitely complex with everything interacting. One can discuss it intelligently, therefore, only bit by bit."[41]

In considering the multiple levels of analysis of any problem, as we do in the empirical parts of this volume, we can avoid an overcommitment to pet theories in order to embrace the largest possible explanatory framework. The aim of the present study is to determine which factors within all domains most completely account for the presence of international conflict.

1.5   THEORETICAL APPROACHES

Science progresses when theoretical speculation keeps pace with empirical investigations, such that deductively derived theories are tested, results are assessed inductively to determine whether specific hypotheses are confirmed or disconfirmed, and corrections in initial formulations are registered. Theory without appropriate data tends to serve only normative purposes, and data isolated from theory can provide only a low-level guide to reality.

To some, bubonic plague was evidence of God's wrath (theory without data). Everyone was accustomed to observe both deaths from the plague and the presence of rats (data without theory), but until the theory arose

41 Sidney Verba, "Assumptions of Rationality and Non-Rationality in Models of the International System," *The International System*, eds. Klaus Knorr and Sidney Verba (Princeton: Princeton University Press, 1961), p. 105; Werner Levi, "The Concept of Integration in Research on Peace," *Background*, IX (August 1965), 126; Sigmund Neumann, oral communication, February 12, 1962; Rudolph J. Rummel, "Dimensions of Conflict Behavior Within and Between Nations," *General Systems Yearbook*, VII (1963), 24; J. David Singer, "Inter-Nation Influence: A Formal Model," *American Political Science Review*, LVII (June 1963), 423 (emphasis added); Charles P. Kindleberger, "Scientific International Politics," *World Politics*, XI (October 1958), 86.

that rats in some way might account for the plague, no one thought of collecting evidence to test the hypothesis. In peace research a somewhat similar situation exists at present. There is much theoretical speculation and a great deal of data, but very little linkage between the two.

Cutting across the three main levels of analysis, nine broad-gauge theoretical schemes have been applied to the analysis of international conflict. Rather than constituting theories with an X-is-related-to-Y structure, the various schemes are in actuality *metatheories,* that is, conceptual and high-level propositional maps that organize a large body of indicators and hypotheses. The existence of several metatheories does not attest to any indecision as to which is best; rather, each alternative provides a unique handle for grasping the complexities of reality.

The earliest and least well-articulated metatheory may be referred to as *cognitive rationalism.* Diplomatic historians since the time of Thucydides have characterized international politics in terms of a quest by leaders of states to achieve particular objectives. Some of the main concepts of cognitive rational theory are goal, reason, means, objective, plan, issue, dispute, agreement, and many legal terms that refer to such devices as treaties, alliances, and ententes. The cognitive rationalist seeks to set forth reasons that prompt decisionmakers to act as they do. And the specific types of "reasons" on which they focus attention are the private objectives that are sometimes masked behind publicly acceptable justifications. To use an illustration from the writing of David Jayne Hill, Prussia's aggression against Saxony in 1756 is explained as follows:

> Frederick II had become convinced of the existence of a conspiracy for his overthrow and the dismemberment of the Prussian monarchy. Believing that the impending peril was inevitable, but that the moment for his enemies to strike had not yet arrived, he had resolved to invade Saxony. . . . He had counted first of all upon proving by the capture of the Saxon archives at Dresden that a coalition had been formed against Prussia in which Saxony was a guilty partner, and then upon dissolving the hostile league by the force and rapidity of his military action.[42]

Cognitive rationalism, hence, is the theory that is brought to bear when we weigh issues, pro and con, in a debate or election campaign. The model of the Oxford debate in part serves to order reality for the cognitive rationalist but "real" reasons for actions, namely, those which are unannounced publicly but are actually operative, are also within the province of cognitive rationalist research. Some well-known cognitive rationalists who have been

---

[42] David Jayne Hill, *A History of Diplomacy in the International Development of Europe* (New York: Longmans, Green, 1914), III, 533, 537.

concerned with war and peace are Samuel Bemis, Herman Finer, Harold Nicolson, A. J. P. Taylor, C. K. Webster, and Allen Whiting.[43]

Genetic theory is a second type of metatheoretical orientation. Historians have been inclined to engage in a genetic approach when they trace the flowering of trends over time, using many organic metaphors. The key concepts of genetic theory are origin, genesis, development, decline, maturity, precursor, growth, and other words reminiscent of evolutionary and social Darwinist thinking. Genetic theorists employ a legal-institutional form of analysis in which structures are hypothesized to be based upon incrementally developed foundations. That which persists has deep roots; ephemeral trends or phenomena lack genetic significance and, thus, remain unreported, even though there may be much in such material for the cognitive rationalist. Some of the most celebrated genetic theorists concerned with international conflict title their volumes in the familiar jargon—*The History of the Decline and Fall of the Roman Empire* by Gibbon, and *The Origin of the War of 1914* by Luigi Albertini.[44] Herbert Feis, Herbert Temperley, and many writers on international organization in the League of Nations era qualify as genetic theorists insofar as they use organic analogies self-consciously.[45]

Power theory, as popularized by Hans Morgenthau and others,[46] regards the outcome of international conflicts as the resultant of a parallelo-

43 Samuel F. Bemis, *A Diplomatic History of the United States,* 5th ed. (New York: Holt, Rinehart and Winston, 1965); Bemis, *Diplomacy of the American Revolution,* rev. ed. (Bloomington: Indiana University Press, 1957); Herman Finer, *Dulles over Suez* (Chicago: Quadrangle, 1964); Harold Nicolson, *Diplomacy,* 3d ed. (New York: Oxford University Press, 1963); A. J. P. Taylor, *The Struggle for Mastery in Europe, 1848–1918* (Oxford: Clarendon, 1954); C. K. Webster, *The Foreign Policy of Castlereagh, 1812–1815* (London: Bell, 1925); Webster, *The Foreign Policy of Palmerston, 1830–1841* (London: Bell, 1951); Allen S. Whiting, *China Crosses the Yalu* (New York: Macmillan, 1960). A more extensive presentation of international relations metatheories is found in Michael Haas, "International Relations Theory," *Approaches to the Study of Political Science,* eds. Haas and Kariel, Chapter 15. A *metatheory* is formally defined as consisting of three components–an analytic frame of reference, a conceptual scheme, and an integrated body of tested propositions.

44 Edward Gibbon, *The History of the Decline and Fall of the Roman Empire,* 7 Vols. (London: Methuen, 1909–13); Luigi Albertini, *The Origin of the War of 1914,* 3 Vols. trans. Isabella M. Masser (London: Oxford University Press, 1952–57).

45 Herbert Feis, *The Road to Pearl Harbor* (Princeton: Princeton University Press, 1953); Herbert Temperley, *The Foreign Policy of Canning, 1822–1827,* 2d ed. (Hamden, Conn.: Archon, 1966). See also William E. Rappard's assertion "The League [of Nations], as all living organisms, cannot remain as it is. It must either die, or grow and change." Rappard, "The League of Nations as an Historical Fact," *International Conciliation,* CCXXXI (June 1927), 300.

46 Morgenthau, *Politics Among Nations;* John H. Herz, *Political Realism and Political Idealism* (Chicago: University of Chicago Press, 1951).

gram of forces. The resources of a state are converted into active capabilities from time to time in order to counter actions or threats by other states. The strongest set of pressures wins in any contest. The recurrent concepts are mechanical and Newtonian—force, struggle, settlement, monopoly, balance of power, and security. A once-active debate between "realists" and "idealists" can, in this light, be interpreted as one between members of the same school, for the same type of analysis undertaken by such realists as Kenneth Thompson and George Kennan is mirrored in the work of Raymond Aron and Arnold Wolfers; only the normative conclusions are different.[47] Power theory builds directly upon cognitive rationalism, for it treats policies and objective reality in much the same terms. The identification of power as the dominant motive of world politics, and an analysis of capabilities as predictors of future constellations of forces, are the unique contributions of power theory, even though such calculating leaders as Frederick II may fail to measure up to expected standards of rationality.

Cognitive rationalist, power, and genetic theories constituted the main approaches to international conflict up to the middle of the present century. The majority of textbooks, documentary accounts, and analytical discussions in the field still retain one of the three outlooks, which remain as ideologies because they are untested empirically. Between 1954 and 1957 a veritable storm broke loose in the field of international relations with the publication of three ambitious and self-conscious metatheoretical volumes. Richard Snyder's decisionmaking approach, Karl Deutsch's communication theory, and Morton Kaplan's system-theory approach for the most part constitute the major research alternatives today.[48]

The *decisionmaking* approach focuses on determinants of individual decisions. The decision to go to war in Korea, for example, is explained in terms of various organizational and role factors.[49] Conditions that possibly might account for a decision are classified into three groups of variables.

[47] Kenneth W. Thompson, *Political Realism and the Crisis of World Politics* (Princeton: Princeton University Press, 1960); George F. Kennan, *American Diplomacy 1900–1950* (Chicago: University of Chicago Press, 1951); Raymond Aron, "The Quest for a Philosophy of Foreign Affairs," *Contemporary Theory in International Relations*, ed. Stanley H. Hoffmann (Englewood Cliffs, N. J.: Prentice-Hall, 1960), pp. 79–91; Wolfers, "The Pole of Power and the Pole of Indifference"; Wolfers, "Statesmanship and Moral Choice," *World Politics*, I (January 1949), 175–95.

[48] Snyder, Bruck, and Sapin, *Foreign Policy Decision Making;* Karl W. Deutsch, *Nationalism and Social Communication* (New York: Wiley, 1953); Deutsch, *Political Community at the International Level* (Garden City, N. Y.: Doubleday, 1954); Deutsch et al., *Political Community and the North Atlantic Area* (Princeton: Princeton University Press, 1957); Kaplan, *System and Process in International Politics.*

[49] Glenn D. Paige, *The Korean Decision* (New York: The Free Press, 1968); Paige, "Comparative Case Analysis of Crisis Decisions: Korea and Cuba," *International Crises*, ed. Charles F. Hermann (New York: The Free Press, 1973), pp. 41–55.

Spheres of competence is a category containing such structural and organizational notions as division of labor, authority structure, professionalization, and decision latitude. *Communication and information factors* include foci of attention, competitive role demands, and the informal channels through which messages travel. *Motivation* deals with psychological states, perceptual selectivities, attitudes, and socialization factors. Decisionmaking theorists search for the ways in which elements involved in the process of deciding in fact determine the course of events. Charles Hermann, Glenn Paige, James Robinson, and James Rosenau have tended to emphasize structural factors in their applications of the decisionmaking approach, drawing upon developments in organization theory.[50] Chadwick Alger, Richard Brody, and Lloyd Jensen have paid particular attention to communication patterns.[51] Robert North, Dina Zinnes, and Ole Holsti have examined motivational states of decisionmakers, finding that in World War I there was much concern with matters of "hostility" and "friendship" in documentary statements, while the preoccupation with capabilities that one might expect on the basis of power theory was conspicuously absent.[52]

[50] In addition to the citations in note 48, see Charles F. Hermann and Margaret G. Hermann, "An Attempt to Simulate the Outbreak of World War I," *American Political Science Review*, LXI (June 1967), 400–16; James A. Robinson and Richard C. Snyder, "Decision-Making in International Politics," *International Behavior*, ed. Herbert C. Kelman (New York: Holt, Rinehart and Winston, 1965), pp. 433–63; James A. Robinson and R. Roger Majak, "The Theory of Decision-Making," *Contemporary Political Analysis*, ed. James Charlesworth (New York: The Free Press, 1967), pp. 175–88; James N. Rosenau, *The Scientific Study of Foreign Policy* (New York: The Free Press, 1970); Charles F. Hermann, *Crises in Foreign Policy* (Indianapolis: Bobbs-Merrill, 1969).

[51] Chadwick F. Alger, "Personal Contact in Intergovernmental Organizations," *International Behavior*, ed. Kelman, pp. 521–47; Alger, "Decision-making Theory and Human Conflict," *The Nature of Human Conflict*, ed. McNeil, pp. 274–95; Alger, "Interaction and Negotiation in a Committee of the United Nations General Assembly," *Peace Research Society Papers*, V (1966), 141–60; Richard A. Brody, "Some Systemic Effects of the Spread of Nuclear Weapons Technology: A Study Through Simulation of a Multi-nuclear Future," *Journal of Conflict Resolution*, VII (December 1963), 663–753; Brody, "Cognition and Behavior: A Model of International Relations," *Experience, Structure and Adaptability*, ed. O. J. Harvey (New York: Springer, 1966), pp. 321–48; Lloyd Jensen, "Soviet-American Bargaining Behavior in the Postwar Disarmament Negotiations," *Journal of Conflict Resolution*, VII (September 1963), 522–41; Jensen, "Military Capabilities and Bargaining Behavior," *ibid.*, IX (June 1965), 155–63.

[52] Dina A. Zinnes, Robert C. North, and Howard E. Koch, Jr., "Capability, Threat and the Outbreak of War," *International Politics and Foreign Policy*, 1st ed., ed. James N. Rosenau (New York: The Free Press, 1961), pp. 469–82; North et al., *Content Analysis;* Ole R. Holsti and Robert C. North, "The History of Human Conflict," *The Nature of Human Conflict*, ed. McNeil, pp. 155–71; Holsti, Brody, and North, "Affect and Action in International Reaction Models," *Journal of Peace Research*, I, No. 3–4 (1964), 170–90; Holsti, "The 1914 Case," *American Political Sci-*

A more specific metatheory, which in many ways could be regarded as derivative of the decisionmaking orientation, is *strategy* theory. As developed by Herman Kahn and Thomas Schelling, the events and interactions of world affairs have been treated in terms of game theory.[53] Alternative means are assessed in terms of relative payoff by strategy theorists; bluffing and arranging to be caught bluffing are viewed as instrumental to certain goals, especially if the adversary is likely to be deterred from aggressive moves when confronted with seemingly randomized maneuvers. Such concepts as saddle point, optimality, utilities, zerosum, and the notion of a "prisoner's dilemma" are unique to strategy theory. In a sense, strategy theory is merely a more rigorous form of power analysis, though nonmonetary and nonpower parameters are more easily handled when treating deterrence and disarmament. The latter problems have concerned such strategy theorists as Kenneth Boulding and Anatol Rapoport,[54] who thereby have been able to transcend the earlier rigidities of the game model. Simulated decisional settings constitute one of the most promising devices for obtaining data to test strategy theory, as Harold Guetzkow has been demonstrating.[55]

Communication theorists deal less with the content or gaming aspects of statements and behavior than with the aggregate flows of goods, persons, and messages across territorial boundaries. By constructing communication maps of mail flow, airline traffic, trade, exchanges of diplomats, and other instances of state interchange, one can observe communication nodes,

---

ence Review, LIX (June 1965), 365–78; Holsti, "External Conflict and Internal Consensus: The Sino-Soviet Case," *The General Inquirer*, eds. Philip J. Stone et al. (Cambridge: MIT Press, 1966), pp. 343–58; Zinnes, "A Comparison of Hostile Behavior of Decision-Makers in Simulate and Historical Data," *World Politics*, XVIII (April 1966), 474–502; Zinnes, "The Expression and Perception of Hostility in Pre-War Crisis: 1914," *Quantitative International Politics*, ed. J. David Singer (New York: The Free Press, 1968), pp. 85–119.

53 Herman Kahn, *On Thermonuclear War* (Princeton: Princeton University Press, 1960); Kahn, *On Escalation* (New York: Praeger, 1965); Schelling, *The Strategy of Conflict;* Schelling, *Arms and Influence* (New Haven: Yale University Press, 1966). The foundations for game theory are found in John von Neumann and Oskar Morganstern, *Theory of Games and Economic Behavior*, 3d ed. (New York: Wiley, 1964). See also Morganstern, *The Question of National Defense* (New York: Random House, 1959), and Glenn Snyder, *Deterrence and Defense* (Princeton: Princeton University Press, 1961).

54 Boulding, "The Economics of Human Conflict," *The Nature of Human Conflict*, ed. McNeil; Boulding, *Conflict and Defense* (New York: Harper, 1962); Rapoport, *Fights, Games and Debates;* Rapoport, *Strategy and Conscience* (New York: Harper, 1964); Rapoport and Albert M. Chammah, *Prisoner's Dilemma* (Ann Arbor: University of Michigan Press, 1965). See also Phillip Green, *Deadly Logic* (Columbus: Ohio State University Press, 1966).

55 Harold Guetzkow et al., *Simulation in International Relations* (Englewood Cliffs, N. J.: Prentice-Hall, 1963).

clusters, and isolates.[56] One of the major hypotheses of communication theory, which is in part based on cybernetics and information theory, is that units interacting with each other at a very high level over a long period of time tend to develop positive affect for each other if mutual rewards for continuing to communicate exceed costs and loads. Positive affect leads to a harmonization of foreign policy goals and to the development of permanent institutions for handling interstate problems; on occasion, two or more units constituting a very dense communication net will unify politically. Karl Deutsch uses the term *integration* to refer to a class of efforts including low-level harmonization of foreign-policy goals as well as political mergers. Hayward Alker, Amitai Etzioni, Donald Puchala, and Bruce Russett have followed up Deutsch's imaginative notions concerning determinants of cooperative state behavior in a variety of contexts.[57]

System theorists insist upon analytical precision at all levels, for one cannot begin a systems analysis until the units are defined and enumerated fully; and the boundaries separating the phenomenon under examination from its environment are justified on the basis of a set of rules or assumptions. Only after these preliminary tasks are completed can a system theorist begin to delimit the appropriate variables and parameters of the inquiry. In contrast with the interest in *general systems theory* as a means for developing a unified theory of human behavior, such systems analysts as Kaplan, Rosecrance, and Singer in actuality sketch a form of systems analysis which we may call *equilibrium* theory. In searching for ways in which normative principles and power distributions can be preserved over time, equilibrium theorists seek to determine homeostatic patterns and conditions under which one type of system is transformed into another.[58] *Field* theorists, such as

---

[56] Karl W. Deutsch, "Shifts in the Balance of Communication Flows: A Problem of Measurement in International Relations," *Public Opinion Quarterly*, XX (Spring 1965), 143–60; Deutsch and Alexander Eckstein, "National Industrialization and the Declining Share of the International Economic Sector, 1890–1959," *World Politics*, XIII (January 1961), 287–99; Deutsch, Chester I. Bliss, and Eckstein, "Population, Sovereignty, and the Share of Foreign Trade," *Economic Development and Cultural Change*, X (July 1962), 353–66.

[57] Hayward R. Alker, Jr., "Supranationalism in the United Nations," *Peace Research Society, Papers*, III (1965), 197–212; Alker and Donald Puchala, "Trends in Economic Partnership in the North Atlantic Area," *Quantitative International Politics*, ed. Singer, pp. 287–316; Amitai Etzioni, *Political Unification* (New York: Holt, Rinehart and Winston, 1965); Bruce M. Russett, *Community and Contention* (New Haven: Yale University Press, 1963).

[58] See Kenneth N. Waltz, "Stability of the Bipolar World," *Daedelus*, XCIII (Summer 1964), 881–909; Karl W. Deutsch and J. David Singer, "Multipolar Power Systems and International Stability," *World Politics*, XVI (April 1964), 390–406; Michael Haas, "International Subsystems: Stability and Polarity," *American Political Science Review*, LXIV (March 1970), 98–123.

Quincy Wright, Rudolph Rummel, and Michael Haas attempt to locate actors within n-dimensional coordinates on the basis of empirical attributes.[59] By intercorrelating variables that describe nation-states, propensities to international conflict can be assessed in terms of a state's position within an empirically derived set of dimensions, known collectively as a "field." *Structural-functional* theory, finally, looks upon systems as arrangements for accomplishing various generic tasks. When functions are performed in particular ways by structures, a system is able to adapt to its environment properly, achieve various developmental goals, integrate its constituent parts, and maintain its autonomy vis-à-vis the environment.[60] To date structural-functional formulations have been proposed only as classificatory schemes for subsuming concepts, rather than as ways of sorting out significant variables for research. Nevertheless, structural-functional guides can serve to relate particular inputs into systems with such outputs as the launching of aggressive wars.

Any of the previous metatheories could become combined within the framework of an eclectic theory. Indeed, Robert North attempts an integration of decision and general systems theory,[61] and genetic theory notions have been absorbed to some extent into structural-functional analysis.[62] The pretensions of general systems theory are to serve as a unifying framework for all of the sciences, and to provide an identical set of concepts for

[59] Quincy Wright, "The Form of a Discipline of International Relations," *The Study of International Relations* (New York: Appleton-Century-Crofts, 1955), Chapter 32; Rudolph J. Rummel, "A Social Field Theory of Foreign Conflict Behavior," *Peace Research Society, Papers,* IV (1965), 131–50; Rummel, "A Field Theory of Social Action with Application to Conflict Within Nations," *General Systems Yearbook,* X (1965), 183–211; Michael Haas, "Types of Asymmetry Within Social and Political Systems," *ibid.,* XII (1967); 69–79; Haas, "Dimensional Analysis in Cross-National Research," *Comparative Political Studies,* III (April 1970), 3–35.

[60] These are the four functions explicated in Parsons, *The Social System.* For applications in international relations see George Modelski, "Agraria and Industria: Two Models of the International System," *World Politics,* XIV (October 1961), 118–43; Chadwick F. Alger, "Comparison of Intranational and International Politics," *American Political Science Review,* LVII (June 1963), 406–19; Karl W. Deutsch, "Integration and the Social System: Implications of Functional Analysis," *The Integration of Political Communities,* eds. Philip E. Jacob and James V. Toscano (Philadelphia: Lippincott, 1964), pp. 143–78; Michael Haas, "A Functional Approach to International Organization," *Journal of Politics,* XXVII (August 1965), 498–517; Herbert J. Spiro, *World Politics in the Global System* (Homewood, Ill.: Dorsey, 1966), Chapter 3; Paul Smoker, "Nation State Escalation and International Integration," *Journal of Peace Research,* IV, No. 1 (1967), 61–75.

[61] North et al., *Content Analysis,* pp. 147–58.

[62] Cf. Martin Landau, "Functionalism and the Myth of Hyperfactualism in the Study of American Politics: A Historical Note," paper presented to the annual convention of the American Political Science Association, New York, September 1966.

analyzing all domains of inquiry.[63] Each metatheory has its own self-contained vocabulary in many respects, and translation from one language to another is often difficult. At the present time each theoretical approach constitutes a distinct island of theory amid a sea of nonconvergence.

Within the present volume a multiple theoretical strategy will be pursued, partly to achieve a degree of synthesis, but also to suggest some new departures. The interpersonal level of analysis will be handled in terms of decisionmaking theory, as initially conceived by Snyder. The societal level of analysis is treated in terms of field theory, and a new schema is proposed to facilitate coordination between deductive and inductive efforts to delineate dimensions. The international level will be examined by placing the concepts from equilibrium theory within a structural-functional categorization. One might expect the author to pursue only one metatheory through all three levels of analysis, a possibility that was considered at one time. Instead, three different formulations were chosen because they incrementally build upon existing preferences to treat decisionmakers in terms of decisionmaking theory, societies as composed of fields, and international arenas as composed of interacting actors and equilibrating processes.

1.6   METHODOLOGICAL APPROACHES

Metatheories contain both propositions and concepts. A *proposition* suggests that phenomena to which concepts refer exhibit a measurable pattern of correlation. *Measurement* involves assigning numbers to variables after performing some sort of counting operation. The task of testing propositions, then, is one of specifying concepts in terms of data-collection operations; of deciding upon an appropriate sample for assembling data; and, finally, of determining how to manipulate data once it is available. The three problems may be referred to as data collection, sampling, and data manipulation.

1.6.1   Data

Should one wish to measure such a concept as "stability," one must first decide upon a datum which, when counted, will indicate lesser and greater amounts of "stability." Social scientists collect many different kinds of *data,* and in diverse settings, so the choice of an indicator hardly is dictated by a scarcity in available methods.[64] Instead, one must be careful to

[63] Ludwig von Bertalanffy, *General System Theory* (New York: Braziller, 1969).

[64] In the quest for a scientific body of knowledge in the social sciences, the test of hypotheses by all possible methods can ascertain whether results of any particular investigation are artifacts of the setting or idiosyncracies of the research design. Such methods of analysis as survey research, experimentation, and content analysis are complementary, rather than competing, procedures for collecting data.

link specific empirical measures with theoretical concepts, whether in the form of questions in a survey, experiments in the laboratory, or information extracted from documents in the library (see Section 2.3.2). Method is secondary to theory, since it is by pyramiding tested propositions that science can develop. Much data fill almanacs and pages of computer output, but they are only scientifically useful when applied to test theories. We now review five sources of data for students of international conflict.

Verbal symbols are probably the most elementary form in which social data appear. *Content analysis* is a procedure in which titles, words, and themes are counted as indicators of such notions as cognitive foci of attention, perceptual images, and psychological moods.[65] Verbal symbols are the most familiar means by which international conflict is articulated and understood, so it is not surprising that a content analysis can be conducted within such sources as newspapers, diplomatic documents, interview protocols, messages passed during simulation runs, and open-ended questionnaire responses. Some of the most significant content analyses relevant to war and peace have attempted to ascertain the images and moods of decisionmakers, as undertaken by Robert Angell, Ole Holsti, Harold Lasswell, Ithiel Pool, Robert North, J. David Singer, and Dina Zinnes.[66]

The *event* is a second source of data. Events are forms of behavior that must be inferred and coded from verbal statements or observed activities. Declarations of war, announcements of diplomatic protests, votes in the United Nations, and instances where deterrence works and fails can be counted per country and over time. Data sources vary from newspapers and historical chronicles to laboratory simulations, wherein subjects are free to make alliances, hold conferences, and issue orders for the massing of troops on a country's borders. Events have been the raw data for such investigators as Charles McClelland, Rudolph Rummel, Bruce Russett, Muzafer Sherif, and Quincy Wright.[67] War as an event is the main dependent variable of this volume.

[65] See Michael Haas, "Image and Mood Content Analysis," *Report to the Ford Foundation,* Stanford Studies in International Conflict and Integration, 1963; North et al., *Content Analysis.* Content analysis may involve frequency or nonfrequency procedures. See Ithiel de Sola Pool, ed., *Trends in Content Analysis* (Urbana: University of Illinois Press, 1959); George Gerbner et al., eds., *The Analysis of Communication Content* (New York: Wiley, 1969); Ole R. Holsti, *Content Analysis for the Social Sciences and Humanities* (Reading, Mass.: Addison-Wesley, 1969).

[66] In addition to references cited in note 51, see Harold D. Lasswell, *Propaganda Technique in the World War* (New York: Knopf, 1927); Ithiel de Sola Pool, *Symbols of Internationalism* (Stanford: Stanford University Press, 1951); Robert C. Angell, Vera S. Dunham, and J. David Singer, "Social Values and Foreign Policy Attitudes of Soviet and American Elites," *Journal of Conflict Resolution,* VIII (December 1964), 329–491.

[67] In addition to references cited in notes 9, 10, and 28, see Charles A. McClel-

Survey data consist of responses to projective or scaling exercises, and to interviews or questionnaires. Most attitude studies prefer to sample public, rather than elite, opinion because of the greater accessibility of the former. Elite statements indicative of attitudes are treated by content analysts. Johan Galtung and Jerome Laulicht have been major exponents of survey data in research on war and peace.[68] Unfortunately very little survey research exists for cross-national comparisons.

Scaled data are perhaps the most elusive. The clearest illustrations are the judgmentally scaled characteristics of states appearing in *A Cross-Polity Survey* by Arthur Banks and Robert Textor.[69] Intuitively, Sweden appears to be a much more democratic country than Haiti, so it seems reasonable to record such a ranking even though no finely calibrated scale may be available to validate one's hunch. One can then ascertain whether democracies tend to be peaceful. The distinction between external and internal war seems clear analytically; yet when sorting individual cases the opportunity for borderline situations reminds one that in sorting "internal" from "external" conflict, one is really assigning crude scale scores or ranks, thereby "making" variables. Scaling may be used to measure such concepts as decision latitude; extent of surprise involved in a decision problem; unipolarity, bipolarity, or multipolarity in an international system; and alliance types such as ententes, nonaggression pacts, or defensive pacts. In a deterrence situation the extent to which deterrence is a "success" or "failure" is determined with reference to a set of criteria for categorizing. In order for an investigator to be reasonably confident of his arbitrary codings, he should be prepared to read much descriptive, qualitative writing on the subjects or cases to be handled. Agreement among a panel of experts on individual ratings is the preferred method for establishing the validity of categorizations. Glenn Paige and Richard Rosecrance are the principal theorists who have

---

land, "Access to Berlin: The Quantity and Variety of Events, 1948–1963," *Quantitative International Politics*, ed. Singer, pp. 159–86; Quincy Wright, "The Escalation of International Conflicts," *Journal of Conflict Resolution*, IX (December 1965), 434–49; Bruce M. Russett, "The Calculus of Deterrence," *ibid.*, VII (June 1963), 97–109.

[68] Johan Galtung, "Foreign Policy Opinion as a Function of Social Position," *Journal of Peace Research*, I, No. 3–4 (1964), 206–31; Jerome Laulicht, "Public Opinion and Foreign Policy Decision," *ibid.*, I, No. 2 (1965), 147–60; John Paul and Laulicht, *In Your Opinion* (Clarkson: Canadian Peace Research Institute, 1967); Laulicht, "Comparative Studies of Foreign Policy Opinions," *Proceedings of the International Peace Research Association, Second Conference*, I, 401–16.

[69] Arthur S. Banks and Robert B. Textor, *A Cross-Polity Survey* (Cambridge: MIT Press, 1963). Any coding operation performed on events, symbols, and survey responses involves fitting cases into categories. "Scaled data" is used here to denote data and variables that are created only by means of category construction and lack any other raw form.

experimented with judgmentally scaled data as major sources for variables in studying international conflict.[70] A major effort to follow their example appears in the present volume in Part II; scaled data are used as some of the variables in Parts III and IV.

When censuses are conducted of large numbers of persons or inanimate objects, the composite result is an *aggregate* statistic for a territorial unit, individual responses having been placed into a single lump in the findings. Gross national product, suicide rates, foreign trade volume, and total radios for a particular country are some familiar forms of aggregate data, all of which may be related to military expenditure levels. Even an individual's annual income is an aggregation of monthly or bimonthly paycheck sums. But we could also consider factor scores, correlation coefficients, beta weights, and Gini indices to be types of aggregate data,[71] since individual cases are added up and their identity as separate cases is subsequently lost when the results of data manipulation are summarized by a single number. Aggregate data, thus, are not in an unprocessed or primitive form; they emerge only after primary data have been collected. Data sources are statistical yearbooks. The aggregate analyses of Karl Deutsch, Michael Haas, Rudolph Rummel, Paul Smoker, and Raymond Tanter are most directly relevant to the subject of international conflict.[72] Parts III and IV below employ an analysis of aggregates.

1.6.2 Sampling

Since any empirical investigation is necessarily finite, a choice must be made concerning what and what not to study. A *sample* of subjects, territorial locations, and time periods must be selected.

[70] Paige, *The Korean Decision;* Rosecrance, *Action and Reaction in World Politics.* For a study in which a panel of experts is asked to scale the friendliness between pairs of nations prior to World War II, see Frank L. Klingberg, "Studies in Measurement of the Relations Among Sovereign States," *Psychometrika,* VI (December 1941), 335–52. See also J. David Singer and Melvin Small, "National Alliance Commitments and War Involvement, 1815–1945," *Peace Research Society, Papers,* V (1966), 109–40.

[71] These types of data are outputs from multivariate analysis techniques, which are discussed briefly in Section 1.6.3 and more extensively in Section 2.4.2.

[72] In addition to references cited in notes 9, 10, and 55, see Michael Haas, "Societal Approaches to the Study of War," *Journal of Peace Research,* II, No. 4 (1965), 307–23; Haas, "Social Change and National Aggressiveness, 1900-1960," *Quantitative International Politics,* ed. J. David Singer (New York: The Free Press, 1968), pp. 215–46; Paul Smoker, "Fear in the Arms Race: A Mathematical Study," *Journal of Peace Research,* I, No. 1 (1964), 55–64; Smoker, "Trade, Defense and the Richardson Theory of Arms Races: A Seven Nation Study," *ibid.,* II, No. 2 (1965), 161–76; Smoker, "A Time Series Analysis of Sino-Indian Relations," *Proceedings of the International Peace Research Association, Second Conference,* I, 250–74.

Two alternative forms of inquiry are followed in the sampling of *subjects,* whether the cases are individual decisionmakers, members of the informed public, nation-states, international organizations, or international subsystems. *Case analysis* focuses on details of a single subject to achieve a deeper understanding of internal dynamics and tendencies. Experts on Mao, Germany, the United Nations, or international relations of East Asia often engage in single-case analysis. Studies on the Korean War, 1914, and Suez are the most prominent recent illustrations of the case approach to international conflict.[73]

Comparative analysis entails examining several cases systematically along a specific number of characteristics or dimensions. If the subjects under study constitute a representative and random sample from the respective universe, as in much survey research, conclusions from comparative analysis can be generalized to an entire population of cases. If the total universe is small in number, exhaustive comparative analysis may be undertaken with ease, as in studies on the societal level of analysis treating all one hundred-odd sovereign states in a particular year. But when the size of a total universe is not known, such as the sum of all decisions to go to war or the total number of international subsystems, a comparative analysis will yield tentative results.[74] Parts II and IV below consist of comparative analyses that lack adequate scientific sampling procedures because the size of the respective universes is unknown; in Part III a nearly full sample of all sovereign states is compared.

A second sampling problem is *geographic* and *ethnographic.* There is a need to take all cultures and regions of the world into account in any comprehensive theory of human behavior. A group of Western scholars can be expected to produce culture-bound theory and scholarship. Attitude surveys outside the United States and selected countries of Europe unfortunately are not abundant. Decisionmaking analyses tend as well to focus on the United States, the home country of the decisionmaking approach. In addition, statistical data are most available for industrialized countries. International relations is regarded by many myopic scholars to be centered in the North Atlantic region, while other countries and international subsystems are somewhere on the periphery of present investigations.

Time sampling is the most neglected problem of all in research on international conflict. *Cross-sectional* slices for individual years have been in vogue recently. Many theories of international conflict posit differences between types of states, for which comparative cross-sectional data are appropriate; and studies of Maurice East, Phillip Gregg, Rudolph Rummel, and

[73] Paige, *The Korean Decision;* Holsti, "The 1914 Case"; Finer, *Dulles over Suez.*
[74] See Michael Haas, "Comparative Analysis," *Western Political Quarterly,* XV (June 1962), 294–303.

Jonathan Wilkenfeld have made substantial contributions.[75] From the point of view of reforming political systems, however, cross-sectional analysis provides an awkward guide for intervening into processes that breed war. Most exciting and practical social theories deal with changes in decisionmakers, states, and international systems over time. Adaptation to change is the main concern of governmental leaders and policymakers in all polities, so a cross-historical analysis would be preferable in order to derive useful knowledge for the normative aims of peace research. In practice, however, *longitudinal* analyses tend to focus only on single cases, thus making an even smaller theoretical contribution. The cost of assembling comparative time-series data for many countries is often prohibitive. Only a few comparative longitudinal analyses relevant to peace research have appeared so far.[76] The three empirical studies undertaken anew in this volume are mainly cross-sectional. Some longitudinal elements are fed into each analysis, but the need to demonstrate the wide utility of three new theoretical schemes has assumed priority over the particular time sample of the data involved. A more careful comparative longitudinal analysis is an objective for the future.

1.6.3 Manipulation

Once data are in the form of numbers, they can be stored on punch cards or on sheets of paper. In either place the data are susceptible to three major forms of processing.

Univariate analysis consists of assembling trend information, sorting cases into yes-no and presence-absence categories, or citing an individual datum to prove a point. Robert North's 1914 study for example, is presented in a univariate form when perceptions of various kinds are plotted over time and fluctuations are noted.[77] If we plot the number of war deaths for each year from 1900 to 1970, we can note the univariate crests and troughs; the same procedure can be used to observe trends in suicide rates over time.

[75] In addition to references cited in notes 9 and 10 see Phillip M. Gregg and Arthur S. Banks, "Dimensions of Political Systems: Factor Analysis of *A Cross-Polity Survey*," *American Political Science Review*, LIX (September 1965), 602–14; Maurice A. East and Gregg, "Factors Influencing Cooperation and Conflict in the International System," *International Studies Quarterly*, XI (September 1967), 244–69; Jonathan Wilkenfeld, "Domestic and Foreign Conflict Behavior of Nations," *Journal of Peace Research*, V, No. 1 (1968), 56–69.

[76] Michael Haas, "Social Change and National Aggressiveness, 1900–1960"; Deutsch and Eckstein, "National Industrialization and the Declining Share of the International Economic Sector, 1890–1959"; Smoker, "Trade, Defense and the Richardson Theory of Arms Races: A Seven Nation Study."

[77] Zinnes, North, and Koch, "Capability, Threat and the Outbreak of War"; Holsti and North, "The History of Human Conflict," *The Nature of Human Conflict*, ed. McNeil.

If the two distributions have identical shapes, however, we may wish to ascertain whether the two variables parallel each other so closely as to be highly interrelated; we must turn to bivariate analysis in order to answer questions of association between variables.

In *bivariate* analysis, correlations are computed between pairs of variables. Correlation coefficients summarize such information as the direction, degree, and form of association between variables in a precise, comparable manner. One of the most interesting illustrations of the contrast between univariate and bivariate analysis is Clinton Fink's reexamination of Russett's study of deterrence cases. Fink's bivariate results challenge some of the conclusions based on Russett's original univariate study, which looked for necessary and sufficient conditions of deterring aggression across several historical cases.[78]

Multivariate procedures move in the direction of determining causality. Some forms of multiple-regression analysis enable one to determine the smallest number of variables that account for the largest amount of variance in a dependent variable. It would be an exciting theoretical breakthrough to discover that four variables predict to war in 95 percent of the cases under examination and to establish causal paths. Causal models can be tested by various procedures, as we will illustrate in the following chapter. Factor analysis, one of the most frequently used multivariate techniques in peace research to date, locates independent clusters of variables. Many other multivariate forms of analysis are possible, now that computers perform in seconds operations that formerly took months or years.

In the present volume, existing studies are summarized at each of the three analytical levels of analysis (in Parts II, III, and IV). Multivariate procedures will be undertaken after reporting bivariate correlations between variables collected in accordance with explicit conceptual and theoretical formulations.

1.7 RECAPITULATION

The purpose of this chapter has been to indicate alternative ways in which international conflict may be studied. An author's preference for a particular approach is arbitrary to a considerable extent. One person's enthusiasm for a special kind of analysis need not be followed by others. Nevertheless, what is to follow may serve as a guide for peace research in the years to come. Three different conceptual schemes are derived from theoretical bearings at the interpersonal, societal, and international levels so as to indicate

[78] Russett, "The Calculus of Deterrence"; Clinton F. Fink, "More Calculations about Deterrence," *Journal of Conflict Resolution,* IX (March 1965), 54–65.

how broad-gauge theory can be useful. And by erecting large frameworks for analysis one can truly comprehend how unfortunate it is that there is a scarcity of theoretically relevant data. The volume, thus, consists of a preface to research and a statement of tentative conclusions.

International conflict indicators will be the dependent variables, while measures from each of the three levels of analysis will serve as independent variables. A decisionmaking orientation will pervade analysis on the interpersonal level; field theory will be deductively developed for the societal level; and the equilibrium metatheory will be used to study international subsystems. Scaled and aggregate data will be subjected to bivariate and multivariate manipulations. Sampling choices will be discussed in more detail in each major section of the book. With its explicit formulation of theoretical and methodological choices, glossary of terms and variables, and report of bivariate and multivariate findings, this volume may be regarded as a blueprint for future construction of peace research theory at the level of decisionmakers, states and societies, and international systems and subsystems. In the following chapter we explain the specific design of the research in more detail.

chapter 2
Normative, Theoretical, and Methodological Perspectives

2.1 CURRENT STATE OF INTERNATIONAL CONFLICT RESEARCH

The existence of many distinct and popular approaches to the study of international conflict might appear to assure eventual progress toward the goal of isolating predictors of the onset of war. Competition between exponents of each approach, after all, could encourage Stakhanovite efforts and empirical breakthroughs. Were our knowledge of international conflict sufficiently comprehensive, this volume would attempt to summarize extant findings. Three main difficulties impede efforts to increase our knowledge about international conflict. First of all, there is normative dissensus and confusion among international conflict researchers. As a result, many advocates of the scientific method with strong ideological convictions have lapsed on occasion into oversimple diagnoses, panaceas, and polemics. The second problem is the tendency for methodologically sophisticated researchers either to collect data endlessly or to demonstrate the utility of a variety of research strategies on trivial questions; what is lacking is the commitment to accumulate a body of tested propositions within the framework of an organized body of knowledge. The failure of metatheories to guide empirical efforts is the third and most serious difficulty. Empirical investigators of international conflict tend to be atheoretical because of the poverty of stimulating and useful conceptual maps specifically applied to guide the collection of data. Because the findings of research are almost unrelated to existing theoretical formulations, the codifications of present conflict research, such as those appearing in Chapters 3, 7, and 9 of this volume, will necessarily be thin in content.

38

How can we liberate the study of international conflict from its three-fold difficulties? The state of self-awareness with respect to one's problems is a first step toward their resolution; and the aim of this chapter is to sketch disparate normative orientations, unexamined theoretical dilemmas, and alternative methodological strategies. In the process a comprehensive rationale for the structure and content of this volume will be delineated.

2.2 NORMATIVE ORIENTATIONS

If research even implicitly fails to stimulate the drawing of normative implications, a major purpose of science and systematic inquiry remains unfulfilled. As a social enterprise, science enables man to come to terms with reality. Among some primitive peoples, seemingly unexplainable and uncontrollable occurrences are conceived of as emanating from gods. With the advance of science, theological cosmologies have been viewed as poetic statements that enable man to achieve greater psychological adjustment to his lot. Just as moral philosophy was once based on theological and metaphysical speculation concerning the nature of man and the universe, the results of scientific investigations have nearly always been inputs into the thinking of persons with a social conscience. Science has much to say about the most appropriate means for achieving certain ends, but the choice between penultimate goals remains outside the jurisdiction of science; analytically, values and facts are two separate realms. Psychologically and practically, however, the decision to study particular phenomena is not determined by science, but instead by the importance attached to the subject. The current attention to the subject of international conflict is due to such considerations as the overkill military capabilities by existing world powers, the precariousness of skirmishes short of war, and the costly and wasteful diversion of human and material resources into military purposes. A student of peace research, therefore, hopes to facilitate the reduction of the destructiveness and incidence of warfare. Within this general normative orientation there is much variety in specific ideological stances, if the term *ideology* is used in its classical sense as consisting of a system of beliefs along with a program of action to bring about a desired state of affairs. Inasmuch as the research focus of a conflict researcher is to a very large extent determined by his normative outlook, adherents of similar ideological positions have tended to form separate communities of scholars. It is useful to enumerate the main alternative views in order to understand why there is often a lack of interchange between each school of thought, which leads to stagnation and insularity among many productive and original students of international conflict.

Conflict between states is such an omnipresent feature of world politics that nearly every student of international relations has undoubtedly had something to say on the subject. Scholars who display a strong and continuing commitment to increase our knowledge of international conflict belong to one of five ideological camps.

The most prominent international conflict analysts are U.S. State Department intelligence analysts who espouse the ideology of *national interest* as set forth most eloquently by Hans Morgenthau.[1] In collecting basic data and estimating capabilities and intentions of allies and potential adversaries, various employees of foreign ministries are by far the most knowledgeable persons on day-to-day changes in the international arena. Capabilities analysts are aware of shifts in military emphases, in deployment of troops and weapons, and they may be in a position to advocate decisions to initiate wars or to undertake negotiations. Such analyses (with information sources labelled "secret") are under the direction of executive officials, who may be prisoners of images of the world constructed for them by intelligence reports that presuppose the desirability of attaining various state goals. One of the more enduring goals, which may at any time be jeopardized by actions of external actors in the international arena, is the preservation of a nation's security. War and power struggles, according to Morgenthau, are an inevitable feature of world politics for which one's country always must be prepared. By focusing on military capabilities, researchers oriented to the ideology of national interest can propose the acquisition of new weapons or recommend that leaders should threaten to use superior force in order to gain various nonmilitary foreign-policy objectives. But the stress on power for its own sake means that a military-science orientation tends to eclipse a thorough evaluation of nonpower and nonmilitary factors in world politics. Practitioners of the ideology of national interest will muddle through various crises: because war and conflict are believed to be inevitable, they feel that one must expect a succession of modi vivendi settlements as a result of the operations of war or from the astute bargaining of diplomats at international conferences. It seems axiomatic to increase national capabilities indefinitely in order to ensure the fullest advancement of a nation's interests. Inasmuch as the ideology of national interest lacks a clear vision of the future, little incentive is provided to encourage systematic examination of data across a large number of crises in order to prevent, control, or manage the incidence of conflicts. Instead, the ideology of national interest goes hand in hand with routine and "agonizing" reappraisals concerning realities of world politics in order to ensure that a particular country will be able to maximize its values. The ideology of national interest does not constrain decisionmakers

---

[1] Hans J. Morgenthau, *Politics Among Nations*, 4th ed. (New York: Knopf, 1967).

to reflect on the ultimate consequences of policy, having militated against long-range planning.

The second ideological orientation focuses on *deterrence.* This second group is found largely within organizations engaged in contract research for the U.S. Defense Department. It is no surprise, therefore, that deterrence advocates accept continuing military preparations as a given. Deterring an adversary is regarded primarily as a psychological problem, one best handled in terms of Schelling's strategy theory.[2] Simulation, small-group laboratory experiments, content analyses, and occasionally aggregate statistical data are used by this group. Deterrence ideology has tended to be compatible with the established views of government leaders, but the results of deterrence research support more long-range planning than do the policies of national interest. In tandem, the two ideologies provide a defensive posture that promises to withstand decades of trial. But in phrasing every research question as a deterrence equation, the negative or preventive aspect is emphasized at the expense of a more creative and positive approach. The chess game of move and countermove, for which deterrence theory is well suited, still does not provide an answer to the more venturesome question, How can we prevent crises that force us to invoke deterrence strategies? The ideology of deterrence, in short, assumes that conflict is inevitable but war avoidable, so the task of these researchers has been to develop a sane and workable set of rules for playing the dangerous game of deterrence.

In contrast to the national interest and deterrence ideologies, which support the "cold war," a third ideology that enjoys widespread acceptance is *Marxism,* which regards war as a transitory phenomenon so long as classes still struggle with each other in the precommunist stage of history.[3] The current Sino-Soviet ideological debate, insofar as it touches upon international conflict, is between Maoists, who favor wars of national liberation,[4] on the one hand, and Sovietists, who prefer a more peaceful but competitive form of temporary coexistence with capitalism, on the other hand.[5]

A new perspective to the study of international conflict is being provided by advocates of *peace research.* Once one assumes that man is a creature who can cooperate, as confirmed by such evidence as the continu-

---

[2] Thomas C. Schelling, *The Strategy of Conflict* (New York: Oxford University Press, 1963); Schelling, *Arms and Influence* (New Haven: Yale University Press, 1966).

[3] Karl Marx and Friedrich Engels, *The Communist Manifesto* (New York: Appleton-Century-Crofts, 1955).

[4] Mao Tse-tung, *On the Correct Handling of Contradictions Among the People,* 7th ed. (Peking: Foreign Languages Press, 1966).

[5] Karel Kára, "On the Marxist Theory of War and Peace," *Journal of Peace Research,* V, No. 1 (1968), 1–27.

ing presence of viable large political units beyond the community and family, the main research question becomes one of determining why the loyalties and positive identifications of men tend to stop at the level of the nation-state. Why are persons outside a country's borders sometimes regarded as adversaries, sometimes as friends?

Peace researchers, however, do not agree with one another on all matters. Indeed, the division between pacifist and nonpacifist peace researchers grew sharper during the period of the Vietnam War. Because governments have tended to ignore the efforts of peace research and will continue to do so, as long as statesmen find it meaningful to think of world politics in terms of cold-war images, peace researchers have maintained a high degree of consensus in order to urge a change in the prevailing imagery. Differences in ideological perspective have come to the fore only in terms of the subjects of analysis and theories selected for testing. Nevertheless, differences between two types of peace research ideologies are worth exploring.

Pacifist peace researchers look upon international conflict as a special case of human conflict, so for them the study of intranational conflict is as important as that of international conflict. They emphasize conflict as a generic form of behavior because they prefer a mutually supportive, harmonious life for man in his social environment. Johan Galtung clarifies this view most vividly in contrasting "positive peace," with "negative peace."[6] *Negative peace* is defined as the absence of war, whereas *positive peace* exists when all of human society is able to cope with its problems creatively and nonviolently. Pacifist peace researchers, thus, are concerned with aggressiveness as a characteristic of man in general, and they operate within nearly every discipline in the social sciences. Because they see thermonuclear war as the most urgent problem facing mankind today, pacifists in all fields have concentrated on the international level very often, but they also see racial and class tensions within countries as proper subjects for an analysis of human aggression. Because pacifist peace researchers are concerned with man and his role in society, they tend to engage in survey research and to aggregate case studies on such subjects as international sanction imposition, summit conferences, technical assistance experiences, and the like. Pacifist peace researchers, hence, avoid the ivory tower of overdetachment as much as do the power and deterrence schools. The aim, to bring about positive peace, becomes so attractive that the zest for policy-relevant research often impels a peace researcher to propound normative formulations that lack sound empirical support. In so doing, the pacifist peace researcher is in

---

6 Johan Galtung, "An Editorial," *Journal of Peace Research*, I, No. 1 (1964), 1–4. See also Galtung, "Entropy and the General Theory of Peace," *Proceedings of the International Peace Research Association, Second Conference* (Assen: Van Gorcum, 1968), I, 3–37.

good company, since the pro-establishment students of international conflict, whom we have mentioned above, are under a similar pressure to advocate measures on the basis of incomplete information. The vision of the pacifist is basically chiliastic, so his prescriptions tend to be much more fundamental in character.

Nonpacifist peace researchers constitute the most amorphous of the five groups. This camp is not only the largest of the ideological schools, but the most fragmentary; its scholars have simply never assembled together nor have they individually given much thought to clarifying their own normative positions. There are few documents to quote in describing this fifth ideology; only a fuzzy intellectual climate of opinion seems present. Certainly the nonpacifist peace researcher does agree with what Galtung has called the principle of "negative peace." To engage in peace research presupposes an opposition to most modern wars, especially thermonuclear war. But the pejorative connotations built into Galtung's term tend to overlook positive, constructive beliefs which, from time to time, become manifest in the form of an ideology best labelled *world pluralism*. The nonpacifist peace researcher would like to see a wide range of social, economic, political, cultural, scientific, and humanistic goals maximized among all peoples of the world (Table 2–1). Pluralism consists of ensuring that no one value crowds out others, and that each goal is achieved to the fullest degree for the largest number of human beings. Unlike the pacifist focus on a single-value cluster—integration and harmony—the pluralist is content to cope more incrementally with violent conflict at the international level. He wishes to establish a more peaceful world order so that each unit of world politics can make its own internal decisions in any fashion it chooses. The world pluralist applies the values of nineteenth-century English utilitarianism to the international level. The "greatest good for the greatest number" becomes the "broadest maximization of values for the largest number of countries." The principle that "an individual's liberty stops where another's nose begins" is transformed into the view that states should be free to make domestic allocations of values so long as the impact upon other states is not debilitating. And since war is one of the most damaging enterprises on which a state can embark, world pluralists seek to construct institutional devices for restraining the use of war as an instrument of national policy.

Probably the most famous world pluralist is Woodrow Wilson, who as a son of a Southern Presbyterian minister combined

> the missionary zeal of the Covenanters and the devotion of the Southern Democrats to Popular Sovereignty or self-determination. Enthusiasm for the political regeneration of mankind was uneasily yoked with a stern insistence on the maintenance of the rights and liberties of individual states and peoples. Thus internationalism and Democracy shared his allegiance.

TABLE 2–1
Comparison Between Pacifist and Pluralist Peace Research Preferences[a]

Pacifist Preferences	Pluralist Preferences
Similarity between nations	Dissimilarity between nations
Maximum interdependence	Differential interdependence
Classless world	Class systems world
Disarmament	Arms control
Multilateralism	Bilateralism as well as multilateralism
Universalism	Regionalism as well as universalism
World state	Intergovernmental organizations

[a] Adapted from Johan Galtung, "Entropy and the General Theory of Peace," *Proceedings of the International Peace Research Association, Second Conference* (Assen: Van Gorcum, 1968), I, 36–37.

There was no necessary incompatibility between the two. But their respective spheres needed to be carefully delimited.[7]

In keeping with the later utilitarian socialist tradition, world pluralists generally favor planning and reforms that promise to make value maximization more possible and the sphere of private action freer from external constraints. World pluralists would like to take action on such problems as overpopulation, nuclear proliferation, the unequal distribution of resources among states, and colonial and neocolonial tyranny; their aim is to enlarge the sphere of state freedom.[8] Because man's most diabolic oppressor has been his ignorance of interconnections between aspects of social reality, the mainstay of the nonpacifist peace researcher has been contemporary social science. Interested in uncovering relationships that explain the rise of such problems as well as their solution, world pluralists tend to support "pure science." Many world pluralists prefer to engage in basic research, leaving practical applications to others as soon as closure in knowledge about a particular subject has been achieved. They are committed to employ the canons of logic and the most rigorous methods of science in order to build theory. Many of the deterrence and pacifist peace research scholars are adherents of the scientific method as well, but insofar as the first two ideologies

[7] Alfred Zimmern, *The League of Nations and the Rule of Law, 1918–1935*, 1st ed. (London: Macmillan, 1936), p. 216. Zimmern goes on to assert that "It was because this task was not undertaken, because President Wilson never fully thought out his political philosophy and brought its elements into harmony, that confusion ensued."

[8] Cf. Ernst B. Haas, "Toward Controlling International Change: A Personal Plea," *World Politics*, XVII (October 1964), 1–12. Haas uses the term "pluralism" on p. 1; although he does not explicitly subscribe to the ideology herein presented under the label of "world pluralism," his essay is one example of a statement of goals that a world pluralist would advocate.

steer their champions away from developing a general theoretical science of human behavior, their conclusions tend to be ad hoc and incomplete with respect to the overall goals that they seek to promote. (Research scientists usually operate to advance the frontiers of knowledge, so they are least able to advocate policies based on their own ongoing preliminary research.) Multivariate approaches are most congenial to the world pluralist ideology, which seeks to advance the simultaneous attainment of many values. The strong commitment of world pluralists to theory building probably sets them apart most clearly from the other groups. It is appropriate, therefore, to discuss the theoretical and empirical operations that should be followed in order to establish normatively oriented peace research within the context of modern social science theory and methods, and thus hasten the day when a more peaceful and pluralistic world can be brought into being.

2.3   THEORY

The perspicacious reader may wonder why it is necessary to theorize on the subject of international conflict. After all, it is possible to collect and manipulate large numbers of variables to ascertain correlates and noncorrelates of various types of external state behavior. Such an empirical exercise might yield results that would fill large and impressive volumes, thereby accumulating information while bypassing the subtleties and imprecisions of literary and deductive language. The first issue, then, is the utility of theory.

2.3.1   Levels of Theory

Let us suppose that we want to know whether countries frequently involved in wars are more or less likely to have high rates of death due to domestic violence. Positing such a relation between two variables is known as a *narrow-gauge hypothesis,* and if we calculate a correlation coefficient between quantitative measures of two pertinent variables, our result will be an *empirical generalization.* Yet what can we predict from such a limited finding? Certainly we cannot immediately state that one variable causes another, for the notion of causation is a model that we use in ordering reality. In order to infer causality, data must be so manipulated that we find a particular model which fits closely with our data. Canons of logic guide our attempts to infer from data, for data do not speak for themselves. Correlations between 1,000 variables cannot tell us anything beyond the data unless they are chosen in accordance with a theoretical guide that builds results from a logical structure. For purposes of prediction as well as the need to ferret out causes and effects, we need to operate on a higher level of abstraction.

Accordingly, *middle-gauge propositions* relate concepts to each other. We could explain a relation between war participation and fatal domestic violence by asserting that the concept of "foreign conflict" is related to the concept of "domestic conflict." Yet "foreign conflict" could be measured by many possible variables. A typology of indicators of foreign conflict might include troop movements, border clashes, massacres of foreign nationals, assistance to foreign insurrectionaries, as well as entries into war. In addition to deaths from domestic violence, a checklist of types of "domestic conflict" would contain such activities as acts of terrorism, revolutions, riots, suspensions of a country's constitution, and executions of political prisoners. With five variables measuring the concept of foreign conflict and six for domestic conflict, the corresponding 30 narrow-gauge hypotheses are subsumed by our middle-gauge proposition that there is a relation between foreign and domestic conflict. When one of the hypotheses has been tested, we might provisionally expect that the other 29 will yield similar results; as our findings expand to include all 30 hypotheses generated from the two typologies, our confidence in the truth or falsity of the initially formulated middle-gauge proposition increases to the point that we feel capable of asserting predictions about as yet unspecified and unmeasured variables.[9] The gain in level of abstraction from the individual cases is considerable, and if we succeed in intercorrelating all possible measures of various concepts, we might eventually state a *law* concerning the relationship between our two key concepts. But, on the other hand, we cannot do so conclusively, since "all possible" refers to an infinite quest.

To rescue empirical research from the blind alley of brute empiricism, to be able to generalize results of research to uninvestigated situations and thereby apply our research to policy calculations, we must develop *broad-gauge theory*. Broad-gauge theory, which is sometimes called *metatheory*, consists of three elements—a paradigmatic frame of reference, a systematic body of knowledge, and a conceptual classificatory scheme. Each of these components needs to be discussed in some detail.

First of all, metatheory necessarily has a *frame of reference;* there is a focus on a particular level of analysis and on a generic behavioral paradigm. Each of the levels of analysis, from the interpersonal, the societal, to the level of the international system, as discussed in Section 1.4.3, are explored by means of paradigms appropriate to the study of international conflict. Decisionmaking metatheorists, for instance, perceive international conflict exclusively as hinging upon situations in which choices are to be made; field theorists try to position states within empirically derived coordinate systems; equilibrium analysts look for stability in inputs and outputs. In an effort to

---

[9] Cf. Hans L. Zetterberg, *On Theory and Verification in Sociology*, 3d ed. (Totowa, N. J.: Bedminster, 1965).

develop broad-gauge theory in a manner most appropriate for the analysis of international conflict, these three paradigms are to be utilized in Parts II, III, and IV, respectively, of this volume.

A second aspect of broad-gauge theory is that it houses and organizes a set of interpreted empirical findings, which we may call a *systematic body of knowledge*. Such knowledge is acquired by following canons of scientific inquiry; to enable theory to pyramid cumulatively, it is useful to codify propositions, tested as well as untested, before operating on the frontiers of research. A comprehensive body of knowledge permits accurate prediction, guides policy, stimulates further research, and is subject to correction as new findings and more factors are taken into account.

The third element of metatheory is a *conceptual framework,* or more precisely a classificatory scheme, which contains a set of mutually exclusive, exhaustive categories for subsuming middle-gauge concepts. Of the three elements, this one is probably the least explored, and it could be argued that the lack of rigorous, comprehensive, conceptual formulations accounts for the current atomistic, noncumulative output among conflict researchers. Because words are the basic elements in any theoretical discourse, and concepts are the starting points for empirical research, much attention should be paid to the method and logic when designing conceptual schemes; this will be discussed in the next section.

2.3.2 Metaconceptualization[10]

Just as a large number of indicators may be subsumed under the conceptual label "foreign conflict," we may think of a *metaconcept* as a term that is used to subsume concepts.[11] A metaconceptual framework consists

---

[10] A source to consult on conceptualization is Carl G. Hempel, *Fundamentals of Concept Formation in Empirical Science* (Chicago: University of Chicago Press, 1952). For an essay that parallels broad-gauge conceptualization with narrow-gauge operationalization, see Michael Haas, "Comparative Analysis," *Western Political Quarterly,* XV (June 1962), 294–303. See also Arthur L. Kalleberg, "The Logic of Comparison: A Methodological Note on the Comparative Study of Political Systems," *World Politics,* XIX (October 1966), 69–82; Llewellyen Gross, ed., *Symposium on Sociological Theory* (New York: Harper, Row, 1959), esp. Robert Bierstedt, "Nominal and Real Definitions in Sociological Theory," pp. 121–44; Morris R. Cohen and Ernest Nagel, *An Introduction to Logic and Scientific Method* (New York: Harcourt, Brace, 1934), Chapter 12; Richard Robinson, *Definition* (Oxford: Clarendon, 1950).

[11] When a concept subsumes other concepts it is called a *metaconcept*. Accordingly, a simple metaconcept might also be subsumed by third- and fourth-order metaconcepts. One might prefer such qualifying adjectives or a pileup of prefixes ("metametaconcept") for purposes of clarity, but once the reader is aware of this subtlety he will not need to be reminded by a special term, and he may even appre-

of a number of primitive, undefined notions that are posited to exhaust a class of phenomena and are mutually exclusive of one another in a logical sense. The word "behavior," for example, is a metaconcept inasmuch as it is a rubric under which many more specific subtypes can fall. Since all definitions eventually regress to a foundation that is intuitively grasped and logically circular, there is bound to be much debate on which set of metaconcepts is most fundamental. In Chapter 4 the metaconceptual dimensions consist of communication levels and functions; in Chapter 6, attributes, dimensions, and patterns are explicated; in Chapter 10, the focus is on functions and styles of function performance. In each case, it is inherently impossible to move directly from the basic terms of a classificatory scheme to the level of variables; metaconcepts suggest and order concepts but are a step removed from reality.

If a metaconcept is an overarching, generic type of concept, what is a "concept"? We may informally define a *concept* as a category for characterizing phenomena in the real world. Since concepts are supposed to apply to an observable reality, they are useful if they are susceptible to measurement procedures, though in their purely analytical form they may be conceived of as suggesting a *continuum* stretching from low to high levels. At each endpoint as well as in the middle of a continuum, it is possible to affix a verbal label (Figure 2–1). Let us take as an example the concept of "foreign conflict" defined in terms of "intensity." A high level of "foreign conflict" could be called *turbulence;* a low level of conflict, *quiescence*. The midpoint could be a halfway mark between "turbulence" and "quiescence" or could exhibit features of both endpoints in some manner.[12] A concept is more precise in meaning than a "notion" or a "conception," and it is measurable insofar as it refers to phenomena and "things." A metaconcept, however, is not

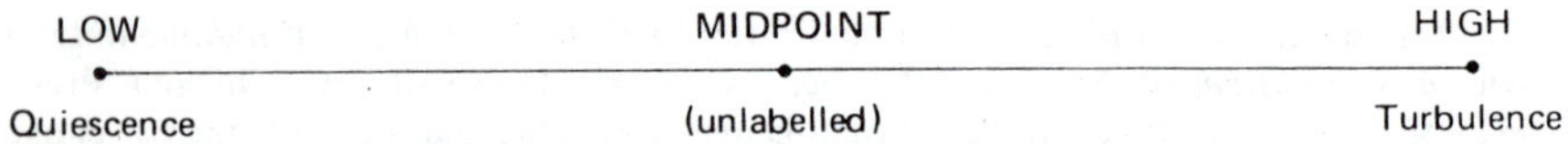

LOW	MIDPOINT	HIGH
Quiescence	(unlabelled)	Turbulence

FIGURE 2–1
Foreign Conflict Intensity Continuum

---

ciate some parsimony in generating strange-appearing words. For a more concrete discussion of this subject, which is often referred to as "property space," see Allen H. Barton, "The Concepts of Property-Space in Social Research," *The Language of Social Research*, eds. Paul F. Lazarsfeld and Morris Rosenberg (New York: The Free Press, 1955), pp. 40–53.

[12] Fred Riggs has coined many words to refer to midpoints that blend features of polar opposites in his *Administration in Developing Countries* (Boston: Houghton Mifflin, 1964). This is entirely appropriate for multidimensional broad-gauge formulations; but in narrow-gauge empirical research it is essential to work with unidimensional scales, the midpoints of which are mathematically halfway between the extremes. Cf. Haas, "Comparative Analysis."

measurable; it can only serve to supply criteria that make variables appropriate or inappropriate for testing propositions suggested by a metatheory. All of the above may seem very abstract. A concept may seem to us to have an intuitively obvious meaning. One might ask, therefore, Why have metaconcepts? The answer seems to be that a concept presupposes a prior formulation of two or more metaconcepts. More concretely, when we classify and define terms there are two major components that enable us to establish the meaning of what we wish to express. We must first identify the *class* to which an element belongs; we then proceed to distinguish what we are trying to define from other *members* of the same class. The existence of a class implies that there are other classes and, hence, a classificatory scheme of some sort would group the classes together. The need to differentiate one member of a class from another challenges us to formulate yet another independent scheme of classification. Both "class" and "membership" schemes inevitably are composed of metaconcepts, since they are one level above ordinary concepts. A concept, thus, is located at the intersection of two metaconcepts (Table 2–2). A properly formed metaconcept will contain a set of concepts that exhaust the metaconceptual common denominator, yet each concept will not overlap into any other when the set is applied to reality. An a priori manner for affixing meaning to a particular concept is to have agreement on the metaconceptual foundations that underpin a technical, specialized language.

The fact that so few researchers have ventured into the task of metaconceptualization accounts for two problems that plague peace research today. Some areas of investigation have a rich conceptual potpourri, but the words are used loosely and inconsistently, thus hindering communication among scholars; many different definitions of "crisis," "integration," and "system" cloud a larger understanding in research on international conflict. In other domains of peace research there is a poverty of concepts because it seems fashionable to let intercorrelations between variables speak for themselves, which as we have seen above is an enterprise that leads nowhere. Let us recall for a moment our hypothetical 30 hypotheses on conflict, with five indicators for one concept and six for another. How can we know whether domestic conflict is related to foreign conflict after we have tested one, 30, or even 1,000 narrow-gauge hypotheses? The answer is that we can only assess how completely we have exhausted the universe of possible hypotheses by referring to a metaconceptual framework, wherefrom the rationale for selecting our variables is derived. Metaconcepts, in short, supply the boundaries around the universe of possible concepts in a metatheory. The specification of variables for each concept is a problem in sampling.

One special problem is associated with self-conscious conceptualization, namely, the necessity of labelling concepts with verbal symbols. A

TABLE 2-2
Conceptual Space

	Metaconcept I	*Metaconcept II . . .*	*Metaconcept N*
Metaconcept A	Concept 1	Concept 4	Concept n
Metaconcept B	Concept 2	Concept 5	Concept $n + 1$
Metaconcept C	Concept 3	Concept 6	Concept $n + 2$
. . .	*. . .*	*. . .*	*. . .*
Metaconcept M	Concept m	Concept $m + 1$	Concept $m + n$

word is an inescapable shorthand device for evoking similar images to different persons, so it is particularly important to select labels that are theoretically appropriate and mnemonically satisfactory. Such relatively esoteric metaconceptual labels as "communication function," "entropy," "demotype," and "articulation" can best be established by giving numerous examples, and by so defining them that they are distinguished sharply from other metaconceptual notions. Because concepts are closer to reality than metaconcepts, the former tend to lose a precise meaning as they slip into common parlance. One might, therefore, wish to be extremely cautious in assigning words to concepts. But in part, the type of labelling employed depends upon the nature of the theoretical problem. For Sigmund Freud *innovative* labelling was exigent: previous psychological theory had been unusually barren with respect to the affective processes that Freud sought to investigate. In a culture that had been largely anti-intraceptive, the use of such poetic concepts as id, ego, and superego constituted a radical departure in human thought. The so-called revisionists of Freud were, hence, in a position to engage in *developmental* labelling by incrementally adding new words to the psychoanalytic vocabulary, such as the "archetypes" of Jung.

In contrast with Freud's problem of awakening others to totally new ideas, the researcher on international conflict is equipped with a very rich vocabulary indeed, even if dictionary definitions are often unenlightening. The use of common parlance has been sufficient to generate an intuitive awareness of a large number of concepts. Until the present, however, conceptualizers in the social sciences have all too often assumed that the existence of dictionary meanings cancels the necessity for precise definitions of concepts. A *conventionalist* school of thought, espoused most stridently by Stuart Chase, even urges that systematic advances in the social sciences must always be communicable to the intelligent layman.[13] But the idea that language is so sacrosanct that it cannot be adapted to suit our changing needs is fundamentally a nonscientific, primitive view.

Accordingly, for the purposes of the present volume, the most unsatisfactory choice would be to coin new words and start afresh within the entire

[13] Cf. Stuart Chase, *The Tyranny of Words* (New York: Harcourt, Brace, 1938).

area of inquiry. There is a degree of self-consciousness in the words already used within conflict research. The intention here is to start with a set of conventional terms that refer, albeit fuzzily, to certain kinds of concepts. It will then be possible to clarify these concepts by specifying common denominators of terms that are used rather sloppily on occasion, thereby enabling our use of the available language to be more precise. The aim in exercising such care over words is not a scholastic quest to develop a dictionary for its own sake, though a glossary of terms and definitions for variables is provided in Appendices A and B, respectively. Instead, we should regard verbal symbols as our only means for coping with a reality that probably cannot be reduced to observable electrons, molecules, and the like. In a science, classification enables us to understand what we are talking about and to discriminate among the various elements of our theories. When a science develops workable causal theories and is able to discard concepts that do not have explanatory power, baroque terminological edifices can crumble more easily; as a necessary though ultimately expendable means for arriving at knowledge, the rise of metaconceptual formulations represents a stage in scientific inquiry that is full of optimism over its own demise.

One of the reasons for looking for metaconcepts is to prepare the way for *dimensional analysis*. Progress within the field of physics has often been attributed to the existence of standard units of measurement. But it has been the combining of various units at different levels of analysis into equations that has enabled physicists to move beyond the primary data of an experiment to develop laws.[14] Each level of analysis, such as length and mass, may be considered as a *dimension*. Within the social sciences, the problem of analytically deriving a set of fundamental dimensions has hardly been acknowledged, but such a task is a necessary counterpart to a self-conscious effort to build metaconceptual frameworks. In the chapters to follow, a search for dimensions is undertaken so that we may arrive at the basic elements needed in order to predict the onset of war in particular times and places.

2.4 METHODS

The logic of theory building demands that one begin an empirical investigation by defining one's terms, formulating propositions, and reviewing extant findings before moving to the frontiers of research, as does the logic of

---

[14] Cf. Percy W. Bridgman, *Dimensional Analysis* (New Haven: Yale University Press, 1922); E. W. Jupp, *An Introduction to Dimensional Method* (London: Cleaver-Hume, 1962); Henry L. Langhaar, *Dimensional Analysis and Theory of Models* (New York: Wiley, 1951); H. E. Huntley, *Dimensional Analysis* (New York: Dover, 1967).

normal scientific inquiry.[15] In moving from theory to research it is customary to engage in *operationalization;* specific hypotheses are derived from propositions, concepts are broken down into variables, and procedures are selected to determine relationships among variables. Each of these aspects of the research process deserves some elaboration.

2.4.1 Index Construction

A *proposition* contains two or more concepts together with a postulated linkage between the concepts, whereas a *hypothesis* consists of two variables and a prediction concerning how one relates to the other. To move from a proposition to a hypothesis, therefore, entails finding variables that can stand for concepts, a task known as *index construction.*

Variables are categories to which we can assign numbers by collecting data for particular cases. *Indicators* are variables that are used as measures of a concept; and they are assessed in terms of such standard criteria as validity, reliability, objectivity, comparability, sensitivity, and utility. That is, indicators should be logically and empirically demonstrated to refer to the concept that one wishes to measure (validity); they should be collected systematically and reproducibly (reliability) and without bias from the data collectors (objectivity); they must have no cross-cultural or cross-case disparities in functional meaning (comparability); they should be refined enough to register even the smallest increments in magnitude (sensitivity); and they should be assembled without an inordinate expenditure of cost and time (utility). But such ideal conditions do not prevail within the social sciences, so one must often take steps to estimate error and to compute and correct for any artifacts produced by inadequacies in the data.

Validity is the most important criterion for evaluating an indicator. At the same time it is the most elusive, and there are several alternative methods for demonstrating validity. To be *valid* an indicator must in fact yield data appropriate to a concept. This requires that the meaning of a concept be clear in the first place; conceptual clarity requires metaconceptualization so that the primitive concepts underlying a term will be set forth in an explicit manner. For example, how do we know that the diversity (concept) of a country is indexed by the number of religions (indicator) present within its borders? We must first decide what we mean by "diversity." An arbitrary definition will not do, since another scholar may come up with a different definition for the same term with equal arbitrariness. We

---

[15] There are, of course, many scientific methods rather than one kind of orthodoxy to which researchers adhere rigidly. Cf. Morton Kaplan, *The Conduct of Inquiry* (San Francisco: Chandler, 1964). The logic suggested in this section represents a cross-breed between neo-Kantianism and instrumentalism.

may decide that diversity refers to demographic characteristics of a population, rather than other types of attributes of societies. But this is insufficient: demographic attributes change over time, are located geographically, and are found in other dimensions. By "diversity" we imply that a type of attribute is manifest in at least two different forms from a logical point of view. Thus, if all persons in a country are Catholics, we encounter religious similarity; but if there are several religious groups with dissimilar beliefs about God, diversity is said to exist. By continuing to specify the meaning of our concept we demonstrate its *internal* validity, that is, we bridge a lexical gap between a concept (diversity) and a real-world phenomenon (religious membership). Still, how do we establish whether an individual is a member of a religious group? He may be an infiltrator, pretending to act as if he were a member of the group in order to spy for the Communist Party or planted there to throw off statistics used by social scientists. As we look at genuineness in the behavior of each person, we are looking for *external* validity—that is, we try to bridge the gap between the functions being performed by human behavior and our conceptual rendering of those functions. We can never really know how each individual perceives his role when we use aggregate statistics about religious membership any more than when we aggregate behaviors of an individual (how frequently he goes to church, how much he contributes in tithes) and say that Mr. A is a Catholic. We are caught by the dilemma of *conceptual dualism:* the world of concepts and the world of reality cannot be bridged except by an act of faith. A further problem must be solved. Let us say that we agree that the number of religious groups is satisfactory as an index of diversity. Is the number of language groups also an index of diversity? On the basis of our specification of the concept "diversity," it would seem so; but empirically the variable called "number of religious groups" may not be associated at all with the variable designated "number of language groups." If the two variables are unrelated, how can they satisfy the test of empirical validity? Obviously they would have to be called subtypes of diversity in order to survive within our conceptual scheme. But why not correct our conceptual scheme instead, to reflect empirical evidence? Because of conceptual dualism, there is no easy answer to this last, and most vexing, question.

Because aggregate indicators are used to measure some 200 concepts in this volume, it will be helpful to the reader to trace the cat-and-mouse game between concepts and empirical data, as schematized in Figure 2–2. One starts with fuzzy, isolated, and overlapping concepts (Figure 2–2A). The next step is to establish at least two metaconceptual axes, with at least one concept for each cell where the metaconcepts intersect (Figure 2–2B). *Operationalization* consists of selecting an empirical counterpart for each concept; although it would be preferable to have as many indicators as possible for each concept, in practice this is not possible, so at least one variable

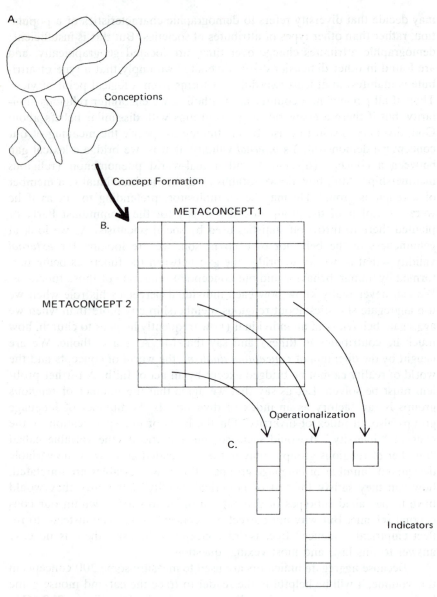

A.

Conceptions

Concept Formation

METACONCEPT 1

B.

METACONCEPT 2

Operationalization

C.

Indicators

FIGURE 2-2
The Formation of Analytical Concepts and Empirical Indicators

will be selected for each concept (Figure 2–2C). The next step is to find
interrelationships between the variables, using statistical techniques that are
to be explained in Section 2.4.2.

Within the present volume, focused as it is on widening metatheoretical horizons, existing quantitative data will be utilized so far as possible. But when no quantitative measures are available, cases will be coded relative to each other in terms of concepts derived from various metaconceptual foundations.

2.4.2 Correlational Analysis

Having discussed empirical aspects of building a metatheory, the next task is to test propositions. As we have discussed in Section 1.6.3, a purely univariate examination of cases is almost as unproductive for theory as reading pages of an almanac. Bivariate and multivariate procedures are preferred because they enable the researcher to discover how strongly a set of variables is related to each other, and to place a system of variables within a causal model.

The basic component of bivariate analysis is the *correlation*. A correlation coefficient supplies a numerical representation of the form, strength, significance, and accuracy of prediction concerning a relationship between at least two variables. Linear correlations are expressed along a scale extending from $- 1.00$ to $+ 1.00$. Relationships are stronger when magnitudes are closer to 1.00 (plus or minus); a 0.00 correlation is interpreted as no correlation between variables. A negative sign means that variables are inversely related; a positive sign indicates that as variable A decreases or increases in magnitude, variable B behaves likewise. In computing a rank-difference correlation, for example (Table 2–3), cases are ranked for two variables; and differences between the rankings that cases receive for variable A and variable B are summed across all cases and standardized into the $- 1.00$ to $+ 1.00$ scale by dividing through by a figure that represents a measure of the total number of cases.[16] Thus, if rankings for two variables are almost identical for all cases, the correlation will approach $+ 1.00$.

There are several formulas for computing correlations, and the nature of the data governs one's choice of a particular correlation coefficient. The most powerful bivariate measure of interrelation is the *Pearsonian product-moment correlation*, which provides more accurate information when there is a *bivariate normal* distribution. In practice, the normality assumption is met when there is a bell-shaped pileup of cases about the mean value for distributions of the variables being intercorrelated (Figure 2–3). When variables do not conform to the normality assumption, one may *transform* the distribution mathematically into a more normal shape. For example, logarithms of values for a particular variable tend to normalize distributions skewed on the left side of the mean; square roots, arcsines, and other functions may be used to normalize, depending upon the type of distribution. But

---

[16] The actual formula is $p = 1 - 6 \Sigma D^2 / N (N^2 - 1)$.

TABLE 2–3
Computation of Spearman Rank-Difference Correlation

Countries	*Variables* Ranks for V_1	Ranks for V_2	*Differences* D	D²
Afghanistan	3	1	2	4
Albania	4	2	2	4
Argentina	10	10	0	0
Australia	8	4.5	3.5	12.25
Austria	5	6	—1	1
Belgium	9	11	—2	4
Bolivia	1	3	—2	4
Brazil	2	7	—5	25
Bulgaria	13	13	0	0
Burma	11	4.5	6.5	42.25
Cambodia	7	8.5	—1.5	2.25
Canada	6	8.5	—2.5	6.25
Chile	12	12	0	0
Sums	13 countries		0	105

$$\text{Correlation} = 1 - \frac{6\,(105)}{13\,(169) - 1} = 0.71$$

transformations might make a nonnormal reality appear normal, and thus distort the results. One might prefer to bypass the complicated question of normality by using a somewhat less powerful correlation, such as the *Spearman rank-difference* formula, which is especially recommended when distributions defy all possible methods of transformation.

A second assumption shared by the Pearsonian and Spearman correlations is that the two variables are related to one another in a *linear* way. An entirely different type of correlation formula must be selected if a cross-plot of two variables reveals a curvilinear relation.[17] The best way to check on the assumptions of normality and linearity is to plot scatter diagrams of two variables (Figure 2–4). Relationships are linear in Figures 2–4A and 2–4B, curvilinear in Figure 2–4C. Plots of variables and the computation of correlations are not mathematically difficult, but they are sufficiently tedious to warrant the use of computers. By using "package" programs, in which one need only specify such information as the number of variables and cases in the sample, one can perform all sorts of univariate, bivariate, and multi-variate operations, even though one is unable to understand a single aspect

[17] For a comprehensive discussion of linear and curvilinear regression techniques, see Mordecai Ezekiel and Karl A. Fox, *Methods of Correlation and Regression Analysis*, 3d ed. (New York: Wiley, 1965).

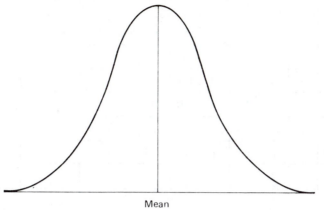

Mean

FIGURE 2-3
Normal Curve

of the computer language in which the programs are written. A little care in assembling data and a few minutes to provide routine information about one's data can produce an enormous output from the computer.

Let us assume that we have 11 variables for 85 countries and we desire to find product-moment intercorrelations between all 11 variables. After checking on the normality and linearity assumptions,[18] one selects the appropriate formula; and results emerge shortly after the problem is submitted to a computer. What conclusions can be drawn from bivariate correlational analysis?

We have already provided a guide to the meaning of various magnitudes of correlations in terms of the direction and strength of relationships between variables. One of the fallacies of interpreting correlation coefficients, however, is to pay too much attention to the statistical information and overlook socially or theoretically significant findings when individual correlations are not statistically strong. It is true that *statistical significance* drops off rapidly for any sample of cases as correlation magnitudes drop, say, below about ± .30. However, zero and low correlation magnitudes may nevertheless be *theoretically significant*. If, for example, 20 correlations between foreign and domestic conflict all turn out to be in the range + .05 to + .25, it is true that there is not much relation between the variables; but the fact that all of the correlations are consistently positive in sign would point toward confirmation of the hypothesis that there is some underlying

---

[18] In addition, the Pearsonian formula assumes *homoscedasticity*, namely, an equality among array dispersions. The distributions in Figures 2–4A and 2–4C are homoscedastic; Figure 2–4B has a heteroscedastic distribution.

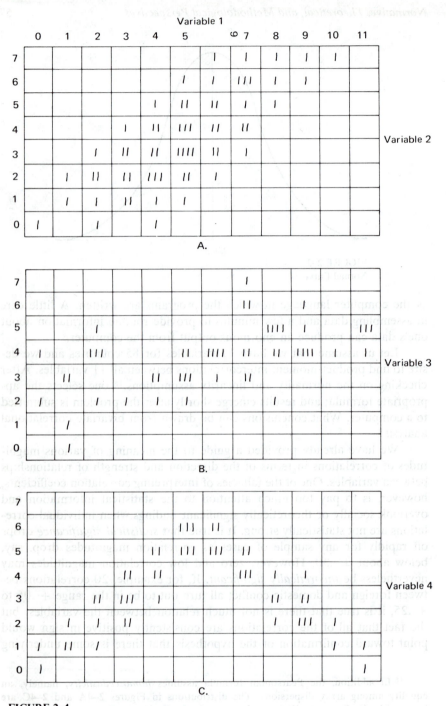

FIGURE 2-4
Scatter Diagrams: Bivariate Cross-Plots

connection between the two concepts.[19] If the correlations are, say, half positive and half negative, then one is challenged to sort out the various indicators into subcategories in order to render the findings meaningful for theory. Low yet consistent correlations between dependent and independent variables often indicate that the variables are related to each other because they are each a function of some third variable which has not yet been brought into the analysis. Correlations that are extremely high may exist between variables that are merely different manifestations of the same phenomenon. In interpreting correlation coefficients, in short, one begins to ask questions concerning causes and effects; and it is wise to be suspicious of any correlation. Nearly everyone knows that correlation is not causation; instead, a correlation enables us to see which variables are so significantly related as to suggest the possibility of a causal relationship. To demonstrate the possibility of causation, which is a logical rather than a statistical or mathematical concept, much more refined multivariate procedures are required.

A simple bivariate correlation is a function of several components: the unique correlation between the two variables under examination is mixed up with spurious relations.[20] Variables A and B, in short, might be highly related in a matrix of correlations because they were both related strongly to C and D as well; a higher interrelation between C and D would boost the coefficient. One reason for such a situation might be that A, C, and D are alternative measures of the same concept, so the respective indicators are empirically indistinguishable from each other. If we choose to sort out our variables into sets before testing our hypotheses, some of the appropriate techniques would be factor analysis, cluster analysis, and smallest-space analysis, which are designed to locate a series of highly interrelated sets of variables.[21] If we postulate that a dozen or so variables are indicators of a

[19] By chance the probability that 1 correlation will be positive is 0.5; that 2 correlations will be both positive, 0.25; that 20 correlation coefficients will all have the same sign is so low that one begins to suspect chance is not involved at all. Cf. William Buchanan and Hadley Cantril, *How Nations See Each Other* (Urbana: University of Illinois Press, 1953), Appendix A; Haas, "Comparative Analysis," pp. 298–99.

[20] *Partial correlation coefficients* compute only the unique bivariate correlation, holding other variables constant. An inescapable additional component in both types of correlations is an error factor, which usually depresses an observed relation.

[21] Reference works for these techniques are Harry H. Harman, *Modern Factor Analysis*, 2d ed. (Chicago: University of Chicago Press, 1967); Louis Guttman, "A General Nonmetric Technique for Finding the Smallest Coordinate Space for a Configuration of Points," *Psychometrika*, XXXIII (December 1968), 469–506; Milton Bloombaum, "Doing Smallest Space Analysis," *Journal of Conflict Resolution*, XIV (September 1970), 409–16. A second-order factor analysis will bring together factors extracted in the initial factor analysis; as one does higher-order analyses one approximates an overall clustering which is provided in a single computer run with cluster analysis.

particular concept, such techniques can determine whether the variables are unidimensional by partialing out some of the spurious relations and bringing together measures that are the most similar empirically.

We can now consider what happens to metaconceptual schemes when data generated therefrom are analyzed empirically (Figure 2–5). We can derive an *empirical taxonomy,* as distinct from a conceptual scheme, by employing multivariate techniques that sort our variables into subsets. In *factor analysis* (Figure 2–5B) each variable is located within dimensions of relatively independent variation: each subset is noncorrelated with every other subset. Thus, if we use ten indicators for one concept, through factor analysis we may find that all ten are highly related with one another and with no other variable or set of variables; alternatively, we may find that the ten variables break down into one subset of six, and another subset of four, with

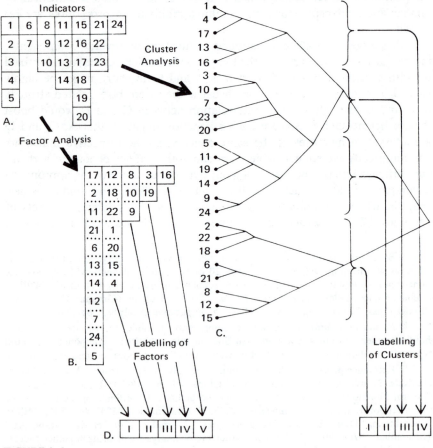

FIGURE 2-5
The Formation of Empirical Taxonomies

variables outside the original ten clinging to either subset (Figure 2–5A). If we use only one variable for each of ten concepts, we can use factor analysis to see whether the concepts, as operationalized, are empirically close or distant from each other. Empirical taxonomies are built up from factors, which contain sets of highly interrelated variables; to make any sense of the results, we must label the factors, putting us back in the realm of concepts again (Figure 2–5D). *Cluster analysis* and *smallest-space analysis* find variable sets and subsets without the stipulation that each cluster must be empirically unrelated to all other clusters, as is required of factors in factor analysis. Clusters require labels, too. In retracing this cycle from fuzzy conceptions to clear metaconceptualizations to operationalized variables to multivariate analyses to the labelling of empirical taxonomies, we find conceptual dualism all over again. It is unlikely that the labels appropriate for factors and clusters will be the same as the concepts or metaconcepts which originally generated the selection of variables. Reality is recalcitrant to a priori conceptual overlays. What, then, should we do?

The *dualistic* approach is to let analytical concepts and empirical taxonomies play separate roles: concepts are used for stimulating diverse operationalizations, but empirical taxonomies yield the raw materials for predictive models of behavior. Dualism sees virtue in continual tension between the two realms; the test of a useful concept that flows from a meta-conceptual scheme lies in how many different ways it encourages us to develop new empirical measures, and the test of a useful empirical taxonomy is whether we can ascertain causal orderings among data.

There are two *monistic* approaches, however. One approach is to regard concepts as sacred and empirical reality as deceptive; conceptual *idealism,* as this view is known, would dictate a continual reanalysis of data until factors or clusters exactly correspond with a priori notions as to the most logical ordering of the universe. The *operationist* approach, finally, would ignore the original conceptual scheme in the first place; variables would be cranked through a multivariate analysis endlessly until similar factors and clusters continued to reemerge as basic substructures of the real world. It is a thesis of this volume, however, that far too much idealism and operationism exists in research on international conflict. A dualistic approach, incomplete as it always will be, is most consonant with ideological pluralism, insofar as it keeps the door open to new metaconceptualizations and new empirical taxonomies and as long as their utility continues to be demonstrated.

All of these stages in conceptualization and empirical taxonomies have been illustrated in Section 1.2 above. It will be recalled that we started with a Parsonian categorization with four cells, derived from two metaconceptual axes, each with two dichotomous categories. We next looked at Rummel's factor analysis of indicators of international behavior, which derived an empirical taxonomy including a factor called Foreign Conflict, which in turn broke down into three subdimensions. Parsons's effort is an example of conceptual idealism, while Rummel illustrates conceptual operationism. Because of my reliance on conceptual dualism, I have not tried to reconcile the two approaches but instead to let the complexity and ambiguity of reality become manifest therefrom.

But whether we use factor analysis, smallest-space analysis, or cluster analysis, demonstrating multidimensionality enables us only to classify our data. In order to build predictive theory we must constitute elements in a causal chain or probabilistic tree. One of the appropriate techniques, known as *causal analysis,* involves postulating a system of interrelations and ascertaining whether relevant partial correlations between the theoretically significant variables in fact fit the model.[22] For example, we could theorize as follows: (1) no noncrisis decisions are ever made to go to war; (2) countries with more self-destructive tendencies are involved in more international crises; (3) multipolarity entails a lesser propensity to interpret small incidents in terms of large-scale consequences and, thus, to wage war; (4) multipolarity and self-destructiveness on the part of countries reinforce each other. One possible model appropriate to such a formulation is represented in Figure 2–6. The solid lines in the system indicate relationships contained in the above four statements. When a relationship is mediated, such as when *O* affects *W* only by way of *C,* the prediction is that *O* and *W* are connected only in accordance with the value for *C* in a particular situation; in short, *O*

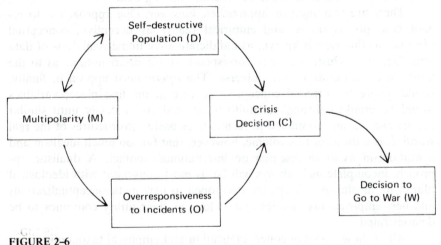

FIGURE 2–6
A Causal Model of International Conflict

22 Hubert M. Blalock, ed., *Causal Models in the Social Sciences* (Chicago: Aldine Atherton, 1971).

and W are postulated to be unrelated when values for C are held constant. One tests the degree of fit by taking the difference between predicted relations and actual correlations (Table 2–4). The correlation between each independent variable and the dependent variable, holding intervening variables constant, is computed. If all bivariate correlations between the five variables in our example are 0.00, then all causal models would be rejected on the a priori ground that there is no relationship of any kind between the variables. Similarly, if the bivariate correlations are 1.00, there are so many possible causal arrow patterns which would be equally satisfactory that we could not choose between them. If variables are intercorrelated between these extreme values, we can compute partial correlations and assess the degree of fit between a theoretical model and empirical reality. Rather than presenting the case of models that fit or fail to fit here, we refer the reader to Sections 5.4 and 8.4, where alternative models are formulated and tested. All that is involved is that differences between expected and actual values are summed, and the departure of observed findings from predicted relations is compared with other possible models to find the system that best fits the data. The data in an acceptable model should not depart too much from expected values.

Causal analysis, in other words, traces the interaction of variables in such a way that we can find whether a system of ordered variables behaves as our causal theories lead us to expect. Causation is never ultimately validated, however, until we rule out all other possible systems of interrelationships. We are once again confronted with a need for metatheory at the most sophisticated level of research methods. For the only way to construct meaningful alternative causal systems is by means of an analytic framework of concepts that have an either/or, rather than a more or less, structure. "Ruling out" calls for the built-in criteria of a classificatory scheme.

2.5 EPILOGUE

The above two chapters have demonstrated that no single approach to the study of international conflict is likely to yield comprehensive knowledge. Each investigator is faced with the necessity of narrowing his focus to a finite scope in order to conduct research. Specialization and division of labor, however, should not preclude an overall balance in approaches; and it is entirely possible that another author might have tried an entirely different tack. For just as a sailboat reaches port against adverse winds by moving first to one side of the harbor and then to the other, dialogue and variety are essential in science. Methods should remain subservient to theoretical demands, which in turn are judged ultimately in terms of their normative impact on civilization.

TABLE 2–4
Testing a Causal Model

Variables to be Intercorrelated	Variables Held Constant	Predicted Relation	Actual Correlation	Difference
DW	C	0.00		
MW	C	0.00		
OW	C	0.00		
MC	D, O	0.00		
OD	M	0.00		

The main purpose of this volume is to enable peace researchers to see major landmarks that must be taken into account when they attempt to explain why wars arise and what steps can be taken to prevent avoidable and unnecessary conflagrations. Because preconditions to such wars could be located on the interpersonal, societal, or international levels, the book is divided into three main substantive divisions. Within each level a parallel series of theoretical and methodological steps is followed. Some of the more enduring theoretical formulations from the time of Plato are discussed and codified at the beginning of each division. Current social science approaches for analyzing each level of analysis are then summarized in terms of key concepts, propositions, and research findings. The metatheoretical terrain of decisionmakers, states and societies, and international systems and subsystems is formally metaconceptualized; concepts and variables are suggested; and data are collected for each concept. The data, in turn, are correlated and analyzed by using factor analysis and cluster analysis to estimate how well the indicators mesh with concepts that began the search for data in the first place. Since the dependent variables in all studies deal with foreign conflict, bivariate correlations with all other variables will be examined across distinct subgroups of the sample with particular care. We shall finally proceed to suggest causal models. Inasmuch as the surface of possible indicators—or even concepts—will be skimmed, the reader is encouraged subsequently to fill in gaps in theory and data collection and to employ even more rigorous research techniques. The integration of provisional knowledge useful to the normatively conscientious peace research community remains a task for the final chapter. The directions outlined here have two goals—contributing toward scientific progress in the field of international relations and enabling man to terminate practices which for centuries have made the international arena a last frontier of human barbarism.

PART II
Decisionmakers

chapter 3
Theories
of Interpersonal
Factors

3.1 INTRODUCTION

One of the basic axioms accepted by students of foreign policy has been that decisions concerning international affairs tend to be made undemocratically.[1] The American Constitution, for example, establishes congressional checkpoints on presidential action with respect to the powers of appropriation, appointment, and treaty ratification; but in practice few congressmen attempt to interfere in the process of making foreign policy. The specific contexts that necessitate foreign policies are ordinarily remote from the everyday concerns of the public; the general public lacks expertise and a knowledge of particulars; even well-informed persons are not in a position to supply quick, flexible advice at crucial times in international bargaining situations. As a result of a lack of public guidance on specific questions, decisionmakers in foreign ministries are very often tempted to regard public articulation of positions as manipulatable or irrelevant. A country, to push this elitist analysis to a logical conclusion, is subject to the whims of its

---

[1] James Bryce, *Modern Democracies* (London: Macmillan, 1921); George F. Kennan, *American Diplomacy, 1900–1950* (Chicago: University of Chicago Press, 1951); Charles O. Lerche, Jr., *Foreign Policy of the American People,* 3d ed. (Englewood Cliffs, N. J.: Prentice–Hall, 1967), pp. 44–57; Walter Lippmann, *The Public Philosophy* (Boston: Little, Brown, 1955); Charles B. Marshall, *The Limits of Foreign Policy* (New York: Holt, 1954). For data on this point, see Warren E. Miller and Donald Stokes, "Constituency Influence in Congress," *American Political Science Review,* LVII (March 1963), 45–56; Miller, "Voting and Foreign Policy," *Domestic Sources of Foreign Policy,* ed. James N. Rosenau (New York: The Free Press, 1967), pp. 213–30; Milton J. Rosenberg, "Images in Relation to the Policy Process: American Public Opinion on Cold War Issues," *International Behavior,* ed. Herbert C. Kelman (New York: Holt, Rinehart and Winston, 1965), pp. 278–334.

leaders. It might seem reasonable, therefore, to assign immediate responsibility for wars to the rational or irrational characteristics of government
leaders. If societal and systemic factors fail to influence the makers of policy,
the only level of analysis remaining is that of man as a psychological being
who plays roles and relies on cohorts for advice and support.

But in examining the nature of international relations, it is clear that
not all men have an equal impact upon events. Most of the public merely
reacts to foreign policy events in a passive way until specific consequences
are vividly brought to bear upon the individual, such as when he is drafted
to serve in a country's armed forces. Some of the public is studiously attentive to major trends and occurrences in foreign relations, but only a fraction
of the attentive public has a modicum of influence over actual choices by
decisionmaking elites.[2] Those persons whom elites allow to advise them,
are, thus, in the best position to influence decisions on war. To rephrase
UNESCO, war begins in the minds of political decisionmakers and their
immediate advisers. Elites alone ordinarily have the power to make foreign
policy decisions that can bind the inhabitants of a country; advisers of elites
supply information and a range of alternatives from which one decision is
selected (Figure 3–1).

3.2 THEORIES OF INTERPERSONAL FACTORS IN WAR AND PEACE

In analyzing the nature of influences on foreign policy elites, political thinkers over the past centuries have concentrated on two main elements—calculation and emotion.[3] Man has been viewed as a rational being who
constantly makes calculations, as well as miscalculations, and who is likely
to be swayed by his passions. The weighting of the two factors in decisionmaking on war and peace has been the subject of much dispute. Many early
thinkers dualistically felt that upper classes were more prone to calculation,
the lower classes to emotion. But even persons with similar social characteristics could receive inaccurate, insufficient, or irrelevant information; so a
second group of theorists has argued that factors related to the cognitive task
of making decisions under conditions of uncertainty largely explain foreign
policy outputs of states. A third view is that the sources of war lie deep

[2] Gabriel A. Almond, *The American People and Foreign Policy* (New York:
Praeger, 1965); James N. Rosenau, *Public Opinion and Foreign Policy* (New York:
Random House, 1961); cf. Johan Galtung, "Foreign Policy Opinion as a Function of
Social Position," *Journal of Peace Research*, I, Nos. 3–4 (1964), 206–31.

[3] Richard R. Fagen, "Calculation and Emotion in Foreign Policy, The Cuban
Case," *Journal of Conflict Resolution*, VII (September 1962), 214–21; see also William A. Scott, "Rationality and Non-Rationality of International Attitudes," *ibid.*, II
(March 1958), 8–16; Sidney Verba, "Assumptions of Rationality and Non-Rationality
in Models of the International System," *World Politics*, XIV (October 1961), 93–117.

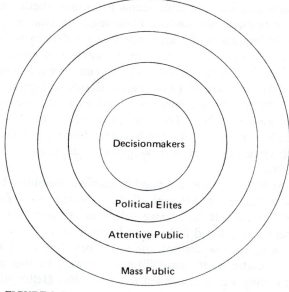

FIGURE 3-1
Foreign Policy Publics

Adapted from Gabriel A. Almond, *The American People and Foreign Policy* (New York: Praeger, 1965); James N. Rosenau, *Public Opinion and Foreign Policy* (New York: Random House, 1961).

within the human psyche, imbedded in the very organization of a personality and its mechanisms of tension management; cognitive processes are regarded as only a superstructure tailored to fit the demands of basic personality needs. The three theories bear closer examination.

3.2.1 Dualistic Theory

In observing the succession of monarchies, aristocracies, and democracies in Greece in the fifth century B.C., Plato and Aristotle came to the conclusion that war was about as likely in one form of government as another. Delineating a continuum in human drives from desire to spirit to reason, Plato argues that populist democracies go to war because of the dominance of base and violent desires; middle-class rule leads to war because of calculations about the probable economic gain or loss from various military contests between states, which involves the use of reason for niggardly desires.[4]

---

[4] Plato, *The Republic*, trans. Benjamin Jowett (New York: Modern Library, n.d.), Book IV, Sections 439–48. Plato discusses three motives in terms of the reason-desire continuum and concludes that spirit or passion, which is at the midpoint of the scale, may be sometimes used in the service of reason, other times arrayed on the side of the concupiscent: Book II, Sections 372–75.

Because the early training of a child seems to dictate whether he will use desires or reason to guide his conduct, Plato urged his students to contemplate what would happen in the ideal war-free republic in which a select few would be so educated that reason in the interest of good would prevail. But Plato realized that his intellectual gentry would never emerge. For his student, Aristotle, the fact that middle classes seek gain, rather than folly, explains why rule by a commercial class would be somewhat more peaceful than mass democracy. The most practicable state for both Plato and Aristotle fails to transcend the fundamental dualism in human motivation, and this becomes the central paradigm in Thucydides' account of the Peloponnesian War.[5]

Because the Hellenic view that mind is unable to dominate body due to improper socialization, Epictetus counselled men to turn away from politics and social conflicts entirely to achieve solace in an inner life.[6] Within a civilization where men refused to be upset by strife and other externals not within their own immediate control, the self-abnegation and purity of the populace would render itself unmobilizable for war. In this manner the Stoics hoped to bring war and conflict to a halt. But Hellenistic thinkers, who would abide an apolitical or anarchistic order, still recognized that reason's struggle with desire had few victors: there would be many failures, some successes, but both rulers and nonrulers were likely to choose war or peace on different occasions.

In the conception of classical thinkers, hence, man is driven by both passion and reason. Sometimes emotions prevail over calculations, only to be overtaken once again by calculations. Both are likely to prompt decisions to go to war. Though reason should ideally chart a course toward a warless world, political life is too volatile to permit the full exercise of higher levels of rationality.

3.2.2 Augustinian Analysis

Largely in opposition to the passivity of the Stoic and Neoplatonist thinkers of his time, Augustine, a bishop of the Christian church, presented a coherent statement of a view that on earth passions always dominate reason.[7] Starting from the premise that man has been inherently sinful since

[5] Plato's essay on the most feasible state is presented in *The Laws*, trans. A. E. Taylor (London: Dent, 1934); Aristotle, *Politics*, trans. Ernest Barker (Oxford: Clarendon, 1961); Thucydides, *The Peloponnesian War*, trans. Richard Crawley (New York: Modern Library, 1951). Cf. William T. Bluhm, *Theories of the Political System* (Englewood Cliffs, N. J.: Prentice–Hall, 1965), Chapter 2.

[6] Epictetus, *The Discourses and Manual*, trans. P. E. Matheson (New York: Oxford University Press, 1938).

[7] Augustine, *The City of God*, trans. Marcus Dods (New York: Modern Library, 1950); Herbert F. Wright, "St. Augustine on International Peace," *Ecclesiastical Re-*

biting the apple in the Garden of Eden, Augustine scoffs at the Greek cyclical view of history in which a Golden Age was expected. Instead, man is seen as progressing toward the day of final judgment with more capacity for an emotional than a rational life: religious conversion as well as decisions to go to war, therefore, are based on sentiments buried in the bosoms of men. Rational calculation takes place only when it serves the passions and desires of men. In seeking power, man loves that which will ultimately hurt himself, and it is the superior attraction of the lust for conquest and other sinful acts that accounts for anarchy and war. With all men socialized to love sin, Augustine argues, there can be neither a particular social class opposed to war nor an ideal state in which war will be less likely. A strong central state may make life somewhat more tolerable by establishing firm restraints on conduct, but rulers of states will not be exempt from the emotions that drive them to prefer war to peace. Writing just after the sacking of Rome by one of the many extant migratory bands, Augustine asserts that the luxuries and comforts sought in prosperous Rome spelled corruption and depravity.

Augustine's analysis is echoed most specifically by Hobbes and Spinoza.[8] Even Locke concurs with the view that reason is the slave of the passions, which is a fundamental tenet of conservative political ideologies, whether expressed in the urbane form of a Burke or the jingoistic predilections of a Nietzsche. In our own day Niebuhr has pointed out the impossibility of controlling war by rational means in characteristic Augustinian theological terms by advocating instead that men turn toward the emotion of love as the key to a genuine peace.[9] Freud, meanwhile, finds war to be man's expression of the death instinct, which can be opposed by only one other fundamental human impulse—eros.[10] Conceiving that love of self is always stronger than love of others, neither Freud nor Niebuhr harbor any illusions that utopias may be brought about on earth.

Unlike Augustine and Hobbes, however, most of the later democratic conservative thinkers feel that the temptation for an absolute ruler to be tyrannical warrants the establishment of a form of government in which the prejudices of men can veto each other. The checks-and-balances system advocated by Locke and the Madisonians is thus grounded in the view that political existence will be less capricious when no one group is able to con-

view, III (September 1917), 744–53; Bluhm, *Theories of the Political System*, Chapter 5.

    [8] Kenneth N. Waltz, *Man, the State and War* (New York: Columbia University Press, 1959), Chapter 2.

    [9] Reinhold Niebuhr, *Christianity and Power Politics* (New York: Scribner's, 1940); Bluhm, *Theories of the Political System*.

    [10] Sigmund Freud, *Civilization, War and Death* (London: Hogarth, 1953).

trol political decisionmaking. War would occur only when the self-interest of many groups happens to converge on the utility of war. Given the hypothesis that interests are themselves conceived through nonrational reflection, conservatives and Augustinians expect no end to war. Because a decision to go to war represents a willingness to make a large investment of resources, some modern conservative international relations theorists argue that such decisions are reached only when interests are most clearly formulated, rather than being based on misunderstandings.[11]

3.2.3 Perfectibility Theory

An assumption that it is futile to expect reason to prevail over the emotions underlies most dualist and Augustinian analysis; and hence utopian, comprehensive, or calculated planning for a more desirable state of affairs is regarded as fruitless and unrealistic. An opposing view, that men can be guided by moral absolutes, and that societies and political processes can be engineered to permit the dominance of man's rational faculties, is characteristic of Enlightenment thinkers.[12] Aquinas is a notable precursor of this view in his attempt to construct a rational basis for religious belief and thus to negate the Augustinian reliance on nonrational appeals. The belief that man can become more and more rational through better educational and social conditions was a vast departure in human thought. For Condorcet, Diderot, Helvetius, and Kant, human existence will be more meaningful and rewarding when society as a whole is reconstructed. But the full implications of the Baconian penchant for trying to harness political reality to serve the noble ends of man remained unrealized until the beginning of modern social science.[13] For the time being, Enlightenment thinkers wished to supplant existing ancient régimes, whose rulers felt free to embark upon frivolous wars to satisfy personal ambitions and dynastic pride.

Assuming that human nature is plastic, and therefore perfectible, this third group of theorists hoped ultimately to isolate conditions that would

---

11 The view that war does not start due to misunderstanding but is instead based upon a clear recognition of conflict is expressed by such theorists as Theodore Abel, "The Element of Decision in the Pattern of War," *American Sociological Review*, VI (December 1941), 853–59; Jessie Bernard, "The Sociological Study of Conflict," *The Nature of Conflict*, ed. International Sociological Association (Paris: UNESCO, 1957), pp. 40–44; and, most recently, by Mancur Olson, discussant paper delivered at the Annual Convention of the International Studies Association, Washington, March 1968.

12 Carl L. Becker, *The Heavenly City of the Eighteenth-Century Philosophers* (New Haven: Yale University Press, 1932).

13 Waltz, *Man, the State and War*, Chapter 3; Irving Louis Horowitz, *The Idea of War and Peace in Contemporary Philosophy* (New York: Paine–Whitman, 1957).

explain why the same decisionmaker might behave emotionally or miscalculate in one situation, while at other times he might calculate accurately and control his emotions. To nearly every perfectibility theorist the main evil is the pursuit of hedonistic goals and the consequent eclipse of rational impulses. A society that brings leisure to its citizens by redistributing wealth also makes it possible for men to transfer their attention to more thoughtful matters, such as how to make their decisions more consonant with an effective attainment of goals. The pacifist and populist socialisms of Tolstoi and Gandhi and the neo-utilitarian instrumentalism of Dewey share this common perspective.[14] They all see aggressiveness as a transitory human trait. Tolstoi and Gandhi regard elite manipulation of the public by deliberate distortions of the truth as the source of hostility toward other countries. Dewey hoped to reorganize the process of governmental decisionmaking, while Gandhi wanted new rulers for his native India, just as Kant two centuries earlier opposed dynastic states as pointlessly warlike. Dewey asserts that decisionmakers are unable to achieve their desires in political and social arenas because they lack knowledge of the linkage between fundamental cognitive processes. Elites experiencing frustration because of their misperceptions and miscalculations resort to war in an act of desperation, not rationality; and to persuade the masses of the wisdom of their deed they believe it necessary to turn to an emotional appeal.

Many modern psychiatrists and psychologists adopt the perfectibility thesis. John Dollard, John Rickman, and Harry Stack Sullivan have hypothesized that wars are caused by immaturities, anxieties, neuroses, maladjustments, misunderstandings due to misperceptions, or by frustrations encountered in the process of socialization.[15] According to depth psychologists, decisionmakers do not always measure up to high standards of rationality and forebearance. Leaders of states respond to daily situations in terms of psychological predispositions and current need deprivations. Cognitive psychologists, more in keeping with Dewey, consider the complexity of decisionmaking so vast that even the level-headed negotiator can scarcely cope with his information load without being subject to such factors as selective perception, time pressure, and failure of previous intelligence estimates.

---

[14] Lev Tolstoi, *The Kingdom of God and Peace Essays,* trans. Aylmer Maude (London: Oxford University Press, 1936); Mahatma Gandhi, *The Story of My Experiments with Truth,* trans. Mahedev Desai (Ahmedabad: Navajivan, 1927); John Dewey, *Human Nature and Conduct* (New York: Holt, 1922); Horowitz, *The Idea of War and Peace in Contemporary Philosophy,* Chapters 5, 11.

[15] John Dollard et al., *Frustration and Aggression* (New Haven: Yale University Press, 1939), pp. 88–90; John Rickman, "Psychodynamic Notes," *Tensions That Cause Wars,* ed. Hadley Cantril (Urbana: University of Illinois Press, 1950), p. 203; Harry Stack Sullivan, "Tensions Interpersonal and International: A Psychiatrist's View," *ibid.,* Chapter 3.

Discovering which decisional factors make for war is left for future research, rather than specified a priori. It is to the results of such investigations that we can now appropriately turn.

3.3 APPROACHES IN INTERPERSONAL ANALYSIS

If we were to accept Augustinian analysis, there would be no reason to proceed any farther. War would be explained by the depravity of men, and the relation between the interpersonal level and the incidence of international conflict would be immutable. For this reason many conservatives are anti-intraceptive, that is, they see no practical reason for probing into the human psyche, where they would expect to find only the basest malevolence and misanthropy.[16] It is from dualistic and perfectibility theorists that we may learn which factors have a constant, which a fluctuating relationship.

In obtaining data on this question two major approaches have gained popularity in the social sciences. One approach is to study propensities for aggressive and warlike postures across various strata of a country's population. The aim of this *public opinion* approach is to determine which strata and categories of persons are prone to favor peaceful resolutions of international disputes. The second approach focuses on *elite decisionmaking* directly, and the quest is for dynamic processes which lead to decision cycles that terminate in war as opposed to peace. The public opinion approach is employed by peace researchers who wish to discover how popular pressures can influence decisionmakers to be less favorable to war as an instrument of foreign policy. But if elites usually enjoy a free reign even in democracies, they are in a far better position to manipulate public sentiments than the peace-minded social scientist. So another facet of the public opinion approach could interpret the results of a public opinion study as a simulate of elite tendencies: if a particular stratum is more likely to choose violent alternatives in the public at large, then one could extrapolate to the conclusion that an elite decisionmaker of the same stratum would be subject to the same propensities. The second approach differs in preferring to study decisions directly. Inasmuch as few decisionmakers will respond obligingly to a series of embarrassing questions posed by an inquiring social scientist, the data for the second approach are generally retrospective or indirect in nature.[17] A review of the findings from both approaches is needed to appraise the quality and convergence of the two.

16 T. W. Adorno et al., *The Authoritarian Personality* (New York: Harper, 1950); Herbert McClosky, "Conservatism and Personality," *American Political Science Review*, LII (March 1958), 27–45.

17 The two approaches are, thus, complementary. Direct data about decisionmaking are of poorer quality, such as content analyses, which are often based upon propagandistic statements; indirect data about simulates of decisionmakers in the

3.3.1 Public Opinion Approach

Among the thousands of questions that have been asked in questionnaires and surveys of public opinion, only a few pertain to international relations. Out of these it will be necessary to select a still smaller set of questions that refer to an individual's preference for war as opposed to peace. In order to establish a criterion for delimiting appropriate questions, we turn to a larger framework that categorizes types or dimensions of foreign policy opinions.

One such effort to classify attitudinal orientations is undertaken by Anthony D'Amato, who distinguishes four themes in foreign policy decisionmaking.[18] The *systemic-personalist* continuum refers to two levels of perception: "systemic" types of decisionmakers perceive themselves as constrained by law, balance-of-power rules, and other objective conditions of international affairs; "personalist" decisionmakers look upon foreign policy choices as involving no such restraints but instead as opportunities for the exercise of unbridled free will. Such a distinction appears to underlie much research on internationalism-isolationism, though either attitude may be consonant with war choices. An isolationist could favor unilateral noninvolvement in war as much as a preemptive strike, and one can favor either military or nonmilitary extensions and still remain an internationalist.[19] The

laboratory or field are of higher quality, but the problem of extrapolating to the "real world" must be handled. Some scholars have claimed more utility for the elite decisionmaking approach, despite efforts of Harold Guetzkow and others to perfect a simulation building in components of the real world that might permit generalization beyond the laboratory. See Guetzkow et al., *Simulation in International Relations* (Englewood Cliffs, N. J.: Prentice-Hall, 1963); Robert C. North et al., *Content Analysis* (Evanston: Northwestern University Press, 1963), and the review by J. David Singer, "Data-Making in International Relations," *Behavioral Science*, X (January 1965), 68–80. An attempt to compare elite and general public opinion patterns is made by John Paul and Jerome Laulicht, *In Your Opinion* (Clarkson, Ont.: Canadian Peace Research Institute, 1963); Herbert McClosky, "Personality and Attitude Correlates of Foreign Policy Orientation," *Domestic Sources of Foreign Policy*, ed. Rosenau, pp. 51–110. One scholar treats the gap between central and peripheral strata as a continuum: Galtung, "Foreign Policy Opinion as a Function of Social Position"; cf. Nils H. Halle, "Social Position and Foreign Policy Attitudes," *Journal of Peace Research*, III, No. 1 (1966), 46–74; Galtung, "Social Position, Party Identification and Foreign Policy Orientation: A Norwegian Case Study," *Domestic Sources of Foreign Policy*, ed. Rosenau, pp. 161–93.

[18] Anthony D'Amato, "Psychological Constructs in Foreign Policy Prediction," *Journal of Conflict Resolution*, XI (September 1967), 294–311.

[19] Leroy Rieselbach, *The Roots of Isolationism* (Indianapolis: Bobbs–Merrill, 1967); Herbert McClosky, "Personality and Attitude Correlates of Foreign Policy Orientation"; Bruce M. Russett, "Demography, Salience and Isolationist Behavior," *Public Opinion Quarterly*, XXIV (Winter 1960), 658–64; Daniel R. Lutzker, "Internationalism as a Predictor of Cooperative Behavior," *Journal of Conflict Resolution*,

incremental-avulsive distinction, secondly, deals with the extent to which decisionmakers conceive of their role as tinkering modestly with existing policy guides, if at all, as opposed to undertaking comprehensive shifts in the direction of policy. The conservative view favors incrementalism, whereas the avulsive choice is fundamentally radical.[20] Incrementalists could favor limited war as much as peaceful change, and the chiliastic component of a rationalistic-comprehensive view might require unilateral disarmament as much as the pursuit of holy wars. The *hawk-dove* continuum differentiates decisionmakers who are more or less reluctant to use force in resolving international disputes, so it is this third orientation that is most relevant to our study of international conflict; tough-soft and tough-minded–tender-minded are alternative phrasings. D'Amato's fourth continuum, *flexibility-rigidity*, deals with the extent to which the preceding three are adhered to in an undoctrinaire or a dogmatic manner.

Although it would be useful to compare D'Amato's self-styled "prefactor analysis" with an analysis of underlying dimensions among a large number of opinion responses, no such study has been conducted to date.[21] We shall proceed, nevertheless, to examine existing findings relevant to the

---

IV (December 1960), 426–30; Charles G. McClintock et al., "Internationalism–Isolationism, Strategy of the Other Player, and Two-Person Game Behavior," *Journal of Abnormal and Social Psychology*, LXVII (December 1963), 631–66; Bernard Fensterwald, Jr., "The Anatomy of American Isolationism and Expansionism," *Journal of Conflict Resolution*, II (June 1958), 11–39; (December 1958), 280–309. Some studies posit internationalism as on the same continuum with nationalism, the latter being defined mostly in terms of isolationism but partly as involving jingoism: William J. Mackinnon and Richard Centers, "Authoritarianism and Internationalism," *Public Opinion Quarterly*, XX (Winter 1956–57), 621–30; Daniel J. Levinson, "Authoritarian Personality and Foreign Policy," *Journal of Conflict Resolution*, I (March 1957), 37–47; Kenneth W. Terhune, "Nationalistic Aspiration, Loyalty, and Internationalism," *Journal of Peace Research*, II, No. 3 (1965), 277–87.

20 The incremental versus rationalistic-comprehensive distinction is from Robert A. Dahl and Charles E. Lindblom, *Politics, Economics, and Welfare* (New York: Harper, 1953). A study on gradualist–absolutist foreign policy stances is reported in Galtung, "Social Position, Party Identification and Foreign Policy Orientation: A Norwegian Case Study," *Domestic Sources of Foreign Policy*, ed. Rosenau.

21 Two preliminary factor analyses of a subset of relevant questions, in which the factors are not labelled specifically, are found in Jerome Laulicht, "An Analysis of Canadian Foreign Policy Attitudes," *Peace Research Society, Papers*, III (1965), 121–36; Davis B. Bobrow and Allen R. Wilcox, "Dimensions of Defense Opinion: The American Public," *ibid.*, VI (1966), 101–42. At least one study finds that attitudes toward international aggression have markedly dissimilar patterns from aggressive attitudes on other issues: Harry A. Grace, "Hostility, Communication, and International Tension: I. The Hostility Inventory," *Journal of Social Psychology*, XXXIV (August 1951), 31–40; but a contrary finding emerges from Arthur I. Gladstone and Martha A. Taylor, "Threat-Related Attitudes and Reactions to Communications about International Events," *Journal of Conflict Resolution*, II (March 1958), 17–28.

hawk-dove continuum. Possible correlates of the desirability of using force may embrace both social position and personality dispositions, which correspond to our division between cognitive and depth psychology, respectively.[22]

Since the findings of any study will be a function of the research design, similar types of questions about war and peace might elicit incongruent responses from the same subjects or from one year or location to another.[23] The studies surveyed for this section of the chapter are based on several types of samples—a representative cross-section of a country[24] or com-

[22] *Ibid.*, p. 103, presents a third category–the impact of a particular situation upon attitudinal propensities. This variable has been neglected, by and large, except in Davis B. Bobrow and Neal E. Cutler, "Time-Oriented Explanations of National Security Beliefs: Cohort, Life-stage and Situation," *Peace Research Society, Papers,* VIII (1967), 31–58. Preferences on maintaining a high military capability are most related to situational factors, but the aggressive use of such forces is not related to the situation when other factors are held constant. Situational variables are considered to be of paramount importance in the elite decisionmaking approach.

[23] The criterion for selecting a study is whether questions ask subjects to choose between either a policy of war or one of nonwar. Many so-called pacifism-militarism questions and attitude scales tap this type of preference, rather than measuring ideological positions as their labelling mistakenly implies. On the other hand, many excellent studies fail to present such a clear choice, such as Bjørn Christiansen, *Attitudes Toward Foreign Affairs as a Function of Personality* (Oslo: Oslo University Press, 1959); and Karl W. Deutsch et al., *France, Germany, and the Western Alliance* (New York: Scribner's, 1967).

[24] Kurt W. Back and Kenneth J. Gergen, "Apocalyptic and Serial Time Orientations and the Structure of Opinions," *Public Opinion Quarterly,* XXVII (Fall 1963), 427–42; Bobrow and Cutler, "Time-Oriented Explanations of National Security Beliefs: Cohort, Life-stage and Situation"; Bobrow and Wilcox, "Dimensions of Defense Opinion: The American Public"; Morris Davis and Sidney Verba, "Party Affiliation and International Opinions in Britain and France, 1947–1956," *Public Opinion Quarterly,* XXIV (Winter 1960), 590–604; Karl W. Deutsch and Richard L. Merritt, "Effects of Events on National and International Images," *International Behavior,* ed. Kelman, pp. 130–87; Galtung, "Social Position, Party Identification and Foreign Policy Orientation: A Norwegian Case Study," *Domestic Sources of Foreign Policy,* ed. Rosenau; Galtung, "Foreign Policy Opinion as a Function of Social Position"; Gergen and Back, "Aging, Time Perspective, and Preferred Solutions to International Conflicts," *Journal of Conflict Resolution,* IX (June 1965), 177–86; Halle, "Social Politics and Foreign Policy Attitudes"; Robert E. Lane, "Political Personality and Electoral Choice," *American Political Science Review,* XLIX (March 1955), 173–90; Jerome Laulicht, "Public Opinion and Foreign Policy Decision," *Journal of Peace Research,* II, No. 2 (1965), 147–60; Laulicht, "An Analysis of Canadian Foreign Policy Attitudes"; McClosky, "Personality and Attitude Correlates of Foreign Policy Orientation," *Domestic Sources of Foreign Policy,* ed. Rosenau; William A. Scott, "Psychological and Social Correlates of International Images," *International Behavior,* ed. Kelman, pp. 70–103; Ross Stagner et al., "A Survey of Public Opinion on the Prevention of War," *Journal of Social Psychology,* XVI (SPSSI Bulletin, 1942), 109–30; Verba et al., "Public Opinion and the War in Vietnam," *American Political Science Review,* LXI (June 1967), 317–33.

munity,[25] and selective samples of college students,[26] of political leaders,[27] college professors,[28] juvenile delinquents,[29] and various adult groups or individuals.[30] Findings of each study should be very modestly generalized unless replicated in parallel studies.[31]

[25] Charles D. Farris, "Selected Attitudes on Foreign Affairs as Correlates of Authoritarianism and Political Anomie," *Journal of Politics*, XXII (February 1960), 50–67; Yasumasa Kuroda, "Peace-War Orientation in a Japanese Community," *Journal of Peace Research*, III, No. 4 (1966), 380–88.

[26] Peter M. Blau, "Orientation of College Students Toward International Relations," *American Journal of Sociology*, LIX (November 1953), 205–24; Hilding B. Carlson, "Attitudes of Undergraduate Students," *Journal of Social Psychology*, V (May 1934), 202–12; Mark Chesler and Richard Schmuck, "Student Reactions to the Cuban Crisis and Public Dissent," *Public Opinion Quarterly*, XXVIII (Fall 1964), 467–82; Stephen M. Corey, "Changes in the Opinions of Female Students After One Year at a University," *Journal of Social Psychology*, XI (May 1940), 341–51; Sidney Crown, "Some Personality Correlates of War-Mindedness and Anti-Semitism," *ibid.*, XXXI (February 1950), 131–43; Daniel Droba Day and O. F. Quackenbush, "Attitudes Toward Defensive, Cooperative, and Aggressive War," *ibid.*, XVI (August 1942), 11–20; D. D. Day. "A Scale of Militarism-Pacifism," *Journal of Educational Psychology*, XXII (January 1931), 96–111; Day, "Political Parties and War Attitudes," *Journal of Abnormal and Social Psychology*, XXVIII (January 1934), 468–72; George J. Dudycha, "The Attitude of College Students Toward War," *Journal of Social Psychology*, XV (February 1942), 75–89; Elizabeth Duffy, "Attitudes of Parents and Daughters Toward War and Toward the Treatment of Criminals," *Psychological Record*, IV (June 1941), 366–72; Stanford C. Ericksen, "A Skeptical Note on the Use of Attitude Scales Toward War," *Journal of Social Psychology*, XVI (November 1942), 229–42; XX (August 1944), 31–38; Maurice L. Farber, "The Armageddon Complex: Dynamics of Opinion," *Public Opinion Quarterly*, XV (Summer 1951), 217–24; Paul R. Farnsworth, "Changes in 'Attitude Toward War' During the College Years," *Journal of Social Psychology*, VIII (May 1937), 274–79; Harry A. Grace and Jack Olin Neuhaus, "Information and Social Distance as Predictors of Hostility Toward Nations," *Journal of Abnormal and Social Psychology*, XLVII (April 1952), 540–45; Vernon Jones, "Attitudes of College Students and the Changes in Such Attitudes During Four Years in College," *Journal of Educational Psychology*, XXIX (January 1938), 14–25; (February 1938), 114–34; E. T. Katzoff and A. R. Gilliland, "Student Attitudes Toward Participation in the War," *Sociometry*, VI (May 1943), 149–55; C. Terrence Pihlblad, "Student Attitudes Toward War," *Sociology and Sociological Research*, XX (January–February 1936), 248–54; Snell Putney and Russell Middleton, "Some Factors Associated with Student Acceptance or Rejection of War," *American Sociological Review*, XXVII (October 1962), 655–66; A. C. Rosander, "Age and Sex Patterns of Social Attitudes," *Journal of Educational Psychology*, XXX (October 1939), 481–96; Milton J. Rosenberg, "Images in Relation to the Policy Process: American Public Opinion on Cold-War Issues," *International Behavior*, ed. Kelman, pp. 277–34; Morris Rosenberg, "Misanthropy and Attitudes Toward International Affairs," *Journal of Conflict Resolution*, I (December 1957), 340–45; Bert R. Sappenfeld, "The Attitudes and Attitude Estimates of Catholic, Protestant, and Jewish Students," *Journal of Social Psychology*, XVI (November 1942), 173–97; William A. Scott, "International Ideology and Interpersonal Ideology," *Public Opinion Quarterly*, XXIV (Fall 1960), 419–35; John Jeffrey Smith, "What One College Thinks Concern-

Turning first of all to social characteristics associated with attitudes favorable to war and unfavorable to peace, the following attributes are associated with hawk orientations toward foreign policy:

1. Lower educational attainments.
2. Catholics (more than Protestants and Jews).
3. Nonconformist females.
4. Males.
5. Years of military experience.
6. Generations reaching maturity during World War I and the Korean War (as opposed to the depression and Vietnam War generations).
7. Urban residence.
8. Businessmen (rather than professionals).
9. Lower social status.

ing War and Peace," *Journal of Applied Psychology,* XVII, No. 1 (1933), 17–28; Ross Stagner, "Some Factors Related to Attitude Toward War," *Journal of Social Psychology,* XVI (SPSSI Bulletin, 1942), 131–42; Stagner, "Studies of Aggressive Social Attitudes," *ibid.,* XX (August 1944), 109–40.

[27] Paul Ekman et al., "Coping with Cuba: Divergent Policy Preferences of State Political Leaders," *Journal of Conflict Resolution,* X (June 1966), 180–97; Morton Gorden and Daniel Lerner, "The Setting for European Arms Controls: Political and Strategic Choices of European Elites," *ibid.,* IX (December 1965), 419–33; Laulicht, "Public Opinion and Foreign Policy Decisions"; McClosky, "Personality and Attitude Correlates of Foreign Policy Orientation," *Domestic Sources of Foreign Policy,* ed. Rosenau.

[28] David J. Armor et al., "Professors' Attitudes Toward the Vietnam War," *Public Opinion Quarterly,* XXXI (Summer 1967), 160–75; Howard Schuman and Edward O. Laumann, "Do Most Professors Support the War?" *Trans-Action,* V (November 1967), 32–35; Smith, "What One College Thinks Concerning War and Peace."

[29] Warren C. Middleton and Paul J. Fay, "Attitudes of Delinquent and Non-Delinquent Girls Toward Sunday Observance, the Bible, and War," *Journal of Educational Psychology,* XXXII (October 1941), 555–58; Middleton and Fay, "A Comparison of Delinquent and Non-Delinquent Boys with Respect to Certain Attitudes," *Journal of Social Psychology,* XVIII (August 1943), 155–58. Delinquency is not itself related to war-mindedness.

[30] Laulicht's sample in both studies cited above in n. 24 consists also of labor leaders, business leaders, and various financial contributors to the Canadian Peace Research Institute.

[31] For detailed summaries of these studies see also Hugh Carter, "Recent American Studies in Attitudes Toward War: A Summary and Evaluation," *American Sociological Review,* X (June 1945), 343–53; M. J. Rosenberg, "Images in Relation to the Policy Process: American Public Opinion on Cold War Issues," *International Behavior,* ed. Kelman; Michael Haas, "Sources of International Conflict," *The Analysis of International Relations,* eds. James N. Rosenau, Vincent Davis, and Maurice A. East (New York: The Free Press, 1972), 252–77.

These findings, however, are based on American samples. Each factor needs to be qualified somewhat. Jewish persons, for example, were hardly pacifistic when Hitler was on the rampage in Europe. "Military experience" includes voluntary participation in ROTC training. The World War I generation is more isolationist than hawklike. The Middle West and South, where one encounters more small towns than in the West and Northeast, score highest on hawk attitudes. Physicians are more dovelike than attorneys, though both are professionals. And persons of lower social standing may fail to understand foreign policy issues sufficiently so as to be consistent in agreeing with belligerent and disagreeing with peaceful foreign policy positions, although their overall score on a military scale would be higher than persons of higher social status.

There is more consistency within studies on personality correlates of war-mindedness, though such studies are not so numerous as those linking social background characteristics with attitudes toward war and peace. The following personality traits are associated with hawk orientations:

1. Authoritarianism.
2. Ethnocentrism.
3. Dogmatism.
4. Concern over status (neuroticism).
5. Cynicism about life in general.
6. Anomie and alienation.
7. Pessimism and low morale.
8. Low intellectualism.
9. Needs for power (rather than a balance between aspiration and achievement levels).
10. Machiavellism (rather than loyalty).
11. Low sociability.
12. High need inviolacy.
13. Hostility (rather than kindness).
14. Obsessiveness.
15. Paranoia.
16. Intolerance of ambiguity.
17. Lack of self-control.
18. Tendency to displace aggression.
19. Recollection of a happy childhood.
20. Unsatisfactory relations with parents.

Two of the above findings require more clarification. Political cynicism in Japan is related to peace-mindedness, but mistrust of politicians is not generalized to cynicism about life as a whole. Displaced aggression is often associated with a tendency to overvalue a friendly attitude object and to greatly undervalue a threatening attitude object; those who like one parent and dislike the other tend to be hawks, whereas doves often can see their own country to be partly at fault in international crisis situations.

Political orientations may be a third source of correlates of warlike attitudes of individuals. The following characteristics are found among hawks:

1. Political-economic conservatism.
2. Nationalism.
3. Low political participation.
4. High expectation of war in the future history of man.
5. Willingness to pay higher taxes to support national defence.
6. Willingness to enlist in the armed forces.
7. Jingoism (rather than humanitarianism).
8. Support for capital punishment.
9. Opposition to world cultural development.

On such variables as political interest, information, and political party preference there is very little difference between doves and hawks as attitude groups.

How can these findings be used to study actual decisionmakers? Using findings from many studies as a simulate to predict the social, personality, and political characteristics of a decisionmaker may be fraught with difficulty. Elite studies, in which such background characteristics of decisionmakers are assembled, are needed to validate the utility of the public opinion approach. To date, however, no such validation study has been attempted, though there are many elite studies and much data on political elites available for such a test.[32] The procedure of relating policy choices of political elites to their background factors is preferable to a priori declarations that personality-oriented factors are irrelevant in foreign policymaking.[33] A focus on specific situational components of foreign policymaking, as reviewed in the next section of this chapter, to some extent discounts personality and attitudes as factors, on the other hand. A bridge between the two approaches remains to be empirically built.[34]

---

[32] John R. Raser, "Personal Characteristics of Political Decision-Makers: A Literature Review," *Peace Research Society, Papers,* V (1966), 101–82; Harold D. Lasswell and Daniel Lerner, eds., *World Revolutionary Elites* (Cambridge: MIT Press, 1965).

[33] Verba, "Assumptions of Rationality and Non-Rationality in Models of the International System," p. 105.

[34] An attempt to provide such a theoretical integration is found in Joseph de Rivera, *The Psychological Dimension of Foreign Policy* (Columbus, Ohio: Merrill, 1968).

3.3.2   Elite Decisionmaking Approach

A major reason for a division between the public opinion and elite decisionmaking approaches is the fact that attitudes may not predict actual behavior. In the less highly structured context in which interviews are administered, stylized verbal responses may result; but in an actual choice situation an individual may decide more on the basis of reality as he perceives it than in accordance with ideological preference or psychological need. On the other hand, if background characteristics predict hawkishness in decision outputs, such a connection between predispositional and actual behavioral characteristics would become evident within actual decisionmaking situations, where such characteristics can be studied together with decisional variables unrelated to background. There are two main sources for data on decisions involving cooperative actions that lead to peaceful resolution of disputes between nations, or noncooperative patterns of behavior that lead toward war. These two alternatives may be called the *simulation* and *comparative decisionmaking case analysis* approaches. The simulation approach involves assigning a foreign policy task to a group of subjects in an experimental setting. The decisionmaking case approach consists of an analysis of decisions made in the real world by foreign policy figures, as reconstructed by historical documents, interviews, and pertinent secondary materials. Although some scholars have argued the superiority of one over the other,[35] in summarizing extant research our interest here will be in the findings and convergences or divergences between the two approaches.

3.3.2.1   SIMULATION APPROACH

Within recent years there has been considerable use of experiments in order to determine factors that account for cooperative and noncooperative behavior among teams of players. The most common form of these experiments has been the "prisoner's dilemma" game, in which teams are asked to compete for payoffs that are arranged to place interteam cooperation or conflict as a critical variable.[36] The results of such experiments are often cited in publications that assess appropriate strategies for achieving disarmament and similar foreign policy objectives. Such prisoner's dilemma experiments are *abstract* games, however, and they differ from *simulations*

[35] See, for example, Singer, "Data-Making in International Relations." Singer reviews North et al., *Content Analysis,* and Guetzkow et al., *Simulation in International Relations.*

[36] Anatol Rapoport and Albert M. Chammah, *Prisoner's Dilemma* (Ann Arbor: University of Michigan Press, 1965). For reviews of research employing the game experiment, see Rapoport and Carol Orwant, "Experimental Games: A Review," *Behavioral Science,* VII (January 1962), 1–37; Philip S. Gallo, Jr., and Charles G. McClintock, "Cooperative and Competitive Behavior in Mixed-Motive Games," *Journal of Conflict Resolution,* IX (March 1965), 68–78.

insofar as the task given to players is prototypic rather than having concrete elements that pertain to a particular subject matter or having an environmental feedback that would incorporate various features of the real-world environment into the decisional setting. Although it has been claimed that results of abstract games are largely similar to those from simulations,[37] for the purpose of this summary of findings, we report only of relationships discovered in simulated foreign policy decisionmaking settings. My preference is to uncover a set of tested propositions that pertain to dovish versus hawkish foreign policy decisions before generalizing to a higher level of abstraction, rather than extrapolating from abstract games to foreign policy issues without first determining in what situations such inferences must be qualified.[38]

There are about eight relevant studies. Richard Brody and Michael Driver start with an initial bipolar international system in the Northwestern Inter-Nation Simulation; the country heading each of the two blocs is in possession of thermonuclear weapons, and they study consequences of the spread of nuclear weapons to other countries.[39] Marc Pilisuk and associates conduct both abstract and simulated games that deal with armament-dis-

---

[37] Pilisuk et al., "War Hawks and Peace Doves: Alternate Resolutions of Experimental Conflicts," *Journal of Conflict Resolution,* IX (December 1965), 491–508, run an *abstract* and a *simulated* game that is identical in form except that in the former poker chips represent dollars, in the latter the same chips are said to represent armament increases and decreases. Results are similar except that players are more dovish in games where there is feedback to every move. No such difference, however, is reported in Pilisuk and Rapoport, "Stepwise Disarmament and Sudden Destruction in a Two-Person Game," *ibid.,* VIII (March 1964), 36–49.

[38] It is equally useful to generalize tentatively from abstract to concrete situations as to inductively generalize from the results of concrete studies toward more abstract levels; the choice of research strategy is one of personal predilection. One example of the former is Jack Sawyer and Harold Guetzkow, "Bargaining and Negotiation in International Relations," *International Behavior,* ed. Kelman, pp. 464–520; Richard H. Walters, "Implications of Laboratory Studies of Aggression for the Control and Regulation of Violence," *Annals,* CCCLXIV (March 1966), 60–72; Muzafer Sherif and Carolyn W. Sherif, *Groups in Harmony and Tension* (New York: Harper, 1953); Muzafer Sherif et al., *Intergroup Conflict and Cooperation* (Norman, Okla.: University Book Exchange, 1961). In the latter two volumes a field experiment takes place in which two boys-camp groups undergo stress, which is resolved by agreeing upon a superordinate goal to pursue jointly. For codification of the inductive studies, see Harold Guetzkow, "Some Correspondences Between Simulations and 'Realities' in International Relations," *New Approaches to International Relations,* ed. Morton A. Kaplan (New York: St. Martin's, 1968), pp. 202–69.

[39] Richard A. Brody, "Some Systemic Effects of the Spread of Nuclear Weapons Technology: A Study Through Simulation of a Multi-Nuclear Future," *Journal of Conflict Resolution,* VII (December 1963), 663–753; Michael J. Driver, "A Structural Analysis of Aggression, Stress, and Personality in an Inter-Nation Simulation" (Lafayette, Ind.: Purdue University, multilith, August 1965).

armament decision options.[40] John Raser and Wayman Crow determine the effects of the presence of one country in an international system with the capacity to delay responses to threats and attacks.[41] Roger Sisson and Russell Ackoff find conditions that may predict military escalation and deescalation.[42] Otomar Bartos correlates variables that account for concession-making in bargaining at simulated international conferences.[43] And Kenneth Terhune, finally, employs the Princeton Internation Game to trace the impact of motivational variables on conflictual and cooperative decisions.[44] All of the findings codified below are based on comparisons among a series of simulation runs.

Bartos's study, conducted with a multiethnic sample at the University of Hawaii, is the only one to treat social background characteristics. In one half of the experiments the subjects are informed in advance concerning the hawkish or dovish characteristics of their opponents, under the code words "tough" and "soft"; and in the other half the subjects were not so informed. One general finding is that hawks are younger in age, and hawkish behavior most often appears when a subject's opponent is female or younger than himself. Subjects uninformed of their opponents' type were hawkish when either Oriental or when facing Caucasian opponents; subjects told about their opponents were hawkish either if Caucasians or playing against non-Caucasians. This curious ethnic difference, that Caucasians are more hawkish when cued that toughness-softness might be present within the experimental setting, suggests that Caucasians are hawkish only when self-conscious about toughness but that Orientals are inclined to be less hawkish when they are alerted that their opponents might be either tough or soft. Similarly, Raser and Crow find that Mexican subjects are less inclined to go to war than Americans, and they attribute the difference to a tendency for Mexicans (like Asians) to be more passive than Americans.

Personality characteristics are handled by several investigators. Comparing hawks, doves, and mugwumps on five scales, Pilisuk and associates find no strong relation between any of the personality characteristics mea-

---

[40] Pilisuk et al., "War Hawks and Peace Doves: Alternative Resolutions of Experimental Conflicts"; Pilisuk and Rapoport, "Stepwise Disarmament and Sudden Destruction in a Two-Person Game."

[41] John R. Raser and Wayman J. Crow, "A Simulation Study of Deterrence Theories," *Proceedings of the International Peace Research Association Inaugural Conference* (Assen: Van Gorcum, 1966), pp. 146–65.

[42] Roger L. Sisson and Russell L. Ackoff, "Toward a Theory of the Dynamics of Conflict," *Peace Research Society, Papers,* V (1966), 183–98.

[43] Otomar J. Bartos, "How Predictable Are Negotiations?" *Journal of Conflict Resolution,* XI (December 1967), 481–98.

[44] Kenneth W. Terhune, "Studies of Motives, Cooperation, and Conflict Within Laboratory Microcosms," *Buffalo Studies,* IV (April 1968), 29–58, esp. pp. 42ff.

sured and the level of cooperative behavior. Hawks score somewhat higher than doves on self-acceptance, internationalism, and on monetary and social risk preferences; doves have a higher tolerance for ambiguity; but mugwumps exhibit no consistent pattern. Bartos uses the California Personality Inventory to determine degrees of adjustment and discovers that well-adjusted subjects are hawks when told that their opponents are either doves or hawks, especially if the opponents are poorly adjusted; whereas well-adjusted subjects in experiments without such information are doves. Bartos also finds that once a subject starts to play a "tough" role, he continues to do so, particularly if the opponent has previously displayed weakness in an experiment where subjects have not been informed of the toughness or weakness of one another. Terhune classifies subjects with high needs for achievement, power, or affiliation. Those with needs for affiliation tend to value cooperativeness for its own sake; other subjects see cooperation as a means toward ends. Nevertheless, subjects with high needs for achievement initiate more cooperative than conflictual acts and have lower military efforts; a high need for power entails more initiation of conflictual acts and military efforts; an equal number of conflictual and cooperative acts are initiated by subjects who have high needs for affiliation, and their overall military efforts are midway between the two other groups. Driver demonstrates a positive relation between authoritarianism and the tendency for aggression, but the frequency of wars and the number of unprovoked arms increases are unrelated to authoritarianism. Ideologism is positively related to wars among major powers but unrelated to the seriousness of aggression and to unprovoked armaments buildups. Liberalism-conservatism is unrelated to all measures of hawkness-doveness in Driver's study.

Driver also examines variables concerning cognitive and informational aspects of the decisionmaking task. War is associated with indicators of perceptual complexity, cognitive simplicity (considering concrete matters rather than abstract elements), and high levels of tension, the latter defined as a composite of low trust, few communications, and high hostility. Unprovoked arms increases and serious (as opposed to minor) acts of aggression are positively related to cognitive simplicity. Sisson and Ackoff, similarly, report that cooperativeness and deescalation are likely to increase when communication among participants is frequent and open. Pilisuk and Rapoport compare results from a "short" and a "long" disarmament game, the former being an experiment in which there is feedback after each move of the game, the latter situation referring to a game wherein feedback is withheld until the final move. The propensity to cooperate is higher in the longer game, in contrast with the Sisson-Ackoff finding on openness of communication. Varying the disarmament game so that subjects can play both games, in either the long-short or short-long order, Pilisuk and Rapoport encounter hawks more often in the short-long combination, which evidently socializes players to a move-countermove scenario wherein subjects are tempted to behave non-cooperatively.

Turning to the nature of the international system, which Coplin has claimed is the most salient aspect of the Inter-Nation Simulation,[45] Brody's analysis reveals that the spread of nuclear weapons beyond bipolar bloc leaders to other countries is not associated with a large number of wars: countries that develop nuclear weapons simply turn to economic issues instead. Among the 5 runs resulting in war, out of a total of 16 runs, 2 remained bipolar and 3 became multipolar. Threat of thermonuclear war correlates positively with war, according to Driver. Raser and Crow discover that once a nation possesses the capacity to delay responses to international threats, the probability of accidental, preemptive, and catalytic war is reduced; wars will be of lower magnitude if they occur at all; and there will be more interest in reaching arms control agreements. Sisson and Ackoff, on the contrary, uncover a domination situation (rather than cooperation) when the level of technology is high.

3.3.2.2   DECISIONMAKING CASE ANALYSIS

Systematic data concerning historical decisions have been unusually skimpy, in contrast to the simulation approach.[46] The reason for the scarcity of studies of this latter approach seems to be that the necessary time and energy required are out of proportion to the research payoff or to the methodological skills of those interested in exhaustively mining historical situations. Lloyd Jensen has collected data on Soviet-American disarmament negotiations between 1946 and 1963.[47] Glenn Paige compares the American decision in 1950 to enter the Korean War with American decisionmaking in the Cuban Missile Crisis of 1962.[48] Dina Zinnes, Robert North, and asso-

[45] William D. Coplin, "Inter-Nation Simulation and Contemporary Theories of International Relations," *American Political Science Review,* LX (September 1966), 562–78; Guetzkow et al., *Simulation in International Relations.*

[46] Two studies employing simulation are not reported here because they replicate findings presented in the next section of this chapter. They are Charles F. Hermann and Margaret G. Hermann, "An Attempt to Simulate the Outbreak of World War I," *American Political Science Review,* LXI (June 1967), 400–16; Dina A. Zinnes, "A Comparison of Hostile Behavior of Decision-Makers in Simulate and Historical Data," *World Politics,* XVIII (April 1966), 474–502.

[47] Lloyd Jensen, "Military Capabilities and Bargaining Behavior," *Journal of Conflict Resolution,* IX (June 1965), 155–63; Jensen, "Approach-Avoidance Bargaining in the Test Ban Negotiations," *International Studies Quarterly,* XII (June 1968), 152–60.

[48] Glenn D. Paige, "Comparative Case Analysis of Crisis Decisions: Korea and Cuba," *International Crises,* ed. Charles F. Hermann (New York: The Free Press, 1973), pp. 41–50. See also his *The Korean Decision* (New York: The Free Press, 1968). In using codings of the two decisions as correlates of war and nonwar outcomes of decisionmaking situations, I am going beyond the inferences by Paige.

ciates compare the same 1962 decision with decisionmaking in 1914 on the part of the Triple Entente and Dual Alliance powers.[49] Bruce Russett derives hypotheses from a number of cases of successful and unsuccessful deterrence, most intensively studying the Pearl Harbor decision of 1941.[50] Quincy Wright reviews 45 international conflicts between 1921 and 1965 to ascertain why some escalate and others fail to do so.[51]

The classic statement on the decisionmaking case analysis approach, by Theodore Abel, is based upon an intuitive survey of 25 decisions to go to war:

> The decision to fight . . . is not reached on the spur of the moment. In every case, the decision is based upon a careful weighing of chances and of anticipating consequences. . . . In no case is the decision precipitated by emotional tensions, sentimentality, crowd behavior, or other irrational emotions. . . . War fever and . . . "the milling of a crowd getting ready to stampede" indeed take place . . . , but they happen after a deliberate decision is reached. Often, the war fever and milling process are intentionally engineered by the power group to win the support of community sentiment.[52]

The contrary view, espoused by some elite decisionmaking theorists, is that war is selected in time of crisis, when emotional tensions are so high that cognitive and perceptual processes break down to some extent. Findings from the more systematic and less intuitive studies of recent years depart

[49] Dina A. Zinnes, Robert C. North, and Howard E. Koch, Jr., "Capability, Threat and the Outbreak of War," *International Politics and Foreign Policy,* 1st ed., ed. James N. Rosenau (New York: The Free Press, 1961), 468–82; Ole R. Holsti, Richard A. Brody, and Robert C. North, "Affect and Action in International Reaction Models," *Journal of Peace Research,* I, Nos. 3–4 (1964), 170–90; North, Brody, and Holsti, "Some Empirical Data on the Conflict Spiral," *Peace Research Society, Papers,* I (1964), 1–14; Holsti, "Perceptions of Time and Alternatives as Factors in Crisis Decision-Making," *ibid.,* III (1965), 79–120; Holsti and North, "The History of Human Conflict," *The Nature of Human Conflict,* ed. Elton B. McNeil (Englewood Cliffs, N. J.: Prentice–Hall, 1965), pp. 155–71; Holsti, "The 1914 Case," *American Political Science Review,* LIX (June 1965), 365–78; Zinnes, "A Comparison of Hostile Behavior of Decision-Makers in Simulate and Historical Data"; Zinnes, "Hostility in International Decision-Making," *Journal of Conflict Resolution,* VI (September 1962), 236–43; Zinnes, "The Expression and Perception of Hostility in Prewar Crisis: 1914," *Quantitative International Politics,* ed. J. David Singer (New York: The Free Press, 1968), pp. 85–119.

[50] Bruce M. Russett, "Cause, Surprise, and No Escape," *Journal of Politics,* XXIV (February 1962), 3–22; Russett, "The Calculus of Deterrence," *Journal of Conflict Resolution,* VII (June 1963), 97–109; Russett, "Pearl Harbor: Deterrence Theory and Decision Theory," *Journal of Peace Research,* IV, No. 2 (1967), 89–106.

[51] Quincy Wright, "The Escalation of International Conflicts," *Journal of Conflict Resolution,* IX (December 1965), 434–49.

[52] Abel, "The Element of Decision in the Pattern of War," p. 855. Abel quotes from Willard Waller, *War in the Twentieth Century* (New York: Random House, 1940).

from Abel's in several respects. The variables examined in the case studies differ in scope from the simulation approach. Social, personality, and political background characteristics of the decisionmakers are not covered at all. Instead, perceptual, cognitive, informational, and international aspects are analyzed.

Message flow and other informational variables are treated by Holsti and Paige. Holsti reports that aggressors tend to experience message overload much earlier than decisionmakers who eventually had to respond to aggression. Fewer messages are sent to future adversaries than to future allies; the aggressor closes off communication channels first. Communication between the heads of state increases as war seems increasingly imminent. The principal targets of hostile pronouncements by decisionmakers who embark upon war are members of the opposing bloc, rather than alliance partners. Aggressors, thus, articulate in an inflammatory manner while seeking to obtain support from close allies. Within the decisionmaking body itself, Paige finds that the American decision on Cuba (nonwar) differs from the Korean (war) decision insofar as the former was characterized by more discussion and even contention over alternatives; consultation with experts and allies was more extensive; more accurate, comprehensive, and documentary information was available; the adversary was better informed on possible contingencies; more information was kept secret from the public, both from the early Soviet forewarnings in 1962 (which had been absent in 1950) to the conclusion of the decisionmaking situation.[53]

North and Holsti focus largely on perceptions; most of their findings are similar to those in the Brody-Driver simulation. Perceptions of hostility, for example, show a considerable rise in frequency and in intensity among decisionmakers prior to military moves and especially within states initiating war. Aggressive decisionmakers decode events as implying consequences harmful or antagonistic to their own state's interests. Perceptions of hostility exceed perceptions of capability, which suggests that a main concern of decisionmakers initiating war is in pinpointing friends and enemies rather than in making calculations about the relative power of contending forces on the battlefield. Aggressors, moreover, are likely to overperceive the actions of their adversaries, erroneously regarding the adversary's level of violence as high and provocative, whereupon the aggressor will overrespond by escalating its response toward higher levels of violence.

As aggressive decisionmakers perceive that other states are behaving in a distressing or hostile manner, they tend to use language containing a hos-

[53] These findings are replicated through simulation in Hermann and Hermann, "An Attempt to Simulate the Outbreak of World War I"; Zinnes, "A Comparison of Hostile Behavior of Decision-Makers in Simulate and Historical Data." The two studies test many of the propositions stated in the above paragraph summarizing the Stanford studies, and there are few divergences.

tile tone. The preoccupation with threats is associated with a mood in which verbal behavior departs from elegance and refinement and instead describes the situation as a stereotypic black-and-white contest between the forces of good and evil. Accordingly, aggressive decisionmakers increasingly perceive that their states are rejected by others before war. If one state seems particularly menacing, hostility is generalized or projected onto many other states; a feeling of persecution develops. As war approaches, aggressive decisionmakers believe that their own states have fewer policy alternatives than do their adversaries and that the alternatives of the latter expand. The aggressor perceives fewer ways of handling the crisis, so primitive methods of dealing with the other country seem attractive. The possible magnitude of the war is deemed more important by decisionmakers who eventually avoid war than by those who opt for war; for the latter, attention to the extent of destruction that might result from a possible war is diverted to a moralistic concern with how much the adversary's misdeeds need to be redressed. Although time is perceived as of greater importance by the aggressor than by a target of aggression, a decisionmaker in a country that initiates aggression will be more concerned with the immediate present than with long-range trends and consequences of his actions. Decisionmakers who stay out of war perceive the actions of their opponents in a neutral, rather than a hostile, manner. Rational discussion of goals decreases among decisionmakers going to war. If a leader perceives that other states constitute potential threats, he will respond by making even more menacing counterthreats. Statements of aggressive decisionmakers are illogically connected and tend to express an affective mood, notably hostility and unfriendliness. Bloc membership results in an inflated estimate of the degree of threat and unfriendliness from decisionmakers in opposing blocs. Leaders of neutral countries are unlikely to be drawn into the spiraling misperceptions and fears of malevolent plots.

The decision to go to war or to avoid war involves the cognitive task of weighing utilities and disutilities of various goals vis-à-vis probabilities that certain events will occur. A longer decision time is recommended by Russett in order to facilitate some experimentation with techniques for resolving disputes short of war. According to Paige, the Cuban decision was deliberated for a longer period of time than the Korean decision, which may account for a number of further peculiarities: in the 1962 case the organizational roles were more heterogeneous and the organizational structure more informal; an elaborate set of contingency plans was developed for many possible Soviet moves. The Cuban decision was regarded to be without precedent, whereas in the Korean case decisionmakers relied on Munich as a source of intellectual capital on which to draw in making a response that would profit from the so-called lessons of history. Korea was much less in the forefront of ongoing debate in 1950 than was Cuba in 1962; vital interests were believed to be much more affected when war was avoided in 1962, though Wright argues that escalation is more likely when both sides consider vital interests at stake in a dispute. Initially, however, the duplicity of Soviet actions that led to the supplying of missiles to Cuba was related to an early preference in Washington for military reprisals; in 1950 no such duplicity was present, and diplomatic efforts were advocated at first. Evidently in the intervening twelve years, American decisionmakers became aware of a principle that early public airing of the most severe among various alternatives being considered in a crisis may prevent later misunderstanding by the adversary on how the situation could eventually be resolved if not mutually tempered.[54] Despite the existence of prior military plans for coping with Cuba, which had been lacking in the Korean case, a peaceful outcome resulted as values thought to be threatened, and symbols used to legitimize American actions, shifted to a more concrete level; many decisionmakers changed their original positions, and others who disagreed found themselves withdrawing from the discussions. In 1950 President Truman revealed more intolerance of ambiguity; legitimating values remained constant; original positions hardened; when diplomatic methods appeared to be failing, war was the final option left. Russett's analysis indicates that deterrence fails to operate either when the utility of war greatly exceeds the utility of peace or when the opponent is vulnerable to an attack, even though the perceived probability of ultimate victory might be slim. Yet in 1962 American decisionmakers were aware of the risk of much stronger counteraction by the Soviet Union than would have been the case in 1950 following the entry of the United States into war. As Wright observes, escalation is avoided if it is too costly for the aggressor.

The nature of the international system figures into case studies on decisions as well. Of Paige's two cases only Cuba involved a direct USA–USSR confrontation, despite Wright's assertion that escalation is more probable when the two parties in contention have a relative parity in available military force. Jensen, meanwhile, finds that a country makes concessions in disarmament negotiations when it has felt weak and is proceeding to catch up by increases in military expenditures; negotiation from a position of strength has meant failure to make concessions. In 1914 the Dual Alliance initiated war, according to North, knowing in advance that it might well lose disastrously. Russett reports that a state will defend a threatened ally to deter aggression only when there is a degree of strong interdependence between the two allies; economic interdependence, moreover, assures success in deterring much more than political or military interdependence. Invocation of assistance by an international organization fails to differentiate the Cuban (nonwar) from the Korean (war) case: the UN was

[54] Cf. Thomas C. Schelling, *The Strategy of Conflict* (New York: Oxford University Press, 1960).

called upon beforehand in 1950, while the OAS was asked to play a role after the storm had passed in 1962. Notwithstanding, Wright suggests that an aroused world opinion can prevent escalation in international disputes.

3.4 INTERPERSONAL DATA

In concluding this section on the public opinion, simulation, and decision-making case analysis approaches, it seems clear that much more systematic research is needed for the latter. The assertions of Wright in particular fail to correspond with Paige's comparative analysis. Reassuringly, the Brody-Driver simulation does parallel the findings from the North-Holsti investigations. What is needed in order to advance the two approaches is much more extensive, overlapping research. In addition, a schema for ordering variables would be helpful in tidying up the haphazard appearance of most of the extant studies so that they can all be related to a single broad framework. In the following chapter a systematic formulation of concepts relevant to the interpersonal level of analysis is presented. Each of the concepts, in turn, will be defined in such a way that one may compare decisions. The concept "decision to initiate violence," for example, can distinguish decisions to go to war from decisions to avoid war by peaceful means; to the former type of decision we could provide a coding of *0,* for the latter a *1* score. In this manner we may code a large number of decisionmaking cases along several conceptual continua.

Because the universe of all possible decisions is nearly infinite, almost any sample of decisionmaking cases would be neither a representative nor a random choice. Criteria for stratifying such a sample, which would have to refer to universes of decisionmaking cases, do not at present exist. We therefore select cases widely, so that no spurious correlations will emerge. Because our principal interest is in foreign conflict, about two-thirds of the cases selected herein deal with foreign affairs. But in order to make the level of a decision a variable as well, domestic cases are included in order to determine whether it really makes a difference to study foreign as opposed to domestic politics. Some other sampling criteria are also used. Half of the sample of both foreign and domestic cases consists of the decisions involving violence; we thereby avoid spurious relationships between foreign and violent decisions. A similar split between institutional and noninstitutional decisions was followed. Beyond these elementary ways of insuring that the variables used in selecting a sample are not spuriously related to other variables that are chosen to shed explanatory light, our selection includes both American and foreign cases and covers a time span from 1887 to 1962.

Some 32 decisionmaking cases are listed below. Dates given in each description pertain to the day when a decision was made. (The last part of each capsule statement, following the word "after," refers to the stimulus for the decision.)

1. *Bohlen.* The decision of the United States Senate to give advice and consent to the nomination of Charles Bohlen as ambassador to the Soviet Union. This decision was made on March 27, 1953, about a month after President Eisenhower submitted Bohlen's name to the Senate.[55]

2. *Quarantine.* The decision of the Kennedy Administration to impose a naval quarantine on shipments of missiles from the Soviet Union bound for Cuba. This decision was made on October 21, 1962, a week after aerial reconnaissance photographs revealed that missile installations were being constructed by Soviet technicians on Cuban soil.[56]

3. *Japan.* Advice and consent by the United States Senate to the Japanese Peace Treaty on July 4, 1952, ten months after President Truman submitted the document to the Senate.[57]

4. *Draft.* The decision of the United States Congress to pass the Selective Service Act on June 19, 1950, thus permitting an involuntary drafting of young men to serve in the army. The measure was debated for three months after President Truman addressed Congress on the subject, urging passage.[58]

5. *Korea.* The Truman Administration dispatches troops to fight North Korea on June 26, 1950, two days after the latter invades South Korea.[59]

6. *Monroney.* The United States Senate resolves that an International Development Association be established to provide loans to underdeveloped countries on a long-term, low-interest basis. The measure was adopted on July 23, 1958, five months after Senator Monroney began hearings on his proposed resolution.[60]

7. *Employment.* The United States Congress passes the Full Employment Act on February 6, 1946, to insure that the American work force would not be underutilized at the end of World War II. The bill was debated for slightly over a year after its introduction by Senator Murray.[61]

[55] James N. Rosenau, *The Nomination of "Chip" Bohlen* (New York: McGraw-Hill, 1960).

[56] Elie Abel, *The Missile Crisis* (New York: Bantam, 1966).

[57] Bernard C. Cohen, *The Political Process and Foreign Policy* (Princeton: Princeton University Press, 1957), Chapters 2–13.

[58] Clyde E. Jacobs and John F. Gallagher, *The Selective Service Act* (New York: Dodd, Mead, 1967), Chapter 3.

[59] Glenn D. Paige, *The Korean Decision,* Chapters 2–11.

[60] James A. Robinson, *The Monroney Resolution* (New York: McGraw–Hill, 1960).

[61] Stephen K. Bailey, *Congress Makes a Law* (New York: Columbia University Press, 1950).

8. *Hiroshima.* The Truman Administration gives an order to have an atomic bomb dropped on a major Japanese city. The order of August 3, 1945, came a week after the failure of Japanese leaders to respond to the Potsdam Declaration.[62]

9. *Suzuki.* The Japanese Privy Council names Suzuki as Prime Minister on August 5, 1945, after a deadlock the previous day within the co-premiership of Koiso and Yonai.[63]

10. *Pearl Harbor.* The Tojo Government assents to an attack on Pearl Harbor. The order, given on November 30, 1941, came five days after the breakdown of negotiations between American and Japanese representatives in Washington.[64]

11. *Norway.* Hitler's staff orders an attack on Norway on April 1, 1940, one and one-half months after the first suggestion that British forces might endeavor to seize Norway.[65]

12. *Vietminh.* The Eisenhower Administration decides not to assist the French by intervening to oppose the Vietminh. The decision, made on April 24, 1954, came one day after an appeal from France for military support.[66]

13. *Aswan.* Secretary of State Dulles turns down Egypt's application for funds to finance a high dam at Aswan on July 19, 1956, three days after the announcement that an emissary, Hussein, would be arriving in Washington for an answer to the request.[67]

14. *Suez.* The British Cabinet agrees to an attack upon Suez. The decision of Eden's government, of October 23, 1956, came nine days after the United Nations failed to support Anglo-French "compromise" measures concerning the operation of the Suez Canal.[68]

---

[62] Robert C. Batchelder, *The Irreversible Decision* (New York: Macmillan, 1961), Chapters 5–9; Louis Morton, "The Decision to Use the Atomic Bomb," *Command Decisions,* ed. Kent Roberts Greenfield (New York: Harcourt, Brace, 1959), pp. 388–410.

[63] Robert J. C. Butow, *Japan's Decision to Surrender* (Stanford: Stanford University Press, 1954), Chapters 2–3.

[64] Roberta Wohlstetter, *Pearl Harbor* (Stanford: Stanford University Press, 1962), Chapter 6; Louis Morton, "Japan's Decision for War," *Command Decisions,* ed. Greenfield, pp. 63–87.

[65] Earl F. Ziemke, "The German Decision to Invade Norway and Denmark," *ibid.,* pp. 39–62.

[66] Chalmers Roberts, "The Day We Didn't Go to War," *Reporter,* XI (September 14, 1954,) 31–35.

[67] Herman Finer, *Dulles over Suez* (Chicago: Quadrangle, 1964), Chapters 1–3.

[68] Leon D. Epstein, *British Politics in the Suez Crisis* (Urbana: University of Illinois Press, 1964), Chapters 3, 5; Terence Robertson, *Crisis: The Inside Story of the Suez Conspiracy* (New York: Atheneum, 1965), Chapters 1–8.

15. *Laos.* The Kennedy Administration backs a neutralist coalition government in Laos on March 21, 1961, some two weeks after Pathet Lao forces won a major battle.[69]

16. *Bay of Pigs.* The Kennedy Administration agrees on April 7, 1961, to supply and to unleash Cuban refugees aiming to attack Cuba at the Bay of Pigs. The decision came 36 days after the Guatemalan President insisted that all training of such refugees cease on Guatemalan soil.[70]

17. *U-Boat.* The German high command resumes unrestricted submarine warfare on January 9, 1917, despite American objections, after the failure by January 2 of Great Britain to respond to peace feelers.[71]

18. *Wilson.* The Wilson Administration asks Congress for a declaration of war against Germany. The April 1, 1917, decision by Wilson came 37 days after the infamous Zimmermann note was decoded.[72]

19. *Murmansk.* The Wilson Administration decides on July 26, 1917, to dispatch American troops to Murmansk, Russia. The decision was urged for several months but delayed until after receipt three weeks earlier of a specific "invitation" for American troops from the Murmansk Soviet.[73]

20. *Siberia.* The Wilson Administration agrees to send American troops to Siberia. This decision, reached on July 6, 1918, came eight days after Czech troops seized Vladivostok.[74]

21. *Poland.* Hitler's staff orders an attack on Poland. The order, issued originally on August 31, 1939, was delayed until after negotiations concerning a possible Nazi-Soviet nonaggression pact took an upturn on August 21.[75]

22. *Stalingrad.* Hitler fails to order a withdrawal from Stalingrad on November 20, 1942, only hours after the Soviet Army began its second offensive, the obvious effect of which would be to encircle 250,000 German troops.[76]

[69] Roger Hilsman, *To Move a Nation* (Garden City, N. Y.: Doubleday, 1967), Chapters 10–12.

[70] Arthur M. Schlesinger, Jr., *A Thousand Days* (Boston: Houghton Mifflin, 1965), pp. 223–79.

[71] Ernest R. May, *The World War and American Isolationism, 1914–1917* (Cambridge: Harvard University Press, 1963), Chapter 19.

[72] Daniel M. Smith, *The Great Departure* (New York: Wiley, 1965), Chapters 1–5.

[73] Leonid I. Strakhovsky, *The Origin of American Intervention in North Russia (1918)* (Princeton: Princeton University Press, 1937), Chapters 4–5.

[74] Betty Miller Unterberger, *America's Siberia Expedition, 1918–1920* (Durham: Duke University Press, 1956), Chapters 2–4; Smith, *The Great Departure*, Chapter 8.

[75] Alan Bullock, *Hitler*, rev. ed. (London: Odhams, 1964), Chapter 9.

[76] Kurt Zeitzler, "Stalingrad," *The Fatal Decisions*, eds. William Richardson and Seymour Freidin (London: World Distributors, 1965), Chapter 4.

23. *Panmunjom.* North Korean and United Nations negotiators agree to move truce talks from Kaeson to Panmunjom, a city in a neutralized area. This October 22, 1951, decision came 47 days after American negotiators objected to Kaeson as a site, in view of its location within territory held by North Korea.[77]

24. *POW's.* North Korean and United Nations negotiators agree to a principle of voluntary repatriation of prisoners of war. The agreement of June 8, 1953, was concluded about six months after a compromise formula was worked out in United Nations sessions in New York.[78]

25. *Truckers.* Pennsylvania Governor Fine vetoes a bill increasing the minimum load haulable by trucks. The veto of January 21, 1952, came a week after the bill's passage.[79]

26. *Steel.* The Kennedy Administration urges the steel industry to rescind price increases. This decision, of April 11, 1962, was reached one day after a representative of the U.S. Steel Corporation announced projected price increases.[80]

27. *Potsdam.* The Suzuki government decides on July 28, 1945, not to comment upon the Potsdam Declaration after its issuance the previous day by the victorious allied powers of Europe.[81]

28. *MacArthur.* President Truman relieves General MacArthur of his command in Korea. This decision, reached on April 6, 1951, came about two weeks after a letter from MacArthur to the Republican House Minority Leader was read aloud by the latter on the floor of the House of Representatives.[82]

29. *Evacuation.* The Roosevelt Administration orders the evacuation of Japanese aliens and Japanese-Americans from the Pacific Coast states. The order of February 19, 1942, came 25 days after the release of the Roberts Commission Report.[83]

30. *Haymarket.* Chicago police chief commands policemen to open fire upon citizens assembled near Haymarket Square on May 4, 1887, only

[77] William H. Vatcher, Jr., *Panmunjom* (New York: Praeger, 1958), pp. 59–75.

[78] *Ibid.,* Chapters 6–7.

[79] Andrew Hacker, "Pressure Politics in Pennsylvania: The Truckers vs. the Railroad," *The Uses of Power,* ed. Alan F. Westin (New York: Harcourt, Brace, World, 1962), pp. 324–75.

[80] Grant McConnell, *Steel and the Presidency* (New York: Norton, 1963), Chapters 5–6.

[81] Butow, *Japan's Decision to Surrender,* Chapters 6–8.

[82] John W. Spanier, *The Truman–MacArthur Controversy and the Korean War* (Cambridge: Harvard University Press, 1959), Chapters 10–13; Harry S. Truman, *Memoirs* (Garden City, N. Y.: Doubleday, 1959), II, Chapters 27–28.

[83] Stetson Conn, "The Decision to Evacuate the Japanese from the Pacific Coast," *Command Decisions,* ed. Greenfield, pp. 88–109.

seconds after a bomb thrown by an unknown person explodes near the approaching police.[84]

31. *Oglesby.* Illinois Governor Oglesby commutes the death sentence to life imprisonment for three Chicago anarchists, while four others remain condemned to be hanged. The Governor's decision of November 11, 1887, came ten days after the U.S. Supreme Court denied a writ of error to review the case.[85]

32. *Bolshevik.* The Bolshevik Central Committee resolves on October 10, 1917, to oust the Provisional Government leaders. The decision is made after the establishment 20 days previously of a date when the Preparliament would meet.[86]

We stop at 32 cases for a very practical reason. The data that will be extracted from each case consist of judgments coding the 32 decisions from low to high for various conceptual variables; one such variable, for instance, is whether the decision is of a domestic, foreign, or mixed domestic-foreign situation. Our data, thus, will follow the example of Paige's comparison of the Korea and Cuba decisions, as reviewed above,[87] except that we scale 32 instead of 2 case studies. In order to provide variables that are distributed normally, measures must be taken to ensure that the scaling assignments provide few extreme high or low cases and a pileup at the midpoints (see Figure 2–3). We can determine how many cases and how many scale positions provide normality in advance, because the concept of normality is based on the *binomial expansion* from probability theory; the formula for the binomial distribution is as follows:

$$(a + b)^n$$

Using this formula we can derive a normal distribution for any number of scale positions. For example, if we have 4 (N) scale positions, the expression expands by substituting 3 ($N - 1$) for the exponent n:

$$(a + b)^3 = (a + b)^2 \, (a + b)^1$$
$$= (a^2 + 2ab + b^2) \, (a + b)$$
$$= a^3 + 3a^2b + 3ab^2 + b^3$$

[84] Ernest B. Zeisler, *The Haymarket Riot* (Chicago: Isaacs, 1956), Chapters 1–11; Henry David, *The History of the Haymarket Affair* (New York: Russell, 1958), Chapter 9.

[85] *Ibid.,* Chapters 19–22.

[86] Leonard Shapiro, *The Origin of the Communist Autocracy* (Cambridge: Harvard University Press, 1955), Chapters 3–4.

[87] Paige, "Comparative Case Analysis of Crisis Decisions: Korea and Cuba," *International Crises,* ed. Hermann.

Now if we count the coefficients in the final expression, we find

$$8 = 1 + 3 + 3 + 1$$

which means that if we have 8 cases and code these cases into a four-interval distribution where there is 1 scaled as "very high," 3 as "high," 3 as "low," and 1 as "very low" for a particular variable, then we automatically have a normal distribution for the variable.[88] We ensure exact normality by limiting the number of cases for scaling to exponents of the number 2, since $2^3 = 8$, $2^4 = 16$, $2^5 = 32$, $2^6 = 64$, and so forth. We choose 32 cases because a total of only 16, with 5 scale positions, would have been too small as a basis for generalization; 64 cases, with 7 scale positions, would have taxed the reliability in coding insofar as a scaler could lose familiarity with each individual decision with such an overload of situations to recall and to evaluate comparatively. The 32 case choice is optimal and yields the following set of coefficients:

$$(a + b)^6 = a^6 + 5a^5b^2 + 10a^4b^3 + 10a^3b^4 + 5a^2b^5 + b^6$$

The data consist of judgments and decisions, similar to Paige's in the Korea and Cuba decisions reviewed above. In order to produce normal distributions in each of the variables along which the 32 cases are to be assigned ratings, a 6-point scale is used, running from low to high. A fixed number of cases must fall into a scale with 6 intervals in order for the distribution to be normal: these frequencies are 1, 5, 10, 10, 5, and 1, respectively. To illustrate, for such a variable as "degree of prior cohesion among the decisionmaking elites" we will code 1 case as extremely uncohesive, 5 cases as generally uncohesive, 10 as somewhat more uncohesive than cohesive, 10 as somewhat more cohesive than uncohesive, 5 as generally cohesive, and 1 as extremely cohesive. The codings will be relative, not absolute: the cases are scaled in comparison with each other for degrees of cohesiveness and are thus forced into a normal distribution through our scaling judgments. The mathematical advantages of normality recommend such a procedure so that we can extract the maximum information from our data.

We now turn to a conceptual framework within which to locate specific concepts and variables for comparing decisions. In Chapter 5 the empirical findings will be surveyed rigorously so that we can determine the extent to which the interpersonal level of analysis enables us to link specific factors with decisions to go to war and to escalate in levels of violent activity.

[88] The logic of scaling into a preselected distribution is presented in William Stephenson, *The Study of Behavior: The Q–Technique and Its Methodology* (Chicago: University of Chicago Press, 1953); Jack Block, *The Q-Sort Method in Personality Assessment and Psychiatric Research* (Springfield, Ill.: Thomas, 1961).

chapter 4
Communication
in Decisionmaking
Cycles

4.1 DECISIONS AND COMMUNICATION

If we define *politics* in accordance with David Easton and Fred Riggs as the process of making authoritative allocations of values to wide numbers of persons in a particular locale or group, the interpersonal aspects of foreign policy behavior necessarily focus on how individuals are able to work together in order to distribute values. Such a collaborative process is permeated by choices and decisions: alternative courses of action are weighed, and one option is adopted by the leaders of a group. Persons terminating the deliberation and assessment of alternative actions for achieving goals are called *decisionmakers*. A decisionmaker is an effective leader, of a state or other political group, who must give assent to a proposed method of value allocation in order for a decision to be authoritative.

Ordinarily a decisionmaker is the top political figure of a state, such as the American president and the Italian premier. A *decisionmaking body* consists of a central decisionmaker plus advisors who take an active role in the deliberation of alternatives; for example, we expect the foreign minister and the defense minister to be consulted in a foreign policy decision involving the use of armed forces. Decisionmaking bodies change in composition according to the issue considered, and the titles of each member of a decisionmaking group can also vary from one country to another; the effective locus of power in such bodies is the main functional element similar across all such groups.[1]

[1] See Richard C. Snyder, H. W. Bruck, and Burton Sapin, eds., *Foreign Policy Decision Making* (New York: The Free Press, 1963); Joseph Frankel, *The Making of Foreign Policy* (New York: Oxford University Press, 1963).

98

A decision is a special kind of choice. A *choice* is the selection of one out of several possible actions; the process of determining a choice may be informal or formal in terms of procedures. A formal choice is a *decision;* in politics, a decision is a terminal state in a process of evaluating authoritative measures that will have an impact upon the overall distribution of values in a society. Informal choice is less self-conscious and has largely private consequences.[2] The sequence of cognitions and actions concerned with choices in general is often referred to as *problem-solving;* a decision, thus, is problem-solving where the level of institutionalization in procedures is relatively high, though of course decisions take place in the context of many informal choices, such as when a decisionmaker smiles, writes notes on a pad of paper, looks at his watch, or elects to make a speech. As Figure 4–1 conceptualizes, the frequency of decisions is much less than that for informal choices. Informal choices lead directly up to decisions and are likely to blossom all the more after decisions. If we consider Figure 4–1 as depicting causal relations, moreover, it is clear that decisions are caused by informal processes and, once made, are the progenitors of new paths of informal choice. In seeking to explain decisions, we therefore need to classify the more ethereal informal processes into meaningful categories.

Our interest in international conflict requires us to study particular types of decisions, namely, those in which violent action is contemplated and even on occasion selected as preferable to nonviolent action. Our focus, accordingly, is not just on the decision, which is an endpoint in a problem-solving process, but is on the nature of predecision calculations and post-decision consequences. In short, we are interested in whole *decisionmaking cycles,* rather than in isolating acts from each other or from their stimuli and effects.[3]

[2] Finding a more technical term appropriate for "informal choice" is not an easy task. *Choice theory* in economics studies both formal and informal choice, the former in microeconomics, the latter in macroeconomics. An aggregate of informal choices in macroeconomics is designated by such phrases as "market demand." Psychologists study informal choices in seeking to understand attitude formation, attitude change, and volitional aspects of motivation. The term *nondecision* has been used to refer to the informal throttling of a decision process by elites who are anxious to avoid public discussion of issues on which they arbitrarily exclude views of non-elites from consideration. See Peter Bachrach and Morton S. Baratz, "Decisions and Nondecisions: An Analytical Framework," *American Political Science Review,* LVII (September 1963), 632–42. We restrict our attention to decisions here, though cases 12, 22, and 27 resemble nondecisions, and variable 63 taps a component of the concept.

[3] Some scholars distinguish between *decisionmaking,* as concerning matters of substance, and *policymaking,* which is defined as dealing with the execution of substantive decisions by administrative staffs. This separation of "politics" from "administration" may be useful to keep in mind because we do not focus intensively here on how substantive decisions are carried out. Cf. George Modelski, *A Theory of Foreign Policy* (New York: Oxford University Press, 1962).

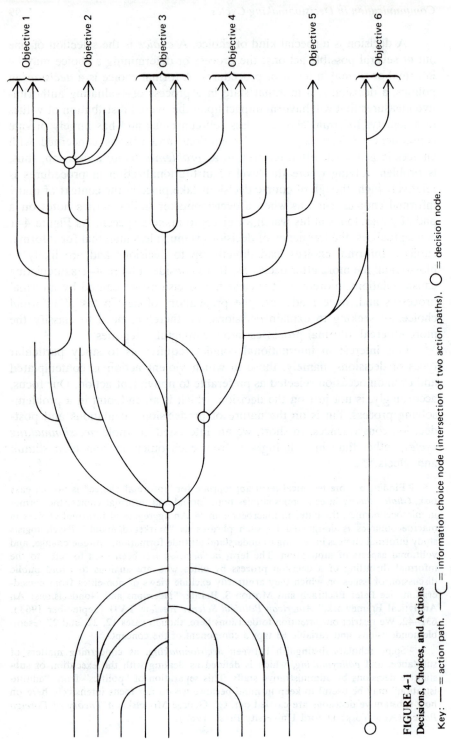

FIGURE 4-1
Decisions, Choices, and Actions

Key: ——— = action path. ⊏ = information choice node (intersection of two action paths). ◯ = decision node.

A decision, in other words, occurs at only one stage in a sequence of actions and choices and concludes a problem-solving quest by specifying that one alternative course of action is to be followed in allocating values. After a decision is made, specific steps are usually taken to implement the objective just selected; and results of the decision are in turn fed back to the decisionmakers, who may then consider whether they have coped with the problem in a satisfactory manner. If politics is composed of decisions, we may also notice that the decisionmaking process is permeated by communication and information. Stimuli must reach decisionmakers in order to trigger them into initiating problem-solving actions; alternative decisions are devised after information about the problem has been collected and evaluated, however imperfectly; a decision itself is a directive form of communication, which is ordinarily recorded and issued as a document so that its contents will be accepted as authentically emanating from the decision-makers. To carry out a decision, still further communication is required. The various elements of the decisionmaking process are linked by communication very much as we have represented them in Figure 4–2. The *agent* is the governing body, which we may regard as a pool of potential decision-makers. The decisionmaking body for each specific problem-solving task will be composed of members drawn from the agent. Ordinarily the *central decisionmaker,* who heads the agent, will draw upon advisers from the agent

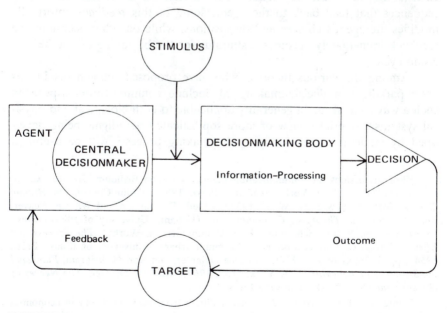

FIGURE 4–2
A Decisionmaking Cycle

according to their perceived competence in relaying information on the issues being considered. Many decisionmaking bodies, thus, are not official institutions; they do not function continuously, since a decision brings their role to an immediate end. Legislatures are the most familiar decisionmaking institutions, but in foreign policymaking they usually play a passive rather than an active role. It is the *stimulus* for a decision that triggers a central decisionmaker into recruiting members for a decisionmaking body to cope with the problem that intrudes into the normal course of activities. A stimulus may come in the form of events perceived in the international arena, domestic pressures, or preferences and desires expressed by advisers to the central decisionmaker; or it may be within the antennae or psyche of the decisionmaker himself. Upon recognition of the stimulus, the central decisionmaker will decompose the agent into a specific decisionmaking body, whereupon materials believed to be useful for arriving at a satisfactory decision will be examined; this *information-processing* stage in the decisionmaking process may be short or long, complex or simple, depending upon intelligence capabilities at hand and needs felt by decisionmakers to calculate options in the light of all obtainable relevant data. A decision simply terminates information processing by enabling an agent to respond collectively to a stimulus. The *outcome* of a decision is the actual consequence of a decision (whether anticipated or unintended) upon a *target,* that is, an external object of the decisional move. Decisions, of course, have consequences that feed back to the agent; some of this *feedback* informally modifies the agent's choices and dispositions, while on other occasions the feedback immediately becomes a stimulus for the beginning of another decision cycle.

Among the various theorists who have proposed refinements in this basic paradigm of decisionmaking, all include communication aspects in such a way as to secure a generality applicable to both biological and physical systems.[4] A brief review of more sophisticated paradigms being developed by students of the foreign policymaking process[5] will be useful in

---

[4] For discussions on communication theory, see Leon Brillouin, *Science and Information Theory* (New York: Academic Press, 1962); Colin Cherry, *On Human Communication* (New York: Wiley, 1957); Claude E. Shannon and Warren Weaver, *The Mathematical Theory of Communication* (Urbana: University of Illinois Press, 1959). See also Wilbur Schramm, "How Communication Works," *The Process and Effects of Mass Communication,* ed. Schramm (Urbana: University of Illinois Press, 1954), pp. 3–26; George A. Miller, Eugene Galanter, and Karl H. Pribram, *Plans and the Structure of Behavior* (New York: Holt, 1960); Karl W. Deutsch, *The Nerves of Government* (New York: The Free Press, 1963).

[5] Foreign policy *decisionmaking theory* differs from *decision theory* in economics and psychology precisely in the latter's deemphasis of process: the nature of the agent,

selecting variables at the interpersonal level that may account for decisions to prefer violent over nonviolent measures.

For Richard Snyder there are six main elements in decisionmaking situations: the internal setting and social structure and behavior (prestimulus), the decisionmaking process and decisionmakers (information-processing), actions (outcomes), the external setting (target), and connections between any two of the first five elements.[6] Each of the categories is broken down into subdivisions, thus encouraging more detailed formulations of narrower segments of foreign policymaking decision cycles. James Rosenau, for example, dissects relationships between opinions held by the public and decisions made by decisionmakers when he specifies such elements as actions, perceptions, opinion-making, opinion-submitting, and decision-making.[7] His paradigm assumes a large role for public opinion; the main feature is more detail on the nature of societal information-processing by decisionmaking bodies, whose members might find that opinions formed and submitted to them within the body politic are either irrelevant or must be taken into consideration in order for the elective officials to remain in office. Robert North and associates, meanwhile, concentrate on the interpersonal and perceptual aspects of information-processing, with a modified stimulus-

---

stimulus, target, and eventual outcome are ordinarily held constant; instead, information-processing (known as *search*) is examined. A major problem is how to achieve the most rational decision, with limited capacities to process relevant information, in evaluating the gap between initial aspirations and the extent to which various alternatives are predicted to lead to satisfactory outcomes. Cf. Charles Wilson and Marcus Alexis, "Basic Frameworks for Decisions," *Journal of the Academy of Management,* V (August 1962), 150–64. A review of decision theory literature is contained in Ward Edwards, "The Theory of Decision Making," *Psychological Bulletin,* LI (July 1954), 380–417; Edwards, "Behavioral Decision Theory," *Annual Review of Psychology,* XII (1961), 473–98; Gordon M. Becker and Charles G. McClintock, "Value: Behavioral Decision Theory," *ibid.,* XVII (1967), 239–86.

Decisionmaking theory is an offshoot from *organization theory,* differing from the latter by taking the entire systemic context of the nature of targets and stimuli into account as well. Organization theory parts company with decision theory by taking one main additional variable into account—the internal organization of the agent while information-processing takes place. See James G. March and Herbert A. Simon, with Harold Guetzkow, *Organizations* (New York: Wiley, 1958); Julian Feldman and Herschel E. Kanter, "Organizational Decision Making," *Handbook of Organizations,* ed. James March (Chicago: Rand McNally, 1965), pp. 614–49.

[6] Snyder, Bruck, and Sapin, *Foreign Policy Decision Making,* p. 72. The equating of Snyder's terms with my own, which are in parentheses, is very approximate, since the original Snyder formulation built in much overlap and ambiguity for heuristic purposes.

[7] James N. Rosenau, *Public Opinion and Foreign Policy* (New York: Random House, 1961).

response model (*SrsR*).[8] External events in the environment (*S*) are included only if they are perceived (*r*) as inputs into a problem-solving task, at the conclusion of which decisionmakers express reactions of various kinds (*s*) toward a target, and eventually take a specific action (*R*) toward the target. The *S* and *R* consist of the stimulus for the decision cycle and the decisional outcome, respectively; the *r* and *s* are two stages within the information-processing stage. James Robinson, thirdly, identifies five variable clusters in an explication similar to our own: situation, participants, organization, process, and outcome.[9]

Using the more formal concepts of information theory, we may regard a foreign policy decision cycle as composed structurally of a set of messages running along channels from a source to a destination. The source of a message in a cycle is the agent; the destination is the target; relevant channels consist of paths taken by messages to and from the agent and decisionmakers. An information-processing channel, in turn, has three elements: an encoder used by a stimulus to broadcast the message, a signal (or the message itself), and a decoder used by decisionmakers at the receiving end of a channel. When a decision is made, decisionmakers encode their message, and the target becomes the new destination. The channels of a complex communication system would include sensors, scanners, samplers, integrators, condensers, filters, monitors, censors, duplicators, degraders, and other such equipment.[10] A more detailed list of functions performed by such equipment would include exposure to inputs, translation, transmission, integration, generation, and the emergence of outputs.[11]

But we are not interested here in a detailed consideration of the specialized parts and functions found within communication channels in decisionmaking cycles. Instead, our focus is on characteristics of decisionmaking that might account for decisions resulting in violent action as opposed to nonviolent. We now turn to a coherent conceptual framework to assist us in locating explanatory variables.

[8] Ole R. Holsti, Robert C. North, and Richard A. Brody, "Perception and Action in the 1914 Crisis," *Quantitative International Politics*, ed. J. David Singer (New York: The Free Press, 1968), pp. 123–58.

[9] James A. Robinson and R. Roger Majak, "The Theory of Decision-Making," *Contemporary Political Analysis*, ed. James C. Charlesworth (New York: The Free Press, 1967), pp. 175–88. See also Craig C. Lundberg, "Administrative Decisions: A Scheme for Analysis," *Journal of the Academy of Management*, V (August 1962), 165–78.

[10] Charles A. McClelland, *Theory and the International System* (New York: Macmillan, 1966), p. 118.

[11] Robert C. North, "The Analytical Prospects of Communications Theory," *Contemporary Political Analysis*, ed. Charlesworth, p. 305; Deutsch, *The Nerves of Government*, pp. 258–61.

4.2 A COMMUNICATION MODEL OF DECISIONMAKING

In the previous section of this essay we have specified four distinct *phases* in decisionmaking cycles; these are the prestimulus, stimulus, information-processing, and outcome stages. A second level of concepts pertains to the types of participants and various facets of their interpersonal activities, which may be referred to as the *definition of the situation*. Four stylistic aspects of decisionmaking situations deserve special attention: structural, cognitive, affective, and evaluative elements (Table 4–1). Decision "phase" and "definition of the situation" are the two basic metaconcepts in our analysis of decisionmaking processes.

The *structural* aspect of decisionmaking consists of the hierarchical level of the agent, stimulus, decisionmaking body, and the target, or what Snyder calls the "sphere of competence." The remaining categories referring to "definition of the situation" owe their origin to Talcott Parson's threefold characterization of motivational orientations in interpersonal relations.[12] *Cognitive* elements deal with object appraisal and other intellectual tasks that equip an individual to handle objective reality on its own terms; Snyder uses "communication and information" to designate this dimension. The *affective* side of life is commonly referred to as emotional in nature, and affective needs become dominant when an individual responds to psychological drives. Because decisionmaking so obviously consists of weighing alternative ends and means, *evaluative* facets of interpersonal relations need to be studied at each phase in the decisionmaking cycle. The affective category corresponds to Snyder's notion of motivation in a psychological sense; the evaluative aspect is relevant to motivation considered from a teleological point of view.

Because outcomes, particularly violent outcomes, comprise the dependent variables to be examined herein, we shall discuss the four major concepts (more properly, metaconcepts) that refer to stages in the decisionmaking process seriatim before explicating the variables appropriate to each cell in the 16-fold matrix of Table 4–1.

But what of our dependent variables? In the prestimulus phase, we would like to know whether a decision takes place while an agent is engaging in violent acts. Is a decision cycle different in such a situation from one that develops under more peaceful conditions? In the stimulus stage, we seek to compare correlates of stimuli that involve a threat of war or violence, with stimuli that are not so threatening, yet trigger a problem-solving quest. Likewise, violence might or might not have been contemplated during information-processing, and a different set of factors might be associated

---

[12] Talcott Parsons, *The Social System* (New York: The Free Press, 1951). In this volume Parsons uses the term "cathective" in place of our "affective." The three Parsonian orientations resemble Freud's ego, id, and superego trichotomy.

TABLE 4–1
A Communication Schema of Decisionmaking

Definition of the Situation	Phases in the Decisionmaking Cycle			
	Prestimulus	Stimulus	Information-processing	Outcome
Structural aspects				
Cognitive aspects				
Affective aspects				
Evaluative aspects				

with one or the other situation. Finally, our main interest is in ascertaining a relation between all of the variables and violent versus nonviolent outcomes. These four conceptual variables relating to violence, one at each stage of decisionmaking, will be used as the set of dependent variables in this section of the volume.

The specific historical cases to be analyzed in terms of our framework have been presented in Section 3.4, with footnotes referring to relevant secondary source material. One of the least accessible arenas for the social scientist continues to be the sequence of events making up decisionmaking cycles, especially on historically critical matters. Control over variables and observational objectivity may be possible in experimental research, but history is not a laboratory for the researcher. Instead, we must often rely on retrospective reconstructions of what happened, as reported by participants whose recall may be faulty due to biases and prejudices of the moment. In addition, such a variable as whether war was considered as an alternative may be kept secret due to its controversial nature. In order to assure reliable judgments as to how to code a particular decision, it is necessary to comb many accounts, being mindful of possible inconsistencies. When actual participants disagree with each other, or scholars feel that decisionmakers actually misperceived, a fundamental methodological problem arises in applying an analytical scheme such as the one that follows. Each concept, therefore, will be tagged as either from the perception of the observer or the participant. Observers and participants may disagree on what they perceive, so some degree of hierarchy in the credibility of judgments will be employed: the central decisionmaker will be given priority in assessing perceptions of participants; the most authoritative scholar will be selected as the main objective observer on the basis of his lack of an ax to grind, noncommitment to a particular fact-distorting ideology, prolific use of documentary source material, academic credentials, and the degree of respect accorded him by other commentators on the same decision.[13]

[13] Three variables have been used for data quality control—extent of documentation (the number of footnotes), academic source (whether the author is either political

Concepts filling the 16 cells of our matrix in Table 4–1 come from several sources. The associates of Richard Snyder have developed his schema to apply mostly to prestimulus and stimulus aspects of decisionmaking cycles under the central concept of "crisis." Although much theorizing on "crisis" decisionmaking has been riddled with apparent tautologies (since there has been no consensus on the meaning of "crisis"), the number of specific variables generated in such discussions has been considerable.[14] Information-processing concepts are largely due to the conceptual innovations of Robert North and his collaborators.[15] Rosenau, finally, has suggested most of the concepts to be used under the rubric of "decision outcome."[16] We now turn to an explication of each of the four sets of concepts,[17] which we will first

---

scientist or a historian, and the length of descriptions (in words) of the decision. Cf. Raoul Naroll, *Data Quality Control* (New York: The Free Press, 1962). None of these 3 variables is correlated above the $\pm$ .60 level with any of the 68 variables coded in this study. The data consist of judgments comparing decisions; accordingly, reliability estimates for the coding of most variables are reported in Table 5–1.

[14] The tautology problem has been that some variables are *defined* as indicative of crisis in one formulation, while the same variables are said to be *correlates* of crisis in other treatises. The relevant literature is ably codified in Charles F. Hermann, ed., *International Crises* (New York: The Free Press, 1973). See also Robinson and Majak, "The Theory of Decision-Making"; James A. Robinson and Richard C. Snyder, "Decision-Making in International Politics," *International Behavior,* ed. Herbert C. Kelman (New York: Holt, Rinehart and Winston, 1965), pp. 433–63. If there is a cluster of variables denoting a "crisis situation," we will determine the identity of variables in that cluster most objectively by operationalizing definitions proposed for "crisis" and factor-analyzing the entire set of variables, an operation performed below in Chapter 5.

[15] Holsti, North, and Brody, "Perception and Action in the 1914 Crisis"; Robert C. North et al., *Content Analysis* (Evanston, Ill.: Northwestern University Press, 1963). See also Jack Sawyer and Harold Guetzkow, "Bargaining and Negotiation in International Relations," *International Behavior,* ed. Kelman, pp. 464–520; Guetzkow et al., *Simulation in International Relations* (Englewood Cliffs, N. J.: Prentice–Hall, 1963). See also Michael Driver, "A Structural Analysis of Aggression, Stress, and Personality in an Inter-Nation Simulation" (Lafayette, Ind.: Purdue University, multilith, August 1965).

[16] James N. Rosenau, *The Scientific Study of Foreign Policy* (New York: The Free Press, 1971).

[17] There are some decisionmaking theory frameworks whose concepts are not used in this section of the book; the reason for this exclusion is that the concepts refer more to the societal level. Knowing whether a decisionmaking body operates within a large or small country, or in one where validator satisfaction is low or high, would be investigated more profitably by selecting aggregate indicators for many countries, as we do in Chapter 7 of this book, than by attempting to apply judgmental coding to the few historically minded foreign policy decisionmaking case studies, most of which pertain to one country, the United States. In time more case material should be available and convergence between the societal and interpersonal levels will be brought about. See *ibid.* and Guetzkow et al., *Simulation in International Relations.*

define, next illustrate with an example from one of the 32 cases, and then finally report bivariate correlations between each conceptual variable and indicators of violent decisionmaking. The main purpose of the rest of the chapter is to familiarize the reader with the basic concepts.

4.3   PRESTIMULUS CONCEPTS

Because the prestimulus stage ordinarily precedes the construction of a decisionmaking body to cope with particular stimuli, concepts relevant to this stage in decisionmaking cycles will be viewed from the standpoint of the observer. Prestimulus variables refer largely to efforts to anticipate the decisionmaking problem.

4.3.1   Structural Aspects

In looking at the agent, before a decisional stimulus emerges, Charles Hermann pays particular attention to the administrative structure of organizations, using the term "precrisis integration" to refer to "the sum of all forces operating to keep units in the organization performing their tasks for the attainment of organizational goals."[18] This concept of *prior cohesion* (1)[19] is broad enough to apply to decisions made in any type of setting. From a structural perspective once again, we may join Harold Guetzkow in delineating *probability of office-holding* (2) as a second structural aspect of prestimulus behavior.

Historically, high cohesion was present during much decisionmaking within the Kennedy Administration and low cohesion within the agent that negotiated the Korean armistice. Probability of office-holding may be calculated as the number of years that a central decisionmaker in fact remains in office after a particular decision, except in the event of an unanticipated death. Our codings for both variables are based on comparative assessments of the cases.

4.3.2   Cognitive Aspects

Expectations are most relevant to cognitive elements in prestimulus stages. Some decisions are more anticipated than others, as Hermann, Robinson, and Snyder have pointed out. A general belief that a stimulus will

[18] Charles F. Hermann, "Some Consequences of Crisis Which Limit the Viability of Organizations," *Administrative Science Quarterly*, VII (June 1963), 67.

[19] Numbers in parentheses refer to numbers of variables, which are defined in Appendix B.

We have used the term "cohesion" rather than "integration" as suggested by Hermann, to conform to a more standard usage to be discussed in Chapter 7, below.

appear may be based upon *correct intelligence estimates* (3) or an *accurate decoding of warning signs* (4).

Information supplied to Hitler just prior to the invasion of Poland and Norway was consistent with past experiences, whereas the discovery of missile installations in Cuba in 1962 produced a dramatic reversal in previous estimates. Despite signals to the contrary, Truman's advisers saw no danger of war in Korea in early 1950, whereas Hitler reached the fjords of Norway just a day or so ahead of Great Britain, having correctly decoded the warning signs.

4.3.3 Affective Aspects

Emotional detachment from a decisionmaking situation is often appraised in terms of the prestimulus attention paid to a particular question or problem area involved. Degree of *prior concern* (5) differed sharply in the cases analyzed by Glenn Paige, for example. A second element, also of interest to Paige, is whether *precedent is invoked* (6) as opposed to de novo consideration of decisionmaking alternatives. Variable 6 has a strong evaluative element, but the use of precedent will depend on how a decisionmaking body feels about a past situation.

One author refers to Wilson's speech asking Congress for a declaration of war as "the great departure," while the nomination of Bohlen as ambassador to the Soviet Union was based largely on a tradition of congressional deference to the executive in such matters.

4.3.4 Evaluative Aspects

Prestimulus evaluation is manifested by *prior planning* (7), such as anticipatory commitments and contingency plans, a variable stressed by Paige, Robinson, and Snyder. An immediate a priori evaluation occurs if it is easy to locate the potential stimulus as an agent's ally, adversary, or neutral, so a further independent variable relevant to the prestimulus stage is *alignment status* (8).

The historical situations we are analyzing range from the lack of planning prior to the Korean War to the carefully worked out set of plans for dropping an atomic bomb on Hiroshima. The appointment of Suzuki as Prime Minister of Japan in 1945 contrasts most strikingly with the Bolshevik decision to initiate the October Revolution when one considers the alignment status of agent and target.

4.3.5 Correlational Results

Along with the appropriate prestimulus dependent variable, *ongoing violence* (9) undertaken by the agent, we may compute correlation coefficients for the first eight independent variables and the four dependent variables used in this chapter (Table 4–2).

We find that within our sample of 32 decisions few of the correlations exceed a level of ± .40, that is, explain more than 16 percent of the variance in indicators of violent decisionmaking. Within this range, we can observe that ongoing violence is most consistently related to lack of prior cohesion. Warning signs are seldom decoded properly before threats of violence. Violent options are most likely to be considered when a central decisionmaker has a high probability of retaining office and has been concerned about the issue prior to a decisionmaking stimulus; prior concern also is related to decisions for violence. But alignment status is the most useful variable here; for if the target is an adversary, there is more likely to be a threat of violence and a violent option considered as well as chosen.

4.4 STIMULUS CONCEPTS

The specific event or situation triggering a decisionmaking cycle is designated as the *stimulus*. There can be no objective stimulus from the standpoint of an observer, since it is the participant who must perceive that some aspect of a situation constitutes a problem that he feels obliged to solve. We shall code stimulus variables as would the main decisionmaking body, even if misperceptions (from an observer's perspective) are involved.

4.4.1 Structural Aspects

Snyder's concept of the "source of requiredness" is central in reviewing structural features of the stimulus to decisionmaking. Consistent with Snyder, we may ask whether a *foreign stimulus* (10) or a domestic stimulus is perceived; for this reason our sample of decisions includes some cases pertaining to domestic and local politics.

Degree of perceived *cultural similarity* (11) on some occasions might be higher if the stimulus is domestic rather than foreign, unless class or ethnic identifications are exclusivistic. A key structural side of decisionmaking, as postulated by power theorists, is the belief on the part of decisionmakers that there is disparity or *power superiority* (12) possessed by the agent vis-à-vis the target. Japanese decisionmakers decided not to comment immediately after the Potsdam Declaration despite obvious weaknesses in their potential to wage further war; in contrast, Truman's firing of General MacArthur was that of an officer who was superior in coercive capabilities.

4.4.2 Cognitive Aspects

As a decisionmaking task is triggered by a stimulus, one of the main intellectual tasks is to determine the scope of issues involved. Rosenau dis-

TABLE 4–2
Correlations Between Prestimulus Indicators
and Violent Aspects of Decisionmaking

		Violent Aspects[a]			
		Ongoing	Threat of	Violence	Decision for
Prestimulus	*Decisional*	violence	violence	considered	violence
Indicators	*Aspects*[b]	9	20	48	65
1. Prior cohesion	S	(—.44)	.35	.32	.23
2. Probability of					
office-holding	S	—.04	.26	(.48)	.36
3. Correct intelligence	C	.14	—.23	.10	—.14
4. Warning signs decoded	C	.07	(—.48)	—.10	—.14
5. Prior concern	A	.17	.38	(.45)	(.42)
6. Precedent invoked	A	—.17	.01	.08	.08
7. Prior planning	E	.19	—.11	.13	.03
8. Alignment status	E	—.12	(—.52)	(—.63)	(—.59)

[a] Correlations greater than ± .40 are enclosed in parentheses.
[b] Key: S = structural aspects
   C = cognitive aspects
   A = affective aspects
   E = evaluative aspects

tinguishes between levels of stimulus complexity using the concept of a *multi-issue* (13) versus a single-issue decisional problem. Wilson, for example, evaluated German moves from a variety of political, economic, ideological, and military perspectives in 1917; but the German takeover of Norway 23 years later was based on military considerations alone.

Turning this notion upside down, or on its side, we may determine the *noise level* (14) within which stimuli are decoded by asking either whether many other issues are all simultaneously the subjects of decisional problem-solving or whether the issue under examination is relegated to a level of priority that crowds out almost all other decisional tasks.[20] The Monroney Resolution was definitely a minor issue; the Bolsheviks were concerned with their very raison d'être in 1917.

4.4.3 Affective Aspects

Stimuli can evoke a variety of cathective perceptions from an agent. A perception of the target emphasized by Driver is the degree of *trust* (15),

---

[20] For a justification of this operationalization of "noise" in a communication system, see James G. Miller, "The Individual as an Information Processing System," *Information Storage and Neural Control*, eds. William S. Fields and Walter Abbott (Springfield, Ill.: Thomas, 1963), pp. 301–28.

which we may define as a belief that the target is well intentioned in its desire to resolve an issue in an honorable manner with the agent. The decision to bomb Hiroshima differs dramatically in the level of trust with the appointment of Suzuki.

Students of so-called crisis decisionmaking have noted two additional affective characteristics. A stimulus may so surprise decisionmakers that they perceive their amount of *control over events* (16) to be low, as did Wilson in his appraisal of the probable impact of American troops in Siberia in 1918; or it may evoke a self-confident perception, as in the case of Hitler's initial view of an attack on Poland after the Soviet-German pact had been concluded. A view that decisionmaking factors are uncontrollable, according to Snyder, Bruck, and Sapin, is largely affective in nature.

Crisis is also supposed to imply *time pressure* (17); that is, decisionmakers may perceive stimuli as restricting their time for making responses, yet feel under considerable pressure to take some sort of action. Police on the scene in the Haymarket Riot felt under an obligation to disperse the crowd quickly; but Senators took their sweet time in passing the Monroney Resolution.

4.4.4 Evaluative Aspects

In decoding stimuli that are responsible for problem-solving activities, one of the basic tasks is to determine the nature of the issue involved. Nearly every student of decisionmaking distinguishes between challenges that involve vital interests from those that threaten nonvital or low-priority values; Snyder and associates refer to this concept as the *cruciality* (18) of a decision. Since what is crucial in a city need not be so perceived at the national or international level, cruciality will be coded relative to the level of the agent. It is useful, therefore, to record how decisionmakers categorize the *level of a problem* (19), from the Haymarket Affair in Chicago to the British decision over Suez in 1956.

4.4.5 Correlational Results

Threat of violence (20) is the dependent variable relevant to the stimulus stage of a decisionmaking cycle. Correlating variables 10 to 20 with the four dependent variables (Table 4–3), we find no high magnitudes associated with ongoing violence. Threats of violence, however, are more likely where there is a foreign stimulus, cultural dissimilarity, lack of mutual trust, a feeling that events are beyond one's control, and cruciality. The same variables are also directly related to whether violent responses are considered and chosen, except that a foreign stimulus and lack of control over the situation are less necessary in contemplating a violent option; and lack of

TABLE 4–3
Correlations Between Stimulus Indicators
and Violent Aspects of Decisionmaking

		Violent Aspects			
Stimulus	Decisional	Ongoing violence	Threat of violence	Violence considered	Decision for violence
Indicators	Aspects[a]	9	20	48	65
10. Foreign stimulus	S	—.02	(.52)	.33	(.42)
11. Cultural similarity	S	—.14	(—.65)	(—.45)	(—.42)
12. Power superiority	S	—.31	—.13	.25	.03
13. Multi-issue	C	.12	.18	.00	.08
14. Noise level	C	—.26	—.35	—.33	—.31
15. Trust	A	—.11	(—.51)	(—.56)	—.33
16. Control over events	A	.00	(—.43)	—.20	—.36
17. Time pressure	A	.00	.28	.35	.31
18. Cruciality	E	.10	(.61)	(.66)	(.58)
19. Level of problem	E	.15	.36	.09	.28

[a] For key to symbols see Table 4–2.

trust of the target is less strongly related to actual decisions for the use of coercive means.

4.5 INFORMATION-PROCESSING CONCEPTS

Although it is preferable to code stimulus concepts from the viewpoint of the decisionmakers, information-processing will not be treated in terms of the lenses used by those who receive and decode inputs. We are more interested here in how messages are actually encoded and transmitted as well as received. An objective rendering of information-processing by scholarly observers can help improve the engineering of foreign policy decisionmaking by enabling us to link actual events, activities, and expressions with the selection of violent outcomes.

4.5.1 Structural Aspects

Among the structural aspects of a decisionmaking body that processes information, we may consider the number of participants, or *size of the decisionmaking body* (21), to provide a clue to the structural complexity of the decisional task. Dulles's announcement that the United States would not finance the Aswan Dam was largely a one-man decision; the Full Employment Act of 1946 had to run the gauntlet of 531 Congressmen. *Decision latitude* (22), a concept used by Guetzkow, refers to the extent to which decisionmakers perceive themselves as sutured off from their validators. Hitler's decision not to allow German soldiers trapped in Stalingrad to retreat represented extreme freedom of action in the face of contrary views expressed by his own commanding general; negotiators at Panmunjom were tied to the instructions of their governments.

Holsti, Paige, and Rosenau stress a distinction between ad hoc and formally constituted decisionmaking bodies, which may be combined into an *officiality* (23) variable. Hitler bypassed formal channels to secure a decision to attack Norway in 1940, whereas a decision by the U.S. Congress is an example of one by an official decisionmaking body. The normal level at which a particular issue is handled may shift upward in some instances, such as when individuals in the original decisionmaking circle are not re-invited to supply advice or information; for this notion Hermann supplies the term *contraction in authority* (24). Lenin preferred to have the Central Committee rather than the plenary body of the Bolsheviks consider whether to begin revolution in 1917, whereas the Senate's solicitation of advice from the executive branch illustrates an upward shift when it considered the Monroney Resolution.

4.5.2 Cognitive Aspects

How communication and information inputs are handled is an important cognitive aspect for us to consider at this stage in a decision cycle. The overall amount of processing may be indexed as *decision time* (25), which will be operationalized by counting the number of days between stimulus and response for each of the decisions coded herein. The Haymarket gunfire erupted in a few seconds upon cue; the Full Employment Bill was debated for approximately one year.

The amount of information processed can be assessed in two ways— by volume of information and by adequacy of information. Volume per se will usually tell us which decisions have *cognitive complexity* (26), namely, have many facets intellectually, necessitating a complicated role structure to filter communication; this variable has been central to studies by Driver, Paige, Robinson, and Snyder, and it distinguishes the elaborateness of the Cuban quarantine decision from the simplicity of Truman's inputs concerning the insubordination propensities of General MacArthur in 1951. Turning to adequacy of information, *input load* (27) will be coded in terms of underload (Stalingrad nonretreat), overload (Panmunjom), and optimum for the task at hand (the ratification of the Japanese Peace Treaty in 1952).

Input intensity (28) may vary from high redundancy to low redundancy in message content, the latter category applying to situations in which messages continue to supply new information to those processing such materials. Hitler was exposed to redundancy after redundancy over his beleaguered Stalingrad army, while Wilson kept seeking out new aspects of the situation in Murmansk before committing troops to North Russia. *Input range* (29) is a variable selected to count the variety of channels used, such as when both oral and written messages are exchanged, and when communications destined for decisionmakers emerge (as it did during the Cuban quarantine decision) from many hierarchical levels in the agent as well as the target.

In attempting to solve a decisional problem, information-processers will on occasion place communication outputs into the range of a target's antennae. Information of this sort, which is the essence of bargaining, needs to be specified in terms of jamming effects; for, if communications fail to carry messages in a manner promoting a mutually agreed-upon solution, we suspect that the interchange was futile. An *input/output ratio* (30) is one way to find asymmetries in communication, though only in terms of total volume. Wilson's entry into World War I followed an excess of inputs; discussions at Panmunjom in 1951–1953 were characterized as "talkathons." Semantic jamming occurs when the *metacommunication level* (31) between an agent and a target is low due to lack of improvement in the fidelity of transmission.[21] The objectives of the Bolsheviks in 1917 were clear to everyone, but the situation at Dienbienphu in 1954 was largely obscure to those in Washington who otherwise might have contemplated American intervention. Asymmetries in input and output range refer to temporal trends as well. Hermann's *reduction in communications* (32) concept enables us to contrast increased information loads due to hearings on Monroney's proposal in the Senate to the tuning out of inputs from Washington by the British, once they found that the United Nations was unwilling to endorse their "compromise" solution over the Suez dispute in 1956.

Communication, nevertheless, might be much ado about nothing. It is a high *learning rate* (33) resulting from information-processing that tells us whether decisionmakers will have an adequate image of the situation, as did Kennedy's advisers in the steel price affair. A low learning rate is the effect of misperceptions and distortions and places a decisionmaker in a position where he cannot cope with the situation, no matter how much information is processed. A low learning rate characterized information-processing in the decision to evacuate Japanese from the West Coast of the United States during World War II.

4.5.3 Affective Aspects

Psychological needs often intrude into the focus of a decisionmaker while he attempts to solve a problem. A central decisionmaker's concern

---

[21] The concept of "metacommunication" is used by Ruesch and Bateson to refer to the process of learning how to communicate effectively—that is, the identification of a set of symbols and expressions which will denote and connote the same semantic import between persons engaged in communication. Jurgen Ruesch and Gregory Bateson, *Communication* (New York: Norton, 1951).

over affective needs is rated by reading observational reports and statements by the information-processers in which their perceptions are candidly reported.[22] To replicate Marc Pilisuk, we should code expressions of *risk propensity* (34), *tolerance of ambiguity* (35), and *self-esteem* (36). The riskless selection of Suzuki as prime minister contrasts with the incredible decision not to withdraw 250,000 ill-supplied troops from Stalingrad; ambiguity led to a search for more information in the Cuban quarantine decision and to premature cognitive closure when Dulles announced that the United States would not finance the Aswan Dam; self-esteem was high when the Illinois governor commuted three anarchist leaders' death sentences for their part in the Haymarket Affair, and it was low in the Americans who were prepared to bomb Hiroshima.

To follow up Terhune's investigation, we will also analyze assertions of decisionmakers that express *desires for achievement* (37), *desires for power* (38), and *desires for affiliation* (39). The Bolsheviks, for example, had high needs for achievement and power in 1917; the Eisenhower Administration demonstrated lower needs of this type in deciding not to intervene at Dienbienphu in 1954. British leaders made many affiliative moves to gain support of allies over Suez in 1956, but Dulles exhibited none of these tendencies in turning down the Egyptian application for a loan to build the Aswan Dam.

As Robert North has demonstrated, verbal assertions are useful in deriving ratings for the following: *perceptions of frustration* (40), in which an agent believes that fulfillment of high-priority goals is blocked; and *perceptions of hostility* (41), in which an agent expresses enmity toward a target. Panmunjom negotiations involved both frustration and hostility; satisfaction characterized the decision to nominate Bohlen; friendship, the appointment of Suzuki. Such affective notions as stress, anxiety, and tension are too diffuse to permit precise codings on a judgmental basis, however important they may be for decisions to go to war; we are therefore unable to code them.

4.5.4   Evaluative Aspects

Evaluation during information-processing involves the selection of certain cues, alternatives, and values as most important in determining the eventual decision. As North has found, evaluation sometimes entails much *stereotypic decoding* (42), such that messages are decoded nonveridically

---

[22] For a discussion of problems in using the content of communication as a basis for inferring psychological characteristics, see Michael Haas, "Image and Mood Content Analysis," *Report to the Ford Foundation,* Stanford Studies in International Conflict and Integration, 1962. See also Louis A. Gottschalk and Goldine C. Gleser, *Measurement of Psychological States Through the Content Analysis of Verbal Behavior* (Berkeley: University of California Press, 1969).

in order to conform to preconceived views and contrary information is filtered out or avoided. Filtering was at a low level when the Kennedy Administration decided to support a coalition government in Laos in 1961; but it was higher the following month when alternatives were presented concerning the Bay of Pigs invasion.

A *structured evaluation* (43) is characterized by little uncertainty in formulating alternatives and in establishing a meaningful image of the situation, according to Snyder. The MacArthur dismissal was a far easier option to devise than what role American troops might play in Siberia in 1918. The *range of alternatives* (44) has been suggested as a concept by North, Robinson, and Snyder, who might operationalize the notion by counting the number of options that are analyzed in terms of pros and cons, utilities and disutilities. Few writers describing decisions are explicit on such a number; yet when Congress passed the Selective Service Act in 1948, it did so after voting on over 100 amendments. The governor of Pennsylvania, on the other hand, was faced with a yes-no choice in 1953, when asked either to sign or to veto a bill raising the minimum weight that a truck could haul.

Intraorganizational consonance (45) occurs when decisionmakers agree at all stages on their evaluations, as did Kennedy's advisers in being astonished at the sudden rise in the price of steel in 1962. If there is disagreement, we speak of *contention* in deliberating alternatives; a classic illustration is the contentious truce talks at Panmunjom.[23]

Two variables concerning how decisions finally come about may be added to this list. *Hierarchical resolution* (46) means that the central decisionmaker's own values and preferences are imposed upon other members of the decisionmaking body, or that they even contradict the pressures of public opinion, as when Dulles turned his back on every adviser in turning down the Aswan loan. Dahl and Lindblom have provided a relevant scale that runs from hierarchy, through bargaining, to polyarchy and indicates the extent to which decisionmakers conclude their business by taking in few, many, or a wide range of interests into consideration.[24] Since polyarchy implies veto power by a set of groups, the appointment of Suzuki is clearly nonhierarchical, for he was acceptable to both civilian and military leaders of Japan in 1945.

Our final variable deals with the rationale invoked to legitimize a

[23] Hermann, "Some Consequences of Crisis Which Limit the Viability of Organizations," uses the term "intraorganizational conflict." Hilsman refers to this concept with the term "disharmony." Roger Hilsman, Jr., "Intelligence and Policy-Making in Foreign Affairs," *World Politics,* V (October 1952), 1–45. The term "consonance" is preferred in order to focus on attitudinal symmetry among members of the decisionmaking body.

[24] Robert A. Dahl and Charles E. Lindblom, *Politics, Economics, and Welfare* (New York: Harper, 1953).

decision. *Pragmatism* (47) instead of *ideologism* is present in evaluation insofar as a decision is selected for the purpose of achieving concrete objectives rather than abstract or moral victories. Ideological tinges pervade our image of Chicago police firing upon the Haymarket crowd; but pragmatic and expediential goals prompted the governor of Illinois to commute death sentences pronounced upon three speakers at that rally.

4.5.5 Correlational Results

The violent aspect in the information-processing stage concerns whether a *violent option was considered as an alternative* (48) by the decisionmakers. This we calculate as the percentage of violent alternatives out of all alternatives considered. In correlating information-processing variables, we find that ongoing violence correlates only with perceptions of frustration at a level above + .40 (Table 4–4). If targets threaten violence, there is a tendency for the information processed to be redundant and cognitively inadequate; target and agent will have a low level of metacommunication. A violent trigger to a decisionmaking cycle also entails a propensity to take risks; and there are perceptions of frustration and hostility and desires for power, all within an unstructured evaluative framework. If a violent alternative is suggested as one among a number of options, we should expect high-risk propensities, desires for power, and much hostility toward the target. If war is actually chosen (or an equivalent form of violence at the national or local level) the decisionmaking body tends to be unofficial, processes an insufficient amount of information for the task at hand, takes risks, desires to achieve a new state of affairs in which the agent will have more power, and views the target in a hostile manner.

4.6 OUTCOME CONCEPTS

Once a decision has been made, our interest shifts to events that follow. The impact made by a particular decision is a matter of historical record and will be coded from the perspective of the observer.

4.6.1 Structural Aspects

The "scope of change" is a general term used by Rosenau in classifying outcomes pertaining to the cognitive dimension. Three specific concepts seem relevant, each looking at how component parts or structures within a target are affected. The *penetration* (49) of a decision is high when structures, attitudes, and behavior are modified; low penetration would affect behavior only. The decision not to intervene in Dienbienphu stands far apart in this respect from the Bolshevik plan to seize power in Russia.

TABLE 4–4
Correlations Between Information-Processing Indicators
and Violent Aspects of Decisionmaking

Information-Processing Indicators	Decisional Aspects[a]	*Violent Aspects*			
		Ongoing violence 9	Threat of violence 20	Violence considered 48	Decision for violence 65
21. Size of decision-making body	S	.06	—.12	—.16	—.11
22. Latitude	S	.04	.27	.24	.23
23. Officiality	S	.19	—.33	—.30	(—.45)
24. Authority contracted	S	.11	.07	.24	.28
25. Decision time	C	—.10	—.35	—.20	—.36
26. Cognitive complexity	C	—.14	.38	.32	.30
27. Input load	C	.00	(—.48)	—.15	(—.42)
28. Input intensity	C	—.02	(.50)	.13	.36
29. Input range	C	—.38	.23	.10	.14
30. Inputs/outputs	C	—.17	—.31	—.30	—.25
31. Metacommunication level	C	—.26	(—.55)	—.20	—.36
32. Reduction in communications	C	.05	.04	.23	.25
33. Learning rate	C	—.11	—.31	—.23	—.28
34. Risk propensity	A	.12	(.48)	(.53)	(.53)
35. Tolerance of ambiguity	A	—.07	.08	—.02	—.03
36. Self-esteem	A	—.06	—.29	—.34	—.17
37. Achievement desires	A	.02	.38	.25	.36
38. Power desires	A	.24	(.52)	(.58)	(.64)
39. Affiliation desires	A	—.14	.01	—.08	—.03
40. Perceptions of frustration	A	(.43)	(.41)	.28	.33
41. Perceptions of hostility	A	.14	(.52)	(.55)	(.53)
42. Stereotypy	E	.07	.04	.28	.25
43. Structuredness	E	.00	(—.48)	—.15	—.36
44. Range of alternatives	E	—.04	.27	—.04	.05
45. Intragroup consonance	E	—.27	—.25	—.01	—.15
46. Hierarchical resolution	E	—.25	.22	.36	.34
47. Pragmatism	E	.05	—.21	.10	—.20

[a] For key to symbols see Table 4–2.

The *transience* (50) of a decisional impact applies most specifically to present versus future impacts, thus distinguishing enduring changes from those which are only momentary or temporary. Police who fired upon the Haymarket crowd merely dispersed those who had been listening to the speakers; the Cuban missiles quarantine has had a more permanent effect upon US–USSR–Cuban relations.

A third concept deals with the *procedurality* (51) of a decision; in the case of the Monroney Resolution the outcome was for mere change or re-affirmation in existing rules and procedures; a more dramatic impact would be substantive and concrete in nature, such as Hitler's attack on Poland. (Rosenau uses the terms "specific" and "general" to apply to substantive versus procedural outcomes.)

A final notion, *formality* (52) in decisionmaking, is present when a decision has been recorded in writing and the document has a high proba-bility of being housed within a historical archive. Statutes, thus, are more formal than military orders, which are in turn more formal than decisions announced merely in speeches.

4.6.2 Cognitive Aspects

Under the rubric "duration of controlled change," Rosenau spells out three variables that refer to cognitive aspects of a completed decision. A high degree of *guidance* (53) refers to a situation in which the agent controls the target like a puppet, or controls it by coercive means, rather than being unable to exercise influence upon the target after the decision is made. Bolshevik seizure of power involved guiding the target, the Provisional Gov-ernment leaders, into prison; self-abnegation characterized the Japanese "no comment" reaction to the Potsdam Declaration.

The *revocability* (54) of a decision refers to Rosenau's irreversible–reversible continuum, differentiating permanent impacts (as upon Hiroshima in 1945) from "changes that can be undone by subsequent counteracts."[25] An additional cognitive aspect is whether a decision represents a *turning point* (55), a concept stressed by Boulding, which may be defined as a "con-vergence of events resulting in new circumstances" or as an "important out-come affecting the future."[26] The nomination of Bohlen is only a minor episode in comparison with the Japanese decision to attack Pearl Harbor, for example.

An indispensable cognitive variable is the degree of *success* (56) achieved. To be successful, the means selected should in fact lead to the desired goals; and the specific goals pursued should result in the attainment of ends of an even higher priority. The success of the quarantine of Cuban missiles in 1962 can be juxtaposed with the failure of Hitler's decision not to withdraw 250,000 soldiers who were eventually surrounded inside the Stalingrad area.

25 Rosenau, *The Scientific Study of Foreign Policy*, p. 227.

26 Kenneth E. Boulding, *Conflict and Defense* (New York: Harper, 1962), pp. 250–51. Cf. James A. Robinson, "Crisis," *International Encyclopedia of the Social Sciences* (New York: Macmillan, 1968), III, 510–14.

Implementation speed (57) is fast if made instantaneously after the appearance of a decision, as when the explosion of a bomb led to police gunfire in the Haymarket affair, whereupon the crowd dispersed. A much slower outcome was the interval between passage of the Monroney Resolution and establishment of the International Development Association.

4.6.3 Affective Aspects

The degree of affect associated with an outcome may be measured by devising concepts that approach the "intensity of change" category of Rosenau. Many decisions unveil *sociometric change* (58) when an agent and a target revise like-dislike perceptions of each other. (Rosenau uses a central-peripheral continuum to refer to this concept.) The Bolsheviks did not change their opinions after seizing power in 1917, but Dulles's rebuff of Egypt reversed an earlier friendly policy toward the Arab world.

Continuousness (59) differentiates "changes that unfold without interruption from those that occur only sporadically,"[27] which Rosenau calls a continuous-intermittent continuum in contrast with a direct-circuitous aspect of the intensity of change, the latter referring to "changes that follow from one another and those that do not unfold interdependently."[28] *Cumulativity* (60) seems the most appropriate label for this latter aspect of a decisional outcome. The decision to move truce talks from Kaeson to Panmunjom had a continuous and cumulative impact; but, though the Full Employment Act had continuous ramifications, its effect was felt independently in various sectors of the economy. Continuousness and cumularity are assessed in terms of the affective responses to decisions.

4.6.4 Evaluative Aspects

An objective desired by decisionmakers may or may not, of course, come to pass. Our focus on the actual impact of a decision now turns to the question of values and intentions, which Rosenau calls the "character of change." *Stabilizing* (61) decisions, using Rosenau's integrative-disintegrative continuum, occur when the agent promotes the coherence and cohesiveness of a target, rather than subverting the target. Wilson justified American intervention in Siberia and North Russia as a move to stabilize a chaotic state of affairs, and this objective was achieved; Hitler's decision not to withdraw from Stalingrad had a disastrous effect upon the target of his decision, namely, the German soldiers trapped therein.

If a decision involves *goal-restructuring* (62), which North and

---

[27] Rosenau, *The Scientific Study of Foreign Policy*, p. 226.
[28] *Ibid.*

associates call a "flip" in decisionmaking, then a new ends-means hierarchy will result from the decision cycle.[29] Voluntary repatriation of prisoners of war in Korea was such a restructuring; the veto of the truck-hauling bill in Pennsylvania reaffirmed older values.

A *promotive* (63) decision differs from a *preventive* one, insofar as in the former case (such as the Monroney Resolution) definite steps are taken to bring about a new state of affairs, whereas in the latter situation (for instance, Stalingrad nonwithdrawal) the decisionmaker maintains a status quo and often waits either for the decisional problem to become obsolete or for the decisionmaking stimulus to disappear. In this sense a "decision not to decide" is a preventive one, whereas a "decision to decide" is promotive.

An evaluative counterpart to the concept of success of a decision is *maximizing* (64) versus *satisficing* outcomes, to use Simon's well-known distinction.[30] The resumption of unrestricted submarine warfare in 1917 was aimed at maximizing Germany's chances for victory, but psychological satisfaction was largely derived from passage of the Monroney Resolution.

4.6.5 Correlational Results

The final variable, a *decision for violence* (65), may now enter into the conceptual framework to indicate the violent aspect of decisional outcomes. Along with the remaining independent variables dealing with outcomes, intercorrelations are computed once again (Table 4–5). Ongoing violence predicts only to a tendency to make decisions with a cumulative impact. Threats of violence are linked to substantive, turning-point decisions with destabilizing impacts. When violence is one of the alternatives discussed, the result is nonprocedural, destabilizing, maximizing, and often a turning point in history. When violence is chosen as the decision, we once again find nonprocedurality, turning points, destabilization, and maximizing, but also cumulativity and a high degree of guidance.

4.7 CONCLUSION

This chapter has attempted to present an orderly analytical framework for subsuming existing concepts that describe decisionmaking. Stages in decision

---

[29] North et al., *Content Analysis*. See also Hermann, "Some Consequences of Crisis Which Limit the Viability of Organizations," p. 73, concerning "modification of standards." The reader will note that two of Rosenau's continua, conscious-unconscious and visible-invisible, are omitted from the discussion because they resemble transience and intermittency, respectively.

[30] March and Simon, with Guetzkow, *Organizations*.

TABLE 4–5
Correlations Between Outcome Indicators
and Violent Aspects of Decisionmaking

Prestimulus Indicators	Decisional Aspects[a]	Violent Aspects			
		Ongoing violence 9	Threat of violence 20	Violence considered 48	Decision for violence 65
49. Penetration	S	—.03	.07	.26	.28
50. Transience	S	—.07	—.04	—.05	.03
51. Procedurality	S	—.14	(—.50)	(—.50)	(—.70)
52. Formality	S	—.01	—.21	.09	.00
53. Guidance	C	.13	.17	.33	(.49)
54. Revocability	C	—.02	—.09	—.20	—.20
55. Turning point	C	.21	(.48)	(.45)	(.46)
56. Success	C	—.05	—.04	—0.3	—.08
57. Implementation speed	C	—.04	.28	.17	.23
58. Sociometric change	A	.02	.16	.08	.03
59. Continuousness	A	.38	—.05	—.04	.16
60. Cumulativity	A	(.53)	.23	.15	(.48)
61. Stabilizing	E	—.16	(—.46)	(—.61)	(—.56)
62. Goal-restructuring	E	—.02	.21	.08	.08
63. Promotive	E	.10	—.26	—.20	—.25
64. Maximizing	E	.10	.28	(.50)	(.42)

[a] For key to symbols see Table 4–2.

cycles and aspects of the definition of the situation constitute the two axes of the framework, with concepts located at the intersections in the resulting matrix. Specific concepts have been located within each cell and defined analytically; 32 case studies have been coded judgmentally in accordance with each definition. Affective elements have by and large predicted violent outcomes much more frequently than cognitive aspects among the four main aspects that define a decisional situation.

Because inferences are only to relationships between variables and not to parameters or universes of all possible decisionmaking cases, we should take the correlational findings more seriously than the codings themselves. We should now ask whether our dependent variables are associated with any significant pattern or combination of variables.

The following variables correlate $\pm$ .40 or better with decisions made by an agent already engaging in violence:[31]

---

[31] The $\pm$ .40 level has been selected arbitrarily as a threshold between higher and lower correlation magnitudes for purposes of convenience. If two variables are intercorrelated at exactly .40, we can explain 16 percent of the variance in one by the

   1. Prior lack of cohesion within the agent.
   2. Perception of frustration during information-processing.

If a stimulus threatens violence, the associated conditions include

   1. Cultural dissimilarity between agent and target.
   2. Cruciality.
   3. Low metacommunication between agent and target.
   4. Agent not aligned with target.
   5. Foreign stimulus to decisionmaking.
   6. High need for power.
   7. Perceptions of hostility.
   8. Agent mistrusts target.
   9. Redundant communications during information-processing.
  10. Substantive, rather than procedural, outcome.
  11. Warning signs improperly decoded.
  12. Information underload during information-processing.
  13. High propensity to take risks.
  14. Unstructured information-processing.
  15. The outcome is a turning point in history.
  16. Destabilizing outcome of the decision.
  17. Agent perceives itself to lack control over events.
  18. Perceptions of frustration.

The strength of the correlation is highest for variables at the top of the list and drops off in magnitude toward the end of the 18 variables.

What factors are found when violence is considered as a possible policy outcome during information-processing? Cruciality has the highest correlation, but cultural similarity drops below the $\pm$ .40 level. There are other differences between the previous list of 18 variables and the 13 correlates of violence as an option:

   1. Cruciality.
   2. Agent not aligned with target.
   3. Destabilizing outcome of the decision.
   4. High need for power.
   5. Agent mistrusts target.
   6. Perceptions of hostility.
   7. High propensity to take risks.
   8. Substantive, rather than procedural, outcome.

---

effect of the other. In the following chapter the aim is to increase the amount of variance explained in the dependent variable, violent decisionmaking; the most successful causal model has almost a 95 percent fit with 1 dependent and 4 independent variables.

9. Maximizing, rather than satisficing, outcome.
10. High probability of office-holding.
11. Prior concern with the issue.
12. The outcome is a turning point in history.
13. Cultural dissimilarity between agent and target.

There are 16 correlates of decisions for violence:

1. Substantive, rather than procedural, outcome.
2. High need for power.
3. Agent not aligned with target.
4. Cruciality.
5. Destabilizing outcome of the decision.
6. Perceptions of hostility.
7. High propensity to take risks.
8. Agent guides the target toward an outcome.
9. Cumulative impact of the decision.
10. The outcome is a turning point in history.
11. The decision is recorded unofficially.
12. Prior concern with the issue.
13. Foreign stimulus to decisionmaking.
14. Cultural dissimilarity between agent and target.
15. Information underload during information-processing.
16. Maximizing, rather than satisficing, outcome.

Once again, the top of the list contains the strongest correlates. Even so, it is worth noting that a decision to use violence seldom is satisfying to a decisionmaker; violence is most likely when an issue between nonaligned disputants is of such a high level of priority that the decisionmaker is preoccupied with a need to become powerful enough to coerce the target.

In the following chapter we will seek to determine the empirical underpinnings of these findings through the application of multivariate techniques. Spurious correlations will be transcended as we begin to build a causal model accounting for why violent decisional outcomes are preferred to nonviolent ones.

chapter 5
Dimensions
and Models
of Decisions for War

5.1 RESEARCH STRATEGY

Interpersonal aspects of decisionmaking have been surveyed so far according to the main currents of philosophic speculation. Concern for structure takes the perfectibility thinkers of the Enlightenment into account; cognitive elements are extracted at the suggestion of the modern perfectibility theorists. Augustinian analysis has thrust affective aspects upon us for consideration; and the dualistic tradition of Greek philosophy recommends the evaluative category. Concepts at four major decision nodes have been specified for each of the four facets of decisionmaking; and we have noted that affective concepts correlate with violent decisionmaking somewhat more often than the others. We now turn to a closer examination of these interrelations.

Factor analysis is a technique that extracts underlying clusters of variables and bypasses spurious relations; it will be employed to uncover empirically irreducible dimensions of the data.[1] Cluster analysis, though based on somewhat different assumptions, is similar to factor analysis and can be used to cross-check its results.[2] Both of these multivariate techniques will be used to analyze cases as well as variables. The case analysis is em-

---

[1] The main source on factor analysis is Harry Harman, *Modern Factor Analysis,* rev. ed. (Chicago: University of Chicago Press, 1967).

[2] The particular clustering procedure to be used is known as Cluster IV, which is based on Joe H. Ward, Jr., "Hierarchical Grouping to Optimize an Objective Function," *Journal of the American Statistical Association,* LVIII (March 1963), 236–44.

ployed to find the heterogeneity of our sample of 32 decisions; the variables are examined to find what combinations of basic variable clusters form necessary and sufficient conditions for violent decisions. After a preliminary screening of the data with factor analysis and cluster analysis, we will be in a position to build causal models. Table 5–1 lists each variable and its corresponding reliability coefficient.[3] Table 5–2 maps each variable into the conceptual matrix.

5.2 DIMENSIONS OF DECISION CASES

In selecting the 32 cases, our aim was to represent as large a spectrum of decisionmaking situations as possible; but our sampling perspicacity was based on hunches rather than an exhaustively compiled list of all decisionmaking cases and their respective strata. No census of the universe of all cases is available, and no random sample could therefore be drawn. One of the results of an investigation of this kind is to provide more definitive clues to the ways in which decisions can be classified. Students of crisis decisionmaking, for example, may claim that their findings are not generalizable to noncrisis decisionmaking situations; yet we lack an authoritative definition of "crisis" as well as a consensus on which decisions fall into a crisis or noncrisis category.[4] We now embark on a *Q-analysis,* treating cases as if they were variables over a single time slice.[5]

5.2.1 Procedure

All of the cases were correlated with each other, producing a 32 × 32 matrix of Pearsonian product-moment correlations.[6] This matrix in turn

---

[3] Reliability coefficients were computed using a coefficient of agreement formula: agreements/agreements + disagreements. The present list of variables was expanded from a smaller trial run; reliability coefficients are reported for the trial run and thus represent a subsample of the total variables.

[4] Cf. Charles F. Hermann, ed., *International Crises* (New York: The Free Press, 1973).

[5] Other ways of analyzing the *data cube,* which consists of occasions, entities, and characteristics, include O-, P-, R-, S-, and T-analysis. Below we employ R-analysis, which involves looking at a number of characteristics for many entities, with time held constant. Both Q- and R-analysis together comprise the main types of what has been called *cross-sectional* analysis, as opposed to *longitudinal* analysis.

[6] The Pearsonian correlation is used because the data are normed and normalized; the scale of each case lies between 0 and 6 for all variables, thus making distortion from *outliers* (extreme values) negligible.

TABLE 5–1
Interpersonal Decisionmaking Variable List

Variable Name	Cases	Reliability[a]
1. Prior cohesion	32	
2. Probability of office-holding	31	.82
3. Correct intelligence	32	
4. Warning signs decoded	32	.77
5. Prior concern	32	
6. Precedent invoked	32	.77
7. Prior planning	32	
8. Alignment status	32	
9. Ongoing violence	32	
10. Foreign stimulus	32	.82
11. Cultural similarity	32	.83
12. Power superiority	32	.89
13. Multi-issue	32	
14. Noise level	32	.76
15. Trust	32	.73
16. Control over events	32	
17. Time pressure	32	.82
18. Cruciality	32	.83
19. Level of problem	32	.82
20. Threat of violence	32	
21. Size of decisionmaking body	32	.55
22. Decision latitude	32	.91
23. Officiality	31	.76
24. Authority contracted	32	.75
25. Decision time	32	
26. Cognitive complexity	31	.76
27. Input load	32	.77
28. Input intensity	32	.64
29. Input range	32	.73
30. Input/output ratio	32	
31. Metacommunication level	32	.77
32. Reduction in communications	32	.91
33. Learning rate	32	.91
34. Risk propensity	32	.74
35. Tolerance of ambiguity	32	
36. Self-esteem	32	
37. Desires for achievement	32	
38. Desires for power	32	
39. Desires for affiliation	32	
40. Perceptions of frustration	32	
41. Perceptions of hostility	32	
42. Stereotypic decoding	32	.82
43. Structuredness	32	.77
44. Range of alternatives	32	.85
45. Intraorganizational consonance	32	.85
46. Hierarchical resolution	32	.82
47. Pragmatism	32	.77

TABLE 5-1—Cont.
Interpersonal Decisionmaking Variable List

Variable Name	Cases	Reliability[a]
48. Violent option considered	32	.91
49. Penetration	32	
50. Transience	32	.86
51. Procedurality	32	.86
52. Formality	32	.91
53. Guidance	32	.77
54. Revocability	32	.77
55. Turning point	32	
56. Success	32	.91
57. Implementation speed	32	
58. Sociometric change	32	
59. Continuousness	32	.77
60. Cumulativity	32	.82
61. Stabilizing	32	.77
62. Goal-restructuring	32	.94
63. Promotive	32	.86
64. Maximizing	32	
65. Decision for violence	32	1.00

[a] See Chapter 5, n. 3.

formed the input for a factor analysis, with communalities set at 1.0.[7] A total of 17 principal components were extracted with eigenvalues over 0.0, 9 with eigenvalues over 1.0. Cattell's scree test[8] was applied, and the appropriate cutoff was determined to be at either 7 or 9 factors. The first 9 factors

[7] Principal components are rotated orthogonally whenever the results depart from *simple structure* criteria—and rotated once again to an oblique solution if orthogonal results are not easily interpretable. In most cases the data have been run through several alternative programs and chunking methods to eliminate artifacts from computation. The factor analysis program uses the Householder method of extracting principal components and Kaiser's varimax method of orthogonal rotation. *Communalities* are the matrix entries corresponding to the correlation of a variable with itself; they depart from 1.0 when there is some error in measuring the variable. An *eigenvalue* is the sum of squared loadings for a factor. See note 9 for the calculation of percentages of variance from eigenvalues. *Simple structure* is present in a matrix of factor loadings if all values are near either .00 or .99, there is at least one high-loading variable for each factor, and no variable loads high on more than one factor; these criteria are seldom met, so factor matrices are *rotated,* that is, postmultiplied in such a way that the matrix begins to resemble simple structure.

[8] Raymond B. Cattell, "The Scree Test for the Number of Factors," *Multivariate Behavioral Research,* I (April 1966), 245–76. The conventional 1.0 cutoff leads to few artifacts when principal components are rotated, so the scree test is only useful diagnostically in locating factors that are likely to be tapping random error. The *scree* line is found where the drop-off in successive eigenvalues assumes a straight-line shape.

TABLE 5–2
Conceptual Map of Interpersonal Variables

Definition of the Situation	Prestimulus	Phases in the Decisionmaking Cycle Stimulus	Information-processing	Outcome
Structural aspects	1–2	10–12	21–24	49–52
Cognitive aspects	3–4	13–14	25–33	53–57
Affective aspects	5–6	15–17	34–41	58–60
Evaluative aspects	7–8	18–19	42–47	61–64
Violent aspects[a]	9	20	48	65

[a] This row contains the dependent variables.

were rotated, using Kaiser's varimax orthogonal solution; and results departed enough from simple structure to suggest the utility of an oblique rotation. The 9 varimax factors were accordingly run on Carroll's oblimin program, and biquartimin solution results based on 30 cycles, 4428 iterations, are presented in Table 5–3.[9] The matrix of loadings for each of the 9 biquartimin factors was intercorrelated; and the corresponding correlation matrix was input, with 1.0 as the communality estimate, to a second-order factor analysis; that is, principal components, varimax rotation, and an oblique rotation were performed again, but this time on the factor-loading matrix itself (Table 5–5). Cluster analysis of the original 32 × 32 correlation matrix was the final empirical operation to determine the dimensionality of the cases (Figure 5–1).

5.2.2 Results

Factor I among the primary or first-order factors appears to be a *demarche* dimension, and it accounts for 18.2 percent of the total variance (Table 5–3). The Cuban quarantine, Korea, Hiroshima, Pearl Harbor, and Suez decisions all involved basic decision nodes with violent outcomes and commitments of troops to new courses of action in which an innovative, risky solution was preferred to muddling through. Violent decisions to send forces to Norway and Murmansk load insignificantly, and these are largely

[9] Carroll's program is used throughout this volume. The options selected are as follows: all vectors are initially normalized; the Hestenes–Karush method of calculating eigenvectors is used; a rotation precision stop of .000001, an eigenvector precision stop of .0000001, and a maximum interfactor correlation of ± .75 are specified on the control card. In presenting the results from oblique rotations, the P (pattern) matrix is reproduced in the tables, but interfactor correlations are based on the S (structure) matrix. *Eigenvalues* are based on the principal axis results. *Percent of total variance* is the eigenvalue for any one factor divided by the total number of variables; *percent of common variance* is computed by summing all eigenvalues over 1.0 and dividing any single eigenvalue for a factor by that sum.

TABLE 5–3
Q–Factor Analysis of Decisionmaking Cases

Decisions	h²	Biquartimin Factors[a]									Cases
		I	II	III	IV	V	VI	VII	VIII	IX	
1. Bohlen	.80	−29	−06	(54)	(86)	26	39	22	07	−08	68
2. Quarantine	.77	(82)	06	−18	−16	46	−15	−01	44	−15	68
3. Japan	.70	−00	−15	(81)	48	29	24	00	−19	27	68
4. Draft	.75	−02	−07	(100)	42	12	22	−05	05	19	68
5. Korea	.84	(81)	14	−27	13	48	−25	−01	07	−06	68
6. Monroney	.71	−13	−13	(71)	12	(61)	−00	−04	−06	34	68
7. Employment	.76	04	−06	(102)	29	09	12	−21	05	11	68
8. Hiroshima	.68	(83)	37	−09	−36	12	06	19	18	12	68
9. Suzuki	.71	−23	17	21	(89)	17	26	−08	17	17	68
10. Pearl Harbor	.78	(81)	44	11	−23	01	26	39	−11	19	68
11. Norway	.80	23	23	−07	26	−01	24	(100)	−03	19	68
12. Vietminh	.72	−02	(58)	−00	07	48	−03	−01	38	37	68
13. Aswan	.69	02	(83)	01	41	−05	−13	12	−09	30	68
14. Suez	.80	(83)	31	10	11	18	01	21	01	(−53)	68
15. Laos	.67	31	15	29	21	(61)	05	07	36	(56)	68
16. Bay of Pigs	.66	44	(71)	08	−09	06	−20	18	02	23	68
17. U–Boat	.66	37	(55)	04	15	−05	47	43	−04	−10	68
18. Wilson	.60	(72)	−14	18	15	31	23	−04	17	01	68
19. Murmansk	.79	16	02	25	24	(89)	18	07	00	04	68
20. Siberia	.80	24	−16	21	11	(90)	−11	−28	−03	−03	68
21. Poland	.73	(51)	40	−08	41	−10	−16	(67)	−04	−13	67
22. Stalingrad	.61	10	(80)	−36	03	−01	13	−03	07	07	68
23. Panmunjom	.76	04	−02	−37	27	03	(87)	11	22	04	68
24. POW's	.74	45	−11	(66)	−11	16	(57)	00	−28	−14	68
25. Truckers	.85	−38	24	35	(84)	−03	−16	21	41	−04	66
26. Steel	.76	25	07	−06	46	07	11	−10	(103)	07	68

TABLE 5-3—Cont.
Q-Factor Analysis of Decisionmaking Cases

Decisions	h²	Biquartimin Factors[a]									Cases
		I	II	III	IV	V	VI	VII	VIII	IX	
27. Potsdam	.77	26	(50)	11	−15	34	22	(−58)	35	−20	68
28. MacArthur	.69	17	16	26	(90)	−10	20	22	48	10	68
29. Evacuation	.65	04	32	39	25	07	−00	27	04	(82)	68
30. Haymarket	.67	30	(68)	−32	22	−37	−04	20	16	15	68
31. Oglesby	.66	08	04	27	(95)	24	−14	21	25	−02	68
32. Bolshevik	.54	(76)	02	09	−11	−14	25	12	18	−14	68
Eigenvalues[b]		5.8	4.8	3.4	2.4	1.9	1.4	1.2	1.1	1.0	
Percent total variance[b]		18.2	15.1	10.5	7.6	6.1	4.4	3.8	3.5	3.1	
Percent common variance[b]		25.2	21.0	14.5	10.5	8.4	6.1	5.3	4.8	4.3	

Correlations between
factor loadings

	I	II	III	IV	V	VI	VII	VIII	IX
I	1.00								
II	−.24	1.00							
III	−.45	−.07	1.00						
IV	−.03	−.45	−.24	1.00					
V	−.33	−.22	.06	−.23	1.00				
VI	−.10	−.24	.02	.09	−.07	1.00			
VII	−.21	.33	.24	−.24	−.14	−.19	1.00		
VIII	−.29	.29	.10	−.45	.11	−.30	.26	1.00	
IX	.20	−.35	−.24	.40	−.16	.14	−.27	−.32	1.00

[a] Factor loadings are multiplied by 100; loadings > ± .50 are enclosed in parentheses.
[b] Based on principal axis factors.

tactical decisions. Variables most highly related to Factor I include desires for achievement and power, cognitive complexity, few important decisions competing for attention (low noise), and a turning-point situation (Table 5–4).[10]

Factor II brings together *debacles,* for in each of the high-loading cases the decision led to very unpleasant consequences. The Stalingrad decision isolated a quarter of a million German troops without means of support; Dulles's decision to turn down the Aswan Dam loan application accelerated a series of events that led to the Suez War of 1956. The variables that correlate most strongly with this factor describe makers of debacles as stereotypic, having small regard for allies, and exhibiting a low learning rate based on a small intake of information about the situation.

Status clarification appears to be the common denominator in Factor III. The Hiroshima and Draft decisions defined power status through coercive means; the Employment, Bohlen, Japan, Monroney, and POW decisions were promotive and reached through collegial means. But all of these positive-loading decisions sharpened status relations much more than the ambiguity of the Stalingrad, Panmunjom, and Haymarket decisions, which load negatively. Status clarification decisions are conceived pragmatically and take a long time to be fully implemented, as we discover from correlations in Table 5–4.

Value reaffirmation situations load high on the fourth factor, and most of these involve recruitment as a common theme. The insubordinate MacArthur decision was demotive, the Bohlen and Suzuki promotive; the Oglesby decision resulted in death for some anarchists but a commutation in sentence for others; and the Truckers decision meant that the railroads would continue to prevail over the trucking industry in the economic life of Pennsylvania. Negative loadings pertain to situations in which violent alternatives, with less predictable outcomes, confronted the decisionmakers. Structuredness correlates + .63 with this factor, control over events + .70.

Target-stabilizing underlies the high-loading cases of American intervention in Murmansk and Siberia in Factor V; and the Laos and Monroney decisions are also relevant to this factor label. The only important negative loading is for the destabilizing Haymarket massacre. Stabilizing is associated with such variables as tolerance of ambiguity, a foreign target, and with increased communications throughout the information-processing stage of decisionmaking.

The last four factors are more specific to individual decisions or closely

---

[10] Correlations between variables and loadings may be considered "poor man's factor scores." Were there no missing data, it would be possible to use a regression approach for calculating *factor scores,* which determine weights for each variable on a factor.

TABLE 5-4
Correlations Between 68 Decisionmaking Variables and 9 Q-Factors

Variables	Biquartimin Q-Factors[a]								
	I	II	III	IV	V	VI	VII	VIII	IX
1. Prior cohesion	.22	.07	-.20	-.12	.13	(-.79)	.10	.41	.06
2. Probability of office-holding	.39	-.00	-.17	.20	-.06	-.27	.37	.13	.27
3. Correct intelligence	-.06	-.00	.50	.04	-.31	.29	.36	-.15	-.15
4. Warning signs decoded	-.28	-.06	(.60)	.05	-.17	.19	.35	-.30	-.18
5. Prior concern	(.58)	.10	-.06	-.42	-.26	-.07	-.02	.26	-.27
6. Precedent invoked	.03	-.04	-.21	.25	.17	-.05	.31	-.17	-.33
7. Prior planning	.18	.05	.45	-.25	-.42	.23	.30	-.11	-.08
8. Alignment status	-.41	.34	.35	(.56)	.05	.10	-.12	-.26	.46
9. Ongoing violence	.17	.06	-.26	-.10	-.10	(.64)	-.14	-.31	.12
10. Foreign stimulus	.22	.29	-.30	-.36	.39	-.28	.18	-.09	-.09
11. Cultural similarity	-.27	-.41	.27	(.55)	-.14	.10	.08	.01	.14
12. Power superiority	.07	-.02	-.04	(.57)	-.43	-.47	.27	-.22	.14
13. Multi-issue	.40	-.31	-.01	.02	.21	.03	-.43	-.31	.02
14. Noise level	(-.64)	.09	.38	.07	.26	-.19	.31	-.04	.21
15. Trust	(-.56)	-.26	.32	.37	.33	.05	-.10	-.12	.17
16. Control over events	-.18	-.19	.13	(.70)	-.40	-.14	.19	-.38	.38
17. Time pressure	.41	.05	(-.51)	.04	-.20	-.23	.13	.25	-.18
18. Cruciality	(.60)	.20	-.33	-.40	-.24	.04	.04	.31	-.41
19. Level of problem	.08	.00	.06	-.44	(.60)	-.19	.06	-.13	-.34
20. Threat of violence	(.60)	.19	-.49	-.43	.09	.08	-.16	-.03	.04
21. Size of decisionmaking body	.01	-.37	(.53)	-.19	.21	-.34	-.19	-.04	-.03
22. Decision latitude	-.10	.37	-.34	-.21	.17	(.71)	.32	.28	-.06
23. Officiality	-.01	-.35	.37	.04	.04	-.08	-.37	(-.59)	.20
24. Authority contracted	.24	.38	-.24	-.14	-.37	.26	.27	.03	-.17
25. Decision time	-.21	-.40	(.80)	-.07	.08	-.04	.14	-.15	.01
26. Cognitive complexity	(.69)	-.36	.12	(-.53)	.22	.26	-.01	-.10	.03
27. Input load	-.21	-.46	.30	.47	.01		.13	-.04	-.09

See Appendix D, pp. 571–73, for complete table.

related pairs of decisions; they account for a much smaller percentage of the total variance, and have low correlations with the 68 variables. Factor VI groups two *armistice* decisions that brought the Korean War to a close; there was, of course, much dissensus between the two governments represented at the official truce talks, and these correlates of the sixth factor appear in Table 5–4. *Aggressive* decisions, notably the Norway and Poland cases, load positively on Factor VII, whereas the Japanese decision not to comment on the Potsdam declaration loads negatively. Kennedy's decision to urge the steel industry not to increase its prices in 1962 receives the only significant loading on Factor VIII, though the MacArthur and Cuban quarantine decisions are close to the + .50 level. All three cases involve having a target eventually rescind an action or power status; the gambits were accepted by the target, and a deescalation resulted, so the factor may be described as one denoting *detente*. The final factor lumps together the Laos and Evacuation decisions, which were preventive moves to forestall future mishaps, whereas the aggressive Suez decision was impetuous and therefore loads negatively. Because the evacuation of Japanese nationals and Japanese-Americans from the Pacific coast during World War II appears in retrospect to have been lacking in prescience, this factor would apply to *overcautious* decisions.

The 9 factors do not comprise a readily identifiable set of categories with a mutually exclusive, exhaustive enumeration. Moreover, communalities are so uniformly low that we might expect to discover many more factors if we continued to label beyond Factor IX, hardly a parsimonious prospect. The initial selection of cases was not guided by a sampling logic because no universe of decisionmaking cases has ever been listed or classified. A second-order factor analysis[11] proves to be useful in rising above the first-order factors to a macroanalytic level; so the matrix of 9 factors for 32 cases was itself factor-analyzed (Table 5–5), yielding 3 factors with eigenvalues over the conventional 1.0 cutoff level, after completing 11 cycles and 232 iterations.

Although half of the common variance is accounted for by the first factor, communalities are low and not all of the total variance has been extracted by the 3 factors together. The 3 factors do not exhaust the 32

---

[11] *First-order* factor analysis works from the raw data correlation matrix or some other configuration of raw data. *Second-order* factor analysis starts with a matrix consisting of intercorrelations between first-order factors. *Third-order* factors would be based on interfactor correlations of second-order factors, and so forth. In using first-order oblique factors, the S-matrix is used as the data input to a correlation program, and so on for any other order. The first-order factors are extracted from variables; any other order extracts factors from lower-order factors. The purpose of higher-order factor analyses is to provide an overview of the primary factors so that clues to causal connections may be gleaned.

TABLE 5-5
Second-Order Q-Factor Analysis

First–Order Factors	h²	Biquartimin Second–Order Q–Factors[a]		
		I	II	III
I. Demarche	.70	04	(−83)	07
II. Debacle	.65	(−57)	−00	(52)
III. Status Clarification	.63	02	(80)	03
IV. Value Reaffirmation	.58	(76)	03	08
V. Target-Stabilizing	.85	−31	19	(−87)
VI. Armistice	.38	(58)	34	−01
VII. Aggressive	.57	−29	35	(55)
VIII. Detente	.54	(−72)	09	−06
IX. Overcautious	.47	(59)	−25	−00
Eigenvalues[b]		2.7	1.5	1.2
Percent total variance[b]		29.9	16.8	13.1
Percent common variance[b]		50.0	28.2	21.9

Correlations between factor loadings	I	1.00		
	II	−.43	1.00	
	III	−.27	−.01	1.00

[a] Factor loadings have been multiplied by 100; loadings > ± .50 are enclosed in parentheses.
[b] Based on principal axis factors.

cases, therefore, even though each of the 9 first-order factors has a high loading on at least one of the second-order factors.

Factor I is the most difficult to label, with such wide-ranging dimensions as Value Reaffirmation, Overcautiousness, and Armistice decisions loading positively, while Debacles and Detentes have negative loadings. An *institutionalization* label is most appropriate because the factors with positive loadings deal with decisions made within bureaucratized bodies; and the Debacles and Detentes were all handled by informal, ad hoc groups of decisionmakers who were brought together to deal with important matters that departed from routine decisionmaking tasks.

Strategic decisions identifies the negative linkage between Demarches and Status Clarifications in Factor II. A demarche involves strategic calculations, but a clarification in status between agent and target is purely a matter of tactics most of the time. And, finally, an *instability* dimension corresponds to the third factor, with high negative loading for Target-Stabilizing and positive loadings for Debacles and Aggressiveness.

We may conclude provisionally that the main criteria to consider when sampling decision cases are the nature of the arena, salience of the decision, and the effect on a preexisting equilibrium. The respective strata are institutional-noninstitutional, tactical-strategic, stabilizing-destabilizing. We now compare these results with a cluster analysis of the same 32 decisions (Figure 5–1).

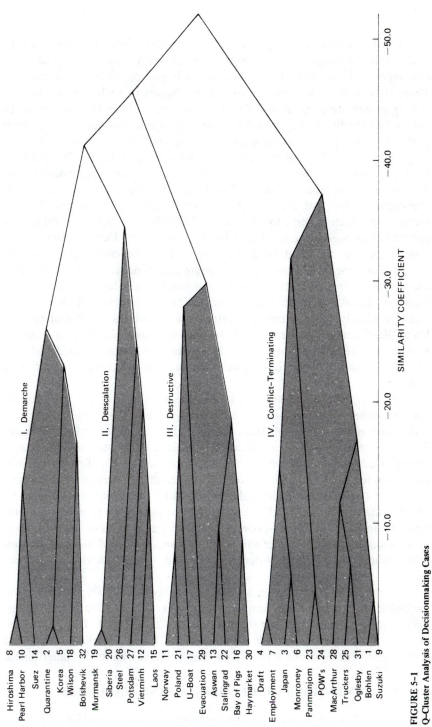

I. Demarche

Hiroshima 8
Pearl Harbor 10
Suez 14
Quarantine 2
Korea 5
Wilson 18
Bolshevik 32

II. Deescalation

Murmansk 19
Siberia 20
Steel 26
Potsdam 27
Vietminh 12
Laos 15

III. Destructive

Norway 11
Poland 21
U-Boat 17
Evacuation 29
Aswan 13
Stalingrad 22
Bay of Pigs 16
Haymarket 30

IV. Conflict-Terminating

Draft 4
Employment 7
Japan 3
Monroney 6
Panmunjom 23
POW's 24
MacArthur 28
Truckers 25
Oglesby 31
Bohlen 1
Suzuki 9

SIMILARITY COEFFICIENT

—50.0   —40.0   —30.0   —20.0   —10.0

FIGURE 5-1
Q-Cluster Analysis of Decisionmaking Cases

137

Cluster analysis decomposes the 32 cases in a binary fashion and supplies a treelike diagram of the point at which each similar group of cases converges with another group until all such groups have finally merged. There is no automatic identification of subclusters in such a procedure, so cutting points are flexible and depend upon one's theoretical interests. In Figure 5–1 the five subclusters that have been shaded do not converge with each other until going beyond a coefficient of similarity of about − 35.0.

Subcluster I, located at the top of the figure, is virtually identical with the highest-loading cases for Factor I in the first-order factor analysis and thus deserves the label *demarche.* Subcluster II brings together the Target-Stabilizing factor and most of the highest-loading cases on the Detente factor; these factors seem to have *deescalation* in common. The third subcluster brings together cases from the Aggressive and Debacle factors; the result looks like the third factor from second-order factor analysis, except for the disappearance of the highest-loading factor, namely, Target Destabilization. A *destructive* label describes the third subcluster most accurately, therefore. Status Clarification and Armistice factors appear in Subcluster IV, followed closely by the final subcluster, which contains cases that tap the Value Reaffirmation dimension. These last subclusters identify a *conflict-terminating* theme that contrasts with the preceding subclusters, which denote situations where conflicts are initiated anew or redefined along different lines.

In short, the cluster analysis locates the first eight of the nine dimensions extracted in the first-order factor analysis, but it puts the clusters together in a manner different from the second-order factor analysis (Figure 5–2). The macroanalytic classification suggested by cluster analysis would appear more oriented toward alternative outcomes. The first three subclusters refer to the magnitude or level of conflict, whether it undergoes escalation (demarche) or deescalation; the final two subclusters inform us whether the conflict was settled destructively or peaceably (conflict termination). Examining the higher-order clusters we find a twofold categorization of decisions—*level of conflict* and *mode of resolution.* And the strata within these rubrics are escalatory-deescalatory and violent-nonviolent, respectively.

We may now proceed to an analysis of the relationship between the variables. A heterogeneous sample permits us to claim that our findings may hold for a large number of cases beyond the sample. But we cannot infer to parameters, since the universe of all cases is unknown and the representativeness of our strata from that universe cannot be determined.

5.3 DIMENSIONS OF DECISIONMAKING VARIABLES

In Chapter 4 we surveyed correlations between the dependent and independent variables, noting which were high enough to warrant a more inten-

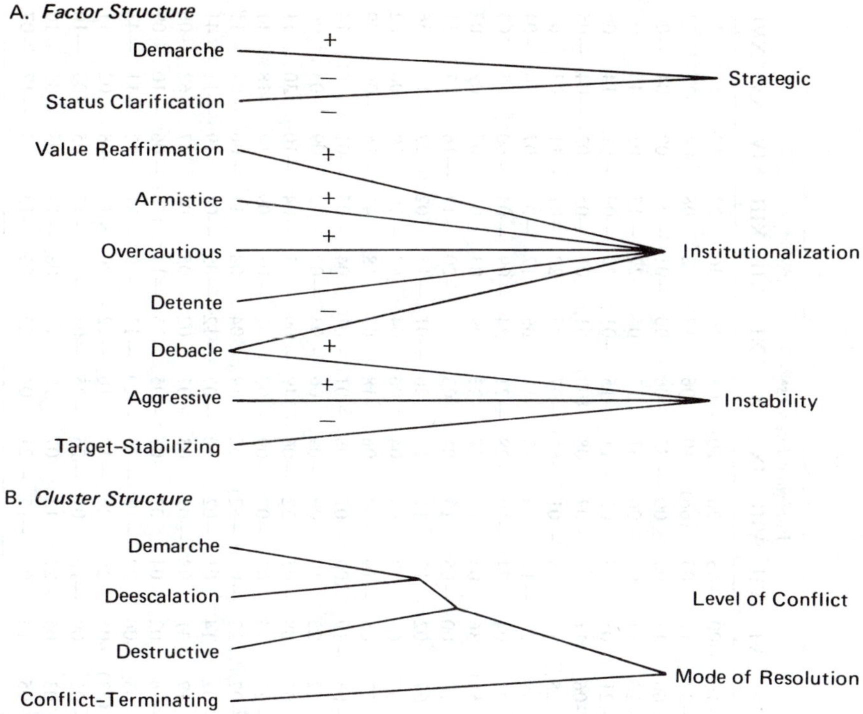

A. *Factor Structure*

B. *Cluster Structure*

FIGURE 5-2
Summary of Q-Factors and Q-Clusters

sive scrutiny. Through factor analysis and cluster analysis we will be able to dimensionalize the variables prior to formulating causal models. We can determine whether the analytic structure used to generate our list of variables is in fact a mapping of empirical factors, as we postulate in Table 5–2.

5.3.1 Procedure

Pearsonian product-moment correlations were computed for all possible combinations of the 68 variables. The resulting 68×68 matrix was factor-analyzed; 35 factors were encountered with eigenvalues above 0.0 and 17 factors exceeded 1.0. According to the scree test, there might possibly be a cutoff at 11 factors, but definitely after 16. A varimax rotation was performed next (Table 5–6), and the results strikingly met simple structure criteria. Oblique rotation was attempted, nevertheless, but all solutions that were attempted had greatly inflated factor loadings in the corresponding P-matrices.[12] The heterogeneity of a 17-factor solution, with the

[12] An *inflated loading* is one exceeding 1.00 by a substantial amount. Inflated loadings and communalities may indicate nonlinearities in the data.

TABLE 5-6
R–Factor Analysis of Decisionmaking Variables

Variables	h²	Varimax Factors[a]																
		I	II	III	IV	V	VI	VII	VIII	IX	X	XI	XII	XIII	XIV	XV	XVI	XVII
1. Prior cohesion	.85	12	−22	−04	06	−16	−00	−46	26	20	−04	19	36	22	12	−11	36	−17
2. Probability of office-holding	.93	27	06	−13	−29	−32	19	05	(66)	10	−06	17	12	08	−04	−25	23	−05
3. Correct intelligence	.85	−06	31	23	−03	−06	13	00	00	(−82)	−06	00	−01	−06	00	−04	−00	−00
4. Warning signs decoded	.90	−24	49	23	−21	−20	−11	02	−06	−41	12	05	−27	−15	01	40	07	08
5. Prior concern	.85	(80)	05	−03	03	−21	−05	−05	02	−11	−15	−01	29	−09	−01	14	06	07
6. Precedent invoked	.86	−03	−02	05	09	−06	11	03	−07	08	(90)	01	−01	−05	−02	−04	−05	07
7. Prior planning	.93	24	37	08	−35	25	12	−13	−01	(−66)	−07	05	22	−01	−11	07	03	07
8. Alignment status	.92	(−63)	13	45	−06	38	20	−10	−09	13	−11	06	12	−08	07	20	−04	−04
9. Ongoing violence	.93	19	−04	−19	−10	22	04	(74)	−19	−28	−21	24	−09	−04	−00	15	03	−04
10. Foreign stimulus	.94	11	04	(−55)	01	(−53)	36	05	−11	27	23	09	03	03	07	09	07	−20
11. Cultural similarity	.88	−26	05	(74)	07	16	00	−05	13	01	03	12	20	−18	−16	27	11	15
12. Power superiority	.96	−11	−03	(62)	−33	−07	−02	−13	11	17	26	−01	−13	02	29	−12	36	−28
13. Multi-issue	.76	14	17	−14	18	03	07	12	−03	−04	−06	−04	(67)	−10	39	00	02	14
14. Noise level	.92	(−73)	18	06	−11	−07	05	−19	−09	06	−18	03	−18	41	−15	−06	09	−13
15. Trust	.96	(−70)	05	22	13	−03	−19	06	−02	08	−01	−01	04	−05	−01	(55)	14	17
16. Control over events	.89	−40	08	(67)	−23	12	25	17	09	−09	06	−03	−07	−12	09	−03	06	−28
17. Time pressure	.94	(52)	−50	03	08	05	08	−07	22	−06	49	09	−03	−04	−10	30	11	−01
18. Cruciality	.94	(85)	−16	−09	12	−23	−14	−07	−03	−09	−00	01	−03	09	14	−18	11	−10
19. Level of problem	.88	04	30	(−52)	36	−02	22	−01	(−52)	−02	19	04	08	11	−06	−01	15	−04
20. Threat of violence	.90	46	−18	(−57)	08	−02	14	01	−02	10	−07	−12	−05	−01	19	−11	41	−23
21. Size of decisionmaking body	.87	−01	(54)	−07	14	17	−31	08	−02	03	−07	02	05	−04	17	62	−06	−02
22. Decision latitude	.86	−02	−26	−19	00	−36	02	04	02	07	−05	05	−14	(70)	−06	−10	09	−30
23. Officiality	.93	−22	(54)	02	05	03	−06	20	−18	−15	−20	−13	−29	−31	17	−11	−43	14
24. Authority contracted	.83	34	−09	02	−39	(53)	−05	25	26	−19	10	−12	20	13	−08	02	−11	−04
25. Decision time	.92	−21	(78)	21	22	−01	−00	−10	01	−26	−25	−05	−06	−13	−05	−03	−10	06
26. Cognitive complexity	.92	45	(58)	−31	19	03	05	−29	13	07	18	17	08	−14	08	09	10	−17
27. Input load	.91	−13	19	(69)	44	05	14	09	−15	−21	04	22	03	−13	03	−17	−07	−04

TABLE 5-6—Cont.
R-Factor Analysis of Decisionmaking Variables

Variables	h²	I	II	III	IV	V	VI	VII	VIII	IX	X	XI	XII	XIII	XIV	XV	XVI	XVII
										Varimax Factors[a]								
28. Input intensity	.90	03	07	-39	28	-12	13	00	19	(51)	-12	25	17	-00	23	27	32	-06
29. Input range	.89	11	41	-16	44	-05	-06	-33	-05	17	28	02	32	-11	32	-09	17	-08
30. Input/output ratio	.95	-13	(64)	26	32	-04	14	11	-06	-03	10	-33	20	-34	04	-14	-09	12
31. Metacommunication level	.93	07	27	(78)	26	-14	-22	-06	04	-13	11	-04	-02	-04	04	10	-15	17
32. Reduction in communications	.94	20	(50)	26	(-68)	-18	08	04	00	-14	07	-07	12	13	-06	07	11	-04
33. Learning rate	.88	-12	25	17	(56)	20	15	06	05	17	24	28	07	42	-01	01	-08	22
34. Risk propensity	.94	(65)	14	-23	-13	-27	04	10	-12	09	-07	-08	04	(52)	15	-06	04	-02
35. Tolerance of ambiguity	.88	13	21	-22	(78)	-09	-13	-03	00	10	04	05	21	-22	08	11	-06	08
36. Self-esteem	.89	-25	-11	45	-26	00	47	26	11	05	29	-33	-14	13	08	09	-05	03
37. Desires for achievement	.92	(66)	23	00	17	23	26	-01	33	13	02	-20	13	-02	06	21	22	02
38. Desires for power	.95	(78)	-08	-02	-32	01	11	19	13	25	05	-03	-16	04	09	-04	24	-02
39. Desires for affiliation	.91	-03	25	-05	(54)	20	-21	03	-01	12	42	12	37	-00	34	04	07	-01
40. Perceptions of frustration	.93	(76)	-06	-22	03	37	15	22	-02	-07	11	01	04	-20	-13	02	-11	-08
41. Perceptions of hostility	.97	(65)	-17	-26	-32	10	-04	03	08	-22	10	-24	02	12	00	-44	09	-05
42. Stereotypic decoding	.89	08	01	-15	(-83)	-22	-05	-00	-16	-00	04	-03	02	-19	-12	-11	00	-16
43. Structuredness	.90	-14	-13	(77)	-20	01	19	06	-03	-17	-08	-07	-30	13	16	-04	-13	07
44. Range of alternatives	.83	10	41	-25	13	40	17	-16	13	01	-33	-30	13	-22	20	15	11	-06
45. Intraorganizational consonance	.91	-04	-40	40	-16	-02	-14	-15	01	44	10	35	14	-23	20	-01	-00	30
46. Hierarchical resolution	.93	11	-19	-07	-19	(-87)	04	-16	-09	07	-06	02	-04	13	05	-02	16	-07
47. Pragmatism	.82	-11	08	12	19	-01	05	-03	09	03	01	(86)	-01	03	-01	03	-04	-06
48. Violent option considered	.87	(57)	-01	-16	-14	-22	-05	-05	01	-14	04	27	-16	02	19	-25	44	-16
49. Penetration	.94	38	18	32	06	-14	25	24	29	07	34	-11	07	05	40	16	25	20
50. Transience	.85	-06	(-66)	00	-19	-14	07	-16	-16	-09	-09	-10	37	-18	-26	19	02	-01
51. Procedurality	.90	-42	13	11	42	04	-26	-03	06	-00	-11	20	-01	-25	-06	-11	(-55)	-04
52. Formality	.95	04	(91)	03	02	-03	-06	-04	-05	-16	09	14	15	01	-02	06	14	03
53. Guidance	.92	30	(52)	11	06	-02	11	25	13	-08	20	11	13	-08	10	03	(59)	15
54. Revocability	.91	-07	-03	-01	34	-14	-26	-06	-36	34	(-55)	12	11	-09	-26	06	-19	-07

141

TABLE 5-6—Cont.
R–Factor Analysis of Decisionmaking Variables

Variables	h²	Varimax Factors[a]																
		I	II	III	IV	V	VI	VII	VIII	IX	X	XI	XII	XIII	XIV	XV	XVI	XVII
55. Turning point	.83	(71)	09	-12	-10	02	05	10	04	16	-26	-07	19	14	29	13	13	10
56. Success	.94	19	07	12	35	18	05	09	(84)	-00	06	07	-06	-03	-02	07	-04	-02
57. Implementation speed	.91	11	(-84)	-06	-15	-18	-11	03	04	13	06	-09	-13	-15	-06	-23	03	-03
58. Sociometric change	.93	01	-09	-02	13	-02	(86)	-05	08	-29	06	08	04	16	-06	-09	04	-15
59. Continuousness	.91	02	13	22	15	04	-03	(83)	15	18	04	-16	-02	03	13	-10	09	10
60. Cumulativity	.90	20	-15	-07	-10	-12	-07	(83)	13	07	16	-01	15	04	-05	-05	09	-13
61. Stabilizing	.85	(-65)	12	07	-19	14	03	-07	-04	-15	08	04	26	-13	13	14	-16	40
62. Goal-restructuring	.93	17	20	02	-24	-01	(78)	-07	02	09	13	00	03	-21	30	-09	09	08
63. Promotive	.84	-05	(63)	05	-05	21	12	06	28	-17	-02	-11	03	-10	11	26	-08	40
64. Maximizing	.91	(63)	31	21	02	02	18	02	28	07	16	25	03	-09	02	18	34	-08
65. Decision for violence	.96	48	-07	-35	-11	-17	-03	23	-06	03	08	-07	-01	05	-02	-01	(68)	-10
66. Extent of documentation	.80	14	10	04	10	-08	11	19	-03	-02	-07	16	06	-19	(71)	04	34	09
67. Academic source	.90	-20	21	16	37	11	-13	-03	-05	03	-00	-09	04	-21	-02	01	-03	(75)
68. Length of description	.94	14	08	11	14	03	05	-11	01	09	07	-12	13	11	(88)	03	-15	-08
Eigenvalues[b]		13.3	9.7	6.6	5.0	3.7	3.0	2.7	2.6	2.4	2.2	1.9	1.8	1.5	1.4	1.3	1.2	1.1
Percent total variance[b]		19.6	14.3	9.1	7.3	5.5	4.5	4.0	3.8	3.5	3.2	2.7	2.6	2.3	2.0	1.9	1.8	1.6
Percent common variance[b]		21.7	15.7	10.7	8.1	6.0	4.9	4.8	4.3	3.8	3.8	3.0	2.9	2.4	2.2	2.1	2.0	1.8

[a] Factor loadings have been multiplied by 100; loadings > ± .50 are enclosed in parentheses.
[b] Based on principal axis factors.

TABLE 5-7
Correlations Between 32 Decisionmaking Cases and 17 R–Factors

See Appendix D, pp. 574–75, for table text.

first factor accounting for only about 20 percent of the total and common variance, meant that a second-order factor analysis was in order (Table 5–8). Cluster analysis rounds out the search for dimensions within the decisionmaking variables (Figures 5–3 and 5–4).

5.3.2 Results

Despite the large variety of definitions of "crisis" that abound in theoretical writings, no empirically based definitions have yet been constructed. When a questionnaire containing definitions of crisis was administered to State Department personnel, the responses fell into a wide distribution.[13] Yet with the 68 variables employed in this study, many of which were chosen from theoretical writings on crisis decisionmaking, it may perhaps not be so surprising that *crisis* is the first factor extracted (Table 5–6). The label crisis seems suitable for encompassing such notions as cruciality, prior concern, desire for power, perceptions of frustration, and low noise level; the factor accounts for 19.6 percent of the total variance. Each of the 32 cases was intercorrelated with loadings from this factor (Table 5–7); and we find that situations that most resemble crises as defined by this factor are the Quarantine, Bolshevik, and Hiroshima cases; the Bohlen, Japan, Monroney, and Suzuki decisions are noncrisis decisions. Most concepts represented on this factor are from the affective and evaluative categories. One of the dependent variables loads moderately high (+ .57)—consideration of violence as a decisional alternative. Crises tend to be associated with violent stimuli and outcomes, but this relationship is not a strong one.

In Factor II structural and cognitive variables at the information-processing and outcome stages load most significantly. *Bottlenecked* decisions are best described by such variables as formality, implementation lag, and a lengthy decisionmaking process. Bureaucratic channels are usually selected for more cognitively complex matters so that they may be broken down into small, specialized tasks. These channels are more likely to allow increases in communication and more inputs than outputs; they also provide the formal machinery to assure that the impact will be more permanent and will guide the target toward a specific goal. Indeed, the situations with the most bottlenecking from our sample were the Draft, Monroney, Employment, and POW decisions; the Haymarket decision, in contrast, was reached on the spot. Bottlenecking is unrelated to decisions for violence.

Clientele decisionmaking emerges as the third factor because it involves both cultural similarity and power superiority of the agent vis-à-vis the target; the agent is able to maintain a high degree of control over domestic

---

[13] Howard Lentner, "The Concept of Crisis as Viewed by the United States Department of State," *International Crises,* ed. Hermann, pp. 112–35.

rather than foreign events. Because of the high loading for structuredness, the label administrative almost seems appropriate; but this would fail to depict some of the cases that correlate most highly (Truckers and Bohlen), and it fails to convey the predominance of stimulus variables on this factor. There is a moderate and negative loading for a decision to use force, so it would appear that a fiduciary role relationship inhibits violence.

Information-processing variables indicating *rationality* load on Factor IV. A high degree of communication, high learning rate, tolerance of ambiguity, and a lack of stereotypy conform to specifications of rationality that have prevailed throughout the administrative science literature.[14] In accordance with this labelling, we find that the most rationally calculated decision among our 32 cases was Wilson's dispatching of American troops to Siberia; the most irrational are Dulles's refusal to finance the Aswan Dam project and the Haymarket massacre, but there is not much of a connection with either violent or nonviolent decisions.

Collegial negotiations between plenipotentiaries as opposed to hierarchical decisionmaking is found on Factor V. Certainly the Korean Armistice decisionmaking body was one of the most collegial in day-to-day operations, whereas the Aswan and Stalingrad decisions were made with very slight consideration for the target and for long-range consequences. Violent decisions load only − .17 on this factor.

A "diplomatic revolution" usually takes place when a country abandons traditional alliance ties and becomes allied with a former adversary. In the sixth factor we encounter both sociometric change and goal-restructuring, and these features make the term *watershed* most appropriate. Examples of watersheds in Table 5–7 are the Pearl Harbor, Vietminh, and Poland decisions; the Truckers and Potsdam decisions involved refusals to cross just such watershed frontiers. Surprisingly, violent outcomes need not be watersheds.

Factors VI and VII are concerned with outcomes; but if change is the motif of the Watershed factor, continuity is the essential element in Factor VII. Impacts that are continuous and cumulative, notably those made in wartime, possess *implementation complexity*. The Stalingrad decision was the most difficult to execute, especially in sending food and supplies to the beleaguered army; the veto of the Truckers legislation obviated any administrative follow up. Given the + .23 loading for a decision to use coercion, it appears that such a choice can often be difficult to implement.

Beyond the seventh factor, the choice of names is simplified because one variable has such a high loading on the factor that it is uniquely identified with that dimension. Factor VIII, for example, has only one high loading

14 Cf. Paul Diesing, *Reason in Society* (Urbana: University of Illinois Press, 1962).

(+ .84 versus + .66 and − .52). If we tag the factor as *successful* decision-making, we can observe that success is most likely when the decisionmaker has been in office for a long time, and when the target is domestic rather than foreign. Such an interpretation enables us to account for the high correlation between this factor and the Bolshevik decision to seize power, which was eminently successful against a domestic target and was made by persons who remained long in power. Japan's Potsdam nondecision, patently unsuccessful vis-à-vis a foreign adversary, was announced by Suzuki, who had only recently assumed the precarious role of the premiership. Aggressive decisions are unrelated to success across the entire sample of cases.

Unexpected decision situations, with incorrect prior intelligence and a lack of prior planning, correspond to Factor IX. The Korea and Quarantine decisions involve the highest degree of surprise, but the public nature of protracted truce talks in Korea made the Panmunjom and POW decisions much easier to foresee. Surprise need not evoke violence, for the loading of the decision for violence variable is close to .00.

History-mindedness links the invocation of precedent with irrevocability in Factor X. Although the precedent-invoking variable loads + .90, much higher than the − .55 loading for revocability, it is clear that the latter implies precedent setting. In addition, if we examine cases that correlate negatively and positively, it is difficult to conceive of any in which more attention was paid to the past than in Eden's obsession with the parallels between Nasser and Hitler when he decided to use force at Suez; in the Employment and Potsdam cases, there was no source of past wisdom to guide the decisionmakers. But, contrary to the counsel of Edmund Burke, violence is unrelated to history-mindedness.

Pragmatism codings comprise the unique element in Factor XI. Whereas the Hiroshima and Steel decisions were conceived to be pragmatic, the Haymarket decision concerning anarchists and Wilson's calculations prior to entering the "war to end all wars" had definite ideological elements. Violent decisions are neither wholly pragmatic nor ideological, however.

The *multi-issue* variable is highest on Factor XII, but the low magnitude of that loading (+ .67) accounts for the fact that this variable has the lowest communality among the 68 variables. Wilson's decisions are the highest correlated cases, which is consistent with his well-known penchant for bringing as many ramifications as possible into consideration. Decisions for violence are found equally as often among single- and multi-issue situations.

Imperious decisions seem to be defined by a high loading for decision latitude (+ .70) and a moderate loading for risk-taking (+ .52) in Factor XIII. The Stalingrad decision was imperious to a considerable extent, in contrast to the mutual deference that prevailed in the armistice negotiations

that ended the Korean War. An aggressive decision is unrelated to impe-
riousness, nevertheless.

Two of the data quality control variables load on Factor XIV, number
of footnotes and total wordage. That this factor, which may be called
ethnographic extensiveness, is separate from all other factors indicates that
the structure of relationships between variables has not been an artifact of
information available for coding. The Korea decision, presented with documentary richness by Glenn Paige, tops the list of cases that correlated
positively with this factor; the skimpiest case-study material dealt with the
American decision not to assist the French in fighting the Vietminh at
Dienbienphu.

Consensus decisions appear on the fifteenth factor, which underlies
both target-agent mutual trust and agents with many persons in the decisionmaking body. The Draft, Monroney, and Suzuki decisions were made
through much discussion with the relevant interests; initially divergent preferences finally came together into acceptable compromise solutions of the
decisional tasks. The Aswan and Stalingrad decisions involved unilateral
actions despite the dissenting views of advisers. Violent decisions are unrelated to the degree of consensus.

Aggressiveness is found on Factor XVI as a dimension, with violent
decisions loading + .68, guided outcomes + .59, and procedurality − .55.
A decision to use violence entails guiding a target in a substantive manner.
The Panmunjom and Japan decisions were deescalatory and correlate negatively with this factor; Hitler's decision to attack Poland has the highest
positive correlation. Of most interest to us here is that a decision to initiate
aggression does not necessarily involve Crisis, Bottlenecked, Clientele, Rational, or the other types of decisionmaking that are specified by the remaining factors extracted in this analysis.

The final factor has one main variable uniquely loading at a high level
—*academic source.* Negative correlations with this case are found in studies
that were published by persons who were neither historians nor political
scientists. Considered as a separate factor, it follows that the nature of a
writer's academic credentials does not necessarily distort the description of
a case study by consistently prejudicing the evaluation by an observer in
any consistent direction.

Extracting 17 factors from 68 variables is only possible if there is much
heterogeneity in the data, despite the relatively narrow range of 6-point
scales used for the variables. The utility of a second-order factor analysis is
immediately evident, especially since the dependent variable in which we are
most interested ended up almost isolated from the rest on Factor XVI. The
results of the second-order analysis are presented below (Table 5–8). A
Pearsonian correlation matrix with 1.0 in the diagonal was factor-analyzed.
The first 17 factors, all with eigenvalues over 0.0, accounted for 100 percent

TABLE 5–8
Second–Order R–Factor Analysis

		Biquartimin Factors[a]					
First–Order Factors	h²	I	II	III	IV	V	VI
I. Crisis	.67	—07	(75)	—21	—04	—03	21
II. Bottlenecked	.60	(79)	00	10	—17	13	—15
III. Clientele	.73	02	(—79)	—04	—01	—03	28
IV. Rationality	.68	34	—07	28	15	(53)	—26
V. Collegiality	.50	(64)	—16	—00	—01	10	18
VI. Watershed	.58	31	04	07	(—70)	08	26
VII. Implementation Complexity	.51	—12	—08	(—72)	06	11	—03
VIII. Success	.59	—03	07	04	07	—00	(78)
IX. Unexpected	.69	(—53)	08	12	35	(56)	04
X. History-Mindedness	.41	—09	—14	—07	—21	43	31
XI. Pragmatism	.59	—17	—19	(75)	—06	03	07
XII. Multi-Issue	.52	17	44	10	49	12	16
XIII. Imperious	.46	(—59)	—03	19	—17	10	02
XIV. Ethnographic Extensiveness	.57	16	11	—15	—14	(73)	—05
XV. Consensus	.54	16	—06	09	(60)	—16	43
XVI. Aggressiveness	.57	—18	(54)	04	—08	08	41
XVII. Academic Source	.59	27	—28	—32	49	14	11
Eigenvalues[b]		2.8	1.9	1.6	1.4	1.1	1.0
Percent total variance[b]		16.6	11.1	9.6	8.0	6.4	6.0
Percent common variance[b]		28.6	19.4	9.8	14.3	11.3	10.2

Correlations between factor loadings

I	1.00					
II	—.40	1.00				
III	.01	.03	1.00			
IV	.54	—.28	.34	1.00		
V	—.04	.22	.21	.16	1.00	
VI	—.28	.07	—.32	—.49	—.28	1.00

[a] Factor loadings are multiplied by 100; loadings > ± .50 are enclosed in parentheses.
[b] Based on principal axis factors.

of the total variance, but 6 factors had eigenvalues over 1.0. The 6 principal components were rotated orthogonally, using Kaiser's varimax criterion; an oblique solution was attempted, and the biquartimin factors are based on 30 cycles, 2536 iterations.

Decisions that are Bottlenecked, Collegial, Expected, but not Imperious load on Factor I, which may be called a *channelled* dimension. This factor brings together mostly structural attributes and information-processing variables.

Factor II appears to have *disputatiousness* as the common denominator, with high loadings for the Crisis, Nonclientele, and Aggressive dimensions, and a moderate loading for Multi-Issue situations. There is a broad representation from the conceptual map of Table 5–2, with somewhat more affective variables.

Tactical decisions are defined by the linkage between Implementation Simplicity and Pragmatism in Factor III. Only four variables are relevant to this second-order factor; half are from affective aspects of the outcome stage, but the other half are from different stages and facets.

The fourth factor combines the Nonwatershed, Multi-Issue, Consensus, and the Academic Source factors, with variables from a wide variety of cells in the conceptual map of Table 5–2. Bargaining or *polyarchic* decision-making covers the first three factors, but the appearance of a data quality control factor (Academic Source) demonstrates that a political scientist or historian is more likely to analyze this type of decision than a military scientist or theologian.

Information-processing and prestimulus stages are most clearly associated with Factor V, which has high loadings for the Rational, Unexpected, History-Mindedness, and Ethnographic Extensiveness factors. Rational responses to unexpected situations, which are perceived in terms of precedents from the past, seem to have *adaptiveness* in common. And such decisions are written up much more extensively in the sample examined in this study.

The final second-order factor has a very high loading for Success but moderate loadings for Consensus and Aggressiveness. This would lead to the inference that one way to ensure successful aggressive moves is to receive widespread support from decisionmaking bodies. But this observation does not assist us in labelling the factor, which the word *coup* describes most adequately, though not entirely satisfactorily.

Because an overview classification of these 6 decision types is not readily apparent, one procedure is to examine the interfactor correlations. From a third-order factor analysis, based on a quartimin rotation of 11 cycles, 29 iterations (Table 5–9), a two-fold classification emerges. *Incremental* or stopgap decisions are suggested by the first third-order factor, which has positive loadings for Tactical and Adaptive decisionmaking but a negative loading for Coups. *Resolvative* or conflict-terminating variables are grouped together in the second of the two third-order factors: Channelled and Polyarchic decisions that are not Disputatious imply a concerted effort to routinize, to apply fair procedures of bargaining, and to avoid an ideological freezing of options for a peaceful resolution of conflict. The main dimensions of decisionmaking, in short, involve a contrast between settlements and modi vivendi. Some decisions are made once and for all, with full agreement among the respective parties, but in other cases a more ambiguous process leads to a temporary outcome until the basic conflict erupts anew. Aggressive decisions are associated more with the resolvative

TABLE 5–9
Third–Order R–Factor Analysis

		Quartimin Factors[a]	
Second–Order Factors	h^2	I	II
I. Channelled	.69	03	(—83)
II. Disputatiousness	.64	31	(78)
III. Tactical	.47	(69)	04
IV. Polyarchic	.75	49	(—66)
V. Adaptiveness	.55	(72)	29
VI. Coup	.61	(—68)	31
Eigenvalues[b]		2.2	1.5
Percent total variance[b]		36.8	25.1
Percent common variance[b]		59.5	40.5
Correlations between	I	1.00	
factor loadings	II	—.29	1.00

[a] Factor loadings are multiplied by 100; loadings $> \pm .50$ are enclosed in parentheses.
[b] Based on principal axis factors.

than with the incremental category, and aggression decreases the chances for conflict resolution.

But before postulating a causal interpretation of the antecedents of international conflict, a cluster analysis of the 68 decisionmaking variables will shed considerable light (Figures 5–3 and 5–4). We note, first of all, that the variables cluster at much higher coefficients than do the cases; and the two main clusters merge at the — 129.37 level. With — 65.00 as an approximate cutting point for delineating subclusters, we find that 11 groups can be shaded.

The uppermost subcluster in Figure 5–3 contains most of the variables that load high and positively on Factor II from the factor analysis, so the *bottleneck* label applies here as well. Subcluster II looks like the fifth second-order factor, uniting elements from the Rationality, Ethnographic Extensiveness, and Multi-Issue factors. We might conclude that well-documented decisions are more likely to appear rational and involved because of a selection process in which only complicated decisions attract scholarly interest— or the rhetorical skill of a writer of a large monograph may find a rationality and complexity that is not immediately apparent to the author of a shorter study. The label *cognitive differentiation* seems especially appropriate because of the multi-issue variable. A subset of the variables that load on the Crisis factor are found together in Subcluster III, mostly those with negative loadings. We find, for example, that political scientists and historians are more apt to write up decisions in which the target and agent are not adversaries. We might call the subcluster one of "amity"; the respective outcomes are usually favorable to both target and agent, and they are planned amid

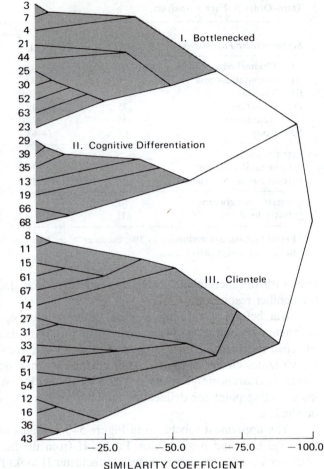

Correct intelligence	3
Prior planning	7
Warning signs decoded	4
Many decisionmakers	21
Many alternatives	44
Long decision time	25
High inputs per output	30
Formality	52
Promotive	63
Officiality	23
Wide input range	29
Affiliation desires	39
Tolerance of ambiguity	35
Multi–issue	13
International problem	19
Many footnotes	66
Many words	68
Aligned status	8
Cultural similarity	11
High trust	15
Stabilizing	61
Academic source	67
High noise	14
Many inputs	27
Metacommunication	31
High learning rate	33
Pragmatism	47
Procedurality	51
Revocability	54
Power superiority	12
Control over events	16
High self–esteem	36
Structuredness	43

I. Bottlenecked

II. Cognitive Differentiation

III. Clientele

−25.0   −50.0   −75.0   −100.0

SIMILARITY COEFFICIENT

FIGURE 5-3
R–Cluster Analysis of Decisionmaking Variables: I

other more pressing matters. Had the subcluster contained variables that indicated the agent's fiduciary capability, we would have had the Clientele factor all over again. Many such variables of administrative decisions do appear in the fourth and fifth subclusters, so there is no escaping the *clientele* label for Subclusters III to V together.

Having now reached the end of the first major cluster, the theme underlying Bottlenecking, Cognitive Differentiation, with Clientele decision-making, is Weberian rationality.[15] We observe an administrative structure

---

[15] Cf. Max Weber, *Theory of Social and Economic Organization,* trans. A. M. Henderson and Talcott Parsons (New York: The Free Press, 1968).

which perceives its constituents in a benign manner while it plays routine roles in a complex social process; political fences are mended, and nearly everything looks proper. Our second main cluster, on the other hand, contains ingredients of decisions made under conditions of uncertainty and suspense. It is in the latter type of situation where violence is found.

Solidarity is found on the first subcluster in Figure 5–4, which contains two of the three key variables that load negatively on Factor V and a third that indicates agent likemindedness. Variables that load negatively on the Rationality factor show up in Subcluster II in Figure 5–4 along with two

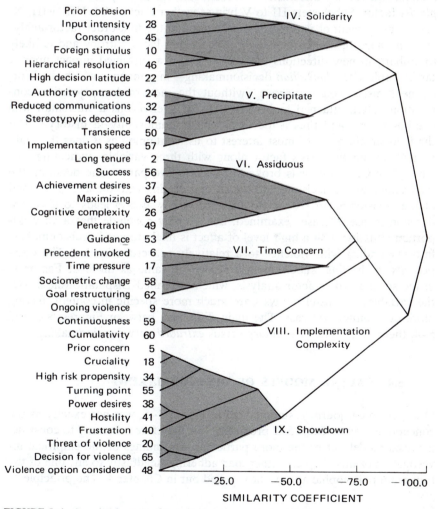

FIGURE 5–4
R–Cluster Analysis of Decisionmaking Variables: II

variables that have negative loadings on the Bottlenecking factor: *precipitate* decisions involve fast implementation, contraction of authority, reduction in communications, stereotypy, yet a short impact on the target. The merger of these first two subclusters results in an *imperative* cluster. In the third sub-cluster, two variables from the Success factor merge with a set that portrays a decision in which the agent considers many intellectual facets in order to maximize his values by manipulating the target to some degree; the adjective *assiduous* becomes an appropriate label. *Time concern* emerges on the fourth subcluster as the union of the Watershed and History–Mindedness factors, and the tiny Subcluster V is identical with the *implementation complexity* factor. Subclusters III to V bring together Factors VI, VII, VIII, X, and an assortment of variables from Factor I in the first-order factor analysis. An image of a decisionmaking process that lacks entropy and is likely to embark in new directions in order to effect a sustained impact upon a target implies *Machiavellian* decisionmaking—in a manner which the Florentine himself would approve (without the modern-day pejorative connotations often attached to his name)—for it envisions a statesman who manifests virtù and thus achieves a secular immortality in history.[16] But the final subcluster is of most interest to us, containing as it does the main variables from the Crisis factor along with three variables indicating violence. The Crisis factor is broken down into two parts—one denoting the importance of the decision, and the second dealing with the affective mood of the decisionmaker. A violent stimulus nearly always leads to a violent decision in the 32 cases examined, but we may conclude that a very important situation with a high level of affect is likely to goad decisionmakers into responding with violence to a relatively peaceful stimulus. The components of the final subcluster are nearly the same as those of Factor II in the second-order factor analysis, which we called Disputatiousness. But the variables of cluster analysis are much more specific in content, having more of a *showdown* cast. The main difference between Figures 5–3 and 5–4, therefore, is one of *ordinary* versus *extraordinary* decisionmaking.

5.4   CAUSAL MODELS OF DECISIONMAKING

Our conceptual journey, summarized in Figure 5–5, was not exactly as the conceptual map of Table 5–2 predicted. It is therefore necessary to construct a causal model out of the more particularistic findings of the empirical investigation of this chapter, rather than adhering steadfastly to any one of the four main philosophic approaches spelled out in Chapter 4. The principle of

---

[16] Cf. Sheldon S. Wolin, *Politics and Vision* (Boston: Little, Brown, 1960), Chapter 7.

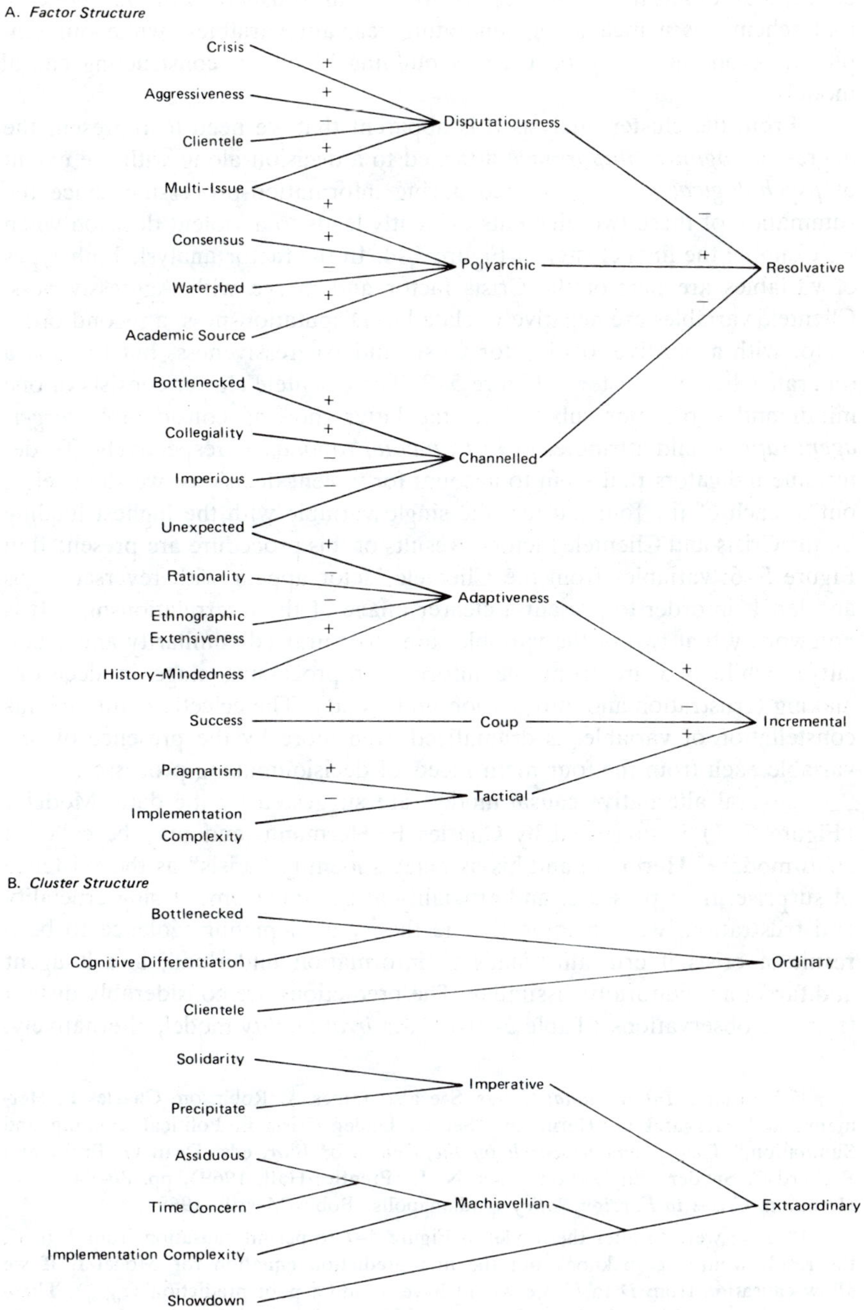

A. *Factor Structure*

Crisis ⟍ +
Aggressiveness ⟍ +
Clientele ⟍ −   Disputatiousness
Multi-Issue ⟍ +
Consensus ⟍ +
Watershed ⟍ −   Polyarchic ————— + ————— Resolvative
Academic Source ⟍   Watershed +   −

Bottlenecked ⟍ +
Collegiality ⟍ +   Channelled
Imperious ⟍ −
Unexpected ⟍ +
Rationality ⟍ −   Adaptiveness
Ethnographic ⟍ +
Extensiveness
History–Mindedness ⟍   +
Success ———— + ———— Coup ———————— − ———————— Incremental
Pragmatism ⟍ +   +
Implementation ⟍ −   Tactical
Complexity

B. *Cluster Structure*

Bottlenecked ⟍
Cognitive Differentiation ⟍   Ordinary
Clientele ⟍

Solidarity ⟍   Imperative
Precipitate ⟍
Assiduous ⟍
Time Concern ⟍   Machiavellian   Extraordinary
Implementation Complexity ⟍
Showdown ⟍

FIGURE 5-5
Summary of R-Factors and R-Clusters

153

conceptual dualism encourages us to remain satisfied with our conceptual scheme as a means for generating relevant variables, while our empirical taxonomies may be used as building blocks in constructing causal models.

From the cluster analysis it is apparent that we need to represent the degree of *cognitive importance* attached to a decision along with the extent of *psychological affect* generated during information-processing, since the summation of these two elements evidently leads to a violent decision when we examine the final cluster in Figure 5–4. In the factor analysis both types of variables are part of the Crisis factor and merge with Aggressiveness. Clientele variables are negatively related to Disputatiousness, a second-order factor with a positive loading for Crisis and Aggressiveness, but there is a separate Clientele cluster in Figure 5–3. The Clientele cluster consists of one minor and two major subclusters, the latter showing considerable *target-agent rapport* and attributes of *instrumental rationality,* respectively. To determine indicators that seem to account for violent decisions, we shall select out of each of the four clusters the single variable with the highest loading on the Crisis and Clientele factors. Results of this procedure are presented in Figure 5–6; variables from the Clientele factor appear with reversed signs and labels in order to present a clearer image of the interrelationships. It is noteworthy that two of the variables are structural (dissimilarity and cruciality), while two are from the information-processing stage in decision-making (frustration and information underload). The eclectic nature of this constellation of variables is dramatized even more by the presence of one variable each from the four main facets of decisionmaking processes.

Several alternative causal models are suggested by the data. Model I (Figure 5–7) is suggested by Charles F. Hermann, and may be called a *crisis* model.[17] Hermann and his associates identify "crisis" as the existence of surprise, time pressure, and cruciality at the same time. Using cruciality and frustration, we can interpret the theory as depicting violence to be a result of crisis if cruciality leads to information underload, and if agent and target are culturally dissimilar. The predictions are considerably distant from the observations (Table 5–10).[18] An *irrationality* model, alternatively,

[17] Hermann, *International Crises.* See also James A. Robinson, Charles F. Hermann, and Margaret G. Hermann, "Search Under Crisis in Political Gaming and Simulation," *Theory and Research on the Causes of War,* eds. Dean G. Pruitt and Richard C. Snyder (Englewood Cliffs, N. J.: Prentice-Hall, 1969), pp. 80–94; C. F. Hermann, *Crises in Foreign Policy* (Indianapolis: Bobbs-Merrill, 1969).

[18] If we were to alter the model in Figure 5–7 to permit causation from F to C, the result would be to knock out the first prediction equation for Model I. If we allow causation from D to U, we would have to add a poor prediction $(r_{dv \cdot u})$. These permutations would not be inconsistent with Hermann's model, but they clearly would not improve the degree of fit.

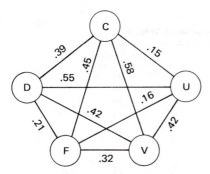

FIGURE 5-6
Variables Selected for Models of Violent Decisionmaking

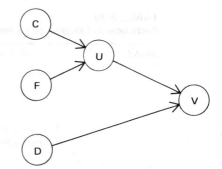

FIGURE 5-7
I Crisis Model of Violent Decisionmaking

Key:

Numbers represent correlations.
C = cruciality (var. 18).
D = dissimilarity (var. 11).
F = frustration (var. 40).
U = underload (var. 27).
V = violent decision (var. 65).

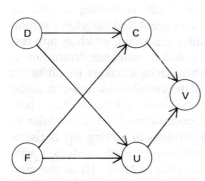

FIGURE 5-8 II
II Irrationality Model of Violent
Decisionmaking

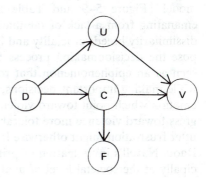

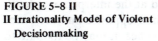

FIGURE 5-9
III Cultural Exchange Model of Violent
Decisionmaking

may be constructed from the writings of Robert North and his collaborators
(Figure 5-8).[19] Perceptions of frustration and cultural dissimilarity jointly
produce violence if intervened both by information underload and by cruciality in Model II, but only half of the results are empirically satisfactory

---

[19] These references are cited in Chapter 3, n. 53. See also the appendix to Robert
C. North et al., *Content Analysis* (Evanston, Ill.: Northwestern University Press,
1963).

TABLE 5–10
Predictions and Degrees of Fit for Interpersonal Models

Model	Prediction	Observation
I	1. $r_{cf} = 0$	.45
	2. $r_{cd} = 0$	.39
	3. $r_{df} = 0$	.21
	4. $r_{du} = 0$	.55
	5. $r_{cv} \cdot {}_u = 0$	.58
	6. $r_{fv} \cdot {}_u = 0$	.28
II	1. $r_{df} = 0$	.21
	2. $r_{fv} \cdot {}_{cu} = 0$	.04
	3. $r_{dv} \cdot {}_{cu} = 0$	.05
	4. $r_{cu} \cdot {}_{df} = 0$	—.12
III	1. $r_{dv} \cdot {}_{cu} = 0$	.05
	2. $r_{df} \cdot {}_c = 0$	.04
	3. $r_{fv} \cdot {}_c = 0$	.08
	4. $r_{cu} \cdot {}_d = 0$	—.08
	5. $r_{fu} \cdot {}_d = 0$	.05

(Table 5–10).[20] A better fit results from application of a *cultural exchange* model (Figure 5–9 and Table 5–10), in which everything is seen as emanating from a lack of familiarity between agent and target.[21] Cultural dissimilarity breeds cruciality and information underload, which in turn dispose the decisionmaking process toward a violent outcome; frustration is seen as an epiphenomenon that results when decisionmakers let off steam while making important decisions, but it is the calculations rather than the emotion which point toward violence. An emotional outlet could make progress toward violence more tolerable at a subconscious level; a condition of utter frustration might otherwise lead to a paralysis in making any decision. Raoul Naroll's investigation of primitive warfare,[22] though conducted principally at the societal level of analysis, substantiates Model III as the most satisfactory among the causal models constructed at the interpersonal level. As decisionmakers gain more empathy toward their opposite numbers, violence should decline. Once a decisionmaker is in office, it may be too late to bring about such an expansion in his horizons; so the voter casting his

20 If we change the position of *D*, such that it points causally only to *F*, the fit would be much poorer.

21 Such a theory has been espoused most eloquently by Robert Angell, especially in "Discovering Paths to Peace," *The Nature of Conflict*, ed. International Sociological Association (Paris: UNESCO, 1958), pp. 204–23; Angell, *Peace on the March* (Princeton: Van Nostrand, 1969).

22 Raoul Naroll, "Deterrence in History," *Theory and Research on the Causes of War*, eds. Pruitt and Snyder, pp. 150–64.

ballot for peaceful decisionmakers should take into account the candidate's broadness of exposure to different cultural patterns. This finding, incidentally, accords with our summary of characteristics of doves in the public opinion studies cited in Section 3.3.1.

Even so, the fit between prediction and observation is hardly perfect,[23] and points the way toward refining our conceptions of how violent decisions are made. Mathematically, Model II is overidentified; but reality, too, may be overdetermined.[24]

What is missing from the models is a more thorough treatment of prestimulus factors, many of which are societal in nature. We now turn to a fuller examination of conditions present in societies that might predispose their respective decisionmakers to embark upon war. International behavior may be analyzed at several levels at the same time, and variables pertaining to each level may make their own distinct contributions to the incidence of international violence.

[23] It is utopian to expect perfect fit between theories and data in any case, so one ordinarily accepts models in which one does not encounter a "significant" difference between predictions and observations. But the meaning of the concept of significance is contingent upon both internal and external checks. The *internal* check consists of comparing degrees of fit between alternative models and accepting the one with fewer differences between actual and expected values; the *external* check is concerned with whether use of the model will lead to desired consequences, such as alerting decisionmakers to sources of violent decisions which could be avoided. A third check might be to employ *another research technique*. Accordingly, the Simon-Blalock analysis was cross-checked with Boudon's dependence analysis, and no differences were observed. See Hubert M. Blalock, Jr., *Causal Inferences in Nonexperimental Research* (Chapel Hill: University of North Carolina Press, 1961); Raymond Boudon, "A New Look at Correlation Analysis," *Methodology in Social Research*, eds. Hubert M. Blalock, Jr., and Ann B. Blalock (New York: McGraw-Hill, 1968), pp. 199–235.

[24] Blalock states the requirement of proper *identification* for any equation in a causal model as follows: "the number of endogenous variables appearing in this equation cannot exceed by more than one the number of exogenous variables that have been left out of the equation." See Hubert M. Blalock, Jr., "Theory Building and Causal Inferences," *ibid.*, p. 164. Meanwhile, Karl Deutsch has suggested that there is no way to avoid overidentification (overdetermination) in causal models of human behavior. For example, an automobile accident may be caused by any one of the following elements: road conditions, traffic engineering on the highway, mental state of driver X, mental state of driver Y, weather, condition of car X, condition of car Y. Only one of these factors might account for an accident on one occasion, but on some occasions a multiple set of conditions might be responsible; none is a necessary condition, but any set of them might constitute sufficient conditions. Despite such a formalization of the possible causal paths, two drunkards driving jalopies during foggy weather might fail to perceive all sorts of signs and yet reach home safely. See Karl W. Deutsch and Dieter Senghaas, "Towards a Theory of War and Peace: Propositions, Simulations, and Reality," paper presented to the Annual Convention of the American Political Science Association, New York, September 1969.

PART III
States and Societies

chapter 6
Theories
of Societal Factors

6.1 INTRODUCTION

An analysis which focuses on personality and role factors that account for the development of crisis and noncrisis situations into wars, will never transcend idiosyncratic characteristics of decisionmaking situations. Why do crises develop in the first place? Why do decisionmakers prone to bellicosity or compromise come to power at various times? In the United States, for example, one of the familiar charges against the Democratic party has been that it is the "war party" because Democratic presidents have served during the two world wars and the Korean and Vietnamese conflicts. What is often forgotten, however, is that reformist leaders are more apt to be elected during times of domestic stress, which in an economically interdependent world are likely to be times of external disturbances.

A decisionmaker, in short, occupies a role with functions and expectations that vary according to the preferences of the electorate or a set of individuals capable of removing him from office and who, reciprocally, lend support to policies believed to be worthwhile. Although nonspecific public moods have little direct impact on foreign policy decisions, leaders undoubtedly read public opinion polls and other indicators of mass sentiments in order to appraise which alternative courses of action are likely to be tolerable or intolerable to the public at large. The public does set some constraints on policymakers insofar as it narrows the range of possible foreign policies. It has been claimed, for example, that public sentiment in England and in the United States in the mid-1930s so constricted the range of choices that government leaders were unable to cope effectively with the threat of

161

Hitler's Germany.[1] When public moods are pacifistic, a government's bellicose stand can only be an empty bluff, particularly in a democracy.

Appraising public aspirations may indeed be the most important
cognitive problem that confronts an elite, since failure to fulfill various
expectations will mean a more precarious tenure in office. Preferences, in
turn, depend upon social conditions and cultural values. One would anticipate very few changes in cultural norms over a unit of time in contrast with
the greater fluctuations in social factors. Within a country the probability
of war may be hypothesized to relate to variations in aspects of social reality
that stimulate changes in public moods. But what sorts of conditions must
be present in societies to make an aggressive foreign policy appear as a
useful escape from, or fulfillment of, national problems?

Since the dawn of civilization many societal conditions have been perceived to be related to fluctuations of war and peace. Among preliterate
peoples the factor cited most often as responsible for propensities to external aggression is the desire to preserve tribal solidarity.[2] Armed clashes of
the ancient empires of Egypt, Assyria, Babylon, Persia, Macedon, and Rome
were conscious attempts to suppress insurrections and external sources of
potential imperial disunity.[3] In the sixteenth and seventeenth centuries, when
religious sentiments and dynastic claims were invoked to legitimize European wars, more outbreaks of international aggression occurred than in any
previous era of history.[4] One of the reasons for such turbulence in foreign
affairs was that European monarchs were consolidating control over states
wherein the papacy and Emperor lost an authoritative role. From 1618
until the middle of the seventeenth century, the Thirty Years War erupted
as a culmination of the period of the Wars of Religion; in order to negotiate
peace, a conference was convened in the province of Westphalia in 1648.
The Peace of Westphalia terminated the long series of wars by sanctioning
the legitimacy of sovereign territorial states independent of the Holy Roman
Empire and of the papacy. The territorial state system agreed to at Westphalia initially made it possible for religious differences to be resolved short

---

[1] E. H. Carr, *The Thirty Years' Crisis*, 2d ed. (London: Macmillan, 1954);
George L. Grassmuck, *Sectional Biases in Congress on Foreign Policy* (Baltimore,
Md.: Johns Hopkins Press, 1951), pp. 113–32; Frederic R. Sanborn, *Design for War*
(New York: Devin–Adair, 1951); William L. Langer and S. Everett Gleason, *The
Challenge to Isolation, 1937–1940* (New York: Harper, 1952).

[2] Quincy Wright, *A Study of War*, 2d ed. (Chicago: University of Chicago Press,
1965), p. 78; Robert F. Murphy, "Intergroup Hostility and Social Cohesion," *American Anthropologist*, LIX (December 1957), 1018–35.

[3] Abba B. Bozeman, *Politics and Culture in International History* (Princeton:
Princeton University Press, 1960).

[4] Pitirim A. Sorokin, *Fluctuations of Social Relationships, War, and Revolution*
(New York: American Book Company, 1937), pp. 297–98.

of war by an acceptance of the Erastian principle that a secular ruler's religious preference constituted the official faith for the realm. By the end of the eighteenth century there was a fading away of purely dynastic quarrels as limited monarchies and constitutional forms of government became more widespread. Nationalism and imperialism flourished in the nineteenth century and encouraged decisionmakers to use military means for seemingly just goals. Ideologies extolling particular forms of political and economic arrangements have been utilized in the twentieth century to sanction both internal and external war.[5]

Parallel with the changing course of international history, writings of prominent theorists from Plato through Lenin have linked societal conditions within states to the aggressive behavior of governments in foreign affairs. A brief codification of such theory may serve as a useful step in setting the stage for research.

6.2   THEORIES OF SOCIETAL FACTORS IN WAR AND PEACE

Throughout writings of theorists who relate domestic conditions of states to warlike behavior, various internal factors have been stressed at different times. We may divide the thinkers into three groups. The earliest theorists lacked full knowledge of the consequences of industrialization. A second group, the utopian socialists, wished to reject dehumanizing aspects of industrial society. Marxists, thirdly, felt that war is a concomitant of the historical process until the arrival of the final stage in history, the communist epoch. The most common arguments among all three groups of thinkers have been that war is a function of governmental or of economic conditions.

6.2.1   Early Theorists

Plato advised Greek city-states that one of the best ways for avoiding war would be to have a cohesive people and an economic system with a moderate level of consumption.[6] A loyal citizenry would be necessary to deter attacks, whereas a moderate level of prosperity would mean that a state would have little marginal economic utility to gain from war and at the same time would not be attractive bait for states desiring booty.

Although Plato regarded democracy as an unstable and warlike form of government, to such philosophers of the Enlightenment as Immanuel Kant,

[5] Raymond Aron, *The Century of Total War* (Garden City, N. Y.: Doubleday, 1954).

[6] Plato, *The Republic,* trans. Benjamin Jowett (Garden City, N. Y.: Doubleday, n.d.), pp. 64–67.

Jeremy Bentham, and Thomas Paine, the lesson that the hypertrophy of dynastic war taught was that republics with representative institutions are more peaceful than monarchical despotisms.[7] Aristocratic elites are warlike and oppressive, so new elites must be installed, the argument went. By reducing governmental restrictions on the citizenry and by establishing popular sovereignty, with a share in decisionmaking extended to all young men who might be conscripted into a country's armed forces, chances of war would decrease. There would be fewer internally generated political tensions to release externally, and no sane man would vote to go to a frivolous war that might mean his death.

The economic aspect of Plato's advice also was modified by later thinkers. Advocates of economic liberalism believed that profits are more abundant when the international environment is stable. Internally, capitalist nations would be so preoccupied with economic development that foreign adventures would be unnecessary diversions from ordinary business pursuits. Indeed, according to classical economists and sociologists such as Adam Smith, Saint-Simon, Auguste Comte, and Herbert Spencer, conquests for economic gain seemed to characterize poor agrarian countries rather than industrial societies, where enrichment is secured most efficiently through extensive economic production and trade.[8]

The overall consensus among early nineteenth-century theorists of interstate relations, then, was that democracy and capitalism would be harbingers of international tranquility. But there was dissent from this view from two camps—from utopian socialists and from communist theorists. Representatives of these two schools of thought never analyzed international conflict at length in any single book, but their critiques of previous speculation rested on entirely new premises and perspectives.

6.2.2 Utopian Socialists

Utopian thinkers apotheosized the tranquil life of villages as contrasted with harsher aspects of urban industrialization. Believing in Rousseau's theory of the desirability of small polities, wherein democracy alone had been thought possible, utopian socialists sought to establish small industrial communities.[9] Communal living would be more enriching intellectually and meaningful personally, and social pressures to conform would be more effec-

---

[7] Kenneth N. Waltz, *Man, the State, and War* (New York: Columbia University Press, 1959), pp. 82–83.

[8] Edmund Silberner, *The Problem of War in Nineteenth Century Economic Thought*, trans. Alexander H. Krappe (Princeton: Princeton University Press, 1946).

[9] Jean-Jacques Rousseau, *The Social Contract*, trans. G. D. H. Cole (New York: Dutton, 1950); Robert L. Heilbroner, *The Worldly Philosophers* (New York: Simon and Schuster, 1953).

tive and acceptable than the sterile, impersonal forces that keep large industrial societies in operation. If decisionmakers far removed from the concerns of the working man could so easily impose decisions to go to war upon a population under capitalism, the phalanstères of Fourier and the communities of Robert Owen promised to abolish elites entirely. An equality among men in material goods and resources, as well as in social standing, would assure democracy and peace. The utopian socialist attack on capitalism was largely moral: dehumanization of man, according to the utopian socialists, seemed too high a price to pay in order to bring prosperity to a few. But the ideal life was envisioned as a return to a style of life that had long since disappeared irreversibly wherever capitalism had become established.

6.2.3 Marxist Theory

Except for the youthful lapse into utopianism in *The German Ideology* (1846), Karl Marx and Friedrich Engels realized that a return to the community was impossible.[10] The allegedly honest village peasant had been transformed into a cog in industrial society along with the city dweller. Thomas Hardy's rural Tess of the D'Urbervilles was as much victimized by forces beyond her control as Charles Dickens's urban Oliver Twist.

According to the Marxian dialectical view expressed in the *Manifesto* (1848), one economic system will be more peaceful than its antecedents, but that system has not yet arrived. War accompanies class struggles of precapitalist and capitalist societies; but in a communist world there are no classes, so there are no wars. Under communism both aristocratic tyranny and bourgeois democracy will be transcended. The most peaceful political system is one with no visible government at all. Under communism there will be no elites to compel men to fight, and there will be no states to attack or to defend. But, unlike the utopians' ideal, industrial progress will continue at a more democratic pace in large-scale communist societies.

Even as bourgeois society progresses toward communism, war will be less of a problem. Marx acknowledges that capitalism is more peaceful than feudalism. His reasoning is based on the view that communism can emerge only when capitalism has developed to the fullest extent. As soon as bourgeois society's internal contradictions reach a maximum, capitalism will collapse. While capitalism spreads globally, its inner logic for the establishment of a single world market economy will result in a breakdown of na-

[10] Karl Marx and Friedrich Engels, *The German Ideology*, ed. R. Pascal (New York: International Publishers, 1965); Marx and Engels, *Manifesto of the Communist Party* (New York: International Publishers, 1948); Marx, *Capital*, trans. Samuel Moore et al. (Chicago: Encyclopaedia Britannica, 1952).

tional barriers for the movement of goods and persons across territorial boundaries. The need for the multistate system sanctioned at Westphalia will disappear as capitalism becomes more internationalistic. Separate national characteristics will vanish, and close economic and political cooperation between capitalists in many lands will give rise to a universal bourgeois culture. In a world of fewer differences and more interdependence among states, wars will decline for both social and economic reasons.

At the same time, war-breeding economic crises may occur due to internal contradictions of bourgeois principles. According to Marx's data presented in *Capital* (1859), crises do not result from a worsening of economic conditions for the working class. Economically, the proletariat actually improves before crises. But because capitalism is not coordinated by altruistic men, there are times when more goods are manufactured for consumers to buy than their wages permit. Overproduction triggers economic collapses, which on occasion lead to war. Why so? According to bourgeois economics, Marx and Engels point out, demand in a "free" market cannot be controlled—by definition. The volume of supply is determined by capitalists' crystal-balling about the size of consumer needs. But there are only four ways of restoring to equilibrium an economic system with a surplus of supply over demand. Supply may be decreased (1) by destroying goods, or (2) by wrecking means of production; but since such action diminishes future sources of profits, capitalists usually prefer to increase demand (3) by exploiting old markets more thoroughly, being careful that the proletariat does not become too powerful, or (4) by seizing new markets through war. International violence may take the form of colonial acquisitions or forcing other nations to adopt bourgeois methods.

Marx evidently predicted that the operation of the dialectical process in history would mean that some day all states would become capitalist. To Lenin, the process should and could be shortened. By the early twentieth century, he commented in *Imperialism* (1917), few of the four techniques for handling crises were available any longer.[11] Competition among giant economic units had advanced so far that all available markets had been exploited. Even with members of the upper proletariat "bribed" by the bourgeoisie with generous wages, thereby expanding profits obtainable in the so-called free market, "trustworthy" internal markets had at last become saturated with economic goods. Greed for more profits could be satisfied only by subjugation of other countries, in other words by stealing markets from capitalists of other lands. A tranquil international arena had become impossible: wars were fought by each newly emerging capitalist state for redivisions of economic spoils. Unlike Marx, Lenin was suggesting that capitalism would entail more, not fewer, instances of international aggression,

---

[11] Vladimir I. Lenin, *Imperialism* (New York: International Publishers, 1939).

since one by one each country would adopt capitalist economic methods and, when more economically developed, engage in war to further its own commercial ends.

The First World War, to Lenin, was an imperialist attempt to "seize lands and to conquer foreign nations, to ruin competing nations, to pillage their wealth," and it was also a war "to divert the attention of the laboring masses from the domestic political crises."[12] The effect of the war in ineptly ruled and discontented Russia was to exacerbate social unrest. When Lenin came to power in 1917, he withdrew the Soviet state from the war in order to consolidate the socialist revolution in his native land. Observing participation by members of socialist parties on both sides of the European conflict, Lenin realized that the war fulfilled yet another function: namely, "to disunite the workers and fool them with nationalism, to annihilate their vanguards in order to weaken the revolutionary movement of the proletariat." Why did revisionist socialists in Europe allow nationalist loyalties to override ideological convictions that capitalist states are unworthy of support? The answer seems to be that in England, France, and Germany alike, opposition by socialist parties to entry into the war would have been interpreted by the public at large as treason; the popular appeal of the socialist movement in each country would otherwise have been undermined, so doctrine yielded to expediency. For Lenin, however, a "betrayal of socialism" was possible because the proletariat failed to become class conscious. As he foresaw, when socialists attempted to set up workers' states in Germany and Hungary after the war, the communist movement proved too weak and was defeated easily.

As class conflicts have been minimized in the twentieth century by the gradual acceptance of socialist and welfare-statist ideas in countries with large capitalist classes, it is true that Marxist and Leninist theory may have lost much of its relevance as a diagnosis of modern problems. Indeed, as economic prosperity has risen throughout developed countries, Daniel Bell has argued, attention to ideology appears to have declined.[13] But the Marx who saw historical trends as superstructures varying with underlying changes in social and economic conditions does remain influential. Subsequent theoretical analyses of war's relation to societal factors have done little more than to expand, to rephrase, or often to negate Marxist hypotheses.

12 Vladimir I. Lenin, "The War and Russian Social-Democracy," *Selected Works*, ed. J. Fineberg (New York: International Publishers, 1935), V, 123.

13 Daniel Bell, *The End of Ideology* (New York: Collier, 1962); cf. Seymour Martin Lipset, *Political Man* (Garden City, N. Y.: Doubleday, 1960), Chapter 13. For a statement that brings Marx up to date, see Karel Kára, *Journal of Peace Research,* V, No. 1 (1968), 1–27. It should be noted that ideology is reasserting itself in the world today in the form of an antiestablishmentarianism: see Henry S. Kariel, ed., *The Political Order* (New York: Basic Books, 1970).

6.3 APPROACHES IN SOCIETAL ANALYSIS

Despite the fact that Marx pioneered in developing concepts, models, and propositions now widely used within sociological theory, there is some ambiguity in his original formulation. On the one hand, he talks of ruling classes as welcoming war to forestall impending revolution or to extend the scope of capitalism. On the other hand, he assigns primacy to the type of economic system, inasmuch as he believes that capitalism requires antagonistic relationships between men in order to operate. In short, there are at least two perspectives on the possible relation between internal factors and war, each of which involves a very different analytical approach. Focusing on objectives invoked by elites or non-elites to legitimize the use of force may be referred to as the *functional approach*.[14] A functionalist searches for a link between various types of goals espoused by decisionmakers and the relative necessity of using war to achieve these goals. The second approach, a search for societal conditions that dispose elites to perceive that aggression is necessary or legitimate, is the *prerequisites* approach. The functional approach is used to analyze individual cases; but, as will be seen shortly, it is not very useful in discovering regularities in behavior. The prerequisites approach concentrates on aggregate characteristics present in countries that enter war but which are absent among countries avoiding war.

6.3.1 Functional Approach

According to functionalists, especially those prominent in the time of German Chancellor Bismarck, war is a technique of internal statecraft to be employed when states find it either useful to increase cohesiveness or profitable to be victorious.[15] In other words, war is justified in terms of social and Realpolitik consequences. Let us examine some of these arguments more specifically.

Because morale is an important component of national power, cohesive states are often in an advantageous position if they wish to go to war. Similarly, potential aggressors may avoid combat with states that possess internal solidarity. On the other hand, countries may be so content internally

---

[14] The *functional* approach differs sharply from the *structural-functional* approach. The former seeks to discover relationships between variables of any sort, while the latter asks what functions for a system are performed by particular structures. Robert K. Merton is an exponent of the functional approach in his *Social Theory and Social Structure*, rev. ed. (New York: The Free Press, 1957). Gabriel Almond and others have employed structural-functionalism, which is discussed more intensively in Chapter 10 of this volume.

[15] Georg Simmel, *Conflict*, trans. Kurt Wolff (New York: The Free Press, 1955), pp. 92–93; Friedrich von Bernhardi, *Germany and the Next War*, trans. Allen H. Powles (London: Arnold, 1914).

that no excuse for international misbehavior will present itself. Apparently disagreeing with Chinese views on the subject at one time, Soviet Russian ideologists do not want internal social progress to be interrupted by wars with no constructive purposes.[16] The "new Soviet man" is supposed to be more humanistic because socialist methods of economic production are not based on the antagonisms that are supposed to beget brutishness in capitalism.

Domestic disturbance is associated with war and peace, too. Societies with internal difficulties can be confronted with war because of military weakness. When political demonstrations broke out in Switzerland in 1802, Napoleon dispatched 20,000 men to obtain an "armistice," which brought the Alpine land under French domination.[17] Large nation-states with vexing domestic problems (modern Asian countries, for example) are difficult for another country to control by bayonets. In short, in some cases internal weakness appears to invite war, and in others it deters external aggression.

War may have a different effect upon elite and non-elite groups in a society. One theory is that the masses alone improve their lot in wartime at the expense of the ruling classes. To ensure wartime unity, an elite may feel compelled to grant political and religious concessions and to distribute income more equitably.[18] If an elite fails to provide tangible rewards, it may be overthrown by a more radically attuned counterelite, as in Russia in 1917. In class struggles of the Greek city-states a discontented faction out of power sometimes would make common cause with external enemies; the former would go on strike as foreign soldiers approached the city's gates, forcing the ruling faction to capitulate.

An alternative hypothesis, namely, that economic elites use international aggression to their own selfish advantage, is a central theme in Marxist theory. Wars are supposed to enable elites to emphasize patriotic feelings over class consciousness, hence delaying and obscuring class conflict and social revolution. Imminence of war can be a justification by elites for jailing potential dissenters and for discouraging opposition so that a country does not appear divided. A state in constant readiness for war can make infringement of liberties seem necessary, though anxiety created by governmental surveillance may reduce internal support, leading to even further restrictions.[19] Because expert elite leadership is needed more in a crisis than

[16] Nikita S. Khrushchev, *The Worker* (New York), July 28, 1963.

[17] J. F. Maurice, *Hostilities Without Declaration of War* (London: Her Majesty's Stationery Office, 1883), p. 35.

[18] David Ricardo's thesis that income is distributed more equitably in wartime is examined in Silberner, *The Problem of War in Nineteenth Century Economic Thought,* Chapter 2.

[19] Harold D. Lasswell, *World Politics and Personal Insecurity* (New York: McGraw-Hill, 1935).

in normal times, rulers also might consider it to their own best interest to make themselves indispensable by engineering a popularly supported war. Another postulated function of war is that of a safety valve to drain off tension that might be dangerous to an elite.

Finally, one could point out that war can be either beneficial or detrimental to elites and non-elites at the same time. Victory may be profitable, and defeat may have a latent function of triggering industrialization in order to recover what has been lost in territory or prestige.

In summary, all of the above considerations, or "reasons of state," could be taken into account equally well by leaders of countries in justifying either a peaceful course of action or entry into war. If the nature of political arguments is unrelated to substantive policy decisions, we may conclude that the functional approach does not lead very far scientifically. The underlying conditions which prompt war, rather than the verbal rationale for war, may instead be linked more closely to the roots of international aggression. It is to these factors that we now turn.

6.3.2 Prerequisites Approach

Theories concerning necessary and sufficient societal conditions for international aggression have not been tested until very recently. Types of political and economic systems have been discussed as prerequisites to war from Plato through Lenin, but the Marxist concept of internal contradictions has seldom been analyzed in rigorous terms.

For each of the types of societal factors there is a growing body of theory. It has been claimed that democratic, authoritarian, and totalitarian political systems have more or less congeniality to decisions to enter war. The wealth of a country and the role of government in the economy have been hypothesized to relate to propensities for international aggression. Asymmetrical societal conditions—such as economic depressions, revolutions, or very rapid social change—are assigned primacy by other theorists.

Unlike functional theory, however, much of prerequisites theory has been undergoing a thorough examination, made possible by advances in techniques of data processing. Methodological advancement, however, has outdistanced the ability of researchers to make conceptual sense out of their findings. A review of the empirical literature will be postponed until the following chapter, in order to explicate the basic concepts here.

6.4 SOCIETAL CONCEPTS

What are the main dimensions of social and political reality? One of the most perplexing obstacles that impedes the systematic study of societal factors in international relations is the absence of a parsimonious conceptual map of the terrain. Inquiries concerned with the relation between various characteristics of societal systems and international behavior all too frequently talk past each other because a Babelish confusion in language has arisen, albeit unwittingly. To those employing various social theories, the conceptual horizon superficially appears rich.[20] One can deal with such notions as "heterogeneity," "diffusion," "instability," "disorganization," "dissensus," "disharmony," and many more such terms and their antonyms. But on closer examination we find that some words are used interchangeably, often merely for the sake of literary variety; and definitions vary widely even when they are made explicit. Investigators fail to communicate with one another because the same terms evoke different or confused meanings. Cumulative research into a very large body of related scholarship has been almost impossible on an interdisciplinary basis, since the various conceptual formulations have failed to build upon each other.

To take one of the better examples, Robert Dahl and Charles Lindblom hypothesize the following:

> Disparities in income are often a source of tension in society, and this in turn is a source of political instability through a breakdown of agreement.[21]

But what precisely are "disparities," "tension," "instability," and "breakdown of agreement"? The task of operationalization, Dahl and Lindblom would argue, is a separate and important problem but one different from that of suggesting testable propositions. On the other hand, many possible indicators could be selected to represent each concept in concrete, measurable terms. Inevitably, an inference that the findings of a particular study are consistent or inconsistent with the Dahl–Lindblom hypothesis runs into trouble because their formulation is ambiguous in the first place.

In a critique of the term "integration" in international relations, Werner Levi points out that seemingly well "integrated" societies contain, nevertheless, many less "integrated" features:

> Citizens cherish varying and sometimes contradictory verbal symbol systems, engage in competitive activities, or extend no concern whatever to each other in their daily behavior. Moral values and practices differ. Economic ideals and goals clash. There are race hatreds and minority discrim-

---

[20] The most significant conceptual schemes and compendia are as follows: Arthur S. Banks and Robert B. Textor, *A Cross-Polity Survey* (Cambridge: MIT Press, 1963); Karl W. Deutsch, *Nationalism and Social Communication* (New York: Wiley, 1953); Amitai Etzioni, *Political Unification* (New York: Holt, Rinehart and Winston, 1965); A. D. Hall and R. R. Fagen, "Definition of System," *General Systems Yearbook*, I (1965), 18–28; Fred W. Riggs, *Administration in Developing Countries* (Boston: Houghton Mifflin, 1964).

[21] Robert A. Dahl and Charles Lindblom, *Politics, Economics and Welfare* (New York: Harper, 1953), p. 139.

ination. Political ideologies are in conflict. There is even the occasional use of violence without serious damage to the continuity and viability of the basically peaceful society.[22]

Again, we find such phrases as "contradictory," "competitive," "differences," "clashes," "hatreds," "discriminations," "conflict," "damage," and "continuity." Since the terms are left undefined, they will succeed in communicating the same message only if their sense is somehow held in common within the scholarly world. Unfortunately, no such clarity exists at present; the purity of lexical definitions has been eroded because of uncoordinated efforts by individual researchers within a plethora of noncumulative, ad hoc, single-concept studies.

Such terminological difficulties arise because there are few a priori conventions for distinguishing between concepts. Once again, we find that it is necessary to construct a property space that will subsume concepts. Seventy or more words that are commonly used by researchers in the societal level of analysis are reducible to three analytically independent types of notions that may be applied to the analysis of any system:

1. Attributes.
2. Dimensions.
3. Patterns.

The words "attribute," "dimension," and "pattern" are primitive terms that may be grasped most vividly by examining their generic subtypes. Formally, an *attribute* is analytically conceived as a basic property of a system. A *dimension* is a conceptual locus for an attribute. A *pattern* refers to a mathematically expressible arrangement of units within a system.[23] The patterns of "symmetry" and "asymmetry" are used for a comparative analysis of societal characteristics of states and international behavior. A more detailed presentation of each of the three sets of metaconcepts is contained below.

6.4.1 Attributes

An *attribute* of a system is a basic element common to all actors or units with systems. Within social and political systems there would appear to be at least six fundamental attributes:

---

[22] Werner Levi, "The Concept of Integration in Research on Peace," *Background,* IX (August 1965), 111.

[23] The usual interpretation of such terms as "attribute," "dimension," or "pattern" in analysis theory is that they constitute analytical constructs. "Attributes," in other words, are not real in a metaphysical sense but are merely categories invented as convenient handles to facilitate systematic analysis. See David Easton, *A Framework for Political Analysis* (Englewood Cliffs, N. J.: Prentice-Hall, 1965); Hall and Fagen, "Definition of System."

1. Resources.
2. Demotypes.
3. Attitudes.
4. Behavior.
5. Functions.
6. Structures.

A *resource* is a nonhuman element, or reservoir of human brawn, that can be energized to perform work on behalf of a system.[24] Income, uranium, untapped water power, and other physical means to achieve abstract ends are examples of resources.

When a statement is made about the racial composition, sex differences, age levels, or aggregated level of group activity, it deals with human genotypes or phenotypes. Lacking a word in our vocabulary to refer to macroanalytic characteristics of groupings of individuals, we propose the term *demotype*. A demotype is a general category (of which genotypes and phenotypes are subtypes) that refers respectively to constitutional features of human beings which originate either through heredity or are acquired within a particular culture. Race, for example, is genotypic because it is determined by unchangeable genes, whereas the educational exposure of an individual is a phenotypic measure of achievement since birth.

Attitudes are general, verbalizable statements and intellectual positions that guide an individual in making congruent responses to similar stimulus situations. To use a more formal definition, an attitude may be viewed as "an enduring, learned predisposition to behave in a consistent way toward a given class of objects."[25] Anti-Semitism, for example, is said to characterize an individual who evaluates Jewish persons and customs negatively and often seeks irrationally to pin some blame for unpleasant happenings on "Jewishness." A pacifistic attitude, similarly, disposes an individual to decide upon nonviolent action in a variety of situations.

Behavior is the meaningful physical action (or its absence) of a living organism. The standard behavior of social man is to communicate with others; economic man exchanges commodities; political man expresses preferences, often by voting, on proposals for regulations that affect a wide range of individuals within a particular system. Behavior is not observed directly

[24] Compare with the notion of "influence resources" used by Dahl in "The Analysis of Influence in Local Communities," *Social Science and Community Action,* ed. Charles R. Adrian (East Lansing: Michigan State University Press, 1960), pp. 35–39, and the use of the concept of "capabilities" in the writings on international relations, such as Charles O. Lerche, Jr., and Abdul A. Said, *Concepts of International Politics* (Englewood Cliffs, N. J.: Prentice-Hall, 1963), Chapter 3.

[25] Horace B. English and Ava Champney English, *A Comprehensive Dictionary of Psychological and Psychoanalytical Terms* (New York: Longmans, Green, 1958), p. 50; Marie Jahoda and Neil Warren, eds., *Attitudes* (Baltimore: Penguin, 1961).

but is abstracted from a sequence of observed movements in an organism: actions become meaningful to the observer only when he recognizes that they correspond to an analytically established category, or form of behavior.[26]

The term *function* is used in systems analysis to denote a generic task, the performance of which is postulated to be one among a number of necessary steps for a complete cycle in the operation of a system. Since styles and frequencies of function performance differ so much from one system to another, we include "function" as an additional attribute. Such metatasks as goal attainment, pattern maintenance, coordination, and adaptation, which are applied to international systems in Chapter 10, are necessary activities for any behavioral or action system.[27] An alternative view is that "functions" are merely broad conceptual terms for coding purposive behavior. A system often must solve needs for self-expression, preserve its distinctiveness from its environment, have a coordinated sequencing in its internal operations, and must keep in step with changes in external and internal constraints on its operations; various actions fulfill these four tasks to a greater or lesser degree. Whatever the list of possible functions, the concept of function implies only that there are larger ends toward which specific classes of behavior lead.

A *structure* refers in general to a social phenomenon describable in terms of meetings, number of members, rules of procedure, and a defined sphere of competence. One standard formal definition seems, however, to equate structures with institutions: "a structure is a pattern, i.e., an observable uniformity of action or operation."[28] Nevertheless, some structures are situational or temporary, and the degree of "uniformity" may vary considerably. Using the degree of and style of institutionalization as variables, courts and army platoons may be distinguished from church picnics and lynchings; all are types of structures.

6.4.2 Dimensions

Until the twentieth century the physical sciences customarily charted phenomena with respect to the two dimensions of distance and mass. Ein-

---

[26] A distinction between "attributes" and "behavior," in other words, is a false dichotomy. One effort to apply this so-called distinction appears in Rudolph J. Rummel, "A Field Theory of Social Action With Application to Conflict Within Nations," *General Systems Yearbook,* X (1965), 185–88. Behavior is one attribute among others.

[27] The four metatasks are actually not functions until they are specified in terms of their relation to decision cycles, a point to be clarified in Chapter 10.

[28] Marion J. Levy, Jr., "Some Aspects of 'Structural-Functional' Analysis and Political Science," *Approaches to the Study of Politics,* ed. Roland Young (Evanston, Ill.: Northwestern University Press, 1958), p. xv.

stein's theory of relativity and Heisenberg's uncertainty principle have expanded the number of dimensions to include a third and a fourth, namely, time and electrical charge. Dimensions are primitive notions that one must intuit in order to achieve a complete socialization in most cultures, and agreement on the meaning of each dimension has been nearly universal. Fortunately for physicists, who deal with matter as their concrete unit, a few dimensions are sufficient for mapping such basic physical attributes as motion, heat, light, sound, and energy.[29]

In the behavioral sciences, where the basic unit is action, the field-theory notion of dimension has been employed only recently. Many preliminary applications have appeared to be procrustean exercises.[30] A *dimension* is a coordinate or baseline in terms of which elements may be positioned within a system;[31] a set of dimensions constitutes a coordinate system or *field* within which one can map one's basic conceptual units. Field theorists in psychology have made some progress in the derivation of independent dimensions,[32] whereas little closure has been achieved in the various inchoate efforts to delineate societal dimensions, because the analytical concept of dimension has not been examined or explored in its true philosophic sense. Instead, there has been a confusion between the need to establish conceptual distinctions and the empirical task of deriving interrelated clusters of variables. Clearly, an empirically discovered *factor,* the name for a cluster determined through factor analysis, may serve to test whether sets of variables consist of one or several empirical clusters; but one cannot so easily argue that a large number of capriciously selected variables will somehow collapse into a pattern that has the conceptual neatness of a metaconceptual framework. And indeed, labels of many factors have been assigned without much consideration for the more intriguing philosophic issues involved. Nevertheless, many studies using factor analysis, cluster analysis, and smallest-space analysis have appeared. The societal data that

[29] Cf. Hans Reichenbach, *The Philosophy of Space and Time,* trans. Maria Reichenbach and John Freund (New York: Dover, 1958), pp. 273–83; G. J. Whitrow, *The Structure and Evolution of the Universe* (New York: Harper, 1959), pp. 199–201; David Hawkins, *The Language of Nature* (Garden City, N. Y.: Doubleday, 1967), pp. 160ff; Arnold Koslow, ed., *The Changeless Order* (New York: Braziller, 1967).

[30] Quincy Wright, *The Study of International Relations* (New York: Appleton-Century-Crofts, 1955), Chapter 32, is particularly vulnerable to this charge, though heuristic.

[31] Cf. Karl Menger, "What Is Dimension?" *American Mathematical Monthly,* L (January 1943), 2–7; Michael Haas, "Dimensional Analysis in Cross-National Research," *Comparative Political Studies,* III (April 1970), 3–35.

[32] See Raymond B. Cattell, "Personality Theory Growing from Multivariate Quantitative Research," *Psychology: A Study of a Science,* ed. Sigmund Koch (New York: McGraw–Hill, 1959), III, 257–327.

have been analyzed include cultural and social characteristics of sovereign states,[33] frequency counts of international behavior,[34] international participation,[35] magnitudes of economic resources of individual countries,[36] and judgmental categorizations for cultures and polities.[37]

Since rules for distinguishing analytically between dimensions have yet to be examined by philosophy of science scholars,[38] the acceptability of four physicial dimensions must be explained on grounds of pragmatic utility

[33] Raymond B. Cattell, "Dimensions of Culture Patterns by Factorization of National Characters," *Journal of Abnormal and Social Psychology*, XLIX (October 1949), 443–69; Cattell, H. Bruel, and H. Parker Hartman, "An Attempt at a More Refined Definition of the Cultural Dimensions of Syntality in Modern Nations," *American Sociological Review*, XVII (August 1952), 408–21; Alvin W. Gouldner and Richard A. Peterson, *Notes on Technology and the Moral Order* (Indianapolis: Bobbs–Merrill, 1962); Cattell and Richard L. Gorsuch, "The Definition and Measurement of National Morale," *Journal of Social Psychology*, LXVII (October 1965), 77–96; Bruce M. Russett, *International Regions and the International System* (Chicago: Rand McNally, 1967), Chapter 2. See also a series of P-analyses: Cattell, "A Quantitative Analysis of the Changes in the Culture Pattern of Great Britain 1837–1937, by P-Technique," *Acta Psychologica*, IX, No. 2 (1953), 99–121; Cattell and Marvin Adelson, "The Dimensions of Social Change in the U.S.A. as Determined by P-Technique," *Social Forces*, XXX (December 1951), 190–201; Cecil A. Gibb, "Changes in the Culture Pattern of Australia, 1906–1946, as Determined by P-Technique," *Journal of Social Psychology*, XLIII (May 1956), 225–38.

[34] Rudolph J. Rummel, "Dimensions of Conflict Behavior Within and Between Nations," *General Systems Yearbook*, VIII (1963), 1–50; Rummel, "Dimensions of Conflict Behavior Within Nations, 1946–59," *Journal of Conflict Resolution*, X (March 1966), 65–73; Raymond Tanter, "Dimensions of Conflict Behavior Within and Between Nations, 1958–60," *ibid.*, 41–64.

[35] Russett, *International Regions and the International System*, Chapters 7–9; R. J. Rummel, "Some Dimensions in the Foreign Behavior of Nations," *Journal of Peace Research*, III, No. 3 (1966), 201–24.

[36] Brian J. L. Berry, "A Statistical Analysis," *Atlas of Economic Development*, ed. Norton Ginsburg (Chicago: University of Chicago Press, 1961), Part VII; Irma Adelman and Cynthia Taft Morris, "A Factor Analysis of the Interrelationship Between Social and Political Variables and Per Capita Gross National Product," *Quarterly Journal of Economics*, LXXIX (November 1965), 555–78; Vincent Farace and Lewis Donohew, "Mass Communication in National Social Systems: A Study of 43 Variables in 115 Countries," *Journalism Quarterly*, LXII (Spring 1965), 253–61.

[37] Phillip M. Gregg and Arthur S. Banks, "Dimensions of Political Systems: Factor Analysis of *A Cross-Polity Survey*," *American Political Science Review*, LIX (September 1965), 602–14; Banks and Gregg, "Grouping Political Systems: Q-Factor Analysis of *A Cross-Polity Survey*," *American Behavioral Scientist*, IX (November 1965), 3–5; Banks, "Grouping Political Systems: A Preliminary Analysis," paper presented at the annual meeting of the American Political Science Association, Chicago, September, 1964; Russett, *International Regions and the International System*. See also Harold E. Driver and Karl F. Schuessler, "Factor Analysis of Ethnographic Data," *American Anthropologist*, LIX (August 1957), 655–63.

[38] Personal communication with Herbert Feigl, March 13, 1967.

alone. But in the social sciences a more optimistic prospect for arriving at a dimensional approach is in sight. The pioneering theorizing of Kurt Lewin, in particular, involves treating the psychological field of an individual as "life space."[39] Louis Guttman's current attempt to develop facet theory, using various notions from logical set theory, tends toward a more formal and analytically self-conscious approach to the problem of dimensions.[40] In the realm of political phenomena, however, metaconceptual schemes have failed to guide a recent proliferation of factor-analysis studies, with the consequence that the factors extracted have been hard to label on occasion and have been viewed more as curious mathematical oddities than as inputs into theoretical speculation.

In order to initiate a dialogue between empirical dimension-hunting and theoretical concept-mapping, the following are proposed as underlying societal dimensions:

1. Spatial.
2. Temporal.
3. Kinetic.
4. Entropic.
5. Allocational.
6. Transactional.

Each of the six dimensions will be defined and justified below.

Space is probably the most elementary societal dimension, referring as it does to the geographic location of entities. Many units are fixed territorially, but some entities lack a spatial anchor, such as the set of displaced persons. In treating societal units, the spatial dimension will be relatively unambiguous, for today only groups of preliterate or nomadic tribesmen are unconcerned with territorial boundaries. In correlational analyses of societal variables, the spatial dimension is usually an analytic "given"; United Nations statistical data, for example, are reported by territorial unit. Subdimensions of space may be determined by the Q-technique. Though the results of a number of studies[41] are not convergent, one use of the Q-technique is to provide a set of empirically derived classes of countries that can serve as strata for sampling purposes. Space corresponds to the physical dimension of distance (length, width, and depth).

[39] Kurt Lewin, *Field Theory in Social Science,* ed. Dorwin Cartwright (New York: Harper, 1951).

[40] Louis Guttman, "A Structural Theory for Intergroup Beliefs and Action," *American Sociological Review,* XXIV (June 1951), 318–28.

[41] Banks and Gregg, "Grouping Political Systems: Q–Factor Analysis of *A Cross-Polity Survey";* Banks, "Grouping Political Systems: A Preliminary Analysis"; Russett, *International Regions and the International System.*

The second societal dimension, *time,* is identical with another physical dimension. In collecting data for countries, the time element ordinarily is the year; in cross-sectional comparisons, it is common to have the same dates for observations of each case, and as a result the temporal dimension is a second "given" in factor-analysis probes. In common-sense discussions, sub-dimensions of time usually are considered to be two in number: so-called normal times are contrasted with crisis periods. In a discussion of patterns of social development, Hornell Hart observes that eras of war and revolution alone upset normal logistic growth rates in many social variables.[42] To determine temporal subdimensions, the P-technique is appropriate; and three extant studies[43] have delineated independent eras for British, American, and Australian data from the mid-nineteenth century to the present.

The remaining four societal dimensions are probably less obvious to the intuition of a layman and more familiar to a student of general systems theory. The kinetic, entropic, allocational, and transactional dimensions deal with system potentialities, organization, stratification, and exchange with the environment, respectively.

The *kinetic* dimension refers to the fact that attributes may be located along active-passive or dynamic-static continua.[44] Water resources may be potential and unexploited, or they may be kinetic and transformed into electricity. The British political system has been used as a model of dynamic performance of political functions, whereas in the French Fourth Republic veto groups effectively blocked innovative governmental programs. The dimension of electrical charge in physics is similar to our kinetic societal dimension.

The fourth societal dimension is *entropy.* In physics, entropy refers to the extent of disorganization or randomness within a system. The entropic dimension at the societal level is concerned with whether there is any departure from an organized, efficient arrangement of parts within a system. What is "organized" is, of course, an a priori judgment; departures from ideal models can be seen as imperfections, without pejorative connotations. Samuel Huntington's models of civilian and military life serve as illustra-

---

[42] Hornell Hart, "Depression, War, and Logistic Trends," *American Journal of Sociology,* LII (September 1946), 112–22.

[43] Cattell, "A Quantitative Analysis of the Changes in the Culture Pattern of Great Britain 1837–1937, by P-Technique"; Cattell and Adelson, "The Dimensions of Social Change in the U.S.A. as Determined by P-Technique"; Gibb, "Changes in the Culture Pattern of Australia, 1906–1946, as Determined by P-Technique."

[44] The independence of this dimension has been exploited most effectively in Charles E. Osgood, George J. Suci, and Percy H. Tannenbaum, *The Measurement of Meaning* (Urbana: University of Illinois Press, 1957).

tions: military life is portrayed as neat, orderly, and rational, but civilian life is supposed to be sloppy, disorganized, and badly linked together.[45] But departures from either model constitute degrees of entropy in a system. Another illustration would be Max Weber's conception of a rational bureaucracy.[46] Whether one prefers military or civilian models of living depends upon one's values, of course, so entropy can be perceived as either good or bad. The choice of Huntington's entropic model, of Weber's notion of rational-legal authority, is governed by the research question or pattern under investigation.

The fifth dimension is labelled *allocational,* and it deals with the subsystems within a particular behavioral unit. Some strata have more of a particular resource than others; functions are performed more frequently by certain strata than others. If one unit in a system dominates other units, one would expect the dominant unit to possess more resources. The allocational dimension, in short, pertains to distributions of values among the strata of a population.

The sixth postulated dimension is the *transactional* aspect of a system. Countries, cities, individuals, and steam engines must exchange with their environment to survive as systems. Similarly, the environment has an impact upon a system, so the two-way nature of relationships between a system and its environment is implied by the term transaction.

Having completed the inventory of possible societal dimensions, the next task is to specify in what manner appropriate data for each dimension could be analyzed. But the mathematical form in which data are collected depends upon one's theoretical aims, so we now turn to a discussion of alternative patterns of data.

6.4.3 Patterns

Each societal attribute may vary across all six dimensions of societal space. Resources are distributed over time and space, in terms of potentiality, by organizational consistency, in relative magnitudes within subsystems, and vis-à-vis an environment. Each of the basic attributes could be placed within a six-dimensional field of analytical coordinates, but the result would only be literary. A third element is needed to delimit the conceptual terrain. Measurement procedures should be applied to the conceptual field in order

[45] Samuel P. Huntington, *The Soldier and the State* (Cambridge: Harvard University Press, 1957). See also Johan Galtung, "Entropy and the General Theory of Peace," *Proceedings of the International Peace Research Association, Second Conference* (Assen: Van Gorcum, 1968), I, 3–37.

[46] Max Weber, *The Theory of Social and Economic Organization,* trans. A. M. Henderson and Talcott Parsons (New York: Oxford University Press, 1947).

to yield mathematical patterns. By defining a *pattern* as a representation that enables two or more elements to be compared, one can hope to delineate many quantitative relationships. An individual, a nation, a discount department store, or any other unit may be observed to exhibit a number of possible patterns, any of which may indicate underlying mechanisms that account for various societal events. Some patterns that interest social scientists are the following:

1. Magnitude.
2. Homeostasis.
3. Equifinality.
4. Recursiveness.
5. Multiplicativeness.
6. Stochasticity.
7. Scalarity.
8. Asymmetry.

A full treatment of all eight (or additional) patterns would take us far afield. But it may be argued that most theoretical speculation on societal factors in war and peace has concentrated on the eighth pattern, asymmetry, as Sections 6.2 and 6.3 attest.

Two or more elements in a system are *asymmetrical* when they are related in such a way that the converse of their relationship is logically impossible. To say that *"A is the husband of B,"* for example, is to state an asymmetrical relationship, for it is not also the case that *"B is the husband of A."* A *symmetrical* relationship is two-way: *"A is married to B"* is compatible with *"B is married to A."* Mathematically, symmetry exists when units are equal to each other: for if $a = b$, then $b = a$. Asymmetry is said to be present when units differ in magnitude: if $a > b$, then it is never true that $b > a$.[47] Since "symmetry" and "asymmetry" patterns are relevant to all six dimensions (Table 6–1), each intersection between the attributes of dimensions will be labelled in Chapter 7 in terms of the asymmetry-symmetry continuum.

6.5 SOCIETAL DATA

To describe societal systems in empirical terms, one must have access to various types of data. The units of societal analysis consist of the aggregate

---

[47] Susanne Langer, *Introduction to Symbolic Logic,* 2d ed. (New York: Dover, 1953), p. 247. See also Hermann Weyl, *Symmetry* (Princeton: Princeton University Press, 1952). My use of the concept of asymmetry follows the suggestions of Lewis F. Richardson, *Statistics of Deadly Quarrels* (Chicago: Quadrangle, 1960), p. 28.

TABLE 6-1
Societal Concepts

Dimensions	Resources	Demotypes	Attributes			
			Attitudes	Behavior	Functions	Structures
Temporal						
Spatial						
Kinetic						
Entropic						
Allocational						
Transactional						

181

characteristics of a population—its social organization, economy, and polity. Whereas population and economic data are amply provided in national statistical yearbooks, political data are too often found scattered unsystematically throughout biographies, newspapers, or nonreplicated surveys of public opinion. And in using such data, researchers have concentrated on the magnitudes of figures almost exclusively, which hampers the theoretical analysis of international conflict in terms of symmetry and asymmetry.

How can the data be demonstrated to be symmetrical or asymmetrical? Assembling data for any pattern requires one to select a *recording unit*. Symmetry is present if each member in a system is identical (Table 6–2). In temporal symmetry, the recording unit is a time period (ordinarily the *year* in statistical compilations), so annual change rates would index asymmetry. The spatial dimension within a society system is recorded less precisely, usually only in terms of urban versus rural *areas;* differences between the two areas will indicate asymmetry. The measure for the kinetic dimension is a *ratio between potential and actual* estimates; the raw recording unit, which is included in both numerator and denominator, cancels out. Entropic asymmetry involves comparing an actual characteristic in a population with an ideal model, so the appropriate asymmetric datum for a dichotomous characteristic would be the *deviation from a 50–50 percent distribution*. Allocational symmetry focuses on individual units and the extent to which there is a disproportionate sharing among elements of the system on particular attributes; *subunit percentages* are the recording units to be selected in most cases. Transactional data are measures of *input-output ratios,* with the original recording units cancelling out; transactional symmetry exists when a country's inputs equal its outputs.

In selecting indicators for each of the 36 empty cells in Table 6–1, the preferred procedure would be a random sample of all possible measures. Government agencies and social scientists, however, have concentrated so far on only a few types of data relevant to the concept of asymmetry, despite a preponderance in theoretical attention. For some of the 36 continua, the number of indicators is large; but for other types of asymmetry, there is a scarcity of data. The most convenient sources on which the investigator can rely, in addition to various United Nations statistical yearbooks,[48] are the following: *A Cross-Polity Survey* (1963), by Arthur Banks and Robert Textor; Norton Ginsburg's *Atlas of Economic Development* (1961); the Yale Political Data Program's *World Handbook of Political and Social Indicators* (1964); and data collected from various sources by the Dimen-

---

[48] United Nations, Statistical Office, *Demographic Yearbook;* United Nations, Statistical Office, *Statistical Yearbook;* Food and Agriculture Organization, *Production Yearbook;* International Labor Office, *Yearbook of Labor Statistics;* United Nations, *Statistical Papers,* Series T.

TABLE 6-2
Symmetry and Asymmetry Patterns for Societal Dimensions

Dimension	Recording Unit	Symmetry Pattern	Asymmetry Pattern
Temporal	Time period	Change rate $= 0.0$	Change rate > 0.0
Spatial	Areas (rural, urban)	$\dfrac{\text{Rural attribute}}{\text{Urban attribute}} = 1.0$	$\dfrac{\text{Rural attribute}}{\text{Total attributes}} \begin{array}{l}> .50 \\ <\end{array}$
Kinetic	System attributes	$\dfrac{\text{Actual attribute}}{\text{Potentialities}} = 1.0$	$\dfrac{\text{Actual attribute}}{\text{Potentialities}} < 1.0$
Entropic	System attributes	Actual attribute $=$ Ideal attribute	Actual attribute $\neq$ Ideal attribute
Allocational[a]	Subunits $(A, B, \ldots N)$	Subunit $A =$ Subunit B (etc.)	$\dfrac{\text{Subunit } A}{\text{Subunit } A + \text{Subunit } B} \begin{array}{l}> .50 \\ <\end{array}$
Transactional	System, environment	Inputs $=$ Outputs	$\dfrac{\text{Inputs}}{\text{Inputs} + \text{Outputs}} \begin{array}{l}> .50 \\ <\end{array}$

Key to symbols: $>$ means that departures in absolute values (with $+$ and $-$ signs removed) constitute degrees of asymmetry.
$\wedge$
$<$ means that figures either larger than or smaller than the value for symmetry constitute degrees of asymmetry ($+$ and $-$ signs should be removed).

[a] If there are more than two strata, A and B, then the asymmetry pattern should reflect this (for example, if there are three strata, subunits A, B, and C should be plugged into a coefficient of variation computation, as are change rates across more than two time periods).

sionality of Nations Project.[49] A sample of 85 countries for the years 1955–1960 yields the largest amount of data across all of the pertinent variables. A survey of research on societal factors and national aggressiveness, which was postponed at the end of Section 6.4, may now proceed. Each of the variables derivable from the 6×6 matrix of concepts (Table 6–1) are specified in the following chapter, and current research findings are reported. Chapter 8 contains a more systematic test of the relation between national asymmetry and international aggression.

[49] Banks and Textor, *A Cross-Polity Survey;* Norton Ginsburg, ed., *Atlas of Economic Development* (Chicago: University of Chicago Press, 1961); Bruce Russett et al., *World Handbook of Political and Social Indicators* (New Haven: Yale University Press, 1964); Rummel, "Dimensions of Conflict Behavior Within and Between Nations"; Tanter, "Dimensions of Conflict Behavior Within and Between Nations."

Some data are also derived from the following: Joseph D. Coppock, *International Economic Instability* (New York: McGraw–Hill, 1962); Ted Gurr, *New Error-Compensated Measures for Comparing Nations* (Princeton: Center of International Studies, 1966); William Buchanan and Hadley Cantril, *How Nations See Each Other* (Urbana: University of Illinois Press, 1952); Michael Haas, *Some Societal Correlates of International Political Behavior* (Stanford: multilithed Ph.D. dissertation, Department of Political Science, 1964); Raymond B. Nixon, "Factors Related to Press Freedom in National Press Systems," *Journalism Quarterly,* XXXVII (Winter 1960), 13–28; Hadley Cantril, *The Pattern of Human Concerns* (New Brunswick: Rutgers University Press, 1963); *Statesman's Year Book;* Council on Foreign Relations, *Political Handbook of the World;* United States, Department of State, *World Strength of Communist Party Organizations.*

chapter 7
Symmetry and Asymmetry in Societal Systems

7.1 DEFINITIONS, PROPOSITIONS, AND INDICATORS

Having proposed three analytically distinct types of notions that may be applied to the analysis of societal systems, we must now put the pieces together. With 6 attributes and 6 dimensions that may be either symmetrical or asymmetrical, 36 continua are generated. At one end of each continuum rests a label that corresponds to a symmetrical pattern; at each pole lies a word that refers to an asymmetrical pattern. This chapter defines 72 concepts; it discusses appropriate propositions that link each concept with a system's propensity to violent foreign-state behavior; and it proposes illustrative indicators for each continuum. The discussion proceeds one dimension at a time. Because the 3 metaconceptual axes are more fundamental than the 72 particular concepts, each of the terms defined below should be regarded as an imperfect verbal symbol; every term is cautiously selected to stand for a condition more precise than conventional usage of the word has allowed hitherto. One cannot easily undo the damage to precision that accrues from a natural growth in language; one can only hope to point out distinct concepts and to avoid semantic traps in future research.

Theoretical and empirical linkage between each of the continua and the incidence of international aggression has been burgeoning within recent years. Much societal theory has been tested, and an empirical review of several studies is possible in the delineation of the 72 concepts. It may, therefore, be useful to preview the statement of findings by enumerating the studies from which they are extracted.

Some of the extant studies are factor analyses. Raymond Cattell has performed one relevant study using cultural variables—a 69-country analysis with 72 variables over the years 1837–1937.[1] Twenty-four political variables have been factor-analyzed by Rudolph Rummel and Raymond Tanter, the former collecting data for 77 countries for 1955–1957, the latter choosing 88 countries for the years 1958–1960.[2] Rummel also has factor-analyzed 238 variables, with a sample of 82 countries, principally for the year 1955.[3] Using simple correlation techniques, Michael Haas has correlated frequencies of participation in war and levels of military expenditures in 10 countries since 1900, with unemployment, electricity production, homicides, suicides, and death rates due to alcoholism.[4] Data from *A Cross-Polity Survey* of Arthur Banks and Robert Textor are utilized in two studies, one by Haas and the other by Banks and Phillip Gregg.[5] Raoul Naroll, finally, intercorrelates 32 variables for each of 30 world civilizations as well as 22 traits across 43 primitive cultures.[6]

Some of the data from these sources are combined with newly collected indicators for treatment in this volume, so a comparison between our

[1] Raymond B. Cattell, "Dimensions of Culture Patterns by Factorization of National Characters," *Journal of Abnormal and Social Psychology,* XLIV (October 1949), 443–69. The same patterns emerge in two subsequent studies: Cattell, H. Bruel, and H. Parker Hartman, "An Attempt at a More Refined Definition of the Cultural Dimensions of Syntality in Modern Nations," *American Sociological Review,* XVII (August 1952), 408–21; Cattell and Richard L. Gorsuch, "The Definition and Measurement of National Morale," *Journal of Social Psychology,* LXVII (October 1965), 77–96.

[2] Rudolph J. Rummel, "Dimensionality of Conflict Behavior Within and Between Nations," *General Systems,* VIII (1963), 1–50; Raymond Tanter, "Dimensions of Conflict Behavior Within and Between Nations, 1958–60," *Journal of Conflict Resolution,* X (March 1966), 41–64; see also Rummel, "Dimensions of Conflict Behavior Within Nations, 1946–59," *ibid.,* pp. 65–73.

[3] Findings from the Dimensions of Nations Project are summarized in Rummel, "Some Empirical Findings of Nations and Their Behavior," *World Politics,* XXI (January 1969), 226–41.

[4] Michael Haas, *Some Societal Correlates of International Political Behavior* (Stanford: Stanford Studies in International Conflict and Integration, multilithed Ph.D. dissertation, 1964); Haas, "Societal Approaches to the Study of War," *Journal of Peace Research,* II, No. 4 (1965), 307–23; Haas, "Social Change and National Aggressiveness, 1900–1960," *Quantitative International Politics,* ed. J. David Singer (New York: The Free Press, 1968), pp. 215–44.

[5] Arthur S. Banks and Robert B. Textor, *A Cross-Polity Survey* (Cambridge: MIT Press, 1963); Haas, "Societal Approaches to the Study of War"; Phillip M. Gregg and Banks, "Dimensions of Political Systems: Factor Analysis of *A Cross-Polity Survey,*" *American Political Science Review,* LIX (September 1965), 602–14.

[6] Raoul Naroll, "Deterrence in History," *Theory and Research on the Causes of War,* eds. Dean G. Pruitt and Richard C. Snyder (Englewood Cliffs, N. J.: Prentice–Hall, 1969), pp. 150–64; Naroll, "Does Military Deterrence Deter?" *Trans-Action,* III (January–February 1966), 14–20.

findings and those obtained in the other studies will permit a broad overview of the relation between societal asymmetry and international conflict. Accordingly, some discussion of the indicators of international conflict is in order before we survey correlational results. Four measures are chosen. *Participation in war* is defined as military action vis-à-vis another country in which troops constitute two or more percent of the country's population. *Foreign clashes* are military actions involving fewer soldiers. *Foreign killed* refers to persons dying from direct foreign military action; to standardize this figure, another index is constructed by taking a *foreign killed per population* ratio for each country.[7] Each of these four indices of foreign violence is correlated with 179 variables selected as indicators for the 36 concepts explained below.

Because it is possible to pinpoint exactly one concept for each cell defined by the three metaconceptual axes of attribute, dimension, and pattern, bivariate correlations are reported in the aggregate for 36 separate tables in the chapter. The range beyond $\pm$ .30 is selected as a boundary for demarcating stronger from weaker correlations. But even if every correlation is below $\pm$ .30, when the signs all point in the same direction it is possible to infer that there is a consistent relationship, as we have discussed this adaptation of Bayesian statistics in Section 2.4.2. As correlations fall below $\pm$ .10, even consistent relationships, however, lose significance, so in presenting our findings we will count the number of correlations in the range + .10 to − .10. We shall now review correlations between each type of asymmetry and the four dependent variables.

7.2 TEMPORAL ASYMMETRY

Temporal symmetry implies that attributes remain fixed with the passage of time. When a system changes from year to year, or from minute to minute, it exhibits asymmetry on the time dimension. Terms appropriate to each of the six societal attributes are listed in Table 7–1. Because the variability of a system from one unit of time to another is the operational measure of temporal asymmetry, an elementary procedure for deriving appropriate indicators would be to sum values over time and to ascertain departures from the mean value. Annual increases in magnitude and coefficients of variation (standard deviations divided by means) are two of the most precise de-

---

[7] Full definitions are supplied in Appendix B. Data sources are supplied in notes 2 and 4 above. Correlations reported in this chapter are based on a wider sample of countries than in my "Societal Asymmetries and World Peace," *Proceedings of the International Peace Research Association, Second Conference* (Assen: Van Gorcum, 1968), II, 70–110.

TABLE 7–1
Temporal Concepts

	Concepts	
Attributes	Asymmetry	Symmetry
Resources	Fluctuation	Constancy
Demotypes	Cosmopolitanizing	Inbreeding
Attitudes	Tides	Normalcy
Behavior	Instability	Stability
Functions	Discontinuity	Continuity
Structures	Situational	Persistent

scriptive measures.[8] The most convenient recording unit is the year, since most cross-national economic and demographic data compilations contain annual figures.

7.2.1 Fluctuation–Constancy

If a particular resource does not vary over time, as in the case of an undiscovered raw material, we would refer to such a condition as one of *constancy*. Most resources *fluctuate:* they may proliferate or become depleted—the former is usually the case with manufactured goods, and the latter is characteristic of raw materials. A familiar hypothesis in theory on international conflict is that war is sought as an outlet when rapid industrialization is arrested in hard times; societies static in resources are often assumed to contain such a well-coordinated balance of internal political and social tendencies that war would be opposed by elites as a disruptive departure from "business as usual."[9]

To study economic fluctuation variables, a number of indicators are appropriate: the ratio between percentage increases in national income and population (1),[10] per capita annual changes in commercial energy consumption (2), gross national product (3), radios (4); coefficients of variation in annual figures for telephones per capita (5), railroad freight ton-kilometers (6), and in per capita electricity production (7). Some

---

[8] For an ingenious codification of ways of measuring temporal change, see Panos D. Bardis, "Synopsis of Theories of Social Change," *Social Science,* XXXVII (June 1962), 181–87.

[9] A. F. K. Organski, *World Politics,* 2d ed. (New York: Knopf, 1968). Level of economic development correlates + .30 with the incidence of both military and nonmilitary foreign conflict behavior, as reported in Haas, "Societal Approaches to the Study of War." The technological advancement of an army correlates + .36 with war participation by world civilizations in Naroll, "Deterrence in History."

[10] Figures in parentheses refer to variable numbers, which are listed in Tables 8–1 and 8–2 and defined in Appendix B.

additional indicators, not necessarily pertinent to industrialization, could be selected to index changes in human and economic resources: annual rate of population increase (8); changes in per capita caloric intake (9) and in per capita protein grammage intake (10); growth in per capita government budgets (11); and Joseph Coppock's national income instability index (12). Nearly all change within our 85-country sample is in the positive direction for these variables.

With about as many negative as positive correlations between indicators of fluctuation and national aggression (Table 7–2), we may conclude tentatively that change has no consistent relation to war incidence.

7.2.2 Cosmopolitanizing–Inbreeding

Within a societal system the distribution of genotypes and phenotypes is nearly always in flux: children are born, thereby altering the age distribution of a population; education proceeds, resulting in stratification of the knowledge held by members of the country. The rates of change, however, can vary markedly from years in which social conditions encourage conceiving and educating children to eras of hard times, when birth control is practiced and offspring try to enter the job market rather than pursuing further schooling. Marriage rates across racial and socioeconomic lines may also be asymmetrical within systems over time. Conventionally, *inbreeding* refers to a condition in which the demotypic composition of a population does not change with time, and when access to certain strata is closed. A *cosmopolitanizing*[11] society undergoes demotypic mixing and is therefore always asymmetrical temporally until a "melting pot" operates so that each individual is identical with one another—or a situation similar to a *Brave New World* arrives in which the demotypic composition of a society is always the same due to a complete control of social processes. In Nathan Glazer's images of immigrant cultures in a host environment,[12] the "nation of nations" concept refers to inbred miniature cultures established side by side, with Chinatowns, silk-stocking Wasp (white Anglo-Saxon Protestant) neighborhoods, "little Italies," and so forth. If population growth and phenotypic change were to remain constant temporally, a "nation of nations" would be symmetrical; the "melting pot" concept is asymmetrical insofar as new hybrid combinations of genotypes and phenotypes are always

---

[11] The word *cosmopolitan* is used colloquially in Hawaii to refer to an individual of mixed racial parentage.

[12] Nathan Glazer, "America's Ethnic Pattern: 'Melting Pot' or 'Nation of Nations'?" *Commentary*, XV (April 1953), 401–8. See also Glazer and Daniel P. Moynihan, *Beyond the Melting Pot* (Cambridge: MIT Press, 1963).

TABLE 7–2
Correlations Between Fluctuation
and National Aggression

| | Conflicts | | Foreign Killed | |
| | Wars | Clashes | Total | Per capita |
Indicators of Fluctuation[a]	180	181	182	183
1. Annual change in national income/ annual change in population	—.11	—.28	—.09	—.18
1d. Annual change in national income/ annual change in population	.20	—.29	—.02	
2. Annual change in per capita electricity consumption	—.26	(—.31)	—.26	—.23
3. Annual change in per capita GNP	.22	—.26	.04	—.03
4. Annual change in per capita radios	.08	—.09	.01	.02
5. Annual change in per capita telephones	.00	.05	—.07	—.09
6. Annual change in per capita rail freight ton-kilometers	—.17	—.22	—.25	—.23
7. Annual change in per capita electricity production	—.16	—.04	—.21	—.14
7c. Late increase in industrial production	—.19	—.13		
7h. Per capita electricity production annual increments	(—.32)			
8. Annual change in population	.06	.21	.11	.18
9. Annual change in per capita caloric intake	.10	—.20	.09	.28
10. Annual change in per capita protein grammage intake	.06	—.29	—.01	.12
11. Annual change in per capita government budget	.09	.12	.13	.09
12. National income in stability	.09	.10	—.00	.04

Positive correlations = 24. Correlations in ± .10 range = 24.
Negative correlations = 30.

[a] Sources for societal variables used in this volume are listed in Table 8–1. Findings from other studies is denoted by the letters following each variable number, as follows:
c   Cattell, "Dimensions of Culture Patterns by Factorization of National Characters" (1949).
d   Rummel, Dimensionality of Nations Project.
g   Gregg and Banks, "Dimensions of Political Systems: Factor Analysis of *A Cross-Polity Survey*" (1965).
h   Haas, "Social Change and National Aggressiveness, 1900–1960" (1968).
r   Rummel, "Dimensions of Conflict Behavior Within and Between Nations" (1963).
t   Tanter, "Dimensions of Conflict Behavior Within and Between Nations, 1958–60" (1966).

arising. More simply, if rates of literacy, death, and other demotypic characteristics are constant over time, symmetry is present; if there are drastic variations from year to year, temporal-demotypic asymmetry exists.

According to Nazi racist theory, violence is necessary from time to time in order to weed out impure or defective genotypes within a society. Converting the Nazi ethic into a testable proposition, the implication is that cosmopolitanizing societal systems are confronted with war more often, since "race-mixing" provides an opportunity for inbred countries to gain from conquest.[13] Population pressure theory, similarly, suggests that the average annual increase of persons in cities (13) indexes a claustrophobic source of tension that can result in a demand for a Lebensraum. Though population density is related positively to war frequency,[14] the impact of asymmetrical cumulative increases in density over time has not yet been subjected to empirical analysis.

Some further indicators that would test the relation between national aggressiveness and inbreeding-cosmopolitanizing are as follows: annual changes in percent agricultural employment (14) and in literacy (15).

Results show that demotypic symmetry is related to war in 75 percent of the computations (Table 7–3). Only half of the magnitudes are over ± .10, however. Although asymmetry in yearly industrial output tends to be unrelated to wars, increases and decreases in population variables are associated with fewer wars and clashes.

7.2.3 Tides–Normalcy

Attitudes, too, may change over time. Within a culture there are eras of *normalcy,* when underlying values and symbols are reaffirmed. But as Arthur Schlesinger, Sr., suggests, there are also political *tides* in which public sentiment swings from equalitarian to inequalitarian extremes in the political pendulum.[15] Attitudes are more likely to be symmetrical over time on "style" than "position" issues, the authors of *Voting* contend, for orientations on such fundamental questions as equalitarianism-inequalitarianism and libertarianism-restrictionism are likely to be more firmly rooted in personality structure than are views on such specific legislative questions as medical care for elderly persons or the noncommunist "loyalty" oath.[16] One conception of the outbreak of war is that a ground swell of "war fever" propels leaders of states to enter foreign conflicts as belligerents,

[13] Adolph Hitler, *Mein Kampf,* trans. Ralph Manheim (New York: Reynal and Hitchcock, 1939).

[14] The contingency correlation between population density and foreign conflict is + .24; between urbanization and foreign conflict, + .20; Haas, "Societal Approaches to the Study of War." Using the presence of topographical natural barriers between peoples as a characteristic of 43 primitive cultures, Naroll finds a + .03 correlation with war frequency among primitive cultures and a + .18 among world civilizations; Naroll, "Deterrence in History"; Naroll, "Does Military Deterrence Deter?"

[15] Arthur Schlesinger, Sr., "Tides of American Politics," *Yale Review,* XXIX (Winter 1940), 217–30.

[16] Bernard Berelson, Paul F. Lazarsfeld, and William N. McPhee, *Voting* (Chicago: University of Chicago Press, 1954).

TABLE 7–3
Correlations Between Cosmopolitanization
and National Aggression

	Conflicts		*Foreign Killed*	
	Wars	Clashes	Total	Per capita
Indicators of Cosmopolitanization	180	181	182	183
13. Annual change in urbanites	−.11	−.27	−.21	−.07
14. Annual change in agricultural employment	−.01	.17	.04	.03
15. Annual change in per capita literacy	−.07	−.03	−.15	−.25

Positive correlations = 3.   Correlations in ±.10 range = 6.
Negative correlations = 9.

and "war weariness" is said to precipitate a movement to bring about peace.[17]

To choose indicators for tides, we would have to be better supplied with cross-historical and cross-national survey data. At this time almost nothing is available. The most easily collected measure is the coefficient of variation for annual figures of percent Communist Party strength (16), which is inversely related to nearly all of the foreign conflict indicators (Table 7–4). Where Communist Party strength is rising or falling, war is evidently precluded. However, since the data are gathered on the basis of intelligence reports that could be unreliable, it could be concluded that where intelligence estimates are least revised over time war is more likely, whereas a low amount of foreign conflict characterizes countries where intelligence estimates change over time.

7.2.4 Instability–Stability

Changes in behavior over time on the part of individuals, groups, or governmental leaders are referred to as *instabilities*. Arthur Banks's governmental instability (17) variable, for example, is defined in terms of "when a constitution is suspended or when an elected president is forcibly ousted from office."[18] *Stability* is equated with an absence of temporal change in

[17] Lewis F. Richardson, *Arms and Insecurity* (Chicago: Quadrangle, 1960), pp. 232–52; Frank L. Klingberg, "Predicting the Termination of War: Battle Casualties and Population Losses," *Journal of Conflict Resolution*, X (June 1966), 129–71.

[18] Banks and Textor, *A Cross-Polity Survey*, p. 84. See similar definitions in Richard N. Rosecrance, *Action and Reaction in World Politics* (Boston: Little, Brown, 1963); Joseph D. Coppock, *International Economic Instability* (New York: McGraw-Hill, 1962); Michael Brecher, "Political Instability in the New States of Asia," *Comparative Politics*, eds. Harry Eckstein and David E. Apter (New York: The Free Press, 1963), pp. 617–35; Charles G. McClintock et al., "A Pragmatic Approach to International Stability," *International Stability*, eds. Dale J. Hekhuis, McClintock, and Arthur L. Burns (New York: Wiley, 1964), pp. 3–26; A. D. Hall and R. R. Fagen, "Definition of System," *General Systems Yearbook*, I (1965), 23.

TABLE 7-4
Correlations Between Tides
and National Aggression

	Conflicts		*Foreign Killed*	
Indicator of Tides	Wars 180	Clashes 181	Total 182	Per capita 183
16. Annual change in percent communist strength/population	—.11	—.20	—.18	—.16

Positive correlations = 0. Negative correlations = 4.	Correlations in ±.10 range = 0.

behavior—that is, with a continuation in routine patterns of human conduct from one day to the next.

Aristophanes' *Lysistrata* advances a proposition that wars would stop if wives were to change their behavior patterns by denying sexual favors to their husbands. Internal system instability (18) has often been regarded as an impediment to external peace, for an interruption in normal expectations may provoke war as an escape from social problems underlying unforeseen changes, which Marx assumed would be prevalent in capitalist societies. Other indicators of instability are the average age of the latest two governments (19), years independent per chief executive (20), and coefficients of variation in annual rates of birth (21), death (22), and marriage (23).

In regressing the various proposed measures onto foreign conflict data (Table 7–5), there is only a modicum of support for the theory that instability at home leads to trouble abroad. Naroll, meanwhile, discovers that rulers in power for nine years or more are slightly more likely to be involved in war.[19]

7.2.5 Discontinuity–Continuity

Political and social functions are seldom performed at a uniform rate. When function performance occurs at a regular rate (even though to a minimal extent), the system may be described as *continuous,* but when functions cease to be performed on schedule, *discontinuities* appear. Gabriel Almond distinguishes "primitive" from "developed" political systems in these very terms: in a primitive system, such as an atomistic tribe, his seven or so functions are hypothesized to be performed intermittently, and formal aspects of a political system are barely detectable; in a developed system each function is performed more regularly.[20] Should function per-

[19] The correlation is + .14 in Naroll, "Deterrence in History."

[20] Gabriel A. Almond and G. Bingham Powell, Jr., *Comparative Politics* (Boston: Little, Brown, 1966), p. 43.

TABLE 7-5
Correlations Between Instability
and National Aggression[a]

Indicators of Instability	Conflicts		Foreign Killed	
	Wars 180	Clashes 181	Total 182	Per capita 183
17. Government instability	—.09	.03	.05	.12
17g. Government instability		.	.29	
18. System instability	.05	.21	.28	(.31)
18g. System instability			(.36)	
19. Average age of latest 2 governments[b]	.04	—.09	—.04	.05
19d. Average age of latest 2 governments[b]	.08			
20. Years independent/chief executives[b]	—.02	.04	.11	.20
21. Annual change in birth rate	—.04	—.07	—.12	—.12
22. Annual change in death rate	.09	—.08	.00	—.12
23. Annual change in marriage rate	.12	—.26	—.14	—.20

Positive correlations = 18.   Correlations in ±.10 range = 16.
Negative correlations = 13.

[a] For key, see notes to Table 7-2.
[b] Signs are reversed to be indicators of asymmetry.

formance come to a standstill, either within developed or primitive systems, a Napoleon-like "man on horseback" may offer an alternative to the painful effects of discontinuities; and the result could be such drastic departures as embarking upon foreign conquest. Edmund Burke's *Reflections on the French Revolution* asserts that discontinuities fail to improve the quality of governmental operations and often bring about international complications.

Three indicators of a paralysis in governmental functioning are the number of major government crises (24), illegitimacy of the present government (25), and the absence in legality of the latest two governmental changes (26).[21] In correlating all three with foreign conflict variables (Table 7-6), there is considerable consistency. War is evidently associated with discontinuities in the procedural functioning of systems as a whole, much as Sorokin finds that eras of warfare among European societal units coincide with times of domestic disturbances.[22]

Some additional measures of discontinuity could be derived from budget expenditures, inasmuch as the amount of money allocated to specific

21 Though other indicators of temporal asymmetry are operationalized in terms of such measures as the coefficient of variation, frequency counts of variables 25 to 27 generally yield dichotomous (presence-absence) distributions that serve admirably as measures of asymmetry.

22 Pitirim A. Sorokin, *Fluctuations of Social Relationships, War, and Revolution* (New York: American Book Co., 1937), pp. 297–98.

TABLE 7-6
Correlations Between Discontinuity
and National Aggression[a]

| | Conflicts | | Foreign Killed | |
| | Wars | Clashes | Total | Per capita |
Indicators of Discontinuity	180	181	182	183
24. Major governmental crises	—.04	.19	.18	(.32)
24r. Major governmental crises	.09	.11	.13	
24t. Major governmental crises	.01	.06	.12	
25. Illegitimacy of present government	.20	.08	.10	—.02
25d. Illegitimacy of present government	.04	.11	.10	
26. Legality of latest 2 governmental changes[b]	.09	.17	.07	.05
26d. Legality of latest 2 governmental changes[b]	—.07	.14	.09	
27. Annual change in per capita defense expenditures	—.16	—.24	—.21	—.09
28. Annual change in per capita education expenditures	—.09	(—.32)	(—.34)	—.28
29. Annual change in per capita welfare expenditures	.03	—.28	—.17	—.27
30. Annual change in per capita total government expenditures	.06	—.05	—.13	.01

Positive correlations = 24.   Correlations in ±.10 range = 20.
Negative correlations = 16.

[a] For key, see notes to Table 7-2.
[b] Signs are reversed to be indicators of asymmetry.

ministries determines whether existing functions will be curtailed or expanded in scope. The coefficients of variation in yearly per capita defense (27), education (28), welfare (29), and total government budget expenditures (30) are almost uniformly related inversely to the dependent variables; and the higher magnitude of the correlations as compared with variables 24 to 26 suggests that an expansion or contraction in budget allocations for specific functions paves the way for fewer wars. Budgetary continuity is associated with deadly foreign conflict.

7.2.6 Situational–Persistent

Once a structure is established, it has a tendency to persist even after the purpose for which it was designed is fulfilled or is performed subsequently by some other structure. But when structures are not *persistent,* they are temporary and *situational* within politics. Such a distinction is what Banks has in mind in his party system instability raw characteristic (31). At one end of a continuum are systems in which political parties are situational, personalistic, or ad hoc; at the other end are those containing permanent and organizationally nonsituational parties. David Easton's notion of "persistence of the system" similarly stresses the continuing presence of formal governmental structures.[23] Variables that might be used to indicate structural asymmetry are coefficients of variation in number of government ministries (32) and in the number of political parties with seats in parliament (33). With about two-thirds of the correlations between these indicators and foreign conflict below $\pm$ .10, however, it is clear that no strong relation exists between structural-temporal asymmetry and international conflict (Table 7–7).

7.3 SPATIAL ASYMMETRY

The law of the conservation of matter, when applied to social phenomena, axiomatizes the fact that there will always be some degree of spatial asymmetry within social and political systems. Resources, demotypes, attitudes, behavior, functions, and structures are not spread evenly across the terrain of a system (Table 7–8). Spatial symmetry may be said to exist when each territorial subdivision within a societal system is, as it were, a mirror image of the contents of every other spatial unit. Useful data on spatial symmetry are quite troublesome to assemble, since statistical compilations tend to report aggregate national figures rather than information about all of the counties, cities, or states within a country. In a biregional societal system with complete asymmetry, half of the country would possess trait A, while the other half would have a trait other than A. Abraham Lincoln's conception of a nation "half slave and half free" is of an asymmetrical society, one that could expect considerable internal strife. Lincoln's Secretary of State, William Seward, in fact, counseled that preservation of the union might require embroilment in foreign conflict in order to deflect attention from domestic problems.[24] The events of the early 1860s in the United States suggest that a society of feuding Capulets and Montagues is seldom in a position to wage war so long as internal adversaries are matched evenly.

One procedure for deriving spatial asymmetry indicators from demographic data, therefore, is to treat the 50 percent level as pure asymmetry for dichotomous variables; the extent of departure from the 50–50 level, in either direction, will index spatial symmetry. If city dwellers equal the number of rural inhabitants in a country, maximum asymmetry exists:

[23] See David Easton's notion of "persistence of the system" in *A Framework for Political Analysis* (Englewood Cliffs, N. J.: Prentice–Hall, 1965); and *A Systems Analysis of Political Life* (New York: Wiley, 1965).

[24] William Seward, "Some Thoughts for the President's Consideration," *Documents of American History*, ed. Henry Steele Commager, 7th ed. (New York: Appleton-Century-Crofts, 1962), I, 392.

TABLE 7–7
Correlations Between Situationality
and National Aggression[a]

| | Conflicts | | Foreign Killed | |
| | Wars | Clashes | Total | Per capita |
Indicators of Situationality	180	181	182	183
31. Party system instability	—.07	.17	.06	.21
31g. Party system instability			(.34)	
32. Annual change in number of government ministries	.04	.02	—.06	—.09
33. Annual change in number of parliamentary parties	.04	—.03	.01	.05

Positive correlations = 9.	Correlations in ±.10 range = 10.
Negative correlations = 4.	

[a] For key, see notes to Table 7–2.

symmetry increases as a country becomes either mostly urban or mostly rural.

7.3.1 Agglutinated–Equalitarian

A fundamental characteristic that distinguishes types of societal systems is the extent to which various resources are located nonrandomly. Bauxite, orchids, salmon, and various marketable commodities are found in varying density across the surface of the earth. The process of collecting resources into particular domains constitutes *agglutination,* whereas the *equalitarian* situation would exist if resources were distributed in such a manner that they could be found in every hamlet, ship at sea, on every street corner, and so forth.[25]

Since a direct measure of agglutination is not available for cross-

TABLE 7–8
Spatial Concepts

| | Concepts | |
Attributes	Asymmetry	Symmetry
Resources	Agglutinated	Equalitarian
Demotypes	Segregation	Desegregation
Attitudes	Sectionalism	Systemization
Behavior	Variation	Uniformity
Functions	Centralization	Decentralization
Structures	Concentration	Deconcentration

[25] For a discussion of the concept of "agglutination," see Harold D. Lasswell and Morton Kaplan, *Power and Society* (New Haven: Yale University Press, 1950).

national comparison, some indirect indicators must be constructed such as the differential use of land. One use of land preempts another use, and some types of cultivation are more profitable than others. Urban environments, for example, tend to have a larger concentration of wealth than do rural or desert areas. The wickedness attributed by Thomas Jefferson and others to city life is based upon the view that money changers and persons employed in other tertiary occupations survive best by trickery, while the simple farmer who makes a decent and honest living from the soil is supposed to be a more peaceable individual. Classical economists observed, on the contrary, that wars are common among rural civilizations, particularly those with large nomadic elements; an unfettered pursuit of agglutination might therefore be so engrossing an enterprise that war would be shunned as an unprofitable interruption in a country's economic development.

The impact of industrialization has indeed produced spatial-resource asymmetry. Though agricultural pursuits can be undertaken even on medial strips of Los Angeles freeways, calculation of the percentage of land area under cultivation (34) will indicate the extent to which urban areas have crowded out the necessary (albeit often less profitable) production of food. Taking the absolute difference between 50 percent and the particular value for each country, spatial resource symmetry is consistently associated with foreign clashes, wars, and battle casualties (Table 7–9), but the correlations range between $-.08$ and $-.16$.

7.3.2 Segregation–Desegregation

Human beings live asymmetrically spatially. When particular demo-types are clustered together, instead of being scattered more randomly, the situation is called *segregation,* which in common parlance refers to a condition in which members of underprivileged minority groups live in ghettos and find that districting is arranged to keep their offspring out of the "better" schools. The existence of silk-stocking districts constitutes segregation as well, though richer persons have more free choice of possible residential locations. When many races and national groups live together, the popular term in use is "integration." But since Karl Deutsch and others use "integration" in a special manner to be discussed in Section 7.5.6 below, it would be preferable to substitute the related term *desegregation* to refer to a symmetrical demographic-spatial distribution.

In contrast to the communal utopias of Fourier and Owen in the nineteenth century, where war was not foreseen as possible, desegregated pictures of totalitarian rule presented by such twentieth-century writers as Aldous Huxley and George Orwell have been less sanguine. They believe that a fully desegregated society will never arise from a natural evolu-

TABLE 7–9
Correlations Between Agglutination
and National Aggression

	Conflicts		Foreign Killed	
	Wars	Clashes	Total	Per capita
Indicator of Agglutination	180	181	182	183
34. Difference between cultivated/total land ratio and 50%	—.08	—.13	—.16	—.16

Positive correlations = 0.	Correlations in ±.10 range = 1.
Negative correlations = 4.	

tionary social process but instead must result from comprehensive planning. The ease with which subjects of a scientistic despotism are manipulated, the two writers warn, guarantees instant obedience to a call for battle according to the whims of the elites.

Spatial-demotypic symmetry would be present if every person in a population were located equidistant from his nearest neighbors, a condition possible only for persons employed in agriculture, or for members of a city-state in which every inhabitant of a polity resides in the capital city. Though population density and degree of urbanization have been found to be positively related to foreign conflict, little attention has focused on possible curvilinear relationships.[26] Countries with either more rural or urban employees (35) are asymmetrical. Some additional indicators include departure from the 50 percent level in the following per capita variables: agricultural population (36), population in cities over 20,000 (37), and the primacy of the major city as compared with the next largest urban centers (38). Foreign conflict tends to emerge from countries that are symmetrically settled (Table 7–10), but again correlation magnitudes are low.

7.3.3 Sectionalism–Systemization

When certain regions of a polity differ in clusters of attitudes, the term most generally employed is *sectionalism*. Banks defines sectionalism as "a phenomenon in which a significant percentage of the population of a nation lives in a sizable geographic area and identifies self-consciously and distinctively with that area."[27] The main difference between his definition and the one proposed here is that he does not specify the kind of identification involved, which he undoubtedly intended to be attitudinal in

[26] Haas, "Societal Approaches to the Study of War," p. 314, Table IV.
[27] Banks and Textor, *A Cross-Polity Survey*, p. 88.

TABLE 7–10
Correlations Between Segregation
and National Aggression[a]

	Conflicts		Foreign Killed	
	Wars	Clashes	Total	Per capita
Indicators of Segregation	180	181	182	183
35. Difference between agricultural/total workers ratio and 50%	—.03	—.02	.02	—.01
36. Difference between agricultural/total population ratio and 50%	.14	.10	.15	—.02
37. Difference between urbanites/total population ratio and 50%	—.14	—.06	—.07	—.04
38. Population of largest city/population of 4 largest cities	.03	—.06	—.01	.15
38d. Population of largest city/population of 4 largest cities	.11	—.20	—.02	

Positive correlations = 7.   Correlations in ±.10 range = 13.
Negative correlations = 12.

[a] For key, see notes to Table 7–2.

character. The opposite of sectionalism is the embracing of similar attitudes by all persons in all geographic regions of a societal system, for which Hall and Fagen supply the word *systemization*.[28]

   Problems associated with sectionalism have received wide attention since World War II. Samuel Lubell has stated that a significant aspect of postwar American politics is the decline of sectional loyalties and the development of a truly national electorate.[29] Because many former colonies in Africa and Asia achieved independence before they attained a sense of nationhood, the problem of coping with spatial-attitudinal asymmetry has been studied by many scholars under the heading of "nation building."[30] Societal systems with distinct attitudinal regions, one could argue, are more prone toward internal than external violence, as in the case of the American Civil War.

   At least two indicators of spatial attitudinal asymmetry may be used: Banks's lack of sectionalism (39) and Gurr's potential sectional separatism (40), the latter recoded somewhat to ensure that a spatial dimension is involved. As the data reveal, sectionalism is not a strong predictor of war (Table 7–11).

   [28] Hall and Fagen, "Definition of System," p. 22.

   [29] Samuel Lubell, *The Future of American Politics*, 2d ed. (Garden City, N. Y.: Doubleday, 1956).

   [30] See Karl W. Deutsch and William J. Foltz, eds., *Nation-Building* (New York: Atherton, 1963).

TABLE 7–11
Correlations Between Sectionalism
and National Aggression[a]

| | *Conflicts* | | *Foreign Killed* | |
| | Wars | Clashes | Total | Per capita |
Indicators of Sectionalism	180	181	182	183
39. Lack of sectionalism[b]	—.09	.08	.07	—.12
39g. Lack of sectionalism[b]			.03	
40. Potential sectional separatism	—.03	.21	.22	.10

Positive correlations = 6. Correlations in ±.10 range = 6.
Negative correlations = 3.

[a] For key, see notes to Table 7–2.
[b] Signs are reversed to be indicators of asymmetry.

7.3.4 Variation–Uniformity

One characteristic of governmental legal regulations in Westernized legal-rational societies is that they generally tend to be applicable at every locale within a particular jurisdiction. Legal commands prescribe, in other words, that there shall be *uniformity* in certain kinds of behavior. Some rules, however, establish different kinds of standards for special areas within a system, zoning laws being familiar examples in modern cities. One way of obtaining an exception to a law in order to benefit from spatial stratification in behavior is to obtain a "variance permit." Much in the manner that a composer's score directs musicians to play variations upon a theme, the many-roads-to-socialism doctrine is a form of ideological justification for varied strategies employed within the communist orbit for achieving governmental control over economic life. Accordingly, it seems reasonable to use *variation* as the term for spatial asymmetry in behavior.

A relevant variable is Gurr's sectional group discrimination measure (41), which provides a list of minority subcultures to facilitate rescaling the variable on purely spatial grounds. The correlational findings, however, are of low magnitude (Table 7–12).

7.3.5 Centralization–Decentralization

The fifth spatially stratified attribute is function performance. If functions are performed only within a single geographic sector of a system, the system is referred to as *centralized*. If there are a number of constituent units within a system that have autonomous powers of function, such as states or provinces under federalism, the system is *decentralized* (Riggs's phrase is "localized"). That a decentralized government, one "closer to the people," is inclined to be more pacific in external affairs was a contention

TABLE 7–12
Correlations Between Variation
and National Aggression

	Conflicts		Foreign Killed	
	Wars	Clashes	Total	Per capita
Indicator of Variation	180	181	182	183
41. Sectional group discrimination	.07	.04	—.01	—.13

Positive correlations = 1.	Correlations in ±.10 range = 3.
Negative correlations = 3.	

of proponents of small, democratic city-states, notably Jean-Jacques Rousseau. James Madison's argument in *Federalist No. 10* in favor of representative government in a larger polity, on the contrary, implies that a larger state can better defend itself from foreign assault as well as avoid the evils of overcentralization.

Three indicators of centralization-decentralization have been collected in scale units—Banks's vertical power centralization (42), Rummel's unitary system (43) and political decentralization (44). Because the data are not entirely consistent (Table 7–13), it appears that if a society is more geographically centralized, it is not necessarily closer to the warlike propensities of decisionmakers. Naroll, however, finds that there is a + .34 correlation between centralization of political authority in world civilizations and the extensiveness of participation in war.[31]

7.3.6 Concentration–Deconcentration

Structures are *concentrated* ("unified" is the term of Amitai Etzioni) if they are located in a small geographic area within a larger system. If structures are more evenly distributed spatially, the system is *deconcentrated* (or "dispersed," another of Riggs's terms). Both Britain and France, for example, have unitary (centralized) systems, but the British have deconcentrated their political structures within various units of local government. The French maintain most of the governmental apparatus in Paris, away from the countryside and small towns which together contain a majority of the population.[32]

[31] Naroll, "Deterrence in History."

[32] For the distinction between "centralization" and "concentration," see Herman Finer, *Governments of Greater European Powers* (New York: Holt, 1956), p. 241. For an attempt to operationalize, see Steven J. Brams, "Measuring the Concentration of Power in Political Systems," *American Political Science Review,* LXII (June 1968), 461–75.

TABLE 7–13
Correlations Between Centralization
and National Aggression[a]

| Indicators of Centralization | Conflicts | | Foreign Killed | |
	Wars 180	Clashes 181	Total 182	Per capita 183
42. Vertical power centralization	.13	.06	.16	.12
43. Unitary system	.15	.03	.01	—.01
43d. Unitary system	—.05	—.08	—.01	
44. Political decentralization[b]	—.12	—.08	—.23	—.09
44d. Political decentralization[b]	.24	.23	.19	

Positive correlations = 11.   Correlations in ±.10 range = 9.
Negative correlations = 7.

[a] For key, see notes to Table 7–2.
[b] Signs are reversed to be indicators of asymmetry.

The symmetrical utopia presented by Marx and Engels in *The German Ideology* is one in which government does not exist because its former functions are performed by the well-socialized human being. Due to the altruistic ethic of communism, violent methods for resolving differences of opinion are unknown. On the other hand, a concentrated state is for Marx inevitably war-prone, because government necessarily is the tool of a social class seeking victory in the class struggle. For Lenin, war is a necessary concomitant of overconcentrated imperial systems.

To test the Marxist conception of the war-breeding nature of structural-spatial asymmetry, three measures are used. Political systems with overseas colonies (45) are by definition concentrated, the dependency abroad being ruled by a so-called mother country. The extent of concentration may be measured by calculating the relative size of national (home) versus colonial and dependent areas and populations, so the percentage of national area (46) and the percentage of national population (47) may provide independent checks upon the "colonies" variable.

Results that correlate structural asymmetry on the space dimension with indicators of violent international conflict contain little ambiguity (Table 7–14). Asymmetry is consistently related to aggressiveness, thereby supporting our intuitive view that colonialism breeds war. An imperial world civilization is likely to have its capital city at some distance from its nearest international rival, and Naroll reports that the duration of war correlates — .21 with the propinquity to a rival and — .10 with the distance between a civilization's capital city and its frontiers.[33]

[33] Naroll, "Deterrence in History."

TABLE 7–14
Correlations Between Concentration
and National Aggression[a]

| | Conflicts | | Foreign Killed | |
Indicators of Concentration	Wars 180	Clashes 181	Total 182	Per capita 183
45. Colonial powers	.05	—.02	—.01	—.09
45d. Colonial powers	.11	—.02	.02	
46. National area/national and colonial land area[b]	.13	.03	.07	—.02
46d. National area/national and colonial land area[b]	.21	.03	.12	
47. National population/national and colonial population[b]	.19	.12	.16	.05
47d. National population/national and colonial population[b]	(.30)	.14	.21	

Positive correlations = 16.   Correlations in ±.10 range = 11.
Negative correlations = 5.

[a] For key, see notes to Table 7–2.
[b] Signs are reversed to be indicators of asymmetry.

7.4 KINETIC ASYMMETRY

There is no law concerning conservation of energy in social and political systems. The potentialities of human resources, behavior, function performance, and the like never seem to be exploited fully; upsurges in levels of performance remain latent until triggered by charisma or through dedication to abstract goals. Systems differ in the extent to which each of the six attributes is in flux, and the ratio between inactivity and activity is what is measured by indicators of the *kinetic* dimension (Table 7–15). The measure that is compared to determine asymmetry is neither a unit of time nor a territorial unit but, rather, a ratio of actualities to potentialities. A one-to-one ratio is symmetrical; as the actualities/potentialities ratio approaches zero, asymmetry increases, and the society becomes less developed.

The kinetic dimension differs from the temporal one in that asymmetries over time are mere changes, which may be explained by a variety of influences. Increased potentialities or dramatic changes in resources, as when Germany was divided into four zones after World War II, are fluctuations, but they are not relevant to the kinetic dimension. A kinetic change is one in which potentialities are assumed to be fixed, while the actualization of various resources, demotypes, attitudes, behavior, functions, and structures shifts on an activity-passivity continuum.

TABLE 7–15
Kinetic Concepts

	Concepts	
Attributes	Asymmetry	Symmetry
Resources	Slack	Mobilization
Demotypes	Immobility	Mobility
Attitudes	Alienation	Identification
Behavior	Uncohesive	Cohesive
Functions	Immobilist	Dynamic
Structures	Bottlenecked	Streamlined

7.4.1 Slack–Mobilization

We are familiar with charity drives in which nonprofit-making organizations solicit contributions from all possible sources in a community. Similarly, a politician and a power behind the throne may try to marshal resources of a political system to gain certain ends; what remains untapped has been described by Robert Dahl as *slack* in the system.[34] The opposite case, when potential resources are being fully utilized, is a *mobilized* situation. Mobilized arrangements exist when any change in the resource distribution of a system involves a definite loss in resource utilization; systems containing slack offer opportunities for all exploiters of resources to gain simultaneously. A problem in operationalization, however, is that the concept of slack implies that there are unmobilized elements that at some future time can be mobilized, which is difficult to demonstrate before the fact. Nevertheless, the theory of "have-not" nations is stated in terms of slack and mobilization: countries with limited resources at home (or capitalists who exhaust domestic markets) are said to have little choice but to seize resources and markets abroad in order to avoid depression and turmoil at home.

Two direct measures of the utilization of potential resources are ratios between potential to actual electric energy (48) and percent development of exploitable waterpower (49). A ratio between energy generation and consumption (50) measures loss of potential electric generation, since a discrepancy would be due to transmission inefficiency (or, in some cases, to station use). Traffic density and utilization of transportation facilities also index kinetic resource asymmetry: we use ratio of motor vehicles to road length (51), and ratio of rail freight to total rail length (52). Ratios of road length to land area (53) and rail length to land area (54) measure

[34] Robert A. Dahl, "The Analysis of Influence in Local Communities," *Social Science and Community Action,* ed. Charles R. Adrian (East Lansing: Michigan State University Press, 1960), pp. 35–39.

the extent to which land is committed to the transportation network of a country; though such facilities might be under-utilized and there may be topographical barriers to road building, the land on which roads and rails rest is nonetheless more efficiently developed than previously. But in correlating all of these variables with national aggressiveness one finds that extent of slack and mobilization is generally unrelated to degree of involvement in war (Table 7–16).

7.4.2 Mobility–Immobility

Demographic properties also vary along the kinetic dimension. Higher education enables one to change occupations more readily, and marriage between a person of low status and one of high social status often helps to upgrade one or downgrade the other. Persons increasing or decreasing in social status are called *mobile;* those staying at the same level are *immobile.* "Inbreeding" and "cosmopolitanizing" refer only to changes that have actually occurred, whereas "mobility" and "immobility" are concerned with the relation between successful mobility and potential mobility. Systems with enforced immobility are asymmetrical; kinetic symmetry exists if there is a high degree of demotypic change, for under such conditions individuals are actualizing their own aptitudes and self-images in order to climb to higher rungs on phenotypic ladders. A common observation concerning social systems closed to mobility in underdeveloped areas is that increases in status are achieved with more certainty by persons pursuing a military career. In such countries middle-class occupations often are unrewarding and require educational skills provided through an expensive education that only wealthy parents can afford; or the entrepreneurs belong to a pariah social group.[35] If military life is esteemed socially, one could hypothesize, the likelihood of war is high. Naroll's data demonstrate that war is somewhat more likely when societies invest many resources in military preparations,[36] but he does not provide an indicator concerning military careers as avenues for social mobility.

Direct measures of intragenerational and intergenerational mobility exist mainly for the United States,[37] so a cross-cultural mobility indicator will necessarily be indirect. Inasmuch as educational exposure contributes to

[35] Morris Janowitz, *The Military in the Political Development of New Nations* (Chicago: University of Chicago Press, 1964); Fred W. Riggs, *Administration in Developing Countries* (Boston: Houghton Mifflin, 1964), pp. 188–94.

[36] The correlation is + .19 for military readiness in primitive cultures but only + .07 for world civilizations: Naroll, "Deterrence in History"; Naroll, "Does Military Deterrence Deter?"

[37] See Seymour Martin Lipset and Reinhard Bendix, *Social Mobility in Industrial Society* (Berkeley: University of California Press, 1960).

TABLE 7–16
Correlations Between Slack
and National Aggression[a]

| | Conflicts | | Foreign Killed | |
| | Wars | Clashes | Total | Per capita |
Indicators of Slack	180	181	182	183
48. Electricity potential/electricity generation	.03	—.06	—.03	—.03
49. Waterpower developed/potential waterpower[b]	—.07	.07	.01	.09
50. Energy generation/consumption	—.01	.23	.23	.14
51. Motor vehicles/road length[b]	—.02	.18	.09	.01
52. Rail freight/rail length[b]	.13	—.17	—.17	.05
52d. Rail freight/rail length[b]	(—.36)	—.15	(—.33)	
53. Road length/land area[b]	—.05	.06	.00	.05
53d. Road length/land area[b]	—.04	.06	.00	
54. Rail length/land area[b]	—.07	.00	—.10	—.08
54d. Rail length/land area[b]	.05	—.03	—.08	

Positive correlations = 20.   Correlations in ±.10 range = 27.
Negative correlations = 17.

[a] For key, see notes to Table 7–2.
[b] Signs are reversed to be indicators of asymmetry.

mobility, the following indicators may be useful: percent illiteracy (55), primary school students as a percentage of children between the ages of 5 and 14 (56), primary and secondary school enrollment as a percentage of persons aged 5 to 19 (57), per capita education expenditures (58), and percent students in secondary and higher education (59). It is of course possible to conceive of educated persons unable to secure employment; and persons with special skills may not be able to advance their social status. But by and large the majority of skilled persons do find jobs, and the demand for skilled personnel is higher than the supply.[38] About half of the correlations between education indices and foreign conflict are positive, half negative, and most magnitudes are low (Table 7–17).

7.4.3 Alienation–Identification

Marx's conception of the *alienation* of the proletariat from the capitalist economic system best describes the attitudinal-kinetic continuum. The workingman's views were not taken into consideration in the early stages of industrialization, as the novels of Dickens vividly portray. The poorer strata had neither familiarity with nor enthusiasm for the middle-class ethic.

[38] Otis Dudley Duncan and Robert W. Hodge, "Education and Occupational Mobility: A Regression Analysis," *American Journal of Sociology*, XLVIII (May 1963), 629–44.

TABLE 7-17
Correlations Between Immobility
and National Aggression[a]

Indicators of Immobility	*Conflicts*		*Foreign Killed*	
	Wars	Clashes	Total	Per capita
	180	181	182	183
55. Illiterates/population	—.04	.12	.02	.00
55c. Illiterates/population	—.09	—.08		
55d. Illiterates/population	.12	—.17	.02	
56. Primary school pupils/population aged 5–14[b]	—.12	.06	.03	.03
56d. Primary school pupils/population aged 5–14[b]	—.24	.14		
57. Primary and secondary school enrollment/population aged 5–19[b]	—.16	.09	—.03	—.06
57d. Primary and secondary school enrollment/population aged 5–19[b]	—.12	—.00	—.09	
58. Education expenditures/population[b]	—.00	.25	.14	.03
58c. Education expenditures/population[b]	.10	.10		
59. Students in secondary and higher education/population[b]	—.01	.04	—.06	.01

Positive correlations = 17.   Correlations in ±.10 range = 22.
Negative correlations = 15.

[a] For key, see notes to Table 7–2.
[b] Signs are reversed to be indicators of asymmetry.

Identification of all members of a population with any system, for Marx, is impossible in the absence of true economic and political democracy. Capitalists can afford to identify with a system in which they emerge as victors in an often cutthroat struggle for profits; and, in the age when Malthusian ideas became popular, lower classes were treated cavalierly as little more than animals unfit for survival. If an alienated proletariat at home would not work arduously enough, the so-called white man's burden could be carried: war would be regarded as a legitimate means for obtaining more workers to employ as capitalist slaves, whether as indentured servants, workhouse orphans, or as assembly-line wage earners. As social theorists attest, alienation seems to go hand in hand with impotence in the determination of policy.[39]

[39] Emile Durkheim, *Suicide*, trans. John A. Spaulding and George Simpson (New York: The Free Press, 1951); John P. Clark, "Measuring Alienation Within a Social System," *American Sociological Review*, XXIV (December 1959), 849–52; Anthony Davids, "Alienation, Social Apperception, and Ego Structure," *Journal of Consulting Psychology*, XIX (February 1955), 21–27; Dwight G. Dean, "Alienation: Its Meaning and Measurement," *American Sociological Review*, XXVI (October 1961), 753–58; Lewis Feuer, "What Is Alienation? The Career of a Concept," *Soci-*

Since potentially an entire population of a country could identify with a societal system in various symbolic and verbal ways, a departure from the 100 percent level in national identification constitutes asymmetry. Lenin's complaint that the upper proletariat had been bribed by the bourgeoisie referred to increased identification by trade-union leaders with the capitalist system. But it was Lenin's successor in power, Joseph Stalin, who pursued the alienation argument to its logical conclusion by demoting or executing members of the bourgeoisie in the USSR at a time when they could only be alienated as "anomalous" participants in a worker-peasant democracy.

Naroll's codings of the tendency to suppress negative opinions, a sociocultural indicator of alienation, has a $+.25$ related to war frequency in his cross-cultural study.[40] Banks's low political enculturation (60) characteristic is unrelated to international conflict (Table 7–18). Lack of a developmental ideology (61) evidently lowers the level of foreign disputes. Articulation by anomic interest groups (62) is directly related to war frequency. Two inconsistently related indicators are percent voter turnout (63) and unionization, that is, the percentage of nonagricultural workers in trade unions (64). Lack of concern for (65) and fear of politics (66) are prevalent where countries abstain from aggression. Overall, however, results are quite uneven.

7.4.4 Uncohesive–Cohesive

Well-coordinated behavior is described as *cohesive;* uncoordinated efforts are *uncohesive.* The clearest illustration of the two concepts is provided in the Pepitone–Reichling small-group experiment concerning the relationship between cohesiveness and articulation of tension.[41] High and low cohesiveness groups were induced experimentally by informing subjects in

---

ology On Trial, eds. Maurice Stein and Arthur Vidich (Englewood Cliffs, N. J.: Prentice-Hall, 1963), pp. 127–47; Melvin Seeman, "On the Meaning of Alienation," *American Sociological Review,* XXIV (December 1959), 783–91.

[40] Naroll, "Does Military Deterrence Deter?"

[41] Albert Pepitone and George Reichling, "Group Cohesiveness and the Expression of Hostility," *Human Relations,* VIII, No. 3 (1955), 327–37. My definition of *cohesiveness* in terms of the ability of parts of a system to stick together behaviorally is approximately equivalent to one employed by Schacter and associates, in which the key element is the extent of attraction toward, rather than repulsion from, group activity: Stanley Schacter et al., "An Experimental Study of Cohesiveness and Productivity," *ibid.,* IV, No. 2 (1951), 229–30; Stanley E. Seashore, *Group Cohesiveness in the Industrial Work Group* (Ann Arbor: Institute for Social Research, University of Michigan, 1954). Often "cohesiveness" is equated with "morale," but the latter element is reclassified here under the concept of "consensus." "Cohesiveness," then, may be associated with Durkheim's "mechanical solidarity"; and "morale" is closer to "organic solidarity."

TABLE 7–18
Correlations Between Alienation
and National Aggression[a]

| | Conflicts | | Foreign Killed | |
| | Wars | Clashes | Total | Per capita |
Indicators of Alienation	180	181	182	183
60. Low political enculturation	—.08	.08	—.11	—.08
60g. Low political enculturation			.03	
61. Lack of developmental ideology	—.26	—.16	—.13	—.23
61g. Lack of developmental ideology			—.18	
62. Articulation by anomic interest groups	.13	.29	.26	.20
62g. Articulation by anomic interest groups			.16	
63. Voters/persons of voting age[b]	—.02	.11	—.03	—.02
64. Trade unionists/nonagricultural workers[b]	—.09	.16	—.07	—.05
65. Persons concerned with politics/sample[b]	.16	(.39)	.26	.02
66. Persons fearful of politics/sample	—.28	.11	—.11	—.18

Positive correlations = 14.   Correlations in ±.10 range = 11.
Negative correlations = 17.

[a] For key, see notes to Table 7–2.
[b] Signs are reversed to be indicators of asymmetry.

one set of matched groups that they were selected in such a way as to maximize group cooperativeness (hi-co), while a second set of groups was told (also nonveridically) that they were unfortunate leftovers who did not fit together but were urged to make the best of the situation (lo-co). The findings are that hi-co groups accomplished more and released more tension and hostility than did the lo-co groups. In short, a cohesive system is one in which individuals coordinate behavior maximally for a joint end; to lack cohesion is to duplicate or to scatter efforts, thereby detracting from full effectiveness in group activities.

A realization of military potentialities is one illustration of the cohesive-uncohesive continuum. Countries that invest money and conscript men to serve in an army demonstrate cohesiveness in achieving a goal, whether a foreign danger is perceived to be present or absent. Indicators of military cohesiveness are of course simultaneously useful in testing the theory that preparations for war do not deter but are undertaken by societies that are more prone to resolve international conflicts by violent means. Comparing percentages of military population (67) with the number of armed forces mobilizations (68), one finds that military cohesiveness is definitely related to the tendency to go to war (Table 7–19). The catchphrase "if you want peace, prepare for war" has little basis in fact.[42]

[42] In both of Naroll's studies, military preparedness is positively correlated with participation in war.

TABLE 7–19
Correlations Between Lack of Cohesiveness
and National Aggression[a]

| | Conflicts | | Foreign Killed | |
| | Wars | Clashes | Total | Per capita |
Indicators of Cohesiveness	180	181	182	183
67. Military personnel/population aged 15–64[b]	(—.37)	—.24	(—.41)	—.30
67c. Military population/total population[b]	—.10	.16		
68. Military mobilizations[b]	(—.41)	(—.51)	(—.41)	—.28
68r. Military mobilizations[b]	(—.37)	(—.54)	(—.41)	
68t. Military mobilizations[b]	(—.43)	(—.41)	(—.38)	
69. Divorces/population	—.25	.13	.24	.02
70. Marriages/population[b]	.04	—.05	.03	—.03
70d. Marriages/population[b]	(—.30)	—.06	—.27	
71. Divorces/marriages	.21	.13	.26	.06
71c. Divorces/marriages	.10	.20		
71d. Divorces/marriages	.16	—.02	.10	
72. Religious parties' votes/religious adherents[b]	.07	.16	.15	.08
73. Communist votes/Communist strength[b]	—.20	.06	—.00	.13

Positive correlations = 20. Correlations in ±.10 range = 15.
Negative correlations = 24.

[a] For key, see notes to Table 7–2.
[b] Signs are reversed to be indicators of asymmetry.

A somewhat different kind of cohesiveness indicator is the extent to which marriages hold together within a society. Divorce rates (69), marriage rates (70), and ratios of divorces to marriages (71), when correlated with national aggressiveness (Table 7–19), reveal that when marriage is more subject to disruption, decisionmakers in foreign affairs are less able to avoid violent outcomes.

Since subgroup solidarity in behavior is the concept being measured, two more indicators are suggested. One is the extent to which religious adherents vote for religious political parties (72). A second indicator is the ratio between the number of Communist votes in national elections and the estimated real Communist Party strength (73). This final pair of cohesiveness variables is not consistently related to the incidence of war.

7.4.5 Immobilist–Dynamic

Whereas Almond and others claim that there are certain functional requisites for the optimum performance of political systems, there are occasions when domestic pressures impede the rate of political outputs. In France an inability to convert inputs into outputs, which was characteristic of the Third and Fourth Republics, is designated as *immobilism.* Few protocoalitions[43] were capable of forming temporary winning coalitions, despite many political activities by the bureaucracy, which was authorized by earlier laws and carried out less controversial functions. Immobilism, in other words, does not mean that political functions are performed infrequently; a system is immobilist insofar as social disputes remain unresolved. The opposite of immobilism is the operation of a *dynamic* polity, in which outputs do indeed emerge to correspond to inputs. In comparative government textbooks the British system appears to receive such a designation: once a political party has a clear majority, leaders of a government ordinarily can count on the loyalty of its rank-and-file members to support nearly all of their proposals. The continuity-discontinuity continuum differs from immobilism-dynamism in that the latter terms deal with the extent to which governmental operations attain goals, adapt to the environment, maintain patterns, and integrate structures, to use Talcott Parsons's four functional requisites.[44]

Banks's variable called "nonmobilizational system style" (74) is a qualitative index of immobilism. Quantitative indicators focus on the ability of a government to tax in order to execute governmental operations: percentage of gross national product devoted to governmental expenditures (75), and the percentage of the gross national product expended on public administration and defense (76), defense (77), education (78), welfare (79), general government (80), and on the central government (81). Since correlations between these variables and foreign conflict are largely negative (Table 7–20), it would appear that functional dynamism is a prerequisite for warlike state behavior. Judging from military expenditure variables, deterrence from a "position of strength" does not work.

7.4.6 Bottlenecked–Streamlined

Excessive bureaucratic restrictions slow down potentialities of structures. Indeed, checks-and-balances systems are designed deliberately to so lack a horizontal concentration of power (82) that activity of one structure may be *bottlenecked* by another structure with considerable ease. Bicameral legislative systems (83), for example, often are characterized by blockage, except in totalitarian polities. *Streamlined* systems are arranged structurally to allow maximum passage through structural channels. To index structural-kinetic asymmetry one might wryly suggest measuring the length of red tape in a system. A political system that is tied up in bureaucratic knots would not be expected to provide much of a military threat. We shall use the ratio

[43] William Riker, *The Theory of Political Coalitions* (New Haven: Yale University Press, 1962).

[44] Talcott Parsons, *The Social System* (New York: The Free Press, 1951).

TABLE 7–20
Correlations Between Immobilism
and National Aggression[a]

| | *Conflicts* | | *Foreign Killed* | |
| | Wars | Clashes | Total | Per capita |
Indicators of Immobilism	180	181	182	183
74. Nonmobilization system style	(—.33)	.26	(—.30)	—.22
74g. Nonmobilization system style			—.11	
75. Government expenditures/national income[b]	—.09	.10	.07	.03
75d. Government expenditures/national income[b]	—.23	—.22	—.28	
76. Public administration and defense expenditures/GNP[b]	(—.46)	(—.37)	(—.41)	(—.44)
76d. Public administration and defense expenditures/GNP[b]	(—.37)	(—.39)	(—.39)	
77. Defense expenditures/national income[b]	—.21	—.27	—.25	—.18
77d. Defense expenditures/national income[b]	(—.31)	—.12	—.29	
77h. Defense expenditures/total expenditures[b]	(—.40)			
78. Education expenditures/national income[b]	—.01	.07	.06	.00
79. Welfare expenditures/national income[b]	.01	(.36)	.28	—.18
80. General government expenditures/GNP[b]	—.21	.21	—.06	.11
81. Central government expenditures/GNP[b]	(—.36)	—.18	(—.42)	(—.31)

Positive correlations = 12.   Correlations in ±.10 range = 10.
Negative correlations = 31.

[a] For key, see notes to Table 7–2.
[b] Signs are reversed to be indicators of asymmetry.

of government revenue to expenditures (84) as an indicator of the ability of a government to spend its resources, going into debt if necessary to conduct operations perceived as useful. The first three streamlining variables are consistently related to foreign conflict (Table 7–21).

When press censorship (85–86), freedom of political opposition (87–88), executive weakness (89), and legislative weakness (90) are selected, correlations turn out more consistently positive (Table 7–21): restrictions on newspapers and political parties go hand in hand with wars, though executives are by no means hamstrung in making decisions for war.

As a general characteristic of a societal system, structural blockage exists if many restrictions, either legal or social, are imposed on various institutions. A high legal voting age (91), high legal marriage age, and restrictions on divorce and prostitution are almost consistently negatively related to national aggressiveness (Table 7–21).[45] A tendency to restrict,

[45] Cattell finds that restrictions on divorce correlate — .23 with war participation and — .16 with the number of foreign clashes; restrictions on prostitution correlate — .00 and — .13, respectively; the minimum legal marriage age correlates — .02 and — .25 with the same two variables. Cattell, "Dimensions of Culture Patterns by Factorization of National Characters."

TABLE 7–21
Correlations Between Bottlenecking
and National Aggression[a]

Indicators of Bottlenecking	Conflicts		Foreign Killed	
	Wars	Clashes	Total	Per capita
	180	181	182	183
82. Horizontal concentration of power[b]	—.11	—.19	—.15	—.01
82g. Horizontal concentration of power[b]			.08	
83. Bicameral legislature	—.17	—.11	—.03	—.12
83g. Bicameral legislature			—.10	
84. Government revenue/expenditure	—.06	—.22	—.10	—.20
84d. Government revenue/expenditure	—.06	—.21	—.11	
85. Press censorship	.21	(.32)	.26	.21
85c. Press censorship	.03	.10		
86. Press censorship	.09	.15	.17	.09
86d. Press censorship	—.10	—.09	—.16	
86g. Press censorship			—.19	
87. Political opposition restricted	.04	.20	.13	.05
87g. Political opposition restricted			.05	
88. Political opposition unrestricted[b]	.11	.05	.03	—.05
88d. Political opposition unrestricted[b]	—.12	.10	—.07	
89. Executive weakness	—.16	(—.33)	—.21	—.09
89g. Executive weakness			.17	
90. Legislative weakness	.14	.21	.19	.08
90g. Legislative weakness			.17	
91. Minimum voting age	—.12	—.11	—.11	—.20
91d. Minimum voting age	.02	—.14	.01	

Positive correlations = 28.   Correlations in ±.10 range = 25.
Negative correlations = 32.

[a] For key, see notes to Table 7–2.
[b] Signs are reversed to be indicators of asymmetry.

in short, appears to be a cultural characteristic that applies equally to restraint in entering both wars and in other areas of social activity.

7.5   ENTROPIC ASYMMETRY

In delineating types of entropic asymmetry, the basic characteristic is a contradiction between various kinds of organizational properties in a system, such that efficiency in operation is lower than it otherwise might be. In systems with *negative entropy* each unit meshes closely with other units; *positive entropy* is present if the elements are arranged randomly (Table 7–22). A system of high positive entropy is disorganized and inefficient; if negative entropy is found in a system, then it is geared in such a way that minimal work is required to generate maximum output.

TABLE 7–22
Entropic Concepts

	Concepts	
Attributes	Asymmetry	Symmetry
Resources	Strain	Adequacy
Demotypes	Diversity	Similarity
Attitudes	Contention	Consonance
Behavior	Conflict	Cooperation
Functions	Diffraction	Fusion
Structures	Fragmentation	Integration

Who is the judge of randomness, efficiency, or proper organization? Because the concept of entropy implies an ideal-typical model of a societal system, assignment of concepts to an entropic symmetry-asymmetry continuum may appear to involve distortable value judgments. The basic recording units are social values, and entropy will be noted wherever contradictory values exist side by side. Whether one wishes to tolerate a situation in which values are out of phase with one another (entropic asymmetry) is a profound moral question, but the existence of such a state of affairs is an empirical question.

7.5.1 Strain–Adequacy

Unplanned social systems lack the social resources to fulfill culturally approved purposes. Propagation of certain goals can be out of step with efforts to provide means for the attainment of goals. Robert K. Merton refers to such entropic-resource asymmetries as *strain,* citing the fact that American cultural norms prescribe upward social mobility as a goal, while individuals of higher social status so restrict the social allocation of resources that most persons cannot achieve mobility; strata publicizing a goal of social advancement do little to provide resources for climbing social ladders.[46] One may regard such a situation as badly organized in an objective sense, even if the social elites are not deliberately two-faced. When there is no discrepancy between aspiration and achievement levels, resources are *adequate* for attainment of cultural goals.

One of the most obvious illustrations of strain is the percentage of unemployment (92). When the economic system encourages a pool of laborers but does not tailor manpower needs to existing resources, blame probably does not rest with individual workers or employers; there is no systemic organization because of nonexistent or faulty corporate or governmental planning. The pupil-to-teacher ratio (93) is another indicator of strain, for

[46] Robert K. Merton, *Social Theory and Social Structure,* rev. ed. (New York: The Free Press, 1957), Chapter 4.

the social value placed on education is often out of proportion to its availability, effectiveness, and quality in small, face-to-face instructional settings. Similarly, one could use a ratio between a country's population and its physicians (94) as well as a ratio between hospital beds and physicians (95). A final indicator is nutritional adequacy, when caloric intake is above medically established minimum daily requirements (96).

One could speculate that systems with entropic-resource asymmetry would be incapable of organizing themselves for battle. Alternatively, inability to eliminate disorganization might be a precondition for paranoiacally believing that internal difficulties are due to machinations of foreign countries. The data provide only a possible answer that both theories are correct (Table 7–23), since there is little consistency among the signs of the correlation coefficients.

7.5.2   Diversity–Similarity

The presence of many ethnic groups in a country may contribute to a rich cultural life; but in conducting collective societal operations, *diverse* cues at some point must be decoded in order to facilitate a group product. In a system composed of persons with *similar* genetic and cultural backgrounds, individuals usually do not talk past one another: they are able to understand most of each other's messages, even if their own personal values are somewhat different. A diverse system is beset with many meanings attached to words, different styles of behavior, and divergent value systems. Aristotle, in his recommendation for a large middle class, recognized that a system which is largely demographically symmetrical will tend to be more dynamic, streamlined, integrated, and symmetrical in other respects.

The presence of diversity is often associated with a tolerance for diversity. Urbanites, who generally live amid more demotypic groups than ruralites, have a more permissive attitude toward deviant behavior.[47] Can we extrapolate this finding to the international level? Toleration of domestic diversity is likely to soften a country's perception of its international rivals, for its diplomats may possess the ability to cope with multiple operational codes.[48]

Diversity may be indexed by counting the number of groups comprising more than one percent of the total population: ethnic groups (97), language communities (98), nationality groups (99), religious groups

---

[47] Samuel Stouffer, *Communism, Conformity and Civil Liberties* (Garden City, N. Y.: Doubleday, 1955).

[48] Cf. Alexander L. George, "The 'Operational Code': A Neglected Approach to the Study of Political Leaders and Decision-Making," *International Studies Quarterly*, XIII (June 1969), 190–222.

TABLE 7–23
Correlations Between Strain
and National Aggression[a]

| | *Conflicts* | | *Foreign Killed* | |
| | Wars | Clashes | Total | Per capita |
Indicators of Strain	180	181	182	183
92. Unemployed/labor force	—.10	—.24	—.12	—.00
92c. Unemployed/labor force	.00	(.33)		
92d. Unemployed/labor force	.23	—.16	—.24	
92h. Unemployed/labor force	(.33)			
93. Pupils/teachers (primary schools)	—.06	.00	—.08	—.08
93d. Pupils/teachers	.26	—.06	.02	
94. Population/physicians	—.06	.09	.07	—.06
95. Hospital beds/physicians	.13	.18	(.35)	(.36)
96. Excess of calories consumed over calories required/calories required[b]	—.08	.01	—.06	.05
96d. Excess of calories consumed over calories required/calories required[b]	—.16	.10	—.08	

Positive correlations = 16.   Correlations in ±.10 range = 19.
Negative correlations = 16.

[a] For key, see notes to Table 7–2.
[b] Signs are reversed to be indicators of asymmetry.

(100), and racial groups (101). Since the indicators are consistently related to foreign conflict (Table 7–24) and most correlations are outside the ± .10 range, it is necessary to negate the finding that there is a degree of toleration for nonconformity in societal systems with diversity: external violence is associated with internal diversity.

7.5.3 Contention–Consonance

Societal systems tend to contain a number of attitudinal clusters with various degrees of inconsistency among them. If several attitudinal configurations are internally consistent or synthesize otherwise contrary views, they are known as *consonant;* competing and inconsistent value systems and ideologies are called *contending.* In writings on the subject of supranationalism, the concept of "community" implies attitudinal consonance, whereas an absence of a community is contention.[49] Asian philosophies are usually thought to be syncretic, or consonance-prone, while European systems of

[49] Cf. Bruce M. Russett, *Community and Contention* (Cambridge: MIT Press, 1963); Leon Festinger, *A Theory of Cognitive Dissonance* (Stanford: Stanford University Press, 1957); Werner Landecker refers to this continuum as "cultural integration" in "Types of Integration and Their Measurement," *American Journal of Sociology,* LVI (January 1951), 332–40.

TABLE 7–24
Correlations Between Diversity
and National Aggression[a]

		Conflicts		Foreign Killed	
		Wars	Clashes	Total	Per capita
Indicators of Diversity		180	181	182	183
97.	Ethnic groups over 1% of population	.08	.07	.13	.06
97d.	Ethnic groups over 1% of population	.20	—.29	—.02	
98.	Language communities over 1% of population	.14	.16	.18	.18
98c.	Language communities over 1% of population	.07	.19		
98d.	Language communities over 1% of population	—.03	(.33)	.19	
99.	Nationality groups over 1% of population	.23	.26	.19	.23
99d.	Nationality groups over 1% of population	.24	.23	.23	
100.	Religious groups over 1% of population	.22	.29	(.34)	(.35)
100d.	Religious groups over 1% of population	.21	.16	(.32)	
101.	Racial groups over 1% of population	—.18	—.13	—.20	—.07

Positive correlations = 27.   Correlations in ±.10 range = 7.
Negative correlations = 7.

[a] For key, see notes to Table 7–2.

thought have been notoriously contentious. To measure these variables, one immediately thinks of such efforts as Charles Morris's *Varieties of Human Values* (1956).[50] In a political system of generally consonant values, new ideas will tend to be absorbed eventually by all of the major interests; but where political parties are ideologically rigid, values will be in contention with each other. A contentious societal system could be so overly consumed with internal disputation that little energy is left for foreign sadism. But it is also possible to hypothesize that an inability to resolve contentious viewpoints entails such a sense of frustration that at times only violent conflict will provide a framework for patching up differences in domestic issues.

If there is a relation between verbal contention and foreign conflict, such indicators as the duration of strikes (102), percentage of a population engaging in strikes (103–105), number of general strikes (106), and number of antigovernment demonstrations (107) could be used. Correlations between these indicators and foreign conflict measures are overwhelmingly positive, though low in magnitude (Table 7–25). A country that is contentious at home carries its disputes to the battlefield abroad, and vice versa.

[50] Charles Morris, *Varieties of Human Value* (Chicago: University of Chicago Press, 1956).

TABLE 7–25
Correlations Between Contention
and National Aggression[a]

| | | Conflicts | Foreign Killed | |
| | Wars | Clashes | Total | Per capita |
Indicators of Contention	180	181	182	183
102. Days lost due to strikes	—.03	.11	.08	.14
103. Strikers/population	.06	.02	.01	.05
104. Strikers/work force	.18	.13	.14	.11
105. Strikers/unionists	.07	.25	.18	.11
106. General strikes	—.05	.07	.04	.16
106r. General strikes	—.01	.01	.04	
106t. General strikes		.03	.06	
107. Antigovernment demonstrations	.01	.13	.20	.22
107c. Antigovernment demonstrations			.07	
107r. Antigovernment demonstrations	.16	.20	.21	
107t. Antigovernment demonstrations	.10	.02	.15	

Positive correlations = 34.   Correlations in ±.10 range = 19.
Negative correlations = 3.

[a] For key, see notes to Table 7–2.

7.5.4 Conflict–Cooperation

Among terms pertaining to asymmetry, perhaps the most misused is "conflict," which in its Latin and French derivatives clearly refers to a physical or behavioral clashing. *Conflict* implies a behavioral opposition between forces; *cooperation* means that behavioral vectors point in the same direction. Lewis Coser, developing a definition based on Georg Simmel's conception, has indicated that conflict is a physical struggle between opponents and rivals, as we have seen in Section 1.2. A similar formulation is presented by Ralph Goldman, in which conflict is identified even more unambiguously as a form of human behavior.[51] Cooperation occurs when behavior of two or more persons is symmetrical—that is, if common means are pursued in tandem.

[51] Lewis A. Coser, *The Functions of Social Conflict* (New York: The Free Press, 1956), p. 8; Georg Simmel, *Conflict and the Web of Group-Affiliations*, trans. Kurt H. Wolff (New York: The Free Press, 1955), pp. 92–93. Robert North, however, refers to "conflict" in terms more appropriate to our use of "contention": North, Howard E. Koch, Jr., and Dina A. Zinnes, "The Integrative Functions of Conflict," *Journal of Conflict Resolution*, IV (September 1960), 355–74. Rummel and Tanter select indicators appropriate to both interpretations (see above, note 2). Ralph Goldman, "Conflict, Co-operation and Choice: An Exploration of Conceptual Relationships," *Decisions, Values and Groups*, ed. Norman F. Washburne (New York: Macmillan, 1962), II, 410–39. See also Quincy Wright, "The Nature of Conflict," *Western Political Quarterly*, IV (June 1951), 193–209.

The clearest examples of domestic conflict are revolution (108) and guerrilla warfare (109), inasmuch as such behavior by definition is at odds with normal government operations. Assassinations (110), purges (111), riots (112), and the death rate due to domestic violence (113) are some other domestic conflict behavior indicators. Though most of the correlations are positive (Table 7–26), the most serious threats to a domestic polity— revolutions and guerrilla wars—are not consistently related to foreign wars.[52] Less serious forms of conflict are almost always positively related. One might infer provisionally that concerted attempts to restructure a national society attract foreign aggressiveness, but that conflict expressed sporadically and anomically is more of a wellspring for war. The pattern of relationships, however, leaves unexamined possible conditions that might mediate between citizen unrest and elite decisions to opt for war. It may be that elites, fearing that their tenure will be cut short in periods of high domestic conflict, decide to select an outside target for the population to displace its aggression; contrariwise, foreign opponents may bide their time until potential adversaries are torn by strife before launching aggressive attacks.

7.5.5 Diffraction–Fusion

Function performance can also be entropically asymmetrical. The functional *diffraction* model depicts a system in which one and only one structure performs a particular function; in *fused* systems a single structure performs many functions, or single functions are performed by many overlapping and competitive structures.[53] In the *Mikado* by Gilbert and Sullivan the character Pooh-Bah illustrates functional fusion, for he is Chancellor of the Exchequer, Prime Minister, Leader of the Opposition, Minister of Justice, Commissioner of Police, and (with the exception of the post of Lord High Executioner) Lord High Everything Else. The Executioner alone has a functionally specific task within a delightfully fused polity.

Such abstract notions as diffraction and fusion would seem difficult to measure in any concrete manner; but if we accept the validity of scaled data supplied by Banks and Textor, there is a possibility of constructing a composite index from several of their raw characteristics. The interest articulation function, for example, has been coded according to five structural alternatives: extent of articulation by associational groups, institutional groups, anomic groups, nonassociational groups, and by political parties. In a system with diffracted function performance, the degree of articulation by

[52] Civil wars correlate + .25 with interstate wars in Naroll, "Deterrence in History."

[53] Almond and Powell, *Comparative Politics;* Riggs, *Administration in Developing Countries.*

TABLE 7–26
Correlations Between Conflict
and National Aggression[a]

Indicators of Conflict	Conflicts		Foreign Killed	
	Wars 180	Clashes 181	Total 182	Per capita 183
108. Revolutions	—.14	.14	.05	.17
108c. Revolutions	—.10	.15		
108r. Revolutions	—.04	.12	.12	
108t. Revolutions	—.02	.06	.23	
109. Guerrilla warfare	—.10	.14	.11	.19
109r. Guerrilla warfare	—.10	—.10	—.04	
109t. Guerrilla warfare	—.05	.05	(.30)	
110. Assassinations	.04	.17	.15	.23
110c. Assassinations	.28	.18		
110r. Assassinations	.19	.15	.18	
110t. Assassinations	.00	.05	(.34)	
111. Purges	—.01	.27	.19	.27
111r. Purges	.17	(.30)	(.34)	
111t. Purges	.03	.19	.25	
112. Riots	—.04	.12	.18	.22
112c. Riots	(.48)	(.49)		
112r. Riots	.12	.08	.19	
112t. Riots	.01	.12	.24	
113. Deaths from domestic group violence/population	—.02	.06	.09	.15
113g. Deaths from domestic group violence			.29	
113r. Deaths from domestic group violence	.07	.02	.22	
113t. Deaths from domestic group violence	.07	.12	.27	

Positive correlations = 55.   Correlations in ±.10 range = 25.
Negative correlations = 12.

[a] For key, see notes to Table 7–2.

associational groups, for example, would be coded as "significant," while all other structures would be "negligible" articulators. Fusion is present if all four types of structures do some amount of articulation. To estimate fused function performance, which exists characteristically within executive structures of developing political systems, the most complete data exist for diffraction in articulation (114) and diffraction in aggregation (115). The highest scale score is assigned to polities in which one structure is a significant performer of the function while other structures are limited or negligible performers of the function. The lowest score is appropriate for polities in which all of the functions are performed in a limited or negligible manner by all possible structures. David Ricardo's expectation that a desire for efficiency through diffraction makes foreign conflict an unattractive sideshow is not borne out by the data (Table 7–27). Diffraction consistently

TABLE 7–27
Correlations Between Diffraction
and National Aggression

	Conflicts		Foreign Killed	
	Wars	Clashes	Total	Per capita
Indicators of Diffraction	180	181	182	183
114. Diffracted articulation	.18	.06	.12	.08
115. Diffracted aggregation	.19	.05	.06	—.03

Positive correlations = 7.   Correlations in ±.10 range = 5.
Negative correlations = 1.

entails a greater extent of participation in international conflict, though only three of the individual correlations exceed .10.

7.5.6 Fragmentation–Integration

If structures are well linked within a system, the system has negative entropy; poor linkage means that structures are related almost randomly. A system in which there is considerable rationality in the linkage of structures is called *integrated;* nonlinked systems are *fragmented.* The term integration has been used in such a variety of ways by social scientists that its Latin derivation is often forgotten: the word denotes a situation in which separate parts have been connected within a single whole. The progressive increase of systemic structural linkage constitutes the "integration process" for Etzioni. One special kind of high-level integration is unification, in which previously independent governmental structures are merged; deunification is the breakup of single political structures into two or more sovereign entities. Much confusion over the term integration exists because it is used as an elementary notion of structural linkage that indicates a "sense of community,"[54] which is an attitudinal notion.

Political integration is to be distinguished from social integration. A polity is integrated if structures perform single functions in concert, somewhat the same notion as diffraction, turned sideways. Social integration

[54] Karl W. Deutsch et al., *Political Community and the North Atlantic Area* (Princeton: Princeton University Press, 1957). Amitai Etzioni in his *Political Unification* (New York: Holt, Rinehart and Winston, 1965) uses "integration" to refer to the endpoint of the continuum toward which the process heads. But, as he suggests, a relation between attaining a sense of "community" and achievement of "integration" is not at all clear; it is possible, in fact, for integration to take place even in the absence of community, as when Germany annexed Alsace and Lorraine between 1871 and the end of World War I. Landecker ("Types of Integration and Their Measurement") refers to our use of "integration" as "communicative integration."

exists when persons are in communication with one another, even when they are hurling obscene epithets at each other. Because some minimal level of coordination is a precondition to waging modern war, one might expect indicators of political and social integration to be positively correlated with national aggressiveness. On the other hand, societies at high levels of integration might prefer a more routinized or peaceful posture in foreign affairs.[55]

Indices of political fragmentation may be constructed by determining whether particular structures perform more than one function in a significant manner, thus overloading facilities for coordination of activities. For example, a fragmentation in functions performed by political parties (116) exists when parties both articulate and aggregate interests. A condition of weak executives with weak legislatures (117) indicates a lack of central drive to accomplish goals within the polity. Military interventions into politics (118) and police interventions into politics (119) characterize politically fragmented systems, since the structures in question—the army and the police—thereby scatter their attention across many functional tasks and exercise their power to negate operations of existing structures. Fragmented polities are more likely to engage in foreign war (Table 7–28), so an active use of strong-arm tactics in place of a strong polity at home signals a move on the part of agents of coercion to embark upon war abroad. Where structures are relegated to narrow spheres of competence, war is avoided.

Measuring the use of communication channels may indicate social integration: per capita cinema attendance (120), library book circulation (121), newspaper circulation (122), telephones (123), pieces of domestic mail (124), radio receivers (125), television sets (126). Correlating social integration measures with national aggressiveness, one finds that the use of communication facilities tends to be high in countries frequently at war, lower for countries not engaged in violent military actions (Table 7–28).

7.6 ALLOCATIONAL ASYMMETRY

The fifth way in which an attribute of a system may be symmetrical or asymmetrical is through *allocation* to various strata of a societal system (Table 7–29).[56] Allocations that are skewed are asymmetrical; lack of stratification is symmetrical.

---

[55] Charles McClelland, "The Acute International Crisis," *World Politics*, XIV (October 1961), 182–204; George Liska, *International Equilibrium* (Harvard: Harvard University Press, 1957), pp. 200–201.

[56] This dimension has been labelled "distributive" in Oran R. Young, *Systems of Political Science* (Englewood Cliffs, N. J.: Prentice-Hall, 1968), Chapter 5.

TABLE 7–28
**Correlations Between Fragmentation
and National Aggression**[a]

| | *Conflicts* | | *Foreign Killed* | |
| | Wars | Clashes | Total | Per capita |
Indicators of Fragmentation	180	181	182	183
116. Fragmentation in party functions	.07	.06	.06	.06
117. Weakness of executive and legislature	.06	.21	.12	.10
118. Military interventions into politics	—.00	.21	.09	.18
118g. Military interventions into politics			.28	
119. Police interventions into politics	—.03	.21	.09	.06
119g. Police intervention into politics			.15	
120. Cinema attendance/population[b]	—.09	—.05	—.06	—.11
120d. Cinema attendance/population[b]	—.26	.04	—.12	
121. Library book circulation/population[b]	.17	.14	.19	(.33)
121d. Library book circulation/population[b]	—.12	.20	—.05	
122. Newspaper circulation/population[b]	—.04	.11	.06	.08
122d. Newspaper circulation/population[b]	—.25	.11	—.03	
123. Telephones/population[b]	—.01	.17	.17	.26
123c. Telephones/population[b]	.03	—.07		
123d. Telephones/population[b]	—.16	.18	.10	
123h. Telephones/population[b]	(.33)			
124. Domestic mail pieces/population[b]	.13	.24	—.06	.13
124d. Domestic mail pieces/population[b]	—.12	.25	.13	
125. Radio receivers/population[b]	—.05	.17	.13	.09
125d. Radio receivers/population[b]	—.22	.21	.06	
126. Television sets/population[b]	.00	.03	—.00	.08

Positive correlations = 46.   Correlations in ±.10 range = 32.
Negative correlations = 21.

[a] For key, see notes to Table 7–2.
[b] Signs are reversed to be indicators of asymmetry.

7.6.1   Disparity–Equality

The meaning of the allocational dimension is quite clear when applied to resources. If income, horses, or matchboxes are distributed evenly throughout a system, the condition is one of *equality;* an uneven allocation of resources constitutes *disparity.* Extremist solutions for international problems, it may be argued, enjoy an appeal not because of the magnitude of resources within a system but because a coexistence of very rich and very poor elements serves to emphasize the wide gap between them.

In evaluating 12 possible measures of inequality, Hayward Alker and Bruce Russett decided that the Gini index of land ownership inequality (127) is preferable,[57] though one could also use the smaller percentage of

[57] Hayward R. Alker, Jr., and Bruce M. Russett, "Indices for Comparing Inequality," *Comparing Nations,* eds. Richard L. Merritt and Stein Rokkan (New Haven: Yale University Press, 1966), pp. 349–82.

TABLE 7–29
Allocational Concepts

	Concepts	
Attributes	Asymmetry	Symmetry
Resources	Disparity	Equality
Demotypes	Heterogeneity	Homogeneity
Attitudes	Cleavage	Consensus
Behavior	Deviance	Conformity
Functions	Discrimination	Nonpreferential
Structures	Differentiated	Undifferentiated

the population owning half of the land (128), or the slope of a Lorenz curve at 95 percent of land ownership (129). The Gini index has also been applied to individual income before taxes (130) and after taxes (131). A final index is the percentage of total farms being rented (132), a measure of absentee landlordism. To determine whether business enterprises bear the brunt of taxation, as opposed to individuals, a useful measure is the percentage of tax revenues accounted for by customs fees (133). The data reveal that inequality is not consistently associated with international conflict (Table 7–30).

7.6.2 Heterogeneity–Homogeneity

If demotypic characteristics across each individual in a population are symmetrical, the system is *homogeneous*. If distinct demotypes are numerous, the composition of a population is described as *heterogeneous*. Whereas heterogeneity and homogeneity are measured by percentages of a population belonging to the most numerous group, in Section 7.5.2 diversity and similarity indices tabulate the number of sizable demotypic strata within a system.

Glazer's "nation of nations" concept is appropriate for a heterogeneous system. Where many cultures live side by side, as in the Soviet Union, it may be possible to maintain a system in accordance with Zipf's law—that cohesion will exist so long as group sizes decline exponentially from the largest to the smallest demotype.[58] The problem of preventing many groups from centrifugally seceding may so exhaust internal resources that warfare is neither welcome nor contemplated.

Heterogeneity has been coded by Banks and Textor for religious (134), racial (135), and linguistic (136) groups; a composite rating (137) is provided as well. The largest group has been percentaged out of total population for the following: religion (138), ethnicity (139), language communities (140), native-born inhabitants (141), and the largest racial

---

[58] George K. Zipf, *Human Behavior and the Principle of Least Effort* (Cambridge: Addison-Wesley, 1949).

TABLE 7–30
Correlations Between Disparity
and National Aggression[a]

Indicators of Disparity	Conflicts		Foreign Killed	
	Wars 180	Clashes 181	Total 182	Per capita 183
127. Land ownership inequality (Gini index)	—.02	.10	—.06	.12
127d. Land ownership inequality (Gini index)	—.02	.12	—.01	
128. Population owning half of land/total population[b]	.02	.13	.03	.23
128d. Population owning half of land/total population[b]	.15	.16	.00	
129. Slope of Lorenz curve at 95% of land ownership	—.16	—.03	.19	.20
129d. Slope of Lorenz curve at 95% of land ownership	.01	—.13	—.13	
130. Income inequality before taxes (Gini index)	(—.35)	(—.47)	(—.34)	.16
131. Income inequality after taxes (Gini index)	(—.30)	(—.47)	(—.31)	—.08
132. Farms on rented land/total farms	.01	.15	.11	.05
133. Customs taxes/total taxes[b]	—.01	—.05	—.18	—.11
133d. Customs taxes/total taxes[b]	.04	—.26	—.21	

Positive correlations = 19.   Correlations in ±.10 range = 16.
Negative correlations = 21.

[a] For key, see notes to Table 7–2.
[b] Signs are reversed to be indicators of asymmetry.

group (142). We find that in general heterogeneity is associated with a lower incidence of international aggression (Table 7–31); the problem of internal maintenance mentioned above may not be so severe after all. Countries that weld together a large number of demotypic groups are evidently inclined to cooperate with peoples of other nations, too.

7.6.3 Cleavage–Consensus

If the distribution of an attitude is universal within a system, *consensus* is said to exist. "Consensus" is used in some theoretical writings to pertain only to agreement on whether a regime rules legitimately,[59] but the scope of its applicability herein extends to all socially and politically relevant attitudes. When an attitude is distributed unevenly, with contrary views present, *cleavage* exists.

[59] Herbert J. Spiro, *World Politics* (Homewood, Ill.: Dorsey, 1966), Chapter 3; Seymour Martin Lipset, *Political Man* (Garden City, N. Y.: Doubleday, 1960). One comprehensive explication is that of Irving Louis Horowitz, "Consensus, Conflict and Cooperation: A Sociological Inventory," *Social Forces*, XLI (December 1962), 177–88.

TABLE 7–31
Correlations Between Heterogeneity
and National Aggression[a]

| | Conflicts | | Foreign Killed | |
| | Wars | Clashes | Total | Per capita |
Indicators of Heterogeneity	180	181	182	183
134. Religious heterogeneity	—.10	—.19	—.06	—.17
135. Racial heterogeneity	—.19	—.22	—.25	—.14
136. Linguistic heterogeneity	.01	—.00	.05	—.02
137. Religious, racial, linguistic heterogeneity	—.10	—.02	.03	.03
138. Largest religious group/population[b]	.05	.09	.11	—.06
138d. Largest religious group/population[b]	—.07	—.02	.04	
139. Largest ethnic group/population[b]	—.17	—.06	—.04	—.06
139d. Largest ethnic group/population[b]	—.19	—.03	—.07	
140. Largest language group/population[b]	.08	.10	.02	.09
140d. Largest language group/population[b]	—.03	.20	.06	
141. Native born/population[b]	—.01	.18	.01	—.01
141d. Native born/population[b]	.01	.09	.07	
142. Largest racial group/population[b]	—.20	—.17	—.23	—.14

Positive correlations = 19. Correlations in ±.10 range = 33.
Negative correlations = 29.

[a] For key, see notes to Table 7–2.
[b] Signs are reversed to be indicators of asymmetry.

Consensus undoubtedly ensures a continuation in foreign policy positions over time, while widespread societal cleavage may provide the party out of power with an opportunity to use a "get tough" campaign pledge in order to attract a majority of the electorate. One-party rule, on the other hand, may entail an elitist control over foreign policy, in which leaders can go to war for any capricious reason because attitudinal asymmetry has been indoctrinated or imposed upon a population.

The extent of competition among political parties may be indexed in several ways. The number of political parties with a membership of more than one percent of the total population (143) is represented qualitatively by Banks's two- or multi-party system (144) and Rummel's multiparty voting system (145) judgmental codings. A more complicated index would be the total number among three distinct types of political parties—Communist, religious, and non-Communist secular (146). More of the asymmetry indicators correlate positively with foreign conflict indicators (Table 7–32), but the magnitudes are too low to infer that cleavage is clearly related to foreign conflict.

7.6.4 Deviance–Conformity

Symmetrical and asymmetrical behavior patterns along the allocational dimension involve notions of *conformity* and *deviance,* respectively. Talcott

TABLE 7–32
Correlations Between Cleavage
and National Aggression[a]

	Conflicts		Foreign Killed	
	Wars	Clashes	Total	Per capita
Indicators of Cleavage	180	181	182	183
143. Political parties over 1% of population	.13	.09	.11	.22
143c. Political parties over 1% of population	.00	—.03		
143d. Political parties over 1% of population	—.06	—.14	.04	
144. Two- or multi-party systems	—.23	—.26	—.23	—.11
144d. Two- or multi-party systems	.21	.16	.32	
144g. Two- or multi-party systems			.01	
145. Multiparty system	.04	.01	.06	.01
145g. Multiparty system			.01	
146. Support for Communist religious, non-Communist secular parties (party types with over 1% of electorate)	.10	—.11	—.09	—.08

Positive correlations = 16.   Correlations in ±.10 range = 14.
Negative correlations = 10.

[a] For key, see notes to Table 7–2.

Parsons defines the latter as "a motivated tendency for an actor to behave in contravention of one or more institutionalized normative patterns," and he goes on to hypothesize that deviance results from a failure of mechanisms of social control.[60]

Behavior constituting a potential threat to the organization of a societal system has been referred to as conflict in Section 7.5.4, and conflict has often been treated as a type of deviant behavior.[61] To maintain a sharp distinction, "conflict" and "deviance" will both be regarded as subdivisions of a larger concept, *nonconforming behavior* (Table 7–33). Deviance then becomes a somewhat less general term, subsuming only assaultive, escapist, and self-destructive activities. Though indicators of domestic conflict have been found to be tridimensional,[62] parallel work on the three categories of deviant behavior—assault, escapism, and self-destructiveness—has not yet been attempted.[63] Provisionally, one may use homicides (147) and motor vehicle

[60] Parsons, *The Social System,* Chapter 7. Equivalent concepts are Landecker's ("Types of Integration and Their Measurement") "normative integration" and Angell's "moral integration." Robert Angell, *The Integration of American Society* (New York: McGraw-Hill, 1941).

[61] The present formulation constitutes a partial recantation of the labelling in my "Societal Approaches to the Study of War," p. 316, Table VII.

[62] See the references cited in note 2. In Tanter's factor analysis, however, two of the three dimensions collapse into one.

[63] Cf. Michael Haas, "Toward the Study of Biopolitics: A Cross–Sectional Analysis of Mortality Rates," *Behavioral Science,* XIV (July 1969), 257–80.

TABLE 7-33
A Classification of
Nonconforming Behavior[a]

Attention Focus	Personality Types	
	Active	Passive
Norms	Conflict	Escapism
Persons	Assault	Self-destructiveness

[a] Adapted from Talcott Parsons, *The Social System* (New York: The Free Press, 1951), Chapter 7.

accident death rates (148) to indicate assaultive tendencies; liver cirrhosis (149), syphilis death rates (150), and illegitimacy ratios (151) indicate escapism; suicides (152), accidents (153), and ulcer (154) death rates measure self-destructiveness. Two-thirds of the correlations between measures of nonconformity and war aggressiveness reveal a negative relation (Table 7-34), so all three forms of deviant behavior (and thus just one of the four types of nonconforming behavior) are prevalent where foreign conflict is absent.

7.6.5 Discriminatory–Nonpreferential

Political systems in which functions are performed selectively are *discriminatory;* the *nonpreferential* performance of a function for all members of a system is a symmetrical characteristic. To perform a function in one manner for a redhead, another for a blonde, and in yet another way for a brunette, may be simply a matter of taste. This kind of performance of a function enables us to detect positive or negative discrimination when it is directed toward specific members of minority or majority groups.

The discriminatory-nonpreferential continuum is basically the same as the undemocratic-democratic distinction, though democracy is defined more commonly by referring to the process of selecting office-holders than by the extent to which governmental functions are performed without favoritism to special interests or persons.[64] Elitist arguments for the superiority of pre-twentieth-century diplomacy often imply that the warlike passions of man can best be held back under undemocratic yet responsible rule.[65] Since peace-minded attitudes are more often held by better-educated and upper-status persons,[66] the elitist view seems to be confirmed, despite Kant's plea that

[64] Robert A. Dahl, *A Preface to Democratic Theory* (Chicago: University of Chicago Press, 1956), adopts the former definition and has been attacked for ignoring the nature of policy outputs in Jack L. Walker, "A Critique of the Elitist Theory of Democracy," *American Political Science Review*, LX (June 1966), 285–95.

[65] Walter Lippmann, *The Public Philosophy* (New York: Mentor, 1956).

[66] Herbert McClosky, "Personality and Attitude Correlates of Foreign Policy Orientation," *Domestic Sources of Foreign Policy*, ed. James N. Rosenau (New York: The Free Press, 1967), pp. 51–110.

TABLE 7-34
Correlations Between Deviance
and National Aggression[a]

Indicators of Deviance	Conflicts		Foreign Killed	
	Wars 180	Clashes 181	Total 182	Per capita 183
147. Homicides/population	—.03	.03	.05	.19
147c. Homicides/population	—.11	—.05		
147h. Homicides/population	—.11			
148. Motor vehicle accident deaths/population	—.16	(—.30)	—.23	—.23
149. Liver cirrhosis deaths/population	—.05	—.19	—.11	—.06
149c. Alcoholism deaths/population	.00	.00		
149h. Alcoholism deaths/population	.14			
150. Syphilis deaths/population	—.08	—.23	—.12	—.16
150c. Syphilis deaths/population	—.03	.00		
151. Illegitimate births/population	—.23	—.14	—.16	.03
152. Suicides/population	.10	—.11	—.03	—.25
152c. Suicides/population	.06	.04		
152h. Suicides/population	.02			
153. Accidental deaths/population	—.03	—.01	—.16	—.25
153d. Accidental deaths/population	.06	—.14	—.07	
154. Ulcer deaths/population	—.03	—.12	.11	.04

Positive correlations = 15.   Correlations in ±.10 range = 23.
Negative correlations = 31.

[a] For key, see notes to Table 7-2.

popular control of foreign affairs would lessen wars, since no sane man if given the choice would choose to go to battle. Several scaled indicators of discrimination may be used if we affirm a tendency for democratic systems to be nonpreferential: constitutional status (155–157), nonpolyarchic representativeness (158), non-elitist political recruitment (159), and lack of personalismo in political parties (160), the latter concept referring to voting for a party due to personal, family, or individual preferences toward the leader of that party. Gurr's group discrimination measure (161), which was used in Section 7.3.4 to indicate variation-uniformity, is relevant here, though the measure will be used without attention to the geographic dimension. Correlations between discrimination indicators and foreign conflict behavior are usually positive though of low magnitude (Table 7–35), so democratic forms of government are indeed somewhat more peaceful.

7.6.6 Differentiated–Undifferentiated

One major way in which governments differ is in the nature of their structural organization. If there are many structures, a system is referred to as *differentiated;* if only a few structures, the system is more symmetrical

TABLE 7–35
Correlations Between Discrimination
and National Aggression[a]

| | *Conflicts* | | *Foreign Killed* | |
| | Wars | Clashes | Total | Per capita |
Indicators of Discrimination	180	181	182	183
155. Constitutional regime[b]	.09	.18	.11	.01
155g. Constitutional regime[b]			.05	
156. Nonauthoritarian regime[b]	—.05	.18	—.04	.04
156g. Nonauthoritarian regime[b]			—.16	
157. Nontotalitarian regime[b]	.13	.02	.09	—.04
157g. Nontotalitarian regime[b]			.11	
158. Nonpolyarchic representativeness	.11	.18	.14	.03
158d. Nonpolyarchic representativeness	—.02	.10	.08	
158g. Nonpolyarchic representativeness			.05	
159. Non-elitist political recruitment[b]	.01	.02	.05	—.11
159g. Non-elitist political recruitment[b]			.06	
160. Lack of personalismo in political parties[b]	.04	.07	—.01	.01
160g. Lack of personalismo in political parties[b]			—.20	
161. Group discrimination	.04	.25	.25	.08

Positive correlations = 29.　　　　Correlations in ±.10 range = 24.
Negative correlations = 8.

[a] For key, see notes to Table 7–2.
[b] Signs are reversed to be indicators of asymmetry.

and *undifferentiated,* to use a pair of terms that Riggs has explicated. One way of indicating differentiation is to count the number of autonomous political structures within a polity (162). Undifferentiated polities lack autonomous interest groups, political parties, legislatures, executives, bureaucracies, and courts; differentiated polities contain each of these structures, and every structure operates independently, rather than being controlled by pervasive elites. Max Weber's model of rational-legal bureaucracy contains considerable differentiation in structure; given Parkinson's laws of agency survival and structural proliferation, differentiation knows no quantitative bounds.[67]

Much Weberian theory suggests that freedom from political pressures is a goal toward which civil servants strive. With a successful separation of administration from politics, a political system might stay out of wars: the onerous burden placed upon a bureaucracy to conduct a war fails to con-

[67] Max Weber, *The Theory of Social and Economic Organization,* trans. A. M. Henderson and Talcott Parsons (New York: Oxford University Press, 1947); Weber, *From Max Weber,* trans. H. H. Gerth and C. Wright Mills (New York: Oxford University Press, 1947); C. Northcote Parkinson, *Parkinson's Law and Other Essays in Administration* (Boston: Houghton Mifflin, 1957).

form to the incrementalist ideology of the civil servant, but his value neutrality prevents him from resisting or counseling against possible violent courses of action in the international arena. In short, an efficient, differentiated bureaucracy may make decisions to enter wars more executable, but bureaucracies that prefer a gradual continuation of the prevailing situation might, contrariwise, be opposed to rash foreign policy ventures. If the two tendencies cancel each other out, there would be no correlation between foreign conflict and differentiation. Banks's bureaucratic traditionalism characteristic (163) permits a test of these hypotheses (Table 7–36). Evidently there is a sharp difference between modern bureaucracies and those falling short of the legal-rational standard set by Weber. Countries with modern bureaucracies stay out of war more consistently than polities with less differentiated administrative structures.

7.7 TRANSACTIONAL ASYMMETRY

The ability of a system to exchange goods, services, and symbols with the environment is essential to its survival. Very often, however, inputs into a system are out of proportion to outputs from a system. If an input/output ratio is unity (1.0), the condition is symmetrical; asymmetry exists to the extent that an input/output ratio approaches zero or infinity (Table 7–37).[68]

Transactional data enable one to test theories concerning dominant and dependent countries, on the one hand, and countries that keep internal and external flows in balance, on the other. In isolationist countries inputs are more likely to equal outputs. An asymmetry in either direction indicates a potential source of war, since both imperialistic and exploited countries are likely to encounter international grievances.

7.7.1 Imbalance–Balance

Economists refer to asymmetries in input and output resources as *imbalances* (or as "favorable" and "unfavorable" balances). A *balanced* flow is one in which inputs equal outputs.

Any kind of imbalance may indicate a future war. A surplus in resources may encourage the cornering of more markets by aggressive means, as Marxist theory predicts. Have-not nations may seek to enrich themselves by achieving military victory over richer but militarily weak neighbors. Using

---

[68] Naturally the direction in which an input/output ratio leans is of significance to many theories on war and peace; the reason that directionality is ignored in the present formulation is the desire to look only at the pattern of asymmetry, rather than the pattern of magnitude.

TABLE 7–36
Correlations Between Differentiation
and National Aggression[a]

| | *Conflicts* | | *Foreign Killed* | |
Indicators of Differentiation	Wars 180	Clashes 181	Total 182	Per capita 183
162. Political structures	—.18	—.16	—.16	—.03
163. Bureaucratic traditionalism[b]	.12	.00	—.08	—.01
163g. Bureaucratic traditionalism[b]			—.08	

Positive correlations = 2.	Correlations in ±.10 range = 5.
Negative correlations = 7.	

[a] For key, see notes to Table 7–2.
[b] Signs are reversed to be indicators of asymmetry.

indices computing departures from the 1.0 level in inputs divided by outputs, the following indicators are proposed: lack of trade dependence (164), exports/trade (165), and the balance of foreign investments contributed or received (166) as well as the balance of donations, namely, of foreign aid sent or received (167).

Imbalance is related to foreign conflict in five-eighths of the correlations (Table 7–38). In focusing on individual variables it is clear that trade and aid transaction partners are involved in more foreign conflict if there is an unbalanced flow.[69] On the other hand, peaceful countries tend to engage in investments abroad, or they are host countries for foreign private development capital. As Burke once said, the giving of charity corrupts the almsgiver as well as the almsreceiver.

7.7.2   Migration–Curtaining

A unique feature of modern totalitarian governments is the effort to enclose a population securely within national boundaries and to prohibit migration. The Berlin Wall is the most celebrated illustration of the Iron Curtain phenomenon. A political system that allows *migration* is likely to have some lack of correspondence between the number of persons leaving and entering its borders, while the effect of *curtaining* is to restrict traffic only to that which always returns to the home country.

Though the departure from 0.5 of a ratio between immigrants and migrants (168) is a valid and feasible indicator of migration, the low magnitudes in three out of four correlations with international conflict suggests a need for more specific data on types of persons crossing borders (Table

[69] Warfare is correlated — .40 with general exchange, — .27 with cultural exchange, and — .17 with trade between rivals in Naroll, "Deterrence in History."

TABLE 7–37
Transactional Concepts

| Attributes | Concepts | |
	Asymmetry	Symmetry
Resources	Imbalance	Balance
Demotypes	Migration	Curtaining
Attitudes	Incongruity	Congruity
Behavior	Unidirectional	Bidirectional
Functions	Nonpenetration	Penetration
Structures	Unreciprocated	Reciprocated

7–39). Asymmetry consisting of a departure of intellectuals, such as the "brain drain" from England to the United States after World War II, is different demotypically from the emigration of English Quakers to America in the seventeenth century. Richardson's study on intermarriage between cultures indicates that migration can be a pacifying influence among nations.[70]

7.7.3 Incongruity–Congruity

If misunderstandings lie at the root of difficulties in diplomatic interchange, then transactional-attitudinal asymmetry is a precursor of international conflict. If country *A* perceives other countries in a manner symmetrical to other countries' perception of *A,* then *A* enjoys attitudinal *congruity*. If *A*'s attitudes toward the outside world are not comparable to the outside world's attitudes toward *A, incongruity* is present. The terms "congruity" and "incongruity" may be different, but the concepts are nearly the same as those which Fritz Heider explicates in his theory of "structural balance."[71]

Countries with congruent attitudes perceive foreign powers in a manner identical to the way those foreign powers perceive them. For example, if the United States believes that Communist China is aggressive, while the People's Republic of China feels that it is not aggressive at all, an incongruent

[70] Lewis F. Richardson, "War and Eugenics," *Eugenics Review,* XLII (April 1950), 25–36.

[71] Fritz Heider, *The Psychology of Interpersonal Relations* (New York: Wiley, 1958). Cf. Festinger, *A Theory of Cognitive Dissonance;* Milton J. Rosenberg et al., *Attitude Organization and Change* (New Haven: Yale University Press, 1960); Robert B. Zajonc, "The Concepts of Balance, Congruity and Dissonance," *Public Opinion Quarterly,* XXIV (Summer 1960), 280–96. The personification of country *A* as a "perceiver" is purely a literary convenience, standing for perceptions either of decisionmakers that can bind their states to foreign actions or of the public at large, as measured by sample survey techniques. The specific indicators used in this section draw upon the latter operationalization.

TABLE 7–38
Correlations Between Imbalance
and National Aggression

	Conflicts		Foreign Killed	
	Wars	Clashes	Total	Per capita
Indicators of Imbalance	180	181	182	183
164. Lack of trade dependence[a]	.01	—.13	—.04	—.13
165. Difference between exports/ total trade ratio and 50%	.08	.18	.20	.25
166. Investments (absolute value)	.05	—.17	—.04	—.11
167. Donations (absolute value)	(.35)	(.39)	(.46)	.28

Positive correlations = 10. Correlations in ±.10 range = 5.
Negative correlations = 6.

[a] Signs are reversed to be indicators of asymmetry.

situation exists, despite the possibility that one perception may be more "correct" than another.

In *How Nations See Each Other* (1952), William Buchanan and Hadley Cantril construct two indicators that might be useful as a source of cross-national congruity data.[72] Persons in Australia, England, France, Germany, Italy, Holland, Norway, and the United States are interviewed concerning national perceptions. A "stereotype" score was derived by averaging the number of positive adjectives applied to another country, minus twice the number of negative adjectives; a "friendliness" score was expressed as a percentage of respondents designating themselves "most friendly" toward a particular people, minus the percentage regarding themselves as "least friendly" toward the same country. Considering the transactional dimension as a system-environment relationship, composite ratings from dyadic stereotypy (169) and friendliness (170) scores are summed. Stereotypy is unrelated, but friendliness predicts to lower magnitudes of foreign conflict (Table 7–40).

7.7.4 Unidirectional–Bidirectional

A country that is the target of behavior as often as it is the initiator is *bidirectional* on the transactional-behavioral dimension. If a system impinges too much onto the environment, or the converse, behavioral transactions are asymmetrical, that is, *unidirectional* in nature. An exchange of human beings across national boundaries does involve a behavioral component, but an effect of such movement is to alter the demotypic more than the behavioral composition of "donor" and "recipient" systems. Exchange of communica-

[72] William Buchanan and Hadley Cantril, *How Nations See Each Other* (Urbana: University of Illinois Press, 1952).

TABLE 7-39
Correlations Between Migration
and National Aggression

Indicator of Migration	Conflicts		Foreign Killed	
	Wars	Clashes	Total	Per capita
	180	181	182	183
168. Difference between immigrants/migrants ratio and 50%	.11	—.01	—.08	—.03

Positive correlations = 1.	Correlations in ±.10 range = 3.
Negative correlations = 3.	

tions is more relevant to a unidirectional-bidirectional continuum, for such traffic does not involve any necessary connection with resource, demotypic, attitudinal, functional, or structural exchanges. One might expect that countries sending more messages than they receive are engaging in some form of political or economic proselytization, and recipients of too many messages could be in a dependent relationship to some other country. Countries with a one-to-one ratio between intake and output are undoubtedly able to maintain themselves as autonomous entities in world politics. Dominating and submissive countries, one could hypothesize, are more likely to be at war than are autonomous polities. The departure from 0.5 of a ratio between foreign mail sent and all foreign mail received (171) enables one to test the relationship. But results are inconsistent (Table 7–41).

A second type of directional indicator is war itself, which involves physical movement and is definitely a societal characteristic. An indicator of military directionality would be the number of times that a country's borders are crossed by invaders, divided by the frequency of invasions that the country itself undertakes. Unfortunately most of the data on foreign conflict so far collected have not been oriented toward intakes and outputs. Four indicators are being used as dependent variables in this part of the volume— war frequencies (180), foreign military clashes (181), foreign conflict deaths (182), and foreign conflict deaths as a percentage of a country's total population (183).[73]

7.7.5 Nonpenetration–Penetration

Within international history the concept of sovereignty has enjoyed a relatively short span in popularity. That a boundary line between national

[73] The gap between variable number 172 and 180 is fixed to separate the independent variables (1–179) from the major dependent variables under investigation (180–183).

TABLE 7–40
Correlations Between Incongruity
and National Aggression

	Conflicts		Foreign Killed	
	Wars	Clashes	Total	Per capita
Indicators of Incongruity	180	181	182	183
169. Stereotypy score	.00	.00	.01	.00
170. Friendliness score[a]	(—.42)	—.20	—.19	.09

Positive correlations = 5.	Correlations in ±.10 range = 5.
Negative correlations = 3.	

[a] Signs are reversed to be indicators of asymmetry.

political systems may from time to time be fixed territorially has not simplified the observer's task of detecting when authoritative decisions that
affect a particular polity result from internal or external influences. The
case of colonies and "mother countries" may have been reasonably clear in
previous centuries, for the former were legal appendages of the latter, functions being performed by an elite and a bureaucracy controlled by the imperialistic power. Satellites, protectorates, and such cases as South Vietnam
today provide ambiguous clues for determining the locus of sovereignty.

Several scholars refer to a political system in which there is a mixture
of internal and external influences as a *penetrated* polity, which is defined as
"one in which nonmembers of a national society participate directly and
authoritatively, through actions taken jointly with the society's members, in
either the allocation of its values or the mobilization of support on behalf
of its goals."[74] Penetrated political systems are much closer to unity in the
ratio of internal to external function performance. *Nonpenetrated* polities

TABLE 7–41
Correlations Between Unidirectionality
and National Aggression

	Conflicts		Foreign Killed	
	Wars	Clashes	Total	Per capita
Indicator of Unidirectionality	180	181	182	183
171. Difference between foreign mail sent/ total foreign mail ratio and 50%	—.03	.12	.05	—.01

Positive correlations = 2.	Correlations in ±.10 range = 3.
Negative correlations = 2.	

[74] James N. Rosenau, *The Scientific Study of Foreign Policy* (New York: The
Free Press, 1971), p. 116. See also Andrew Scott, *The Revolution in Statecraft* (New
York: Random House, 1967).

are of two major types: some are functionally autonomous and fully sovereign; others are operated entirely by an outside power, such as colonial possessions and puppet regimes which constitute distinct political units only formally and operate in a manner similar to the so-called independent republics within the Soviet Union. One rough indicator of penetration would be bloc prominence (172), for elites within a bloc of nations are likely to intervene in the affairs of bloc followers. Communist and quasi-Communist states (173), with the exception of the Soviet Union, are the major examples of penetrated polities in Rosenau's formulation. But a few countries outside the Soviet orbit in the late 1950s qualify as penetrated, such as the Congo (Leopoldville), Cyprus, Finland, Laos, Luxembourg, Saudi Arabia, South Vietnam, and Yemen; Guatemala's economic penetration by the United Fruit Company and Panama's penetration by dint of the isthmian canal have political overtones, too. This coding for penetrated polities (174) will serve as another indicator of functional-transactional symmetry. The data accord with findings presented in Section 1.2—namely, that major powers are most frequently embroiled in international conflict. Communist satellites, however, have been much more consistently involved in wars than one would expect on the basis of their national power (Table 7–42). Penetrated polities are in general likely to become involved in wars.

One purpose of staying out of blocs and coalitions may be to escape penetration from abroad, so membership in international power blocs (175) is yet another asymmetrical type of transactional function performance situation. Countries aligned with some but not all countries have asymmetrical sociometric patterns in the world polity; neutrals are symmetrical in role functions with respect to each other, and with aligned states. The professed aim of neutralist powers to increase world peace by staying out of entangling alliances is partly consistent with the data in Table 7–42. Bloc followers and nonpenetrated countries are able to avoid embroilment in foreign war, but there is no clear relationship between alignment and foreign conflict.[75]

7.7.6 Unreciprocated–Reciprocated

Governments exchange many structures within international environments. When a government exchanges a structure with another government, then a symmetrical, *reciprocated* situation exists. A structure without such sharing exhibits an *unreciprocated* transactional pattern.

After a country has achieved membership in a family of nations, by concluding agreements with other powers to exchange diplomatic represent-

---

[75] An alliance between the leader of a world civilization and its rival will inhibit war: there is a − .11 correlation between such alliances and months of warfare for a civilization, according to Naroll, "Deterrence in History."

TABLE 7–42
Correlations Between Nonpenetration
and National Aggression[a]

| | Conflicts | | Foreign Killed | |
| | Wars | Clashes | Total | Per capita |
Indicators of Nonpenetration	180	181	182	183
172. Bloc prominence	(.42)	(.42)	(.47)	.14
172d. Bloc prominence	(.45)	(.34)	(.50)	
173. Communist and quasi-communist polities (except USSR)[b]	—.01	—.18	—.27	—.22
174. Penetrated polities[b]	—.27	—.13	—.21	—.08
175. Bloc membership[b]	.03	.10	.10	—.10
175d. Bloc membership[b]	—.12	—.16	—.07	

Positive correlations = 10. Correlations in ±.10 range = 7.
Negative correlations = 12.

[a] For key, see notes to Table 7–2.
[b] Signs are reversed to be indicators of asymmetry.

atives, a conventional expectation is that an equal number of ambassadorial personnel will be exchanged between capitals. Temporary asymmetry between diplomats at home and those abroad exists in cases of the expulsion or recall of diplomats (176) and severances of diplomatic relations (177). Such cases are restored to a symmetrical situation by replacing a persona non grata or by withdrawing a diplomatic mission, respectively. Table 7–43 shows that nonreciprocating structural transactions are generally associated with foreign military conflict, and severance of diplomatic relations often constitutes a first step toward an eventual outbreak of war.[76]

When the number of embassies and legations at home exceeds those abroad over a longer time span, it may be because the host country is too poor to afford a diplomatic corps yet holds something of value to the outside world. When a country has more representatives stationed abroad than at home, it may desire a higher status than it deserves. The departure from 0.5 in the number of embassies and legations abroad, divided by the total at home and abroad (178), yields a figure that can be used as a measure of asymmetrical structural exchange. A final measure of transactional—structural asymmetry is the departure from 0.5 in the ratio of the number of headquarters of international organizations located at home to the number of such organizations that a country has joined (179). Both indices are subtracted from the 50 percent level, and the absolute value of the difference is an indicator of asymmetry. Neither of these final indicators corre-

[76] Wars correlate + .29 with diplomatic activity but — .21 with diplomatic agreements in *ibid.*

TABLE 7–43
Correlations Between Nonreciprocation
and National Aggression[a]

| | *Conflicts* | | *Foreign Killed* | |
| | Wars | Clashes | Total | Per capita |
Indicators of Nonreciprocation	180	181	182	183
176. Expulsions and recalls of diplomats	.12	.20	(.30)	.26
176g. Expulsions and recalls of ambassadors			—.02	
176r. Expulsions and recalls of ambassadors	.01	—.08	.02	
176t. Expulsions and recalls of ambassadors	.25	.28	.22	
177. Severances of diplomatic relations	.00	.27	.05	.05
177r. Severances of diplomatic relations	.07	(.54)	(.31)	
177t. Severances of diplomatic relations	.08	.05	.13	
178. Difference between embassies and legations abroad/total home and abroad ratio and 50%	.04	.05	—.02	.03
179. Difference between international organization headquartered at home/total international organization memberships ratio and 50%	—.14	—.08	—.15	—.06

Positive correlations = 22.   Correlations in ±.10 range = 16.
Negative correlations = 7.

[a] For key, see notes to Table 7–2.

lates strongly with foreign conflict, though diplomatic nonreciprocation tends
to be somewhat more closely associated with belligerence, and international
organization nonreciprocation with peaceful state behavior.

7.8   SUMMARY

Reviewing the labelling for each of some 72 concepts (Table 7–44), one
can locate nearly all of the terms being discussed by theorists who focus
on the societal level of analysis. If some labels seem not to have been fixed in
a precise manner, it should be emphasized that the basic definitional components are the respective dimension, attribute, and pattern of symmetry or
asymmetry. (A possible refinement would be to specify terms at the midpoint of the continua, which has been a major contribution of Riggs within
political development theory.)

The most important reason for devising such an elaborate scheme is to
prevent theorists and researchers from falling into semantic traps. If such
terms as "consensus" and "integration" denote different concepts, then one
would be cautious in the future about using indicators of one to index the
other. This was one eventual difficulty when Deutsch's monumental *Nationalism and Social Communication* (1953) was applied by students of

TABLE 7-44
Types of Asymmetry Within Systems[a]

Dimension	Resources	Demotypes	Attitudes	Attribute Behavior	Functions	Structures
Temporal	*Fluctuation* Constancy	*Cosmopolitanizing* Inbreeding	*Tides* Normalcy	*Instability* Stability	*Discontinuity* Continuity	*Situational* Persistent
Spatial	*Agglutinated* Equalitarian	*Segregation* Desegregation	*Sectionalism* Systemization	*Variation* Uniformity	*Centralization* Decentralization	*Concentration* Deconcentration
Kinetic	*Slack* Mobilization	*Immobility* Mobility	*Alienation* Identification	*Uncohesive* Cohesive	*Immobilist* Dynamic	*Bottlenecked* Streamlined
Entropic	*Strain* Adequacy	*Diversity* Similarity	*Contention* Consonance	*Conflict* Cooperation	*Diffraction* Fusion	*Fragmentation* Integration
Allocational	*Disparity* Equality	*Heterogeneity* Homogeneity	*Cleavage* Consensus	*Deviance* Conformity	*Discrimination* Nonpreferential	*Differentiated* Undifferentiated
Transactional	*Imbalance* Balance	*Migration* Curtaining	*Incongruity* Congruity	*Unidirectional* Bidirectional	*Nonpenetration* Penetration	*Unreciprocated* Reciprocated

[a] Asymmetrical terms are italicized.

241

international politics. A linkage between empirical research and theoretical speculation is made more possible by an explicit conceptual scheme.

But it might be preferable, in fact, to avoid using any words at all to describe each of the 72 concepts. First of all, the use of an extra set of labels is not a parsimonious procedure; second, once words are applied to a concept, terminology may tend to acquire an independent existence of its own, taking on meanings borrowed from other concepts, a situation in which we now find ourselves enmeshed.

Turning to results of existing studies, we find that an asymmetrical pattern is as likely to be associated with military resolutions of foreign policy disputes as a symmetrical pattern (Table 7–45). In about a third of the cases no discernible pattern emerges, and there are no rows of columns of consistent relationships.

Entropic asymmetries seem more consistently related to participation in wars; an exception is resource entropy, which is related at a chance (50 percent) level. Using an entry in Table 7–45 between 40 and 60 percent as a level of nonrelationship, we do find some isolated concepts predicting to foreign conflict. War is likely to result from temporal-attitudinal symmetry, spatial-resource symmetry, kinetic-functional asymmetry, entropic-demotypic asymmetry, entropic-behavioral asymmetry, and transactional-resource asymmetry. From these findings one can draw the following conclusion: societies with normalcy, nonagglutination, immobilism, diversity, domestic conflict, and imbalance enter war more often than those with tides, agglutination, dynamic polities, demotypic similarity, domestic cooperation, and balanced foreign transactions.

Looking at individual variables whose correlations with foreign conflict are computed within this chapter, there are 23 variables over the $\pm$ .30 range; only 5 of these correlations exceed $\pm$ .40. We may summarize our findings by enumerating these correlates, from the strongest to the weakest relations, across all four measures of foreign conflict:

1. Bloc prominence.
2. Military mobilizations.
3. Perceptions of internation hostility.
4. Public administration and defense expenditures as a percentage of total GNP.
5. Foreign aid sent or received.
6. Percentage of population in armed forces.
7. Equality in income levels before taxes.
8. Percentage of population apathetic toward politics.
9. Low ratio of welfare expenditures to total national income.
10. Equality in income levels after taxes.

TABLE 7–45
Percentage of Positive Correlations Between Asymmetries
and National Aggression[a]

			Attribute			
Dimension	Resources	Demotypes	Attitudes	Behavior	Functions	Structures
Temporal	44.4	25.0	(00.0)	58.1	60.0	61.5
Spatial	(00.0)	36.8	66.7	25.0	61.1	76.2
Kinetic	54.1	53.1	(45.2)	(45.5)	(27.9)	46.7
Entropic	50.0	(79.4)	91.9	(83.6)	87.5	68.7
Allocational	(45.0)	39.8	61.5	32.6	78.4	22.2
Transactional	(62.5)	25.0	62.5	50.0	45.5	74.8

[a] Parentheses denote situations where more than 60 percent of correlations exceed ±.10.

11. Central government expenditures as a percentage of total GNP.
12. A high ratio of hospital beds to physicians.
13. Many religious groups (over 1 percent of the total population in size).
14. Low library book circulation per capita.
15. Strong executive.
16. No change in per capita expenditures on education.
17. Press censorship.
18. Major government crises.
19. Mobilizational system style.
20. System instability.
21. No change in per capita electricity production.
22. Expulsions and recalls of diplomats.
23. Low motor vehicle accident death rate.

Some of these 23 variables are so highly intercorrelated that we will discover them to be spurious relationships when multivariate techniques are employed to ascertain underlying empirical dimensions in Chapter 8.

7.9 CONCLUDING REMARKS

Explication of a conceptual scheme, suggestion of relevant hypotheses, specification of 183 variables, and a report of existing findings set the stage for a comprehensive analysis in the following chapter. Yet a sense of incompleteness lingers.

One would prefer to have many more indicators to study each continuum, whereas only a few appropriate measures are available to index each concept. But an advantage of an explicit theoretical scheme is that one is not victimized by having to use raw data naively. Brute empiricists too often enslave themselves to that which is manifest and at the surface. The use of coefficients of variation and other manipulations generate data that is meaningful in the context of a specific theory. And by knowing what one wants in advance, it is possible to channel one's frustrations over unavailable measures into well-reasoned recommendations that governments and social scientists collect new types of data.

chapter 8
Dimensions
and Models of
Warmaking Countries

8.1 RESEARCH STRATEGY

Although societal symmetry has been regarded as a proper foundation for a peaceful foreign policy throughout the writings of many philosophers since the time of the Greeks, the data surveyed in Chapter 7 fail to support such a view on a broad basis. Temporal asymmetry and kinetic symmetry, favored by Adam Smith and the early exponents of capitalism, were supposed to reduce the probability of war while the goal of economic productivity was being pursued. But such is not the case: neither symmetry nor asymmetry is related consistently to warfare. A socialist preference for spatial and allocational symmetry is not completely consistent with the correlational findings either. Plato and Aristotle, apostles of entropic harmony and balance, would also be chagrined to discover that a nothing-too-much domestic ethic can mean either war or peace. Incorrect also is the Humean conception of international relations as an autonomous sphere, in which nonmilitary allocational asymmetries lead to international aggression.

Combinations of some variables might multiply account for the incidence of violent international conflict, so we now turn to a more intensive scrutiny of the data, using factor analysis and cluster analysis. Having operationalized so many of what Marxist theorists would call "internal contradictions," it is possible to take stock of philosophic currents which have posited relationships between warfare and certain societal attributes that are more complex than mere bivariate relationships.

Table 8–1 lists all of the variables, providing their sources and more technical descriptions. Table 8–2 maps variables into the property space

245

TABLE 8-1
Societal Asymmetry Variable List
See Appendix D, pp. 576–83, for table text.

TABLE 8-2
Conceptual Map of Societal Variables

| Dimension | Resources | Demotypes | Attribute | | Functions | Structures |
			Attitudes	Behavior		
Temporal	1–12	13–15	16	17–23	24–30	31–33
Spatial	34	35–38	39–40	41	42–44	45–47
Kinetic	48–54	55–59	60–66	67–73	74–81	82–91
Entropic	92–96	97–101	102–107	108–13	114–15	116–26
Allocational	127–33	134–42	143–46	147–54	155–61	162–63
Transactional	164–67	168	169–70	171,180–83[a]	172–75	176–79

[a] The gap between 171 and 180 is due to the fact that 180–83 are dependent variables, which for convenience appear at the end of the enumeration.

based upon postulated dimensions and attributes of societal systems. The reader will note that attitudinal variables are in short supply, and four of the variables located in the attitude column have so few cases (only 9 or 11) that they will have to be deleted from most of the multivariate analyses conducted in this chapter.

But even with these variables excluded from the analysis, it is a fact that statistical sources are more extensive, reliable, and accessible for modernized countries than for nations which emerged only yesterday from colonial or traditional rule. The sample of 85 countries on which the data in this chapter are based is, thus, both too small and too large—too small because there are more than 100 states in the United Nations, too large because the amount of missing data entries which cannot be authoritatively estimated or "guesstimated" constitutes approximately 12 percent of the total number of data cells. Accordingly, it will be necessary to run the total sample and then check results with a subsample of countries where there are few missing data. A Q-analysis of the 85 nations, in short, will be used to discover empirically distinct subsamples.

8.2 DIMENSIONS OF NATIONS

One of the major purposes of Bruce Russett's *International Regions and the International System* (1967) was to demonstrate that Q-analysis of nations extracts different sets of subsamples and strata depending upon an initial data base.[1] Similar types of variables could lead to an isolation of differing Q-Factors during different time periods, so our results will identify strata of countries within the international arena for the years 1955 to 1960.

8.2.1 Procedure

All of the cases were intercorrelated, using the Spearman rank-difference formula in view of the fact that the scales of each variable are so different from one another.[2] Correlations were based on all of the 183 variables except those with fewer than 20 cases, namely, variable numbers 65, 66, 130, 131, 169, and 170. The resulting 85×85 matrix was factor-analyzed, with communalities set initially at 1.0.[3] Exactly 50 principal

---

[1] Bruce M. Russett, *International Regions and the International System* (Chicago: Rand McNally, 1967).

[2] In *ibid.*, Russett norms variables first by fitting each variable into a distribution between 0 and 100. Such a procedure was tried here but the resulting product-moment Q-correlations were greatly inflated in value and thus unacceptable (insofar as the input to factor analysis should range outside of a distribution from correlations of $\pm$ .95 to $\pm$ .99).

[3] The computation procedure is the same as the one discussed in Chapter 5.

components had eigenvalues over 0.0, but only 8 exceeded 1.0; Cattell's scree test pointed to a cutoff after Factor XVII, but Factors IX through XVII are not easily interpretable and hence are not reported. Factors I to VIII were rotated due to a marked departure of principal components from simple structure. An astonishingly high eigenvalue appeared for Factor I: a dropoff from 55.7 to 5.4, followed by 3.8, 2.7, 2.1, 1.6, 1.3, and 1.2, would ordinarily indicate one major factor with a lot of smaller, idiosyncratic factors, whereas intuitively we would expect to find several strata with somewhat equal weights within a sample of 85 countries located at various levels of economic development and on all continents of the globe. A varimax orthogonal rotation was used; Factors I–III account for about the same amount of total variance while extracting together most of the common variance among all 8 factors. As a result, eigenvalues were recomputed by multiplying the percentage of total variance for each factor by 85, the total number of observations in the same sample.[4] The varimax solution did not yield simple structure, for some countries loaded above ±.50 on more than one of the first 3 factors. Oblique solutions of various sorts were attempted, but all had inflated factor loadings in their respective P-matrices, so the varimax results are retained for presentation in Table 8–3. Eventually second-, third-, and fourth-order factor analyses proved necessary. A cluster analysis of the 85×85 matrix based on the same 177 variables was performed (Figures 8–1 and 8–2) so that ambiguities in the varimax loadings can be reconciled theoretically as well as empirically.

8.2.2 Results

The first-order factors neither resemble those of Russett nor lend themselves to easy interpretation. Accordingly, correlations between the 8 primary factors and all 183 variables were computed for additional diagnostic assistance (Table 8–4). The number of variables was increased to 184 by totaling the instances of missing data for each country.

Centrifugal best describes Factor I, which accounts for 22.5 percent of the total variance. Countries loading high on this factor have difficulties in internal maintenance problems; some of these countries are underdeveloped (Afghanistan), but some are advanced (Canada) or developing rapidly (Argentina). Countries with high loadings contain minority groups which are discriminated against, although the form of discrimination is social more than political. Variables correlated with the factor show fragmentation and suppression amid smoldering conflict. There are positive correlations above ± .30 with fears about politics, system and government instability, sectional discrimination, revolutions, land ownership inequality, and illegitimate gov-

---

[4] This procedure is performed only here in the volume. It is customary to report eigenvalues based on principal components.

TABLE 8-3
Q-Factor Analysis of Nations

Country	h²	I	II	III	IV	V	VI	VII	VIII	Cases
					Varimax Factors[a]					
1. Afghanistan	.85	(78)	-34	-20	-17	02	-12	-15	19	106
2. Albania	.90	(68)	-42	-39	03	08	-29	-06	-14	123
3. Argentina	.83	(65)	-15	-42	35	09	-06	-08	26	160
4. Australia	.88	43	-19	(-78)	-06	10	-01	-19	01	170
5. Austria	.89	38	-21	(-75)	08	33	-07	-05	12	172
6. Belgium	.89	48	-09	(-72)	02	22	-07	07	27	172
7. Bolivia	.81	(72)	-17	-36	20	22	-05	-20	07	146
8. Brazil	.91	(60)	-16	-49	35	39	01	04	02	163
9. Bulgaria	.90	(60)	-39	-45	01	22	-33	13	-06	148
10. Burma	.85	(75)	-39	-35	03	08	07	-01	03	130
11. Cambodia	.90	(60)	-49	38	-10	37	04	06	-11	125
12. Canada	.91	(51)	-31	(-72)	04	08	00	13	-01	171
13. Ceylon	.90	(69)	-26	-47	20	19	-04	21	05	159
14. Chile	.82	(52)	-16	(-63)	30	18	-04	02	04	167
15. China	.85	(78)	-38	-15	02	14	-20	12	-02	117
16. Taiwan	.89	46	-30	(-51)	10	44	-33	09	-05	124
17. Colombia	.81	(65)	-14	-37	39	17	-13	-06	13	163
18. Costa Rica	.81	(57)	-26	(-52)	33	11	-03	01	-16	158
19. Cuba	.87	(61)	-00	-32	46	26	-24	-11	20	124
20. Czechoslovakia	.88	(56)	-33	-48	-04	24	-39	11	02	148
21. Denmark	.92	41	-21	(-81)	04	11	-21	04	-00	175
22. Dominican Rep.	.85	(64)	-20	-40	36	20	-21	-12	07	149
23. Ecuador	.86	(65)	-30	-41	36	20	-06	08	-03	158
24. Egypt	.79	49	-33	-44	16	39	-25	-09	04	157
25. El Salvador	.93	(58)	-35	-46	30	40	-05	-02	-08	157
26. Ethiopia	.88	(74)	(-50)	-24	-07	06	-04	-08	-08	117
27. Finland	.90	(50)	-21	(-73)	14	17	-13	-02	-05	171

249

TABLE 8-3—Cont.
Q-Factor Analysis of Nations

Country	h²	I	II	III	Varimax Factors[a] IV	V	VI	VII	VIII	Cases
28. France	.81	45	−11	(−69)	27	12	−14	06	11	167
29. E. Germany	.89	45	−23	(−58)	−00	23	−44	−21	−00	143
30. W. Germany	.90	48	−19	(−76)	06	15	−15	−02	−00	172
31. Greece	.87	(62)	−20	(−60)	12	15	−21	−01	−01	161
32. Guatemala	.94	(75)	−21	−38	42	10	01	−06	−03	153
33. Haiti	.89	(58)	−25	−28	21	32	−02	−44	25	122
34. Honduras	.84	(70)	−34	−39	21	04	−07	−10	16	155
35. Hungary	.87	(55)	−32	−42	23	05	−47	−04	09	145
36. India	.83	(72)	−20	−31	18	13	−09	31	13	161
37. Indonesia	.81	(75)	−23	−26	18	17	−07	06	24	133
38. Iran	.92	(64)	(−50)	−32	01	33	−05	02	20	124
39. Iraq	.80	(68)	−32	−30	14	23	00	−11	27	140
40. Ireland	.86	38	−22	(−74)	13	25	−16	−06	−11	171
41. Israel	.85	40	−21	(−70)	17	28	−06	−08	19	168
42. Italy	.87	39	−14	(−71)	20	25	−16	06	24	174
43. Japan	.92	46	−10	(−77)	17	18	−11	−05	19	172
44. Jordan	.95	(68)	−36	−32	11	41	−01	13	22	139
45. N. Korea	.94	(55)	−35	−38	−13	26	−45	−28	−12	94
46. S. Korea	.94	31	−17	−31	29	(79)	−06	−08	01	137
47. Lebanon	.95	28	−14	−30	20	(80)	−01	10	27	137
48. Liberia	.94	23	−31	−31	−01	(80)	−16	−11	−06	108
49. Libya	.75	36	(−59)	−35	06	36	−09	03	11	111
50. Mexico	.82	29	−42	(−53)	35	31	−05	13	21	163
51. Nepal	.85	19	(−78)	−17	13	14	−09	−34	14	94
52. Netherlands	.96	13	−49	(−80)	20	07	−04	−02	12	175
53. New Zealand	.93	20	(−56)	(−74)	18	05	−08	00	04	172
54. Nicaragua	.86	31	(−55)	−38	47	15	−11	−20	12	140

TABLE 8–3—Cont.
Q–Factor Analysis of Nations

Country	h²	I	II	III	IV	V	VI	VII	VIII	Cases
					Varimax Factors[a]					
55. Norway	.95	17	(−50)	(−77)	14	23	−08	−05	01	174
56. Mongolia	.95	21	(−80)	−38	14	10	−26	−12	−11	100
57. Pakistan	.81	42	(−63)	−23	22	24	08	19	19	136
58. Panama	.79	33	−42	−38	(55)	23	−07	02	02	154
59. Paraguay	.82	42	(−52)	−10	33	29	−25	−20	24	132
60. Peru	.82	36	(−59)	−38	40	19	−00	−01	07	150
61. Philippines	.85	30	(−54)	(−58)	33	17	−01	−07	01	169
62. Poland	.92	29	(−56)	−43	34	18	−41	02	08	158
63. Portugal	.85	35	−37	(−50)	16	28	−47	−03	14	164
64. Rumania	.89	36	(−60)	−48	−04	09	−40	03	10	132
65. Saudi Arabia	.84	15	(−83)	−24	06	05	−15	−20	−10	98
66. Spain	.78	19	(−56)	−39	16	09	−43	13	20	162
67. Sweden	.94	16	−46	(−77)	11	27	−14	−08	08	172
68. Switzerland	.88	23	−47	(−73)	14	18	−08	03	04	170
69. Syria	.79	32	(−65)	−26	29	15	05	09	28	125
70. Thailand	.89	32	(−74)	−38	22	18	−02	−00	11	155
71. Turkey	.84	31	(−63)	−46	19	22	−01	15	16	166
72. South Africa	.83	39	−44	−46	25	18	−01	06	42	164
73. USSR	.84	28	(−69)	−39	20	16	−20	17	05	133
74. UK	.89	23	−44	(−72)	19	23	−03	16	10	174
75. USA	.88	22	(−50)	(−69)	20	12	−08	10	18	175
76. Uruguay	.84	20	−42	(−75)	14	02	−07	−19	07	139
77. Venezuela	.90	35	−36	−44	(60)	25	−01	07	18	169
78. Yemen	.92	25	(−91)	−04	02	−14	−11	00	−08	69
79. Yugoslavia	.91	33	(−66)	(−51)	06	16	−28	07	−01	157
80. Laos	.84	28	(−74)	−06	10	15	38	−10	16	105
81. N. Vietnam	.95	16	(−78)	−27	−15	34	−21	22	−03	83

251

TABLE 8–3—Cont.
Q–Factor Analysis of Nations

Country	h²	Varimax Factors[a]								Cases
		I	II	III	IV	V	VI	VII	VIII	
82. S. Vietnam	.84	24	(−79)	−33	−04	20	−11	03	05	109
83. Morocco	.78	20	(−51)	−20	11	11	−07	−08	(64)	98
84. Sudan	.74	36	(−69)	−09	06	04	08	03	33	83
85. Tunisia	.79	06	(−56)	−47	21	11	−44	−02	04	96
Eigenvalues[b]		19.1	17.2	21.8	4.3	5.7	3.1	1.4	2.1	
Percent total variance[b]		22.5	20.3	24.5	5.1	6.7	3.7	1.6	2.5	
Percent common variance[b]		25.6	23.0	29.0	5.8	7.9	4.2	1.9	2.9	

Correlations between factor loadings

	I	II	III	IV	V	VI	VII	VIII
I	1.00							
II	.56	1.00						
III	.20	−.41	1.00					
IV	−.02	.21	−.01	1.00				
V	−.05	.28	.06	.06	1.00			
VI	.07	−.05	.12	.19	.03	1.00		
VII	.00	−.06	−.10	.01	.05	.06	1.00	
VIII	−.09	.06	.18	.23	.01	.25	.04	1.00

[a] Factor loadings are multiplied by 100; loadings > ±.50 are enclosed in parentheses.
[b] Based on varimax factors.

TABLE 8–4
Correlations Between 8 Q–Factors and 183 Asymmetry Variables

See Appendix D, pp. 584–90, for table text.

ernmental succession. Negative correlations are found for such variables as nutritional adequacy, percentage of children in primary schools, general government expenditures divided by national income, lack of personalismo in political parties, and several measures of per capita media exposure. The population in such countries, thus, is unenlightened and mobilizable for separatist political and social movements. Almost all of the asymmetry variables correlate positively with this factor, but missing data is not related.

Factor II involves *politicoeconomic development*. Since there are a variety of definitions for "development,"[5] the meaning of this factor should be rendered as specific as possible. Since all loadings have a negative sign, the factor is defined by the negatively loading countries, the six highest of which are Yemen, Saudi Arabia, Mongolia, the two Vietnams, and Nepal. These countries are noted for having unmobilized and undifferentiated political systems run by oligarchies astride populations that are partly apathetic and partly contentious. As we examine the correlations with our 183 variables, we spot a tendency for the higher correlations to be along the entropic dimension and to reflect asymmetries in structure. Entropically, the factor reveals that such countries possess a considerable gap between potential and exploited hydroelectric power, have few railroads and roads for automobiles. This failure to fully tap or harness resources corresponds to Jacob Viner's definition for lack of "development."[6] Rigg's definition of "development" stresses the presence of specialized and effective political and administrative structures in a polity.[7] Factor II gives evidence of this type of development in having positive correlations with number of political parties, weak executives, and the use of strikes; yet it also has negative correlations with elitism, weak legislatures, press censorship, traditional bureaucracy, horizontal power concentration, nonpolyarchic representation, restrictions on the political opposition, and police intervention into politics. The factor reveals some anomic activity, such as assassinations and riots, but no sectional separatism, suggesting that conflict is less likely to be fundamentally divisive within developed countries than among polities loading high on Factor I. Whereas conflict and structural differentiation are asymmetrical concepts, declining entropy means increased symmetry, so it is not surprising that the development factor is related to both symmetrical and asymmetrical concepts. There

[5] See Lucian W. Pye, *Aspects of Political Development* (Boston: Little, Brown, 1966), Chapter 2.

[6] Jacob Viner, *International Trade and Economic Development* (Oxford: Clarendon, 1964).

[7] Fred W. Riggs, "The Dialectics of Developmental Conflict," *Comparative Political Studies,* I (July 1968), 197–226; Riggs, *Administration in Developing Countries* (Boston: Houghton Mifflin, 1964); Riggs, "The Theory of Political Development," *Contemporary Political Analysis,* ed. James C. Charlesworth (New York: The Free Press, 1967), pp. 317–49.

is only a moderate positive correlation between Factor II and missing data.

In Factor III most countries with high though negative loadings are Western European, North American, or are the most Westernized among non-European countries (Chile, Taiwan, Costa Rica, Israel, Japan, Mexico, Philippines, Uruguay). Correlations with the 183 variables are high with nearly the same variables that were associated with Politicoeconomic Development, except that the signs are consistently reversed. There are few highways and railroads, and waterpower remains unexploited; there is police intervention, press censorship, anomic articulation, a restricted political opposition, horizontal concentration of power, a weak executive and legislature, and a very few IGO's or NGO's are located in the relevant countries; negative correlations are present for multipartism and constitutional regime. A third set of indicators, concerned with social development, is clearly evident as well: positive correlations exist for rural populations, revolutions, and low political enculturation; but negative correlations show up for media circulation, high percentages of national income devoted to education and welfare, and changes in death and marriage rates. Though unrelated to symmetry-asymmetry, the factor correlates − .77 with extent of missing data. The variables with highest correlations come from the immobility, bottlenecked, fragmented, and discriminatory conceptual domains. The most appropriate label would seem to be *lack of modernization,* a term that denotes an absence of an appropriate social base from which to start developmental processes in either the economy or the polity.[8]

Factors IV through VIII merit only passing attention due to the small amount of variance for which they account. *Latin American* countries load highest on Factor IV, which is associated with multiracial populations, high illegitimacy and homicide rates, low divorce and suicide rates, inequality, rapid urbanization, activist domestic conflict, government crises, and a low rate of economic growth. Factor V links Lebanon, Liberia, and South Korea, a set of countries with no apparent relation to one another, but correlations in Table 8–4 reveal considerable export-import imbalance, suggesting the existence of a *neocolonial dependency* stratum within the sample. Factor VI contains *open* (as opposed to closed) *societies,* for it has highest negative loadings for Hungary, North Korea, Portugal, and Spain; variables with which the factor is most associated possess not only such democratic features as a free political opposition, several political parties, bicameralism, press freedom, and lack of group discrimination but also weak executives, short elite tenure, many homicides, revolutions, party instability, nonmobili-

8 Cf. J. P. Nettl and Roland Robertson, *International Systems and the Modernization of Societies* (New York: Basic Books, 1968).

zational style, nonpolyarchic representation, lack of unionization, and a traditional bureaucracy. A completely open society, in short, has few coercive capabilities of any sort, and political life therein resembles Hobbes's state of nature: there is an intense expression of conflicts and cleavages. Factor VII contrasts countries with minority groups who pursue separatist goals (India and Pakistan) from those having fewer breaks in social communication patterns (Haiti and Nepal); *lack of intergroup accommodation* will be used to refer to this factor, which is the only one having consistently positive and moderate correlations with foreign conflict variables. The final factor correlates positively with high domestic conflict and negatively with six indicators of temporal change, indicating that intense political conflicts throttle political continuity and economic growth and that stagnation leads to conflict; in either case the factor points to overall *societal paralysis,* in which contending forces strive to achieve dominance in internal wars of mutual attrition. Morocco and South Africa have high positive loadings; Costa Rica and Mongolia are among countries with higher negative loadings.

Putting the correlations between the eight factors into a second-order factor analysis, five factors emerge with eigenvalues over 1.0 (Table 8–5). Factor I pulls together the Latin American, Open Society, and Societal Paralysis factors, and thus seems to represent a *dionysian* dimension, while an *apollonian* dimension appears on Factor II as the common element uniting Centrifugal Asymmetry and Politicoeconomic Development.[9] The second-order factor analysis, however, leaves Lack of Modernization, Neocolonial Dependency, and Lack of Intergroup Accommodation as unique factors. They do merge in a third-order analysis, nevertheless (Table 8–6). The first third-order factor depicts countries that are neither modernized nor have much intergroup accommodation and lack trade dependency, or perhaps any important form of trade at all; such countries would be so amorphously put together that the label *disunited* would be appropriate. The second-order factors, Apollonian and Dionysian, which together denote *activism,* end up on the second and final third-order factor. A basic contrast between countries, thus, is whether they contain strata that pursue definable goals, or whether the society is almost entirely acephalous.

Results from the factor analysis closely resemble a cluster analysis of the same data (Figures 8–1 and 8–2). Using a cutoff of about 35.0, there are seven main subclusters. Subcluster I contains the core of non-Western countries from the first factor in the factor analysis, justifying a *non–Western centrifugal* label. The second subcluster is composed of Latin American countries plus Greece, Taiwan, and Egypt; if we overlook these three countries, the *Latin American* label would be most descriptive if procrustean.

[9] Cf. Ruth Benedict, *Patterns of Culture* (Boston: Houghton Mifflin, 1934).

TABLE 8–5
Second–Order Q–Factor Analysis

First–Order Factors	h²	*Quartimin Factors*[a]				
		I	II	III	IV	V
I. Centrifugal	.97	—11	(99)	21	01	—11
II. Politicoeconomic Development	.95	13	(70)	—43	—08	22
III. Lack of Modernization	.91	02	07	(101)	—15	17
IV. Latin American	.58	(73)	00	—27	—10	02
V. Neocolonial Dependency	.97	—05	—04	26	08	(105)
VI. Open Society	.54	(59)	11	18	25	—11
VII. Lack of Intergroup Accommodation	.93	—04	—02	—19	(99)	09
VIII. Societal Paralysis	.58	(74)	—11	13	—06	02
Eigenvalues[b]		1.7	1.2	1.5	1.0	1.0
Percent total variance[b]		21.3	15.0	18.8	12.5	12.5
Percent common variance[b]		26.6	18.8	23.6	15.6	15.6
Correlations between	I	1.00				
factor loadings	II	—.44	1.00			
	III	—.00	—.41	1.00		
	IV	—.19	—.38	.15	1.00	
	V	—.25	.08	—.58	—.36	1.00

[a] Factor loadings are multiplied by 100; loadings $> \pm .50$ are enclosed in parentheses.
[b] Based on principal axis factors.

TABLE 8–6
Third–Order Q–Factor Analysis

Second–Order Factors	h²	*Varimax Factors*[a]	
		I	II
I. Dionysian	.90	—09	(—94)
II. Apollonian	.61	—46	(63)
III. Lack of Modernization	.60	(75)	—21
IV. Lack of Intergroup Accommodation	.61	(75)	23
V. Neocolonial Dependency	.58	(—73)	20
Eigenvalues[b]		2.1	1.2
Percent total variance[b]		41.1	24.8
Percent common variance[b]		63.9	36.1
Correlations between factor loadings	I	1.00	
	II	—.21	1.00

[a] Factor loadings are multiplied by 100; loadings $> \pm. 50$ are enclosed in parentheses.
[b] Based on principal axis factors.

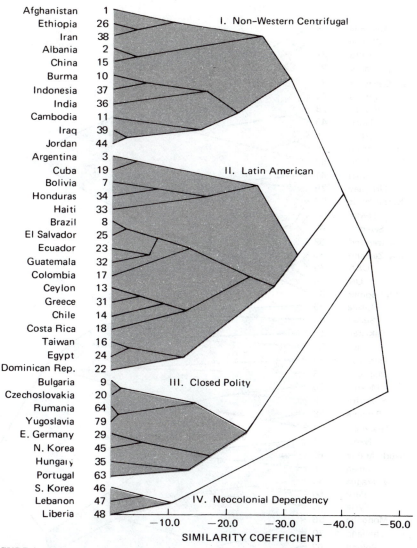

FIGURE 8-1
Q–Cluster Analysis of Nations: I

The merger of the first two subclusters clearly identifies a *centrifugal* stratum. *Closed polities,* though only a subset of Factor VI, appear together on Subcluster III. The fourth subcluster in Figure 8–1 consists of the three countries loading highest on the *neocolonial dependency* factor. The entire cluster of Figure 8–1 presents a common thread—countries beset with *pattern maintenance* problems.

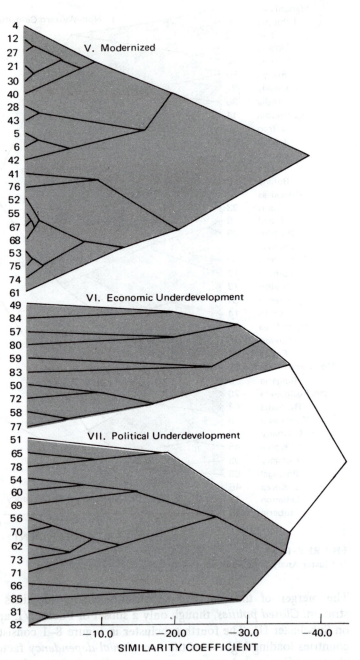

FIGURE 8-2
Q–Cluster Analysis of Nations: II

Three subclusters are present in Figure 8–2. Subcluster V consists of *modernized* countries and is the reverse of Factor III; countries most representative of this factor are Western European and Anglo-American plus Finland, Israel, Japan, the Philippines, and Uruguay. The final two subclusters house countries that are underdeveloped, politically or economically. Subcluster VI brings together *economically underdeveloped* nations, along with Mexico and South Africa, which have less well-developed political infrastructures in light of one-party and one-race rule, respectively. *Politically underdeveloped* countries appear in Subcluster VII; the Soviet Union, for example, is administratively advanced but lacks interest groups and contending political parties.

Subclusters build up incrementally, rather than collapsing into tightly insulated strata. In Figure 8–1 each of the four subcultures joins the whole without first building up into larger subclusters. Subclusters I and II come together at a coefficient of − 39.9. Closed Polities enter the larger cluster at − 44.2, and the tiny Neocolonial cluster completes the merger at − 46.8 coefficient of similarity. Modernized countries (Figure 8–2) join the cluster of Figure 8–1 at − 52.1, and the final two subclusters, after combining at − 41.6, enter the combined 85-country cluster at − 59.5. This scheme of subcluster mergers appears in Figure 8–3 (along with results of primary and higher-order factor analyses). Since modernization implies stressing goal attainment activities, the link between Modernized and Pattern Maintenance clusters represents *system-wide planning,* in contrast to the final distinct subcluster, *underdevelopment.* In summary, factor analysis discovers two main types of countries—those with disunity or unity and those differing on the nature of their activism (either apollonian or dionysian orientations). The cluster structure also discovers two classes of countries: it contrasts the extent of societal planning and levels of development.

8.3 DIMENSIONS OF ASYMMETRY VARIABLES

Because correlations with the four dependent variables, as reported in Chapter 7, are uniformly of low magnitude, one of the advantages of undertaking a multivariate analysis of asymmetry variables will be to find which sets of variables together predict international aggression. In addition, we may determine the extent to which the variables selected collapse in a manner similar to the variable map of Table 8–2; if so, we would expect 36 distinct factors—one pertaining to each cell at the intersection between the 6 dimensions and 6 attributes, though because we are deleting variables 65, 66, 130, 131, 169, and 179 from the factor analysis, it will be impossible for a separate attitudinal-transactional dimension to appear. As an alternative,

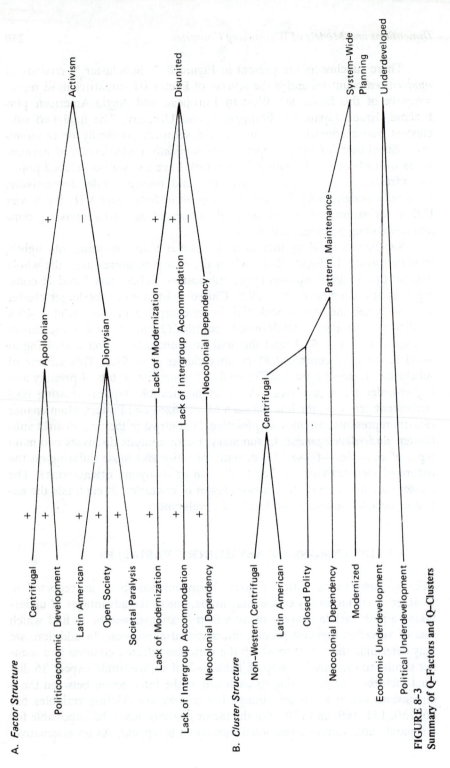

FIGURE 8–3
Summary of Q–Factors and Q–Clusters

we might derive the 6 postulated dimensions intact, either initially or after a second-order analysis.

8.3.1 Procedure

Due to the missing-data problem, intercorrelations between 177 variables were computed for two samples of countries—the full 85 and a subsample of countries with the least amount of missing data. This second sample represents the entire membership in the Modernized cluster of Figure 8–2, some 21 countries in all. In the full sample of countries, 98 principal components were extracted with eigenvalues over 0.0; 43 of these were over 1.0, although the scree test suggests a cutoff at 29 factors. Communalities were very low for some variables that failed to appear with high loadings on any of the 43 factors; however, other variables had communalities far in excess of 1.0, whether they were computed for 29 or 43 factors.

The percent of total variance explained by the first 37 factors sums to 99.8; the last 6 factors cause it to exceed 100. Upon closer examination, it was evident that a cutoff of 16 or so factors would have more respectable communalities, but many significant factors would be overlooked. Inflated communalities often are merely an artifact of missing data or of a matrix in which there are more variables than cases. The Modernization subsample was factor-analyzed next to determine which of these interpretations would be correct. One result of this factor analysis of modernized countries was the appearance of inflated communalities as well, but the total number of principal components over 0.0 and 1.0 was halved in comparison with the total sample. Factors failing to appear in the smaller factor analysis describe characteristics that differentiate unmodernized countries from one another and thus logically are not relevant as factors to be extracted from the sample of 21 modernized countries. The results of the full sample are presented below, along with Pearsonian correlations between factor loadings and the 85 countries (Table 8–8). The first 10 factors extracted from the 177 variables are presented in Table 8–7. In view of the visually cumbersome nature of reproducing a matrix of 43 factors based on 177 variables, the 10 variables loading most prominently on Factors XI through XLIII are placed in separate tables (Tables 8–9 to 8–41). A cluster analysis of all 183 variables is possible because cluster analysis results are subject to fewer artifacts when based on variables for which there is missing data (Figures 8–4 to 8–6).

It is the novelty of the factors that is of most interest in attempting to achieve a broad-gauge dimensional theory for the social sciences. Including some variables from previous studies evidently has not guaranteed their re-

TABLE 8-7
R-Factor Analysis of Asymmetry Variables

Variables	h^2	I	II	III	IV	V	VI	VII	VIII	IX	X
						Varimax Factors[a]					
1. Δ National income/pop.	.93	-44	24	-09	04	22	-03	15	-10	-07	-12
2. Δ Elec. consumption/pop.	1.19	-13	02	-08	-12	-18	-10	10	04	-17	01
3. Δ GNP/pop.	.95	-43	29	06	02	16	-04	(52)	-10	08	-22
4. Δ Radios/pop.	.57	(-54)	-01	08	02	-12	07	04	-19	-01	-18
5. Δ Phones/pop.	.33	-25	-24	-05	-00	09	00	-14	06	-05	-04
6. Δ RR ton-km.	.81	-21	-27	-03	-22	08	18	-07	27	-14	13
7. Δ Elec. production/pop.	.67	-39	-27	01	-08	-14	00	-24	15	-17	-02
8. Δ Population	1.00	(61)	-06	01	07	-25	-17	01	04	-12	-05
9. Δ Caloric intake	1.01	-06	-03	-06	-03	-02	-09	(92)	05	01	-01
10. Δ Protein intake	1.07	01	-14	10	-09	-08	-26	(88)	-01	13	09
11. Δ Government budget	.23	-06	26	-02	07	28	-07	-06	03	01	-05
12. Δ National income	.66	26	04	-12	-20	09	-23	-01	29	13	-39
13. Δ Urban population	.97	07	10	02	-10	(-58)	-31	36	17	28	-12
14. Δ Agr. employment	1.06	-10	01	09	-02	21	22	-05	-07	04	05
15. Δ Literacy rate	1.23	14	25	25	-06	07	-05	35	07	19	-10
16. Δ % Communist Party strength	.72	-31	-06	-00	03	13	08	07	-17	-35	-30
17. Government instability	.76	(50)	07	-32	06	-06	-25	08	10	-11	-02
18. System instability	1.00	41	15	(-65)	19	-14	-10	09	16	-02	-01
19. Government tenure	1.07	-03	24	07	06	-10	02	01	-00	-00	-03
20. Elite tenure	.81	07	24	28	00	07	17	13	06	16	10
21. Δ Birth rate	.74	-22	-45	03	05	-15	29	-08	13	-02	18
22. Δ Death rate	.72	(-56)	-41	15	-03	-04	11	-14	-08	-06	-03
23. Δ Marriage rate	.39	-30	-23	21	-09	06	17	01	01	05	-15
24. Government crises	.81	22	-15	-48	-08	06	09	01	31	-08	00
25. Government illegitimacy	.21	07	19	03	-08	-12	01	-11	06	-06	-05

See Appendix D, pp. 591–97, for complete table.

262

TABLE 8-8

Correlations Between 43 R–Factors and 85 Countries[a]

Country	I	II	III	IV	V	VI	VII	VIII	IX	X	XI	XII
						Varimax Factors						
1. Afghanistan	.01	.06	.19	−.11	.02	−.06	.15	−.00	.07	.05	−.00	.04
2. Albania	−.08	.09	.21	−.10	.10	−.02	.33	.00	.20	.03	−.05	.02
3. Argentina	−.08	−.01	.13	−.06	−.02	.07	.01	.01	−.25	.07	.02	−.02
4. Australia	−.14	−.05	.16	−.01	.02	.05	−.01	−.09	−.17	.02	−.07	.03
5. Austria	−.08	−.04	.10	−.09	−.01	−.02	.09	−.02	−.15	.00	−.11	−.01
6. Belgium	−.15	−.05	.11	−.01	.05	.14	.02	−.05	−.21	.04	−.08	−.02
7. Bolivia	.03	.01	.03	−.09	−.11	−.02	.06	.05	−.27	.03	.04	−.05
8. Brazil	−.01	−.05	.10	−.07	−.08	−.04	.01	.03	−.30	.00	.01	.01
9. Bulgaria	−.11	.05	.14	−.09	.06	−.05	.28	−.03	.13	−.01	−.06	.00
10. Burma	−.09	−.02	.12	−.13	.04	−.09	.23	.02	.02	.04	−.22	−.05
11. Cambodia	.04	.03	.08	−.13	−.02	−.11	.10	−.02	−.01	−.02	.04	.05
12. Canada	−.18	−.05	.14	.00	.05	.06	−.00	−.17	−.01	.00	−.12	.03
13. Ceylon	−.04	.03	.11	−.10	−.01	−.08	.14	−.03	.09	.00	−.04	.00
14. Chile	.03	.00	.10	−.07	−.10	−.03	.04	.05	−.24	.02	.09	−.02
15. China	−.01	.04	.12	−.17	−.01	−.19	.12	−.07	.01	−.12	.02	.06
16. Taiwan	−.00	.15	.17	−.04	.08	.08	.16	.06	.08	.12	.08	.03
17. Colombia	−.01	−.00	.09	−.05	−.09	−.02	−.00	.05	−.32	.02	.08	−.02
18. Costa Rica	.03	−.01	.08	−.07	−.09	−.06	.07	.02	−.22	.01	.06	.01
19. Cuba	−.04	.05	.02	−.06	−.06	.03	.05	−.05	−.14	.05	.02	−.07
20. Czechoslovakia	−.15	.00	.14	−.05	.06	.00	.18	−.15	.11	−.01	−.20	.03
21. Denmark	−.16	−.05	.14	−.03	.04	.06	.01	−.13	−.10	.01	−.10	.04
22. Dominican Rep.	.03	.03	.11	−.07	−.07	−.01	.14	.04	−.17	.04	.07	.00
23. Ecuador	.06	−.01	.07	−.06	−.12	−.03	.02	.05	−.31	.01	.10	.01
24. Egypt	.04	−.02	.06	−.08	−.08	−.02	−.02	.06	−.33	.01	.03	.01
25. El Salvador	.06	−.00	.07	−.08	−.12	−.05	.03	.03	−.26	.00	.09	.01

See Appendix D, pp. 598–608, for complete table.

emergence in these studies, although the first two factors do resemble the first factors in the studies of Russett, Gregg–Banks, and Rummel;[10] the remaining factors are new. Unlike most of the prior factor analyses, there is no dimension labelled *size,* and this would appear to be a direct result of weeding out all variables expressed as magnitudes. The hypothesis that six major dimensions would emerge, or perhaps that a separate factor would be extracted to correspond to each cell in Table 8–2, proved incorrect. There is a tenuous mesh between empirical results and analytically postulated dimensions. The property space designed in Chapter 6 does not conform to empirical results based on indicators selected to represent cells in the conceptual matrix in Chapter 7. The cantankerousness of reality reminds us of conceptual dualism. Our conceptualization succeeded in generating a large number of variables and provided data for an entirely new set of empirical taxonomies.

The first factor accounts for about 20 percent of the total variance; Factor II extracts 10 percent, the remaining factors very gradually taper off. Summing the first set of factors cumulatively, it takes 7 factors to account for more than half of the total variance. Interfactor correlations are uniformly low. We may conclude that the data are extremely heterogeneous in terms of factors. Once again a multiaxis conceptual scheme has been useful in arriving at a complex representation of dimensions, and higher-order factor analyses are necessary.

8.3.2 Results

The first two factors resemble findings in previous factor-analytic studies, whose data are used herein. Factor I contains indicators of immobility and fragmentation, as we have defined these concepts; it appears similar to the first factor in the studies of Rummel and Russett. Although these two authors label their first factor as "economic development," it is evident that our Factor I is concerned principally with aspects of what Karl Deutsch has called "social mobilization."[11] Because the correlations between Factor I and such variables as radios per capita, percent students, library book and

---

[10] Russett, *International Regions and the International Systems,* Chapter 2; Rudolph J. Rummel, "Some Empirical Findings of Nations and Their Behavior," *World Politics,* XXI (January 1969), 226–41; Phillip M. Gregg and Arthur S. Banks, "Dimensions of Political Systems: Factor Analysis of *A Cross-Polity Survey,*" *American Political Science Review,* LIX (September 1965), 602–14.

[11] Karl W. Deutsch, "Social Mobilization and Political Development," *American Political Science Review,* LV (September 1961), 493–514; Deutsch, *Nationalism and Social Communication* (Cambridge: MIT Press, 1953).

newspaper circulation are negative here, the label *sparse social communication* seems most appropriate. The factor distinguishes between high and low density in social communication; variables with high loadings indicate the technological paraphernalia necessary to maintain a dense system of communication. In Table 8–8 we can observe that the countries corresponding to these two extreme positions on the social communication density continuum are Canada, Sweden, and the USSR on the one hand (− .18 correlation) and Guatemala and Iraq (+ .07 correlation) on the other. But there is no relationship between the foreign conflict variables and this first factor.

Many variables from the "access" factor of Gregg and Banks show up in Factor II with negative codings—nonconstitutional governments, horizontal power concentration, nonpolyarchic representation, and a weak legislature with a strong executive. The ranking and number of these variables, as well as their negative correlation with the factor, suggests a *despotism* factor. Authoritarian rule without much structural differentiation is associated more with this factor than totalitarian rule, wherein the need for efficient goal attainment leads to internal propaganda programs and formalistic participation in political processes. The whole continuum, hence, starts with authoritarianism (Taiwan) shades off into totalitarianism, and ends with constitutionalism (Japan). Despotism has no clear relationship with foreign conflict at this point in our analysis, but we shall soon find that there is a connection when we perform higher-order factor analyses and look at the results from our cluster analysis.

Nonconflictual domestic political behavior is the third factor, corresponding to the fifth factor in Rummel's study.[12] Antigovernment demonstrations, riots, assassinations, general strikes, government crises, guerrilla warfare, and purges all have high negative loadings along with one stray variable—polities that are Communist satellites. During the 1955–1960 period evidently Communist satellites (especially Cuba) were much more plagued with domestic conflict behavior than any other type of polity. Yemen, stable during the time period in question, has the highest positive correlation with this factor. Domestic conflict, like Despotism, has a weak but positive relationship with foreign conflict and shows up in subsequent analyses of the data.

---

[12] See also Rummel, "Dimensions of Conflict Behavior Within and Between Nations," *General Systems Yearbook,* VIII (1963), 1–50. The label for this factor is changed from "Domestic Cooperation" in my earlier summary of the factor analysis: Haas, "Dimensional Analysis in Cross-National Research," *Comparative Political Studies,* III (April 1970), 3–35. Some other labels are changed, as for example Factor III from "irredentism" to "separatism." The changes are based on the broader conceptualization presented herein.

Entirely novel factors begin to appear after Factor III. Group discrimination, sectionalism, and multiethnicity point toward *separatism* as the common thread of Factor IV. Countries least associated with this factor have territorial boundaries more or less coinciding with the limits of where a particular nation resides, whereas separatist countries contain peoples seeking to detach themselves or to gain more local autonomy. Canada, Sudan, and the USA have the only positive correlations with this factor; Nepal is the least separatist. In higher-order factors, foreign conflict is related to separatism which is not entirely a domestic problem in the contemporary world of Vietnams.

Factor V is not easily interpretable, having highest loadings for number of racial groups and an assortment of seemingly unrelated variables. In a factor analysis by Cattell and Gorsuch,[13] however, two of these variables are part of a factor called "anomie versus channelled emotionality." The label *monoracial unity,* hence, seems most appropriate. The factor refers to small countries, such as Laos, in which resources are tapped but limits are not yet reached in the amount of arable land, waterpower, and profitable locations for urban centers; because of the small size of these countries and their somewhat spartan economies, which are partially dominated by absentee landlords, few persons from foreign racial groups have migrated to resettle. Perhaps it is the staid, institution-dominated existence which leads to high rates of divorce in these countries, but we should be aware that this lone form of social conflict proceeds through legal channels. Latin American countries, which contain three or four racial groups (Caucasian, Indian, Negro, and mestizo) and permit no divorce, correlate negatively with this factor. There is no connection between *monoracial unity* and the incidence of foreign conflict.

A *centripetal* factor is found in Factor VI. Such indicators as percent colonial area and population, international organizations headquartered at home, absentee landlordism, and political decentralization portray countries that seek to bring resources or other attributes in closer juxtaposition to a central hub. Belgium, the smallest country with a large colonial empire in the 1950s, correlates strongly with this factor; many former colonies have negative correlations.

W. W. Rostow's theory of economic growth specifies a set of conditions which, once attained, are hypothesized to permit rapid progress toward eco-

---

[13] Raymond B. Cattell and Richard L. Gorsuch, "The Definition and Measurement of National Morale," *Journal of Social Psychology,* LXVII (October 1965), 77–96. In "Dimensional Analysis in Cross-National Research," I use the venturesome label "Monoracial Channelled Emotionality."

nomic maturity.[14] Because so many of these conditions (urbanization and increased literacy) and related variables (adequate food intake, unionization, high voter turnout) load highly on Factor VII, the best descriptive label would be *takeoff stage*. From Table 8–8 we may infer that Tunisia is among those fulfilling takeoff preconditions in the 1955–1960 period, whereas negative correlations with the factor appear for both pre-takeoff (Egypt) and post-takeoff countries (USA). Contrary to Adam Smith's theory, there is no positive or negative relation between this factor and foreign conflict.

Politicoeconomic paralysis underlies variables with high loadings on Factor VIII, including stationary government budgets, government crises, income and party instability. South Africa has the highest correlation, no doubt due to its apartheid policy in the late 1950s. Canada and the United States are among the least paralyzed in economic growth and political goal-attainment capabilities. Politicoeconomic Paralysis entails neither a paralysis in military operations nor a hyperactive armed forces.

Factor IX brings together indicators of *equalitarian* land ownership, where Communist Party voting is also high. Surprisingly, however, Communist countries correlate less highly with the factor than agrarian, unmodernized societies. The high loadings of Liberia and Yemen may be more due to a cultural disinterest in acquisitiveness than to an ideology of equalitarianism. Inequality characterizes some of the larger Latin American and Arab countries most acutely. Contrary to the theme of the second biennial conference of the International Peace Research Association held at Tällberg, Sweden, in 1967, inequality breeds neither warlike nor peaceful state behavior.

The tenth factor is too elusive to interpret on first inspection. A country with as many immigrants and emigrants would appear to be a way station that collects refugees, who move on to other countries after a brief stop. The fact that much taxation is imposed on trade, while the economic sector remains almost constant, suggests that such countries contain major ports where goods are docked temporarily and then reexported. *Permeability*, used in the manner proposed by John Herz,[15] seems to be the main theme, for access to these countries seems to be especially easy to obtain. It is to be expected that Lebanon would be highly correlated positively, while the People's Republic of China would correlate negatively. The "bamboo curtain" in Asia, in other words, is less permeable than the "iron curtain" in Europe.

---

[14] W. W. Rostow, *The Stages of Economic Growth* (Cambridge, England: Cambridge University Press, 1964).

[15] John H. Herz, *International Politics in the Atomic Age* (New York: Columbia University Press, 1959); for an essay on informal penetration, see Andrew M. Scott, *The Revolution in Statecraft* (New York: Random House, 1967).

But whether such a curtain is open or closed matters little in predicting international conflict between nations.

One of the major types of political capabilities stressed by Gabriel Almond is the ability of a government to extract resources from members of the population.[16] As we see in Factor XI (Table 8–9), a *nonextractive* factor is empirically independent of other factors derived so far. Many of these variables, though with negative signs, also appear on Russett's second factor, which he labels Communism. Nevertheless, we find herein that non-Communist countries might be as equally over- or underextractive as Communist states. Burma and Czechslovakia are among the former; North Korea and Sudan extract lesser amounts of tax revenues from their citizens. Although taxes are usually needed to pay for the operations of armed forces, there is no connection between the capacity to extract taxes and military capabilities.

Absentee landlordism sums up Factor XII (Table 8–10), inasmuch as countries described by these variables would have a great need for land reform. But in these countries large educational expenditures substitute for land redistribution, in order to build consensus for the secularized regime. The economy, meanwhile, remains stagnant, the government balances its budget, and food production has increased. Poor Communist countries correlate positively (Mongolia, North Korea), but so does Mexico. Cuba, Hungary, and Indonesia have high negative correlations. The wisdom of the stress on educational development appears to be that otherwise such a polity is headed for domestic unrest.[17] There is no clear propensity among such countries to engage in foreign conflict at low or high levels.

Factor XIII is composed of indicators of *rural austerity,* which include at least a 50–50 split between rural and urban sectors along with caloric deficiency and few government expenditures (Table 8–11). Saudi Arabia, Sudan, and Yemen are highly correlated; rural populations in all three countries are generally neglected by elites residing in their respective capital cities. Much more opulent farmers are to be found in France, Italy, and the Soviet Union. Foreign conflict is unrelated to this factor.

A high level of *political competition* is portrayed in Factor XIV (Table 8–12) by many political parties, government crises, and rising Communist Party votes. The competition not only involves many different parties but also counterelites plotting forcible takeovers. Israel, according to correla-

---

[16] Gabriel A. Almond and G. Bingham Powell, Jr., *Comparative Politics* (Boston: Little, Brown, 1966).

[17] In Haas, "Dimensional Analysis in Cross-National Research," the label "Ideological Development" was used for this factor.

NOTE: See Appendix D, pp. 609–19, for Tables 8–9 through 8–41.

tions in Table 8–8, is the most competitive country; Yemen lacks political competition entirely. Levels of competitiveness are not correlated with foreign conflict.

In Factor XV negative correlations are highest for indicators of foreign conflict. The reverse of casualties in foreign conflict, wars, military clashes, military mobilizations, and military expenditures is not necessarily cooperation, but instead *nonconflictual foreign behavior* (Table 8–13). As with the third factor, Nonconflictual Domestic Political Behavior, variables with high loadings here indicate merely an absence of overt conflict. Diagnostic clues are meager in Table 8–7, in view of the overall lower correlations; isolationistic countries (Yemen and Mongolia) have high correlations with the factor. Foreign conflict is prevalent among bloc leaders and countries that donate or receive large amounts of foreign aid. Using correlations between a country and this factor as an approximate scale of intensity of foreign conflict, we find that Laos and North Korea were the most prone toward war during 1955–1960, the years covered by our study.

Factors XVI through XLIII are presented below, but in the interest of brevity their labels are neither justified nor discussed (Tables 8–14 to 8–41), except by indicating countries that are most and least associated. The first fifteen factors account for about 75 percent of the total variance, and unique factors are common after Factor XX.

Factor XVI groups together indicators of *unguided development,*[18] from guided Pakistan to unguided Iraq during the late 1950s. Factor XVII differentiates *modernizing oligarchies,* such as Jordan, from standpatist countries, such as Sudan. *Societal tension* (XVIII) is high for Canada but low for Jordan. Hungary and Indonesia are high on *discontentment with laxity* (XIX), but Yemen is low. Factor XX contrasts countries like South Africa, which are *developmentally reactionary,* with the more radical policies of a Tunisia. *Elite scapegoatism* (XXI) is high in Laos, low in Greece. *Developmental slowdown* (XXII) was present for the USA during the late 1950s, absent for Albania. North Korea has high *domestic disengagement* (XXIII) in contradistinction with Tunisia. Liberia, South Vietnam, and Tunisia have a high degree of *internationally guided development* but this same factor (XXIV) is very low for South Africa. *Patriarchical rule* (XXV) is present in Liberia, absent in the People's Republic of China. Sudan has a *lack of professional expertise* (XXVI), Czechoslovakia decidedly does not. Iraqis live in *unstructured* situations (XXVII) in contrast with Thais. Variables on Factor XXVIII suggest *modernizing welfare statism,* but a positive correlation for South Africa and a negative correlation

---

[18] For purposes of the higher-order factor analysis I have reversed this factor from "Unguided Development" in *ibid.*

for North Korea are somewhat surprising. The USA is characterized as having *labor unrest amid affluence* (XXIX), a set of conditions quite different from those in Bolivia. *Governmental philistinism* (XXX) is present in Uruguay and the USSR, absent in Jordan. North Korea exhibits more *solidarity* (XXXI) than Yemen. North Korea also has much *cathective involvement* (XXXII), but this is not true for Cambodia. Conditions associated with *bourgeois revolution* (XXXIII) were brewing in Cuba, absent in Yemen. There is much *phenotypic symmetry* (XXXIV) in Jordan, little in Morocco. A *developmental junta* (XXV) has been in charge in Burma, but not in Yemen. *Evenness in development* (XXXVI) has been characteristic of Laos, but not of Nepal. Canada and Switzerland have been *reorganization-minded* (XXXVII), but not North Vietnam. *Incorporative articulation* (XXXVIII) has been present in Nicaragua and Poland, rather than in Nepal. *Unenlightened rebellion* (XXXIX) took place in Cuba, but these conditions were not present in the Soviet Union during the late 1950s. The United States has achieved a stage of *sustained industrialization* (XL), but Liberia is far from that level of economic growth. Yemen fulfills conditions for being a *neocolonized* (XLI) country, but Burma and the People's Republic of China have been able to avoid this state of affairs. Sukarno's notion of *guided democracy* (XLII) is realized best by Tunisia, least by Nepal. Much *entrepreneurial development* (XLIII) is present in Nepal, little in Jordan.

A second-order factor analysis is clearly needed to reduce the large number of factors into a smaller set of dimensions. Accordingly, product-moment correlations between the 43 factors were computed and put into a principal axis factor analysis. Some 16 factors were extracted with eigenvalues over 1.0; a varimax rotation was performed, but oblique solutions failed to improve upon the approximation to simple structure of the orthogonal solution (Table 8–42). A second-order factor including foreign conflict ranks fifteenth in eigenvalues.

The first second-order factor is *political asymmetry,* bringing together principally Politicoeconomic Paralysis, Domestic Conflict, and Lack of Professional Expertise. Factor II, *societal expansiveness,* is composed of the Takeoff factor and the opposite of the Reactionary Development factor. *Social symmetry,* Factor III, has negative loadings for Separatism and Societal Tension, a positive loading for Phenotypic Symmetry. *Laissez-faire development* shows up on Factor IV as a positive loading for the Unguided Development factor and a negative loading for Solidarity, suggesting that the population is having much difficulty in achieving developmental goals. In Factor V we discover that countries receiving foreign aid for purposes of development are likely to have high scores on Monoracial Unity and Centripetal factors; since these primary factors have negative signs, an appropriate label is *volatility*. *Directive rule* results from a merger of Despotism and Nonincorporative Articulation in Factor VI. Although Factor VII has a lone high-loading primary factor, Uneven Development, loadings in the + .30 to + .40 range indicate Centrifugal, Politically Competitive, Nonpatriarchical polities lacking Unenlightened Rebellion but having Developmental Slowdowns and Entrepreneurial Development. Fred Riggs's image of *dialectical development,* oscillating between liberal and conservative trends, seems to be present;[19] countries with low loadings for this factor would be likely to follow a more unilinear path of development. Reorganization-Mindedness alone has a high negative loading on Factor VIII; *political incrementalism* describes the opposite end of this continuum. *Neocolonialism* enjoys a high loading on Factor IX, and this is the only loading above + .40. *Nontraditional rule* in Factor X represents a union of Absentee Landlordism with several factors having much lower positive loadings, such as Equalitarianism and Domestic Disengagement, with a negative loading for Guided Democracy. *Modernizing clique rule* appears in Factor XI, where there is a very high loading for Developmental Junta, and moderate loadings for Modernizing Oligarchy as well as Modernizing Welfare Statism.

Factors VII through XI are associated mainly with one of the 43 primary factors; most of these factors are beyond Factor XXV, where one might expect residuals or random error rather than meaningful sources of variance. The last few factors, however, have several high-loading entries and include some primary factors between I and XVI, one of which enables us to trace foreign conflict. Factor XII in the second-order analysis has negative loadings both for Labor Unrest amid Affluence and for Governmental Philistinism; there are smaller positive loadings for Politicoeconomic Paralysis and for Development Slowdown; lack of a *redistribution crisis,* a notion conceived by Lucian Pye,[20] incorporates most of the common features of these factors. In Factor XIII Permeability and Sustained Industrialization have negative loadings, which could only be true for an *autarkic economy.* *Disunited scarcity,* similarly, seems to bind together the four main elements of Factor XIV—Rural Austerity, Unenlightened Rebellion, Unstructuredness, and a negative loading for Monoracial Unity. Foreign Conflict combines in Factor XV with Discontentment with Laxity and, to a much lesser extent, with Despotism, Domestic Conflict, Separatism, Elite Scapegoatism, Domestic Engagement, lack of Modernizing Welfare Statism, Bourgeois Revolution, and Incorporative Articulation; an omnibus *aggressiveness* factor is appropriate, and we see that correlates of foreign conflict are quite

TABLE 8-42
Second-Order R-Factor Analysis

First-Order Factors	h²	Varimax Factors[a]															
		I	II	III	IV	V	VI	VII	VIII	IX	X	XI	XII	XIII	XIV	XV	XVI
I. Sparse Social Communication	.75	41	−04	−33	−01	31	40	19	−07	29	04	04	−08	00	21	08	17
II. Despotism	.69	01	15	−14	−16	03	(71)	−05	04	−01	−00	03	11	05	05	30	−01
III. Nonconflictual Domestic Political Behavior	.73	(−59)	13	14	02	−04	17	00	−10	01	−07	−24	19	06	−31	−25	22
IV. Separatism	.68	05	−15	(−71)	−17	04	16	−12	06	04	01	−07	−02	−05	−12	22	−10
V. Monoracial Unity	.72	−14	04	09	09	(−63)	01	−06	03	10	05	−03	13	11	−46	13	−11
VI. Centripetal	.65	00	−35	15	−20	(−50)	−27	−30	−02	−18	−02	03	−04	−06	−02	−12	−01
VII. Takeoff Stage	.64	−10	(65)	20	11	−03	14	−13	14	13	−03	05	07	13	10	−10	−19
VIII. Politicoeconomic Paralysis	.63	(65)	06	01	05	15	−03	01	−07	05	06	05	32	−11	02	−11	20
IX. Equalitarian	.61	−27	23	−02	09	−34	08	−07	−06	18	42	12	−17	19	00	−03	−24
X. Permeability	.61	−06	−02	−04	−08	−05	23	−04	−10	10	−26	14	−09	(−58)	26	−13	11
XI. Nonextractive Polity	.56	37	20	−20	−34	18	24	−06	04	−08	02	−22	−17	−07	21	−02	03
XII. Absentee Landlordism	.63	−06	12	−05	10	01	00	03	−02	11	(−75)	−04	−01	09	02	00	−11
XIII. Rural Austerity	.65	23	25	13	−13	−09	11	04	05	−01	04	−06	−05	01	(67)	−16	−09
XIV. Political Competition	.62	45	07	−06	09	−02	−15	39	38	08	−16	06	−03	05	11	−02	19
XV. Nonconflictual Foreign Behavior	.61	−06	−08	06	−09	24	00	04	−23	−16	−01	−10	−04	10	−02	(−64)	−11
XVI. Unguided Development	.65	07	16	05	(74)	04	−08	−02	05	−00	−09	−00	−03	−13	06	17	04
XVII. Modernizing Oligarchy	.62	01	12	25	−03	−02	39	16	−07	26	12	46	00	−06	−00	−10	24
XVIII. Societal Tension	.59	−27	06	(−51)	−07	−03	−17	−20	14	−23	−14	06	−06	04	−22	−11	16
XIX. Discontentment with Laxity	.54	02	−01	−13	08	12	11	−01	−20	02	−02	01	−05	09	−09	(66)	−04
XX. Reactionary Development	.67	−08	(−74)	21	03	−00	00	−08	18	06	04	−03	−07	02	04	−11	−02

272

TABLE 8-42—Cont.
Second–Order R–Factor Analysis

First–Order Factors	h²	I	II	III	IV	V	VI	VII	VIII	IX	X	XI	XII	XIII	XIV	XV	XVI
												Varimax Factors[a]						
XXI. Elite Scapegoatism	.54	07	−03	−01	16	25	−16	−13	06	16	11	−19	−09	−19	22	28	40
XXII. Development Slowdown	.70	−09	−22	−19	−00	−45	−18	39	−05	19	19	−28	25	03	03	−10	10
XXIII. Domestic Disengagement	.54	41	01	−23	17	09	03	−13	−19	01	30	−08	−05	−11	−13	−29	−12
XXIV. Internationally Guided Development	.55	02	04	−07	01	(−71)	−02	−01	−03	−05	−03	−05	−16	−02	10	03	04
XXV. Patriarchical Rule	.58	−29	22	−07	−28	−24	14	−32	−23	−15	15	−11	−03	−19	03	−02	18
XXVI. Lack of Professional Expertise	.49	(52)	02	12	00	−14	12	07	−12	−01	−21	−15	−18	−03	09	12	17
XXVII. Unstructured	.54	−17	−11	−08	09	14	−10	08	09	04	−20	16	17	−18	(51)	18	−15
XXVIII. Modernizing Welfare Statism	.63	−48	04	−14	13	06	−09	07	−23	26	−17	34	−08	−07	08	−24	12
XXIX. Labor Unrest amid Affluence	.65	−15	−11	03	−02	−06	−12	02	−06	28	03	−09	(−68)	15	10	09	−00
XXX. Governmental Philistinism	.56	13	−01	06	−01	−04	04	03	02	−22	03	−01	(−64)	−20	−12	−07	09
XXXI. Solidarity	.61	10	35	08	(−51)	21	−14	17	−05	11	−04	−08	−16	−16	18	01	13
XXXII. Cathective Involvement	.54	09	−08	−04	−03	−04	05	09	02	−03	05	03	−04	07	−13	01	(70)
XXXIII. Bourgeois Revolution	.52	15	04	06	25	06	09	21	−16	−32	03	01	−00	−34	21	28	06
XXXIV. Phenotypic Symmetry	.62	−05	−17	(72)	−11	06	−05	−03	10	04	−01	08	−13	03	−11	−03	−07
XXXV. Developmental Junta	.61	−03	02	06	02	07	−03	06	02	−13	05	(75)	08	−04	01	10	−04
XXXVI. Evenness in Development	.65	−04	−04	−16	06	−05	−09	(−75)	01	15	03	−12	05	02	−01	04	−07
XXXVII. Reorganization-Mindedness	.75	04	07	−01	−06	−04	−07	00	(−85)	02	−04	02	−02	01	−02	02	−01

273

TABLE 8-42—Cont.
Second-Order R-Factor Analysis

First-Order Factors	h²	Varimax Factors[a]															
		I	II	III	IV	V	VI	VII	VIII	IX	X	XI	XII	XIII	XIV	XV	XVI
XXXVIII. Incorporative Articulation	.64	10	02	05	−39	−16	(−54)	−18	−15	−03	03	13	09	17	07	22	−01
XXXIX. Unenlightened Rebellion	.66	16	−15	07	26	−02	−00	−32	−13	−19	11	−10	17	34	47	−01	00
XL. Sustained Industrialization	.65	22	−03	−03	16	01	−04	−05	09	15	18	04	01	(−69)	−12	03	−13
XLI. Neocolonialism	.70	02	06	08	−02	03	04	−09	−01	(80)	−07	−08	01	−13	−03	13	−00
XLII. Guided Democracy	.60	18	−24	04	00	−13	38	−14	−15	−13	−39	−01	12	−17	−07	−09	−28
XLIII. Entrepreneurial Development	.60	−13	−21	−06	−03	22	−24	31	−05	−26	14	−17	05	−44	10	07	−08
Eigenvalues[b]		3.6	2.3	2.2	2.0	1.9	1.8	1.6	1.6	1.4	1.4	1.3	1.2	1.2	1.1	1.1	1.0
Percent total variance[b]		8.5	5.4	5.1	4.6	4.4	4.1	3.8	3.7	3.3	3.2	3.0	2.9	2.8	2.6	2.5	2.4
Percent common variance[b]		13.6	8.7	8.3	7.3	7.1	6.6	6.1	6.0	5.3	5.2	4.9	4.6	4.5	4.3	4.0	3.9

[a] Factor loadings are multiplied by 100; loadings > ± .50 are enclosed in parentheses.
[b] Based on principal axis factors.

TABLE 8-43
Third-Order R-Factor Analysis

Second-Order Factors	h²	Biquartimin Factors[a]					
		I	II	III	IV	V	VI
I. Political Asymmetry	.49	(62)	—15	—03	14	14	—24
II. Societal Expansiveness	.56	07	—15	(74)	—05	—02	01
III. Social Symmetry	.62	04	—13	—15	—02	01	(78)
IV. Laissez-faire Development	.52	—06	(57)	—16	—01	48	05
V. Volatility	.49	(52)	05	19	36	—05	—04
VI. Directive Rule	.49	10	17	(63)	04	—08	—20
VII. Dialectical Development	.55	13	—03	01	(69)	04	25
VIII. Political Incrementalism	.44	13	—03	—16	05	(62)	11
IX. Neocolonialism	.52	—16	—12	45	04	(50)	08
X. Nontraditional Rule	.22	—20	—26	—13	09	05	—23
XI. Modernizing Clique Rule	.49	—14	38	19	23	05	48
XII. Lack of a Redistribution Crisis	.45	—16	(66)	01	—10	—05	—12
XIII. Autarkic Economy	.41	—22	—26	21	—44	11	07
XIV. Disunited Scarcity	.65	(81)	—18	06	—11	06	18
XV. Aggressiveness	.49	13	13	12	—07	(58)	—39
XVI. Subjectivism	.61	—16	—31	03	(69)	03	—16
Eigenvalues[b]		1.9	1.3	1.3	1.3	1.2	1.1
Percent total variance[b]		11.6	8.4	7.9	7.9	7.5	6.7
Percent common variance[b]		23.0	16.7	15.6	15.5	14.8	13.3

Correlations between							
factor loadings	I	1.00					
	II	.22	1.00				
	III	—.07	.05	1.00			
	IV	.21	.01	—.09	1.00		
	V	—.18	—.13	—.31	—.12	1.00	
	VI	—.17	.01	.03	—.15	—.06	1.00

[a] Factor loadings are multiplied by 100; loadings > ± .50 are enclosed in parentheses. Solution took 20 cycles, 1125 iterations.
[b] Based on principal axis factors.

complex. Factor XVI has a high loading for Cathective Involvement and a moderate loading for Elite Scapegoatism; this would appear to involve a *subjectivist* dimension.

In evaluating the 16 second-order factors, we find that the postulated dimensions from Chapter 6 fail to appear. Instead, political variables tend to merge together independently of economic and social variables; the polity, economy, and society appear as empirically independent sectors within a country. Occasionally some spillover does take place, notably on the Aggressiveness factor. A third-order analysis is performed (Table 8-43) for an even more parsimonious overview. The resulting six factors were also factor-analyzed to yield two fourth-order dimensions (Table 8-44 and Fig-

TABLE 8–44
Fourth–Order R–Factor Analysis

		Varimax Factors[a]	
Third–Order Factors	h²	I	II
I. Disintegrative	.59	—26	(72)
II. Administrative Inactivity	.26	—42	29
III. Elite Development	.58	(—69)	—31
IV. Ideologism	.39	—03	(63)
V. Change Orientation	.66	(80)	—10
VI. Harmonizing	.35	—18	(—56)
Eigenvalues[b]		1.5	1.3
Percent total variance[b]		24.9	22.4
Percent common variance[b]		53.6	46.4
Correlations between	I	1.00	
factor loadings	II	.00	1.00

[a] Factor loadings are multiplied by 100; loadings > ± .50 are enclosed in parentheses.
[b] Based on principal axis factors.

ure 8–4). Labelling of third-order factors reveals less about overall structure than the fourth-order division into a familiar distinction by Robert Bales between two modes of orientation by persons in small groups.[21] The first fourth-order factor is concerned with *task orientation,* and it has a high loading for Change Orientation, which in turn is composed of Aggressiveness, Neocolonialism, and Political Incrementalism. From the negative loadings, we may infer that a Task Orientation is unlikely to be found where Administrative Inactivity is high or Elite Development is present. Factor II portrays the *social-emotional orientation,* with a high loading for Disintegrative tendencies (Political Asymmetry, Volatility, and Disunited Scarcity), Ideologism, and Nonharmonizing Rule. International conflict turns out to involve more task orientation by dint of its merger with Political Incrementalism, Laissez-faire, and Neocolonialism on the Change-Oriented third-order factor.

A cluster analysis of the 183 symmetry variables reveals a much clearer structure (Figures 8–5 to 8–7).[22] The identity of the first 15 or so

[21] Robert F. Bales, *Interaction Process Analysis* (Reading, Mass.: Addison–Wesley, 1950). The distinction is almost the same as the apollonian-dionysian.

[22] It has been necessary once again to devise abbreviations for each variable. If the first symbol is "*A,*" we refer to "asymmetry between," and this symbol usually precedes a ratio which is standardized to set 50–50 distributions at 0.0 so absolute departures from 50–50 index asymmetry; △ means "change in."

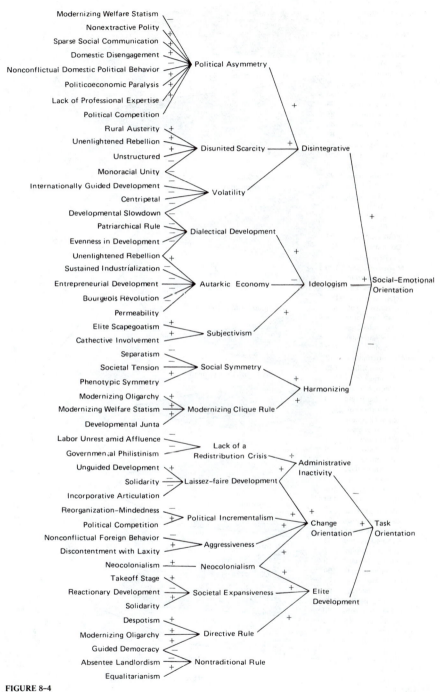

FIGURE 8-4
Summary of R-Factors

277

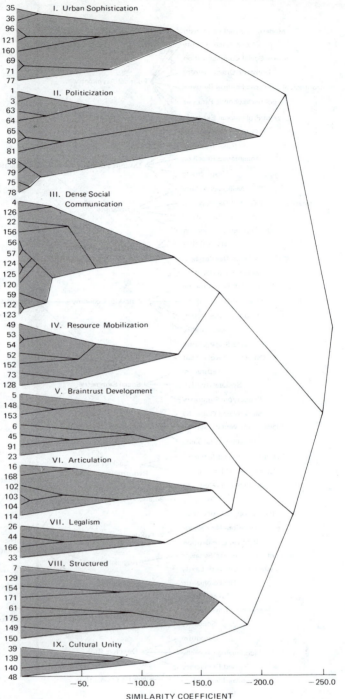

FIGURE 8-5
R–Cluster Analysis of Asymmetry Variables: I

278

factors is preserved within the cluster analysis, and indeed most variables collapse into groupings that correspond to the main dimensions of the factor analysis. Three major clusters emerge. Variables characteristic of prosperous and democratic westernized nations occupy all of Figure 8–5 and the first set of variables in Figure 8–6. The balance of Figure 8–6 contains indicators that one would expect to find within underdeveloped, newer states of Asia and Africa. Variables most related to foreign conflict are described by the cluster in Figure 8–7. A total of 28 subclusters form, merging with one another only beyond the level of a − 150.00 co-efficient of similarity.

Examining subclusters, we encounter *urban sophistication* at the top of Figure 8–5. Asymmetry between urban and rural sectors usually means a high degree of urbanization; library book circulation, lack of personalismo, and high divorce rates suggest sophistication, urbanity, and selectivity. Moreover, the cluster is composed of variables that load negatively on Rural Austerity, which was Factor XIII in the factor analysis. Large government expenditures in relation to gross national product and large chunks of annual budgets devoted to education and welfare are associated with large increases in national income and gross national product; when high voter turnout and unionization are added, Subcluster II is best labelled *politicization*. Most variables have negative loadings on Nonextractive Polity (Factor XI).

Dense social communication, the reverse of Factor I, shows up quite clearly in Subcluster III. It is noteworthy that authoritarian polities have the least emphasis on education and lowest levels of literacy and communication media usage.

Road-mile density, rail-mile density, exhaustion of waterpower potential, and a high percentage of Communist Party members actually voting for Communist candidates all come together in Subcluster IV, hence indicating a high degree of *resource mobilization*. One cost of reducing entropy across various societal sectors appears to be a high rate of deaths due to suicides, however.

The fifth subcluster contains a disparate collection. A colonial power with a high legal voting age suggests elements of paternalism; rapidly increasing railroad tonnage and more telephones per capita would go hand in hand with an upsurge in industrial expansion. *Braintrust development* may express the essence of these four variables, but just how accident proneness and high marriage rates fit into this picture is not obvious.

Interest group *articulation,* particularly from the working class, is a prevailing aspect of Subcluster VI. There is no clue as to whether demands are being met, as in Factor XXXVIII, which we label Incorporative Articulation. Instead, we find that strikes are common in countries with influxes of new immigrants (or departures of emigrants in large numbers), and we see

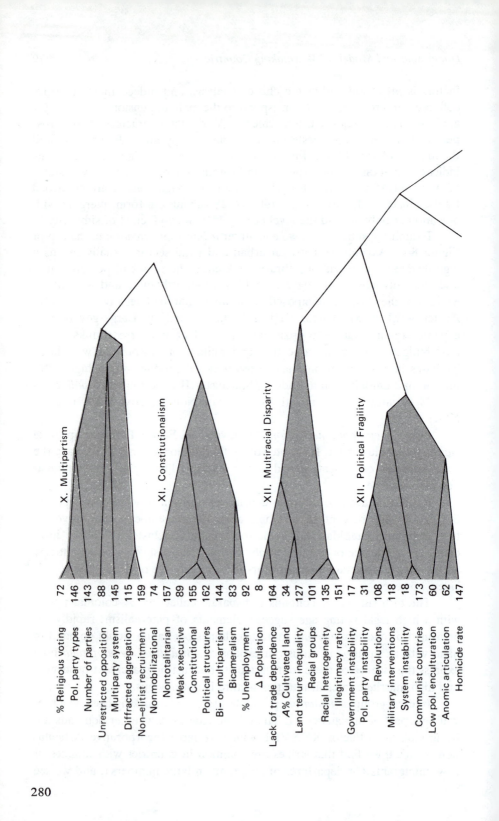

X. Multipartism

% Religious voting — 72
Pol. party types — 146
Number of parties — 143
Unrestricted opposition — 88
Multiparty system — 145
Diffracted aggregation — 115
Non–elitist recruitment — 159

XI. Constitutionalism

Nonmobilizational — 74
Nontotalitarian — 157
Weak executive — 89
Constitutional — 155
Political structures — 162
Bi- or multipartism — 144
Bicameralism — 83
% Unemployment — 92
Δ Population — 8

XII. Multiracial Disparity

Lack of trade dependence — 164
A% Cultivated land — 34
Land tenure inequality — 127
Racial groups — 101
Racial heterogeneity — 135
Illegitimacy ratio — 151

XII. Political Fragility

Government instability — 17
Pol. party instability — 31
Revolutions — 108
Military interventions — 118
System instability — 18
Communist countries — 173
Low pol. enculturation — 60
Anomic articulation — 62
Homicide rate — 147

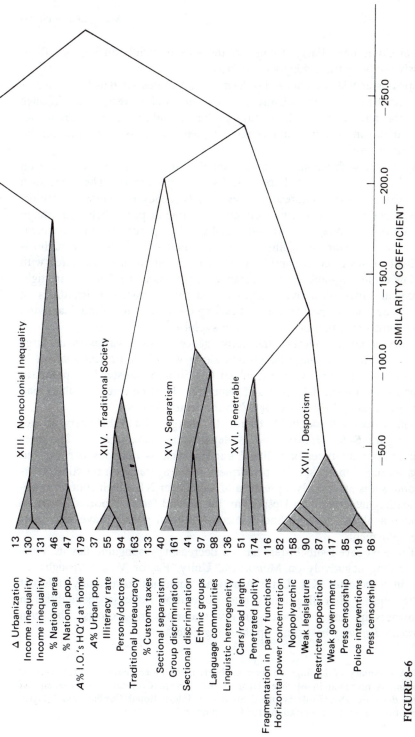

FIGURE 8–6
R–Cluster Analysis of Asymmetry Variables: II

also that Communist Party strength changes dramatically during periods of successive—though not general—strikes.

Subcluster VII is composed of *legalistic* attributes, such as legal governmental succession, decentralization of governmental powers, and a change in the total number of parliamentary parties. In addition, countries whose citizens invest in foreign ventures seem to require the stability afforded by a legal framework.

Variables with negative loadings on Factor XXVII reappear here on Subcluster VIII, so the label *structured* seems appropriate. There are such direct evidences of structured cultures as a tendency to belong to a bloc, increased per capita electricity production, a large disparity between foreign mail sent and received, and wide ownership of property. But indirect measures are all the more revealing, for we find that ulcers and liver cirrhosis are salient causes of death; and both of these conditions are associated with a feeling of inadequacy and internalized aggression resulting from tight hierarchical supervision over employees in bureaucracies.[23] Rigidities in family structure, or perhaps anxieties expressed through sexual activity, may account for a high death rate from syphilis.

Cultural unity underlies the convergence of such variables as large dominant ethnic and linguistic groups along with lack of sectionalism in Subcluster IX. A fourth variable, which falls into the cluster last, points to an exhaustion in potential sources of electricity. The first three variables load negatively on Separatism, Factor IV in the factor analysis.

Subclusters I through IX eventually merge with Subclusters X and XI in Figure 8–6. *Multipartism* is depicted in Subcluster X, for there are many different types of political parties, such as religious parties; and parties are functionally specific performers of the aggregation function. *Constitutionalism* is an underlying feature of Subcluster XI, which contains variables loading negatively on Despotism, the second factor reported above in the factor analysis. We also find that constitutional polities have high rates of unemployment.

The next seven subclusters have a decreasingly sanguine flavor. Variables loading negatively on Monoracial Unity, Factor V, are brought together in Subcluster XII. Latin American countries have many different racial groups, a high illegitimacy rate, population increase, inequalities in land ownership, and imbalances in raw materials and exports. The term *multiracial disparity* best sums up these ingredients.

---

[23] A summary of findings on liver cirrhosis in its more common form, chronic alcoholism, is provided in Michael Haas, *Some Societal Correlates of International Political Behavior* (Stanford: Stanford Studies in International Conflict and Integration, multilithed Ph.D. dissertation, 1964), Chapter 2.

Political fragility in Subcluster XIII involves such variables as system, government, and party instability, as well as revolutionary and military interventions into the political process. Where polities are likely to succumb to extraconstitutional inputs, political enculturation is at a low level, and there is a high homicide rate. The connection with communist countries during the 1955 to 1960 period is more incidental; during these years uprisings in Hungary, Poland, and Cuba gained considerable worldwide attention.

Subcluster XIV is a merger of two sets of variables, one referring to inequality, the other to noncolonial powers. This *noncolonial inequality* is also associated with rapid urbanization and a lack of international organizations headquartered in the home country.

High illiteracy, a predominantly rural population, a traditional bureaucracy, a high proportion of indirect taxes, and few physicians per capita are almost classic conditions of *traditional society*. Moving from Subcluster XV to XVI, *separatism* appears once again as a sum of sectionalism and ethnic-linguistic heterogeneity.

The final two subclusters in Figure 8–6 actually merge before the − 150.00 level, but they develop so separately up to that point that it seems useful to distinguish between them in an analysis of elementary yet coherent subclusters. High automobile density for available roads, political parties performing more functions than just aggregation, and penetrated polities comprise Subcluster XVII, and perhaps the label *penetrable* will preserve the identity of this peculiar configuration. Subcluster XVIII reincarnates the *despotism* factor from our factor analysis.

Turning to Figure 8–7, we discover that Factor XXVIII and Subcluster XIX both capsulize conditions of *bourgeois revolution*. Once again, signs of economic prosperity provide a backdrop for purges, violent domestic conflict, and seizure of power by illegitimate channels. And it is no clearer here whether revolutionaries are agitating for or against bourgeois rule.

Variables that load negatively on Factor III constitute Subcluster XX. Because the variables indicate extreme types of domestic conflict, *disruptive political activism* seems appropriate in tying together riots, general strikes, assassinations, guerrilla warfare, and government crises.

Only a venturesome conception could compress such variables as stereotypy, fears concerning politics, many rented farms, and a high proportion of trade-unionists on strike into a single term. It is for this reason that Subcluster XXI, if pushed to its logical conclusion, may be interpreted to outline attributes of an ongoing *class struggle* in which landlords and employers are unable to bridge a gap between themselves and tenants and employees, respectively. With perceptual images dichotomized, and the outcome of a class struggle uncertain (otherwise, violence would be more

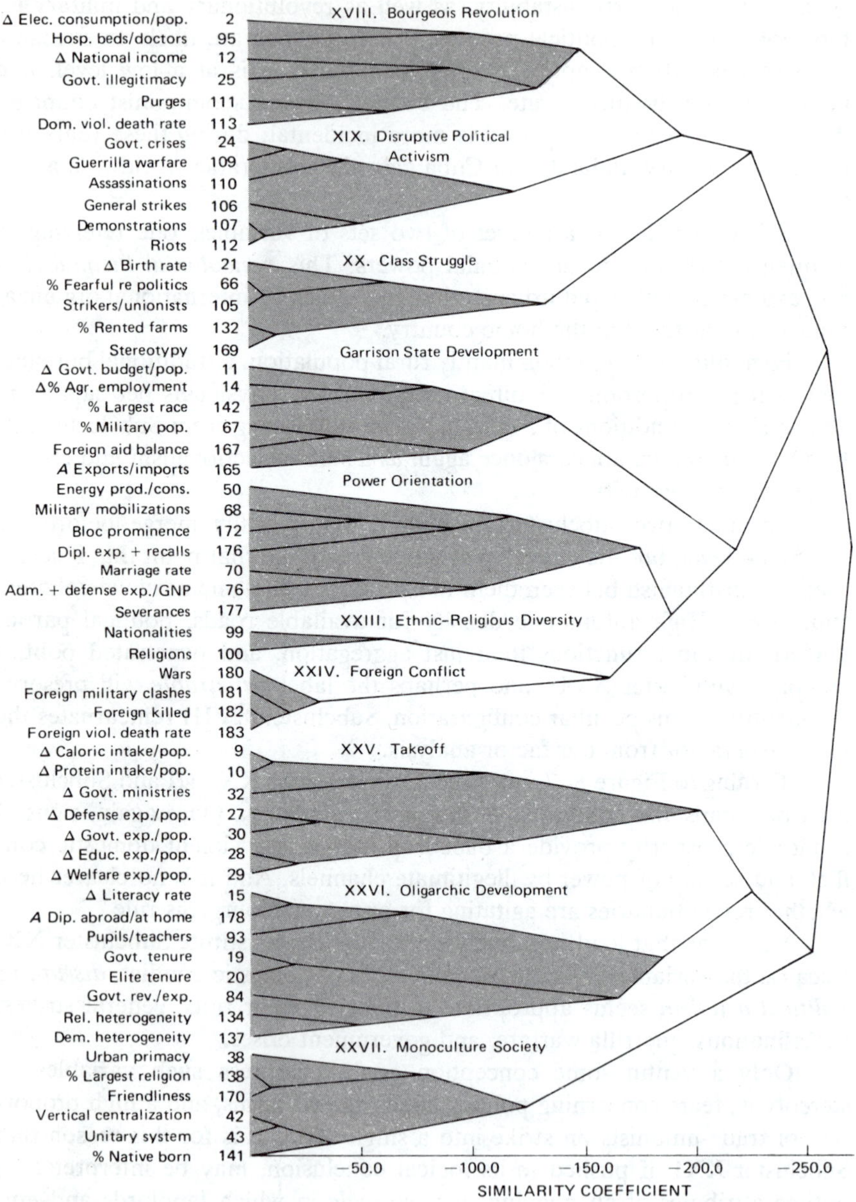

Δ Elec. consumption/pop.	2	XVIII. Bourgeois Revolution
Hosp. beds/doctors	95	
Δ National income	12	
Govt. illegitimacy	25	
Purges	111	
Dom. viol. death rate	113	
Govt. crises	24	XIX. Disruptive Political
Guerrilla warfare	109	Activism
Assassinations	110	
General strikes	106	
Demonstrations	107	
Riots	112	
Δ Birth rate	21	XX. Class Struggle
% Fearful re politics	66	
Strikers/unionists	105	
% Rented farms	132	
Stereotypy	169	Garrison State Development
Δ Govt. budget/pop.	11	
Δ% Agr. employment	14	
% Largest race	142	
% Military pop.	67	
Foreign aid balance	167	
A Exports/imports	165	
Energy prod./cons.	50	Power Orientation
Military mobilizations	68	
Bloc prominence	172	
Dipl. exp. + recalls	176	
Marriage rate	70	
Adm. + defense exp./GNP	76	
Severances	177	XXIII. Ethnic–Religious Diversity
Nationalities	99	
Religions	100	
Wars	180	XXIV. Foreign Conflict
Foreign military clashes	181	
Foreign killed	182	
Foreign viol. death rate	183	
Δ Caloric intake/pop.	9	XXV. Takeoff
Δ Protein intake/pop.	10	
Δ Govt. ministries	32	
Δ Defense exp./pop.	27	
Δ Govt. exp./pop.	30	
Δ Educ. exp./pop.	28	
Δ Welfare exp./pop.	29	
Δ Literacy rate	15	XXVI. Oligarchic Development
A Dip. abroad/at home	178	
Pupils/teachers	93	
Govt. tenure	19	
Elite tenure	20	
Govt. rev./exp.	84	
Rel. heterogeneity	134	
Dem. heterogeneity	137	
Urban primacy	38	XXVII. Monoculture Society
% Largest religion	138	
Friendliness	170	
Vertical centralization	42	
Unitary system	43	
% Native born	141	

−50.0   −100.0   −150.0   −200.0   −250.0

SIMILARITY COEFFICIENT

FIGURE 8-7
R–Cluster Analysis of Asymmetry Variables: III

284

manifest), it follows that political affairs would lead to less than benign outcomes. A rapid increase in births may be a clue toward one way of overcoming tensions of class struggle.

Garrison state development emerges in Subcluster XXII.[24] Not only
are some variables from Internationally Guided Development, Factor
XXIV, present within the subcluster, but a large military population is a
tipoff that countries receiving or giving foreign aid usually have military
objectives in mind. Government budgets increase when aid is absorbed, and
levels of underemployment decline.

Some variables loading positively on Elite Scapegoatism (Factor XXI)
appear in Subcluster XXIII, but in addition, bloc prominence, military mobilizations, and marriage rates are part of the picture. Needs to dominate, or
perhaps to choose friends and enemies with care, add up to *power orientation.*

Subcluster XXIV is the smallest in the number of variables, for it has
just two members and can only be called *ethnic-religious diversity.* Adjacent
is another easily identifiable subcluster, namely, *foreign conflict.*

The final three subclusters are similar to factor analysis results. Subcluster XXVI resembles *takeoff,* Factor VII, with all of the variables indicating change. Subcluster XXVII is a combination of Patriarchical Rule
(Factor XXV), Nonreactionary Development (Factor XX), and two indicators of heterogeneity: the label *oligarchic development* unites the traditionalist and the elitist aspects, and heterogeneity is a correlate. The final
subcluster is one of a *monoculture society* with a unitary system, one major
city, many native-born inhabitants belonging to the same religious group,
and a spirit of mutual friendliness.

The subclusters merge with one another in three waves (Figure 8–8).
Eleven clusters form from the merger of twosomes or threesomes of the
microclusters described above. The 11 clusters collapse eventually into two
main clusters, though some intermediate categories are delineated within
each of the two, corresponding to *liberal democratic sustained modernization* on the one hand and *directive but faltering modernization* on the other.
We now examine components of these two types of societal system.

Within the Liberal Democratic Sustained Modernization cluster, there
are 11 microclusters. Urban Sophistication and Politicization merge into a
secularization cluster. Dense Social Communication and Resource Mobilization give rise to a *technological development* cluster, thus reproducing the
main outlines of the first factor in analyses by Rummel and Russett. Brain-

---

[24] Cf. Harold D. Lasswell, "The Garrison State," *American Journal of Sociology,*
XLVI (January 1941), 445–68; Lasswell, *World Politics and Personal Insecurity* (New
York: McGraw-Hill, 1935).

trust Development, Articulation, and Legalism come together next; all three of these terms suggest a preference for *formalism,* that is, a use of institutional channels and frameworks for conducting affairs of state. A *unified society* is described by a convergence of the Structured and Cultural Unity subclusters; *polyarchy* is an inescapable label linking together Multipartism and Constitutionalism.[25] As Figures 8–5 and 8–8 reveal, these five molar attributes do not collapse together immediately after their formation. Technological Development, Formalism, and the Unified Society clusters meet first in what might be called a *bureaucratized productivity* cluster; but we find that neither Secularization nor Polyarchy are intimately connected with this large cluster. This pattern indicates the inevitable need for developing countries to solve problems of social identity while establishing a differentiated structural apparatus in order to regularize operations of government. Bureaucratized Productivity and Secularization come together at a similarity coefficient of − 273.44, but Polyarchy does not join the rest of the aggregation until − 304.49.

The path of mergers in the Liberal Democratic Sustained Modernization cluster permits some speculation on which priorities to assign to the various problems of political development within the newer states of Africa and Asia. Indeed, Lucian Pye has suggested that developmental change is achieved when states are able to solve six basic societal tasks,[26] all of which are depicted in Figure 8–8. An *identity crisis* is solved when societies are homogenized by means of an interpenetration of social life with political and universalistic structures; the Unified Society cluster pulls together these elements. A *legitimacy crisis* is overcome when legal and formal mechanisms are accepted as authoritative and utilized adaptively, and this is a theme of our Formalism cluster. But we can also observe that the solution of identity and legitimacy crises goes hand in hand with Technological Development. The next two crises are solved without any necessary connection between each other and are unrelated to the Bureaucratized Productivity cluster. Polyarchy represents a solution of a *participation crisis,* at which time political parties are viable and intrastructural groups have a great deal of access to decisionmaking by political elites. A *penetration crisis* is solved when conditions in the Secularization cluster are present: most inhabitants are urbanized and politicized in outlook. Variables pertaining to a *distribution crisis* are closely related to Secularization as well. Within this framework of findings from the cluster analysis, we may argue that an *integration crisis* is passed when all of the above crises have been solved; thus a country be-

---

[25] Robert A. Dahl, *A Preface to Democratic Theory* (Chicago: University of Chicago Press, 1956).

[26] Pye, *Aspects of Political Development.*

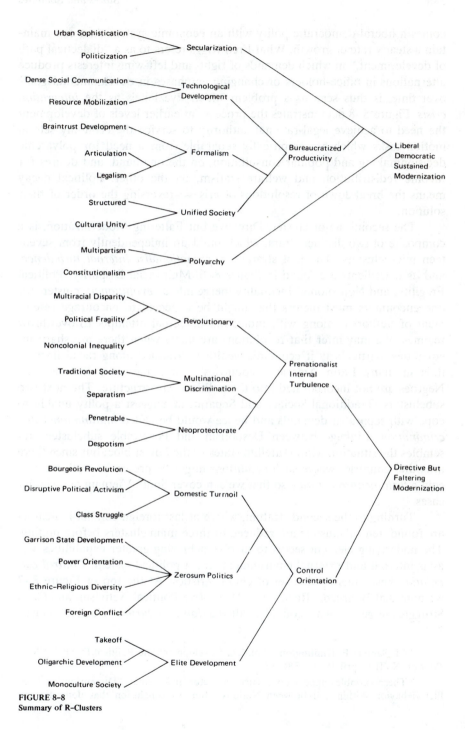

FIGURE 8-8
Summary of R-Clusters

287

comes a liberal-democratic polity with an economic system than can maintain a steady rate of growth. What Fred Riggs refers to as a "dialectical path of development," in which demands of right- and left-wing interests produce alternations in office-holders or changing emphases in developmental goals over time, is thus seen as a problem which Pye labels as the *integration crisis*. Figure 8–8 demonstrates the process: at earlier levels of development the need to achieve legal-rational authority to service the economy sets in motion tasks which are empirically separable from a need for polyarchic decisionmaking and popular consultation, on the one hand, and desires for income redistribution and welfare statism, on the other. Political decay means the breakdown of resolutions of crises—reversing the order of their solution.[27]

The second major cluster, Directive but Faltering Modernization, is a composite of two distinct strata, which build up independently from seventeen microclusters. The first stratum is *prenationalist internal turbulence,* and its ingredients are found in Figure 8–6. Multiracial Disparity, Political Fragility, and Noncolonial Inequality merge into a *revolutionary* cluster, for one encounters most factors that might be expected to encourage resentment of authority, along with indicators of actual attempts to overthrow regimes. We may infer that revolutions are likely when there are sharp inequalities, particularly if economic wealth is stratified along racial lines as it is in many Latin American countries, where mestizos, Indians, and Negroes are not incorporated into the political infrastructure. The next two subclusters, Traditional Society and Separatism, suggest a polity unable to cope with separatist demands and hence would be called *multinational discrimination*. Linkage between Despotism and Penetrable subclusters resembles the situation within satellite states of the Soviet bloc; but since there are other countries where such conditions might be present as well, we may coin a term *neoprotectorate* so that we can cover South Vietnam and similar cases.

Turning to the second stratum, where at last foreign conflict indicators are found, ten subclusters are reduced to three main clusters before uniting. The underlying element seems to involve achieving greater capabilities vis-à-vis internal and external environments for a political system. *Control orientation* best sums up this set of characteristics. At the top of Figure 8–7 we note that Bourgeois Revolution, Disruptive Political Activism, and Class Struggle merge into what could be called a *domestic turmoil* cluster.[28] Garri-

---

[27] Cf. Samuel P. Huntington, "Political Development and Political Decay," *World Politics,* XVII (April 1965), 386–93.

[28] These variables appear on a Turmoil factor in Rummel, "Dimensions of Conflict Behavior Within and Between Nations." But his conclusion that domestic and

son State Development, Power Orientation, Ethnic-Religious Diversity, and Foreign Conflict form the next cluster, which suggests a propensity to engage in all-or-nothing *zerosum politics*. The four foreign conflict variables are joined by number of national and religious groups first; and since large countries are more likely to stretch across many ethnic and linguistic groups, we may regard the proximity of these two subclusters as a clue that large countries (leaders of international power blocs) are more likely to become involved in foreign conflict than small, mono-ethnic countries with fewer borders. The etiology of international aggression may be traced from Power Orientation and Garrison State Development subclusters more clearly. First of all, diplomatic moves before wars often entail expulsions and recalls of diplomats and, ultimately, severances in diplomatic relations. War-prone countries are likely to contribute to arms races, for they have large proportions of their citizens in uniform, and their budgets are heavily committed to military expenditures; such countries send or receive large amounts of military foreign assistance, and a troop mobilization is an obvious military precondition to war. If we desire to prevent war in such countries, the entire social and economic fabric would have to be restructured. Our attention should be directed at variables that might be altered more easily and in the short run; a useful counsel would be to suggest measures likely to implement an immediate end to arms races.

One of the variables in the Garrison State Development factor has the highest loading on the Discontentment with Laxity factor (XIX) from our factor analysis—electricity production greatly in excess of consumption. And we see here as well that where electric transmission is inefficient, or there is a foreign trade imbalance, the Domestic Turmoil cluster is not far away. A high marriage rate might seem peculiar, but we could reflect that mismatches might be more common within multi-ethnic societies, where dissimilar social backgrounds will hamper resolutions of marital conflicts; a high marriage rate represents new marriages with different partners. Educational systems that integrate schools and give attention to principles of social psychology in the context of ethnic studies programs (which are now beginning in the United States) might tend to reduce stereotypic perceptions held toward peoples of other countries as well. And, as linkages are traced to the next main cluster, we may conclude that Domestic Turmoil is a frequent con-

---

foreign conflicts are independent, because they do not converge in a factor analysis that pools indicators of internal and external conflict, is premature. In one other investigation, which uses causes of death indicators, I have found that foreign and domestic conflict merge when one performs second-order analyses; see Michael Haas, "Toward the Study of Biopolitics: A Cross Sectional Analysis of Mortality Rates," *Behavioral Science*, XIV (July 1969), 257–80.

comitant of foreign conflict. The final set of subclusters, Takeoff, Oligarchic Development, and Monoculture Society, combine into an *elite development* cluster at the bottom of Figure 8–7. Prenationalist Internal Turbulence and Control Orientation, two conditions found most frequently in underdeveloped regions of the world, merge at − 319.52, which is about where the *liberal democratic sustained modernization* cluster is formed. The second stratum, which is described by another cumbersome compound phrase, is one of *directive but faltering modernization*. In short, countries unable to achieve cultural unity or political institutions with a high degree of legitimacy, while harboring desires for technological advancement, have so far been unsuccessful in maintaining democratic forms. Authoritarian or even totalitarian direction of the modernization process occurs when it is realized that ultrastable leadership alone can secure technological growth and suppress domestic unrest amid economic privation.[29] The two clusters finally meet at a − 363.83 coefficient of similarity. The classification provided by cluster analysis is twofold—between liberal democratic polities that have reached a level of sustained economic modernization and authoritarian systems where modernization processes are faltering. But a different set of classes emerges from the factor analysis—variables indexing task completion, on the one hand, and social-emotional problems, on the other.

8.4 CAUSAL MODELS OF SOCIETAL PROCESSES

A selection of variables for a causal model of the paths from societal factors toward war propensity is a more complex task than was the case with decisionmaking variables. First of all, few correlations with war frequency and casualty measures are very high in the summary reported in Chapter 7; no single variable unlocks a guide to plausible models. Second, although a foreign conflict dimension does emerge quite distinctly in both the factor analysis and the cluster analysis, variables adjacent to foreign conflict in the cluster diagram are not identical to the variables that load at the top of higher-order factors merging with the foreign conflict factor. Factors that merge with the Aggressiveness factor in Table 8–43 account for very little of the total variance extracted from the 180-odd societal variables.

Such considerations necessitate more complex causal models at the

---

[29] The term *ultrastable* refers to systems which "search" for new levels of homeostasis when old ones break down. Cf. W. Ross Ashby, *Design for a Brain* (New York: Wiley, 1952).

societal level than those postulated at the interpersonal level of analysis. More variables will have to be manipulated, and criteria of inclusion will have to be specified in greater detail than in Section 5.4.

The dependent variable, *international violence,* is one among four indicators of war propensity; the highest loading variable in Factor XV is deaths due to foreign conflict (Table 8–13). Other variables are chosen on at least two of three grounds. Some variables have high loadings on Factor XV but are not types of foreign conflict per se; if we use these variables, we end up with *bloc prominence* and an index of the size of a country's *military-industrial complex*—the variable military and public administration expenditures as a percentage of total gross national product. Second, variables adjacent to the Foreign Conflict cluster in Figure 8–7 are combed for possible inclusion; this criterion justifies all variables picked so far and nets three additional components for causal models. Subcluster XXII, Garrison State Development, is best summed up by measuring changes in governmental budgets as percentages of total gross national product; we thereby obtain a dimension of *government expansion* for our roster of critical variables. Ethnic-Religious Diversity, Subcluster XXIV, is composed of two variables; we choose *ethnic diversity* because it loads higher on the Phenotypic Asymmetry factor than the variable religious diversity. Subcluster XXIII contains several possible candidates for inclusion in a causal model, so we must invoke a third criterion: a variable loading highest on a factor that merges with Foreign Conflict in a higher-order factor analysis is deemed acceptable. Accordingly, we will select *electricity inefficiency,* which tops Factor XIX (the Discontentment with Laxity factor) and merges with Foreign Conflict in the second-order factor analysis (Table 8–17). The second-order factor containing both Discontentment with Laxity and Foreign Conflict factors is named Aggressiveness, and in the third-order factor analysis. Aggressiveness merges with two other factors—Political Incrementalism and Neocolonialism (Table 8–43). Taking the highest loading factor of the two, Political Incrementalism, and decomposing it to its principal factor, Reorganization-Mindedness (Table 8–42), we can isolate the variable loading highest on the Reorganization-Mindedness factor—lack of change in the number of government ministries between the years 1955 and 1960 (Table 8–35); this latter variable is used to index *administrative stagnation.* In all, our search nets seven variables for a causal model of societal factors that dispose countries to become involved in war (Figure 8–9). Each attribute is represented with the exception of the attitudinal, for which data is the most difficult to locate. Four of the six postulated societal dimensions are included in the seven variables to be fit into the causal model; only spatial and allocational dimensions are left out.

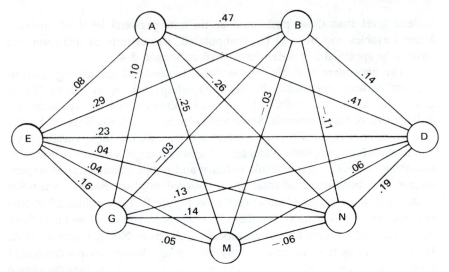

FIGURE 8-9
Variables Selected for Models of War Propensity

Key:

   Numbers represent correlations.

   A = military–administrative budget/GNP (var. 76).

   B = bloc prominence (var. 172).

   D = deaths due to foreign conflict (var. 182).

   E = energy production ≠ consumption (var. 50).

   G = Δ government budget per capita (var. 11).

   M = unchanged number of government ministries (var. 32).

   N = number of nationalities (var. 99).

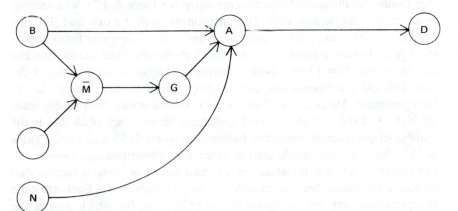

FIGURE 8-10
I Polis Model of War Propensity

   The symbol M̄ indicates that the sign of the variable is reversed.

TABLE 8-45
Predictions and Degrees of Fit for Societal Models

Model	Prediction	Observation
I	1. $r_{bn} = 0$	—.11
	2. $r_{en} = 0$	.04
	3. $r_{mn} = 0$	.06
	4. $r_{be} = 0$	.29
	5. $r_{gn} = 0$	.14
	6. $r_{dn} \cdot a = 0$	.34
	7. $r_{dg} \cdot ab = 0$	.10
	8. $r_{eg} \cdot \overline{m} = 0$	.16
	9. $r_{ae} \cdot g = 0$	.80
	10. $r_{am} \cdot bg = 0$	.30
	11. $r_{bg} \cdot \overline{m} = 0$	.03
	12. $r_{bd} \cdot a = 0$	—.06
	13. $r_{de} \cdot a = 0$	—.18
	14. $r_{d\overline{m}} \cdot a = 0$	.05
II	1. $r_{bm} = 0$	—.03
	2. $r_{mn} = 0$	—.06
	3. $r_{en} \cdot b = 0$	.08
	4. $r_{gn} \cdot b = 0$	.14
	5. $r_{gm} \cdot e = 0$	.04
	6. $r_{am} \cdot eg = 0$	.37
	7. $r_{dm} \cdot a = 0$	—.05
	8. $r_{bg} \cdot e = 0$	—.02
	9. $r_{ab} \cdot egn = 0$	.41
	10. $r_{bd} \cdot a = 0$	—.07
	11. $r_{de} \cdot a = 0$	—.18
	12. $r_{dn} \cdot a = 0$	.34
	13. $r_{dg} \cdot a = 0$	.10
III	1. $r_{bd} \cdot ae = 0$	—.10
	2. $r_{dm} \cdot a = 0$	—.05
	3. $r_{dg} \cdot an = 0$	.04
	4. $r_{bm} = 0$	—.03
	5. $r_{bg} = 0$	.03
	6. $r_{bn} = 0$	—.11
	7. $r_{em} = 0$	.04
	8. $r_{gm} = 0$	.05
	9. $r_{mn} = 0$	—.06
	10. $r_{eg} = 0$	.16
	11. $r_{en} = 0$	.04
IV	1. $r_{bd} \cdot aen = 0$	—.10
	2. $r_{dm} \cdot a = 0$	—.05
	3. $r_{dg} \cdot aen = 0$	.13
	4. $r_{bm} = 0$	—.03
	5. $r_{bg} = 0$	.03
	6. $r_{gm} = 0$	.05
	7. $r_{en} \cdot bg = 0$	.05

293

Our first model, the *polis,* tests Plato's theory of war (Figure 8–10). We encounter three paths leading to a high incidence in war deaths. Plato suggests that middle powers are least likely to engage in war, so one path starts with bloc prominence and is mediated only by the level of expenditures on armed forces and public administration. A poor country with an inefficient conversion of electricity from production to consumption ends up in war, according to the theory, if it is also administratively active and undergoes a rapid increase in government expenditures. Bloc leaders, similarly, might become administratively overactive, yet when government budgets soar, the outcome is a higher military-administrative budget and thence war. Plato's preference for cohesive states, finally, is represented by a third major path: countries with a large number of national groups are prone to enter war if, and only if, they devote a large proportion of their gross national product to military-administrative purposes. Despite some plausibility for this argument, however, many predictions generated by the polis model are far from actual observations with the data we obtained from 85 countries in the late 1950s (Table 8–45). Of 14 predictions, only 7 are less than $\pm$ .10 within the range of our predicted .00 correlation.[30]

A second alternative is a *bourgeois capitalist* model, which grafts on elements of both Marx and Lenin (Figure 8–11). Economic inefficiency, as indexed by the electricity input-output disequilibrium variable, is seen as coming from two main sources: capitalist states do not take wishes of workers into serious consideration, so the number of government ministries remains frozen, and government structures are not encouraged to accommodate demands of the working class; second, bloc leadership exacerbates internal contradictions within capitalism most severely. Economic inefficiency, in turn, means that capitalists will try to use government to bail them out of financial disaster; more money will be spent for administrative and military services necessary for conquering peoples of foreign lands. Yet another consequence of being topdog in the international system is that a country will eventually grow larger and more diverse in ethnic composition, posing problems for internal maintenance; and a larger army will be needed to quell possible internal revolt. But a country with a large army will be tempted to employ it in foreign arenas in order to build national patriotism and to divert attention from pressing domestic problems. This second model has a somewhat better fit than the polis model but is off the mark in 5 of the 13 predictions (Table 8–45).

An alternative to an emphasis on overdevelopment as a prime source

---

[30] The direct link $N \rightarrow D$ would yield a prediction of $r_{an} = 0$, whereas the actual bivariate correlation between these two variables is $-$ .26.

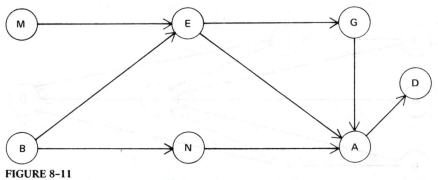

FIGURE 8-11
II Bourgeois Capitalist Model of War Propensity

of tension in societies is to divide our sample of countries into three groups: least developed and traditionalist states, developing countries which are using state-capitalist methods of achieving new economic levels, and highly developed countries. These three categories resemble some of the typologies derived from our Q-analyses of the 85-country data in Section 8.2. In one analysis based on a comparative analysis of longitudinal trends in ten countries between 1900 and 1960, three distinct causal paths are suggested.[31] In all countries an arms buildup is seen as preparatory to warfare. Advanced countries can slip into war as well if they happen to be inefficient for a time, whence they might go to war immediately or after some military preparations. The least developed countries, if stagnant administratively, go to war so long as they devote a high proportion of their national wealth to military expenditures. Developing countries, thirdly, avoid war if they are homogeneous in ethnic composition; if not, internal maintenance problems bring about a war-prone garrison state. The 11 predictions that follow from this moderately overidentified *development* model are very close to actual observations, with eight of the predictions at the $\pm$ .06 level or lower and the three higher predictions topped only by a .16 correlation (Figure 8–12 and Table 8–45).[32]

Because of the relative success of the third model, a more *eclectic*

---

[31] See Michael Haas, "Social Change and National Aggressiveness, 1900–1960," *Quantitative International Politics*, ed. J. David Singer (New York: The Free Press, 1968), esp. pp. 238–42.

[32] When the model was originally constructed, the $B \rightarrow A$ and $G \rightarrow A$ links were not drawn so as to avoid an overidentified model. The predictions $r_{ab \cdot e} = 0$ and $r_{ag \cdot n} = 0$ were so far from actual observations, however, that it was necessary to add these two arrows to improve the fit.

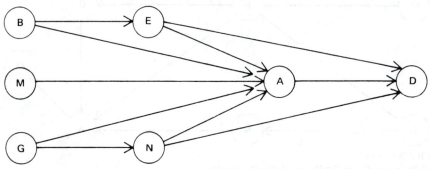

FIGURE 8-12
III Developmental Model of War Propensity

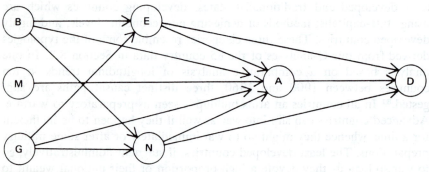

FIGURE 8-13
IV Eclectic Model of War Propensity

model seems possible (Figure 8–13). The aim in this final model is simply to patch up the incorrect predictions of the third model by adding more causal linkages, thus controlling for more variables. Every exogenous variable is filtered through the level of military-administrative expenditures, although ethnic heterogeneity and economic inefficiency may also set off a war for the developing and developed countries. The increase in causal arrows entails an overidentified structure of equations, though the number of predictions is simplified; and in only two of the seven cases do we encounter results higher than the ± .05 level (Table 8–45). The average difference between predictions and observations, derived by summing absolute partial correlations for each prediction and dividing by the total number of prediction equations, is nearly identical for Models III and IV; so parsimony will be invoked to decide in favor of the *developmental* model.

Once again, readers should be cautious in accepting a model which does not completely fit all predictions. And, just as we focused on only one level of analysis in our examination of interpersonal models of violent decisionmaking, we should be aware of our artificial elimination of relevant variables that may be operating on other levels of analysis. We might conclude, in other words, that a cultural perception model should be juxtaposed with a developmental model in order to achieve a high degree of predictive power. We now turn to factors at the systemic level, which seem particularly appropriate now that we have found that a country's level of development may be crucial in assessing its propensity to enter war. Levels of development, after all, are relative to attainments of other countries in the international arena.

PART IV
International
Systems

chapter 9
Theories
of Systemic Factors

9.1 INTRODUCTION

It is quite conceivable that well-adjusted leaders at the helm of internally tranquil states may find themselves at war, not due to any fault of their own decisionmaking or because of characteristics of the states which they govern, but by dint of the presence of other less fortunate states elsewhere in the international arena. A third level of explanation for international aggression would seem to be required to account for targets of aggression, the impact of international stratification of power, and for the fact that war frequencies differ so much in various historical eras. By analyzing international systems as a whole one may be able to explain why crises and domestic conflicts arise with varying intensities and frequencies over time and among different clusters of states.

According to international system theory, the probability that a set of interacting countries will become an arena for war is a function of the kind of environment in which they operate. An environment with very scarce resources, for example, might be more likely to be associated with sharp disagreements between states; haphazardly fixed boundaries may be subject to dispute more often than borders drawn in accordance with rationally agreed-upon principles; international systems lacking neutral peace-keeping arrangements are often hypothesized to be more explosive than those with institutionalized regulators of international conduct.

International system theorists analyze the arrangement of parts, distribution of resources, presence of cultural norms, and other aggregate aspects of international society. Though it might be possible to plot such variables over time, system theorizing so far has been built upon insights from selected

301

historical cases, usually drawn from European history, rather than being subjected to systematic comparative empirical testing. An overattention to the European international scene, though culturally myopic, has established the precedent for analyzing international *subsystems:* the notion of a "world political system" appears to be a reification in view of tendencies for regional clusters of countries to stratify their political activity to the exclusion of clusters located elsewhere on the globe.[1]

In writings on historical international systems, references to successful and peaceful international cooperation often seem dwarfed by more dramatic accounts of state intransigence, warfare, and transformations of international systems. Earlier interstate systems often had only one power center and regarded a rival empire as an intolerable threat. At the close of the second millenium B.C. the previously isolated civilizations of Egypt, Assyria, Chaldea, and Persia were brought into contact with each other due to improvements in military and civilian administration.[2] When empires found that they could maintain control over larger territorial expanses, borders began to touch. Since each empire maintained distinctive religious beliefs and modes of social organization, penetration by another international entity was interpreted as a challenge. When war broke out, victors extended imperial rule over the vanquished and demanded absolute allegiance.

As multistate systems arose in China, Greece, and, much later, in Western Europe, a secular orientation to world politics seemed reasonable. But both sacred and profane orientations have made rich contributions to international system theory. A brief propositional résumé will prepare us for more systematic inquiry.

9.2 THEORIES OF SYSTEMIC FACTORS IN WAR AND PEACE

Historically the most frequent, longest lasting, and, undoubtedly, the most peaceful international systems have been those dominated by a single elite state. The war-torn multiple states in China of the seventh century B.C. and

---

[1] An empirical investigation of homogeneous subsets of states is reported in Bruce M. Russett, *International Regions and the International System* (Chicago: Rand McNally, 1967). Russett's identification of countries with similar profiles over a large number of variables does not correspond to analytical procedures for delineating "subsystems" to be used in this chapter, especially as set forth in Section 9.4. For an alternative view, see Stanley Hoffmann, *The State of War* (New York: Praeger, 1965).

[2] Adda Bozeman, *Politics and Culture in International History* (Princeton: Princeton University Press, 1960); William H. McNeil, *A World History* (New York: Oxford University Press, 1967); cf. Raoul Naroll, "Imperial Cycles and World Order," *Peace Research Society, Papers,* VII (1967), 83–102.

the Hellenic state system two centuries later were engulfed by the imperial Ch'in and Macedonian armies, respectively. Most earlier writers, accordingly, comment approvingly on unistate international systems as having been stable. The multistate European subsystem, which was merely inchoate in the Middle Ages, did not crystallize until after the Thirty Years War and Wars of Religion of the early 1600s, an era that constitutes a watershed dividing quite different theories on the systemic nature of interstate relations.

9.2.1 Early Theorists

In the classical Greek conception of a polytheistic universe, gods were thought of as active troublemakers in the affairs of man. An implication of the Greek cyclical view of history was that any distribution of power in the world, whether unipolar, bipolar, or multipolar, is bound to flower, wither, and regrow in an inexorable if unpredictable manner. Socrates and Plato generally preferred the polis, as did Aristotle, despite his role as tutor to Alexander the Great. But the Greek city-state system was internationally turbulent, as descriptive accounts of Thucydides remind us.[3]

Monotheism was concomitant with a view of history as a struggle between "forces of light" and "forces of darkness."[4] Disturbers of a secure, legitimate, imperial realm were branded as interlopers from a nether world, fit only for extermination or slavery. As wars between Eastern totalist civilizations exhausted a previous world power, each new empire proceeded to assert similar absolutist claims anew.

In Augustine's City of God model, however, warfare is inconceivable; a shared belief in spiritual values would be capable of transcending mundane conditions that lead the City of Man to wars and to other injustices and calamities.[5] Since Augustinian man is inherently sinful, no social order can perfect his nature; but an authoritarian or elitist political regime that effectively constrains vile and malevolent human tendencies can make existence in the City of Man somewhat more tolerable than anarchy. An international order managed by one powerful state (to follow Augustinian logic to a conclusion not reached explicitly) would be preferable to continual warfare, which is argued to be inevitable whenever international power is decentralized and the greed of man rampant. In the era after the fall of man, Augus-

---

[3] Thucydides, *The Complete Writings of Thucydides,* trans. Richard Crawley (New York: Modern Library, 1934); Peter J. Fliess, *Thucydides and the Politics of Bipolarity* (Baton Rouge: Louisiana State University Press, 1966); Karl W. Deutsch, "Changing Images of International Conflict," *Journal of Social Issues,* XXIII (January 1967), 91–92.

[4] *Ibid.,* pp. 96–100.

[5] Augustine, *Basic Writings* (New York: Random House, 1948); Deutsch, "Changing Images of International Conflict," pp. 93–94.

tine argued, firm authority and policed restrictions of man's freedom are the best guarantees for the continuity of human existence.

The unity achieved by Rome under the Antonines collapsed in the fifth century A.D., when Italy, Gaul, Britain, the Iberian peninsula, and North Africa were occupied by Germanic peoples who migrated westward and southward. Uninfluenced by Greco-Roman culture, the tribes sacked and looted as they traveled, breaking down secular communication networks that had enabled the Roman Empire to operate. In time, the spread of Christianity among the new masters of the former imperial realm produced a certain degree of cultural uniformity, and the prestige of the Holy See enabled popes to gain widespread recognition of their spiritual authority. Throughout the Middle Ages, the papacy worked to increase the politic al and social influence of the church, while Charlemagne and early secr ar rulers of the Holy Roman Empire—the formal successor to the sec lar Roman state—attempted to establish unified domains of their own. During the medieval period the only truly international organization was the Church, which was considered to be a hierarchical entity that extended from Rome to abbeys, bishoprics, and other divisions. Prominent leaders of the Church, indeed, began to envision feasibility for a City of God on earth under the devout overlordship of the papacy, notably from the eleventh to the thirteenth century. The Cluniac Order and the institution of the Peace of God originated a drive to circumscribe secular powers of the Holy Roman Empire in order to establish a Christian Commonwealth, on the principle that a community among Christians would guarantee a more tranquil life for all.[6] Crusades, in which European warriors fought to liberate the Holy Land from Saracen rule, to some extent kept Christian monarchs from attacking one another by diverting their ambitions and frustrations against the infidel. In due course, the Holy See became an international state with its own system of taxation, law, education, and even its own armed forces. The Church had control over practically all media of communication and information, and armies of the Crusaders were, at least in theory, at the disposal of the pope to bring recalcitrant Christian rulers, as well as pagans, to heel. But growth of new centers of power in developing national states— among traders and merchants, and even among Christian military and monastic orders—gradually reduced the power and prestige of the papacy. Because the foundations of papal unity were crumbling, there were pleas for restoration of the medieval Christian community. Frequent wars prompted Dante in the early fourteenth century to advocate a return of

---

[6] August C. Krey, "The International State of the Middle Ages: Some Reasons for Its Failure," *American Historical Review*, XXVIII (October 1922), 1–12; Stefan Possony, "Peace Enforcement," *Yale Law Journal*, LV (August 1946), 910; Bozeman, *Politics and Culture in International History*, Chapter 8.

peace under the sway of a single, hierarchical secular government.[7] His contemporary, Pierre Dubois, suggested a major revival of the Crusades, which might unite Europe in behalf of a common goal.[8] Dubois foresaw the possibility of a European interstate council, giving somewhat equal power to various rulers of Europe, a scheme that was the first proposal for international organization in the modern sense. But Europe was bent upon a development of separate national states that would not band together to form an international organization for some 500 years. A multistate European subsystem was arising.

9.2.2 Multistate Theorists

The failure of plans of Dante, Dubois, and those of the papacy left Europe halfway between a community of like-minded souls and a totally anarchical aggregation of states. Warfare could be mitigated somewhat because of a common Christian heritage, but jealously rising national states would never go so far as to agree upon a merger of their realms under a central authority. Three hundred years after Dubois's suggestions were published, the Reformation and Counter-Reformation movements threatened to destroy any sense of religious affinity. During the period of the Wars of Religion, the nature of international politics was examined more carefully than ever before. Four thinkers—Emeric Crucé, Thomas Hobbes, Hugo Grotius, and the duc de Sully—each had their own diagnosis and remedies.[9]

Crucé, an obscure French monk, felt that a redirection of energy toward cultural and economic pursuits might supply requisites for peace. Common interests would be more lasting if states were to base their transactions on esthetic and economic sentiments; war would thus be regarded as too costly and frivolous an enterprise.

Hobbes urged absolute monarchies within states. A sovereign with full power to weed out dissent could guarantee internal peace, but an international sovereign would simply lack power to subjugate all territories of Europe. Excessive contests between dominant and challenger states would be an unnecessary consequence of following a policy of international alli-

---

[7] Dante Alighieri, *On World Government*, trans. Herbert W. Schneider (Indianapolis: Bobbs-Merrill, 1957).

[8] Pierre Dubois, *The Recovery of the Holy Land*, trans. Walther I. Brandt (New York: Columbia University Press, 1956).

[9] Emeric Crucé, *The New Cyneas*, trans. Thomas Willing Balch (Philadelphia: Allen, Lane, Scott, 1909); Thomas Hobbes, *The Leviathan* (New York: Dutton, 1950); Hugo Grotius, *De Jure Belli ac Pacis*, trans. Francis W. Kelsey (Oxford: Clarendon, 1925); duc de Sully, *The Grand Design of Henry IV* (London: Sweet and Maxwell, 1921).

ances or hegemony. Hobbes's preference for strong national states with a minimum of collaboration paved the way for the later popularity of the concept of the "balance of power."

For Grotius, whose native Dutch Republic was dedicated to the principle of national independence, a peaceful equilibrium in Europe might be maintained by a general recognition of a code of interstate law. The code, which he derived from natural and Roman law, would protect rights of weak and powerful nations alike. Grotius ventured that the work of establishing rules for the behavior of states in specific instances and of settling disputes could be carried out either by conferences of nations or by tribunals of arbitration. But Grotius was writing at a time when states, proudly guarding their newly proclaimed sovereignty, were hardly likely to draw up a code that surrendered their own absolute power.

The most insightful analysis of conditions responsible for European warfare was penned by the duc de Sully, finance minister and closest adviser to Henry IV of France. Attributing ideas contained in his "Grand Design" to his royal master, Sully argued for a complete reshuffling in European boundaries. There were to be fifteen major powers of roughly equal strength, with an equal number of hereditary kingdoms, elective monarchies, and republics. The purpose was to prevent an easy combination between any two or more states into a preponderant coalition along religious, cultural, ideological, or geographic lines. A council of Europe, with local subsidiary councils in major cities, would arbitrate disputes and regulate international transactions; there would be an international police force, to which each ruler would contribute men and matériel. Sully's proposals were largely ignored because they involved stripping the house of Habsburg of all its possessions on the European mainland except Spain; but his view that power dispersion is essential for peace was a most original contribution to international system theory.

As the territorial state system of Europe took form, a contest between the Bourbon and Habsburg dynasties continued; many states found themselves waging wars to determine successors to deceased monarchs. For proponents of representative forms of government, such as Immanuel Kant, a reason for continued war seemed to be that republics were outnumbered by monarchies.[10] Kant hoped that the formation of an international organization including only republics might shame the peoples of Europe into establishing entirely new forms of government with representative institutions. Kant's contemporary, the Abbé de Saint-Pierre, worked these ideas into a

---

[10] Immanuel Kant, *Perpetual Peace,* trans. Helen O'Brian (London: Sweet and Maxwell, 1927); Kenneth N. Waltz, "Kant, Liberalism, and War," *American Political Science Review,* LVI (June 1962), 331–40; Deutsch, "Changing Images of International Conflict," p. 95.

comprehensive and elaborate plan, which he addressed to statesmen at the Conference of Utrecht in 1714.[11]

The thoughts of Kant and Saint-Pierre, according to Jean-Jacques Rousseau (as well as the delegates at Utrecht), were based upon the fallacious premise that men are guided by moral absolutes and reason more than by self-interest and passion. Rousseau's observations constituted the most coherent theory of international politics yet articulated.[12] In answer to Kant, first of all, an Augustinian "rotten apple in the barrel" argument was delineated. Since man is by nature not a social animal, he will be corrupt within any form of government; the potential existence of one malefactor in a society always keeps man on his guard. Similarly, a self-abnegating foreign policy is foolish so long as at least one state remains free to behave selfishly. To expect an end to self-centered perspectives at some future time is utopian. Even a condition of economic interdependence arises out of rational calculation, rather than from a growth in community spirit; so communication "breeds not accommodation and harmony, but suspicion and incompatibility."[13] International conflict, in turn, provides leaders of states with a reason to restrict liberties: political tyranny and war are causes of one another. For Rousseau, manipulation of symbols of international legal mumbo jumbo may serve to beguile leaders, fooling them with altruism; therefore, the international organization of Saint-Pierre would be dangerous insofar as mischievous countries would use the framework to further their own ends—only selfish or naive countries would join the body. The "balance of power," moreover, is only a temporary expedient that tends to make war seem more legitimate than the consciences of ordinary men would otherwise condone. Dissatisfied with the pessimistic nature of his analysis, the volatile Rousseau next offered a solution that resembled the power dispersion feature of the Grand Design. Since it may be possible to reach a consensus and to resolve conflict peacefully in urban or rural communities, Rousseau recommended the establishment of small, self-sufficient polities, where the "good life" could be achieved by bringing the moral judgment of a community to bear on the selfish few. Self-sufficiency, economically and socially, would mean that no state's vital interests could rest under a Damoclean sword of any other state. A loose confederation with a permanent international structure would handle any of the nonvital disputes that might arise from time to time. Rousseau, in short, had much in common with the utopian

[11] Abbé de Saint-Pierre, *Perpetual Peace,* trans. H. Hale Bellot (London: Sweet and Maxwell, 1927).

[12] Jean-Jacques Rousseau, *A Project of Perpetual Peace,* trans. Edith M. Nutall (London: Cobden-Sanderson, 1927).

[13] Stanley Hoffmann, "Rousseau on War and Peace," *American Political Science Review,* LVII (June 1963), 321.

socialists: his prescriptions could be adopted only by reversing irreversible trends.

Statesmen of Europe, meanwhile, constructed a much more workable theory in order to preserve the multistate arrangement that survives to the present day. The theory was in reality just a set of principles for playing the game of power politics; the rules are known collectively as the *balance of power*. David Hume was the first thinker to supply a coherent rationale to the practice of coalition formation in order to prevent aggressive states and their allies from achieving predominant strength.[14] The most masterful exponents were such men as William III, George II, Alexander I, Woodrow Wilson, and Franklin Roosevelt, whose respective policies checked the ambitions of Louis XIV, Frederick II, Napoleon, Kaiser Wilhelm, and Hitler. But, of course, operation of the balancing process left much room for continued war, both for the temporary rewards and temptations accruing from misbehavior and because of the resulting necessity to restrain disturbers of the European equilibrium.

Because of the Napoleonic wars, in which power balancing operated in a grossly inefficient manner, theorists who preferred international law and organization grew in number and in popularity,[15] though leaders of the great powers continued to pay lip service to the idea of balancing power to preserve the European multipolar equilibrium. Drawing upon a body of theory developed in previous centuries, the reformist and practical orientations constituted two very different analytical approaches to the subject of war. It will be necessary to make more detailed examination of these two schools of thought before proceeding with any further research on dynamics of international systems and subsystems.

9.3   APPROACHES IN SUBSYSTEM ANALYSIS

The tendency for thinkers and scholars to subscribe to somewhat different models of international affairs has given rise to a variety of approaches in the study of international systems (Figure 9–1). Borrowing from the distinction made by Ferdinand Tönnies, we may conceive of a continuum

---

[14] David Hume, "Of the Balance of Power," *Political Essays* (New York: Liberal Arts, 1953), pp. 142–44. For further discussions on the balance of power, see Ernst Haas, "The Balance of Power: Prescription, Concept, or Propaganda?" *World Politics, V* (July 1953), 442–77; Morton A. Kaplan, *System and Process in International Politics* (New York: Wiley, 1955); Dina A. Zinnes, "An Analytical Study of the Balance of Power Theories," *Journal of Peace Research,* IV, No. 3 (1967), 270–88.

[15] See Merle Eugene Curti, *The American Peace Crusade* (Durham, N. C.: Duke University Press, 1929); F. H. Hinsley, *Power and the Pursuit of Peace* (Cambridge, England: Cambridge University Press, 1963), Chapters 6–7.

ANARCHY	SOCIETY	COMMUNITY
(Ephemeren	(Gesellschaft)	(Gemeinschaft)
Vereinigungen)		

FIGURE 9-1
Models of International Systems

extending from a stage of complete "anarchy" to the closely knit "community," with "society" in between.[16] A *community* exists when members of a system share many common values and identify their raison d'être with the destiny of a system. An illustration of such a Gemeinschaft in international politics is the notion of a Christian Commonwealth as espoused by the Cluniac Order. *Societies* are looser associations, formed because of a coincidence of interests to accomplish certain definite goals. In international relations a Gesellschaft is equivalent to a set of countries that recognize each other diplomatically, trade and exchange tourism, and occasionally become alliance partners; such a conception accords with Grotius's preferred mode of state interaction. *Anarchy,* finally, is a condition in which units of a system are only in sporadic contact and lack a structural basis for their interaction. One instance of an anarchical system is the Roman Empire just after the time of its decline; Hobbes's model of world politics is closest to an anarchy image.

From the three models, two theoretical approaches have arisen. The *community* approach conceives of many harmonized,[17] goal-seeking, and permanent structural arrangements between states, basing its aspirations on sentiments expressed by Crucé and the Abbé de Saint-Pierre. Exponents of a *stratification* approach look upon war as a consequence of types of power

[16] Ferdinand Tönnies, *Community and Society,* trans. Charles P. Loomis (East Lansing: Michigan State University Press, 1957); René König, ed., *Soziologie* (Frankfurt: Bücherei, 1958), p. 38. The distinction of "society" from "community" is discussed also in Werner Levi, *Fundamentals of World Organization* (Minneapolis: University of Minnesota Press, 1950), p. 209, n. 11. A similar distinction, one between "organic" and "mechanical" solidarity, is made in Emile Durkheim, *The Division of Labor,* trans. George Simpson (New York: Macmillan, 1933). Johan Galtung distinguishes between the two notions in terms of greater or lesser amounts of entropy in his "Entropy and the General Theory of Peace," *Proceedings of the International Peace Research Association Second Conference* (Assen: Van Gorcum, 1968), I, 3–37.

[17] Etzioni locates a concept "harmonization" between "community" and "society," whereas the continuum proposed here is itself one of harmonization from lower to higher levels. Amitai Etzioni, *Political Unification* (New York: Holt, Rinehart and Winston, 1965), p. 282. In this respect Guetzkow's hypotheses are also relevant to the community approach. Harold Guetzkow, "Isolation and Collaboration: A Partial Theory of Internation Relations," *Journal of Conflict Resolution,* I (March 1957), 48–68.

distributions and alliance configurations, building upon insights of Sully and Hume. Community theorists try to isolate conditions that dispose two or more independent states to achieve political or economic unification. From a global perspective the community approach promises to suggest a formula by means of which greater cooperation may be achieved within interacting sets of countries. Stratification theorists conceive of international affairs as involving more of a distinct struggle for resources; elements of disharmony are weighed as predictors of levels of conflict. But whether one prefers to investigate internally peaceful, Gemeinschaftish collections of states such as the Scandinavian subsystem of modern times, or Gesellschaftish confrontations such as those made in the century after the settlement of Westphalia, a comparison between empirical findings derived by the two approaches involves turning sides of the same coin.

9.3.1 Community Approach

The immediate antecedents of the contemporary community approach are the nineteenth-century nationalist propagandizers. Aroused by ideas popularized by the French Revolution, various peoples of Europe agitated to make the political boundaries of states coincide with the domain of distinct social communities. In Germany and Italy, the impact of nationalism encouraged a welding of smaller states into a whole; other nationalist movements set out to detach subject peoples from rule by elites of a differing nationality, resulting, for example, in a breakdown of the Austrian and Ottoman empires. Giuseppe Mazzini and Woodrow Wilson foresaw peace as an inevitable outcome of a restructuring of nations so that they could achieve a common destiny, unhindered by foreign control.[18]

Probably the first academic exponent of an empirically oriented community approach to international subsystems is Karl W. Deutsch. In his seminal *Nationalism and Social Communication* (1953),[19] concepts of cybernetics are applied to an analysis of the success and failure of national unification in Finland (1749–2000), Czechoslovakia (1900–1971), India and Pakistan (1850–2000), and Scotland (1707–1907). Setting out to apply communication theory to the international level,[20] Deutsch was also rapporteur for a team investigation of international communities in the

[18] Giuseppe Mazzini, *The Duties of Man* (New York: Dutton, 1961); Woodrow Wilson, *State Papers and Addresses* (New York: Doran, 1918), pp. 348–56, 468–70. For a bibliography on nationalism and pannationalism, see Karl W. Deutsch, *An Interdisciplinary Bibliography on Nationalism* (Cambridge: MIT Press, 1956).

[19] Karl W. Deutsch, *Nationalism and Social Communication* (New York: Wiley, 1953).

[20] Karl W. Deutsch, *Political Community at the International Level* (Garden City, N. Y.: Doubleday, 1954).

North Atlantic area.[21] A second community theorist, Amitai Etzioni, combining "a traditional power analysis with the Parsonian theory of action and with conceptions of cybernetics and communication theory introduced by Karl Deutsch,"[22] analyzes two cases from European and two from non-European efforts at political mergers.

The Deutsch and Etzioni studies focus on two types of structural integration (see Table 9–1). *Pluralistic* integration involves an establishment of common interstate structures, such as customs unions, military alliances, or a formation of permanent intergovernmental organizations; *amalgamated* integration occurs when two or more previously independent states merge political structures into a single larger unity.[23] Deutsch comments that either the pluralistic or the amalgamated path may lead to a decline in the use of military means to resolve disputes among constituent parts of an integrated subsystem. He states that most cases of successful amalgamation have occurred in the premodern era, despite the highly selective and nonrandom sample reported in Table 9–1. Etzioni, on the other hand, asserts that conditions are ripest in modern times for the formation of transnational structures, inasmuch as a higher level of political and administrative skill is attainable through modern education and social-scientific research. A mass-based loyalty to an integrative structure is only possible where literacy and educational levels permit the spread of information about such integrating structures, and more international business is transacted by the most highly developed political and economic systems.[24] Data assembled by Deutsch, however, clearly reveal that developed countries have a high volume of communications with other countries but proportionally fewer are international, since internal transactions skyrocket in later stages of economic and political development.[25] According to Deutsch, the pluralistic form of integration seems to be a more feasible choice wherever domestic problems begin to overload administrative capabilities of national governments. Moreover, Bruce Russett has

[21] Karl W. Deutsch et al., *Political Community and the North Atlantic Area* (Princeton: Princeton University Press, 1957).

[22] Etzioni, *Political Unification*, p. ix.

[23] Deutsch's confusing definition of "integration" has been discussed above in Section 7.5.6.

[24] Deutsch et al., *Political Community and the North Atlantic Area;* Etzioni, *Political Unification*, pp. 318–21.

[25] Karl W. Deutsch et al., "Is American Attention to Foreign Research Results Declining?" unpublished manuscript, 1954; Deutsch, "Shifts in the Balance of Communications Flows: A Problem of Measurement in International Relations," *Public Opinion Quarterly*, XX (Spring 1956), 143–60; Deutsch and Alexander Eckstein, "National Industrialization and the Declining Share of the International Economic Sector, 1890–1959," *World Politics*, XIII (January 1961), 267–99.

TABLE 9-1
Successful and Unsuccessful International Integration[a]

Type of Integration	Successes	Failures
Pluralistic	Switzerland (1291–1847)	*German Confederation (1815–1866)*
	England–Scotland (1570–1707)	Austria–Germany (1867–1932)
	United States (1781–1789)	
	North German Confederation (1867–1871)	
	Britain–Netherlands (1815–)	
	United States–Canada (1819–)	
	United States–Britain (1871–)	
	Sweden–Denmark (1900–)	
	Denmark–Norway (1900–)	
	Britain–Norway (1910–)	
	Britain–Denmark (1910–)	
	Britain–Sweden (1910–)	
	Norway–Sweden (1907–)	
	Britain–Belgium (1928–)	
	Belgium–Netherlands (1928–)	
	United States–Mexico (1930–)	
	England–Ireland (1945–)	
	Nordic Council (1953–)*	
	European Economic Community (1958–)*	

found that civil violence within states is historically more prevalent than interstate warfare,[26] an observation consistent with a preference for pluralistic integration as a pathway to peace. Parts of existing states with only a rudimentary sense of community can settle disputes most efficaciously by secession. Differences between members of highly integrated structures often seem to be resolvable through an application of coercive measures, such as through revolution or by attempting mass arrests of dissenters.

Summarizing hypotheses generated by the North Atlantic study, there are about four types of conditions relevant to the chances for successful integration (Table 9–2).[27] *Identitive* factors are present when similar

[26] Bruce M. Russett, *Trends in World Politics* (New York: Macmillan, 1965), p. 56.

[27] The factors in Table 9–2 are derived from Deutsch et al., *Political Community and the North Atlantic Area,* Chapter 4. The distinction between four classes of

TABLE 9-1—Cont.
Successful and Unsuccessful International Integration[a]

Type of Integration	Successes	Failures
Amalgamated	England (1215–)	*Habsburg Empire* *(1526–1918)*
	England–Wales (1542–)	*Austria–Bohemia* *(1620–1917)*
	England–Scotland (1707–)	*Britain–United States* *(1607–1776)*
	Switzerland (1848–)	*United States* *(1789–1861)*
	Italy (1860–)	*England–Ireland* *(1801–1918)*
	Germany (1871–)	Norway–Sweden (1814–1905)
	United States (1877–)	Austria–Hungary (1867–1918)
	Canada–Newfoundland (1948–)	*France–Algeria* *(1830–1962)*
		United Arab Republic (1958–1961)*
		Federation of the West Indies (1958–1962)*

[a] Asterisked cases are studied by Amitai Etzioni, *Political Unification* (New York: Holt, Rinehart and Winston, 1965); all others are cited by Karl W. Deutsch et al., *Political Community and the North Atlantic Area* (Princeton: Princeton University Press, 1957). Italicized cases were accompanied by internal warfare, particularly near the date of termination.

values, preferences, and common attachments to symbols are shared within each unit of an integrating subsystem (conditions 1–4). *Coercive* assets deal with capabilities of governments to achieve their ends through military force, such as when an outside foreign threat is present (conditions 5–7). *Utilitarian* assets include all forms of economic resources (conditions 8–10). *Communication* factors indicate the extent to which there is an international flow of symbols, goods, and persons (conditions 11–14).

Consonance in major values seems to be the most essential precondition to integration. Politically active strata of successfully integrated polities would be unable to agree upon specific goals and means without a high level of cultural compatibility. An understanding to depoliticize questions on

factors is based upon Etzioni, except that his "identitive" category is broken down here into attitudinal and communication factors, the former reclassified as "identitive," the latter as "communication" assets. Etzioni, *Political Unification*, p. 331.

TABLE 9-2
Conditions Conducive to International Integration[a]

Conditions	Type of Integration	
	Pluralistic	Amalgamated
1. Compatibility of main values	E[b]	E
2. Distinctive way of life	h	E
3. Mutual responsiveness	E	E
4. Reluctance to wage war	h	h
5. Core area with rising capabilities	h	E
6. Broadening of elites	h	E
7. Joint foreign threat	h	h
8. Strong economic ties	h	h
9. Expectation of economic gain	h	E
10. Economic growth	h	E
11. Unbroken social communication	h	E
12. Mobility of persons	h	E
13. Wide range of transactions	h	E
14. Ethnic or linguistic assimilation	h	h

[a] From Karl W. Deutsch et al., *Political Community and the North Atlantic Area* (Princeton: Princeton University Press, 1957).

[b] Key:
E = essential condition (necessary but not sufficient).
h = helpful condition (neither necessary nor sufficient).

which the units will continue to differ is a corollary. Beyond a mere verbal attachment to a similar intellectual position, a "we-feeling" seems to be necessary in order to assure a mutual perception of needs and responsiveness in political decisionmaking, as local foci for loyalties gradually come into competition with a higher-level structure. The tendency for peoples of an integrated framework to perceive potential war as almost unthinkably fratricidal is perhaps a special case of this development of a cultural distinctiveness. Indeed, data of L. F. Richardson demonstrate that an alliance partnership reduces the likelihood of war between countries, though the effect wears off in time after the alliance has been dissolved.[28]

Political amalgamation requires leadership by particular elite units, who are located in a "core area." Elite countries generally possess a more advanced political system. If political and administrative economic capabilities are steadily rising within the core, each non-elite unit is assured of the capacity of the amalgamated polity to act decisively. An alternation in majority and minority roles by units of the integrated structure helps to overcome localism and solidification of strong or privileged positions that may resist social change. A recent broadening of strata from which political or social elites emerge enables an integration effort to appear mass-based,

[28] Lewis F. Richardson, *Statistics of Deadly Quarrels* (Chicago: Quadrangle, 1960), pp. 194, 197.

thereby attracting support from all strata. Extension of suffrage after unification can be a disintegrative factor, for political strata that were passive before might well see that their self-interest is promoted by secession; closure in an established political elite might encourage a rise of revolutionary counterelites. If other conditions favorable to integration are present, an outside military threat may serve to trigger structural mergers between countries, but pragmatic wartime alliances are notoriously short-lived once a threat has passed.

Politically relevant strata must perceive that integration will lead either to increased economic gain or to an expansion in political and social rights and liberties. Economic stagnation or excessive military burdens, contrariwise, may suggest the utility of secession by the most secure units. A delay in the granting of political reforms may provide time for a revolutionary spirit to rise. If there is superior economic development in the core units, an expectation of economic gain is enhanced, provided that each unit is able to cash in on benefits of integration. Previous strong economic linkages between members of an integrating subsystem indicate success in future efforts to achieve international cooperation, but if other essential conditions are present this prior experience is not an indispensable element in integration.

To ensure that integration is felt evenly across a subsystem, there should be solid horizontal and vertical communication networks, that is, both geographically between territories and socially between the politically relevant strata of each country. Increasing linguistic or ethnic diversity may result in barriers to communication that will militate toward a schism in political attitudes. Channels of communication must not only be open but also used frequently, an observation that negates Rousseau's disdain for international communications. A high volume of mail, cultural and educational exchange, scientific integration, trade, intermarriage, and tourism is essential for political amalgamation.

In a critique of the North Atlantic study, Ernst Haas points out that the findings should be qualified inasmuch as nearly all cases under analysis antedate nuclear weapons systems, Cold War bipolarity, the industrial revolution, mass democracy, mass society, and totalitarianism. The six conditions bound entirely different eras, he feels. Haas then checks Deutsch's conclusions by referring to an extensive discussion in *The Uniting of Europe* (1958), in particular to the period just prior to the establishment of the European Coal and Steel Community in 1950.[29] The major import of the ECSC case is to demote condition 3 (mutual responsiveness) to the level

[29] Ernst B. Haas, *The Uniting of Europe* (Stanford, Cal.: Stanford University Press, 1958); Ernst B. Haas, "The Challenge of Regionalism," *International Organization*, XII (Autumn 1958), 440–58.

of a nonessential though helpful factor in pluralistic integration. The common intergovernmental framework within the ECSC greatly assisted in bringing many conditions to higher levels through a "spillover" process. As one substantive issue opened up for cooperation, ramifications flowed into other problem areas; and the ECSC's effects were felt by increasing numbers of groups and persons throughout Europe. The fulfillment of most of Deutsch's predictions in the case of the European Common Market in 1958 was possible only because of steps taken by the Coal and Steel Community in steering its own course, despite an initial lesser fulfillment of the 14 background conditions.

Criticisms of the North Atlantic study implied in Amitai Etzioni's *Political Unification* (1965) are even more incisive and lead to conceptual innovations.[30] For Etzioni, the dependent variable *success,* the duration of integration, is only one parameter of the community approach. One may also assess *decisiveness,* the effectiveness with which goals to broaden operations in accordance with statutory aims are accomplished; *commitment,* the degree of affective attachment to an integrated subsystem; *acceleration,* the speed of growth in scope and level of function performance; and *evenness,* the extent to which all units share in dividends of higher performance levels. Etzioni's focus is much broader than either Deutsch's or Haas's, and his conclusions are often iconoclastic. He asserts, for example, that violence can promote and sustain integration. Contrary to Deutsch, he finds that *equalitarian* integration—that is, absence of a dominant elite element—can be just as successful as *mono-elite* integration. If two elites are in coalition, the effect is similar to mono-elite unification; but otherwise unions with fewer elites endure longer than those with more. Equalitarian unions generate higher commitments than unions with elites, although a core area ensures more decisiveness. The use of coercive assets often serves to prolong unification. Weak unions may decay from lack of enforcement of norms, which makes the structure seem to be purely a formalistic anachronism. Too much exercise of naked power, however, will also jeopardize success, so an application of force should be within some optimal range.

In an empirical study of community formation at the international level, Roger Cobb and Charles Elder test Deutsch's propositions to see whether levels of international interaction can be predicted from the factors specified in Table 9–2.[31] They find that increasing levels of political and economic development predict to high levels of interaction, but there is little attitudinal spillover therefrom: favorable views toward a country, or its policies,

---

[30] Etzioni, *Political Unification.*

[31] Roger W. Cobb and Charles Elder, *International Community* (New York: Holt, Rinehart and Winston, 1970).

are not especially affected by increased transactions, contrary to the hypotheses of Deutsch.

9.3.2 Stratification Approach

The interest of community theorists in structural merger is matched by the vision of international organization held by many stratification theorists. If strong interstate machinery were able to counterbalance the power of individual states, war would be deterred within international society to a much greater degree. Jeremy Bentham, for instance, argued for decolonization, open diplomacy, and free trade as conditions that promote a more peaceful international society.[32] Colonies easily become subjects of disputes; secret diplomacy enables rulers to ignore public opinion; tariffs occasion reprisals, autarky, and unnecessary competition for markets. All these practices are likely to affect the distribution of power, directly or indirectly.

When stratification theorists treat international conflict, one of the main issues is whether stability accrues from various distributions of power. For Augustine and Dante, unipolar (mono-elite) systems are more peaceful. Multipolarity is preferred by Sully, Hobbes, Rousseau, and balance of power theorists. Yet the twentieth century has witnessed a dramatic increase in bipolar arrangements, starting with the years preceding World War I, including the era of Hitler's aggression, and reaching an apex in the contemporary cold and thawing war between the Soviet Russian bloc and the Western alliance system headed by the United States. Bipolarity has been assessed as the most dangerous condition by many writers. According to E. H. Carr, the existence of have and have-not powers in the same arena is alleged to breed constant international turmoil.[33] The modern age, for A. F. K. Organski, is experiencing an era of "power transition," in which existing topdogs are under constant challenge by newer, rapidly developing industrial giants.[34] The premodern world polity had a more equalitarian distribution of power, according to Organski, inasmuch as economic wealth was then derived from subsistence agriculture; but an age of uneven growth in industrial power within countries assures a sporadic if persistent flow of new challengers to contest transitory orders. When all states reach a maximum in political, economic, and administrative assets, a more stable

[32] Jeremy Bentham, *Plan for an Universal and Perpetual Peace* (London: Sweet and Maxwell, 1927). See also William Penn, *The Peace of Europe* (New York: Dutton, 1915).

[33] E. H. Carr, *The Twenty Years Crisis* (New York: Macmillan, 1939).

[34] A. F. K. Organski, *World Politics*, 2d ed. (New York: Knopf, 1968), pp. 300–33. A somewhat similar view is advanced by Toynbee. See Kenneth W. Thompson, "Toynbee and the Theory of International Politics," *Political Science Quarterly,* LXXI (September 1956), 365–86.

era will reappear, Organski claims, in sharp disagreement with W. T. R. Fox's prediction that internal development within today's superpowers is sufficient to preclude the rise of more than a few "squirrels" to the rank of "elephants."[35]

Morton Kaplan's classification of various international systems in terms of performance norms agrees with the classical view that multipolarity is more peaceful than bipolarity, as does a formal analysis by Karl Deutsch and J. David Singer.[36] But Kenneth Waltz, in a vigorous dissent from balance of power theory, sagely observes that current bipolarity has been remarkably long in duration and free from debilitating wars.[37]

The most systematic efforts to examine stratification theory have been undertaken by Richard Rosecrance, J. David Singer, and Melvin Small.[38] Rosecrance's focus is on power stratification. Guided by elementary notions of general systems theory, he establishes time boundaries for nine historical "international systems" between 1740 and 1960, each defined in terms of power stratification. After delineating a number of qualitative categories for describing an international system, he supplies codings for each of nine systems (Table 9–3).[39] In a manner similar to community theorists, Rosecrance conducts a necessary-and-sufficient-condition analysis of preconditions to "stability," which he defines as the ability of a regulator to cope

[35] W. T. R. Fox, *The Super-Powers* (New York: Harcourt, Brace, 1944). Waltz's calculations support Fox. Kenneth N. Waltz, "Stability of the Bipolar World," *Daedelus*, XCIII (Summer 1964), 881–909. Cf. Johan Galtung, "A Structural Theory of Aggression," *Journal of Peace Research*, I, No. 2 (1964), 95–119.

[36] Morton A. Kaplan, *System and Process in International Politics;* Kaplan, "The Systems Approach to International Politics," *New Approaches to International Relations,* ed. Kaplan (New York: St. Martin's, 1968), pp. 381–404; Karl W. Deutsch and J. David Singer, "Multipolar Power Systems and International Stability," *World Politics,* XVI (April 1964), 390–406. See a similar argument concerning economic oligopoly in Kenneth E. Boulding, *The Organizational Revolution* (New York: Harper, 1953).

[37] Waltz, "Stability of the Bipolar World."

[38] Richard Rosecrance, *Action and Reaction in World Politics* (Boston: Little, Brown, 1963). J. David Singer and Melvin Small, "Alliance Aggregation and the Onset of War, 1815–1945," *Quantitative International Politics,* ed. Singer (New York: The Free Press, 1968), pp. 247–86; see also Zinnes, "An Analytical Study of the Balance of Power Theories."

[39] Rosecrance's form of presentation consists of a series of charts rather than a statistical table; Rosecrance, *Action and Reaction in World Politics,* Chapter 11. The semiquantitative and historical approaches are abandoned later in his "Bipolarity, Multipolarity, and the Future," *Journal of Conflict Resolution,* X (September 1966), 314–27. For critiques of Rosecrance's procedures, see Zinnes, "The Requisites for International Stability," *Journal of Conflict Resolution,* VIII (September 1964), 301–305; and George Liska, "Continuity and Change in International Systems," *World Politics,* XVI (October 1963), 118–36.

with disturbances that threaten to undermine an existing power distribution. With respect to power distribution, the lone unipolar system in his sample is fairly stable, but multipolarity is clearly more stable than bipolarity. Considering "resources" either as areas ripe for colonial and imperial expansion or as new states that may be targets for ideological or political proselytization, Rosecrance's codings reveal that an availability of unappropriated resources makes for stability; scarcity, for instability.[40] The existence in a system of contending or non-status-quo ideologies means that conflict will be intense, but a divergence in elites' ethos is neither a necessary nor a sufficient condition for instability, thus agreeing with Waltz's views concerning the insignificance of ideological aspects of the contemporary bipolar world. Insecurity of elites' tenure at home is always associated with instability abroad, as Rousseau predicted. But in contrast with community theorists, such as Mazzini and Wilson, the drawing of boundaries such that allegiances are now more nationalist than dynastic has not resulted in a more benign international arena; in fact, unstable systems have been encountered more frequently since the rise of nationalism and the use of citizen forces. Increasing world levels in economic development, as Organski has hypothesized, bring more disturbers into confrontation with elites, rather than providing more power for regulators of international systems. And no single regulator, whether balance of power, concert of great powers, alliance system, or international organization, has been able to maintain stability in all of the cases. The record of the Concert of Europe in maintaining stability is better, but the breakdowns of 1848 and 1914 were too extraordinary for informal summit conferences to avert or to resolve. Whenever the disturbance level has been high, regulators have proved inadequate.

Systematic case comparisons, using a set of concepts central to systems analysis, to some extent bridge a gap between community and stratification approaches, for codings of values (ideological conflict, dynastic versus national control) are treated along with stratification elements (poles, resources, capabilities). One of the strengths of multipolarity is supposed to be a higher probability of cross-cutting loyalties; a polypolar system is hypothesized to avoid serious conflict because of reduced stratification in attention and responsiveness capabilities.

In attempting to operationalize Rosecrance's notion of *polarity,* however, there appear to be two major elements. One aspect is the degree of national power of individual states; the other is the extent to which individual units are clustered into alliances and blocs.

---

[40] According to Waltz an absence of a periphery for expansion makes for stability; Kaplan attributes earlier stability in Europe to an existence of vast areas for colonization where a no-holds-barred contest could be pursued. Waltz, "Stability of the Bipolar World," p. 882; Kaplan, *System and Process in International Politics.*

TABLE 9-3
Rosecrance's Codings of Nine European Subsystems[a]

Variables	Years Bounding Subsystems								
	1740 1789	1789 1814	1814 1822	1822 1848	1848 1871	1871 1890	1890 1918	1918 1945	1945 1960
POLES[b]	4+	2	4+	2/4+	4+	1	2	2	3
RESOURCES									
Availability[c]	++	–	++	+++	–	++	–	++	++
Fixed	+	+	–	+	+	+	+	+	+
IDEOLOGICAL CONFLICT	–	+	–	+	–	+	–	+	+
CONTROL									
Secure[d]	++	–	+++	+⧺⧺	+++	++	++	⧺–+	⧺–+
Dynastic	+	⧺	++	⧺⧺	=	=	+	–	–
National	–	⧺	–	⧺	–	+	+	+	+
CAPABILITIES									
Citizen forces	+	+	+	+	+	+	+	+	+
Mobilization[e]	–	–	–	–	=	=	+	⧺	⧺⧺
Technology[f]	–	–	–	–	–	+	+	+	⧺⧺
REGULATOR									
Balance of power	+	+	+	+	+	+	–	–	–
Concert	–	–	+	+	+	+	+	–	–
Alliance system	–	–	–	–	–	+	+	–	–
International organization	–	–	–	–	–	–	–	+	+
Neutral bloc	–	–	+	=	–	+	–	+	+
Powerful	–	=	+	–	–	–	–	–	=
Growing	–	–	–	–	–	+	–	+	–
DISTURBANCE									
Considerable	–	++	–	=	++	=	++	++	–
Growing	+	+	++	+	–	–	+	–	–
STABILITY[g]	+	–	++	+	–	+	–	+	+

TABLE 9-3—Cont.
Rosecrance's Codings of Nine European Subsystems[a]

[a] Source: Richard Rosecrance, *Action and Reaction in World Politics* (Boston: Little, Brown, 1963), Chapter 11.

[b] Exact number of poles except:
2/4+ = quasibipolarity.
4+ = multipolarity.

[c] Remaining data are coded in terms of presence (+) and absence (—). Here the gradations are as follows:
++ = abundance.
+ = adequacy.
— = scarcity.

[d] The symbol ± means that two poles had opposite codings.

[e] Key:
— = slow.
—/— = one pole slow, other pole gradual.
— = gradual.
= = moderate.
+ = rapid.
±± = one pole moderate, two poles continuous.

[f] Key:
— = primitive.
— = elementary.
— = developing.
= = transitional.
+ = early modern.
++ = modern.
±±± = one pole transitional, two poles contemporary.

[g] Key:
— = highly unstable or well outside stable range.
— = outside stable range.
= = within stable range or barely stable.
+ = well within stable range.

321

Singer and Small pay close attention to alliance configuration patterns. Starting with a hypothesis that the onset of war is associated with an increase in alliance commitments between countries, they assemble an impressive array of data on wars and alliances in order to test balance of power theory empirically. For the years between 1815 and 1945 they collect statistical indicators for each member of the family of nations. The measures are as follows:

1. Indicators of international violence (dependent variables):
   a. Number of wars (all countries).
   b. Battle deaths (all countries).
   c. Battle deaths (major powers).
   d. Duration of wars (all countries).
   e. Duration of wars (major powers).
2. Indicators of alliance aggregation (independent variables):
   a. Countries allied/all countries.
   b. Major powers allied/major powers.
   c. Countries in defense pacts/all countries.
   d. Major powers in defense pacts/major powers.
   e. Major powers allied with minor powers/major powers.
   f. Extent of exhaustion of bilateral defensive pact links between major powers.

Singer and Small derive a sample of international systems in a manner somewhat similar to the procedures employed by Rosecrance, for they analyze four subsamples of international systems—a "central system" composed mostly of European countries for two eras, 1815–1899 and 1900–1945, and a "total system" of central and peripheral countries for the same two eras. Although intercorrelations between independent and dependent variables are mostly positive when data are aggregated across all years for total and central systems, the two eras exhibit opposite patterns when results for the nineteenth century are compared with twentieth-century findings. For the 1900–1945 period most correlations are positive, demonstrating that wars have been preceded by a formation of alliances; between 1815 and 1899, in contrast, correlations are mainly negative, revealing that alliance involvement may have served as a deterrent to international military conflict.

To summarize at this point, we can observe considerable consensus among theoretically oriented investigators of power stratification. Rosecrance, Singer, and Small delineate a number of factors that seem central to an analysis of international systems as a whole. Both the Rosecrance and Singer-Small studies find a time-slice breakdown to be necessary for a more precise study of the impact of power distribution upon the incidence and expression of international conflict. Rosecrance codes both community and stratification variables. Singer and Small seek quantitative measures for individual countries and years, thus supplying data for a more specific analysis of trends.

Nevertheless, the analytical procedures followed by Rosecrance, and Singer and Small need to be clarified and tightened, especially in the criteria for selecting international "systems." One question to pose is whether Rosecrance's nine and Singer's and Small's four systems are really "international." To be sure, Rosecrance makes occasional references to events in North America and Japan, but most of his attention is directed to European interstate politics. Singer and Small explicitly acknowledge that their "central" systems are European in composition. A second problem is in dating separate eras. Rosecrance finds nine eras between 1740 and 1960, while Stanley Hoffmann turns up three subsystems for the years 1648–1960.[41] Singer and Small arbitrarily divide the data into two sets, 1815–1899 and 1900–1945. Thirdly, as Zinnes has pointed out, there is a need to construct a much larger number of indicators in order to study many different facets of power stratification.[42] The first two of these three tasks are considered in the remaining sections of this chapter; a classificatory scheme for systematically generating variables will be presented in Chapter 10.

9.4 THE CONCEPT OF INTERNATIONAL SUBSYSTEM

Ordinarily a *system* is thought to consist of parts that are related in some way to one another. Formally, "a system is a set of objects together with relationships between the objects and between their attributes."[43] In social

---

[41] Stanley Hoffmann, "International Systems and International Law," *World Politics,* XVI (October 1961), 205–37.

[42] Dina A. Zinnes, "An Analytical Study of the Balance of Power Theories."

[43] A. D. Hall and R. R. Fagen, "Definition of System," *General Systems Yearbook,* I (1956), 18. A common semantic trap is to say that a system exists only when it reaches some threshold level of frequency in interaction. Certainly it is more consistent with general systems theory to define a *system* as any set of parts that are related in some way; and a classification of types of relations would clearly be incomplete without the category "interacting," for which one could assemble data to differentiate systems interacting at high and low levels. Entities, in short, are to be described with reference to conceptual variables, instead of being defined in terms of thresholds. Such an approach is consistent with the "constructivist" systems approach advocated by David Easton, *A Framework for Political Analysis* (Englewood Cliffs, N. J.: Prentice-Hall, 1965), pp. 30–34. Our interest in international *political* subsystems focuses our attention upon interactions dealing with authoritative allocations of values in order to determine members of the subsystems studied in this volume. Cf. Peter Nettl, "The Concept of System in Political Science," *Political Studies,* XIV, No. 3 (1966), 305–38. A somewhat different attempt to carve out subsystems is presented in Paul Smoker, "A Preliminary Empirical Study of an International Integrative Subsystem," *International Associations,* XVIII (November 1965), 638–46.

systems the *objects* are referred to as the "actors" or "members." *Relationships between objects* are ways in which actors are linked, and this serves to distinguish members from nonmembers. *Attributes* are conceptual variables that describe each object, and *relationships between attributes* are the hypotheses under investigation. Since the notion of a system is analytic, imposed by the mind upon the so-called real world, it is technically possible to consider as systems the set of kangaroo courts, white nylon carpets, and Italians whose last names do not end with the letter "i." Such a choice would be branded a *complex,* or loose collection of entities, by most persons. Still, features of a realistic or concrete system remain to be specified. If we consider any set of related parts to be a system, then the most important distinction between systems is the nature of the relationship. A typology of interrelationships enables us to classify systems more meaningfully.

Intuitively, the idea of a world international polity seems to be an abstraction with little empirical foundation; an "international system" resembles a "complex" more than a "concrete" system. Representatives of Ecuador and Ethiopia, for instance, do have an opportunity to communicate with each other at the United Nations, but they seldom have anything of importance to say to one another; their destinies are bound up with political activities of very different sets of countries. Some nations have global interests, which means that they transact business in two or more sets of international arenas; middle and minor powers have primary interests only within a localized regional system. That regional systems appear to be more "real" in many respects than global systems has been the thesis of recent essays on international regions in the Middle East, Asia, Africa, Renaissance Italian city-states, multistate China, and to the more isolated international systems of the Aztecs and Incas.[44] Michael Brecher, in fact, has suggested a comparative coding of three "subordinate" and four "dominant" subsystems (Table 9–4).[45]

For the sake of clarity, an *international system* may be defined as an aggregation of all politically autonomous and semiautonomous societal systems; any subset of such entities thus constitutes an *international subsystem.* The empirical task is to differentiate between systems and subsystems that have greater or lesser degrees of linkage, and it seems plausible so far to regard an Ecuador-Ethiopia subsystem as a loosely related subsystem, just as a potpourri consisting of all international actors for the year 1453 would be a curious choice. A more realistic political linkage may be found at the regional level between the micro- and macro-extremes. More formally, since

[44] Louis J. Cantori and Steven L. Spiegel, *The International Politics of Regions* (Englewood Cliffs, N. J.: Prentice-Hall, 1970).

[45] Michael Brecher, "International Relations and Asian Studies: The Subordinate State System of Southern Asia," *World Politics,* XV (January 1963), 211–35.

TABLE 9-4

Brecher's Codings of International Systems[a]

Variables	Dominant Systems				Subordinate Systems		
	Multistate Greece	Multistate China	19th-Century Europe	Current World System	South Asia Today	Middle East Today	America Today
Level of power	+			++	-	-	+
Power stratification		+	-	=	=	-	++
Political organization			++	+++	-	=	++
Military organization			++	+++		-	=
Economic organization					+	=	+
Frequency of interaction					-	+++	+
Completeness of interaction					+	+++	=
Penetration by dominant system					-	+	=
Penetration of dominant system					+		=
Level of communications					-	-	-
Homogeneity of values			=		-	+	+
Diversity of polities	+		+		+	+	++
Domestic instability					+	++	=

[a] Source: Michael Brecher, "International Relations and Asian Studies: The Subordinate State System of Southern Asia," *World Politics*, XV (January 1963), 211–25.

Key:
++ = very high.
+ = high.
= = medium.
- = low.
-- = very low.
(blank) = not coded.

"relationships between objects" is an essential feature in defining a system, precise criteria for determining membership in international subsystems must be phrased in terms of how member states relate to each other. Michael Brecher takes an impressive step in postulating six features of what he calls a "subordinate" system. Though the notion of "subordinate" systems collapses upon closer examination, as we shall see shortly, his list is an excellent starting point for a delineation of criteria useful in locating boundaries between international subsystems:

1. Scope is delimited, with primary stress on a geographic region.
2. There are at least three actors.
3. Taken together, they are objectively recognized by other actors as constituting a distinctive community, region, or segment of the global system.
4. The members identify themselves as such.
5. The units of power are relatively inferior to units in the dominant system, using a sliding scale of power in both.
6. Changes in the dominant system have greater effect on the subordinate system than the reverse.

One consequence of the sixfold formulation is to deny by definition that the United States was a member of an Asian subsystem during the late 1960s, even though some 500,000 of its citizens were participating in a military enterprise in Vietnam. The idea of a "subordinate" system is as procrustean as the formerly myopic equation of European interstate politics with world politics. Although it is justified as a corrective for an overly broad focus on the states in control of the world polity, the "subordinate" system concept excludes from membership the very elephants who are responsible for the destiny of the squirrels:[46] an overly microscopic conceptualization replaces the overly macroscopic. If major powers of Europe determine who gets what, when, and how[47] within many regional clusters of states, then such countries indeed belong to international political subsystems outside Europe. Since a systematic analysis of determinants of conflict should deal with all of the major factors operating in international arenas, one can hardly exclude from the scope of one's inquiry the very actors pulling the strings. A reanalysis and reformulation of Brecher's criteria is in order.

Criterion 1 seems reasonable, for the concept of "subsystem" does

[46] Brecher, however, relents by admitting Communist China to membership in his South Asia Subsystem on the ground that "it is the low level of power in Southern Asia that gives China, an extra-area actor [*sic*], virtual carte blanche access to the system, as well as de facto membership in it." *Ibid.,* p. 222. The same argument obviously applies to any country maintaining a military presence outside its home territories.

[47] Harold D. Lasswell, *Politics* (New York: McGraw-Hill, 1936).

imply a regional cluster of countries, most but not all of which are roughly contiguous or separated by short distances. Criterion 2 specifies that there should be at least three members of a subsystem, thereby excluding all possible dyadic systems. Nevertheless, the Rome–Carthage subsystem might well have had only two principal actors, so a lower limit of two would seem less arbitrary. Criteria 3 and 4 embody most fully the heart of the problem of determining membership, and they will be discussed more extensively below. Criterion 5 depoliticizes the notion of international subsystems, for it assumes that dealings between small powers can be autonomous and are somehow isolated from the tentacles of major powers of the dominant systems. Item 6 states a proposition rather than a criterion, and one counter-example can serve to dispel any aura of sanctity that the assertion may have: while changes in European subsystems had very little impact upon East Asian subsystems until 1914, cooperation between China and Russia after the Sino–Japanese War so alarmed Great Britain that it decided to forego its traditional policy of "splendid isolation" and conclude an alliance with Japan in 1902 as a check upon the Asian ambitions of St. Petersburg. Moreover, if some powers belonging to the European subsystem happened to be strong in the East Asian subsystem, it would be a fallacy to syllogize therefrom that the European system as a whole was somehow dominant, the East Asian subordinate. Many powerful members of the European sub-system had no interest whatever in Asia, and such countries made no attempt to delegate authority to the European states (strong and weak) who chose to enter Asian political arenas. Several centuries earlier, China was considerably stronger than the few European nations that ventured into the Orient, but no one claims that an Asian subsystem was then dominant, the European subordinate. Europe and Asia have remained distinct and separate arenas.[48] Criteria 5 and 6 will therefore be dropped.

Returning to criteria 3 and 4, which deal with "recognition" and "identification," respectively, a more operational guide is needed. For example, what is "objective recognition"? If the criterion refers to a condition in which nonmember states believe that certain countries belong to a subsystem, then a reputational measure is involved. A few misperceptions by "outside" or "inside" actors will suffice to distort results of a survey on reputed subsystem membership.[49] A more convincing case can be made instead for the conferring of "objective recognition" when states in fact interact with each other, which is the focus in criterion 5. To exchange

---

[48] A *subordinate* subsystem would more properly consist of a set of puppet states within a subsystem. The Eastern European Soviet satellites in the time of Stalin were such a subordinate subsystem within the North Atlantic subsystem.

[49] For a critique of reputational indicators, see Raymond E. Wolfinger, "Reputation and Reality in the Study of 'Community Power'," *American Sociological Review,* XXV (October 1960), 636–44.

ambassadors, to trade, or even to conduct military operations objectively constitutes a recognition by one international actor of another's existence. Whether one actor regards another as "illegitimate" is independent of the concept of objective recognition. When Great Britain began to subdue the Indian subcontinent, the government in London was not accepted by all tribal elements; but whether Baluchis and other actors were displeased with the peculiar way in which the "white man's burden" was borne, the British, the Baluchis, and others all belonged to a South Asian subsystem. Interaction between actors entailed a perception of common subsystem membership. The Baluchis did not belong to another subsystem, for their communications with actors outside the region were minimal.

Accordingly, an international subsystem could be isolated empirically as a dense network of communications and transactions between states. If one were to construct a map of transactional exchanges between all countries, the densest clusters would be between subsystems within the total network.[50] But are all types of communications equally appropriate? According to James Rosenau there could be as many analytical systems as there are *issue areas*.[51] In factor analyses of roll-call votes in the General Assembly, several studies demonstrate that countries align themselves quite differently on at least two issue areas, political security and social-economic questions.[52] Positions taken within both issue areas tend to fall into overlapping polarizations: an East-West alignment on resolutions dealing with "guns" is empirically independent of a North-South divergence on the subject of "butter." A solution to the membership criterion problem involves choosing whether one wishes to study military-political or socioeconomic subsystems, a contrast that underlies our distinction between stratification and community approaches. The focus of this book is on violent conflict between states, so membership will be defined herein on the basis of military actions and perceptions. An *international conflict subsystem* may be defined as composed of a set of actors with a relatively self-contained pattern of

[50] Russett, *International Regions and the International System*, does not deal with political interactions per se. See Steven J. Brams, "Transaction Flows in the International System," *American Political Science Review*, LX (December 1966), 880–98; Chadwick F. Alger and Brams, "Patterns of Representation in National Capitals and Intergovernmental Organizations," *World Politics*, XIX (July 1967), 646–63.

[51] James Rosenau, *The Scientific Study of Foreign Policy* (New York: The Free Press, 1971). See also Roger Fisher, "Perceiving the World Through Bipolar Glasses," *Daedelus*, XCIII (Summer 1964), 910–15.

[52] Hayward R. Alker, Jr., "Dimensions of Conflict in the General Assembly," *American Political Science Review*, LVIII (September 1964), 642–57; Alker and Bruce M. Russett, *World Politics in the General Assembly* (New Haven: Yale University Press, 1965); Russett, *International Regions and the International System*, Chapters 4–5.

military articulation and aggregation of state interests, along with interstate plan-making, implementation, and any other functions characteristic of autonomous polities.[53] Brecher's original criteria, now revised for detecting an international political subsystem, are as follows:

1. Scope is delimited, with primary stress on a geographic region.
2. There are at least two actors.
3. There is a relatively self-contained network of military interactions between the members, involving such activities as goal attainment, adaptation, pattern maintenance, and coordination.

9.4.1 Subsystem Membership

Our three criteria for determining conflict subsystems will help to delimit subsystems in Europe, Asia, Africa, America, or even Hawaii. But two problems remain. Which criteria are most useful for determining membership of an actor in a particular subsystem? Second, inasmuch as density in international conflict fluctuates from one historical epoch to the next, what are the time boundaries for international subsystems?

Turning first of all to membership criteria, one would potentially wish to include city-states, secessionist revolutionaries, duchies, principalities, nation-states, subnational states, multinational empires, alliances, blocs, the papacy, international organizations, concerts of great powers, international conferences, and so forth. A major common denominator is structure, for all of the above entities contain political hierarchies that persist over some unit of time. Nevertheless, looser collections of persons with structural coherence may, from time to time, act within a system yet fail to perform at the same level as a full-fledged member. What criteria will inform us whether an international *actor* is a *member* of a conflict subsystem? In order for an investigator to exclude such actors as the International Political Science Association, Andorra, the International Telecommunication Union, peace marchers in Central Park, rumrunners in the Caribbean, and the good ship *Titanic,* there must be some reasonable cutoff point; otherwise our list of members will become lengthy, uneven, and bizarre. Ideally we would seek quantitative data on stratification for all entities over the globe and then

---

[53] The structural-functional approach to international relations is applied more fully in Chapter 10 in this volume. The use of Weber's definition highlights conflict, which is only one phenomenon of interest to a student of international subsystems; definitions by Easton and Riggs that are mentioned in earlier chapters embrace a broader perspective of the nature of politics than does Weber. The same functions mentioned here are repeated in Section 9.4.1 in delineating subsystem membership, but the terms themselves are defined in Chapter 10.

determine clusters of states. However, since such data are not available for long historical sweeps, it will be necessary to proceed analytically.[54]

One of the essential characteristics of an *actor* in a conflict subsystem is communication with other members of that system on political matters. What, then, is a member? A *member* of a conflict subsystem may be defined as an actor that engages in a high level of interaction relevant to international conflict, both from a quantitative and a qualitative point of view. An actor could be either a hasty visitor or a relatively dormant entity that happens to be located within the geographic region in question. More concretely, the intensity of a mere actor's interactions will necessarily be shallow, whereas a member is an active participant in the attainment of goals, adaptation to changes in exogenous conditions, maintenance of the pattern of the subsystem, or coordination of the subsystem; because security issues are the concern herein, the substance of interactions should deal at least with power transformations that are likely to be affected by war or threat of war. But there is an arbitrary step that must be taken at an early stage in delineating subsystem members: one must select core units around which other members can be said to revolve. France, for example, has been at the core of European politics for centuries; in East Asia it would be unimaginable to construct subsystems without including China. But in making choices in order to establish more peripheral members on the basis of communication linkage, it is possible to formalize intuitively applied criteria. France and China have been continuously active, have possessed many military resources, and have been either major or middle powers for most of modern history. A *core member* of a conflict subsystem, therefore may be defined as a militarily powerful state located within a particular geographic region that appears to qualify as a subsystem. Countries possessing some minimal amount of military resources that are interacting significantly with core members of an international subsystem would therefore seem to be reasonable candidates for members.

Accordingly, it is necessary to define levels of power among international actors. *Major powers* are elite or dominant members of a system whose behavior is capable of upsetting an existing power distribution or

---

[54] Methods of deriving subsystems from quantitative transactional data are described in several sources: Russett, *International Regions and the International System;* Brams, "Transaction Flows in the International System." Unfortunately relevant data are not available for long periods of time in international history for each actor who manifests conflict. Other attempts to isolate regions are discussed in the following essays: Donald J. Bogue, "Nodal Versus Homogeneous Regions, and Statistical Techniques for Measuring the Influences of Each," *Institut Internationale de Statistique,* IV (1957), 377–92; Mary Megee, "Problems in Regionalizing and Measurement," *Peace Research Society, Papers,* IV (1965), 7–35; Brian J. L. Berry, "A Method for Deriving Multi-Factor Uniform Regions," *Polish Geographer,* XXX, No. 2 (1961), 263–79.

placing a power equilibrium in jeopardy. *Middle powers* are locally prominent actors, who may be sought as allies by major powers but who are never leaders of a subsystem; the only comfort of a middle power is that it can put minor powers in their place. A *minor power,* then, is a minimally viable military entity that is incapable of defending itself effectively when attacked by two or more actors but can hold its own against one power below the middle rank. A *satellite* is a minor power that formally operates as an independent entity but in actuality is controlled by a major or middle power.[55]

Such criteria as military viability and significant interactive participation are rather fuzzy guides to threshold levels on two distinct scales. Further specification is necessary. Singer and Small use a similar set of rules, so it may be useful to examine their cutting points.[56] *Military viability* is equivalent to their requirement that a member state have a population of at least 500,000. *Significant interaction* is approximated by diplomatic recognition by either of two so-called legitimizers, Britain or France. Unfortunately, population and recognition data are not available as far back as the seventeenth century for the subsystems examined here, so Singer's criteria would have to be applied in many eras on the basis of impressionistic accounts. Nevertheless, even if data were available for all countries and years, a rigid application of the Singer–Small criteria would overlook quite a number of militarily active participants within subsystem regions. For example, as soon as a secessionist movement begins, a rebel group both demonstrates its military viability and engages in rather significant conflictual interactions. Belgians acted independently when they began their fight to achieve autonomy from the Netherlands in 1830, whereas their status as a fully sovereign state was not recognized until later. Similarly, members may lose their status due to war; Saxony was removed as an independent actor by Napoleon's armies in 1806 but was restored to full sovereignty in 1814. A third case is a politically cohesive community or group, such as the Carbonari of Piedmont and Sicily in 1821, which undertakes an internal revolt that attracts intervention from an outside power. And a final situation is a country outside a geographic region that dispatches troops to engage in war, at the end of which

[55] Compare with the concepts of *elite, lieutenant,* and *follower* units in Etzioni, *Political Unification.* The rationale for such a threefold division is presented by George Liska, *Nations in Alliance* (Baltimore: Johns Hopkins University Press, 1962), pp. 161–67. Categorization of specific countries follows the delineation of Singer and Small, "Alliance Aggregation and the Onset of War," p. 260, which in turn is based on Hans J. Morgenthau, *Politics Among Nations,* 2d ed. (New York: Knopf, 1954), p. 324.

[56] J. David Singer and Melvin Small, "The Composition and Status Ordering of the International System," *World Politics,* XVIII (January 1966), 236–82; Bruce M. Russett, Singer, and Small, "National Political Units in the 20th Century: A Standardized List," *American Political Science Review,* LXII (September 1968), 932–51.

the troops are withdrawn, such as when the Commonwealth countries fought in World Wars I and II. The rules of Singer and Small, in short, are so formal that they would exclude actors that are in the very center of arenas of military conflict yet are somewhat less visible than the more powerful states. It is particularly important to avoid the legalistic trap of including only so-called sovereign states, especially in an age when contests involving such entities as the Vietcong guerrillas may continue to threaten the very survival of the human race. Accordingly, once core members are determined, the following criteria for determining membership in an international political subsystem would seem provisionally useful:

1. A member must interact more or less continually with core members in a manner relevant to political-military goal attainment, adaptation, pattern maintenance, and coordination (see Section 10.2).

   a. The existence of diplomatic interaction neither confers nor denies membership per se, but actors within dense regional diplomatic-exchange clusters are automatically members of subsystems.

   b. An entity entering into a defensive alliance with a core member gains membership if geographically on the same continent or subcontinent.

   c. Members must have a minimal level of internal political organization. (A rebel political faction may qualify, but a social group or ethnic community is excluded.)

2. A member must possess military viability.

   a. All units with a population exceeding 500,000 are members.

   b. All sovereign states engaging in war within the relevant region are members.

   c. Membership ceases when an actor is absorbed or conquered and occupied by another unit, unless the new status is that of a peacetime satellite.

   d. A domestic military faction is a member if it is a participant in an initially internal war in which one or more major and middle powers have intervened, or if it eventually succeeds in achieving political autonomy as a separate state.

In applying these criteria to some difficult cases, we can see by criterion 1b that Parma, which was not a militarily significant entity, achieved membership when Austria contracted a defense pact with it in 1851; if a major power desires to curry the support of such a state, then it is judged forthwith to have significant interaction and some military importance. By insisting that an actor be organized politically in criterion 1c, we can eliminate social groups, such as Bosnian Moslems, Indonesian Chinese, or Chinese Christians, who became parties to nondomestic conflicts in 1875, 1947, and 1900, respectively. A militarily organized subnational group achieves membership under criterion 2d, such as the Carbonari and the preindependence belligerent Belgians. Extraregional actors become members of a subsystem when they send troops to fight wars under criterion 2b; examples are the governments of South Africa during both world wars and Brazil in World War II. Membership, however, lapses as soon as troops are withdrawn by extraregionals or when subnational factions cease military operations without achieving statehood, though they must attract outside intervention to be deemed participants in "international" subsystems.

9.4.2 Dating of Subsystems

Inasmuch as international subsystems are specified in terms of military-political issue areas, time boundaries for historical eras that contain distinct parties and issues in conflict need to be determined. Power stratification and alliance configuration hardly remain constant over time; an impact of certain wars between major powers has often been to transform stakes of conflict dramatically among countries in subsystem regions.[57] An appropriate research technique for determining clusters of years is P-factor analysis, but data on alliances and resources of states are not available for the long sweeps of time that a rich comparative analysis of international subsystems would hope to encompass.[58] The concept of system is entirely an analytic one in any case, so an initial task in determining subsystem transformations is to distinguish between qualitatively distinct kinds of stratification relevant to international conflict. A change from one type of stratification to another demarcates the end of an old and beginning of a new subsystem era.

International stratification exists to the extent that some resources possessed by members within a system are used individually or are pooled in coalitions to achieve common goals. *Polypolarity* would exist if each of sev-

---

[57] The "stakes of conflict" criterion is proposed by Hoffmann, "International Systems and International Law"; cf. Robert L. Rothstein, "Power, Security and the International System," paper presented to the American Political Science Association Annual Convention, Chicago, September 1967; Hoffmann, *The State of War*.

[58] For an empirical effort to determine cycles in warfare, see Frank Denton, "Some Regularities in International Conflict, 1820–1949," *Background*, IX (February 1966), 283–96; see also Denton and Warren Phillips, "Some Patterns in the History of Violence," *Journal of Conflict Resolution*, XII (June 1968), 182–95. Singer, who cuts his data into two historical time periods, objects to the "sequence-of-systems" approach in "The Global System and Its Sub-Systems: A Developmental View," *Linkage Politics*, ed. James N. Rosenau (New York: The Free Press, 1969), pp. 21–43. Nevertheless, his specific objections apply most harshly to his own time-slicing, which lacks an explicit theoretical rationale but leads to important results.

eral members of an international subsystem were approximately equally strong. *Multipolarity* is a condition in which there are some alliance constellations or major powers of approximately equal strength, with many minor powers. Kaplan suggests that the presence of five to nine nonaligned major powers makes possible the operation of multipolar balance of power politics in a system with 15 or so members.[59] *Bipolarity* and *tripolarity* characterize systems in which the preponderance of world power is shared among two or three units of a system, respectively. *Unipolarity* is present when one actor or coalition accounts for more than about 40 percent of total capabilities within a system, provided no other unit has a significant proportion in comparison.

In addition to totalling the number of major powers or coalitions within a system, a second aspect of a power distribution is what Kaplan refers to as the "tightness" or "looseness" of a system. A *tight* system exists when there are no members outside the control of major poles and every unit is committed within a bloc. A *loose* system contains independent members that have not joined coalitions or blocs. Most historical international systems have been loose in modern times, even unipolar ones, where a dominant state has tolerated—perhaps temporarily—small independent states on its periphery. Looseness can result from the existence of noncolonized territories, but most often looseness is related to the completeness of membership within blocs: nonaligned states are regarded by Rosecrance as "unappropriated resources." One semantic confusion in the argument over the stability of bipolarity concerns the notion of looseness within the world polity. Those who contend that bipolarity is unstable usually describe loose bipolarity, and those who argue for the stability of bipolarity have a tight bipolar system in mind. In specifying world power stratification one must be prepared to estimate tightness or looseness within the system as a second distinctive conceptual variable.[60]

Thus, should one bloc prove victorious in a bipolar struggle, a move from bipolarity to unipolarity would signal a transformation in subsystems. To demarcate a year that divides two such systems is to determine when a weaker pole actually breathes its last, and the day on which hostilities terminate would usually be used to date the shift. A new subsystem might also begin when regional power has undergone a reconstruction, such that the territorial pie is newly sliced. International systems terminate when mem-

---

[59] Kaplan, *System and Process in International Politics*, p. 22. A multipolar system must have at least several middle and minor powers, so a lower limit of five major powers must be understood to apply to multistate systems only.

[60] See a clarificatory essay by Wolfram Hanrieder, "The International System: Bipolar or Multibloc?" *Journal of Conflict Resolution*, IX (September 1965), 299–308. Hanrieder equates "symmetrical polarity" with our use of "tight" as a feature of a power distribution; "asymmetry," with a "loose" distribution.

bers obtain significantly different power relations, particularly at the conclusion of wars between major powers. One bipolar subsystem, accordingly, could follow another if military roles played by each actor change because of defeat, victory, or termination of conflict.

More formally, subsystem transformation may be defined by either of the following two conditions:

1. A new system begins if there is a change in power distribution, such as the following:

   a. A major power is demoted through military defeat.
   b. One or more middle powers rise to major power status.
   c. A major power enters the system anew or exits from the region.
   d. New military alliances between major powers are contracted.
   e. Existing military alliances involving major powers collapse, or membership reshuffles.

2. A new system begins when a dramatic event precipitates a trend toward tightening or loosening in power distribution, such as the following:

   a. A previously nonaligned major power becomes an exclusive ally of another major power.
   b. An alliance among major powers develops a schism.
   c. A major power enters the system anew or exits from the region. bloc arrangements.
   d. New military alliances between major powers are contracted.

In Section 9.5 some 21 subsystems are delineated in accordance with these criteria, so no further elaboration will be attempted here. It is reassuring to be aware, however, that in Frank Denton's analysis of data on war frequency virtually the same time periods emerge as empirically separate from each other.[61]

9.5 SUBSYSTEM MEMBERS, POLES, AND TIME BOUNDARIES: EUROPE, ASIA, HAWAII

Delineation of territorial and time boundaries for international subsystems in practice involves a great deal of trial-and-error experimentation and the choice of whether to consider members or years as fundamental defining characteristics. The task involves a chicken-and-egg dilemma. Our procedure has been to posit core members for each set of subsystems and then

---

[61] Denton, "Some Regularities in International Conflict."

to fix an arbitrary starting point in time. A consideration of members, timing, and poles may then proceed separately (Table 9–5).

For Europe obvious core members are France, England, Spain, Prussia (Germany), and the former Austrian Habsburg Empire. The date of 1648 may be selected as an initial starting point because in that year the Peace of Westphalia concluded the Thirty Years War by redrawing European boundaries.

China and Japan are central members of any East Asian subsystem. It was in 1689 that China signed its first modern treaty (with Imperial Russia), the effect of which was to slow down Russian expansion in Asia.

Until the unification of the Hawaiian Islands by King Kamehameha I in 1810, various rulers of the islands of Hawaii, Oahu, and Maui controlled the most significant members of Hawaiian subsystems. Foreign penetration, which did not occur until the late eighteenth century, was undertaken by France, Great Britain, and the United States. The lack of early records dictates 1738 as an initial year, when a conference between the kings of Oahu, Maui, and Hawaii resulted in a cease-fire of a war that might otherwise have meant the unification of the islands under the joint rule of Alapainui of Hawaii and his brother, Kamehamehanui of Maui.

9.5.1 European Subsystems (1648–1963)

The territorial multistate system of Europe was sanctioned formally in 1648, when conferences in two cities of Westphalia brought to a conclusion the last of the religious wars arising out of the Reformation and Counter-Reformation. The terms of the Peace of Westphalia applied only to Western Europe from 1649 until the wars of Louis XIV attracted attention from eastern countries; after Louis was subdued, the Peace of Utrecht in 1713 became a fully European settlement. The scope of the European subsystem expanded to include the United States and Canada briefly during World War I, and permanently in a North Atlantic subsystem after World War II (Figure 9–2). Ten subsystems are found between 1649, the first year in which the Westphalia settlement took effect, and 1963. The number of subsystems totals one more than Rosecrance proposes, since he does not consider the years 1649 to 1738.[62]

---

[62] The most useful secondary sources have been David Jayne Hill, *A History of Diplomacy in the International Development of Europe* (New York: Longmans, Green, 1914); R. B. Mowat, *The European States System* (London: Oxford University Press, 1923); and Rosecrance, *Action and Reaction in World Politics*. Many other sources should be consulted for a comprehensive grasp of the ten time periods. The early separation of Northeast from Western European subsystems is treated by Mowat, p. 32.

TABLE 9–5
Time Boundaries of 21 International Subsystems

Region	Dates	Power Distribution
I. Western Europe	1649–1713	Loose bipolarity
II. Europe	1714–1789	Loose multipolarity
III. Europe	1790–1814	Tight bipolarity
IV. Europe	1815–1822	Tight multipolarity
V. Europe	1823–1847	Loose bipolarity
VI. Europe	1848–1871	Loose multipolarity
VII. Europe	1872–1890	Loose unipolarity
VIII. Europe	1891–1918	Tight bipolarity
IX. Europe	1919–1945	Loose bipolarity
X. North Atlantic	1946–1963	Tight bipolarity
XI. East Asia	1689–1842	Loose unipolarity
XII. East Asia	1843–1895	Tight bipolarity
XIII. East Asia	1896–1913	Loose bipolarity
XIV. East Asia	1914–1945	Tight tripolarity
XV. East Asia	1946–1954	Tight bipolarity
XVI. Asia	1955–1963	Tight tripolarity
XVII. Hawaii	1738–1758	Loose tripolarity
XVIII. Hawaii	1759–1782	Tight tripolarity
XIX. Hawaii	1783–1795	Tight bipolarity
XX. Hawaii	1796–1818	Tight unipolarity
XXI. Hawaii	1819–1898	Loose unipolarity

I WESTERN EUROPE 1649–1713

The Peace of Westphalia consisted of three treaties, two signed at Münster and one at Osnabrück. One effect of the treaties was to deprive of any legitimacy the previously vague claims to overlordship on the part of the Holy Roman Empire and the papacy. The Austrian Empire, as a result of several innovations in diplomatic protocol, was no longer *primus inter pares* as a successor to the Roman Empire but, instead, merely a great power on equal footing with France, England, and Spain. The independence of smaller states was sanctioned as well—formally in the case of the United Netherlands and by implication in an agreement to respect religious choices of both Protestant and Catholic rulers. Due to success at Westphalia in confining the House of Habsburg to as small a share of Europe as possible, a multipolar arrangement was created on paper. Louis XIV subsequently embarked upon a series of wars to advance the frontiers of France while Habsburg power was receding and provoked instead a bipolar framework. Several coalitions of states formed to defend the equalitarian nature of Westphalia, only to disperse after Louis conceded to various small-scale settlements, ensuring a looseness to the lingering bipolarity. The War of the Spanish Succession was a different matter. Charles II of Spain had willed his dominions to the Bourbons, a situation that would have rendered

FIGURE 9-2
Map of Europe

France the undisputed master of Southern Europe. Ten years of fighting between Louis and his adversaries ensued and finally resulted in a stalemate. A peace congress met at Utrecht in 1712 and 1713, with a conference the following year at Rastadt, in order to restore a European multipolar equilibrium in a manner not to be contested by Habsburgs or Bourbons for some time to come.

Major powers of the period were Austria, England, France, and Spain. Neither the Ottoman Empire nor Russia sent delegates to Westphalia. Sweden, which for some twenty years had been fighting Russia, was but a middle power on a periphery of the Western European subsystem while acting as a major power in a Northeast European subsystem. The second middle power was the Netherlands, a member of the Triple Alliance (with England and Sweden) against Louis XIV. Brandenburg was consolidating itself to make a bid for a major power status in the next subsystem. Minor powers included Baden, Bavaria, Bremen, Denmark, Genoa, Hamburg, Hanover, Hesse, Lorraine, Mecklenburg, Papal States, Portugal, Savoy, Saxony, Switzerland, Tuscany, Two Sicilies, Venice, Württemberg. Most of these "squirrels" were involved in the Thirty Years War and the subsequent Peace of Westphalia.

II EUROPE 1714–1789

After Utrecht a dualism between Western and Eastern subsystems was impossible; the theater of struggles for power redistribution moved to Central Europe. A haphazard series of wars arose, with no major disturbance to the European equilibrium and few infractions of a balance of power ethic. Prussia's seizure of Silesia in 1740 was an exception, and this signaled its new status as a major power. Sweden's empire eroded to the advantage of Russia and Prussia; the Elector of Hanover acceded to the throne of England; France, chastised for Louis XIV's policy of excess, was anxious to be a peacemaker; Spain endeavored to drive Austria from Italy. A kaleidoscopic web of temporary alliances and abortive machinations kept the system multipolar and loose up to the outbreak of the French Revolution.

The persistence of a balance of power is often attributed to a plethora of great powers, and seven such countries vied during the eighteenth century —Austria, England, France, Prussia, Russia, Spain, and Sweden. Middle powers, the Ottoman Empire and the United Netherlands, were much weaker than the new "elephants" of Europe. Minor powers were Baden, Bavaria, Bremen, Denmark, Genoa, Hamburg, Hanover/Brunswick, Hesse, Lorraine up to the absorption by France in 1766, Mecklenburg, Papal States, Poland, Portugal, Savoy, Saxony, Switzerland, Tuscany, Two Sicilies, Venice, Württemberg.

III   EUROPE 1790–1814

The French Revolution erupted in the midsummer of 1789. Louis XVI was imprisoned and later guillotined. The Revolution challenged not only feudalism but also property rights of foreigners residing in France (which had been guaranteed at Westphalia). Nationalistic propaganda was spread to inflame neighboring states, and French troops were dispatched abroad. In 1796, Austrian threats to Paris provoked the Girondins to war. The Netherlands, many German States, Poland, Switzerland, and most parts of Italy were conquered, and several satellite republics were established. Coalitions among the remaining major powers fought first the Robespierrists and later the armies of Napoleon Bonaparte until his decisive defeat at the Battle of Waterloo.

The major antagonists of France consisted of Austria, England, Prussia, and Russia. A citizen force fighting for the glory of France and for the principle of national determination was a far cheaper and more reliable military instrument than mercenary armies of the monarchical powers; one major power could therefore hold the rest at bay for a while.

Two middle powers, Spain and Sweden, were incapable of thwarting Napoleon's designs. Spain dropped to minor power status in 1796, though later its own nationalism was aroused to stand off the French armies. In Sweden the throne was occupied by the Frenchman Bernadotte, but in 1790 Russia so took advantage of Sweden's poor finances that Stockholm was relegated to a lesser role. A third middle power, the Ottoman Empire, was still active but definitely peripheral in the Napoleonic struggles. The Netherlands fell under French control by 1795.

Most of the minor powers were absorbed into the Napoleonic Empire: Baden in 1806, Bremen in 1809, Genoa in 1806, Hamburg in 1810, Hanover in 1805, Hesse in 1807, Mecklenburg in 1808, Papal States in 1797; Poland was partitioned and disappeared as an independent state in 1795; Saxony disappeared in 1806, Switzerland in 1802, Tuscany in 1807, Venice in 1797, and Württemberg in 1806. Bavaria, Denmark, Sardinia, Portugal, and Sicily remained autonomous.

IV   EUROPE 1814–1822

The defeat of Napoleon necessitated cooperation among the great powers of Europe, and the same powers were agreed that a peace settlement at the Congress of Vienna should be more lasting than Westphalia or Utrecht. "Legitimacy" rather than "nationality" was the basis of the new territorial division; Russia and Austria interpreted the legitimacy principle as bestowing a right upon great powers to decide jointly upon measures for preserving the new order. The Concert of Europe was established to facilitate major power consultation whenever disturbances were perceived to threaten the Vienna settlement. The Concert, in fact, intervened to put down nationalist uprisings in Spain and in Italy, though Great Britain was reluctant to give any sign of support to either venture. The view that the Vienna system should remain intact and multipolarity tightly maintained was not shared at all by Britain, and in France there was a tendency to avoid extremes both of the right and left. When the Concert met at Verona in 1822, Britain severed ties with the Concert as Tsar Alexander attempted to exorcise yet another nationalistic specter in Spain.

Actually, the plenary session of the Congress of Vienna met only to ratify a decision reached by an executive committee composed of the major powers. France, represented by the skillful Talleyrand, was admitted to great power status by the victors, Austria, Great Britain, Prussia, and Russia. The Ottoman Empire was "promoted" to the rank of major power after Vienna as a counterweight to offset the "army of Europe," as Alexander preferred his military force to be called. Sweden, the Netherlands, Spain, and Piedmont emerged as middle powers. The latter was to form a nucleus for the unification of Italy by midcentury. Spain barely retained middle power status.

A large number of minor powers returned to the system: Baden, Bavaria, Bremen, Denmark, Hamburg, Hanover, Hesse (Electoral and Grand Ducal), Mecklenburg, Papal States, Portugal, Saxony, Switzerland, Tuscany, Two Sicilies, Venice, Württemberg. Greece began a successful revolt despite the reactionary Concert in 1821. Montenegro and Serbia, formerly independent, now began to play a more active role against Austria and the Porte. The Carbonari of Piedmont (1821) and Sicily (1821–22) qualify as members, since their use of force in domestic quarrels was counteracted by Concert intervention.

V EUROPE 1823–1847

British departure from the Concert did not serve to terminate the practice of mutual consultation. Only the illusion that the great powers always could reach a consensus was shattered. Britain and France became exponents of a progressive conservatism; the three Eastern powers continued to wave flags of reaction and legitimacy. A very loose bipolar division arose without an open breach.[63] Austria, Prussia, and Russia at one point permitted Britain and France to deal with Spain and Portugal as they wished; France and Austria supervised Germany and Italy; the three emperors watched over Eastern Europe, and the fate of the Ottoman Empire was a

---

[63] Rosecrance refers to the period as "quasibipolar," but perhaps his concept of "bi-multipolarity" is more applicable. If so, the bi-multipolarity of Subsystem V did not enjoy the advantages specified in his later formulation. Rosecrance, *Action and Reaction in World Politics,* pp. 243–47; "Bipolarity, Multipolarity, and the Future."

problem left to Russia until 1839. The two groups had agreed to disagree only in theory, while agreeing in practice by dint of accepting separate spheres of non-influence. Paris began to break its entente with England after the restoration of the French monarchy in 1830, and the three reactionary powers of the East were more concerned in this period with internal problems. The Concert became a looser device, more for ratifying moves of the great powers than for deliberating on new joint policies.

The major powers of Subsystem V were identical with those of the previous subsystem. Internal dissension in Spain reduced that country to minor power status in 1823; the Netherlands split into Belgium and Holland in 1830. Only Sweden and Sardinia (Piedmont) remained as middle powers.

Moldavia and Wallachia became minor powers in 1829. Due to foreign interventions on the Iberian peninsula, short-lived members include Portuguese Liberals (1823–1834), Spanish Republicans (1823, 1833–1840), Basques (1833–1839), Moderate Spanish (1833–1840), and Carlists (1823, 1833–1840). Familiar as minor powers were Baden, Bavaria, Bremen, Denmark, Greece, Hamburg, Hanover, Hesse, Mecklenburg, Montenegro, Papal States, Portugal, Saxony, Serbia, Switzerland, Tuscany, Two Sicilies, Württemberg. Modena became a minor power in 1847, when it entered an alliance with Austria.

VI   EUROPE 1848–1871

The age of legitimacy and conservatism, prolonged artificially since the Congress of Vienna at the behest of the Concert of great powers, was traumatized by a series of revolutionary outbursts in 1848. Austria, France, Germany, Hungary, Italy, Russia, Wallachia, and the Ottoman Empire were involved in one way or another. As a result, liberalism was adopted with enthusiasm in Sardinia, while autocracies became more aware of public opinion. Internal maintenance problems assumed highest priority. By 1871 German and Italian states were unified under the leadership of Prussia and Sardinia, respectively. France under Napoleon III abandoned her entente with England and sought territories on the Rhine, in Mexico, and annexation of Nice and Savoy as a compensation for supporting Sardinia against Austria. The Concert became a nullity, and a go-it-alone multipolarity replaced the former consensus of great powers. The wars of Sardinia (with Austria and France), and Prussia (with Denmark and Austria) were of little concern to other countries, who could find many rewards elsewhere.

Major powers gained a new member in 1860, when most of Italy became unified under Victor Emmanuel of Sardinia. The Ottoman Empire clearly had slumped to middle power status by the outcome of the Crimean War. Sweden remained at a middle level.

Minor powers began to evaporate as Italy and Germany became unified. Parma, after entering as an ally of Austria in 1851, was annexed to Sardinia in 1860 along with Modena, Tuscany, and the Two Sicilies; Venice and the Papal States finally succumbed in 1866 and 1870. Bremen, Hamburg, Hanover, Electoral Hesse, Mecklenburg, and Saxony joined the North German Confederation headed by Prussia by 1866; by 1870 Baden, Bavaria, Grand Ducal Hesse, and Württemberg were absorbed completely. Wallachia and Moldavia merged into the Rumanian state in 1859. Belgium, Denmark, Greece, Holland, Montenegro, Portugal, Serbia, Spain, and Switzerland were still minor powers. A group of revolting Herzegovinans attracted outside intervention in 1862 but were unable to achieve an autonomous position, as was a Hungarian rebel faction in 1848–1849, which was crushed by a joint force of Russians and Austrians.

VII EUROPE 1872–1890

In order to round out the German Empire, Otto von Bismarck felt obliged to unleash the well-disciplined army of Prussia against France in 1870. German armies victoriously entered Paris the following year and occupied France; the territories of Alsace and Lorraine were annexed. The German victory once again failed to evoke the attention of the Concert, and a laissez-faire attitude toward foreign affairs prevailed. As soon as German troops left France in 1871, Bismarck believed, it would be to the advantage of the Reich to erect a new concert and alliance system with its nexus in Berlin; France was to be shut out of the alliance system. Germany thenceforth espoused the cause of peace abroad and semiliberal nationalistic principles at home. The effect was a loose unipolar system; alliances no longer contended with one another, preferring to accord supremacy to an army that had proved itself capable of winning in a matter of weeks.

Though France remained isolated and weakened, Germany stopped short of eliminating her neighbor from the major power category. Major and middle powers were identical with those of the previous period. But minor powers were far fewer in number, owing to the completion of German and Italian unification. Belgium, Denmark, Greece, Holland, Montenegro, Portugal, Rumania, Serbia, Spain, and Switzerland remained. Bulgaria became militarily independent in 1878, although it was not accorded full sovereign status until later.

VIII EUROPE 1891–1918

An entente between France and Russia in August of 1891 signaled a move toward bipolarity, which was consummated by a full-fledged military alliance three years later. Germany looked to England in vain and had to remain content with Austria in 1879 and Italy in 1882 as alliance partners. British neutrality might have kept the situation more fluid, but the Anglo-

French Entente Cordiale of 1904 provided an incentive for Germany to step up development of a strong navy even further. Bipolar rivalry between the Triple Alliance and the Triple Entente tightened but failed to interest middle or minor powers with one important exception, the Kingdom of Serbia. Intent on achieving irredentist ambitions, Belgrade encouraged, supplied, and often intervened on behalf of South Slav peoples, who chafed under Ottoman and Austrian yokes. The assassination of Archduke Ferdinand, who was at the time in disfavor in Vienna, triggered a monomaniacal desire on the part of the Austrians to punish Serbia, to whom the assassination plot was linked. Nothing would stop Austria; and when Germany and Russia stood firmly behind their respective allies, Austria and Serbia, the cataclysm of World War I broke forth.

The major powers of Austria, France, Germany, Great Britain, Italy, and Russia were augmented in 1917 by the entry of the United States into the European war. The Ottoman Empire and Sweden remained as middle powers. The defeat of Austria by 1917 and Germany in 1918 rendered these two countries middle powers.

Belgium, Bulgaria, Denmark, Greece, Holland, Montenegro, Portugal, Rumania, Serbia, Spain, and Switzerland continued as minor powers. Albania became independent in 1912, and Norway broke away from Sweden in 1905. Albania, however, was occupied from 1914 to 1921. World War I attracted the participation of Australia, Canada, New Zealand, and the Union of South Africa in 1914. Four new members were formed and thereby joined the European subsystem in 1917, namely, Czechoslovakia, Finland, Poland, and the Ukraine. The revolution in Russia, which reduced that country to a middle power, gave rise to two new entities: the so-called Red Finns attempted an abortive revolution in Finland in 1917, while groups of Russian émigrés and nobles launched a series of counter-revolutionary attacks on the Bolsheviks in 1918. The Irish began their revolt from the United Kingdom in 1916.

IX   EUROPE 1919–1945

Though the Treaty of Versailles did not actually impose a harsh peace upon Germany, the possibility of a return to multipolarity was marred due to the punitive manner in which the peace was administered. Reparation payments were demanded even when economic conditions deteriorated. Leaders of France, in particular, blamed Germany for the war, and they sought to erect a network of alliances around Germany by becoming aligned with Poland and Czechoslovakia. In Italy the Versailles settlement wounded national pride as well, and Benito Mussolini as early as 1922 assumed the role of a charismatic spokesman for an aggressive nationalism that the League of Nations was not able to constrain. Though Germany resumed major power status by 1925, it was not until after Hitler came to power in Germany in 1933 that the bipolar system concocted by France suddenly turned to devour its maker. Germany moved troops into the Rhineland, annexed Austria without a shot, and gained access to Czechoslovakia through the Munich agreement. Aligned with Italy and the USSR by 1939, Germany declared war and moved into Eastern Europe, Denmark, the Netherlands, Belgium, Norway, France, and North Africa.

American failure to enter the League of Nations as a full member was an indication of its withdrawal from a role in the European subsystem after 1920. Only after France, Germany, Great Britain, Italy, and the Soviet Union were embroiled in war did the United States return as a major power (in the early part of 1942). Canada, however, remained in the League and achieved status as a middle power in 1919 due to its wartime industrialization. The former Austro-Hungarian Dual Monarchy split into two minor powers, Austria and Hungary, with newly independent Polish and Czechoslovak states also attaining a minor rating; Austria was absorbed by Germany in 1938. Sweden, staying out of both world wars, retained middle power status. The USSR, having incorporated the Ukraine in 1920, resumed major power status and defeated the émigrés and nobles in 1922.

Several new minor powers emerged. Three states bordering on the Baltic Sea achieved independence by 1919—Estonia, Latvia, and Lithuania. Luxembourg also became independent in 1919. Ireland continued its war of independence with the British until 1922. Montenegro and Serbia merged in the Kingdom of Serbs, Croats, and Slovenes. Iceland declared its independence from Nazified Denmark in 1944.

Many minor powers were absorbed by the Axis powers. In 1939 World War II broke out, and Albania was seized by Italy; Germany overran Belgium, Denmark, Luxembourg, Holland, Norway, and Poland in 1940; Yugoslavia fell in 1941; Greece and France were absorbed in 1942. Russia seized the Baltic states in 1940. Czechoslovakia was carved up by the Third Reich, though the state of Slovakia was left temporarily carved out. Other minor powers remained autonomous: Bulgaria, Finland, Hungary, Portugal, Rumania, Spain, Switzerland, and Turkey, which had been stripped of most of its European territories. Outside support was dispatched in 1939 by Australia, New Zealand, and the Union of South Africa, and in 1942 by Brazil. Several evanescent members appeared on the scene: Hungarian Communist elements appeared in 1919–1920 and 1944–1945, Spanish Falangists from 1936 to 1939, Greek Communists and Yugoslav Partisans in 1941, Italian Democrats in 1943, Democratic Rumanians and Bulgarians in 1944.

The era concluded with the defeat of Italian fascism in 1944 and German nazism in 1945. Italy was demoted to middle power status; Germany and Austria were occupied by the military forces of the four victorious allied powers.

X   NORTH ATLANTIC 1946–1963

Russian, American, British, and French armies remained in defeated Germany from 1945 until 1949. Western powers could maintain a demilitarized Germany with a skeleton crew of soldiers, but the Soviet army stationed between Berlin and Moscow forced the states of Eastern Europe into the grip of Communist Party governments. In 1946, Albania, Bulgaria, Hungary, Poland, and Rumania were already Soviet satellites. Czechoslovakia fell under in 1947. In a short time an "iron curtain" had descended to demarcate a boundary between contenders in the tightest bipolar struggle of modern times. By 1963 much of the solidarity within both camps was fading, however. Yugoslavia and Albania were no longer even indirectly controlled by Moscow; Rumania was moving to sever ties with Comecon, the Soviet consultative body for economic development in Eastern Europe. France had rejected British entry into the European Economic Community in 1963 and was developing an independent nuclear capability.

The USA and the USSR were the principal clashing superpowers. Britain, a third great power due to its early possession of nuclear weapons, abandoned its role as a nuclear power by the early 1960s. France was consigned to the status of a middle power, along with Canada, Italy, Sweden, and West Germany (after independence in 1949). Minor powers were Albania, Austria (independent in 1955), Belgium, Bulgaria, Czechoslovakia, Denmark, East Germany (no longer officially occupied after 1949), Finland, Greece, Hungary, Hungarian rebels (in 1956), Iceland, Ireland, Luxembourg, Netherlands, Norway, Poland, Portugal, Rumania, Spain, Switzerland, Turkey, and Yugoslavia. Greek Communists were defeated in 1949 after a three-year struggle.

9.5.2   Asian Subsystems (1689–1963)

Probably the first conscious recognition of an East Asian subsystem occurred in 1689, when China contracted the Treaty of Nerchinsk with Russia. After that date it is possible to isolate six subsystems, five within East Asia exclusively, and one modern Asian subsystem. The reason for a bifurcation between East and South Asia was initially that China was dominant in the East and did not move very far in the direction of India; many developments in Central Asia had no impact upon such countries as Japan. The understanding between Britain and France on their respective spheres of influence effectively transformed the Indochinese peninsula into a buffer between South and East Asian politics (Figure 9–3). When new states emerged from French control in 1954, an awareness of Asian politics as a

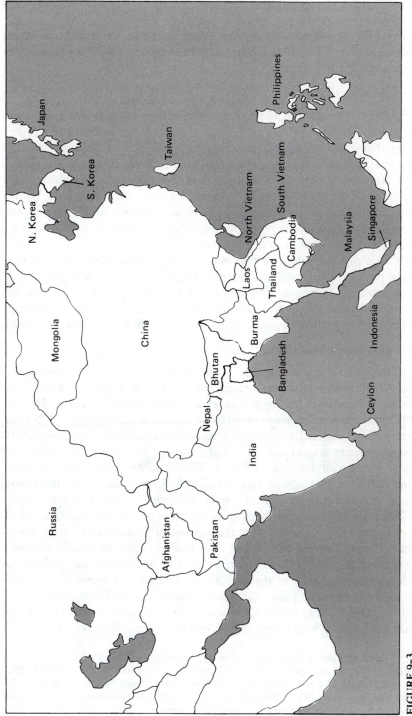

FIGURE 9-3
Map of Asia

347

whole was comprehended in capitals from Tokyo to Kabul. The Bandung Conference of 1955 enabled leaders to consummate a new Pan–Asian spirit in face-to-face interaction.[64]

XI   EAST ASIA 1689–1842

After the abortive Russian Amur Expedition of 1689 the East Asian international subsystem was reaffirmed to be unipolar in character. Japan, having abandoned her interest in continental politics since the sixteenth century, was still pursuing an isolationist policy. Russian expansion slowed down after the Treaty of Nerchinsk. Limited attempts to establish trade were made by the Dutch in the Pescadores, Taiwan, and at Nagasaki, but the Netherlands chose not to colonize. In the later years of China's long hegemony in the Far East, her supremacy was assumed loosely to exist, and there was no concerted attempt to test her strength.

China was the only major power, with Japan and Russia as abdicating middle powers. The so-called "Hermit Kingdom," Korea, was joined as a minor power by France in 1790 and Great Britain in about 1793, when the two countries first sought to establish trading relations with China. Portugal had established itself in Macao in 1557 and strengthened its hold after 1833.

XII   EAST ASIA 1843–1895

The easy victory of England in the Opium War by 1842 changed the East Asian power situation dramatically. Though capitalist states were interested primarily in trading privileges, a decentralization of power throughout China encouraged each country to obtain local commercial concessions, which were tied to political arrangements such as extraterritoriality. Western powers cooperated in a tight bipolar struggle to maintain and enlarge spheres of interest in China. France secured privileges in south China, adjacent to her well-established sphere of influence in Indochina; Britain concentrated on central China; Germany seized Tsingtao; Russia advanced over Siberia and focused its attention on Manchuria. Japan, having emerged from seclusion after the mission of Commodore Perry, moved toward Korea, Taiwan, and Fukien. The United States, proclaiming a most-favored-nation principle, attempted to cash in on incremental concessions made by China to each of the powers. As a result, the arena of East Asia was widened to encompass—the Spice Islands and the Philippines.

The Opium War brought France, Great Britain, and Russia to major power status along with China. Japan remained a middle power until 1895,

[64] Some succinct sources are Harold M. Vinacke, *A History of the Far East in Modern Times*, 6th ed. (New York: Appleton-Century-Crofts, 1959); Harley F. MacNair and Donald F. Lach, *Modern Far Eastern International Relations*, 2d ed. (New York: Van Nostrand, 1955). References cited in both volumes should be perused for a more thorough understanding of Asian subsystems.

when it demoted and exchanged ranks with China. The Netherlands, newly colonizing in the East Indies, and Spain, with control in the Philippines, constituted new middle powers. Several groups who resisted colonization joined Korea and Portugal, the latter now controlling Timor, as minor powers: the Achinese, Balinese (lost independence in 1849), Banjermasinese (up to 1863), Boninese (up to 1860), and the Vietnamese (up to 1885) peoples. During the Meiji Restoration, separatist Satsuma and Choshu clans became an object of both foreign and domestic hostilities (in 1862–1864).

XIII   EAST ASIA 1896–1913

During the years between the Opium War and the Sino-Japanese War of 1894–1895, no important dispute arose among the exploiting powers; with so much of China available for exploitation, a quarrel over a division of bountiful spoils seemed quite unnecessary. When Japan unexpectedly proved victorious in its war with China in 1894–1895, the relative power distribution of members of the East Asian subsystem became more sharply estimable. Japan's rapid industrial development and logistical advantage had propelled her toward a role as the strongest power in Asia, though only a second-class power when compared to major powers within contemporary European subsystems. France, Germany, and Russia together compelled Japan to revise the terms of the Treaty of Shimonoseki in 1895, thereby creating an independent Korea and reducing the likelihood that Japan might use some clauses of the treaty as a shoehorn to further continental domination. Bipolarity resulted. The absorption of Great Britain, Germany, and the United States with matters outside East Asia meant a loose, rather than a tight, stratification of power as the nineteenth century drew to a close. Russia served as a protector of China, and France's European-oriented alliance with Russia constrained any aggressive Asian ambitions the latter might have contemplated. It was assumed that European powers were in favor of a balance between China and Japan, but this required a more active participation by outside powers. Japan continued to industrialize and grow more powerful. Insofar as Russia's cooperation with China appeared to tip scales on the side of a future Russian hegemony in Asia, the British became disturbed as the new century opened. The so-called revolution in Far Eastern politics begun by the Anglo-Japanese Alliance of 1902 was conceived as an effort to contain Russia, rather than to trigger, as it did, Japan's long series of successes until she achieved dominion over most of East and Southeast Asia by the early 1940s. Initially, however, the alliance served to encourage Japan to tackle Russia. The surprising victory by Japan in the Russo-Japanese War foreshadowed things to come, but the Japanese were content to accept American mediation in 1905 for a settlement restoring a loose bipolarity in East Asia.

France, Great Britain, and Japan remained as major powers, Holland as a middle power, but China and Russia were demoted to middle power status due to their respective wartime defeats in 1895 and 1905. The United States entered the system as a middle power by unseating Spain from the Philippines in 1898, though it was first necessary to defeat a Philippine insurrectionary element that until 1902 declared itself independent. Korea fell under the sway of Japan in 1905; and Germany seized the Chinese peninsula of Shantung in 1897, gaining a minor foothold. The Achinese were finally defeated by the Dutch in 1908. Portugal maintained itself as a "squirrel" throughout the period.

XIV   EAST ASIA 1914–1945

The outbreak of World War I in Europe provided an unparalleled opportunity for Japan to increase its power in the East Asian subsystem. Its first move was to seize Germany's Shantung peninsula on a pretext of facilitating the transfer of the German port of Tsingtao to China after the war. As of 1917 both Russia and China ceased temporarily to be unified entities, and European powers were consumed first with world war and then with internal economic reconstruction. France and Britain tended to co-operate more with the United States on Asian matters; but though World War I left the United States in an even stronger position relative to other members of the East Asian subsystem, an American return to "normalcy" implied at most a very slowly growing role in the East Asian international subsystem. Japan, now democratically functioning, agreed at the Washington Conference of 1921 to a distribution of power that could be "balanced." But the 5:5:3 ratio in naval strength, in which Japan was to grow no larger than three-fifths the size of either the British or French navies, still left her the supreme power in East Asia. Japan's Manchurian invasion of 1931 and subsequent establishment of the puppet state Manchukuo were contested only verbally. After moving as far inland as Inner Mongolia, Japanese forces moved southward to conquer China in 1936. The advance on China, how-ever, was occurring as the strength of the USSR began to reassert itself in Asia; and Moscow provided aid for the Kuomintang, thus reenforcing a tripolar constellation composed of Japan, China, and three Western powers —Britain, France, and the United States. After the Pearl Harbor bombing in late 1941, which brought the United States into the Pacific war, Japan was opposed by nearly every other power in Asia, though the major burden of the struggle was borne by Commonwealth countries and the United States and drew the former into the East Asian subsystem for the first time in 1940.

Subsystem XIV involved a major change in power on the part of France and Great Britain, who had retrenched to the middle category in 1914 and dropped to minor power status in 1941. Former middle powers remained at substantially the same level, though Holland was reduced to a minor power by dint of Japanese aggression in 1941. The United States became a major power in 1941, with its forces mobilized for the war; and Japan dropped to the minor power level when it became an American satellite in 1945. The Chinese Revolution supplied some minor power actors due to intervention by the Japanese—namely, the communist faction (1926–1945), and the Sun Chuan-Fang and Wu Pei-Fu groups (1926–1927). Manchukuo emerged in 1932. Mongolia entered the system owing to a treaty with Russia and military combat with Japan, both events taking place in 1936. World War II involved Thailand in 1940 and Australia, Canada, and New Zealand in 1941. Indonesia began its break from the Netherlands in 1945. Portugal retained Macao, but Timor was seized by the Japanese in 1942. German power in East Asia disappeared after 1914.

XV   EAST ASIA 1946–1954

The immediate postwar period consisted of a bipolar contest. The United States established a military presence in Japan and Okinawa; Britain virtually retired from East Asia, maintaining only a precarious hold on Borneo and Hong Kong. France returned to Indochina as a middle power. The increased power of the USSR in Asia became a new factor. The Chinese Communists had achieved victory over the Kuomintang government by 1949. The system tightened by 1950 with the outbreak of the Korean War; and the American involvement revealed that a Western containment of Communist strength would extend even to areas once thought "peripheral." Chinese participation in the war served to remind other powers of the awakening giant of Asia.

The two superpowers, the United States and the Soviet Union, far outdistanced the middle powers—Australia, China, France, Japan (independent as of 1952). The small powers included the newly independent states (with the exception of Holland and New Zealand): the Philippines (independent since 1946); North and South Korea (since 1948); and Taiwan (since 1949). The Vietminh began a successful war of independence from France in 1947; and Indonesians continued their struggle with the Dutch until 1949, when independence was finally granted. Portugal regained Timor at the end of World War II.

XVI   ASIA 1955–1963

Seeds of a three-cornered alignment were sown in 1951, when United Nations forces crossed the thirty-eighth parallel into North Korea over strong objections of India. Delhi immediately withdrew her support from the United Nations' action and began to proselytize throughout the new states of Asia for a policy of nonalignment. Neutralism, India claimed, might succeed in mitigating antagonisms between the two omnipotent blocs of the East and West. The independence of several states in Southeast Asia, and

French withdrawal from Indochina and India by 1954, played into India's hands as she asserted leadership within a new group of states. Following Indonesia's acceptance of a neutralist foreign policy and the Bandung Conference of 1955, tripolarity was established on firmer ground. With the Indochinese buffer gone, the East Asian subsystem merged with the formerly separate South Asian international subsystem. By participating actively at Bandung, establishing supremacy in Tibet in 1959, and later raising the issue of redrawing the Sino-Indian border, the Chinese clearly intruded into the former South Asian subsystem and thereby widened interests of actors in the formerly autonomous bipolar East Asian subsystem. The United States' escalating participation in Vietnam, China's possession of thermonuclear weapons, the Sino-Indian border war, Pakistan's estrangement from the American-sponsored SEATO pact, and a rift between Malaysia and Indonesia brought an end by 1963 to the tripolar house of cards constructed by the neutralist bloc.

The two thermonuclear giants, the United States and the Soviet Union, were major powers. Australia, China, India, and Japan filled the middle position. A large number of minor powers were in various stages of political and economic development: Afghanistan, Burma, Cambodia, Ceylon, Indonesia, North and South Korea, Laos, Malaysia (independent in 1957), Nepal, New Zealand, Pakistan, Philippines, Taiwan, Thailand, Tibet, and North and South Vietnam. The Pathet Lao and Vietcong began concerted guerrilla warfare in 1959, and in the following year the Malayan Communists were defeated. One actor in the Vietnamese revolution was a nationalist element; because it deposed the Diem government in 1963, it merits membership status. Holland departed in 1962, when it agreed to a United Nations settlement awarding West Irian to Indonesia. Portugal lost one of its possessions, Goa, in 1962; British power was restricted to a military presence in Brunei on islands in the Indian Ocean, as it began to phase out its forces on Singapore.

9.5.3 Hawaiian Subsystems (1738–1898)

There were five subsystems in the interstate arena of the Hawaiian islands between 1738, a date from which historical records are more accurate, and 1898, when the United States annexed the islands (Figure 9–4). The initially loose tripolarity of Subsystem XVII broke down into a tight struggle to unify the islands in Subsystems XVIII and XIX. Unipolar dominance, tight in Subsystem XX, was whittled down to a looser form in Subsystem XXI.[65]

---

[65] Major sources are Abraham Fornander, *An Account of the Polynesian Race* (London: Trübner, 1880), II; Ralph S. Kuykendall and A. Grove Day, *Hawaii,* rev.

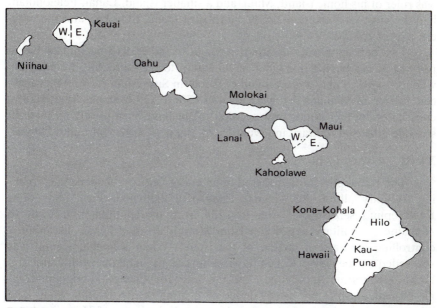

FIGURE 9-4
Map of the Hawaiian Islands

XVII   HAWAII 1738–1758

Alapainui, ruler of the island of Hawaii, nearly succeeded in unifying all of the major Hawaiian islands in 1738. Alongside his brother, who was ruler of Maui, Alapainui's combined military force subdued Molokai and proceeded to Oahu, where victory was almost certain but was contested bitterly by Peleioholani, ruler of Oahu. Rather than pursuing their advantage to obtain what might be a Pyrrhic victory, the rulers of Hawaii and Maui agreed to a cessation of hostilities with Oahu and concluded the Treaty of Naonealaa. Molokai was returned to Peleioholani. The three rulers agreed to establish an informal concert, such that tripolarity would be guaranteed, and any clash between two of the three major powers would be halted at the insistence of the third. A relatively peaceful era, with a loose trifurcation of power, followed until 1758, when the concert arrangement broke down completely as Hawaii and Maui locked horns in the aggressive Kapalipilo Battle.

Domains of the three major powers were roughly equal in size. Alapainui and his successors ruled the largest island, Hawaii. Kamehamehanui

ed. (Englewood Cliffs, N. J.: Prentice-Hall, 1961); Kuykendall, *The Hawaiian Kingdom, 1854–1874* (Honolulu: University of Hawaii Press, 1953); Sylvester K. Stevens, *American Expansion in Hawaii, 1842–1898* (Harrisburg, Pa.: Archives Publishing, 1945).

was ruler of his home island, Maui, and a smaller island, Lanai. Peleioholani had the most far-flung domain, being ruler of Oahu, Molokai, and the western part of Kauai.

Two entities qualify as minor powers. In the eastern portion of Kauai reins of power passed from ineffectual Kaulii to the more wily Kaeokulani, who managed to play a more significant role in Subsystem XIX. An evanescent faction of Mauians that were loyal in 1738–1739 to the usurper, Kauhi, constitutes another minor power: what might have been purely an internal struggle attracted military intervention by rulers of both Oahu and Hawaii.

XVIII   HAWAII 1759–1782

The Kapalipilo Battle ushered in an era of bellicose leaders, each seeking to unify all of the islands. Tripolarity tightened. Five years after Kalaniopuu's seizure of power in 1754 from the legitimate successor to Alapainui, a military expedition from Hawaii invaded Maui, successfully controlling the eastern section of the island. When Kamehamehanui was succeeded by the clever Kahekili, Maui turned its sights on both Oahu and Hawaii, the former for conquest and the latter for revenge. A tripolar struggle ensued. Despite the disadvantage of fighting on two fronts, Maui held its own until the death of its main adversary, Kalaniopuu of Hawaii, whereupon Maui concentrated its forces for the takeover of Oahu. The system became bipolar as of 1782, when Kahekili conquered Oahu.

Once again major powers were Hawaii, Maui, and Oahu. Kauai, a minor power, evidently was unified under Kaeokulani during this period, but records on this point are sketchy. One other minor power deserves mention. Keeaumoku, who was the chief of a local element of the island of Hawaii, became dissatisfied with Kalaniopuu's rule and revolted, most probably in 1763. After the uprising was put down, Keeaumoku fled to Maui, still thirsty for power. Obtaining a following on both Maui and Molokai, Keeaumoku initiated insurrections on both islands in 1767. Rulers of Maui and Oahu buried the hatchet temporarily to bring Keeaumoku to his knees in a joint effort. Only in the latter case was there a definite international implication to the renegade Keeaumoku, so the duration of his faction as a minor power of the subsystem is restricted to the year 1767.

Hawaii, meanwhile, was convulsed with discord. The heir to Kalaniopuu threatened to redistribute land in a manner particularly unattractive to chiefs of the Kona district, and a civil war followed for ten years. The single entity of Hawaii was split up into three minor powers based in the Hilo, Kau and Puna, and Kona and Kohala districts. The latter was led by Kamehameha, who obtained support from a faction led by Kanekoa in 1782 in one of the various battles of the civil war.

Subsystem XVIII, hence, began with three major powers but only Kahekili of Maui survived, Oahu having been defeated and Hawaii trifurcated. Kanekoa and Keeaumoku factions enjoyed their status as minor powers with Kauai.

XIX   HAWAII 1783–1795

The near-victor in an intense bipolar struggle was Kahekili, who solidified his power by taking up residence on Oahu and by establishing a firm alliance with Kaeokulani of Kauai. Molokai fell to Kahekili as spoils of victory over Oahu, and Kamehameha was unable to maintain control of the eastern part of Maui in the Kaumupikai Battle. But with Kahekili no longer a resident on Maui, Kamehameha took advantage of a power vacuum in the middle of the island chain to gain control of Maui, Molokai, and Lanai in 1790, even before his authority had been solidified on his home island. The Kahekili-Kamehameha fight was continued up to 1795, when in the Battle of Nuuanu the army of Kamehameha pushed Kahekili's forces up to the Pali precipice; those who escaped plunging to their death did not contest the new hegemony of Kamehameha. All of the islands except Kauai fell under the rule of Kamehameha I, and opposition on his home island collapsed.

There were two major powers in Subsystem XIX. One was the merged domain of Maui-Oahu-Molokai under Kahekili up to 1795; after 1790 the Kamehameha faction operated as a major power.

Many minor powers were present. The Kanekoa faction ceased to exist in 1783. The Kau and Puna districts under Kiwalao first and later Keoua, and the Hilo district, ruled by Keawemauhili, eventually disappeared in 1795. Kauai remained a minor power that was allied to Kahekili. The penetration by citizens of Great Britain and the United States began in 1785 and 1791, respectively. Though the two countries were major powers at the time in the North American subsystem, their military influence in Hawaii so far was negligible.

XX   HAWAII 1786–1818

Though Kamehameha's unipolar preeminence clearly dates from 1786, the existence of a last independent ruler spurred Kamehameha to sail to Kauai. After heavy storms forced his fleet of warships to turn back on two occasions, Kamehameha soft-pedaled the urgency of a victory that seemed inevitable. His patience was rewarded when Kaumaulii, ruler of Kauai, declared a voluntary surrender of the island in 1810 to the authority of Kamehameha. When a group of Russians, who had been encouraged by Kaumaulii to establish a colony on Kauai in 1796, departed in 1818, Kamehameha I assumed complete dominance of a tight unipolar system.

The sole major power during Subsystem XX was the new Hawaiian Kingdom. Minor powers were Kauai, Russia, Great Britain, and the United

States. Western countries were reluctant to be too imperialistic at a time when Napoleon's European expansionism was still in disrepute.

XXI HAWAII 1819–1898

The position of Kamehameha and his successors loosened considerably during the nineteenth century, though unipolar control was maintained. At various times France, Great Britain, and the United States contemplated forcing Hawaii into an imperialistic cocked hat. France moved first in 1819, but soon realized that conquest would not be so easy. In 1843 an entente was reached between France and Great Britain, in which it was agreed that Hawaii would remain independent. The American president John Tyler was reluctant to go along with the 1843 agreement for fear that his policy of foreign entanglement would be vilified by his opposition party. In the last half of the century American and Oriental settlers arrived in great numbers, gradually taking commercial and economic control of the islands. In due course American settlers sought political arrangements favorable to their economic interests. In 1875 a commercial treaty, known as the Reciprocity Treaty, in effect wedded Hawaii economically to the United States; as the treaty was executed, Hawaii fell into a position of dependency, though still remaining autonomous militarily. In 1887 the United States gained hold over Pearl Harbor by a naval lease, thus elevating Washington to the status of a major power; and two years later American marines were landed at the request of Kamehameha V to suppress the so-called Wilcox Revolt. The monarchy fell in 1893 primarily at the instigation of the American settlers; a republic was declared in 1894; and the islands were annexed by joint resolution of Congress in 1898, terminating the autonomy of Hawaiian subsystems.

Throughout the nineteenth century Hawaii remained a major power. France, Britain, and the United States were middle powers insofar as they could easily have made effective conquest of the islands at almost any time during the period but refrained from doing so. France and Britain were simply too busy with bigger prizes: there was less international competition elsewhere in Oceania. There were no minor powers.

9.6 SUBSYSTEM DATA

The total universe of subsystems is, at this stage, an unknown figure. Multistate China, medieval Europe, Africa, Latin and North America may contain many more cases for analysis. And some of the 21 subsystems so far specified meet our criteria better than others, so a "procrusteanness" measure undoubtedly should be assigned to each case in the sample as a check upon judgmental procedures.

The next step after defining the attributes of each case is to collect data. Conceptual formulations of Deutsch, Etzioni, Rosecrance, and Brecher provide several useful suggestions for comparative subsystem analysis. Indeed, the growing number of ways of categorizing international systems is reaching a point of overload for the researcher. In Chapter 10 a single classificatory scheme, based on structural-functional analysis, is proposed and defined. Data for the 21 subsystems are assembled to map continua that subsume concepts currently in use.

The dependent variable of this volume is the resort to warfare as a means of settling disputes. If particular aspects of international systems, such as alliance configuration, are central to an explanation of wars, it follows that data on alliances and wars need to be assembled. Accordingly, there are some standard compendia containing information on internal and external violence. Pitirim Sorokin enumerates domestic disturbances and foreign wars for national groupings since the sixth century B.C., the time of classical Greece and Rome.[66] Quincy Wright's *A Study of War* (1965) covers military clashes with formal declarations of war, since the year 1480.[67] Lewis F. Richardson's more exhaustive compilation, *Statistics of Deadly Quarrels* (1960), contains nearly all "deadly quarrels" since 1820, except cases with fewer than 316 deaths.[68] More recently, J. David Singer and Melvin Small supplement the three studies for the years 1815 to 1945 along with a list of alliances for the same time period.[69] Hawaiian data are presented in Abraham Fornander's authoritative account.[70] An investigation using these quantitative sources, combined with some judgmental codings, promises to check up on our folklore concerning the functioning of international systems.

---

[66] Pitirim A. Sorokin, *Fluctuations of Social Relationships, War, and Revolution* (New York: American Book Co., 1937), pp. 547–77.

[67] Quincy Wright, *A Study of War*, 2d ed. (Chicago: University of Chicago Press, 1965), pp. 644–49, 1538–40, 1544–47.

[68] Richardson, *Statistics of Deadly Quarrels*, pp. 33–111.

[69] Singer and Small, "Alliance Aggregation and the Onset of War, 1815–1945." In addition, Richardson and Singer and Small are brought up to date with data supplied by Mr. Richard Cady, Bendix Systems Division, Ann Arbor, from a study of low-intensity warfare sponsored by the Office of Naval Research, Contract N00014–66–CO262. See also Small and Singer, "Formal Alliances, 1816–1965: An Extension of the Basic Data," *Journal of Peace Research*, VI, No. 3 (1969), 257–82, which was published after our analysis of the data up to 1945.

[70] Fornander, *An Account of the Polynesian Race*.

chapter 10
Structures and Functions
in International Subsystems

10.1 DESCRIBING INTERNATIONAL SUBSYSTEMS

Power stratification is but one of a number of characteristics useful in describing politically interacting regional clusters of states. In this chapter the aim is to develop a schema for generating and subsuming many variables to differentiate subsystems from one another.

The concept of an "international system" is of recent vintage though the notion was grasped intuitively from time to time by various scholars.[1] During the last few years, however, various conceptual formulations, theoretical models, and proposals for research undertakings have publicized the notion that one may place international systems into qualitative categories and empirical dimensions. One of the earliest explicit pleas for a theoretical guide came from Morton Kaplan, who pointed out that balance of power theory is just a special case of theory concerning power relations among actors of any system.[2] Conceptual innovations of Karl Deutsch and Amitai Etzioni, as discussed in the previous chapter, were the first to focus on subsets of states within the international political arena; though preferring to treat

[1] For a historical perspective on systems analysis, see Charles A. McClelland, *Theory and the International System* (New York: Macmillan, 1966). Use of the term "state system" appears much earlier, however: see R. B. Mowat, *The European States System* (London: Oxford University Press, 1923).

[2] Morton A. Kaplan, *System and Process in International Politics* (New York: Wiley, 1957). Another early plea is in Charles A. McClelland, "Applications of General Systems Theory in International Relations," *Main Currents in Modern Thought*, XII (1955), 27–34.

instances of international collaboration, most of their key variables are applicable to international conflict. Many new terms appear in essays by Fred Riggs and George Modelski in a volume entitled *The International System* (1961).[3] Richard Rosecrance and Michael Brecher have proposed categorizations combining an attention on subsystems with some more traditional notions of balance of power theory; the usefulness of their proposals is demonstrated in a trial coding of a few historical cases. The list of proposed system-theoretical concepts is lengthy indeed and begs for schematization and operationalization.

As the number of formulations increases, dilemmas have arisen. No attempt has been made to harmonize one classificatory scheme with any other, so each proposer in a sense competes to gain acceptance of his virtually untried nomenclature. Any battle to achieve dominance of a classificatory language is likely to obscure the fact that many words have been coined to refer to similar phenomena. Moreover, no feeling of conceptual closure, of having exhausted all possible lacunae, has arrived. The latest framework holds our suspense, as we see newly polished jargon on display. And, more important, the theoretically and empirically oriented behavioral revolution, which encourages conceptual innovations, has yet to deal with a traditional emphasis in international relations on diplomatic history and concrete happenings in the world polity. Indeed, neither traditional chronicles of events nor behavioral games of taxonomic solitaire have moved very far toward producing a systemic theory of international conflict.

As an answer to the need for conceptual consistency, parsimony, and closure in order to launch research on international subsystems, an attempt of Talcott Parsons to formulate a set of mutually exclusive categories that exhaust all components of social systems is relevant.[4] In the field of comparative government, where problems similar to those in international rela-

---

[3] Klaus Knorr and Sidney Verba, eds., *The International System* (Princeton: Princeton University Press, 1961). The essays appeared simultaneously in *World Politics,* XIV (October 1961), 1–239. Fred W. Riggs, "International Relations as a Prismatic System," *ibid.,* pp. 144–81; George Modelski, "Agraria and Industria: Two Models of the International System," *ibid.,* pp. 118–43.

[4] Talcott Parsons and Neil J. Smelser, *Economy and Society* (New York: The Free Press, 1956). See also Charles P. Loomis, *Social Systems* (Princeton: Van Nostrand, 1960), and D. F. Aberle et al., "The Functional Prerequisites of a Society," *Ethics,* LX (January 1950), 100–11. Specific adaptations to political science appear in Robert T. Holt and John E. Turner, *The Political Basis of Economic Development* (Princeton: Van Nostrand, 1966); David Easton, *A Systems Analysis of Political Life* (New York: Wiley, 1965); Karl W. Deutsch, "Integration and the Social System: Implications of Functional Analysis," *The Integration of Political Communities,* eds. Philip E. Jacob and James V. Toscano (Philadelphia: Lippincott, 1964), pp. 179–208. Cf. William C. Mitchell, *Sociological Analysis and Politics* (Englewood Cliffs, N. J.: Prentice-Hall, 1967).

tions have been observed,[5] Gabriel Almond and others[6] have sought to apply Parsonian theory in order to isolate functions common to all political systems, from the most primitive to the most institutionally elaborate. An adaptation of functional theory to an analysis of international subsystems, therefore, is one possible way to order existing partial conceptual frameworks in a theoretically significant fashion. What follows in this chapter is such an attempt.

10.2 FUNCTIONS OF POLITICAL SYSTEMS

Much controversy surrounds the word "function," which often is regarded as metaphysical or as an imputation of teleological notions to nonpurposive phenomena. Clearly neither "function" nor "asymmetry" are actually observed in the real world, so they must be categories understood in the mind of an observer. One confusion concerning the term function is based on the naive view that functions, boundaries, and structures are real, somehow independent of an observer's theories, categories for decoding reality, and prejudices. Instead, structural-functional theory is based on an as-if premise: certain functions are provisionally assumed to exist in order to guide empirical research. By assuming that reproduction, respiration, digestion, excretion, and other such metatasks are biologically required functions for the operation of an organism, the discipline of biology has somewhat more order than might otherwise be the case. And it is conceptual disorder that blocks empirical progress in the study of international subsystems. Just as modern physics rejected the early heuristic wave theory in favor of quantum theory, functional theory in international politics may serve a necessary role in advancing conceptual clarity and empirical progress until a more comprehensive vista can be sketched from a plethora of empirical findings.

In my view, nearly every contemporary attempt to classify systems in terms of operating characteristics has involved certain assumptions about a sequence in which system activities ordinarily proceed in solving a set of

[5] Cf. Roy C. Macridis, *The Study of Comparative Government* (New York: Random House, 1955).

[6] Gabriel A. Almond and James S. Coleman, eds., *The Politics of the Developing Areas* (Princeton: Princeton University Press, 1960); Almond and G. Bingham Powell, Jr., *Comparative Politics* (Boston: Little, Brown, 1966); Modelski, "Agraria and Industria: Two Models of the International System"; Chadwick F. Alger, "Comparison of Intranational and International Politics," *American Political Science Review*, LVII (June 1963), 406–19; Michael Haas, "A Functional Approach to International Organization," *Journal of Politics*, XXVII (August 1965), 498–517. Cf. Don Martindale, ed., *Functionalism in the Social Sciences* (Philadelphia: American Academy of Political and Social Science, 1965); William Mitchell, *The American Polity* (New York: The Free Press, 1962).

elementary problems. Rather than skirting around with merely implicit structural-functional notions because of various difficult assumptions that are supposedly involved,[7] it might be best to be explicit. It would be useful to have a statement outlining structural-functionalism at the international level in any case. Such a model might at least provide something of substance to attack, rather than preserving a shadowy timidity among international system theorists, who venture into structural-functionalism only when no one seems to be looking.

Metaconceptually, nearly everyone would acknowledge that structural-functional theory has few peers in its ability to subsume batteries of concepts within a reasonably orderly set of headings. But before discussing various concepts and hypotheses flowing from structural-functional models, we must first understand the basic terms.

A *function* may be defined as a generic type of activity or task; such a metatask is postulated to be important and necessary for a complete sequence in a system's operations to occur.[8] Functions, in short, have both a behavioral and a temporal aspect. The temporal character is central, since structural-functional theory assumes the existence and paramount importance of behavioral cycles in phenomena. For political systems to be treated in terms of functions, there must be a definable beginning and end to political activities, with a sequence of actions between the two temporal limits; there is a tendency for termination of one task to serve as a trigger for initiation of another task, including a return to a beginning, once all functions have been performed in an appropriate manner. Accordingly, politics is often regarded as a process in which various interests are expressed and pressures exerted to obtain rewards from official or governmental sources;

---

[7] A static equilibrium bias, lack of operationalization, postulates of interdependency, indispensability, and universality are treated most eloquently by proponents. Robert K. Merton, *Social Theory and Social Structure*, rev. ed. (New York: The Free Press, 1957), pp. 19–84; Gabriel A. Almond, "A Developmental Approach to Political Systems," *World Politics*, XVII (January 1965), 183–214. It seems to me that the three postulates constitute superfluous baggage; one can certainly conduct much cumulative empirical research without adhering to a view that functions have some inner logic or necessary patterning, as Chapter 11 will demonstrate. See Ernest Nagel, "A Formalization of Functionalism," *Logic Without Metaphysics* (New York: The Free Press, 1956), Chapter 10.

[8] But there is no reason for complete cycles to occur at all, and only a structural-functional formulation can make analytic sense out of incomplete performance. One can study nondecisions and dysrhythmic processes systematically only with respect to a set of functional categories, for otherwise such notions would elude us. See Peter Bachrach and Morton S. Baratz, "Decisions and Nondecisions: An Analytical Framework," *American Political Science Review*, LVII (September 1963), 632–42; C. S. Whitaker, Jr., "A Dysrhythmic Process of Political Change," *World Politics*, XIX (January 1967), 190–217.

official bodies then deliberate and act; and the behavior of officials eventually feeds back into the body politic, where new demands may originate once again. The notion of a cyclical or sequential character of politics is a familiar analogy, espoused particularly by such group theorists as Earl Latham and David Truman.[9]

Temporally, we may follow a suggestion of David Easton and place functions into three categories (Figure 10–1). Some functions are concerned with *inputs* into authoritative or effective decisionmaking centers; the elites of world politics are generally the major powers. Others are *outputs* from such sources. A third set of functions pertains to *withinputs,* or tasks that take place while elites within these centers convert inputs into outputs, or fail to do so.

Elite-centered activity in international relations, lacking as it does a formal or even effective head of state, will necessarily focus on major powers. Minor powers' actions are not considered to involve a significant political character except in relation to major power confrontations.[10] But such a narrowing of focus provides a more powerful consideration of activities that do involve elites, which we expect to be considered systematically by international relations theorists in terms of systems analysis. The trifurcation of the functional domain, schematized in Figure 10–1, however, does not delineate the content of metatasks; rather, Easton separates distinct phases or loci in the cyclically conceived operation of politics. Accordingly, the

[9] Earl Latham, *The Group Basis of Politics* (Ithaca, N. Y.: Cornell University Press, 1952); David B. Truman, *The Governmental Process* (New York: Knopf, 1951). Cf. Arthur F. Bentley, *The Process of Government* (Bloomington, Ind.: Principia, 1949); Frank J. Goodnow, *Politics and Administration* (New York: Macmillan, 1900); and especially Easton, *A Systems Analysis of Political Life.* Some other important process models include Luther Gulick, "Notes on the Theory of Organization," *Papers on the Science of Administration,* eds. Gulick and L. Urwick (New York: Institute of Public Administration, 1937), pp. 1–46; Harold D. Lasswell, *The Decision Process* (College Park, Md.: Bureau of Governmental Research, 1956); George Modelski, *A Theory of Foreign Policy* (New York: Praeger, 1962); James N. Rosenau, *Public Opinion and Foreign Policy* (New York: Random House, 1961); Herbert J. Spiro, *World Politics* (Homewood, Ill.: Dorsey, 1966), Chapter 3. A group theorist of international relations par excellence is Hans J. Morgenthau, *Politics Among Nations,* 4th ed. (New York: Knopf, 1967).

[10] Similarly, relations between Black Muslim and B'nai B'rith are only of interest to a macroanalysis of a political system when their leaders are involved as actors. One might, however, wish to employ structural-functionalism in a microanalysis of interest groups as a system. So far structural-functionalists have preferred macroanalysis, but such a restraint is not implied by structural-functional analysis per se. Cf. M. B. Nicholson and P. A. Reynolds, "General Systems, the International System, and the Eastonian Analysis," *Political Studies,* XV (February 1967), 12–31; Fred W. Riggs, "Political Development Theory," *Approaches to the Study of Political Science,* eds. Michael Haas and Henry S. Kariel (San Francisco: Chandler, 1970), Chapter 8.

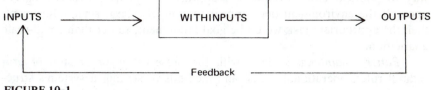

FIGURE 10-1
A Political Cycle

Adapted from David Easton, *A Systems Analysis of Political Life*
(New York: Wiley, 1965).

broad definition of politics espoused in this volume seems quite appropriate, for we are guided by a functional outlook to include all activities pertaining to authoritative allocations of values that affect wide classes of actors within a system.

Ordinarily delineations of functions in social and political systems have ignored the temporal dimension and sought instead to posit on the behavioral or task level exclusively. A result has been lack of clarity and, at the same time, much needless disagreement among structural-functionalists on the content of basic goals of systems. Since functional analyses clarify how actions are instrumental to the fulfillment of fundamental systemic aims, it would seem reasonable to specify some basic problems that all systems must solve in order to remain viable. (Viability, of course, may not be a desirable or necessary outcome of political activity.) Talcott Parsons has recognized this vital need in proposing four "imperatives of any system of action."[11] Because the four imperatives factor out a temporal dimension, they may be explicated independently of inputs, outputs, and withinputs.

Goal attainment is the first of Parsons's imperatives, and it refers to behavior that is directed toward the fulfillment of new blueprints for a system. Political systems are most active when goal attainment is stressed, such as during times of imperialistic take-overs of foreign peoples and territory. Disarmament, decolonization, and the Thousand-Year Reich are further examples of self-consciously utopian conditions toward which countries strive at various times.

Adaptation involves an incremental adjustment of a political system to changes in the environment outside a system. Epidemics, trade imbalances, and developments in nuclear physics may tend to make current politically sanctioned arrangements out of date. Adaptation is involved when demands for quarantining disease carriers, treaty revision, adjustments in currency exchange ratios, and investing in more flexible weapons systems make their

---

[11] Parsons and Smelser, *Economy and Society*. Almond's categories of conversion, responsiveness, regulation, and symbolic capabilities are based on this fourfold Parsonian breakdown. Almond and Powell, *Comparative Politics*.

way to political elites without a reappraisal of goals previously agreed upon. If the environment does appear to compel a large-scale adjustment, then the appropriate task would be goal attainment, rather than small-scale adaptation.

Pattern maintenance deals with the preservation or erosion of procedural rules, operational codes, and methods of staffing a system's structures. Any system, to persist over time, must transmit its values, practices, and procedures to the next generation and to successive occupants of various roles. Of course, socialization of existing and future actors in a system may be imperfect. Demands for a change in current operations may arise when values are themselves dissonant. Activities designed to enculturate new presidents of the United Nations General Assembly, to keep alliance partners together on policy stands in various crises, and to prevent dramatic shifts in international power distributions are aimed at maintaining basic patterns of a system.

Coordination refers to the ability of units of a system to work together, which is, of course, enhanced when there is a high degree of linkage between structures and actors of a system.[12] Acceptance of the International Court of Justice's optional clause, payment of United Nations annual assessments, and arbitration of disputes constitute several ways of producing a more organized arrangement among parts of international subsystems in a procedural sense.

Goal attainment and adaptation are alike insofar as they focus on *substantive* activities; pattern maintenance and coordination are largely *procedural* (Table 10–1). Goal attainment and coordination, however, involve more *comprehensive* matters; adaptation and pattern maintenance are achieved *incrementally* by stopgap repairing of a system in the direction of goals and structural arrangements previously agreed upon. The Parsonian framework, however, does not readily lend itself to operationalization because each metatask is so abstracted from concrete behavior that there would be low agreement among a team of observers as to whether one political act fits into one of the four categories. The lack of time specification renders the fourfold categorization somewhat nebulous. If, however, the term *function* stands for a metatask performed at a particular time point in the political process, with the three temporal and four behavioral elements agreed upon so far, an obvious step is to generate 12 functions from a combined 3 × 4 matrix (Table 10–2). Alternative structural-functional formulations fall into place within the 12-fold categorization, since temporal and behavioral elements are for the first time made explicit and used deductively.

----

[12] Parsons's word for this imperative is "integration," which is less informative than the term "coordination," especially in light of the discussion in Chapter 7 of this volume.

TABLE 10–1
Imperatives of a System[a]

	Scope of Change	
Type of Change	Comprehensive	Incremental
Substantive	Goal attainment	Adaptation
Procedural	Pattern maintenance	Coordination

[a] Adapted from Talcott Parsons and Neil J. Smelser, *Economy and Society* (New York: The Free Press, 1956).

The reader will note that Almond's functional categories are to a considerable extent subsumed within our Easton-Parsons matrix, from which Almond received his original inspiration in the first place.[13]

Somewhat abstract definitions will be supplied for each function. In the following sections of this chapter, illustrations and indicators appropriate to styles of function performance will be specified. Each of the 21 subsystems can then be coded in accordance with the way in which events and situations in a subsystem seem to fall along each conceptual continuum.

Inputs are demands and activities from actors in the polity that are placed before official and unofficial elites, including demands lodged by one elite upon another. *Articulation* is a demand from a single actor in a political system for incremental modifications in existing allocations of values. *Aggregation* is a demand for a new allocation of values placed by many actors in concert; since many different actors are involved, aggregation in-

TABLE 10–2
Functions of a Political System

		Temporal Aspect	
Behavioral Aspect	Inputs	Withinputs	Outputs
Goal attainment	Aggregation	Plan-making	Implementation
Adaptation	Articulation	Gatekeeping	Rule-adapting
Pattern maintenance	Socialization	Recruitment	Enforcement
Coordination	Support	Supervision	Direction

[13] There are some notable differences, which are present possibly because Almond has not sought to anchor his conceptual and theoretical bearings in orthodox Parsonian assumptions. Almond's use of "communication" as a function, rather than as an instrument by which any function may be expressed and perceived, most sharply differs from our view of functions as metatasks specific to stages in a cycle of activities. "Rule application" also seems too loosely employed, for it might imply implementation, adaptation, enforcement, or even direction of plans as well as "rules." As used in the present formulation, a *goal* is an elementary unit of value. A *plan* is a set of goals aimed toward bringing about a concrete change in the allocation of values. See George A. Miller, Eugene Galanter, and Karl H. Pribram, *Plans and the Structure of Behavior* (New York: Holt, 1960).

volves a prior harmonization of differences before stating a unified plan for change. Aggregation involves cooperation in an expression of demands by two or more actors within a political system, wherein mutual inconsistencies are resolved before collective advocacy of a single package of demands. The aim in pooling demands is to enable formerly separate demands to have a greater chance of fulfillment.

Socialization is a process in which actors learn cues, rules, and roles for behaving in an appropriate procedural manner. Ordinarily men learn to respond to stimuli in a manner that they believe will lead to desired rewards, and the same is true of decisionmakers within states, who structure conduct in such a way that their statecraft assumes a distinctive style of behavior. *Support* is a conferring of deference and loyalty to system elites. All of these functions, of course, may be performed negatively: nonarticulation, nonaggregation, malsocialization, and nonsupport would fall under each of the four respective categories and are relevant to all members of political system, whether elites or non-elites, major or minor powers.

Withinputs are metatasks handled by elites, that is, by the effective allocators of values. Major powers, along with middle powers, serve as elites in international subsystems. Elites may be regarded as legitimate or illegitimate, official or unofficial; they may work through formal structures or prefer more informal arenas in which to act. *Plan-making* is a process of arriving at an elite decision to make a substantive reallocation of values. *Gatekeeping* is a task of deciding whether to agree to proposals for incremental change in existing plans for value allocation.[14] To gatekeep is in effect to decide whether articulated demands are questions of "administration" or "politics." In the former case, a routine readjustment may take place; but in the latter situation articulators of demands must be prepared to get backing from other actors in the polity in order to attempt a more major modification in the political functioning of a system. *Recruitment* is a process of selecting and replacing elites in a system. *Supervision* is a task of observing how well political plans work out in practice, especially with a view to determining the impact of a plan, the degree of compliance, and the willingness of actors to obey or to carry out political plans and procedures. Supervision involves observation and fact-finding of the extent to which a polity is coordinated and actions in fact conform to agreed-upon norms.

Outputs are activities by elites and their agents to carry out specific reallocations of value. In international relations, major powers seldom delegate output functions to minor power agents. *Implementation* is an administrative task of translating general plans, as drawn up by elites, into a specific operational sequence of actions. *Rule-adapting* is an incremental

---

[14] The term is based on the concept of "gateway" in Bernard R. Berelson, Paul F. Lazarsfeld, and William N. McPhee, *Voting* (Chicago: University of Chicago Press, 1954, 1966), p. 209, as developed in Easton, *A Systems Analysis of Political Life.*

modification in existing goals and procedures that takes into account various environmental and political conditions arising after plans have been adopted and executed. Rule-adapting, thus, is usually not controversial, for changes with a more fundamental scope would be routed through goal-attainment channels and classified as "implementation" when put into effect. *Enforcement* is a task of maintaining order and a procedural status quo within a system (by overt coercive practices if necessary). *Direction* is a task of keeping the multiple activities in a political system in as well-meshed a flow as possible (by overtly establishing communication linkages or dominance-subordination relationships if necessary).[15] Once again, negations of these functions are relevant activities for each category—nonimplementation, maladaptation, underenforcement, and misdirection have a definite functional significance for a system. Some optimal level of performance in each function might be perceived as "best" by an efficiency expert, but there are occasions when underperformance of a particular function might lead to revolution or overperformance might prevent such a situation from arising; and either condition might be preferable, depending upon one's values.

10.3   STYLES OF FUNCTION PERFORMANCE

In order for a set of international actors to constitute a distinct subsystem within the world polity, all 12 functions must be performed more or less autonomously among them: a strategic-military confrontation must be present. Beyond this basic functional similarity there are many differences between subsystems. The differences consist of diverse styles in which functions may be performed. *Styles*—that is, distinctive ways of performing functions—are classifiable generically under four headings, based on four of Parsons's pattern variables (Table 10–3).[16] As in the case of our delineation of functions, pattern variables are not proposed for distorting our attention, but rather as convenient metaconceptual terms for subsuming

---

[15] The term is used most recently in Norman J. Padelford and George A. Lincoln, *The Dynamics of International Politics* (New York: Macmillan, 1962), p. 258, which is based on the definition in Gulick, "Notes on the Theory of Organization," p. 13.

[16] The four headings are in conformity with Almond and Coleman, eds., *The Politics of the Developing Areas;* Holt and Turner, *The Political Basis of Economic Development.* Parsons, on the other hand, has changed his formulation from time to time. Compare Talcott Parsons and Edward A. Shils, eds., *Toward a General Theory of Action* (Cambridge: Harvard University Press, 1951) with Parsons, Robert F. Bales, and Shils, *Working Papers in the Theory of Action* (New York: The Free Press, 1953). See also Parsons, "Pattern Variables Revisited: A Response to Robert Dubin," *American Sociological Review,* XXV (August 1960), 467–83; Parsons, "The Point of View of the Author," *The Social Theories of Talcott Parsons,* ed. Max Black (Englewood Cliffs, N. J.: Prentice-Hall, 1961), pp. 311–63; Mitchell, *Sociological Analysis and Politics,* p. 31.

TABLE 10-3
Styles of Function Performance

	Pattern Variables			
Functions	Latent–Manifest	Diffuse–Specific	Universalistic–Particularistic	Affective–Instrumental
Articulation				
Aggregation				
Socialization				
Support				
Gatekeeping				
Plan-making				
Recruitment				
Supervision				
Rule-adapting				
Implementation				
Enforcement				
Direction				

particular styles of function performance. Until a more useful set of meta-concepts is proposed, pattern variables will suffice to encourage systematic formulations of styles that may pertain within any function and system. Fred Riggs, for example, deserves much credit for expanding, clarifying, and explicating pattern variables for use in a wide range of political situations.[17] Each style, in turn, could be viewed from at least three perspectives, corresponding to the threefold division of this book. These foci are on decision-making preoccupations, structuring of state behavior in international society, and systemic patterns displayed by international behavior in the aggregate.[18] The result of employing such a division is to generate a 12-cell matrix (Table 10–4). Once again, our purpose in proposing such a broad schema is to subsume current conceptual grab bags in the literature of international system theory.

10.3.1 Manifest–Latent

The first pattern variable pair in our adaptation from Parsons's schema is the manifest-latent continuum. *Manifest* function performance results from behavior undertaken self-consciously to achieve goals of a political

[17] Riggs, "International Relations as a Prismatic System"; Riggs, *Administration in Developing Countries* (Boston: Houghton Mifflin, 1964). See also David E. Apter, *Some Conceptual Approaches to the Study of Modernization* (Englewood Cliffs, N. J.: Prentice-Hall, 1968); Holt and Turner, *The Political Basis of Economic Development.*

[18] Just as the *societal* level includes aggregated state behavior as well as composite profiles of decisionmakers within each state, the *systemic* level combines aggregated profiles of decisionmakers, societies, and characteristics of subsystems as a whole.

TABLE 10-4
Basic Styles of Function Performance

Pattern Variables	Decisionmaking	Level of Focus Societal	Systemic
Manifest–Latent	Unintended–Intended	Formal–Informal	Hyperactivity–Hypoactivity
Diffuse–Specific	Exogenous–Endogenous	Nonspecialized–Specialized	Polyarchical–Hierarchical
Universalistic–Particularistic	Macrocentric–Microcentric	Contract–Status	Multilateral–Unilateral
Affective–Instrumental	Ideological–Pragmatic	Preoccupied–Routinized	Turbulent–Quiescent

system. *Latent* performance occurs when an activity unknowingly accomplishes political goals, as when behavior conceived largely in nonpolitical terms unconsciously has a political implication or by-product. Ordinarily we expect that when functions are performed manifestly they take place much more often than when they are performed in a latent manner. Almond's manifest-latent dichotomy appears to be based upon Parsons's achievement-ascription continuum, since achievement represents manifest behavior toward a goal, while ascription involves such procedures as inheritance, traditional recognition of the rights and duties of persons of varying status, and other such nonbehavioral elements. Riggs points out that in many countries one can find elements of both achieved and ascriptive styles, so he uses the word attainment for the midpoint of the continuum. We more operationally code international subsystems in terms of three major types of variables relevant to manifest and latent styles of function performance.

The self-consciousness with which actors perceive that they are articulating, aggregating, becoming socialized, and so forth is probably the most obvious style. Critics of the structural-functional approach often contend that actors are only dimly aware of the functional consequences of their individual moves. Therefore, it might be useful to rank subsystems along an undeniably significant dimension, which we will refer to as the *intended-unintended* continuum, in keeping with Robert Merton's terminology.[19] Economic activity spilling over into politics is a major form of unintended function performance. An operational measure of intentionality would be the number of times that a particular function is performed, which could be obtained by counting such phenomena as wars and alliances within a system.

The degree of formality with which functions are carried out is a second way to conceive of our manifest-latent continuum. *Formal* conduct is diplomatic, or state-to-state; *informal* international behavior includes rela-

[19] Merton, *Social Theory and Social Structure*.

tions between nonsovereign entities and actors across state boundaries, with official governmental representatives less involved. The number of times that a function is performed may be percentaged in terms of the presence of nonsovereign actors as agents or targets of political interaction.

The volume of function performance is a third variable. We would expect systems to differ in the percentage of total actors performing functions. Hence, we could assess whether functions are being overperformed or underperformed. *Hyperactivity* involves devoting too much attention to one function as opposed to other functions; and one obvious example would be a subsystem elite with a mania for suppressing up-and-coming powers, thereby adhering to a comprehensive orientation to international conflict, rather than adjusting incrementally to demands for broadening of the international elite stratum. *Hypoactivity,* on the contrary, takes place if elites within a system fail to perform a function, whether for ideological or practical reasons. A count of the number of members performing individual functions would index gross activity levels when divided by the total number of members of a system.

10.3.2 Diffuse–Specific

Turning to a second set of pattern variables, functional *specificity* may be said to exist if one and only one structure performs a particular function; when several types of structures perform a given function, or a structure performs several functions, the condition is known as *diffuse* function performance.[20] There are three distinct aspects of diffuse and specific function performance.

One key element is whether functions are performed *endogenously,* that is, within the geographic core of the subsystem; *exogenously,* by members in an area not geographically contiguous to the core of the subsystem; or "mesogenously," Riggs's prismatic midpoint between the two polar concepts, implying participation in function performance by both core and noncore members. The higher the exogenous to endogenous ratio, the more a subsystem has been carved out of the global international system in a procrustean manner. Wars or alliances entered by members of a system may be divided into those outside the region and those inside the region. A ratio between intraregional and extraregional frequencies is an index of endogenousness.

---

[20] A discussion of Riggs's concepts is relevant at this point. A *diffracted* polity is one in which a single structure performs one and only one function; *fusion* exists when one structure is omnifunctional. A *prismatic* polity combines some elements of diffraction and some of fusion, swinging back and forth as leaders, issues, and times change. Since his terms represent an overall assessment of a political system, the more microassessing terms of "diffuse" and "specific" have been preferred for the classification of how individual functions are performed within systems.

Seldom are functions of international subsystems performed by specialized units other than states, the building blocks of most international subsystems. On the national level, we are accustomed to the presence of legislatures, executives, interest groups, and so forth; whereas functionally equivalent structures within international politics include intergovernmental organizations, world courts, peace-keeping forces, and other such intermittently operating structures. It might be useful, therefore, to compare subsystems in terms of institutionalized function performance. The obvious concepts would be *specialized* and *nonspecialized,* and operational counterparts would be counts of institutional linkages between states.

Extent of hierarchy is a third notion implied by the diffuse-specific continuum. Functions could be performed on a strict, *hierarchical* basis or on a more *polyarchic,* disorganized, free-for-all basis.[21] Measures of power stratification, such as monopolization in function performance by elites, are appropriate here.

10.3.3 Universalistic–Particularistic

Turning from quantitative and structural aspects of function performance to a cognitive focus, we may distinguish between universalism and particularism. A *universalistic* performance of a function takes the interest of an entire subsystem into account. In national political systems the term "public interest" is a familiar phrase referring to a universalistic perspective; the term "regional interest" pertains to a more universalistic function performance within international subsystems. *Particularistic* function performance, contrariwise, is behavior that seeks to perform functions for the benefit of the self. Parsons uses another pattern variable, "self versus collectivity orientation" in a manner equivalent to particularism-universalism, at least for the purposes of international subsystem analysis. (Riggs's term "selectivistic" is proposed for the midpoint of the continuum.) Universalism-particularism may be broken down into three types of variables.

One of the most obvious ways in which subsystems differ is in the attention paid by members to foreign as opposed to domestic politics. Foreign affairs may be approached *microcentrically* (isolationalistically and nationalistically), or *macrocentrically* (internationally). Nonaggression pacts, for example, could be expressed as a percentage of all types of alliances to index macrocentrism.

Another implication of the universalism-particularism dichotomy deals with power relations. A particularistic power relation is one in which *status* is a prime element for determining outcomes; a more universalistic orientation would be to have all actors in a subsystem agree to deal with each other

---

[21] This distinction is from Robert A. Dahl and Charles E. Lindblom, *Politics, Economics and Welfare* (New York: Harper, 1953).

on a *contractual,* treaty-like basis. (Riggs uses the term "status-contract nexus" to refer to the condition between status and contract orientations.) Contractual popularity may be measured by computing the number of alliances per member of a system.

Degree of *multilateralism* is a third variable relevant to universalism-particularism. Despite the microcentrism or macrocentrism of foreign affairs, some subsystems may have more members participating in joint interactions, consultations, and institutions; others have a more *unilateral* character. The number of partners in alliances is an obvious indicator of multilaterality.

10.3.4 Affective–Instrumental

Instrumental or "neutral" function performance, finally, is oriented toward getting a job done with the greatest possible efficiency and speed, while denying opportunities for short-run gratification along the way. An *affective* style exists when an agent of function performance prefers to satisfy social and emotional desires and employs means to achieve more immediate gratification, thus postponing fulfillment of long-range goals. The dichotomy is somewhat similar to Herbert Simon's distinction between maximizing and satisficing behavior.[22]

From a decisionmaking point of view, one interpretation of the affective-instrumental continuum would identify subsystems in which vital interests clash, as apart from those with more limited interests. *Ideological* politics involves contention over Weltanschauungen; *pragmatic* politics is concerned with accomplishing finite objectives in a political arena in order to keep nonpolitical (usually economic) activities within bounds. Short wars and alliances of limited duration indicate more pragmatic objectives, as Etzioni has suggested.[23]

The degree of *preoccupation* by states with international affairs is a function of the extent to which vital interests are being contested. If many new wars or alliances appear in each year of a subsystem era, we may argue that levels of affect and concern are greatly in contrast with more *routinized* systems.[24]

The intensity of violence, finally, is a clear indicator of tension and perceived need for speed in fulfilling fervently desired goals. Usually the terms

[22] Herbert A. Simon, *Administrative Behavior,* 2d ed. (New York: Macmillan, 1957).

[23] Amitai Etzioni, *Political Unification* (New York: Holt, Rinehart and Winston, 1965); cf. Edmund Stillman and William Pfaff, *The Politics of Hysteria* (New York: Harper, Row, 1964).

[24] The term *preoccupation* is used to denote degrees of concentration in attention focus. Cf. Karl W. Deutsch, "Transaction Flows as Indicators of Political Cohesion," *The Integration of Political Communities,* eds. Jacob and Toscano, pp. 75–97.

"stable" and "unstable" have been applied here; but because these words have been assigned a more technical meaning above in Section 7.2.4, the more descriptive *quiescent* and *turbulent* are to be assigned as opposite ends of this final continuum of functional styles.

Recapitulating, fundamental styles for performing some 12 functions have been delineated. Each style, in turn, has been specified in terms of three foci. With 12 functions and 12 substyles, a total of 144 concepts emerge for describing international subsystems comparatively. We now move to an operational level, seeking to describe subsystems in terms of quantitative indicators or judgmental codings. The presentation in the remainder of the chapter will be devoted to an explication of variables that operationalize each concept, followed by correlations between these variables, on the one hand, and the two conceptual variables which define our 21 subsystems—number of poles and tightness or looseness of stratification —on the other hand.

10.4 INPUT FUNCTIONS

Inputs consist of demands and predecisionmaking activities proceeding from actors in world politics. If one member of a system establishes hegemony over other members, demands placed upon that actor constitute inputs for the subsystem. If there are several elite units vying for supremacy or equality, demands placed upon one elite by another are also considered to be inputs. Articulation, aggregation, socialization, and support are four specific types of inputs, each of which may be performed in different ways within particular international subsystems.

10.4.1 Articulation

Articulation is the process of making demands upon elites within a system in order to bring about incremental changes in operations of a system. As Almond and Powell observe:

> Interest articulation . . . marks the boundary between the society and the political system. If groups within the society do not find open channels through which to express their interests and needs, these demands are likely to remain unsatisfied. The resultant dissatisfactions may erupt in violence, or may require suppression by the elites.[25]

Voicing demands is, of course, separate from meeting those demands, the latter comprising part of the gatekeeping function to be discussed in Section 10.5.1. Since our concern is with conflictual interactions between

[25] Almond and Powell, *Comparative Politics*, pp. 73–74.

states, articulation will be defined below as it relates specifically to the incidence of warfare. The 12 styles of performing articulation have been accorded much attention in international system theory because few states have been reluctant to make their desires known in the international arena. Politicization is a concept appropriate for a continuum between intended or unintended styles in the performance of the articulation function. International subsystems that self-consciously deal with conflict and security matters are highly politicized, as Werner Levi has suggested;[26] but subsystems that engage in politics only as a by-product of a concern with social, economic, or religious matters are politicized to a lesser degree. Almost by definition we would expect that a less politicized subsystem would be freer from wars, which are the obvious means by which the demands of political-military issues reach the surface. As an indicator of the intentional style of performing the articulation function, the number of wars (1)[27] will be summed for each international subsystem.

Formal articulation is state-to-state; and informal articulation involves entities with less autonomy and sovereignty, such as vassals or insurgent groups. Degrees of sovereignty and nonsovereignty, hence, denote a second style for performing the articulation function. Many observers, such as C. A. W. Manning, feel that the prevalence of the independent nation-state as a basic unit of world politics demarcates the present era of international instability from the previous more tranquil epochs.[28] Such a hypothesis may be tested by percentaging the number of wars involving subnational entities as participants (2).

Hyperarticulation in subsystems would occur if there were a large number of units at war. The fewer members at war in a subsystem, the more likely it is to be comparatively assessed as underactive on military-strategic matters. The percentage of all subsystem members at war (3) will be used to index hyperactive articulation.

Turning to diffuse and specific function performance, we may distinguish between subsystems in which the extraregional actors do the most, least, or an equivalent amount of articulation compared to intraregional members of a subsystem. Where exogenous articulation prevails, the degree of communication linkage with other subsystems—a notion developed by Brecher—is at a very high level. Subsystems that attract considerable inter-

---

[26] Werner Levi, "On the Causes of Peace," *Journal of Conflict Resolution,* VII (March 1964), 23–35.

[27] Numbers in parentheses refer to variable numbers. A complete list is provided in Table 11–2; definitions are supplied in Appendix B.

[28] C. A. W. Manning, *The Nature of International Society* (New York: Wiley, 1962); cf. John H. Herz, *International Politics in the Atomic Age* (New York: Columbia University Press, 1959).

est from outside a region are undoubtedly weaker and, thus, more suscept-ible to defeat in international combat. Percentages of extraregional wars (4) and extra-era wars (5) will indicate the locus of articulation.

One of the central concepts of international stratification theory is that of poles within international systems. A *pole* may be defined as a single major power or set of entities that are militarily viable yet unaligned with any other militarily significant entity within an international subsystem. A pole, therefore, constitutes a specialized form of international articulation; so a count of the number of poles (6) within subsystems would yield a measure of relative diffusion or specificity of power as articulated in a more specialized manner than individual instances of war and disputes. There are four main types of polarities, each of which may exhibit somewhat different patterns; and a separate coding may therefore prove useful: unipolarity (6a), bipolarity (6b), tripolarity (6c), and multipolarity (6d).[29] This variable is one of the two independent variables to be analyzed in this chapter.

Subsystems with many wars and many countries at war may differ in the tendencies of individual countries either to participate in only one war per system or to wage war over and over again. A hierarchical performance of the articulation function, thus, would find some states repeatedly engaging in international aggression, while most others would remain peaceable. When the number of war participants summed across all wars is divided by the number of states in at least one war (7), a recidivism ratio is obtained.

Subsystems tend to differ in the scope of issues raised. It is often said that politics ceases "at the water's edge"—a phrase meaning that there are some issues about which disputation would be unthinkable, for, if contested, a political system itself would be placed in jeopardy. International sub-systems likewise would collapse if there were no common perceptions by one state that another state's membership in the subsystem is legitimate. A macrocentric style of articulation avoids warfare with states which have so many similar characteristics that the conflict would be fratricidal. Percent-ages of all pairs of members at war with similar languages (8), similar bodily characteristics (9), similar clothing (10), and similar religions and philosophies (11) hence index the breadth of the "water's edge" in interna-tional subsystems; for we would expect macrocentric articulation to avoid such confrontations. Contrarily, the percentage of war dyads composed of former enemies (12) indicates a preference for a more microcentric con-tinuation of old disputes and their persistent nonresolution despite the use of arms.

Subsystems in which disputes are settled largely on the basis of status,

[29] Michael Haas, "International Subsystems: Stability and Polarity," *American Political Science Review*, LXIV (March 1970), 98–123.

rather than by contractual means, are likely to have many members at war in several instances. The number of wars per member (13) will be calculated, accordingly.

Unilateral focusing of articulation involves aggressors who attack one and only one opponent; multilateral articulation occurs when a single state attacks several enemies at the same time. The number of participants per war (14) will be used to indicate the multilateral style of articulation.

Pragmatic articulation in the form of war means to seek specific goals, that is, to have a set of grievances; military means are employed in such a case to speed up attainment of goals or to fulfill them at minimum cost. Holy wars, in which articulation focuses on the preservation or extension of one ideology as opposed to another, tend to cast economic considerations aside and are of longer duration.[30] Mean years per war (15) will therefore indicate ideologism in articulation.

Almond and Powell distinguish between low- and high-intensity articulation within systems. Brecher, similarly, refers to intensity of communications as one of the main characteristics of subsystems. If vital interests are at stake, the subsystem will be more intensely concerned with the outcome of disputes than when the scope of conflict involves nonvital interests. If there is a high degree of concern for the outcome of international conflict, the percentage of years with new wars within a subsystem (16) would be expected to be high, and the level of stress on pattern maintenance would be high.

Turning to turbulent and quiescent articulation, we will be concerned with two outcomes of international aggression—whether aggressors succeed in destabilizing conditions and how deadly the battles are. Following Richardson's descriptions of each war in his compilation, it is possible to count the percentage of wars resulting in destabilization (17) and the mean number of battle-related deaths per war (18).

We now turn to survey the relation between the variables described above (Table 10–5) and the measures of international stratification. Despite the small sample size of 21 subsystems, and the even lower number of cases on which some correlations are based due to missing data, several correlations reported in Table 10–5 are high in magnitude.[31] We find in general

---

[30] For findings that wars fought for economic reasons are of shorter duration than those for nonpragmatic reasons, see Lewis F. Richardson, *Statistics of Deadly Quarrels* (Chicago: Quadrangle, 1960).

[31] Spearman correlations are reported because few of the variables are normally distributed. Because of a small sample size (N $\leq$ 21), correlations are seldom statistically significant. The ± .40 level will be used as a cutoff point in distinguishing between stronger and weaker correlations reported in this chapter; this is an arbitrary threshold but appears to be a point where the upper tail of the distribution of correlation magnitudes begins. In computing the correlations, the sample of subsystems for which Richardson's data are most complete will be used, rather than the subsystems

that the number of wars increases with the number of poles, and most of the wars tend to be with countries that are similar in background, rather than with arenas outside the confines of a subsystem. Wars under multipolarity tend to break out in many different years, and there is a tendency for the same countries to send troops to battlefields over and over again. Tight polarity entails a continuation of wars into two subsystem eras, but is associated with no other variable in a consistent or significant manner.

10.4.2 Aggregation

Consistent with Almond's framework, *aggregation* is regarded as a combining of interests of separate actors, such that general policy alternatives are demanded of elites in a polity. When many groups collectively advocate a departure from ongoing operations, the effect is more likely to involve comprehensive, substantive changes. Political parties have not yet emerged in a concrete sense on the international scene as specialized aggregators, but alliances, blocs, summit conferences, and even intergovernmental organizations have functioned in an aggregating role. More data are available on alliances, due to data collection efforts of J. David Singer and Melvin Small.

The number of alliances (19) is the most precise indicator for the extent to which aggregation is performed self-consciously within international subsystems. Findings of Singer and Small indicate that alliance formation sometimes deters and at other times provokes warfare; this variable may be used to determine which trend is most dominant in a larger sample of subsystems.

Informal aggregation can take place in at least two basic ways. Alliances, of course, constitute one of the main formal devices for pooling state demands. But there are times when a strong state so penetrates the political functioning of a weaker state that the latter is best described as a *satellite* of the former. The number of satellites (20) in subsystems serves to index this informal method of aggregation. Alliances may themselves be of three main types: offensive or defensive pacts, nonaggression pacts, or ententes. The terms of a *defensive pact* state conditions under which two or more countries will go to war; the *nonaggression pact* is a joint pledge not to engage in war; an *entente* is merely a gentlemen's agreement that may not bind states that change political leadership. Formalized aggregation involves a document or treaty to codify rules governing a pact relationship. A more formal situation usually involves far-reaching goals, so one would anticipate

---

where Wright focuses his attention; the reason for this selection is that more data is available for the subsystems studied by Richardson—namely, Subsystems 5–10, 12–21. Wright subsamples include no data for Hawaiian subsystems.

TABLE 10–5
Intercorrelations Between International Stratification
and International Articulation[a]

Articulation Variables	Style[b]	International Stratification[a] Poles 6	Looseness of Poles 132	Source[c]
1a. Number of wars	I	(.58)	.06	RFB
1b. Number of wars	I	(.54)	.15	W
2. Percent wars with subnational entities	—F	.23	—.13	RFB
3a. Percent members at war	A	(.60)	—.16	RFB
3b. Percent members at war	A	.19	.16	W
4a. Percent extraregion wars	E	(—.62)	(.43)	RFB
4b. Percent extraregion wars	E	(—.51)	.08	W
5a. Percent extra-era wars	E	.31	(—.46)	RFB
5b. Percent extra-era wars	E	(.42)	(—.40)	W
6. Number of poles	S	(1.00)	—.06	H
6a. Unipolarity (or not)	—S	—.41	.16	H
6b. Bipolarity (or not)		—.35	—.15	H
6c. Tripolarity (or not)		.13	—.22	H
6d. Multipolarity (or not)	S	(.90)	.16	H
7a. War participants per members	H	(.50)	—.21	RFB
7b. War participants per members	H	(.41)	.34	W
8. Percent war dyads between countries with similar languages	—M	(.60)	—.12	R
9. Percent war dyads between countries with similar bodily characteristics	—M	(.86)	.14	R
10. Percent war dyads between countries with similar clothing	—M	(.62)	.10	R
11. Percent war dyads between countries with similar religion and philosophy	—M	(.60)	.24	R
12. Percent war dyads between former enemies	—M	—.10	.17	R
13a. Wars per member	—C	(.59)	—.26	RFB
13b. Wars per member	—C	.28	.36	W

that subsystems with many pacts are more likely to be explosive than those containing mainly low-key ententes. Singer's and Small's data on military pacts, nonaggression pacts, and ententes permit us to express the degree of formality in aggregation in terms of the percentage of all alliances that are pacts rather than ententes (21).

If George Washington had had his way, subsystems would be hypo-active with respect to aggregation, for a nonentanglement policy would keep states apart in the hope that levels of conflict would subside. The percentage

TABLE 10–5—Cont.
Intercorrelations Between International Stratification
and International Articulation[a]

		International Stratification[a]		
			Looseness	
		Poles	of Poles	
Articulation Variables	*Style*[b]	6	132	*Source*[c]
14a. Participants per war	—U	(.45)	.16	RFB
14b. Participants per war	—U	.26	.05	W
15a. Mean years per war	—P	.26	—.12	RFB
15b. Mean years per war	—P	.27	.06	W
16a. Percent years in era with new wars	—R	(.68)	—.28	RFB
16b. Percent years in era with new wars	—R	(.58)	(—.49)	RB
17. Percent destabilizing wars	—Q	.18	.10	RFB
18. Mean deaths per war	—Q	—.01	—.24	RB

[a] Correlations greater than ±.40 are enclosed in parentheses. Correlations are based on the Richardson subsample of subsystems, unless variables are given a "b" suffix.

[b] Key to styles:

I	= intentional.	—I	= unintentional.
F	= formal.	—F	= informal.
A	= hyperactive.	—A	= hypoactive.
E	= exogenous.	—E	= endogenous.
S	= specialized.	—S	= nonspecialized.
H	= hierarchical.	—H	= polyarchic.
M	= macrocentric.	—M	= microcentric.
C	= contractual.	—C	= status.
U	= unilateral.	—U	= multilateral.
P	= pragmatic.	—P	= ideological.
R	= routinized.	—R	= preoccupied.
Q	= quiescent.	—Q	= turbulence.

[c] Key to sources:

B = Bendix System Division, ONR study of low-intensity warfare.
F = Fornander, *An Account of the Polynesian Race* (1880).
H = Haas, this volume.
R = Richardson, *Statistics of Deadly Quarrels* (1960).
Ro = Rosecrance, *Action and Reaction in World Politics* (1963).
Sp = Speeckaert, *The 1978 International Associations Founded Since the Congress of Vienna* (1957).
SS = Singer and Small, "Alliance Aggregation and the Onset of War" (1968).
W = Wright, *A Study of War* (1965).

of members in alliances (22) will be used to measure degrees of entanglement.

Alliance relationships with extraregional actors and members might be found when there is a power vacuum within a particular subsystem. Solicitation of support for an intraregional member's cause may signal the need to bring in "strangers" for an impending showdown within a subsystem. The percentage of extraregional alliances (23) indicates whether a core is really central in aggregation. The percentage of extra-era alliances (24) assesses whether alliances are predominantly specific to issues and confrontations of a subsystem or spill over into adjacent eras.

Aggregation is performed by specialized institutions in international subsystems: the appropriate bodies are the various transnational nongovernmental international organizations (NGO's), such as the International Chamber of Commerce, International Confederation of Free Trade Unions, and so forth. Paul Smoker, in fact, has hypothesized that the rate of formation of NGO's may index periods of international equilibrium and disequilibrium. The number of new NGO's formed during a subsystem (25) may be quantified by consulting Speeckaert's *The 1978 International Associations Founded Since the Congress of Vienna* (1957).[32]

Group membership theory has tended to stress the utility of multiple memberships within a polity in reducing the number of irreconcilable disputes between groups.[33] Similarly, Kaplan has hypothesized that cross-cutting loyalties of states will soften demands and make compromise and bargaining more feasible. Overlapping alliance memberships would, therefore, signify a polyarchic style of performing aggregation, as opposed to a distinctive alliance network, to use a pair of Riggs's terms. If most alliances are made by only two members of a subsystem, then the ratio between alliance partnerships and aligned members (26) will be close to 1.0.

The cross-cutting loyalty thesis of Kaplan would, of course, be more applicable to a subsystem in which alliances are skewed toward the macrocentrism end of the scale. When aggregation has a macrocentric style we expect higher percentages of nonaggression alliances (27), accordingly.

A contractual orientation to aggregation would appear to involve a high ratio of alliances to members (28) within a subsystem. When aggregation is based largely upon status considerations, there is no necessity to verbalize its terms.

The unilateral-multilateral continuum pertains to the number of parties to an alliance. Multilateralism reflects broad aggregation, wherein many members of a subsystem agree to an identical document, usually to establish an intergovernmental organization or to extend its scope. Advocates of "world public opinion" and "functional" approaches to peace advocate multilateralism as a way to eliminate violence on the international level.[34] The average number of partners per alliance (29) will be calculated from Singer's data.

Affective-instrumental patterns have been studied with much care by

[32] G. P. Speeckaert, ed., *The 1978 International Associations Founded Since the Congress of Vienna* (Brussels: Union of International Associations, 1957).

[33] Truman, *Governmental Process*. For a test of overlapping group membership theory pertaining to international relations, see Harold Guetzkow, *Multiple Loyalties* (Princeton: Center for Research on World Political Institutions, 1955).

[34] Inis L. Claude, Jr., *Swords into Plowshares*, 3d ed. (New York: Knopf, 1964).

students of international conflict. Ideological aggregation has been characterized as absolute-value oriented by Almond, as opposed to pragmatic. Alliances seeking to remake a subsystem in terms of an ideal model might tend to avoid compromise and thus promote cold wars, whereas aggregation in which bargaining is an element would be perceived less often to be an extension of an actor's ego. Aggregative ideologism will be indexed by averaging the duration of alliances (30). Morgenthau and other power theorists have implied that limited, shorter alliances are to be preferred to broad ones, inasmuch as austere members of a world polity are less likely to allow emotional considerations to override rational calculations. Accordingly, we might expect subsystems with pragmatic aggregation to be less destructive of human life on the battlefield, for total victory would be less necessary than obtaining concrete objectives.

When aggregation has a routinized aspect, formal or informal aggregation would be torn asunder with a minimal feeling of sorrow, as soon as collective goals are met (or are seen later as unattainable). When there is a preoccupation with the need for pursuing multiple goals in tandem among states, many alliances are likely to be made. Considered as a systematic characteristic, the percentage of years in which at least one alliance is formed (31) differentiates between subsystems with high and low degrees of preoccupation with aggregation.

The final continuum, accordingly, stretches from wars in which many nonaggression pacts are involved to those in which many alliances have a military character. The percentage of so-called defensive pacts (32) serves as one indicator of aggressive aggregation. Another facet of aggressive aggregation is the extent to which aggregation is disrupted, which may be measured by percentages of dyadic confrontations between former allies (33). These two indicators are correlated along with the other styles of aggregation in Table 10–6.

International stratification predicts to aggregation far less than was the case with articulation. As a system has greater dispersion in power among various poles, former allies tend to oppose each other in combat and most alliances that are signed are for military purposes. Alliances become more multilateral, more numerous, and most countries are aligned where there is a loose stratification of power; hence, we could argue that alliances tend to keep stratification fluid.

10.4.3 Socialization

The concept of international *socialization* is an application of Almond's notion of "the process whereby political attitudes and values are inculcated as children become adults and as adults are recruited into roles."[35] In place

---

[35] Almond and Powell, *Comparative Politics,* p. 24.

TABLE 10–6
Intercorrelations Between International Stratification
and International Aggregation[a]

| | | *International Stratification* | | |
| | | Poles | Looseness of Poles | |
Aggregation Variables	*Style*	*6*	*132*	*Source*
19. Number of alliances	I	.11	(.44)	SSF
20. Number of satellites	—F	.37	—.06	H
21. Percent pact alliances	F	(.40)	—.02	SSF
22. Percent members aligned	A	.09	(.59)	SSF
23. Percent extraregion alliances	E	—.28	.07	SSF
24. Percent extra-era alliances	E	—.01	.33	SSF
25. New NGO's formed	S	.13	.31	Sp
26. Ratio between alliance partnerships and aligned members	H	.02	.35	SSF
27. Percent nonaggression alliances	M	.27	.12	SSF
28. Ratio between alliances and members	C	.10	.37	SSF
29. Partners per alliance	—U	.28	(.46)	SSF
30. Durations per alliances	—P	—.06	.24	SSF
31. Percent years in era with new alliances	—R	—.00	.37	SSF
32. Percent defensive pacts	—Q	.36	.03	SSF
33. Percent former allies in war dyads	—Q	(.50)	—.36	R

[a] For key to symbols see Table 10–5.

of "children" and "adults" we could substitute members of a subsystem, inasmuch as the process of learning how to play the game of international politics is a continuing task for member units in a subsystem. Socialization by domestic elites results from processing information that comes from internal sources within their own polity and from events that occur externally.

When international socialization is intentional, actors focus on events in the international arena. One obvious indicator of the scope of socialization is the number of members (34) of a subsystem which must adjust to one another; this variable corresponds to Modelski's notion of the size of an international system. When decisionmakers within a subsystem are bombarded by outer stimuli more than by inner demands, their range of choice seems larger; and there is a degree of flexibility in maneuvering that is lost as soon as the public rigidifies its stands on foreign policy questions. Extent of decision latitude (35) will be assigned as a second index of the degree of self-conscious international stratification, based on Rosecrance's codings.

An informal type of socialization within an international subsystem is that experienced by subnational and nonsovereign entities. Because such members of a subsystem lack customary attributes of sovereignty, they are unlikely to be recognized diplomatically or to have formal channels of communication available to them. The percentage of sovereign members (36) will therefore index the extent of formality in socialization across subsystems.

When an entity slumps from the status of a sovereign member to that of a nonsovereign entity, one consequence is that it will subsequently be less active in performing the socialization function: as a subnational or satellite member, it will adjust mainly to one dominant state, tuning out happenings that are more geographically remote throughout the subsystem arena. The percentage of members retaining sovereignty (37), therefore, seems a precise measure of the extent of hyperactivity in socialization.

When innovating actors of a subsystem lie at the periphery, and core units adjust to these innovations, a condition of exogenous socialization is present. Extraregional actors are likely to be trading and colonizing countries. Toynbee's hypothesis that system transformation occurs owing to a decline of core units could be tested by the percentage of extraregional members (38),[36] a more generic form of Deutsch's "presence of foreign threat" variable.

A specialized method of achieving international socialization is by establishing diplomatic relations. Singer and Small have collected extensive data on the number of officials exchanged by individual countries, weighted according to the level of officials so that exchange involving ambassadors is more significant than exchange of officials of lesser rank; the total score for each country is called a *status score*, since Singer and Small suspect that more prestigious countries will be more active in exchanges of ambassadors. We may use mean status scores (39) for all members of a subsystem to indicate specialization in socialization.

One axiom of international political theory is that weaker powers are consigned to adjust to stronger members of an international subsystem. A ratio between total members and middle and major powers (40) will therefore index the extent of hierarchy in socialization.

When socialization is microcentric, there is little identification by members with a regional cluster of states of which they are a part. Brecher's subsystem identification, Riggs's level of sociocultural similarity, and Modelski's homogeneity concepts are pertinent here, as is Deutsch's finding that a distinctive way of life is necessary before an amalgamated security community will be formed among a set of nations. Diversity in ways of life (41) will be used as a judgmentally scaled indicator of microcentric socialization,

---

[36] Kenneth W. Thompson, "Toynbee and the Theory of International Politics," *Political Science Quarterly*, LXXI (September 1956), 365–86.

since there are no quantitative measures available. A common way of life would indicate macrocentricity.

The extent of power orientation within international subsystems varies with the degree of respect for international law, treaties, and other commitments that have been agreed upon in advance of specific situations where infractions might result in short-run advantages for lawbreakers. Unfortunately data on observance of international law and custom are not available over lengthy historical periods, so judgmental codings for the extent of power orientation (42) will be used instead to index a contractual style of performing the socialization function.

Brecher's notion of incompleteness of interaction (43) and Deutsch's variable, unbroken links of social communication between members of a subsystem, are relevant to our unilateral-multilateral distinction. If interaction among members has few barriers, and if there is a consistent type of response across all members of the subsystem, interaction is complete (or, using Riggs's concept, the system is unicommunal).

To determine whether international socialization has an ideological or pragmatic character, it is necessary to inquire into what Rosecrance calls the "ethos of states" in a subsystem. Nationalism, however, has been conceived both ideologically and pragmatically. Bismarck's drive for unification took the latter course with a more maximizing type of orientation, whereas Italian unification was buttressed with the more intellectual trappings of Mazzini. Maximization and the profit motive might dictate either imperialistic expansion or an "imperialism does not pay" conclusion. Ideologies, too, could be more or less pacifistic in tone. The extent to which a foreign affairs ethos is justified in terms of rational calculations (44) will be used as a judgmentally scaled conceptual variable.

The great popular interest in foreign affairs during the twentieth century, which has given rise to the "new diplomacy," is regarded by W. T. R. Fox as one of the basic features distinguishing contemporary international relations from all previous world history.[37] At the same time, however, Deutsch and Eckstein have found that trade patterns in the later phases of industrialization show decidedly lower proportions of trade as a percentage of gross national product.[38] This finding from the Deutsch–Eckstein study, that advanced countries become more internally preoccupied, suggests adding a variable to distinguish between international subsystems with rou-

[37] William T. R. Fox and Annette Baker Fox, "The Teaching of International Relations in the United States," World Politics, XIII (April 1961), 341; see also Harold Nicolson, Diplomacy, 3d ed. (New York: Oxford University Press, 1966).

[38] Karl W. Deutsch and Alexander Eckstein, "National Industrialization and the Declining Share of the International Economic Sector, 1890–1959," World Politics, XIII (January 1961), 267–99.

tinized versus preoccupied socialization. Codings for extent of internal pre-occupation (45) will indicate the extent to which areas outside the main region of an international system are regarded as of a routine and secondary importance by elites; the variable is assigned judgmentally because of a lack of trade figures for long historical sweeps.

The more wars, the more often will a member of a subsystem have to devote its attention to learning how to cope with military situations. Such turbulent socialization could refer to both international and domestic warfare. The latter condition seems to have caught the interest of most theorizers on international systems.[39] Numbers of internal wars (46), interventions (47), and foreign wars (48) can be rendered socialization variables by dividing each sum by the total number of wars in the subsystem. Another set of indicators would measure intensity of domestic turbulence: deaths per internal war (49) and per intervention (50), as well as Rosecrance's insecurity of elite tenure (51). Richardson and Wright are also consulted to determine percentages of members initiating wars (52).

Intercorrelating independent variables 34 to 52 with stratification variables (Table 10–7), we discover that multipolarity socializes decisionmakers to think in terms of power considerations; foreign wars and interventions are common, and nearly every member of the subsystem, having a broad decision latitude, initiates at least one war. Tight polarity also conditions actors to think in terms of power. But foreign policy elites are less free to act, and they start wars less often; ideological considerations will enter into decisionmaking.

10.4.4 Support

The concept of *support* is borrowed from David Easton, who defines his notion as "actions or orientations promoting and resisting a political system, the demands arising in it, and the decisions issuing from it."[40] Support and nonsupport are inputs in the political process, an effect of which may alter the scope of elites' coordination in political activities.

If scholars have only recently conceived of international systems and subsystems, decisionmakers of states doubtless have even fuzzier images. Nevertheless, on occasion some units rally together to ward off aggressive actions. Instances of alliances between minor powers and major powers enable us to chart the extent to which weaker members are willing to go along with elites of particular subsystems, and vice versa. Similarly, we

---

[39] James N. Rosenau, "Internal War as an International Event," *International Aspects of Civil Strife,* ed. Rosenau (Princeton: Princeton University Press, 1964), pp. 14–44.

[40] David Easton, "An Approach to the Analysis of Political Systems," *World Politics,* IX (April 1957), 390.

TABLE 10–7
Intercorrelations Between International Stratification
and International Socialization[a]

Socialization Variables	Style	International Stratification Poles 6	Looseness of Poles 132	Source
34. Number of members	I	.33	.15	H
35. Decision latitude	I	(.40)	(.57)	Ro
36. Percent sovereign members	F	—.07	.14	H
37. Percent members retaining sovereignty	A	—.26	.19	H
38. Percent extraregion members	E	—.39	.09	H
39. Mean total "status scores"	S	—.05	—.07	SS
40. Ratio of members to middle and major powers	H	—.01	—.07	H
41. Diversity in ways of life	—M	.06	—.06	H
42. Extent of power orientation	—C	(.51)	(—.52)	H
43. Incompleteness of interaction	U	—.03	.38	H
44. Extent of rational calculation	P	—.35	(.62)	H
45. Extent of internal preoccupation	R	.11	—.26	H
46a. Percent internal wars	—Q	—.33	.19	RFB
46b. Percent internal wars	—Q	—.26	.32	W
47a. Percent interventions	—Q	(.46)	—.09	RFB
47b. Percent interventions	—Q	(.53)	—.24	W
48. Percent foreign wars	—Q	(.43)	—.14	RFB
49. Deaths per internal war	—Q	.36	—.19	RB
50. Deaths per intervention	—Q	.39	—.15	RB
51. Insecurity of tenure	—Q	—.33	.05	Ro
52a. Percent members starting wars	—Q	(.68)	—.11	RFB
52b. Percent members starting wars	—Q	.17	(.46)	W

[a] For key to symbols see Table 10–5.

would profit from knowing the extent of membership in *coalitions,* that is, groups of entities fighting on the same side in wartime.

Since the term support refers to the backing of elites who govern polities, indicators of self-consciousness in support would consist of counts of overt manifestations of alliances and wartime coalitions with major powers as partners. Number of minor powers allied with major powers (53), and number of minor powers in coalitions with major powers (54) will be used, therefore.

If ententes are the least formal types of alliances, it follows that the percentage of pacts (rather than ententes) with both major and minor powers (55) will measure formality in support. The percentage of all wartime coalitions with minor powers that include subnational entities (56) can serve as a separate indicator of informal support for elites.

When an international subsystem is supported vigorously, we expect much more warfare than when there is a general level of disinterest. Support hyperactivity might be estimated by percentaging the number of minor powers in alliances containing major powers (57) and the number of wars involving minor powers in which minor powers fight alongside major powers (58).

Exogenous support would exist were members of a subsystem mostly loyal to some second subsystem in which they are also members, a situation resembling xenophilia on the interpersonal level. If overlapping group membership theory is correct, peaceful subsystems combine both exogenous and endogenous loyalties. Extraregional alliances of minor powers, accordingly, will be percentaged from the sum of all alliances contracted by minor powers (59) to determine the extent of multiple loyalties. As a measure of temporal exogenousness, the percentage of wartime coalitions (60) and alliances between major and minor powers (61) which fall into more than one era will be calculated.

Within national systems, specialized situations in which support may be demonstrated are such practices as the singing of a national anthem, saluting of a flag, and expressing symbolic manifestations of the polity as a whole. Nonfestive activity on the other hand, abounds on the international level. In ancient international subsystems, such as the Persian and Mesopotamian imperial subsystems, fealty to an elite unit was imposed upon subject units in the form of religious practices; participation in the Olympic games might qualify as affirmations of the coherence of various Greek subsystems. The mean "status score" for minor powers (62) will permit a quantitative comparison among subsystems on the scope of linkage between non-elite units and the subsystem as a whole, based on diplomatic representation by a country.

We may dichotomize elite countries into those demanding total loyalty and those allowing multiple loyalties, a distinction appropriate to hierarchical support. The concept of alliance overlap is appropriate here to minor powers that support major powers: ratios between partners in major-minor alliances[41] and minor powers so aligned (63) and between partners in major-minor wartime coalitions and minor powers in these coalitions (64) will be used as indicators of whether only one minor power is allied with several major powers (the hierarchical case).

Macrocentric support would be more obvious to an observer when

---

[41] That is, alliances in which major powers are aligned with minor powers.

states contract nonaggression pacts, rather than so-called defensive pacts or mere ententes. Percentages of major-minor nonaggression pacts (65) will enable one to determine, however, whether such agreements are in general a mere ruse to give smaller states an illusion of security, as did Hitler in the 1930s.

One of Grotius's reasons for advocating international law is that contractual state behavior is more likely to evoke mutual trust and respect, whereas a dominant-submissive situation is always precarious, given the possibility that national pride may be asserted eventually. We may assume that legitimization is precarious if changes are bulldozed by superior force, rather than based upon contractual relationships. The number of major-minor alliances per major and minor power (66) would be high when a contractual orientation predominates.

Multilaterality of support is measured by counting the number of partners per major-minor alliance (67). The same countries could be involved in the index, as in the complex alliance network of a bloc arrangement; or various partners could be fairweather friends or fortuitous bedfellows. This difference, irrelevant here, figures into the preoccupied-routinized continuum.

If the basis on which consent is conferred is ideological, a subsystem will tend to focus on questions of formulae. A more pragmatic type of support would stress codes or policies as means to ends, and these could be different throughout the subsystem. Using length of alliances and wartime coalitions as indicators, we may calculate means of the duration of major-minor alliances (68) and coalitions (69).

When support is routine, no challenges are present within the duration of a subsystem: members are "satisfied," to use Organski's notion. Preoccupation occurs when an era is too cluttered with challenges and mobilizations of support to maintain the position of elites. To index intensity of commitment to a subsystem, a variable used by Etzioni, we may calculate the percentage of all years in which minor powers are merely allied with (70) or fight alongside (71) major powers.

Lucian Pye's notion of a systemic "identity crisis"[42] is relevant to the final style of performing the function of support. Within international subsystems, a turbulent era from the standpoint of support is one with much challenge of elites in combat situations. Accordingly, the number of wars initiated by minor powers to upset the status quo will be percentaged out of the total wars for a subsystem (72); as cross-checks, Rosecrance's codings for disturbance level (73), and increase in disturbance (74), and the per-

[42] Lucian W. Pye, *Aspects of Political Development* (Boston: Little, Brown, 1966), p. 63. The identity crisis concept comes from Erik H. Erikson, *Identity and the Life Cycle* (New York: International Universities Press, 1959).

centage of minor-major alliances that are defensive pacts (75) will be used to index turbulent support.

When there are more major powers, each heading a pole in an international subsystem, there is a flurry of cross-status alliance and coalition formation, the latter often lasting through two eras; on the other hand, minor powers tend to upset equilibria, and there is more disturbance in eras of multipolarity (Table 10–8). Loose power stratification is associated only with a high degree of alliance formation on the part of minor powers and a tendency for such subsystems to increase in disturbance over the life-span of the era.

10.5 WITHINPUT FUNCTIONS

As soon as inputs are perceived by elites within a polity, decisions or non-decisions must be made concerning articulated demands, aggregated plans, socializing influences, and the degree of support for elites. If a specific decision is made by an elite, the withinput process may be described as one of converting inputs into outputs. Process is emphasized, rather than product, which is treated in Section 10.6 under "outputs."

10.5.1 Gatekeeping

It could be simpler for elites to agree to any demand. Adaptation to every pressure, however, might undermine the power positions of elite members of a system. When a new demand emerges, only an elite may interpret it as worthy of adoption or to turn down the proposal. An accepted proposal passes along in the flow of politics to the rule-adapting stage; but a rejected proposal could either be dropped, or the member whose ideas have been rejected could seek allies in order to gain more potency by issuing the same demand within an aggregated package. *Gatekeeping,* in short, involves deciding whether a demand shall be handled either administratively or politically; in the former case the demand is approved and passed along to officials capable of putting it into effect, but in the latter case members inputting demands are forced to pressure and maneuver in concert with other members of the system. One of the most important issues handled by gatekeepers, accordingly, is the decision to admit a new actor as a member of a subsystem. Most of the variables to be discussed in this section pertain either to decisions to admit new members as participants in a subsystem or to dismiss former members.

Chinese and Japanese decisions in the early part of the nineteenth century illustrate intended and unintended gatekeeping. Japan opened a door to trading nations, thus allowing political access only indirectly. But the

TABLE 10-8
Intercorrelations Between International Stratification
and International Support[a]

Support Variables	Style	Poles 6	Looseness of Poles 132	Source
53. Number of minor powers allied with major powers	I	.12	.33	SSF
54. Number of minor powers in wartime coalitions with major powers	I	(.46)	—.08	RFB
55. Percent major–minor pacts	F	.05	.14	SSF
56. Percent coalitions with subnationals	—F	(.46)	.09	RFB
57. Percent minor powers allied with major powers	A	.09	(.42)	SSF
58. Percent minor powers in coalitions with major powers	A	(.48)	—.27	RFB
59. Percent extraregion minor power alliances	E	.05	.23	SSF
60. Percent extra-era major–minor coalitions	E	(.41)	—.29	RFB
61. Percent extra-era major–minor alliances	E	.06	.24	SSF
62. Mean minor power "status scores"	S	.10	—.18	SS
63. Ratio between partners in major–minor alliances and minor power alliances	H	—.02	.16	SSF
64. Ratio between partners in major–minor coalitions	H	(.47)	.08	RFB
65. Percent major–minor nonaggression pacts	M	.07	.25	SSF
66. Major–minor alliances per major and minor power	C	.01	.23	SSF
67. Partners per major–minor alliances	—U	.11	.25	SSF
68. Durations per major–minor alliances	—P	.02	.01	SSF
69. Durations per major–minor coalitions	—P	.25	—.19	RFB
70. Percent years in new wars with major–minor alliances	—R	.08	.26	SSF
71. Percent years in era with new major–minor coalitions	—R	(.50)	—.11	RFB
72a. Percent minor powers initiating wars	—Q	(.45)	—.14	RFB
72b. Percent minor powers initiating wars	—Q	—.03	.12	W
73. Disturbance level	—Q	(.48)	.13	Ro
74. Increase in disturbance	—Q	(.71)	(.44)	Ro
75. Percent major–minor defensive pacts	—Q	.06	.15	SSF

[a] For key to symbols see Table 10–5.

Chinese policy of exclusion looked upon economic entry as having political overtones, and the outcome was the Opium War, which resulted in the breaking down of both economic and political barriers. The number of gate-passers (76) accordingly, will be counted within each subsystem.

Gatekeeping with respect to sovereign states is more likely to receive publicity. Nonsovereign entities are handled quite informally, their admission to a subsystem taking place when belligerent subnational groups either begin a successful war of independence or attract interveners to enter the combat situation. We may therefore express the degree of formality in gate-keeping as the percentage of gatepassers that are sovereign states (77).

Hypoactive gatekeeping entails a minimum of decisions on the part of elites in adjusting to changes in the environment. A hypoactive era would be one of contentment with the status quo. The percentage of members who are gatepassers (78) is appropriate here as a measure of hyperactive gate-keeping.

Exogenous gateopening is known popularly as an "open door" policy, which was advocated by the United States as it sought admission to East Asian international subsystems in the nineteenth century. The "closed door" policy of the Chinese was met with armed resistance on the part of Western powers, resulting in the gradual weakening of China as an elite in East Asia. The percentage of new members located extraregionally (79) will index whether Deutsch's mobility precondition is present; and the percentage of gatepassers who are readmitted or deleted during the following era from the membership roster, that is, of re-gatepassers (80) will serve as a measure of temporal exogenousness.

When entry into a system is given international recognition, the new member exchanges diplomatic officials widely. The mean "status score" of gatepassers (81) is a convenient measure of specialization in gatekeeping.

If elites receive demands for adaptation from subordinates, they are likely to interpret the move in terms of their continued ability to maintain a hierarchical control over subunits. A more polyarchical gatekeeping situation would be a collegial decisionmaking process, in which new members would be allowed to enter the subsystem. The net number of gatepassers (82)—that is, the difference between disappearing and new members—has been used by Inis Claude to indicate success in the functioning of the bal-ance of power.[43]

When gatepassers are isolates that enter the system on their own in-itiative rather than enter into an existing power structure, the gatekeeping function is performed microcentrically. Macrocentric gatekeeping may be indexed by percentaging gatepassers who are aligned (83).

---

[43] Inis L. Claude, Jr., *Power and International Relations* (New York: Random House, 1962).

When gatekeeping is performed for contractual motives, there would be a tendency for gatepassers to enter many different kinds of alliances. Alliances per gatepasser (84) may be used to measure nonstatus orientations of those who align themselves in many different kinds of arrangements.

Multilateral gatepassing, similarly, takes place if the number of partners in alliances with gatepassers (85) is large. For new members, alignment means a smoother socialization process in becoming familiar with roles and rules of a subsystem; for members dropping out of a subsystem, though widely aligned, a defeat would imply a multilateral confrontation.

Pragmatic gatekeeping exists when a given member is only temporarily a member or nonmember. Bismarck's Germany, for example, occupied Paris for a comparatively short period of time and withdrew troops as the French indemnity was being paid; there was no pragmatic reason for staying any longer. The sum of durations of postgatekeeping status, divided by number of years in a subsystem era (86) will measure this element of pragmatism in the 21 subsystems to be analyzed.

The number of years in which petitioners for demands confront elites is high in a preoccupied gatekeeping situation. As for admission to a subsystem, we may index routinization-preoccupation in terms of the percentage of years in which new members are admitted or old members evicted (87).

If an international subsystem contains many wars of independence and other violent efforts on the part of actors to achieve recognition or alterations in the status quo, turbulent gatekeeping is taking place. Accordingly, the instances of all gatepassing due to war may be expressed as a percentage of total gatepassers (88).

As we see in Table 10–9, the existence of many poles encourages actors to enter or to leave as members through violent means and then to depart or reenter in the next subsystem period. Most gatepassing in loosely stratified subsystems is associated with alliance activity.

10.5.2 Plan-Making

Plan-making can be defined as deciding whether or how to allocate resources within international subsystems. Allocations could favor elites or non-elites, but they have a comprehensive scope and a concrete behavioral objective in common. *Procedural* rules having been classified under the heading of gatekeeping, plan-making is concerned largely with *substantive* rules of a polity. Our attention here will focus on alliances exclusively entered into by major powers, for it is in such structures that the most specific plan-making will be found; we will call these "major power alliances."

Because elites are a priori plan-makers, the total number of major powers (89) will indicate the extent of self-conscious plan-making. One of the basic postulates of balance of power theory has been that the existence

TABLE 10–9
Intercorrelations Between International Stratification and International Gatekeeping[a]

Gatekeeping Variables	Style	*International Stratification*		Source
		Poles 6	Looseness of Poles 132	
76. Number of gatepassers	I	(.48)	—.06	H
77. Percent sovereign gatepassers	—F	.00	—.18	H
78. Percent gatepassers	A	.21	—.23	H
79. Percent extraregion gatepassers	E	—.24	.08	H
80. Percent gatepassers in next era	E	(.44)	—.32	H
81. Mean "status score" of gatepassers	S	—.07	.31	SS
82. Percent net gatepassers	—H	.14	—.27	H
83. Percent aligned gatepassers	M	—.11	(.64)	SSF
84. Alliances per gatepasser	C	—.03	(.62)	SSF
85. Partners per alliances with gatepassers	—U	.07	(.49)	SSF
86. Durations of postgatepassing status per years in era	—P	.23	—.10	H
87. Percent years of gatepassing	—R	.30	—.14	H
88. Percent violent gatepassers	—Q	(.59)	—.05	H

[a] For key to symbols see Table 10–5.

of many major powers makes for stability, since it is difficult to conceive of any single alliance that would not provoke a counterbalancing combination and thus maintain subsystem equilibrium.

Formal plan-making involves official declarations of aims and intentions by major powers. The percentage of pacts exclusively contracted by major powers (90), as opposed to the ententes agreed to, will serve as an index of formality in plan-making.

Hypoactive plan-making is identical with *immobilism,* a term defined in Section 7.4.5 to embrace the notion of blockage in developmental processes within societal systems. The percentage of major powers aligned exclusively with each other (91) represents a hyperactive situation at the level of international subsystems.

The plan-making process is predominantly exogenous when elites are largely external, to use another Etzioni concept. Although Etzioni analyzes a case in which external elites abandon the scene of their own unification efforts, in many international subsystems no such prospect is often in sight; hence, wars of decolonization often arise. We may index exogenousness by calculating the percentage of major powers joining extraregional alliances (92) and the percentage of major power alliances that spill out into succeeding subsystem eras (93).

In national polities a specialized structure that we ordinarily expect to sanction plans is the legislature. In international subsystems, therefore, we might ask whether assemblies of intergovernmental organizations (IGOs) are present or absent. Another way of proceeding is to count the number of new IGOs (94) within a subsystem, since such bodies tend to have some specialized plan-making activities.

Unity among major powers is relevant to hierarchical and polyarchical plan-making. As soon as a division appears in the ranks of the elites, one would expect more violence within an international subsystem. Etzioni's mono-elite and equalitarian unions are conceived to have both advantages and disadvantages: the former are more effective, the latter more durable. The ratio between the size of exclusive major power alliances and the number of aligned major powers (95) within subsystems can inform us about the broadness or narrowness of programmatic preparations and thus of the extent of hierarchical plan-making.

Macrocentric plan-making has as its target a restructuring of an international subsystem in the interest of all members and potential members. Since it is elites who must decide to embark on such a venture, macrocentric plan-making may be indexed by the percentage of all exclusive major power alliances that are nonaggression pacts (96).

The most contractual way in which plans may be drawn up within international subsystems would be by treaties, resolutions, conventions, and other legal documents. Plans conceived on the basis of status considerations are seldom found in quite so observable a form. An indirect measure of preferences among elites for planning alongside one another would be the percentage of all major power alliances that exclusively have major powers as partners (97).

Plan-making is multilateral when a concert of great powers is established, as in some of the subsystems of Europe and Hawaii reviewed in the previous chapter. The mean number of partners per exclusive major power alliances (98) will yield a measure of bilaterality versus multilaterality.

Once pragmatic plans are brought to fruition, we anticipate disruption of the alliance. In a more ideological plan-making situation a series of plans emerges over time, as a figure representing the mean duration of exclusive major power alliances (99) would demonstrate. On the other hand, of course, some plans do take longer to achieve than others, so the indicator is not entirely satisfactory.

Preoccupied plan-making consists of several simultaneous efforts to restructure political reality; a more routinized plan-making style involves cumulative changes. Planning on many fronts might so drain the resources of even a superpower that it would prefer peace in order to proceed to a successful completion of plans espoused and undertaken; alternatively, a high degree of cumulativity in planning implies a willingness to take things casually and a reluctance to become excited or tempted into entering war. The percentage of years with new exclusive major power alliances (100) will be used to indicate preoccupation in plan-making, in determining whether routinization or preoccupation is a pathway toward peace.

Turbulent plan-making would be associated with wars when elites fight among themselves to divide spoils or to agree upon spheres of influence. The percentage of defensive pacts among exclusive major power alliances (101) indexes the extent to which plan-making is seen as necessary on the level of military-strategic commitments.

None of the 13 variables indexing major power plan-making activity in Table 10–10 is related very strongly to the number of poles. But loose stratification encourages concert-type alliances in which many major powers band together and do not admit middle or minor powers as partners. These concert arrangements tend to persist in two eras more often when power is loosely distributed, evidently because their rationale for existing persists only so long as polarity does not become too rigidified.

10.5.3 Recruitment

In order for elites to maintain patterns of relationships within an international subsystem, which we are defining in terms of military-security issues, some control must be exercised over the selection of new elites or the elimination of existing elites. The function of *recruitment* is central to an analysis of how an existing power stratification is maintained, changed, or undermined.

In international subsystems of the twentieth century, recruitment has been handled in a more ad hoc way than in the early nineteenth century, when Chinese hegemony in Asia and the Concert of Europe clearly stood in a position to admit or dismiss prospective major and middle powers from membership. If the degree of procedural indeterminacy in recruitment is high, there may be higher levels of conflict than in subsystems with major powers who tightly control admission to their own status. The number of *recruitees* (102) may be defined as all powers crossing a threshold from or to middle powers status—in either direction. This variable will index the extent to which recruitment is performed self-consciously.

A formally recruited elite would fulfill various conditions, such as obtaining supremacy in thermonuclear weapons, or may achieve elite status through military prowess, such as by victory or defeat in warfare. Informal

TABLE 10–10
Intercorrelations Between International Stratification
and International Plan-Making[a]

Plan-Making Variables	Style	International Stratification		Source
		Poles 6	Looseness of Poles 132	
89. Number of major powers	I	.12	.29	H
90. Percent exclusive major power pacts	F	.17	(.47)	SSF
91. Percent major powers allied exclusively with each other	A	.18	(.47)	SSF
92. Percent extraregion major power alliances	E	.25	.10	SSF
93. Percent extra-era exclusive major power alliances	E	.23	(.48)	SSF
94. Number of new IGO's	S	.17	.05	Sp
95. Partners per exclusive major power alliance	H	.00	(.40)	SSF
96. Percent exclusive major power nonaggression alliances	M	.18	.19	SSF
97. Percent exclusive major power alliances	—C	.11	.28	SSF
98. Partners per exclusive major power alliances	—U	.33	(.46)	SSF
99. Durations per exclusive major power alliances	—P	.34	.26	SSF
100. Percent years with new exclusive major power alliances	—R	—.07	.29	SSF
101. Percent exclusive major power defensive pacts	—Q	.18	(.53)	SSF

[a] For key to symbols see Table 10–5.

recruitment involves promotion or demotion, which can often be a more subtle process. We shall, therefore, divide formally recruited elites by all those recruited in a particular subsystem (103).

Hypoactive recruitment entails no addition or subtraction from the middle or major power categories when one subsystem succeeds another. The percentage of all members changing from or to elite status (104) will be used as an indicator of hyperactivity.

Recruitment of extraregional major and middle powers is the same kind of situation as penetration on the societal level, as set forth in Section 7.7.5. Nonpenetration exists when a subsystem recruits only endogenously. The percentage of extraregional recruitment (105) will be used to index exogenousness in recruitment.

If we were to analyze national polities, a specialized institution for recruitment would ordinarily be an election. It is true that elections do take place within international organizations; but we are focusing on international subsystems conceived in terms of conflict, and no elections are held for the role of elites. We are forced, therefore, to use "specialization" in a broad sense and to measure mean "status scores" of recruitees (106), indicating whether new or old elites are recognized by other countries or isolated diplomatically. The latter situation, of course, is illustrated by the rise of the People's Republic of China to major power status despite her diplomatic isolation in the 1960s.

The most hierarchical type of recruitment involves the major power category, rather than the middle power rank. The net percentage of major power recruitment (107) will be calculated to determine whether minor-middle or middle-major thresholds are associated with different sorts of conditions. The denominator for this variable is the number of countries gaining or losing the status of major or middle power.

Macrocentric recruitment, like macrocentric gatepassing, would be more in evidence when entities changing status are aligned with other countries, instead of achieving objectives as lone wolves in the international arena. The percentage of recruitees in alliances (108) indexes macrocentrism in recruitment.

Multilateralism in recruitment is highest when each recruitee is allied with many other members of a subsystem. The number of partners per alliance with recruitees (109) will supply a measure of countries attached in some way to the destiny of a recruitee.

Contractuality in recruitment, accordingly, exists when the number of alliances per recruitee (110) is high. A change in a member's status can be bound up with the contractual record of many other member states in this manner.

The duration of postrecruitment status for members varies according to the year in which a member increases or decreases his status during the life of a subsystem. The postrecruitment durations per year in an international conflict subsystem (111) is a variable which indicates whether most recruitment takes place in earlier or later stages of a subsystem era. If the index is high, then pragmatic recruitment is low; recruitment based on ideological criteria would be more likely to persist.

Preoccupied recruitment would take place were an indicator of percent years of recruitment (112) to reveal that changes in status occur very frequently. A more routinized recruitment situation would be to have status changes in one and only one year for a subsystem era.

The process of recruitment may be peaceful or disorderly, depending upon whether means used to bring about change are violent or nonviolent.

The number of violent recruitees, percentaged from the total recruitees in a subsystem era (113), is therefore proposed as an index of turbulent recruitment.

During many years of multipolar systems there are likely to be reshufflings in the composition of elites, and on the basis of victories and defeats in war (Table 10–11). Tight stratification is more likely to have changes in elite status at the conclusion of the era, and to involve countries with a wide range of diplomatic contacts (though based geographically close to the core of the subsystem).

10.5.4 Supervision

Detailed observation by elites of the extent to which activities in a polity are out of phase with each other is *supervision*. Since the concept of supervision is unique to the structural-functional schema presented in this volume,[44] further elaboration is needed. If we regard the main source of innovations as demands placed upon elites, an elite must also have some sort of factual understanding of a situation in order to proceed effectively in considering alternative policies. Similarly, a jury in a courtroom will want to be exposed to relevant information before making its decison. Supervision consists of fact-gathering and observation with an aim of piecing together an organized conception of realities relevant to individual choice situations. It is essential to know how a polity is actually operating before deciding to restructure its operations. Activities designed to yield an integrated view of how political affairs are conducted at an operational level are often referred to as intelligence gathering, but that term usually denotes an accumulation of secret information for processing by elites. Supervision is processing of intelligence data as well as information from more public sources. Whereas plan-making is more properly the business of stronger powers in international arenas, supervision may be performed by both major and middle powers that wish to protect and extend their interests as dominant members of an international subsystem. As a withinput, supervision is primarily an elite activity, since only elites are able to afford the luxury of overseeing the subsystem as a whole.

Serendipitous supervision is an unintentional discovery of information useful to elites in coordinating activities of an international subsystem. Conscious supervision is search behavior,[45] using that term in the technical

[44] The first appearance is in Haas, "A Functional Approach to International Organization." See also E. A. Landy, *The Effectiveness of International Supervision* (Dobbs Ferry: Oceana, 1966).

[45] Cf. James G. March and Herbert A. Simon, with the collaboration of Harold Guetzkow, *Organizations* (New York: Wiley, 1958).

TABLE 10–11
Intercorrelations Between International Stratification
and International Recruitment[a]

Recruitment Variables	Style	International Stratification		Source
		Poles 6	Looseness of Poles 132	
102. Number of recruitees	I	.10	.23	H
103. Percent formal recruitment	F	.02	—.28	H
104. Percent recruitees	A	—.02	.09	H
105. Percent extraregion recruitees	E	.11	(.47)	H
106. Mean recruitee "status scores"	S	.26	(—.43)	SS
107. Percent net major power recruitment	H	—.33	.01	H
108. Percent aligned recruitees	M	—.04	.38	SSF
109. Number of partners per alliance with recruitee	C	.14	.37	SSF
110. Alliances per recruitee	—U	.02	.31	SSF
111. Postrecruitment durations per year	—P	—.05	(.42)	H
112. Percent years of recruitment	—R	(.41)	—.21	H
113. Percent violent recruitees	—Q	(.44)	.13	H

[a] For key to symbols see Table 10–5.

sense established by organization and decision theorists. The number of major and middle powers (114) gives a clue to the scope and magnitude of supervision within a subsystem at the self-conscious level.

Supervision that takes on a formal cast may be recorded on paper or in official transcripts, such as ambassadorial reports and proceedings of conversations. Informal supervision entails a heavier reliance on oral sources of communication.[46] Informal supervision will be judgmentally assessed under the rubric extent of indirect supervision (115).

Hypoactive and hyperactive supervision are direct counterparts to underload and overload situations, as we have explicated them in Chapter 4. An ability to process large amounts of information is related to channel capacity; an appropriate variable indexing hyperactive supervision is Rosecrance's assessments for level of technology (116).

[46] Chadwick F. Alger, "Decision-Making Theory and Human Conflict," *The Nature of Human Conflict*, ed. Elton B. McNeil (Englewood Cliffs, N. J.: Prentice-Hall, 1965), Chapter 13.

Extraregionality of targets of supervision will be coded on the basis of whether elites predominantly supervise intraregion members and situations, rather than supervising largely outside the territorial confine of a subsystem. If a home subsystem is so peaceful that attention can be deflected abroad, one might anticipate a history of long subsystem eras. The ratio of intra-region to extraregion supervision (117) will be coded judgmentally to determine whether it is in fact the case that peace within a subsystem leads to imperial expansion on the part of major and middle powers.

If supervision is performed largely by elites, then specialization in supervision will be indexed by mean "status scores" of middle and major powers (118). Wide official contacts would be contrasted with situations wherein a practice of diplomatic exchange is considered less necessary, due to policies of isolationism or punitive nonrecognition.

Hierarchical supervision exists when most elites are major powers and there are few middle powers. The ratio of major to middle powers (119) will enable us to ascertain whether most supervision is undertaken by mem-bers of subsystems with the power to bring about change in response to observations, or merely by countries that are unable to fully control their own destinies. (The latter countries are middle powers, the former major powers.)

Macrocentric supervision (120) involves the collection of data in order to further goals embracing the subsystem as a whole. Microcentric super-vision is reminiscent of John Foster Dulles's phrase "agonizing reappraisal," a practice that indicated an inability either to predict foreign state behavior or to control entropic tendencies of world politics.

Supervision to determine when members of a subsystem have fulfilled contractual obligations may be called auditing. In a subsystem where there is much suspicion of disobedience from members with inferior status, super-vision would consist of policing; though as soon as police agents introduce a coercive flavor, their activities cease to be solely supervisory. A ratio be-tween auditing and policing by elites (121) will be scaled judgmentally.

Unity among elites is a key characteristic in Kaplan's discussion of the operation of various systems. When supervision is undertaken by each state on its own behalf, however, it has been considered to be a "hidden hand" that supposedly makes for stability; this has been one of the chief views espoused by balance-of-power theorists. A rating of the extent of coopera-tion between major and middle powers (122) will be attempted to take multi- and unilaterality in supervision into account in our subsequent analysis

Supervision focusing on ideology tends to match existing conditions against an ideal type of subsystem—that is, in terms of a substantive type of order to be established. A more pragmatic form of supervision would be concerned with specific demands for decisions for ad hoc adjustments within an existing modus vivendi. The most appropriate variable here would appear to be Rosecrance's ideological consonance (123), for basic differences between "is" and "ought" models in international relations are usually expressed in the jargon of an ideology.

If resources of a subsystem are agreed to consist of territories and peoples, one task of supervision is to assess whether peoples in certain territories are satisfied enough with their respective governments to be ready to defend themselves against outside threats. A reshuffling in resources becomes manifest when boundaries are redrawn, governments are overthrown, or peoples and territories are occupied by foreign elements. But supervision is routine so long as there are neither neutral powers nor unpopulated areas for colonization. Unavailability of resources (124), another Rosecrance notion, would therefore be a measure of lack of preoccupation over supervision as a function.

If members of a subsystem resist efforts to supervise them, a turbulent epoch will ensue if inquisitive elites persist in breaking through barriers. The quotation in Section 1.5 from D. J. Hill concerning Prussia's desire to capture archives in Saxony is a classic example of the danger of secret diplomacy. A nonburglarizing performance of the supervision function, according to Woodrow Wilson, would go hand in hand with a more peaceful era. Paralleling Riggs's notion of ease of legitimization of innovations, we may assume that ease of legitimizing changes of major and middle powers (125) is much more precarious if changes are bulldozed by superior force, rather than based on value compatibility and consultations of non-elites, as Deutsch and associates urge in the formation of security communities.

The more poles, the more supervision will be indirect and microcentric (Table 10–12). Tight polarity is more of a modern phenomenon, since it is highly related to levels of technology and to far-flung diplomatic representation; tightness also entails much cooperation between major and middle powers, but the number of such elites will be smaller than in looser eras.

10.6 OUTPUT FUNCTIONS

After elites of a system have made a decision, their next step is to carry out their intentions. In national politics it is the duty of administrative staffs to perform output functions, but in international subsystems elites very often must do the job themselves.

10.6.1 Rule-Adapting

If a demand placed upon an elite is regarded as worthy of incremental adoption, the withinput process is for the most part short-circuited; an arduous effort to aggregate and to perform the plan-making function is

TABLE 10–12
Intercorrelations Between International Stratification
and International Supervision[a]

Supervision Variables	Style	International Stratification Poles 6	Looseness of Poles 132	Source
114. Number of major and middle powers	I	.10	(.47)	H
115. Extent of indirect supervision	—F	(.64)	—.26	H
116. Level of technology	A	—.02	(—.72)	Ro
117. Ratio of intraregion to extraregion supervision	E	.38	—.26	H
118. Mean major and middle power "status scores"	S	.39	(—.65)	SS
119. Ratio of major to middle powers	H	.05	—.25	H
120. Macrocentric supervision	M	(—.42)	.32	H
121. Ratio between auditing and policing	C	—.28	(.52)	H
122. Extent of cooperation among major and middle powers	—U	.04	(—.41)	H
123. Ideological consonance	—P	.31	—.29	Ro
124. Unavailability of resources	—R	—.17	.13	Ro
125. Ease of legitimizing changes of major and middle powers	Q	.13	.25	H

[a] For key to symbols see Table 10–5.

unnecessary. The adaptation process is usually activated in response to changes in the nonhuman environment; but if a particular plan is difficult to implement within a polity, information on possible noncompliance might lead instead to a minor modification in a plan so that its goals can be achieved with less political friction. Procedural adjustments sometimes have a legal aspect, and one aspect of the judicial process consists of deciding whether vague or outmoded statutes, or even previous court decisions, should be brought up to date in their applicability to contemporary conditions. Administrative law is more directly pertinent to rule-adapting, since decisions on administrative matters tend to be less dramatic and more incremental in scope. Almond has used the broad term "rule adjudication" as a separate function in his framework. However, adjudication involves some performance of the gatekeeping and supervision functions: courts can decide not to hear cases on appeal, and evidence being presented before a court constitutes a report of supervisory activities. Only the terminal process in a judicial proceeding involves applying rules to particular situations—that is, *rule-adapting*. Rule-adapting in international conflict becomes manifest in the form of postwar treaties of peace, so we will develop indicators based on Quincy Wright's data, wherein each war is designated as terminated by treaty or otherwise.

Self-conscious rule-adapting may be indexed by counting the number of postwar treaties (126). Subsystems with many wars, thus, have more opportunities to engage in rule-adapting in military-strategic matters; whether such potential is realized remains an empirical question.

If elites adapt rules mainly regarding sovereign states, the process is more likely to be formalized and overt than when the object of attention is a nonsovereign entity. Secret diplomacy, nevertheless, was so common in the heyday of sovereign states preceding World War I that Woodrow Wilson felt obliged to call for a new era of open diplomacy. Following the terminology of Easton, formal behavioral rule-adapting is "overt," whereas "covert" performance of the function is informal and is performed in secret. A ratio between overt and covert rule-adapting (127) would blend these considerations into a single indicator, though lack of quantitative raw data necessitates a judgmental scaling of the 21 subsystems.

Hyperactivity in rule-adapting entails a growth in international law. But few international subsystems have been so under the influence of Grotius as to accelerate legal aspects of international order. The variable decrease in international law (128) permits us to score diminution separately from stasis.

Adapting primarily with reference to units outside the core region of a system involves moves to penetrate and to dominate. When most adapting is in reference to intraregional members of a subsystem, the system is autonomous. The degree to which one subsystem is dominant or subordinate vis-à-vis another is thus related to exogenousness in rule-adapting. We will use the percentage of extraregional postwar treaties (129) by member states as a quantitative variable. The percentage of extra-era postwar treaties (130) will handle the temporal dimension.

Because tribunals are obvious rule-adapting structures, the absence of subsystem tribunals (131) will serve as a variable appropriate for nonspecialized rule-adapting. Courts perform other functions for a polity, but to a lesser degree; few structures are more specifically expected to adapt rules to changing conditions in international arenas.

One looks for centralized operations to signify hierarchical rule-adapting. Unlike the notion of poles discussed above in Section 10.4.1, centralization here refers to whether the function of rule-adapting is handled by one organization or by many independent entities. The degree of looseness in polarity (132), one of the defining characteristics of subsystems, serves as an index of polyarchy in that elites may effect administrative changes in a system by means other than strict chain-of-command delegation to subordinate units of a subsystem. Initially the loose-tight continuum was proposed by Kaplan to refer to monolithicity in bipolar bloc arrangements. Rosecrance has expanded the scope of our judgmental sensitivities by using the concept of unappropriated resources for both neutralist and unconquered power vacuum situations, though looseness applies somewhat more specifically to the lack of hierarchy in fashioning the rules that guide members of international subsystems.

One of the major debates about how statesmen calculate and operate in the international arena is concerned with whether realism or idealism is an optimal strategy, as has been alluded to in our discussion of power theory in Section 1.5. A ratio between realism and idealism (133), thus, would yield a variable that taps the extent of microcentrism versus macrocentrism in rule-adapting.

If status considerations are paramount in rule-adapting, then elites merely bow to strong pressures. Contractual rule-adapting means revising treaties and other agreements in an atmosphere respectful to international law. The extent of procedural rule-adapting (134) has always been low in international systems, though self-conscious efforts to bring international law into being in some of the earlier European subsystems will result in higher rankings for these periods; and the pursuit of peaceful change[47] will be used as a supplementary guide to the coding.

Deutsch's notion of "mutual responsiveness" between members of an international subsystem or security community is applicable to multilateral rule-adapting. When units are responsive to one another's needs and desires, a multilateral process of adaptation is taking place. Unilateral adaptation, in contrast, occurs when there is a lack of cooperation across poles (135) of a subsystem.

If the basis on which rules are adapted is ideological in nature, the subsystem will tend to focus on absolute values. A more pragmatic type of rule-adapting would stress codes or policies as means to ends that could be different throughout the subsystem. Of the two orientations, delineated by Riggs, disputes over codes appear more amenable to compromise and bargaining. A ratio between instrumental and ideological rule-adapting (136) is to be assigned judgmentally to each subsystem for purposes of quantitative analysis in Chapter 11.

Preoccupation with rule-adapting occurs when the percentage of years with wars concluded by treaties (137) is high. Wars that fail to be concluded by documents asserting new rules suggest that power struggles will

[47] Wolfram Hanrieder, "International Organizations and International Systems," *Journal of Conflict Resolution*, X (September 1966), 297–313.

continue unabated and there will be no attempt to create legally defined modi vivendi.

Wars to secure an adaptation in rules are referred to in the traditional jargon of diplomatic historians as "wars of settlement."[48] A more quiescent form of adaptation occurs when the existing framework of an international subsystem is accepted, and change is effected by a "muddling through" process.[49] The percentage of all wars not concluded by treaties (138) gauges the extent to which turbulent behavior leads to a performance of the function of rule-adapting.

Under multipolarity wars are more likely to be concluded by treaties, and there is less proceduralism, with more overall cross-pole cooperation, based on realistic rather than idealistic values (Table 10–13). Poles fail to cooperate when power is loosely stratified, and it is less likely that wars will be concluded by treaties when tightness is present. We should also note that competing value systems are more likely to clash with each other under tight than under loose polarity.

10.6.2 Implementation

In Almond's structural-functional formulation the term "rule-applying" is approximately equivalent to our use of *implementation*. However, the lexical meaning of "application" is sufficiently broad to subsume "rule-adapting," "enforcement," and even "direction" to a significant extent. A precise word is preferred to denote activities of elites and their agents which carry out substantive plans in a positive sense. Implementation of plans means moving from the drawing boards to operational reality. Implementation via international conflict, therefore, surfaces in warfare involving major powers as participants, which we shall refer to as "major power wars."

Following our convention of indexing intentional styles of function performance with magnitudes, the number of wars with major powers (139) will indicate intentional implementation. Subsystems with many major power wars self-consciously contain more implementation of elite plans. The term "implementation," however, denotes a beginning of efforts to achieve elite aims through military means; to be victorious in such wars is something else again and pertains to our rule-enforcement function.

If implementation involves only sovereign states, the degree of formality is high. Elites, however, may prefer to expand into areas not under the control of established members of a subsystem, so we might anticipate

[48] Cf. Mowat, *The European States System.*

[49] Charles E. Lindblom, "The Science of 'Muddling Through'," *Public Administration Review,* XIX (Spring 1959), 79–88.

TABLE 10–13
Intercorrelations Between International Stratification and
International Rule-Adapting[a]

Rule-Adapting Variables	Style	International Stratification		Source
		Poles 6	Looseness of Poles 132	
126. Number of postwar treaties	I	.24	(.59)	W
127. Ratio of overt to covert rule-adapting	F	—.24	—.35	H
128. Decrease in international law	—A	.14	—.07	H
129. Percent extraregion postwar treaties	E	(—.47)	—.33	WF
130. Percent extra-era postwar treaties	E	.27	(.41)	WF
131. Lack of international tribunals	—S	.16	—.04	H
132. Looseness in polarity	—H	—.06	(1.00)	H
133. Ratio between realism and idealism	—M	(.44)	(—.46)	H
134. Extent of procedural rule-adapting	C	(.70)	—.39	H
135. Cooperation across poles	—U	(.41)	(—.75)	H
136. Ratio of instrumental to ideological rule-adapting	P	—.38	.01	H
137. Percent years with postwar treaties	—R	.23	(.66)	WF
138. Percent wars not concluded by treaties	—Q	(.70)	(—.58)	WF

[a] For key to symbols see Table 10–5.

informal implementation to involve more aggressive elite activity and use the indicator percent major power wars with subnational entities (140).

Hyperactivity in implementation occurs when each major power is a belligerent in several wars and seeks at all times to secure outcomes favorable to the interests of one or more of the elites. The number of war entries per major power (141) will be computed, accordingly.

Kaplan suggests that one of the reasons for European stability and continuing multipolarity was that aggressive energies could be directed toward imperial and colonial expansion outside Europe up to the contemporary era, when former colonies have been granted independence. Exogenous implementation may be gauged by several variables: percentage of what Wright classifies as imperial wars (142), percent extraregional major power wars (143), and percent extra-era major power wars (144).

Presence of a system-wide bureaucracy constitutes a specialized form of implementation. Few such institutions relevant to military-strategic issues, however, have existed in international subsystems. Rosecrance's concept of "regulator" has been proposed as a functional equivalent of a systemic implementation device. But regulators are either specialized or nonspecialized in form. The classical balance of power mechanism did not have an institutionalized form, for it sprang into existence only when some members of a subsystem had to band together in order to check ambitions of a potentially hegemonic force; an alliance regulator, in this light, would be only partly specialized insofar as an alliance often specifies or assumes a date of termination and thus makes the structure too impermanent to be an institution. More specialized forms of regulation are concerts of major powers and international organizations; subsystems with a regulator institution (145) will be coded on a yes-no basis so that permanency in regulation may be correlated with independent variables in this section of the volume.

Hierarchical implementation suggests major powers that subdue middle and minor powers on a battlefield. The percentage of major power wars with major powers fighting on opposite sides (146) and percent exclusive major power wars (147) can be used to ascertain whether most implementation involves power struggles at the top, which are more polyarchical in character, or whether the chain of command itself is being attacked and defended vis-à-vis minor and middle powers.

Another way of looking at implementation is in terms of motives that prompt elites to secure compliance. If intentions are benign, the effect of wars would be expected to be different from the situations in which elites are out for selfish gain. The percentage of major power wars aiming to destabilize (148) can provide a measure of microcentrism.

Plans put into practice to buttress an actor's status in a system are implemented in a discriminatory fashion. Wars per major power (149) may give a clue concerning repeated efforts of elites to assert their status, whereas the percentage of major power wars ended by treaties (150) measures the tendency for such wars to be handled in a contractual manner.

A dyadic war involving one or more major powers may be described as bilateral, for no third parties are present to assist or to oppose the elite states. As the number of participants per major power war (151) increases, implementation is more multilateral in style.

Sometimes plan implementation involves a fulfillment of utopian dreams, based on ideological perspectives. When the mean duration per major power war (152) is short, a pragmatic solution is much more probable than in a knock-down drag-out war in which elites are belligerents.

Similarly, implementation in military-strategic issues is more routine the less often wars erupt. The percentage of years with new major power wars (153) indexes preoccupation with the implementation function.

From time to time, plan implementers run into resistance from constituents within a polity. If implementation within an international subsystem is achieved in a quiescent manner, there are three main possibilities: the scope of implementation could be low and almost unperceivable; elites and their agents could be virtually omnipotent and unchallenged; or implementers could enjoy considerable legitimacy. The percentage of all wars with major powers resulting in destabilization (154) may be used as a rough index of the turbulence with which implementation is performed in international subsystems.

Implementation turbulence is correlated positively with several variables over the ± .40 level (Table 10–14). For example, the major powers are much more likely to go to war under multipolarity, even against each other, in order to destabilize the stratification of power; these wars will be of long duration and will succeed in destabilizing the status quo despite institutional regulators. Major powers will repeatedly initiate wars when there is loose power stratification, also despite regulatory bodies.

10.6.3 Enforcement

When members of a system are insubordinate, it is incumbent upon elites to enforce procedural rules for maintaining a pattern of a system. *Enforcement,* in short, is yet another breakdown of Almond's broad "rule-applying" function, and it implies an exercise of coercion or even violence to quell troublesome conduct. At the international level, counterelite wars are one immediate way in which to evoke enforcement. Unlike implementation, our interest here is not in mere participation by major powers but in initiation of wars by elites of a subsystem.

Enforcement activity is intended when the number of wars initiated by major powers (155) is high. A more intentional performance of the enforcement function would be to engage in aggressive activities in order to ensure that a subsystem is under control.

One must look at targets of elite activity to distinguish between formal and informal enforcement. Formal, state-to-state enforcement is external war. When enforcement activities delve into domestic quarrels, one refers to such less formalized situations as interventions. The percentage of wars started per major power including nonsovereign (156) participants will indicate lack of formality in enforcement.

Etzioni's suggestion that force is useful in welding together a single polity from formerly separate units lends justification to some measure of overall effectiveness in elite enforcement activities. An underresponsive elite fails to enforce when violations might transform an international system; overresponsiveness implies that too much effort is expended to impose conformity in picayune situations. Accordingly, the number of war initiations per major power (157) is one of the best measures of efforts to enforce the will of elites.

TABLE 10–14
Intercorrelations Between International Stratification
and International Implementation[a]

Implementation Variables	Style	International Stratification		Source
		Poles 6	Looseness of Poles 132	
139a. Number of major power wars	I	(.64)	—.01	RFB
139b. Number of major power wars	I	(.43)	.37	W
140. Percent major power wars with subnational entities	—F	.18	.01	RFB
141a. War entries per major power	A	(.75)	—.26	RFB
141b. War entries per major power	A	.32	(.40)	W
142. Percent imperial wars	E	—.25	—.19	W
143a. Percent extraregion major power wars	E	(—.40)	.38	RFB
143b. Percent extraregion major power wars	E	—.22	—.16	W
144a. Percent extra-era major power wars	E	.28	—.39	RFB
144b. Percent extra-era major power wars	E	(.40)	—.23	W
145. Presence of regulator organ	S	(.59)	(.50)	Ro
146. Percent minor power wars with majors on opposite sides	—H	(.49)	.30	RFB
147. Percent exclusive major power wars	—H	(.47)	—.05	W
148. Percent major power wars aiming to destabilize	—M	(.77)	—.27	RFB
149a. Wars per major power	—C	.08	(.64)	RFB
149b. Wars per major power	—C	—.25	(.67)	W
150. Percent major power wars ended by treaties	C	.27	.02	WF
151a. Participants per major power war	—U	.20	—.22	RFB
151b. Participants per major power war	—U	.25	.04	W
152a. Mean duration per major power war	—P	(.71)	—.27	RFB
152b. Mean duration per major power war	—P	(.68)	.03	W
153a. Percent years with new major power wars	—R	.11	.37	RFB
153b. Percent years with new major power wars	—R	(.58)	(.52)	W
154. Percent destabilizing wars	—Q	(.57)	.12	RFB

[a] For key to symbols see Table 10–5.

An international subsystem in which elites engage in extraregional enforcement is clearly a dominant rather than subordinate subsystem. An elite expanding its domain into areas outside the core of a subsystem, hence, is contrasted with one operating solely on a localized home front. Some related notions are impermeability of actors, as developed by Herz, and Boulding's "conditional viability."[50] The percentage of all wars initiated by major powers taking place outside the core or era of a subsystem will be computed as the percent extraregion (158) and extra-era (159) wars initiated by major powers.

Strength of a regulator (160) is an obvious indicator of the extent of specialized enforcement within an international subsystem. This variable has been coded by Rosecrance across his subsystems, and similar ratings are applicable to Asia as well.

Hierarchical enforcement means to impose plans down a chain of command. Polyarchic enforcement takes place when enforcer and enforcee are both major powers. The percentage of wars initiated by major powers opposing other major powers (161) will be used to indicate the extent to which such contests tend to be fought between equals.

Enforcement with a microcentric aim involves elites in warring to upset a status quo for their own ends, rather than to stabilize a subsystem. We may accordingly percentage the number of wars initiated by major powers aiming to destabilize (162).

Elites engaging in enforcement activity may seek to legitimize their efforts through a treaty of settlement. A victory over small powers, after all, may result in domination and thus obviate a need for a contractual conclusion. The percentage of wars initiated by major powers ended by treaties (163) will be used to determine the extent to which enforcement discriminates on the basis of status. Another index is the ratio of wars initiated by major powers to total number of major powers (164).

Collective security is a multilateralized form of enforcement by means of which members of international subsystems may bring a recalcitrant to justice. Self-help, the unilateralized form of enforcement, has been customary in securing compliance within most international subsystems of the past; some thought that the League of Nations might change this pattern, yet it has remained. Instead, it would be useful to know the mean number of partners in coalitions initiated by major powers (165), for this would be a useful measure of multilaterality in enforcement.

Consistent with earlier discussions on pragmatic styles, the mean in durations per wars initiated by major powers (166) is selected to index ideologism in enforcement. Relentless struggles over many years are usually for or against preservation of a way of life, rather than over pragmatic values.

A preoccupied enforcement situation is one in which every year of a subsystem contains at least one war by an elite. Saber-rattling and other nonviolent, even nonverbal, displays of superiority in elite power are much more routine features in enforcement activities, whether international, national, or at the level of local police. The percentage of years containing

50 Kenneth E. Boulding, *Conflict and Defense* (New York: Harper, 1962).

wars initiated by major powers (167) within a subsystem indicates preoccupation versus routinization in enforcement.

Turbulent enforcement implies that an international subsystem stands perilously close to disruption on many occasions. As an indicator we will use the percentage of wars initiated by major powers resulting in destabilization (168).

Multipolarity provides a motivation for major powers to start wars over and over again in order to change the distribution of power to their own advantage (Table 10–15). Tight power stratification discourages major powers from starting wars, especially against each other, and wars in these eras will seldom be ended by treaties.

10.6.4 Direction

An innovation in the present structural-functional framework is our concept of *direction*. The term has a venerable background, for it appears in POSDCORB, and Norman Padelford and George Lincoln describe what they call "policy direction" as

> Washingtonese for the more detailed guidance of the conduct of foreign affairs and the execution of policies which have been formulated.[51]

In the same discussion the authors distinguish "direction" from "policy formulation," which we have called "plan-making" in this volume, and from a third function, "implementation" which coincides with our terminology. Direction, thus, means coordination of operational elements of foreign policy; insofar as international conflict is concerned, a crucial instance of direction is a war won by an elite member of an international subsystem. Ultimately, assertion of directive control is through victory on the battlefield. Richardson's data permit us to code each deadly quarrel participant as either a victor or nonvictor in the struggle. Wars won by major powers (169) is an index of intentional direction.

Victory by major powers in wars leads to a better coordination of various elements in the power structure of an international subsystem, even if major powers are among the defeated belligerents. When elites seek to coordinate each other as well as sovereign states, we have a condition of formal direction. If elements of a subsystem that fail to mesh are nonsovereign territories or peoples, such as piratical bands, then efforts to establish structural and behavioral linkages will have an informal appearance. Targets of coordination, in turn, vary according to the nature of units misbe-

---

[51] Padelford and Lincoln, *Dynamics of International Politics.* Cf. Gulick, "Theory of Organization." POSDCORB is an acronym for the functions of Planning, Organizing, Staffing, Directing, Co-ordinating, Budgeting.

TABLE 10–15
**Intercorrelations Between International Stratification
and International Enforcement**[a]

| | | International Stratification | | |
| | | Poles | Looseness of Poles | |
Enforcement Variables	Style	6	132	Source
155a. Number of wars initiated by major powers	I	.34	.28	RFB
155b. Number of wars initiated by major powers	I	.10	.10	W
156. Percent wars initiated by major powers including subnational entities	—F	(.56)	.04	RFB
157a. War initiations per major power	A	—.33	(.59)	RFB
157b. War initiations per major power	A	—.07	—.19	W
158a. Percent extraregional wars initiated by major powers	E	.30	—.11	RFB
158b. Percent extraregional wars initiated by major powers	E	.15	.18	W
159a. Percent extra-era wars initiated by major powers	E	—.16	—.38	RFB
159b. Percent extra-era wars initiated by major powers	E	—.03	—.34	W
160. Strength of regulator	S	.29	.03	Ro
161a. Percent wars initiated by major powers versus major powers	—H	.39	(.59)	RFB
161b. Percent wars initiated by major powers versus major powers	—H	.27	.35	W
162. Percent wars initiated by major powers aiming to destabilize	—M	(.47)	—.10	RFB
163. Percent wars initiated by major powers ended by treaties	C	.02	(.64)	WF
164a. Ratio of wars initiated by major powers to total major powers	—C	(.56)	.03	RFB

having in the subsystem, as defined by the major powers. The percentage of wars won by major powers involving subnational entities (170) will serve to indicate informal enforcement.

If there is more than one elite in an international subsystem, one can gauge hyperactivity of direction by counting the frequency of summit conferences and other exchanges of delegations among the major and middle powers. Because many international subsystems are unipolar, a somewhat broader variable is called for. Extensiveness in direction will, therefore, be indexed by the mean number of victories achieved per major power (171) in a subsystem.

TABLE 10–15—Cont.
Intercorrelations Between International Stratification
and International Enforcement[a]

Enforcement Variables	Style	International Stratification Poles 6	Looseness of Poles 132	Source
164b. Ratio of wars initiated by major powers to total major powers	—C	(.46)	.30	W
165a. Partners in coalitions with major powers initiating wars	—U	.35	.18	RFB
165b. Partners in coalitions with major powers initiating wars	—U	.13	.31	W
166a. Durations per wars initiated by major powers	—P	(.40)	.20	RFB
166b. Durations per wars initiated by major powers	—P	.28	.26	W
167a. Percent years with new wars initiated by major powers	—R	(.57)	.03	RFB
167b. Percent years with wars initiated by major powers	—R	(.61)	.15	W
168. Percent wars initiated by major powers resulting in destabilization	—Q	.39	.27	RFB

[a] For key to symbols see Table 10–5.

The target of direction is especially relevant to the exogenous-endogenous continuum. If, as in the relatively homogenous Persian Empire, units being coordinated are located well within the core of the subsystem, a set of satraps can be used to hold together a domain. If the core is held securely but a periphery needs watching, as in the Roman Empire, governors will be sent out with armies, though the armies might turn around to attack Rome itself. Exogenousness of direction, thus, may be calculated by percentaging extraregion (172) and extra-era wars won by major powers (173).

Though Padelford and Lincoln assert that the most specialized institution for displomacy in the United States is the State Department, they are thinking more of the field staff than of the bureaucracy at home. On the international level the closest approximation to a specialized organ for the function of direction is Rosecrance's concept of regulator; but, inasmuch as direction deals with potency of elite activity, a judgmental coding for increase in regulator capacity (174) supplied by Rosecrance will suffice to index specialization in the performance of the direction function.

One looks for a distinction between direction by elites and non-elites in focusing upon polyarchical versus hierarchical direction. The percentage of wars won by major powers opposing other major powers (175) is an appropriate way of measuring polyarchy in direction, since the defeat of a minor by a major power is strictly a hierarchical act.

The motive for major power involvement in wars figures into styles of macrocentrism and microcentrism. If a high percentage of wars won by major powers aim to destabilize (176), then direction is microcentric.

Repetitive victories by major powers characterize subsystems in which force is more significant than consensus in bringing about equilibria in relations between members of the system. A ratio between wars with major powers on the winning side and the total number of major powers (177), hence, yields a measure of direction on the basis of status, rather than through contractual means.

If elites have allies, their efforts to suppress international disorder can be pooled. The mean number of partners in winning coalitions with major powers (178) can tell us the extent of multilateralism in direction.

Indicators for pragmatic-ideological and preoccupied-routinized styles follow the pattern of previous functions. Mean durations of wars won by major powers (179) will be computed for the former; percent years with wars won by major powers (180) pertains to the latter.

If the process of directing an international subsystem is turbulent, elites and their agents find it almost impossible to obtain a satisfactory way of dealing with non-elites. Organski's "power transition" notion suggests that so long as economic development proceeds there are bound to be dissatisfied powers that will avoid efforts to coordinate them within a general framework. The percentage of all wars won by major powers resulting in destabilization (181) in an international subsystem will index failure of elites to keep entropy at low levels, which may be cross-checked with Rosecrance's international instability (182) estimates. Duration of a subsystem (183) is a final indicator, though it indicates quiescence rather than turbulence in direction: the longer a subsystem era, the more its regulators and elites are able to keep a power structure intact over time.

A complex pattern emerges when correlations between poles, tightness, and various styles of direction are computed (Table 10–16). According to the data, major powers are more likely to win in multipolar eras, which will be marred with instability and an increase in regulatory capacity. Tight polarity brings impotence to regulatory organs, shortens the life expectancy of a subsystem, and lowers the number of major power victories in extraregional locations.

10.7 CONCLUSION

As in Chapter 7, an effort has been made to generate variables and to hypothesize relationships on the basis of a deductively derived conceptual map. Fewer variables are selected per conceptual cell here than in Parts II and

TABLE 10–16
Intercorrelations Between International Stratification and
International Direction[a]

Direction Variables	Style	International Stratification Poles 6	Looseness of Poles 132	Source
169. Number of wars won by major powers	I	(.59)	.10	RFB
170. Percent wars won by major powers with subnational entities	—F	.12	.17	RFB
171. Victories per major power	A	(.65)	—.03	RFB
172. Percent extraregional wars won by major powers	E	—.14	(.69)	RFB
173. Percent extra-era wars won by major powers	E	.33	—.21	RFB
174. Increase in regulator capacity	S	(.40)	(.63)	Ro
175. Percent wars won by major powers versus major powers	—H	(.46)	—.05	RFB
176. Percent wars won by major powers aiming to destabilize	—M	(.58)	.05	RFB
177. Wars won per major powers	—C	(.69)	.01	RFB
178. Covictors in wars won by major powers	—U	.14	.30	RFB
179. Durations per wars won by major powers	—P	.26	.19	RFB
180. Percent years with wars won by major powers	—R	(.60)	—.01	RFB
181. Percent wars won by major powers ending in destabilization	—Q	.15	.37	RFB
182. International instability	—Q	(.52)	—.14	Ro
183. Subsystem duration	Q	—.01	(.51)	H

[a] For key to symbols see Table 10–5.

III. In many respects, however, the formulations are entirely different. Terms denoting asymmetry have a much older history than do the concepts referring to international subsystems, and terms referring to decisionmaking are also extracted from an older lexicon. Asymmetry concepts, as a result, have been subjected to clarificatory labelling in order to reduce ambiguities of language, but we have specified variables without naming the 144 conceptual cells derived in this chapter. There are at least two reasons why it does not seem unorthodox to bypass labelling. First of all, there is little confusion so far in our use of such terms as "articulation," "routinizing," and "universalistic."

The careful reader will notice that judgmental variables are involved. Approximately 30 are entirely based on a nonquantitative appraisal of how the 21 subsystems rank with respect to a qualitatively defined characteristic; an additional 30 or so variables are quantitative in form, and yet are based on definitions of such terms as "nonsovereign" or "poles." Though it would be preferable to provide an extensive rationale for each qualitative coding, as Rosecrance does so skillfully in *Action and Reaction in World Politics*, this type of discussion would merit a separate volume.[52]

Do our stratification variables relate strongly to any of the functions or styles of function performance? Polarity has consistently high correlations with almost all indicators of articulation and, to a lesser extent, with variables representing implementation and direction by elites. Looseness and tightness are associated with plan-making and supervision. Thus polarity predicts better to inputs and outputs; tightness, to withinputs in international subsystems. Correlations across the pattern variables, however, are not consistently high with either measure of stratification.

Summarizing the results of our bivariate analysis, we find that when the number of poles increases from unipolarity toward multipolarity, the following conditions are increasingly present:

1. War dyads between peoples with similar bodily characteristics.
2. Most major power wars fought to destabilize power stratification.
3. Increasing level of disturbance.
4. Procedurality in rule-adapting.
5. Wars not concluded by treaties.
6. Lengthy wars with major powers as participants.
7. Many war victories on the part of each major power.
8. Indirect international supervision.
9. New wars in many years in the era.
10. War dyads between peoples with similar styles of clothing.
11. War dyads between peoples with similar languages.
12. War dyads between peoples with similar religions and philosophies.
13. Many years with victories by major powers.
14. Members entering or departing from the subsystem primarily through violent means.
15. Presence of a regulatory organ.
16. Many years containing wars started by major powers.
17. Many wars won by major powers.
18. Many wars occur.

[52] Some coding checks were administered, but reliability coefficients are not presented herein.

19. Many wars won by major powers that desire to destabilize power stratification.
20. Many wars with destabilizing outcomes.
21. Many wars started by major powers with nonsovereign participants.
22. Few extraregional wars.

The above findings are based on bivariate correlations running from .77 to .56; the bottom of the list includes those with lower correlations. Some 32 other variables are related above the ± .40 level but are excluded from the summary for the sake of brevity. Taking the ± .55 level as a threshold for reporting correlates of tightness and looseness in power stratification, we discover that tightness is associated with the following characteristics:

1. Lack of cross-pole cooperation.
2. High level of technology.
3. Few wars won by major powers outside the core region.
4. Few years with postwar treaties.
5. Major and middle powers with an extensive diplomatic corps.
6. Major powers involved in only a very few wars.
7. Few wars started by major powers concluded by treaties.
8. Few new or departing members of the subsystem contracting alliances.
9. Regulatory capacity decreasing over time.
10. Ideological calculations overriding pragmatic considerations.
11. Few members entering alliances.
12. Few total postwar treaties.
13. Few wars concluded by treaties.
14. Low decision latitude.

Wars are clearly more common when there are many major powers, each vying for supremacy but failing to form blocs that decrease the number of poles in an international subsystem. Tight power stratification is associated with high levels of diplomatic activity and an advanced technology, but increased economic development heightens rather than ends ideology as a component of international rivalry. Postwar treaties are seldom made in tight eras, and there are relatively few alliances.

We now turn to an analysis of our 183 subsystem variables to decompose them into empirical dimensions. We hope thereby to build predictive models of the dynamics of international conflict at the systemic level of analysis.

chapter 11
Dimensions and Models
of Turbulent Systems

11.1 RESEARCH STRATEGY

What are the major dimensions of international subsystems? In the previous chapter we outlined a matrix of concepts for the analysis of international subsystems as political systems that contain inputs, withinputs, and outputs. Unlike the schemas proposed at the interpersonal and societal levels. a structural-functional classification often is presumed to entail more than just the framework of metaconcepts and conceptual variables at the intersection between two dimensional axes. The use of functional terminology, in other words, is often assumed to imply the author's bias toward functional*ism,* which makes him out to be an adherent of such postulates as a tendency for systems to persist by seeking equilibria, a tendency for behavior within systems to be complementary and interdependent, and an indispensability of a complete cycle in the performance of all functions for all types of systems. Critiques of functionalism[1] usually miss the most important aspect of structural-functional formulations—the comprehensiveness of the conceptual map for empirical research. Functional categories form the basis for theory in anthropology and sociology, and political scien-

[1] The most vigorous critique of functionalism is that of Carl G. Hempel, "The Logic of Functional Analysis," *Symposium on Sociological Theory,* ed. Llewellyn Gross (Evanston, Ill.: Row, Peterson, 1959), pp. 271–307. For a fascinating survey of types of functionalism, see William Flanigan and Edwin Fogelman, "Functionalism in Political Science," *Functionalism in the Social Sciences,* ed. Don Martindale (Philadelphia: American Academy of Political and Social Science, 1965), pp. 111–26. My approach is a type of functionalism which they do not list, however; an appropriate label for what is attempted in this part of the volume is *conceptual* functionalism, for I use categories only as guides for collecting data in an exhaustive and mutually exclusive manner.

418

tists and students of conflict will find that any functional framework suited to their task may of necessity be complex in initial empirical forays. The 183 variables derived from the 144-cell matrix of functions classified by pattern variables only skim the surface of possible indicators (Tables 11–1 and 11–2). Results, hence, will be far less generalizable about the metaconcepts than was the case in our analysis of interpersonal and societal factors, where it was possible to have several variables for each conceptual cell.

Our analysis will proceed in the same manner as in earlier empirical chapters. Sampling strata will be delineated through a Q-analysis, and major dimensions of the variables will be derived in an R-analysis. There will be one major difference in research design, however. Data on wars and internal violence have been assembled by several authors, as we mentioned in Chapter 9; we contrasted findings from Lewis Richardson's data with those for Quincy Wright's data in Chapter 10.[2] A comparison between the Richardson and Wright data will be continued in this chapter as well.

11.2 DIMENSIONS OF INTERNATIONAL SUBSYSTEMS

International systems have been classified in accordance with a variety of criteria. Membership criteria differ between Richardson and Wright. Richardson counts nonsovereign as well as sovereign entities in all types of violent disturbances with more than 315 deaths. From his list of what he calls "fatal quarrels" we will delete purely internal situations. Wright includes in his list of wars only those with formal declarations of war.

For Kaplan and Rosecrance,[3] the number of poles is the basic struc-

---

[2] The main data sources are Lewis F. Richardson, *Statistics of Deadly Quarrels* (Chicago: Quadrangle, 1960); Quincy Wright, *A Study of War*, 2d ed. (Chicago: University of Chicago Press, 1965). The main reason that data from two other compendia, those of Sorokin and Singer, are not used in the analysis in this chapter is that they are not available for enough years and countries to cover the long historical sweep of this study. See Pitirim A. Sorokin, *Fluctuations of Social Relationships, War, and Revolution* (New York: American Book Co., 1937), pp. 547–77; J. David Singer and Melvin Small, "Alliance Aggregation and the Onset of War, 1815–1945," *Quantitative International Politics*, ed. Singer (New York: The Free Press, 1968), pp. 247–86. Intercorrelations between individual variables collected from all four data bases were performed to check on whether different findings might result; Sorokin's data set is least related to the other samples of data, based as it is on an incomplete sample of countries. Singer and Wright are intercorrelated at the + .90 level or higher for nearly every variable, so there would appear to be little information loss in using Wright's data rather than Singer's—and much gain in view of the former's longer historical coverage.

[3] Morton A. Kaplan, *System and Process in International Politics* (New York: Wiley, 1957); Richard N. Rosecrance, *Action and Reaction in World Politics* (Boston: Little, Brown, 1963).

TABLE 11-1
International Subsystems Variable List

See Appendix D, pp. 620–26, for table text.

TABLE 11-2
Conceptual Map of Systemic Variables

Functions	Inten-tional	Formal	Hyper-active	Exoge-nous	Special-ized	Pattern Variables Hier-archical	Macro-centric	Status	Multi-lateral	Prag-matic	Preoc-cupied	Turbu-lent
Articulation	1	2	3	4–5	6	7	8–12	13	14	15	16	17–18
Aggregation	19	20–21	22	23–24	25	26	27	28	29	30	31	32–33
Socialization	34–35	36	37	38	39	40	41	42	43	44	45	46–52
Support	53–54	55–56	57–58	59–61	62	63–64	65	66	67	68–69	70–71	72–75
Gatekeeping	76	77	78	79–80	81	82	83	84	85	86	87	88
Plan-Making	89	90	91	92–93	94	95	96	97	98	99	100	101
Recruitment	102	103	104	105	106	107	108	109	110	111	112	113
Supervision	114	115	116	117	118	119	120	121	122	123	124	125
Rule-Adapting	126	127	128	129–130	131	132	133	134	135	136	137	138
Implementation	139	140	141	142–144	145	146–147	148	149–150	151	152	153	154
Enforcement	155	156	157	158–159	160	161	162	163–164	165	166	167	168
Direction	169	170	171	172–173	174	175	176	177	178	179	180	181–183

tural attribute of an international system, and their suggestion has been adopted in forming units of analysis for this part of the volume. Many theorists claim that the nature of international systems has changed so dramatically since the introduction of nuclear weapons in the mid–1940s that generalizations about previous eras of international politics fail to apply to the present day.[4] David Singer and Melvin Small find that results from their 1815–1945 study vary when an arbitrary cutting point of 1899–1900 is used to demarcate two time subsamples: nineteenth-century international systems operate differently from twentieth-century systems.[5] Our sample of 21 international subsystems, hence, might be composed of a number of distinct strata, as in our analysis of 32 decisionmaking cases; alternatively, there may be considerable homogeneity, as our examination of 85 countries revealed.

11.2.1 Procedure

Two pools of data were assembled, one consisting of all 183 variables using Richardson's data, and a Wright sample, also with 183 variables.[6] When all 217 variables for all 21 subsystems were intercorrelated,[7] two artifacts immediately became apparent: first of all, there is an extensive amount of missing data, which totals about 20 percent of all possible data entries; second, many variables beyond those for which both Richardson and Wright provide data intercorrelate at a ± .90 level or higher, thus rendering factor analysis precarious if an underlying structure is to be uncovered. As a consequence the two subsamples are used separately, limiting the amount of missing data to a more acceptable range. The two pools of data each have 16 cases: Richardson's includes subsystems 5–10 and 12–21; Wright's sample is composed of subsystems 1–16; five subsystems are deleted due to missing data, since the two data sources cover different though partially overlapping time periods. In addition, the number of variables was reduced through the following procedures: the variable most highly related to the others (116 "level of technology") was deleted, then the next most highly correlated variable was eliminated, and so forth until pairs of variables with only one high correlation (namely, with each other) were isolated. Then, one of the two was dropped on the basis of preserving as much equality in

---

[4] The uniqueness of postnuclear eras is claimed by Ernst B. Haas, "The Challenge of Regionalism," *International Organization,* XII (Autumn 1958), 440–58.

[5] Singer and Small, "Alliance Aggregation and the Onset of War, 1815–1945."

[6] Some 34 variables are identical for both subsamples, since differences pertain only to data on wars.

[7] Correlations were calculated using the Spearman formula in view of the small number of cases.

the number of variables within each row and column of the matrix in Table 11–2. Q-analysis, accordingly, was based upon 147 Richardson variables and 153 Wright variables.

When the Richardson sample was intercorrelated (a 16 × 16 matrix) and factor-analyzed, 13 principal components emerged with eigenvalues over 0.0, and 3 factors exceeded a 1.0 eigenvalue; for the Wright sample, there were 12 principal components over 0.0 and 4 over 1.0. The scree test of Cattell agreed with a cutoff at 3 and 4 main factors, respectively. Results of the principal axis factor analysis were not readily interpretable, so varimax orthogonal and biquartimin oblique rotations were performed—12 cycles, 488 iterations for Richardson; 13 cycles, 780 iterations for the Wright sample. Results are presented in Tables 11–3 and 11–4. Cluster analyses based on the two sets of variables are traced in Figures 11–1 and 11–2.

11.2.2   Results

In the Richardson sample, Factor I has lower loadings for recent subsystems and high loadings for *premodern* subsystems (Table 11–3). Variables most highly correlated with Factor I show a paucity of alliances, especially on the part of minor powers (Table 11–5). Factor II reveals a pattern that is almost the reverse of the one for Factor I, so the second factor would be most aptly designated as *modern*. The dividing line between premodern and modern subsystems appears to be the late nineteenth century, almost coterminous with the time boundary fixed by Singer and Small. Twentieth-century subsystems are most noted for high casualty rates in foreign wars and shifts in elite status on the part of countries with wide-ranging diplomatic contacts. Factor III is somewhat more difficult to identify on a chronological basis; it correlates − .71 with Factor I and is unrelated to Factor II. With high loadings for the bipolar North Atlantic subsystem between 1946 and 1963, Bismarckian Europe between 1872 and 1890, and the era of Italian and German unification (1848– 1871), one can identify much external preoccupation and alliance-making; the overall result is of a period of *elite stabilization* in power relationships, and much integrative alliance activity is correlated with this factor.

The premodern period is more differentiated in Wright's data, which extend farther back in time (Table 11–4). Factor I has highest loadings for nineteenth-century Europe along with the 1955–1963 tripolar Asian subsystem; a *concert* label is appropriate for nineteenth-century Europe and approximates the tacit manner in which conflict was limited to brushfire wars in Asia after the departure of the French from Indochina. Correlates of Factor I depict an era of major power victories and pacts headed by major

TABLE 11–3
Q–Factor Analysis of Richardson Sample of Subsystems

Cases	h²	Biquartimin Factors[a]		
		I	II	III
5. Europe 1823–1847	.70	(82)	24	33
6. Europe 1848–1871	.77	(78)	—00	(61)
7. Europe 1872–1890	.94	35	42	(69)
8. Europe 1891–1918	1.02	—23	(101)	13
9. Europe 1919–1945	1.01	—23	(84)	46
10. N. Atlantic 1946–1963	.74	—09	05	(99)
12. E. Asia 1843–1895	.61	(105)	—24	01
13. E. Asia 1896–1913	.86	(61)	(60)	10
14. E. Asia 1914–1945	1.06	29	(89)	—21
15. E. Asia 1946–1954	1.06	25	(91)	—13
16. Asia 1955–1963	.64	(62)	(59)	08
17. Hawaii 1738–1758	.66	(101)	—03	06
18. Hawaii 1759–1782	.76	(88)	24	—30
19. Hawaii 1783–1795	.77	(87)	25	—30
20. Hawaii 1796–1818	.79	(97)	08	—04
21. Hawaii 1819–1898	.61	(102)	—08	09
Eigenvalues[b]		8.4	3.0	1.6
Percent total variance[b]		52.4	19.0	9.8
Percent common variance[b]		64.6	23.1	12.3
Correlations between factor loadings I		1.00		
II		—.40	1.00	
III		—.71	.09	1.00

[a] Factor loadings are multiplied by 100; loadings > ± .50 are enclosed in parentheses.
[b] Based on principal axis factors.

powers, sometimes exclusively with other major powers (Table 11–5). Factor II has high loadings for European and Asian subsystems of the seventeenth and eighteenth centuries and thus is called *early state system,* where there were dynastic rulers, few international institutions, and underdeveloped weapons systems. In Factor III we find a clustering once again of *modern* subsystems, but this time the cluster clearly excludes nuclear eras; high casualty figures stand out as the most important correlate. The fourth factor in Wright's sample resembles Richardson's third factor, *elite stabilization* except that it includes the interwar twentieth-century European subsystem; once again, variables most highly related to this factor indicate high levels of institutionalized international interaction, with the nonaggression pact as a prevailing type of alliance.

Results of cluster analyses are generally similar to the factor analyses. In the Richardson data, the three main subclusters resemble the three factors reported in Table 11–3. The first subcluster contains *stabilizing* subsystems,

TABLE 11–4
Q–Factor Analysis of Wright Sample of Subsystems

Cases	h²	*Biquartimin Factors*[a]			
		I	II	III	IV
1. W. Europe 1649–1713	.99	35	(80)	06	—04
2. Europe 1714–1789	.96	26	(84)	08	02
3. Europe 1790–1814	.81	(66)	35	08	—25
4. Europe 1815–1822	.72	(74)	11	09	—30
5. Europe 1823–1847	.87	(81)	19	09	06
6. Europe 1848–1871	.88	(84)	21	—12	26
7. Europe 1872–1890	.84	(60)	—04	20	(55)
8. Europe 1891–1918	1.01	—09	—10	(100)	15
9. Europe 1919–1945	1.04	11	—16	(73)	(56)
10. N. Atlantic 1946–1963	.79	01	05	01	(89)
11. E. Asia 1689–1842	.95	—06	(97)	11	04
12. E. Asia 1843–1895	.84	05	(92)	—09	06
13. E. Asia 1896–1913	.82	42	24	(57)	—03
14. E. Asia 1914–1945	1.08	05	34	(92)	—10
15. E. Asia 1946–1954	1.08	23	03	(94)	—21
16. Asia 1955–1963	.70	(72)	—00	21	13
Eigenvalues[b]		8.4	3.2	1.6	1.2
Percent total variance[b]		52.5	19.8	9.8	7.7
Percent common variance[b]		58.3	22.2	11.1	8.4
Correlations between	I	1.00			
factor loadings	II	—.50	1.00		
	III	.50	.01	1.00	
	IV	—.01	—.29	.35	1.00

[a] Factor loadings are multiplied by 100; loadings > ± .50 are enclosed in parentheses.
[b] Based on principal axis factors.

which include the three most prominently loading subsystems from Factor I of the Wright subsample (Figure 11–1A). *Modern* subsystems have high loadings on Subcluster II. The third subcluster is composed of subsystems with high loadings on the first Richardson factor but in fact contains only Hawaiian subsystems and East Asia between 1843 and 1895; out of the Richardson sample, these subsystems constitute eras in which there was a dim recognition of the meaning of "sovereignty," and thus an *early state system* label is appropriate.

The cluster analysis of Wright's sample of subsystems conforms exactly to the corresponding factor analysis, even though there are three subclusters in contrast with the four factors of Table 11–4. Subcluster I contains subsystems loading high on Wright's Factor II, which was called *early state system* (Figure 11–1B). Subcluster II brings together all six subsystems with higher loadings on the *concert* factor (Factor I in Table 11–4). The third subcluster has *modern* subsystems most closely embedded together, but Sub-

TABLE 11-5
Correlations Between 183 Subsystem Variables and Q-Factors[a]

Variable	Richardson Sample				Wright Sample		
	I	II	III	I	II	III	IV
1. Wars	−29	26	04	33	25	01	−17
2. % Wars with subnationals	−39	−01	31	−04	−33	−18	19
3. War participants/members	−05	43	−38	−26	27	43	−20
4. % Extraregion wars	−35	−17	49	−35	−05	−16	35
5. % Extra-era wars	−17	(67)	−20	29	−27	43	−11
6. Poles	06	09	−12	41	15	02	−05
7. War participants/members at war	09	13	−33	24	(58)	−27	−38
8. % Dyads with same language	(62)	−43	(−62)	00	(71)	−43	(−74)
9. % Dyads with same body type	−30	27	−18	−13	−06	27	01
10. % Dyads with same clothing	33	00	(−67)	−12	(69)	00	(−64)
11. % Dyads with same philosophy	31	−14	−19	14	05	−14	−19
12. % Former enemy dyads	−30	−18	(79)	30	(−60)	−18	(66)
13. Wars per member	17	12	−48	−09	(75)	−18	−48
14. Participants per war	(−61)	(65)	36	−13	−23	30	20
15. Years per war	−10	40	−14	00	31	12	−10
16. % Years with new wars	−11	36	−13	(52)	−25	37	−14
17. % Destabilizing wars	−10	34	−03	17	(66)	−01	(−66)
18. Deaths per war	(−60)	(90)	−08	−35	−42	(91)	13
19. Alliances	(−90)	(52)	(80)	−05	(−73)	42	(94)
20. Satellites	−47	22	39	17	−35	08	12
21. % Pacts	−30	35	16	42	−44	32	12
22. % Aligned	−39	−12	(51)	−01	−10	−07	49
23. % Extraregion alliances	10	02	−15	(−67)	(64)	20	−33
24. % Extra-era alliances	−44	28	(50)	12	21	−41	−42
25. New NGO's	(−62)	26	(79)	−19	−50	09	(80)
26. Partners per alliance	(−85)	(51)	(68)	(−56)	−39	35	(64)
27. % Nonaggression pacts	−35	46	42	−13	−43	(72)	(72)

See Appendix D, pp. 627–31, for complete table.

425

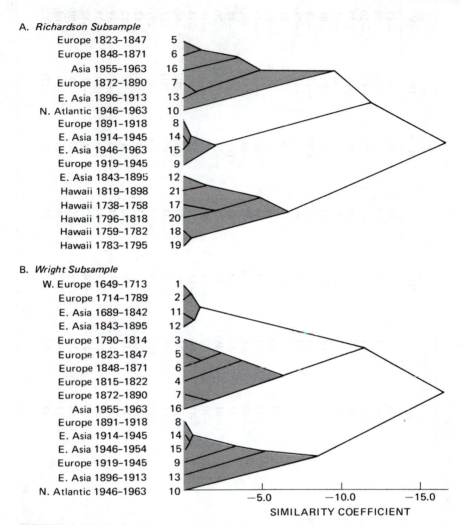

A. *Richardson Subsample*

Europe 1823–1847	5
Europe 1848–1871	6
Asia 1955–1963	16
Europe 1872–1890	7
E. Asia 1896–1913	13
N. Atlantic 1946–1963	10
Europe 1891–1918	8
E. Asia 1914–1945	14
E. Asia 1946–1963	15
Europe 1919–1945	9
E. Asia 1843–1895	12
Hawaii 1819–1898	21
Hawaii 1738–1758	17
Hawaii 1796–1818	20
Hawaii 1759–1782	18
Hawaii 1783–1795	19

B. *Wright Subsample*

W. Europe 1649–1713	1
Europe 1714–1789	2
E. Asia 1689–1842	11
E. Asia 1843–1895	12
Europe 1790–1814	3
Europe 1823–1847	5
Europe 1848–1871	6
Europe 1815–1822	4
Europe 1872–1890	7
Asia 1955–1963	16
Europe 1891–1918	8
E. Asia 1914–1945	14
E. Asia 1946–1954	15
Europe 1919–1945	9
E. Asia 1896–1913	13
N. Atlantic 1946–1963	10

$$-5.0 \qquad -10.0 \qquad -15.0$$
SIMILARITY COEFFICIENT

FIGURE 11-1
Q–Cluster Analysis of Subsystem Samples

system X (which has the highest loading on Factor IV) joins this final subcluster rather late and is the most tenuous component of Subcluster III.

Chronological categories are surprisingly more appropriate in delineating strata of international subsystems than the a priori classifications previously discussed. Nuclear subsystems, for example, do not differ significantly from prenuclear subsystems. Asian and European subsystems are not sorted out into separate clusters that reflect a regionalism factor, although one cluster in Figure 11–1A is almost exclusively formed out of Hawaiian subsystems. Polarity seems to be a far less useful structural attribute than the type of institutional arena in defining whether there is a concert of great powers or whether the modern Western concept of the state system is well or poorly established as a basis for international communications and boundaries. A final important thread differentiating subsystems from one another is a stabilizing-destabilizing dimension, although this factor is less pronounced than the innocuous labels "modern" and "premodern."

11.3 DIMENSIONS OF INTERNATIONAL FUNCTIONS

With two samples of data that contain similar though not identical strata of international subsystems, our next task is to discover whether dimensions of the variables can be found to correspond with either pattern variables or functional categories. In order to ascertain how well reality is mapped by the conceptual scheme, a complicated research design is necessary, as is explained in Section 11.3.1.

11.3.1 Procedure

We have collected two separate sets of data—one composed of Richardson's statistics of deadly quarrels, which relies on an inclusive definition of subsystem membership, and a second set based on Wright's tables, of wars declared and fought principally between sovereign entities. In Section 11.2 we found no dramatic difference between the Richardson and Wright data; we therefore might expect relationships between variables to be similar when comparing results from the two subsamples. A separate analysis of the two sets of data could nevertheless yield different dimensions in an R-analysis, so it is necessary to have two parallel investigations of the 183 variables collected across the international subsystems. But such a research design has two difficulties. First of all, it will be tedious for the reader to review all of the various analyses in detail; an abbreviated summary is therefore presented. Second, Q-analyses were not run on all 183 variables because many had such high intercorrelations: it was imperative to eliminate some variables so that subsystems would not be found homogeneous simply because of a sampling artifact. An analysis of 147 or 153 of the total 183 variables, however incompletely it examines the empirical structure of variables that index all international functions, is therefore necessary. In the following pages we report results based on a factor analysis of data supplied principally by Quincy Wright, because this sample has more variables, yields more Q-factors, and has somewhat less missing data. Unfortunately Wright's sample does not include data for Hawaiian subsystems, but a parallel analysis of

Richardson's data reveals no substantial difference in findings, as we shall see when we perform an R-cluster analysis on the Richardson sample.[8]

Correlations in both analyses are based on Spearman's formula, since our sample of 16 cases contains few normally distributed variables. In a principal axis factor analysis of the 153 Wright variables, 82 factors emerged with eigenvalues over 0.0, although 17 factors exceeded 1.0, and a scree cutoff was indicated at about 19 factors. A varimax orthogonal rotation was attempted inasmuch as the principal components failed to correspond to simple structure criteria. Oblique solutions failed to improve upon the varimax solution. Communalities for the 17-factor solution were in excess of 1.00, largely because of the wide gap between 82 total factors and the 17 that had an ascertainable meaning. Second- and third-order factor analyses were performed with the Wright variables in order to obtain a fuller view of underlying patterns. A cluster analysis, finally, was calculated for all 183 variables using the Richardson sample of indicators; the cluster analysis with this second data base was used to check on results from the factor analysis and to discover any findings peculiar to the Richardson variables, which were, after all, collected according to somewhat different criteria.[9]

11.3.2 Results

Factor I in the analysis of the Wright variables, accounting for about one-fifth of the total variance, appears at first to be an omnibus "size" factor (Table 11–6). Although most of the factor loadings are negative, the factor is associated with a large number of alliances, many new international organizations, and a high level of diplomatic exchange. The bulk of the high-loading variables indicate aggregation; some are indices of support and plan-making. *Alliance nonsaturation* is thus a more precise label for the factor, since the higher codings are negative. An examination of the original

---

[8] Another procedure was to separate out variables pertaining to inputs, withinputs, and outputs. Three subsets of the data were thus factor-analyzed, but the results were not very different from the larger analysis of 153 variables. One advantage of the analysis based on three subsets was that fewer variables were deleted from the total of 183 due to high bivariate correlations within the input, withinput, and output variables. (There are several variables across the three subsets which intercorrelate with each other at the $\pm$ .90 level or higher.)

The reader will notice that communalities are, as usual, based on the varimax factor loadings. But when oblique rotations are applied throughout this chapter, the size of communalities shrinks in order to improve the clarity of the overall patterns.

[9] Similar results for the Richardson and Wright samples were encountered in a study using some 50 of the 183 variables. See Michael Haas, "International Subsystems: Stability and Polarity," *American Political Science Review*, LXIV (March 1970), 98–123.

Spearman correlations for the 30 variables excluded from the factor analysis reveals correlations of — .90 or higher between some of the higher-loading variables on Factor I and variables 28, 31, and 65, all of which are measures of the extent to which members of a subsystem enter alliances. In addition, variable 116 (level of technology) correlates + .90 or higher with several of the variables with loadings of more than — .50 on the alliance nonsaturation factor; subsystems with higher levels of technology, in short, have high densities in alliance networks. The only variables directly relevant to violent international behavior on Factor I are 8 and 172, suggesting that alliance activity may lessen the possibilities for war between countries and peoples with similar languages, both internally and externally. Looking at correlations between Factor I and each of the 16 subsystems in Wright's sample, we find that the recent North Atlantic bipolar system has the most alliance saturation, while some of the older eras for Asia and Europe have been associated with very little alliance formation (Table 11–7).

Factor II also superficially resembles a "size" factor, but most of the higher-loading variables clearly point toward *lack of war disturbance*. The combination of indicators of war incidence, measures of initiation of wars and of destabilizing outcomes adds up to an image of international disequilibrium; once again, the signs are largely negative (Table 11–6). Most variables with loadings in excess of ± .50 indicate the implementation and enforcement functions. Among variables excluded from the factor analysis but highly correlated with one or more high-loading variables on Factor II, all nine (7, 15, 141, 150, 153, 154, 164, 171, and 177) depict instability rather than mere war incidence. Subsystems most related to the factor happen to have positive correlations, and all are eras in which there has been much conscious effort to keep war at a minimum through cooperation between great powers (Table 11–7).

Bloc rivalry sums up the assortment of variables prominent on Factor III, especially recurrence of warfare among former enemies, density of cross-status (major-minor) alliances, and the high positive correlations with Subsystems X and XII. Nevertheless, there is considerable evidence that bloc antipathy is associated with a lessening in overall conflict between nations, since most indicators of violence are low or absent from the higher-loading variables; there are very few promotions or demotions from major power ranks, and most members either are sovereign or retain sovereignty, while there is little extraregional contact. It is also worthy of note that internal wars are rare, according to loadings of variables 10 and 49. Factor III extracts about 14 percent of the total variance among the 153 variables analyzed, and a very gradual decrement in explained variance is characteristic of each successive factor.

Nearly all of the variables with loadings above −.85 on Factor IV indicate gatepassing activity—that is, admission of new members or expul-

TABLE 11–6
First–Order R–Factor Analysis of International Subsystem Performance Data: Wright Sample[a]

| | | | | | *Varimax Factors* | | |
Variable	h²	I	II	III	IV	V	VI
1. Wars	1.23	—16	(—82)	14	—40	08	—01
2. % Wars with subnationals	1.24	—37	16	14	—18	—32	(—71)
3. % Members at war	1.08	—01	—43	(—69)	—04	11	49
4. % Extraregion wars	1.27	—06	41	—06	(54)	15	—17
5. % Extra-era wars	1.04	—09	—07	18	—50	—17	—16
6. Poles	1.12	27	—40	—09	—48	—13	—20
8. % Dyads with similar language	1.59	(54)	—44	—45	—11	21	(—77)
10. % Dyads with similar clothing	1.46	45	—17	(—94)	—10	—03	08
11. % Dyads with similar philosophy	1.59	25	—37	18	—34	11	08
12. % Former enemy dyads	1.42	—35	04	(101)	04	14	13
13. Wars per member	1.30	11	(—75)	—44	27	29	05
14. Participants per war	1.18	—24	(—56)	—24	—26	—05	26
16. % Years with new wars	1.13	05	—14	18	(—82)	—15	17
18. Deaths per war	1.27	—26	—02	—31	—20	20	(56)
19. Alliances	1.27	(—95)	—25	17	—40	11	25
20. Satellites	1.06	08	—09	—03	(—91)	05	—17
21. % Pacts	1.27	27	—09	33	—43	—02	07
22. % Aligned	1.23	(—74)	—04	—29	04	—39	10
25. New NGO's	1.15	(—68)	—19	40	—07	24	—01
26. Partners per alliance	1.19	(—98)	05	—28	07	06	21
27. % Nonaggression pacts	1.13	(—57)	—13	—05	—16	22	17
29. Partners per alliance	1.23	38	01	(69)	—00	—18	—38
30. Years per alliance	1.13	—38	—15	—19	00	—34	(—53)
32. % Defensive alliances	1.24	(85)	—22	26	—31	01	05
33. % Dyads former allies	1.29	—38	—43	—45	—47	32	19
34. Members	1.01	—31	—32	42	(—62)	06	—25
35. High decision latitude	1.68	05	(—80)	05	16	—35	—07
36. % Sovereign members	1.08	03	—06	(62)	43	11	37
37. % Retain sovereignty	1.06	05	15	(55)	41	—44	—09
38. % Extraregion members	1.16	01	33	(—86)	21	16	20
40. Members/major+middle powers	1.01	—29	—16	(52)	(—67)	17	—15
41. Diverse ways of life	1.28	15	39	(—70)	—11	35	02
42. Nonlegalist power orientation	1.30	(68)	13	—24	—06	13	44
43. Incomplete external interaction	1.03	18	10	—07	21	25	—04
44. Rational calculation	1.15	07	03	(57)	47	—07	—19
45. Internal preoccupation	1.11	41	—15	(—60)	30	—05	—07
46. % Internal wars	1.11	11	—17	—03	(71)	41	—02
47. % Interventions	1.17	10	—18	11	—36	—16	(—85)
48. % Foreign wars	1.39	—24	—19	—34	—19	03	11
49. Deaths per internal war	1.40	(52)	10	(—59)	25	—09	—07
50. Deaths per intervention	1.10	—31	02	17	—47	—10	08
51. Insecure domestic elites	1.45	18	18	31	43	(—50)	—38
52. % Starting wars	1.10	02	—23	—37	37	(58)	09
54. Minors in coalition with majors	1.17	—35	—37	12	(—75)	23	08
55. % Formal major-minor alliances	1.21	—09	—09	(87)	—25	—39	—09
57. % Minors allied with majors	1.28	—49	—26	(53)	(—61)	—37	—01

See Appendix D, pp. 634–41, for complete table.

VII	VIII	IX	X	XI	XII	XIII	XIV	XV	XVI	XVII
07	−04	−11	04	42	−27	03	−05	12	−03	26
−05	−30	−23	39	−06	−02	20	10	−14	08	−17
14	−04	−07	10	03	−12	−28	−15	−03	−06	12
17	−42	22	11	(−59)	−01	17	−12	03	13	−30
06	−11	(−80)	10	−00	−06	−13	−06	05	01	10
03	09	−18	−01	−04	−01	06	30	09	−01	(67)
−04	−22	21	−12	−05	−22	29	−06	09	05	05
−06	04	34	−23	−12	−02	17	13	01	00	30
(105)	−05	−09	11	−19	−00	04	05	−03	12	22
08	17	−22	−21	−23	01	17	−13	−07	07	12
21	05	−02	−10	37	−30	13	−08	−06	−06	22
−17	11	19	26	−22	−02	(−58)	−21	08	−10	18
28	−00	−38	10	11	07	18	−20	−13	−02	14
−27	02	(−54)	26	−11	−06	−48	−11	−09	−10	07
09	05	09	09	−06	02	01	−08	−04	03	07
−13	−24	15	−16	−11	06	−12	−14	−11	09	−10
(−79)	22	−15	04	−19	09	−20	−02	−02	−07	35
04	−22	43	−27	−00	02	33	01	04	00	−12
−24	−02	18	18	−39	−08	−28	13	07	07	20
14	−14	−10	−07	−04	−11	−10	−02	−07	00	−14
(−72)	−07	−19	08	−24	−12	−09	−05	−08	06	18
12	−22	−26	(−52)	−12	−05	−03	−08	07	08	−05
(58)	−15	−36	18	−00	−03	03	−04	−02	01	−12
22	05	−14	02	−26	07	−07	07	−02	04	39
07	−03	−02	(55)	−14	−04	−15	03	−06	03	21
−06	−06	−03	19	−16	−05	−23	−00	21	01	13
−09	(−69)	−19	−01	06	−37	20	−09	13	22	34
15	09	−22	−14	−07	−13	18	20	05	06	41
−04	−24	−26	−10	12	−09	08	42	−08	−02	10
−01	−18	−05	08	−40	05	−01	−07	−00	−03	−03
−08	−24	−09	−04	02	−08	−08	10	08	05	−07
34	−31	−00	−05	−31	01	32	05	−03	10	−25
06	−11	−38	08	−38	10	−06	−44	−13	−01	−13
(66)	−26	09	−11	−18	−10	30	42	18	08	10
−21	−28	15	−44	−18	−12	−22	20	25	08	10
04	−34	−06	−36	32	−17	02	28	−09	−03	−05
−16	−08	−23	−18	04	−28	39	−20	−05	09	04
−11	−09	−00	14	−27	02	−26	08	21	−02	12
39	33	−15	(−78)	08	−10	29	−34	03	−01	16
−11	−06	−16	−06	−06	01	(79)	02	−06	−06	13
(−76)	−22	22	11	−07	−01	19	12	02	−02	07
(−56)	−32	−07	−04	−27	01	−04	32	08	08	30
32	13	−13	−01	−22	−18	−21	11	06	03	40
−19	11	−32	26	−00	−08	−04	−05	10	−08	19
−17	−04	−30	04	−20	08	02	−07	03	05	21
−10	−09	20	−27	−01	11	−02	−14	15	05	05

sion of former members of an international subsystem. Because of the additional variables related to warfare, the label *peaceful gatepassing* strongly suggests the factor. Subsystems I, II, XI, and XII have highest positive correlations with Factor IV; and in all four cases new memberships were tolerated, if at all, only toward the end of the subsystem era, and were achieved through war. Endogenous violence occurred in Europe, but the source of wars in Asia was imperialistic expansion. An aim of gatecrashing is not merely to enter into a subsystem as an equal partner, but instead to assert power superiority; there are several variables relevant to treaty-making with high positive loadings, for example.

Lack of concert pacification describes Factor V, which features plan-making variables with high negative loadings. Major powers tend not to be aligned with each other, but major powers in different poles have a high degree of macrocentric cooperative activity. As a result, few wars are started; wars have few cross-status coalitions and seldom end in treaties with major powers as signatories. Variable 17, though not included in the 153-variable factor analysis, is related to this factor because of its high correlation with variable 75; and this provides some evidence that there is a tendency for wars relevant to Factor V to be destabilizing in outcome. There are positive correlations with Subsystems II, V, XI, and XIII; these eras lacked a consensus among major powers sufficient to contain levels of violence and preserve an equilibrium.

Factor VI has high loadings for so-called status scores, which are measures of diplomatic exchanges between states; other high-loading variables portray few interventions, little cross-status but much alliance activity on the part of recruitees. *Elite membership linkage* sums up this collection, and the label is reenforced by variables which, though excluded from the factor analysis, are correlates of variables that pinpoint the nature of Factor VI: variables 31, 39, and 118 have high correlations with variables 62, 81, and 106, respectively. Elite membership linkage is also associated with a high level of technology (variable 116), and this relationship no doubt explains why there is a moderately high positive loading on deaths per war in Factor VI: as Richardson has demonstrated in his own analysis of war data, more efficient instruments of military destruction in modern times account for more deaths per battle.[10] High correlations with Subsystems VI, VIII, IX, XIII, XIV, and XV provide yet another basis for regarding Factor VI as relevant to elite leadership.

Factors VII through XVII are increasingly difficult to label as the number of high-loading variables on each factor decreases. Factor VII is topped by variable 11, a high percentage of violent conflict dyads in which belligerents share similar philosophical or religious outlooks. Other variables

---

[10] Richardson, *Statistics of Deadly Quarrels,* Chapter 3.

TABLE 11–7
Correlations Between 17 R–Factors and Wright Sample of Subsystems

First-Order Factors	Subsystems															
	1	2	3	4	5	6	7	8	9	10	11	12	13	14	15	16
I. Alliance Nonsaturation	.10	.11	.23	.21	.10	–.00	–.12	–.07	–.15	–.26	.22	.20	.00	.01	–.03	.09
II. Lack of War Disturbance	.04	–.04	–.04	.16	.09	.03	.15	.05	.07	.05	.08	.11	.15	.07	.13	.27
III. Bloc Rivalry	–.02	.07	.03	.08	.06	.02	.03	–.05	.02	.16	–.11	–.20	–.18	–.11	–.08	–.04
IV. Peaceful Gatekeeping	.14	.15	–.13	–.09	.03	–.05	–.02	–.03	–.08	–.02	.22	.17	.08	–.01	–.05	–.12
V. Lack of Concert Pacification	.15	.18	.14	.06	.16	.24	.12	.10	.11	.11	.22	.07	.18	.12	.10	.14
VI. Elite Membership Linkage	–.03	–.02	.06	–.11	.05	.16	.21	.18	.16	.01	.06	–.01	.33	.20	.25	.11
VII. Fratricidal Conflict	.05	.09	.03	.02	–.07	–.04	–.30	–.10	–.21	–.14	.09	.01	–.09	–.13	–.14	–.22
VIII. Noncosmopolitan	.01	–.04	.01	.14	–.07	.06	.01	.05	.04	.04	–.09	–.00	–.02	.02	.04	–.08
IX. Temporal Continuity	.14	.14	.21	–.11	.02	.20	.11	–.14	–.03	.12	.06	–.01	.02	–.15	–.19	–.02
X. Aggressive Alliance	–.19	–.07	–.09	–.06	.10	.02	.10	.12	.14	.10	–.08	–.01	.08	.12	.10	.09
XI. Imbalance of Power	.24	.22	.16	.03	.06	.01	–.07	–.05	–.09	–.17	.08	.03	–.05	–.01	–.02	.01
XII. Short Subsystem Duration	–.43	–.36	–.09	.02	–.14	–.04	.00	–.01	–.01	–.01	–.41	–.08	.01	–.01	.00	.02
XIII. Internal Discord	–.03	–.03	–.13	–.17	–.12	–.14	–.12	–.24	–.23	–.17	–.01	.30	–.14	–.16	–.22	.11
XIV. Pragmatism	.25	.22	–.12	.06	.12	.15	.12	–.03	.02	.08	.17	.10	.10	–.02	–.05	.11
XV. Successful Major Power Wars	.22	.17	.03	.07	.04	.05	–.02	–.06	–.05	–.01	.09	–.04	–.05	–.07	–.09	–.05
XVI. Elite Expansion	.15	.07	.07	.02	–.03	–.05	–.11	–.09	–.09	.01	.08	–.07	–.16	–.12	–.07	–.08
XVII. Multipolar Disequilibrium	.04	.10	–.11	–.06	–.06	–.00	–.02	.01	.03	.08	–.07	–.02	–.10	–.01	–.02	–.03

with high loadings pertain to long alliances, alliances exclusively between major powers, a lack of internal conflicts, ententes rather than formal alliances; the associated variable 17 (because of its high correlation with variable 21, one of the variables loading high on Factor VII) indicates that wars connected with this factor point toward destabilizing conditions. The three subsystems least associated with the factor are unipolar Bismarckian Europe, tripolar Asia after the departure of the French from Indochina, and twentieth-century Europe between the two world wars; Subsystems I–IV, XIII, and XIV alone have positive correlations, and these are the earliest time periods in our sample of subsystems from both Europe and Asia. Identification of a common thread is most difficult; Deutsch's notion of *fratricidal conflict* incorporates all of these elements conveniently, but not entirely satisfactorily.

Noncosmopolitan subsystems are described by Factor VIII, which is related to ideological disagreement, low decision latitude, and endogenous alliance linkage by major powers. Within these subsystems elites share a low degree of consensus, and many resources are available for expansion, as Rosecrance suggests in the case of classical eighteenth-century European interstate politics.[11] Glancing at correlations with the 16 subsystems, one finds that cosmopolitanism was least characteristic of the early years of the Concert of Europe and most appropriate to the earliest East Asian and latest Asian subsystems.

Subsystems with little gatepassing and few wars that are either a legacy of a previous era or continue on into future time periods are described in Factor IX. The fact that the highest loading variable deals with a lack of change in total membership of a subsystem dictates a cautious *temporal continuity* designation. Subsystems I–III are the most temporally insular; Subsystems VIII, XIV, and XV are "messier" in keeping their wars within the temporal boundaries that were selected on the basis of our analytical criteria.

Factor X has high loadings for nonaligned gatepassing and multilateral alliance memberships as well as duration of foreign wars won by major powers. The factor is most associated with Subsystems VIII, IX, and XIV and is least related to Subsystem I. A common theme among these variables is an inability of alliance networks to serve in themselves as deterrents to warfare; this finding casts doubt on the theory that alliance commitments may keep international relations more integrated along peaceful methods of interaction.[12] Alliances, after all, can be formed either for aggressive or

---

[11] Rosecrance, *Action and Reaction in World Politics,* Chapter 2.

[12] Cf. Karl W. Deutsch and J. David Singer, "Multipolar Power Systems and International Stability," *World Politics,* XVI (April 1964), 390–406; Singer and Small, "Alliance Aggregation and the Onset of War, 1815–1945."

for peaceful aims; Hitler's nonaggression pacts were devices to provide false assurances against possible attack. An *aggressive alliance* label is therefore appropriate.

Imbalance of power characterizes Factor XI. Subsystems lacking institutional regulators (international organizations) are regulated either by alliances or by balance of power politics, according to Rosecrance. Within the variety of definitions of "balance of power,"[13] one possibility is that of a multistate system harassed with warfare: equilibria will be upset and balanced and then upset all over again. Such is the case particularly with Subsystems I–III; and it is decidedly not the case within the carefully balanced bipolar Cold War of the contemporary North Atlantic subsystem. It is of interest that several variables with negative loadings on Factor XI pertain to extraregional activities, and that many wars go hand in hand with epochs containing few new intergovernmental organizations.

A high negative loading for variable 183 (subsystem duration) dwarfs all other loadings on Factor XII. Moreover, there are high negative correlations between Factor XII and three subsystems which lasted the longest number of years—Subsystems I, II, and XI. The remaining variables with factor loadings over ± .30 may thus be interpreted as concomitants of *short subsystem duration* in international history, when new power constellations are eroded quickly; we should note especially a high number of destabilizing major power and imperial wars and an absence of recruitment and alliances, although decisionmakers are constrained with a narrow decision latitude and international tribunals. Several variables excluded from the factor analysis are nevertheless related to negatively loading variables: these include major power initiations, belligerences, and victories in war as well as a high war recidivism ratio.

An *internal discord* theme pervades most of the variables on Factor XIII, and this concurs with a positive correlation with Subsystem XII and negative correlations with Subsystems VIII, IX, and XV. Internal wars are prevalent, and few countries are involved in foreign wars.

For the first time in the factors thus far examined, a judgmentally scaled variable heads Factor XIV. A preference for realism rather than idealism as a guide to foreign policy decisionmaking is reenforced with a high retention of sovereign status by each country as well as by a low overall level of disturbance. (The latter is a judgmental coding adapted from Rosecrance.) Because this realism is not therefore manifest in the form of the naked aggression of Machiavellian power politics, the term *pragmatism* best denotes the enlightened self-interest depicted by the factor. The most pragmatic

---

[13] For various definitions of "balance of power," see Ernst B. Haas, "The Balance of Power: Prescription, Concept, or Propaganda," *World Politics*, V (July 1953), 442–77.

subsystems, accordingly, turn out to be the earliest—Subsystems I, II, and XI.

Successful major power wars are indicated by Factor XV, which has a concentration of enforcement variables. Perhaps not ironically, this preponderance of wars started by major powers goes hand in hand with elite legitimacy and a growth in international law. Subsystems I and II are most closely associated with this factor.

Variables indexing recruitment, supervision, and rule-adapting load better than ± .30 on Factor XVI. Higher loadings for recruitment variables, however, should be placed in the perspective of much exogenous behavior. An *elite expansion* factor label is appropriate; major powers are most likely to be recruited anew through violent imperial wars, when they venture into geographically noncontiguous regions of the globe, or demoted through wartime defeat. Elite contraction marks the demise of countries in subsystems with high negative loadings—Subsystems XIII and XIV—as opposed to the expansion in Subsystem I.

There is much similarity between Factors XI and XVII, although the latter can be easily assigned a *multipolar disequilibrium* rubric. Articulation, support, and direction variables have the higher loadings, and we see also that a multipolar system is associated moderately with much war and alliance activity. Most of the wars are won by major powers over other major powers, and a result of such victories is to destabilize a subsystem. Subsystems III and XIII are least related to Factor XVII, and Subsystem II is somewhat of a classic case illustrating that fragmentation of power into many different countries and distinct poles is likely to breed wars in which major powers vie for a topdog position.[14]

In order to obtain a wider perspective on the 17 principal components of the international function-performance data, second- and third-order factor analyses are conducted. The matrix of intercorrelations between the 17 first-order factor loadings was itself factor-analyzed. Exactly 17 principal components emerged with eigenvalues over 0.0, seven of which exceeded 1.0. A scree line fell most clearly after 9 factors; but there was some ambiguity, and a cutoff of either 5 or 7 would also have been possible. Adhering to the conventional cutoff of factors with an eigenvalue of at least 1.0, we derive 7 factors. Unrotated factors did not lend themselves to a clear interpretation, so the unrotated factor matrix was rotated into an orthogonal (varimax) solution, and the matrix resembled simple structure even more when an oblique rotation was performed. The biquartimin solution took 30 cycles, 2112 iterations (Table 11–8).

The first second-order factor suggests *incorporativeness,* with the high-

---

[14] The instability of multipolarity is the principal finding in M. Haas, "International Subsystems: Stability and Polarity."

TABLE 11-8
Second-Order R-Factor Analysis of International Subsystem Performance Data: Wright Sample

First-Order Factors	h²	Biquartimin Factors[a]						
		I	II	III	IV	V	VI	VII
I. Alliance Nonsaturation	.65	17	—03	36	16	16	02	(70)
II. Lack of War Disturbance	.68	23	(—77)	—12	—03	06	17	01
III. Bloc Rivalry	.68	—06	—00	—29	(—73)	15	01	—06
IV. Peaceful Gatekeeping	.49	(63)	—05	10	12	05	17	—03
V. Lack of Concert Pacification	.71	06	—01	—15	(80)	22	—09	21
VI. Elite Membership Linkage	.64	—06	—05	—49	(57)	—06	21	—11
VII. Fratricidal Conflict	.52	—11	22	(64)	06	30	01	02
VIII. Noncosmopolitan	.51	(—67)	06	—07	—05	03	10	24
IX. Temporal Continuity	.60	01	15	10	10	—15	(71)	—10
X. Aggressive Alliance	.73	02	17	—02	12	—15	(—81)	—14
XI. Imbalance of Power	.41	10	42	14	—14	—38	07	11
XII. Short Subsystem Duration	.36	—34	—41	15	—19	10	—03	—00
XIII. Internal Discord	.65	17	—23	(74)	—09	—08	15	04
XIV. Pragmatism	.54	(59)	05	—22	—21	02	—06	28
XV. Successful Major Power Wars	.52	04	(59)	—15	—10	35	15	—05
XVI. Elite Expansion	.58	04	03	—19	01	(76)	02	—05
XVII. Multipolar Disequilibrium	.66	—26	02	—09	06	—29	02	(77)
Eigenvalues[b]		2.0	1.7	1.5	1.3	1.2	1.1	1.1
Percent total variance[b]		11.9	10.3	10.0	7.8	6.9	6.3	5.7
Percent common variance[b]		20.2	17.1	15.1	13.1	12.1	11.1	11.0

[a] Factor loadings are multiplied by 100; loadings > ±.50 are enclosed in parentheses.
[b] Based on principal axis factors.

437

est loadings for Cosmopolitanism, Peaceful Gatekeeping, and Pragmatism. Factor II looks like a description of *protracted violence,* with a high level of War Disturbance, Successful Major Power Wars, Imbalance of Power, and lengthy Subsystem Duration.[15] The third factor is composed of indicators of *schismatism,* for subsystems lacking Alliance Saturation and Elite Membership Linkage while being riddled with Fratricidal Conflict and Internal Discord clearly have severe problems in getting together either domestically or abroad. *Hierarchy* represents Factor IV, with much Elite Membership Linkage, very little Bloc Rivalry, and no consequent Concert Pacification; the factor describes a situation with much international contact, no consensus among major powers to keep the peace, yet a preference among rivals to avoid a major confrontation. *Empire-building* emerges in Factor V, which has a very high loading for Elite Expansion, a moderate positive loading for Successful Major Power Wars, and a moderate negative loading for Imbalance of Power. Factor VI brings together *stabilization* from first-order Factors IX and X, Temporal Continuity and lack of Aggressive Alliances. The final second-order factor results from a conjunction of first-order Factors I and XVII: Multipolar Disequilibrium collapses with Alliance Nonsaturation, and suggests that when multipolar systems fail to have alliances, or when there are many alliances under stable bipolarity, then it is necessary for foreign policy decisionmakers to display considerable skill in pragmatic diplomacy; subsystems thereby uncovered may lack cosmopolitan features. An abbreviated name for Factor VII, hence, would be *atomization.*

A third-order factor analysis was run next in an effort to reduce the complexity of findings even more. A principal axis factor analysis yielded 7 factors with eigenvalues over 0.0 and 4 over 1.0; the scree test agreed with a cutoff at 1.0 in eigenvalues. To improve interpretability, the factor matrix was rotated orthogonally and then an oblique (quartimin) rotation was performed. The oblique solution took 18 cycles, 464 iterations. Each of the 4 factors extracted about the same percentage of total variance. Factor I, named *imperial expansion,* brings together Empire-Building as well as Incorporativeness and Stabilization. *Stable stratification* emerges as the second factor from a convergence of Hierarchy and Stabilization. *Disintegration* is described in Factor III; with a very high loading for Schismatism and a moderate loading for Incorporativeness, the factor has positive loadings for both conflictual and cooperative types of behavior, indicating discord in the structures of states themselves as well as fragility in international subsystems of which they are a part.[16] *Polarization,* if seen as a gradual historical

---

[15] Cf. Robert Strausz–Hupé et al., *Protracted Conflict* (New York: Harper, 1959).

[16] Cf. John Herz, *International Politics in the Atomic Age* (New York: Columbia University Press, 1959).

TABLE 11-9
Third–Order R–Factor Analysis of International
Subsystem Performance Data: Wright Sample

| Second–Order Factors | h² | Quartimin Factors[a] | | | |
		I	II	III	IV
I. Incorporativeness	.71	46	09	(69)	07
II. Protracted Violence	.76	—31	23	12	(76)
III. Schismatism	.84	—11	—30	(97)	—07
IV. Hierarchy	.71	—23	(86)	—14	—01
V. Empire-Building	.63	(79)	—08	—00	—02
VI. Stabilization	.57	43	(63)	—06	—03
VII. Atomization	.79	18	—27	—18	(80)
Eigenvalues[b]		1.5	1.2	1.1	1.1
Percent total variance[b]		21.7	17.8	16.5	15.4
Percent common variance[b]		30.6	24.5	22.4	22.3
Intercorrelations between factor loadings	I	1.00			
	II	—.31	1.00		
	III	—.42	.23	1.00	
	IV	—.19	—.45	—.34	1.00

[a] Factor loadings are multiplied by 100; loadings > ±.50 are enclosed in parentheses.
[b] Based on principal axis factors.

process, encompasses both Protracted Violence and Atomization dimensions of international subsystems in Factor IV.

Although the above labels have been chosen inductively, and with some hesitation and tentativeness, it is perhaps not surprising to find ourselves back with four Parsonian categories. Imperial Expansion represents goal attainment; Stable Stratification, pattern maintenance; Disintegration indicates a lack of coordination; and Polarization is relevant to Parson's category of adaptation, for under conditions of Protracted Violence and Atomization there will be a tendency for foreign policies to be reactive rather than innovative.[17]

We now shift our attention to a cluster analysis of all 183 variables collected in accordance with Richardson's criteria. Our aim is to find whether results are similar with those of the factor analysis of Wright's data. Such a comparison is the hardest case, for if differences appear they could be attributed either to a different data base or to a different multivariate procedure for the analysis of the data. A similarity in findings would indicate

[17] Cf. Charles A. McClelland, "The Acute International Crisis," *World Politics,* XIV (October 1961), 182–204; George Liska, *International Equilibrium* (Cambridge: Harvard University Press, 1957), pp. 200–201. When we trace the four factors back to the original variables, we do not discern a one-to-one correspondence between the a priori conceptualization and our empirical taxonomy, however.

that findings are independent of the sampling and criteria used to generate the data.

Cluster analysis results for the 183 variables are far more complex than the cluster analysis of the 16 subsystems in Figure 11–1. If a coefficient dissimilarity of − 200.0 is arbitrarily chosen as a cutoff for determining major clusters, we derive three constellations of variables; a − 180.0 cutoff yields four clusters, but any lower figure would introduce severe complexities into the analysis (Figures 11–2 to 11–5). The cluster in Figure 11–2 is knitted together at − 208.4; the outermost limit of the cluster in Figure 11–3 is − 221.3; clusters in Figures 11–3 and 11–4 fall short of − 200.0 but both merge together at − 235.0. Using a − 50.0 level as a minimum coefficient of dissimilarity for identifying subcluster, there are 32 subclusters in all.

Subcluster I contains variables relevant mainly to wars initiated by major powers, which have been designated indicators of *enforcement* in Section 10.6.3. Most variables in Subcluster I have high loadings on Factor II, War Disturbance, but the specific connection with major powers is too obvious to overlook in naming the subcluster; enforcement activity is elite behavior.

Although indicators of the direction function are concentrated in one half of Subcluster II, the other variables suggest a more generalized *major power victories* subcluster. Many of the variables also load high on Factor XV, Successful Major Power Wars.

A large number of poles, embedded within measures with moderate loadings on the Elite Expansion factor (XVI), are found in Subcluster III. An appropriate designation, hence, is *multipolar jockeying for power.*

War incidence is clearly present among variables in Subcluster IV, which contains several measures of the articulation function. Subcluster V depicts *concert equilibration*—a situation in which major powers are collaborating pragmatically, with an end result that many countries return to membership. This especially recalls the Napoleonic period in which states became satellites and were later restored to sovereignty after the major powers of Europe united to defeat the armies of France. A situation of major powers fighting other major powers, as portrayed in Subcluster VI, resembles a "world war" and corresponds to Morgenthau's often-quoted axiom that all international politics involves a struggle for power,[18] though in this case there is a *violent power struggle.*

International lawlessness characterizes Subcluster VII, while a generalized *elite turbulence* pervades Subcluster VIII. In the first case, international law either is absent or it is not invoked; in the second case, wars are ex-

[18] Hans J. Morgenthau, *Politics Among Nations,* 4th ed. (New York: Knopf, 1967).

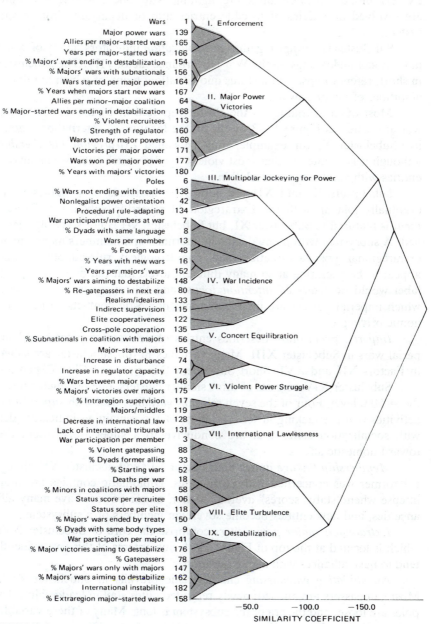

Wars	1	I. Enforcement
Major power wars	139	
Allies per major-started wars	165	
Years per major-started wars	166	
% Majors' wars ending in destabilization	154	
% Majors' wars with subnationals	156	
Wars started per major power	164	
% Years when majors start new wars	167	II. Major Power Victories
Allies per minor-major coalition	64	
% Major-started wars ending in destabilization	168	
% Violent recruitees	113	
Strength of regulator	160	
Wars won by major powers	169	
Victories per major power	171	
Wars won per major power	177	
% Years with majors' victories	180	
Poles	6	III. Multipolar Jockeying for Power
% Wars not ending with treaties	138	
Nonlegalist power orientation	42	
Procedural rule-adapting	134	
War participants/members at war	7	
% Dyads with same language	8	
Wars per member	13	
% Foreign wars	48	
% Years with new wars	16	
Years per majors' wars	152	
% Majors' wars aiming to destabilize	148	IV. War Incidence
% Re-gatepassers in next era	80	
Realism/idealism	133	
Indirect supervision	115	
Elite cooperativeness	122	
Cross-pole cooperation	135	
% Subnationals in coalition with majors	56	V. Concert Equilibration
Major-started wars	155	
Increase in disturbance	74	
Increase in regulator capacity	174	
% Wars between major powers	146	
% Majors' victories over majors	175	VI. Violent Power Struggle
% Intraregion supervision	117	
Majors/middles	119	
Decrease in international law	128	
Lack of international tribunals	131	VII. International Lawlessness
War participation per member	3	
% Violent gatepassing	88	
% Dyads former allies	33	
% Starting wars	52	
Deaths per war	18	
% Minors in coalitions with majors	58	
Status score per recruitee	106	
Status score per elite	118	VIII. Elite Turbulence
% Majors' wars ended by treaty	150	
% Dyads with same body types	9	IX. Destabilization
War participation per major	141	
% Major victories aiming to destabilize	176	
% Gatepassers	78	
% Majors' wars only with majors	147	
% Majors' wars aiming to destabilize	162	
International instability	182	
% Extraregion major-started wars	158	

| | | | |
| −50.0 | −100.0 | −150.0 |

SIMILARITY COEFFICIENT

FIGURE 11-2
R-Cluster Analysis of Richardson Subsystem Data: I

441

tremely bloody, former allies are fighting with one another, and elites are involved in a series of forcible entries into or departures from a subsystem.

Subcluster IX brings together *destabilization* indicators, many of which have moderate loadings on the War Disturbance factor (II). The subcluster, in short, refers to upsets in a status quo situation, many of which are due to ambitions of major powers.

Most of the variables in the cluster reported in Figure 11–2 refer to warfare, whereas Figure 11–3 dwells on the location of international activity. Subcluster X, for example, may be called *extraregion membership,* although it is of interest that most violent dyads in such subsystems involve entities with similar types of clothing.

Subclusters XI and XII are homogeneous triads of variables which eventually join up with the Extraregion Membership subcluster. *Recruitment* is featured in Subcluster XI, but Subcluster XII is not so easily identified. A subsystem with many deaths in internal wars, members having many extraregional postwar treaties, and nonideological rule-adapting would appear to be operating at so many different levels that the only appropriate label would be *scattered attention focus,* and this suggests a situation in which imperial powers are intervening into domestic conflicts to gain economic privileges.

Imperial penetration describes entries of new major powers and imperial wars in Subcluster XIII. Many variables in this subcluster are salient in Factors XII and XVI, Short Subsystem Duration and Elite Expansion.

Subcluster XIV consists of three smaller clusters, one of which exceeds the − 50.0 level. Four of the seven relevant variables deal with *supervisorial* activities that are lacking in tension; most of the remaining indicators deal with socialization styles that are conducive to a supervisory orientation toward domestic affairs.

Membership linkage unites both Factor VI and Subcluster XV, though the former was concerned with more elites. Diplomatic contacts are more intense when "status scores" average higher, minor powers have many alliance ties, and new entities become sovereign members of a subsystem.

Extraregion major power wars comprise the core of Subcluster XVI, which is located at the top of Figure 11–4. Subsystems of this sort evidently tend to have alliances with a long duration.

An *affiliative gatepassing* characteristic prevails in Subcluster XVII. Most gatepassers are aligned; newly recruited elites stay in leadership roles; poles are loose; and the era of the subsystem is long. Many of these variables had negative loadings on the Aggressive Alliance factor (X).

War and alliance continuity sums up Subcluster XVIII. We have seen already that the duration of a subsystem is not far away as a variable but nevertheless is part of a distinctly different constellation. We find several

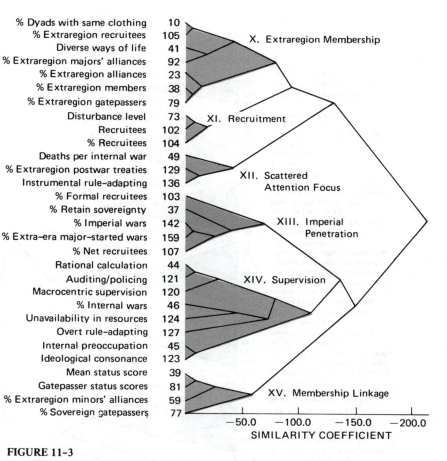

% Dyads with same clothing	10
% Extraregion recruitees	105
Diverse ways of life	41
% Extraregion majors' alliances	92
% Extraregion alliances	23
% Extraregion members	38
% Extraregion gatepassers	79
Disturbance level	73
Recruitees	102
% Recruitees	104
Deaths per internal war	49
% Extraregion postwar treaties	129
Instrumental rule-adapting	136
% Formal recruitees	103
% Retain sovereignty	37
% Imperial wars	142
% Extra-era major-started wars	159
% Net recruitees	107
Rational calculation	44
Auditing/policing	121
Macrocentric supervision	120
% Internal wars	46
Unavailability in resources	124
Overt rule-adapting	127
Internal preoccupation	45
Ideological consonance	123
Mean status score	39
Gatepasser status scores	81
% Extraregion minors' alliances	59
% Sovereign gatepassers	77

X. Extraregion Membership

XI. Recruitment

XII. Scattered Attention Focus

XIII. Imperial Penetration

XIV. Supervision

XV. Membership Linkage

SIMILARITY COEFFICIENT: −50.0 −100.0 −150.0 −200.0

FIGURE 11-3
R-Cluster Analysis of Richardson Subsystem Data: II

variables from Factor V, Lack of Concert Pacification, bunched together in Subcluster XIX, though they are dwarfed by indicators of *major power alliances* and coalitions, either with other major powers or with minor powers.

Treaty-making variables appear in Subcluster XX along with indicators of destabilization. Since the only treaties counted in our 183 variables pertain to those concluding wars, it should be no surprise that such documents would ratify changes in the international status quo.

The high proportion of *temporally exogenous* variables in Subcluster XXI calls to mind Factor IX, Temporal Continuity. And indeed the presence of an institutional regulator alongside few elites in comparison with the total number of members cements an impression that members are extremely active outside analytically defined time boundaries of a subsystem.

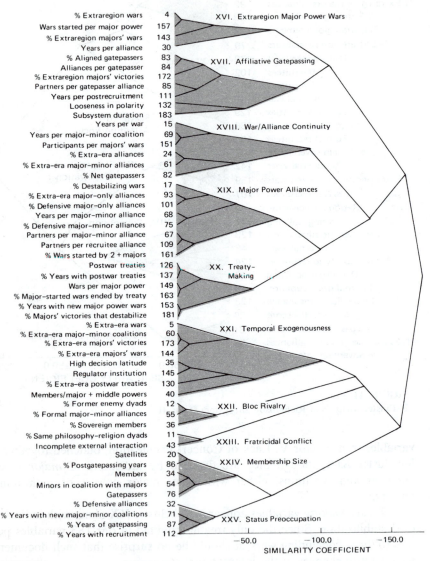

% Extraregion wars	4	XVI. Extraregion Major Power Wars
Wars started per major power	157	
% Extraregion majors' wars	143	
Years per alliance	30	
% Aligned gatepassers	83	XVII. Affiliative Gatepassing
Alliances per gatepasser	84	
% Extraregion majors' victories	172	
Partners per gatepasser alliance	85	
Years per postrecruitment	111	
Looseness in polarity	132	
Subsystem duration	183	
Years per war	15	XVIII. War/Alliance Continuity
Years per major–minor coalition	69	
Participants per majors' wars	151	
% Extra–era alliances	24	
% Extra–era major–minor alliances	61	
% Net gatepassers	82	
% Destabilizing wars	17	XIX. Major Power Alliances
% Extra–era major–only alliances	93	
% Defensive major–only alliances	101	
Years per major–minor alliance	68	
% Defensive major–minor alliances	75	
Partners per major–minor alliance	67	
Partners per recruitee alliance	109	
% Wars started by 2 + majors	161	
Postwar treaties	126	XX. Treaty–Making
% Years with postwar treaties	137	
Wars per major power	149	
% Major–started wars ended by treaty	163	
% Years with new major power wars	153	
% Majors' victories that destabilize	181	
% Extra–era wars	5	XXI. Temporal Exogenousness
% Extra–era major–minor coalitions	60	
% Extra–era majors' victories	173	
% Extra–era majors' wars	144	
High decision latitude	35	
Regulator institution	145	
% Extra–era postwar treaties	130	
Members/major + middle powers	40	
% Former enemy dyads	12	XXII. Bloc Rivalry
% Formal major–minor alliances	55	
% Sovereign members	36	
% Same philosophy–religion dyads	11	XXIII. Fratricidal Conflict
Incomplete external interaction	43	
Satellites	20	XXIV. Membership Size
% Postgatepassing years	86	
Members	34	
Minors in coalition with majors	54	
Gatepassers	76	
% Defensive alliances	32	
% Years with new major–minor coalitions	71	XXV. Status Preoccupation
% Years of gatepassing	87	
% Years with recruitment	112	

−50.0   −100.0   −150.0
SIMILARITY COEFFICIENT

FIGURE 11-4
R–Cluster Analysis of Richardson Subsystem Data: III

The next two subclusters have a small number of variables. Subcluster XXII contains three of the highest-loading variables from Factor III and thus will be called *bloc rivalry* as well. Similarly, *fratricidal conflict* is represented in Subcluster XXIII by two of the higher-loading variables from Factor VII. In both cases it is unusual for factors explaining so much of the total variance to have counterparts in cluster analysis with so few variables as group members.

Membership size underlies Subcluster XXIV, whereas the final subcluster in Figure 11–4 pulls together measures of the pattern variable "preoccupation." A subsystem with much yearly activity in gateopening, recruitment, and coalition formation is certainly eventful from the standpoint of membership status, hence the label *status preoccupation*.

Interventions are indexed by variables falling in subcluster XXVI. Many of these variables have high loadings on Factor VI (Membership Linkage) but are also representatives of the pattern variable "informality" (Figure 11–5).

Plan-making crops up in Subcluster XXVII. There is no particular clue that the impact of such *concert alliances* results in stabilization—even if members of the elite are perceived as legitimate—so the cluster falls short of a Concert Pacification designation, as in Factor V.

The triad of variables in Subcluster XXVIII is indicative of lengthy multilateral wars won by major powers and thus falls neatly under the direction function, as defined in Section 10.6.4; we shall refer to this as a *world war* subcluster. Subcluster XXIX has *formal alliance saturation* at its core but also involves heavy battlefield casualties in interventions and wars which are presumably started by subnational entities but eventually attract outside attention despite a network (or smoke screen) of nonaggression alliances. Subsystems lacking informal ententes between countries, in short, may breed internal wars which are interpreted in the light of existing bloc rivalries rather than being resolved purely as a matter of domestic jurisdiction and concern.

Alliance size appears in Subcluster XXX. It is fascinating to note that alliance activity is so strongly related to levels of technology. The need for countries to have contractual arrangements with one another evidently increases with higher levels of economic and political development.

The final two subclusters are also related to alliance memberships. *Multilateralism* composes Subcluster XXXI. Elite alliance memberships increase with the number of elites, so *elite alliance saturation* is most descriptive of the final subcluster.

Recapitulating the structure of clusters, we find considerable similarity with the factor analysis (Figure 11–6), and variables indexing particular functions emerge on the same clusters together.

Many of the 32 cluster labels are the same as the names given to the 17

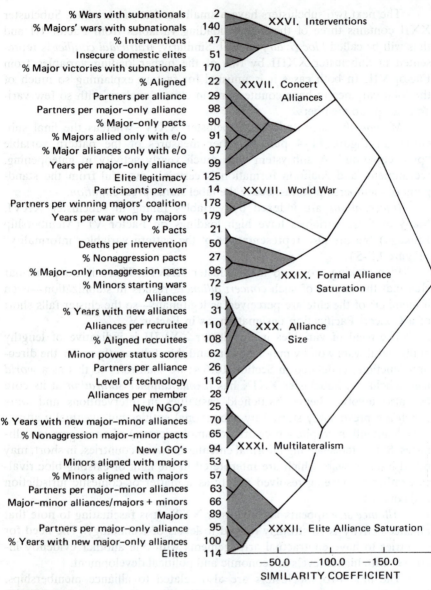

% Wars with subnationals	2
% Majors' wars with subnationals	140
% Interventions	47
Insecure domestic elites	51
% Major victories with subnationals	170
% Aligned	22
Partners per alliance	29
Partners per major–only alliance	98
% Major–only pacts	90
% Majors allied only with e/o	91
% Major alliances only with e/o	97
Years per major–only alliance	99
Elite legitimacy	125
Participants per war	14
Partners per winning majors' coalition	178
Years per war won by majors	179
% Pacts	21
Deaths per intervention	50
% Nonaggression pacts	27
% Major–only nonaggression pacts	96
% Minors starting wars	72
Alliances	19
% Years with new alliances	31
Alliances per recruitee	110
% Aligned recruitees	108
Minor power status scores	62
Partners per alliance	26
Level of technology	116
Alliances per member	28
New NGO's	25
% Years with new major–minor alliances	70
% Nonaggression major–minor pacts	65
New IGO's	94
Minors aligned with majors	53
% Minors aligned with majors	57
Partners per major–minor alliances	63
Major–minor alliances/majors + minors	66
Majors	89
Partners per major–only alliance	95
% Years with new major–only alliances	100
Elites	114

XXVI. Interventions

XXVII. Concert Alliances

XXVIII. World War

XXIX. Formal Alliance Saturation

XXX. Alliance Size

XXXI. Multilateralism

XXXII. Elite Alliance Saturation

−50.0 −100.0 −150.0
SIMILARITY COEFFICIENT

FIGURE 11–5
R–Cluster Analysis of Richardson Subsystem Data: IV

factors because similar variables are involved. We now turn our attention to higher-order clusters as they gradually build up into a single conglomerate (Figure 11–6B).

There are 14 second-order clusters, some of which resemble the 17

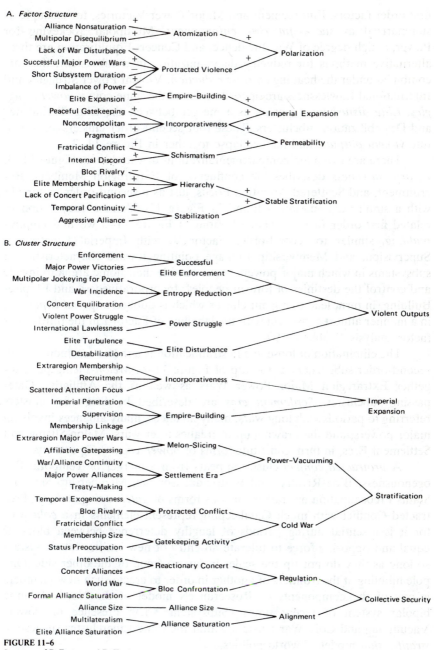

A. *Factor Structure*

Alliance Nonsaturation —(+)
Multipolar Disequilibrium —(+)→ Atomization
Lack of War Disturbance —(−)
Successful Major Power Wars —(+)
Short Subsystem Duration —(−)→ Protracted Violence
Imbalance of Power —(−)
Elite Expansion —(+)→ Empire-Building
Peaceful Gatekeeping —(+)
Noncosmopolitan —(−)→ Incorporativeness
Pragmatism —(+)
Fratricidal Conflict —(+)
Internal Discord —(+)→ Schismatism
Bloc Rivalry —(−)
Elite Membership Linkage —(+)→ Hierarchy
Lack of Concert Pacification —(+)
Temporal Continuity —(+)
Aggressive Alliance —(−)→ Stabilization

Atomization —(+)
→ Polarization
Protracted Violence —(+)

Empire-Building —(+)
→ Imperial Expansion
Incorporativeness —(+)

Incorporativeness —(+)
→ Permeability
Schismatism —(+)

Hierarchy —(+)
→ Stable Stratification
Stabilization —(+)

B. *Cluster Structure*

Enforcement
Major Power Victories → Successful Elite Enforcement
Multipolar Jockeying for Power
War Incidence → Entropy Reduction
Concert Equilibration
Violent Power Struggle
International Lawlessness → Power Struggle
Elite Turbulence
Destabilization → Elite Disturbance
Extraregion Membership
Recruitment → Incorporativeness
Scattered Attention Focus
Imperial Penetration
Supervision → Empire-Building
Membership Linkage
Extraregion Major Power Wars
Affiliative Gatepassing → Melon-Slicing
War/Alliance Continuity
Major Power Alliances → Settlement Era
Treaty-Making
Temporal Exogenousness
Bloc Rivalry → Protracted Conflict
Fratricidal Conflict
Membership Size
Status Preoccupation → Gatekeeping Activity
Interventions
Concert Alliances → Reactionary Concert
World War
Formal Alliance Saturation → Bloc Confrontation
Alliance Size —— Alliance Size
Multilateralism
Elite Alliance Saturation → Alliance Saturation

Successful Elite Enforcement
Entropy Reduction → Violent Outputs
Power Struggle
Elite Disturbance

Incorporativeness
Empire-Building → Imperial Expansion

Melon-Slicing → Power-Vacuuming

Settlement Era

Protracted Conflict → Cold War

Gatekeeping Activity

Reactionary Concert → Regulation

Bloc Confrontation

Alliance Saturation → Alignment

Power-Vacuuming → Stratification
Cold War

Regulation → Collective Security
Alignment

FIGURE 11-6
Summary of R-Factors and R-Clusters

first-order factors. Enforcement and Major Power Victories, for example, is summarized as *successful elite enforcement.* Multipolar Jockeying for Power, a high degree of War Incidence, and Concert Equilibration are three alternative methods for reducing disorganization in a subsystem; they are combined under the heading *entropy reduction.* Violent Power Struggles and International Lawlessness are opposite sides of the same coin—*power struggles.* Elite disturbance appears as a merger between the Elite Turbulence and Destabilization subclusters. These four second-order clusters all constitute *violent outputs,* and they collapse together in Figure 11–2.

There are two main compartmentalizations of variables in Figure 11–3. *Incorporativeness* describes the confluence of Extraregion Members, Recruitment, and Scattered Attention Focus, just as a second-order factor (I) with a similar designation is found in Figure 11–6A at a conjunction of related first-order factors. At the bottom of Figure 11–3 we find *empire-building,* similar to second-order Factor V, with Imperial Penetration, Supervision, and Membership Linkage pointing toward characteristics of subsystems in which major powers probe outside their home arena to invade and control the destinies of foreign peoples. Incorporativeness and Empire-Building, in turn, lead to a giant cluster which is dubbed *imperial expansion* in a manner almost consistent with the labelling of Factor I in the third-order factor analysis (Table 11–9).

The elimination of looseness in stratification is a theme common to both second-order subclusters at the top of Figure 11–4. *Melon-slicing* pulls together Extraregion Major Power Wars as well as the Affiliative Gate-passing subcluster. *Settlement eras* are described by first-order clusters referring to periods with long wars, many alliances, many alliances involving major powers, and the drawing up of treaties after wars. Melon-Slicing and Settlement Eras, in turn, constitute forms of *power-vacuuming* activity.

A *protracted conflict* cluster appears from a merger of Temporal Exogenousness, Bloc Rivalry, and Fratricidal Conflict. Membership Size and Status Preoccupation are rather obvious forms of *gatekeeping activity.* Protracted Conflict with much Gatekeeping represent elements in a *cold war,* for it is essential during periods of lengthy deterrence between blocs of equal and opposing force to tolerate an entry of new entities into a system so long as they do not tip the scales in favor of one or the other side. One pole nibbling at the frontiers of another in order to create such new members is one of the components of Rosecrance's model of the North Atlantic bipolar system of recent times (Subsystem X).[19] Presence of Power-Vacuuming and Cold War clusters within the same supercluster suggests a *stratification* model of world politics.

[19] Richard N. Rosecrance, "Bipolarity, Multipolarity, and the Future," *Journal of Conflict Resolution,* X (September 1966), 314–27.

The final cluster analysis figure also contains two main aggregations of variables (Figure 11–5). If Concert Alliances occur when there are many Interventions, we encounter a *reactionary concert,* however nobly major powers conceive of their task as preserving a power equilibrium in an international subsystem. World War and Formal Alliance Saturation subclusters constitute *bloc confrontations.* Both Reactionary Concert and Bloc Confrontations pertain to a problem of *regulation* and power management in international systems.

Alliance size remains as a separate cluster in the second-order analysis, but Multilateralism and Elite Alliance Saturation resurrect an *alliance saturation* category, which was of course the first factor in the factor analysis. Alliance Size and Alliance Saturation, in turn, are summarized as an *alignment* cluster. And an international system with a high degree of alignment along with active regulatory behavior fulfills minimal conditions for an arena of *collective security,*[20] however imperfectly outputs of such a system may be performed.

The dissimilarity coefficient for Violent Outputs (Figure 11–2) is − 208.5. Expansion appears at − 221.3 (Figure 11–3). The Stratification cluster is formed at − 186.8 (Figure 11–4), and the Collective Security cluster converges at a − 197.3 coefficient of dissimilarity (Figure 11–5). Cluster analysis eventually must pull all four together into one large group. Stratification and Collective Security have the greatest affinity for one another, coming together at − 235.0. The joint Collective Security–Stratification cluster is joined by Expansion at − 261.3. Our Hobbesian cluster, named Violent Outputs, is finally brought together after the other three clusters have become welded; this final combination of conflict-management with conflict-ridden clusters is at the − 302.9 level of dissimilarity.

The major clusters (or superclusters) suggest five alternative forms of international conflict resolution. One model is of a *struggle for power,* as exemplified by the first cluster. A second model is *hegemonization,* under which one or more poles seek to expand and eventually to dominate. Hegemonization drives may be successful in the case of the Pax Romana, or they may generate an environment of transitory leaders and successive challengers.[21] A third type of power management system accepts *stratification* as inexorable and works for a division of spoils or series of modi vivendi that will be acceptable to contending poles; under this approach bloc rivalries are kept "cold" rather than allowed to erupt into hegemonic drives for supremacy. One of the historic conceptions of Stratification subsystems has been the theory of the balance of power; a more recent form is the so-called

[20] Cf. Inis L. Claude, Jr., *Power and International Relations* (New York: Random House, 1962).

[21] Cf. A. F. K. Organski, *World Politics,* 2d ed. (New York: Knopf, 1968).

balance of terror between thermonuclear giants in contemporary world politics.[22] *Collective security* is a final alternative. In such cases the major powers (or all powers) band together in order to halt unilateral threats to international peace. We may interpret these results to suggest that collective security, though its components can become manifest too late,[23] is one method of holding down levels of violence; stratification is almost as effective in dampening war propensities. Hegemonic overseas direction is the least related to the incidence of international aggression. In the factor analysis, four factors emerge, one pertaining to each Parsonian functional imperative; the adaptation function (Polarization) emerges from War Disturbance and Alliance Nonsaturation first-order factors. The factor analysis, in short, agrees with the cluster analysis that peaceful subsystems will contain many alliances and relatively few major powers.

11.4 CAUSAL MODELS OF INTERNATIONAL
SYSTEMIC PROCESSES

Although there is considerable overlap between individual clusters and factors in our analysis of variables of international subsystem performance, guides for causal models of international violence are rather nebulous. Higher-order factors reveal affinities between variables which index Parsonian functional categories; superclusters suggest alternative ways in which subsystems cope with problems of conflict. It would be appropriate to intersperse higher-loading variables from the factor analysis among key variables from the cluster analysis that identify models of conflict management.

Variables appropriate for a causal analysis of systemic processes fall most clearly on Factor IV of the third-order factor analysis, which is labelled Polarization; two second-order factors have high loadings on Polarization, Protracted Violence (II) and Atomization (VII). In the cluster analysis the obvious dependent variables are located on the Violent Outputs supercluster. It is therefore necessary to represent various types of violent outputs while selecting at least one variable from five first-order factors— Lack of War Disturbance (II), Short Subsystem Duration (XII), Successful Major Power Wars (XV), Alliance Nonsaturation (I), and Multipolar Disequilibrium (XVII).

<hr/>

[22] The stability of bipolarity is a principal finding in M. Haas, "International Subsystems: Stability and Polarity," in which a subset of the 183 variables was analyzed. This confirms the expectations of Kenneth N. Waltz, "Stability of the Bipolar World," *Daedalus*, XCIII (Summer 1964), 881–909.

[23] Claude, *Power and International Relations*.

A total of nine variables is necessary to be representative[24] of all aspects of international subsystem behavior. *War disturbance* is indexed somewhat more accurately by counting the number of wars initiated *per country* than by a simple count of the number of wars in a subsystem, so the variable with the second highest loading in first-order Factor II is appropriate; moreover, for subsystems with only a few major powers, variable 156 is less desirable than 164, inasmuch as the latter averages the number of wars started per major power; both variables are located on Subcluster I. *Successful major power wars* is indexed aptly by variable 180, which is part of Subcluster II. *Subsystem duration* is embodied in variable 183 and no other, but it is found in a tiny subcluster with variable 132, *loose poles,* which of course is a defining characteristic of our delineation of subsystems. Turning to factors that compose the Atomization second-order factor, we find that the highest-loading variable in Factor I actually suggests multilateral alliances, whereas the number of alliances per member (variable 28) is more appropriate, and variables 26 and 28 are both found on the same subcluster in Figure 11–5. *Multipolar disequilibrium* has two facets: variable 6 is a count of the number of poles, and disequilibrium is indexed by the variable with the second highest loading—the percentage of major power victories which change a prior status quo (variable 176). Variable 6 is on Subcluster III; variable 176, on Subcluster IX. In order to round out the variables selected so far, at least one should be chosen that assesses the nature of membership in a subsystem, so variable 38 (percent extraregional members) is taken from Subcluster X. Finally, it is essential to differentiate between eras of domestic turbulence and those of internation violence; from Subcluster IV we therefore select variable 48, percent foreign wars. The nine variables are taken from a subset of the various functions and pattern variables (Figure 11–7). About half of the variables are manifestations of input variables, half output variables. There are no withinput variables at all, and this seems less surprising with international subsystems, which lack well-established, powerful institutions and channels for converting inputs into outputs. Three of the four pattern variables are represented. The latent-manifest pattern fails to show up among the nine variables, but the remaining styles of function performance are just about equally represented; the key independent variables come from the diffuse-specific pattern, and dependent variables indicate the affective-instrumental pattern.

Despite our care in selecting variables that are ideal for a causal analysis, results are disappointing. In constructing and testing more than 50 causal models, including one for each mechanism of power management

---

[24] By "representative" I mean the set of independent sources of variation closest to the dependent variable.

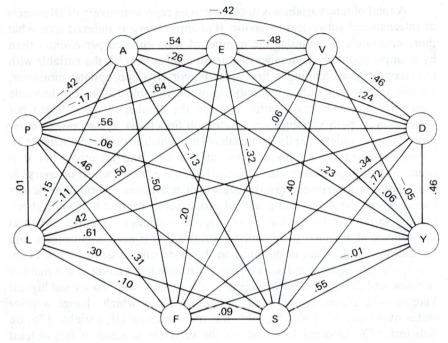

FIGURE 11–7
Variables Selected for Models of Systemic Processes

Key:
   Numbers represent correlations.
   A = alliances per member (var. 28).
   D = % destabilizing major power victories (var. 176).
   E = % extraregion members/members (var. 38).
   F = % foreign wars (var. 48).
   L = looseness in power stratification (var. 132).
   P = poles (var. 6).
   S = wars started per major power (var. 164).
   V = % years with major power victories (var. 180).
   Y = years of subsystem duration (var. 183).

suggested by the cluster analysis, no single model was entirely or even
largely satisfactory. A third of all prediction equations were within acceptable limits (+ .10 to − .10); but another third exceeded ± .50, with the
final third in between. Many alternative variables were tried by substituting
those with high loadings on a particular factor for variables closely related
in the cluster analysis; even the number of variables was reduced below
nine. None of these permutations ever improved the overall fit.

   The thorny notion of cause will thus remain a problem at the systemic
level in the analysis of international conflict. Having widely sampled vari-

ables from assorted variables and clusters, we departed from the practice in Chapters 5 and 8 of using variables that are closely embedded on the same clusters and factors. In so doing we sought to include theoretically relevant facets of systemic processes, for too many of the clusters and factors had almost identical variables with extremely high intercorrelations. In a subsequent study with a larger number of subsystems, sampling artifacts will doubtless disappear and it may be possible to trace causal paths with more success. Fortunately we are able to fall back on the finding that collective security, stratification, and hegemonization systems are likely to avoid a high frequency in violent outputs.

PART V
Conclusion

chapter 12
Implications

12.1 SUMMARY

This final chapter will present a brief codification of research findings and draw policy implications that may make decisionmakers aware of processes leading to war that are reversible. A summary is presented along three levels of analysis in the form of scenarios—that is, reconstructions of findings that may provide dramatists with scripts for a true-to-life representation of conditions conducive or unfavorable to an outbreak of a war. In stating policy implications, unchangeable elements will be separated from reversible conditions so that a decisionmaker desirous of peace can implement achievable objectives (Section 12.3).

12.1.1 Interpersonal Scenario

What kinds of persons are most likely to prefer peaceful rather than warlike options in times of foreign policy crises? In a search for a dove decisionmaker based on the public opinion approach, as reviewed in Section 3.3.1, the casting department of our repertory company would look for a middle-aged Negress with a college education and the status of a physician or college professor. She would reside outside a big city but not too far from her country's capital. She would be nonauthoritarian, nonethnocentric, flexible, achievement-oriented, uncynical, nonalienated, optimistic, and intellectual; and she would be able to tolerate ambiguity. Her political views would be neither conservative nor nationalist; she would be politically active, would not anticipate war as an inevitable feature of world politics, would be disinclined to take risks, and she would not be confident that her country would be victorious in time of war. According to the foreign policy case study approach, summarized in Section 3.3.2, our decisionmaker will prefer peaceful decisions when information inputs are neither perceptually complex nor cognitively simple. She would seek to maintain mutual trust, friendliness, and a high level of communication, though short of an information overload. She would insist on accurate information—and would receive a true picture of a situation without engaging in stereotypic decoding of input messages or in provocative encoding of output messages. Her advisers would be in some disagreement over alternatives; and they would be concerned enough over long-range implications to draw up contingency plans, while she attempts to prolong the duration of the decisionmaking process.

The analysis in Chapters 4 and 5 of this volume mines some 32 decisionmaking case studies in order to distinguish the most violent decisions from those in which violent modes of conflict resolution have been avoided. In a correlational analysis of several aspects of decisionmaking, the following conditions are most strongly related to violent decisions.

1. The decision holds substantive, rather than procedural, consequences.
2. The decisionmaker has high needs for power.
3. The decisionmaker is not aligned with the target of his decision.
4. The decision is perceived as crucial by the decisionmaker.
5. The decision upsets a previous status quo.
6. Many perceptions of hostility are expressed by the decisionmaker.
7. The decisionmaker takes excessive risks.

The same variables are subjected to multivariate analyses. The first step is to classify the 32 decisionmaking case studies on the basis of similarities and differences across 68 variables. In a factor analysis, 9 factors account for almost 75 percent of the total variance; the factors collapse into 3 major groupings in a second-order factor analysis. The following classification summarizes the findings (see Figure 5–2A):

    I.   Strategic decisions.
        A. Demarches.
        B. Decisions that do not entail clarification of status distinctions.

   II. Institutionalized decisions.
        A. Decisions reaffirming values.
        B. Armistices.
        C. Overcautious decisions.
        D. Decisions that do not involve detentes.
        E. Decisions that do not produce debacles.

III. Decisions relating to instability.
   A. Debacles.
   B. Aggressive decisions.
   C. Decisions destabilizing for the target.

In a separate cluster analysis, the 32 decisions are grouped as follows (see Figure 5–2B):

I. Decisions relating to the level of conflict.
   A. Demarches.
   B. Deescalations.
   C. Destructive decisions.

II. Decisions relating to the mode of conflict resolution.
   A. Conflict terminating.
   B. Conflict initiating.

With such heterogeneous strata within the 32-case sample of decision-making situations, we proceeded to delineate factors from the 68 variables. A total of 17 factors extract almost 90 percent of the total variance, and it is necessary to perform a third-order factor analysis to decompose the variables into a parsimonious empirical taxonomy. Two sets of variables are contrasted with each other—those dealing with whether incremental or comprehensive changes are made, and those pertaining to alternative ways of resolving or provoking conflicts (see Figure 5–5A):

I. Resolvative elements of decisionmaking.
   A. Nondisputatiousness.
      1. Absence of a crisis mood.
      2. Nonaggressive outcomes.
      3. Objects of the decision treated as clients.
      4. Few issues involved.
   B. Polyarchic decision process among decisionmakers.
      1. High level of consensus.
      2. A routine, rather than a watershed, decision.
      3. Many issues involved.
   C. Decisions not handled through institutional channels.
      1. Absence of bottlenecking.
      2. Hierarchical, rather than collegial, relationships.
      3. Imperiousness.
      4. An unexpected stimulus for the decision.

II. Incremental elements of decisionmaking.
   A. Adaptiveness.
      1. An unexpected stimulus for the decision.

2. Absence of an application of rational principles of decisionmaking.
3. Decisionmakers are history-minded.
B. Decisions that do not involve coups.
1. Unsuccessful decisions.
C. Tactical Concerns.
1. Pragmatic elements.
2. Implementation simplicity.

A cluster analysis of the same data was much less complicated. The basic contrast is between ordinary and extraordinary aspects of decisionmaking processes (see Figure 5–5B):

I. Ordinary elements.
A. Bottlenecking.
B. Cognitive differentiation of the task.
C. Decisionmaker regarding the object of his decision as a client.

II. Extraordinary elements.
A. Imperative aspects.
1. Solidarity among the decisionmakers.
2. Precipitate processes.
B. Machiavellian aspects.
1. Assiduousness in decisionmaking.
2. Concern for time.
3. Complexity in implementation.
C. Showdown aspects.

From the factor analysis, violent decisions appear as instances of aggressiveness that are flanked by crisis and nonclientele elements; in the cluster analysis, violent decisions are pinpointed as showdown-oriented. Our scenario at the interpersonal level, therefore, indicates that we can avoid violence as an outcome in decisionmaking if decisionmakers avoid moods of crisis and showdown in their deliberations.

The components of violent decisionmaking are strung together in several causal models in Section 5.4. A *cultural exchange* model has the best fit. According to this model, a decisionmaker wishing to avoid war should be most cautious when the target of his decision is an entity with greatly dissimilar values and possesses an unfamiliar cultural background. When agent and target are culturally dissimilar, moreover, it is essential to have adequate information for making a wise choice. An expression of frustration will serve no useful purpose during information-processing and might even drain off tensions in a maladaptive direction if the decisional problem deals with high-priority values, especially those in which the persistence of the agent is at stake.

12.1.2 Societal Scenario

In our search for societal propensities for warmaking, possible prerequisites were difficult to find. If, following Kant, we were to admit to an international organization only states most likely to keep the peace, the data of Part III of this volume would direct us to select small and minor powers. But their pacific tendencies appear related to the obvious fact that they are less likely to participate in international interactions, and that they will prefer to express violence by actions short of war simply because they are unlikely to be victors in a showdown situation. Stated more precisely, the following variables are correlated most strongly with indicators of foreign violence:

1. Bloc prominence.
2. Military mobilizations.
3. Public perceptions of hostility toward peoples of other countries.
4. A high proportion of gross national product devoted to military and public administration expenditures.
5. A large amount of foreign aid sent or received.
6. A high percentage of the population serving in the armed forces.
7. Equality in income levels (before taxation).

Examining the societal variables across 85 countries, the first step in a multivariate analysis was to ascertain independent strata of countries. Eight factors extract somewhat over 87 percent of the total variance in the countries, and a second- and third-order factor analysis is needed before the eight factors can be grouped into a binary classification. Countries differ primarily according to whether they are active or passive, or united or disunited. To sum up the findings, the factors are presented below (see Figure 8–3A):

I. Activism.
   A. Apollonian countries.
      1. Centrifugal characteristics.
      2. High level of politicoeconomic development.
   B. Countries where dionysian values do not prevail.
      1. Countries outside of Latin America.
      2. Closed, rather than open, societies.
      3. Countries lacking societal paralysis.

II. Disunited countries.
   A. Unmodernized countries.
   B. Lack of intergroup accommodation.
   C. Countries that are not neocolonial dependencies.

Development is the basic characteristic that distinguishes countries in a cluster analysis. The structure of the cluster analysis is as follows (see Figure 8–3B):

I.   Underdeveloped countries.
     A. Economic underdevelopment.
     B. Political underdevelopment.

II. System-wide planning.
     A. Modernized countries.
     B. Countries concerned with pattern maintenance.
         1. Centrifugal polities.
             a. Non–Western centrifugal countries.
             b. Latin American countries.
         2. Closed, rather than open, polities.
         3. Neocolonial dependencies.

A factor analysis and cluster analysis are performed on the 183 societal variables in order to locate which characteristics are related more intimately with propensities to enter wars. (A separate factor analysis of the modernized countries that were isolated in the cluster analysis corresponded with an analysis of variables across all 85 countries, except for factors that would distinguish underdeveloped countries from each other.) A total of 43 factors extract the total variance in a principal axis factor analysis, so the 43 factors are themselves factor-analyzed until a compact taxonomy is assembled empirically. The main comparison between factors in a fourth-order factor analysis is derived from a framework of Robert Bales, who distinguishes between social-emotional and task orientations in group situations. The overall structure breaks down as follows (see Figure 8–4):

I.   Social-emotional orientation.
     A. Disintegrative processes.
         1. Politically asymmetric characteristics.
             a. No modernizing welfare statist trends.
             b. Polity unable to extract tax revenues.
             c. Sparse social communication.
             d. Domestic disengagement.
             e. Domestic political conflict.
             f. Politicoeconomic paralysis.
             g. Lack of professional expertise.
             h. Much political competition.
         2. Disunion and scarcity in resources.
             a. Rural austerity.
             b. Unenlightened rebellion.
             c. Unstructured society.
             d. No monoracial unity.

    3. Volatile processes.
      a. No monoracial unity.
      b. No internationally guided development.
      c. Centrifugal characteristics.
      d. Rapid development.
  B. Ideological characteristics.
    1. Dialectical process of development.
      a. Rapid development.
      b. Nonpatriarchical rule.
      c. Uneven development.
      d. No unenlightened rebellion.
    2. Nonautarkic economy.
      a. No unenlightened rebellion.
      b. Sustained industrialization.
      c. Entrepreneurial development.
      d. Bourgeois revolution.
      e. Permeability.
    3. Subjectivist processes.
      a. Elite scapegoatism.
      b. Cathective involvement.
  C. Harmonizing processes absent.
    1. Social asymmetry.
      a. Separatism.
      b. Societal tension.
      c. Phenotypic asymmetry.
    2. Modernizing clique rule absent.
      a. Modernizing oligarchy absent.
      b. Modernizing welfare statism absent.
      c. Developmental junta absent.

II. Task orientation.
  A. Administrative activity.
    1. Redistribution crisis.
      a. Labor unrest amid affluence.
      b. Governmental philistinism.
    2. No laissez-faire development.
      a. Guided development.
      b. Societal solidarity.
      c. Incorporative articulation.
  B. Change orientation.
    1. Laissez-faire development.
      a. Unguided development.
      b. Societal solidarity absent.
      c. Nonincorporative articulation.

    2. Political incrementalism.
       a. Political competition.
       b. Reorganization-mindedness absent.
    3. Aggressiveness.
       a. Foreign conflict behavior.
       b. Discontentment with laxity.
    4. Neocolonial characteristics.
  C. Absence of elite development.
    1. No neocolonial characteristics.
    2. No societal expansiveness.
       a. Pretakeoff stage.
       b. Reactionary developmental process.
       c. Absence of societal solidarity.
    3. Nondirective rule.
       a. Dense social communication.
       b. Nondespotic rule.
       c. Modernizing oligarchic rule absent.
       d. No guided democracy.

In addition to this nested classification of factors, a second-order factor, Traditional Rule, is unrelated to any of the third-order factors and thus drops out of the overall taxonomy. Traditional Rule is a composite of lack of Equalitarianism, lack of Absentee Landlordism, and an absence of Guided Democratic Rule.

In a separate cluster analysis of the same societal variables, a somewhat different structure emerges; societies with liberal democratic sustained modernization processes are contrasted with those having a directive but faltering process of modernization (see Figure 8–8):

   I. Liberal democratic sustained modernization.
    A. Secularization processes.
       1. Urban sophistication.
       2. Politicization.
    B. Bureaucratized productivity.
       1. Technological development.
          a. Dense social communication.
          b. Mobilization of resources.
       2. Formalistic processes.
          a. Development by braintrusts.
          b. Articulation of interests.
          c. Legalism.
       3. Unified society.
          a. Structured society.
          b. Cultural unity.

    C. Polyarchic decisionmaking processes.
       1. Multiparty system.
       2. Constitutionalism.
II. Directive but faltering modernization.
    A. Prenationalist internal turbulence.
       1. Revolutionary tendencies.
          a. Multiracial disparity.
          b. Political fragility.
          c. Noncolonial inequality.
       2. Multinational society with social discrimination.
          a. Traditional society.
          b. Separatism.
       3. Neoprotectorate.
          a. Penetrable sovereignty.
          b. Despotic rule.
    B. Control orientation.
       1. Domestic turmoil.
          a. Bourgeois revolutionary tendencies.
          b. Disruptive political activism.
          c. Class struggle.
       2. Zerosum politics.
          a. Development of a garrison state.
          b. Power-oriented politics.
          c. Ethnic-religious diversity.
          d. Foreign conflict.
       3. Development by elites.
          a. Stage of economic takeoff.
          b. Oligarchic development.
          c. Monoculture society.

Foreign violence is associated with task-oriented trends in societies undergoing directive but faltering modernization. More specifically, Foreign Conflict and Discontented Laxity form a pair of factors that are labelled Aggressive on the second-order factor analysis, while foreign conflict is nested together with the development of a military-industrial complex and the pursuit of power politics, and is found within large countries that have several ethnic and religious groups living side by side. Our scenario of the peaceful country concurs with capitalist theorists of the early nineteenth century, for development and democracy together direct countries toward both internal and external cooperation. There is no direct connection between foreign and domestic conflict, but both are concomitants of an underlying process of disintegration in the extent of democratic consent, which in turn results when there is unsteady economic growth.

In choosing between alternative causal models, a *developmental* model yields the closest fit. By dividing countries into the categories of developed, developing, and undeveloped, three different routes toward war are evident. In all three cases an increase in military expenditures precedes war, but motivations to step up arms production come from different sources. The least developed countries find themselves at war if they are administratively stagnant. Developing countries are tempted to embark upon wars when their population is heterogeneous and are thus prone toward domestic conflicts. Advanced countries enter wars most often during periods of economic downswings.

12.1.3 Systemic Scenario

According to the international community approach, states are more likely to settle their differences peacefully if they share compatible main values, jointly possess a distinctive way of life, are mutually responsive, have an unbroken social communication network with a wide range of transactions, and if there is a strong core area with rising economic capabilities and expectations of even more economic growth. Findings on international stratification are inconclusive on the role of alliances as either precipitants or deterrents to the outbreak of war. Unipolar systems are by far the most peaceful; members of such systems are aggressive only in other arenas, if at all. Historically bipolarity has brought peace, though when wars do occur they tend to be destabilizing and long in duration. Tripolar and multipolar systems contain the most wars, members at war, members per war, deaths per war, and are consistently associated with other indicators of international violence.

Over the last three or four centuries wars have been less prevalent but increasingly costly in terms of lives lost; fewer initiators of war have succeeded in winning wars, when one contrasts the nineteenth with the twentieth century.[1] Contrary to Rosecrance,[2] available and unappropriated resources make for instability; scarcity, for stability. The existence in a system of contending or nonstatus quo ideologies means that conflict will be intense; but a divergence in elites' ethos is neither a necessary nor a sufficient condition for instability: ideological aspects of contemporary bipolar sub-

---

[1] These findings are from Lewis F. Richardson, *Statistics of Deadly Quarrels* (Chicago: Quadrangle, 1960); and Karl W. Deutsch and Dieter Senghaas, "Towards a Theory of War and Peace: Propositions, Simulations, and Reality," paper presented to the Annual Convention of the American Political Science Association, New York, September 1969. The remaining findings summarized in this section are taken from Chapters 10 and 11.

[2] Richard N. Rosecrance, *Action and Reaction in World Politics* (Boston: Little, Brown, 1963).

systems are incidental. However, boundaries drawn so that allegiances are nationalist instead of dynastic have been associated with more, rather than fewer, wars. No single regulator—balance of power, concert of great powers, alliance system, or international organization—has been able to maintain stability in all of the European cases. The record of the Concert of Europe is somewhat better, but the breakdowns of 1848 and 1914 were too extraordinary to be averted.

Because the observations thus far summarized in the international system scenario are based largely on European history, several additional arenas of conflict are delimited in Chapter 9. The data in Chapters 10 and 11 define twenty-one international subsystems in Europe, Asia, and Hawaii in terms of conflictual interactions and military confrontations. Variables most strongly related to multipolarity in an international subsystem are as follows:

1. Many wars occur between peoples with similar bodily characteristics.
2. Most wars involving major powers are fought to destabilize a balance of power.
3. Disturbance to the stability of a system increases over time.
4. There is a procedural, rather than substantive, emphasis in adapting norms of international conduct to new situations.
5. Treaties are seldom written to conclude wars.
6. Wars including major power participants are lengthy.
7. Each major power wins several victories on the battlefield.

Power can be stratified so that every state and territory is aligned with one or another bloc; but when there is a looser power stratification, one encounters neutral powers throughout an international conflict subsystem. Tight power stratification is most intimately associated with the following conditions:

1. There is little cooperation among poles.
2. High levels of technological development prevail.
3. Outside the core subsystem, major powers are seldom victorious.
4. There are few years during the subsystem era in which postwar treaties are concluded.
5. Diplomatic representation by major and middle powers is extensive.
6. Major powers enter few of the wars fought.
7. If a war is started by a major power, the war will not be ended by a treaty.

These two sets of findings depict a scene in which the best guarantee of international peace is to have as few power blocs as possible within the conflict subsystem, keeping the number of major powers to a minimum. A tight stratification of power is more common in recent eras of history, and major powers tend to avoid direct confrontations as much as possible in view of the all-or-nothing implications of a single thermonuclear encounter. An empirical taxonomy of the 21 conflict subsystems is based on 183 variables. In a factor analysis, 81 percent of the total variance is extracted by only 3 factors when one subsample of the data is analyzed; in a second subsample, 4 factors extract almost 90 percent of the variance. The overall classification based on all samples shows that nuclear eras do not differ substantially from all other periods in international history (see Tables 11–3, 11–4; Figure 11–1):

I.   Premodern subsystems.
     A. Concert subsystems.
         1. Europe 1790–1814.
         2. Europe 1815–1822.
         3. Europe 1823–1847.
         4. Europe 1848–1871.
         5. Europe 1872–1890.
     B. Early state systems.
         1. Western Europe 1649–1713.
         2. Europe 1714–1789.
         3. East Asia 1689–1842.
         4. East Asia 1843–1895.
         5. Hawaii 1738–1758.
         6. Hawaii 1759–1782.
         7. Hawaii 1783–1795.
         8. Hawaii 1796–1818.
         9. Hawaii 1819–1898.

II. Modern subsystems.
     A. Europe 1891–1918.
     B. Europe 1919–1945.
     C. East Asia 1896–1913.
     D. East Asia 1914–1945.
     E. East Asia 1946–1954.
     F. Asia 1955–1963.

III. Elite stabilization.
     A. Europe 1848–1871.
     B. Europe 1872–1890.
     C. North Atlantic 1946–1963.
     D. East Asia 1689–1842.

In two cluster analyses of the same data, a very similar classification emerges, so there is no need to summarize the results separately.

When all 183 variables are intercorrelated and factor-analyzed, 17 factors extract all of the variance. A third-order factor analysis finally reduces the number of factors to 4 major sets, one representing each of Talcott Parsons's 4 functional imperatives (see Figure 11–6A):

I. Polarization (adaptation).
   A. Atomization.
      1. Alliance nonsaturation.
      2. Multipolar disequilibrium.
   B. Protracted violence.
      1. High level of war disturbance.
      2. Successful major power wars.
      3. Long subsystem duration.
      4. Imbalance of power.

II. Imperial expansion (goal attainment).
   A. Empire-building.
      1. Elite expansion.
      2. No imbalance of power.
   B. Incorporativeness.
      1. Pragmatism.
      2. Cosmopolitanism.
      3. Peaceful entry of new members.

III. Permeability (coordination).
   A. Incorporativeness.
      1. Pragmatism.
      2. Cosmopolitanism.
      3. Peaceful entry of new members.
   B. Schismatism.
      1. Fratricidal conflict.
      2. Internal discord.

IV. Stable stratification (pattern maintenance).
   A. Hierarchy.
      1. No bloc rivalry.
      2. Elite membership linkage.
      3. No concert pacification.
   B. Stabilization.
      1. Temporal continuity.
      2. Lack of aggressive alliances.

The same 183 variables were cluster-analyzed as well. The clusterings are more complex than the factor structure, unlike most of the previous parallel runs (see Figure 11–6B):

I. Violent outputs.
    A. Successful elite enforcement.
        1. Enforcement.
        2. Major power victories.
    B. Entropy reduction.
        1. Multipolar jockeying for power.
        2. War incidence.
        3. Concert equilibration.
    C. Power struggle.
        1. Violent power struggle.
        2. International lawlessness.
    D. Elite disturbance.
        1. Elite turbulence.
        2. Destabilization.

II. Imperial expansion.
    A. Incorporativeness.
        1. Extraregion membership.
        2. Recruitment.
        3. Scattered attention focus.
    B. Empire-building.
        1. Imperial penetration.
        2. Supervision.
        3. Membership linkage.

III. Stratification.
    A. Power-vacuuming.
        1. Melon-slicing.
            a. Extraregion major power wars.
            b. Gatepassers have alliance partners.
        2. Settlement era.
            a. Continuity in wars and alliances.
            b. Major power alliances.
            c. Treaty-making.
    B. Cold war.
        1. Protracted conflict.
            a. Wars and alliances overlap two subsystem eras.
            b. Bloc rivalry.
            c. Fratricidal conflict.

2. Gatekeeping activity.
   a. Many members in the subsystem.
   b. Status preoccupation.

IV. Collective security.
   A. Regulation.
      1. Reactionary concert.
         a. Interventions.
         b. Concert alliances.
      2. Bloc confrontation.
         a. World war.
         b. Formal alliance saturation.
   B. Alignment.
      1. Alliance size.
      2. Alliance saturation.
         a. Multilateralism.
         b. Elite alliance saturation.

From the factor analysis our scenario of peaceful international subsystems depicts hierarchical relationships that have congealed over time, whether imperial or organized into blocs.

No causal model has a satisfactory fit with the data; we are therefore left with a finding that subsystems with both strong regulators and intense alignments are most distant from anarchical subsystems in which elites are continually winning wars, there is an ongoing power struggle, and the overall level of war incidence is high.

12.2 METHODOLOGICAL IMPLICATIONS

We are now in a position to comment, albeit briefly, on the results of applying a particular logic in conducting research. A codification of classical theories and modern approaches has assisted in pointing out significant models and vistas for bringing together a set of diverse empirical findings. Some possible approaches, which may be very fruitful, were not pursued in depth: the public opinion approach to interpersonal factors has been conducted over the last 40 years, and the principal findings are summarized in Section 3.3.1; the community approach to international systems, surveyed in Section 9.3.1, deals with international cooperation more than conflict.

Each part of this volume employs cross-sectional instead of longitudinal analysis. This choice was deliberate and was based on previous experience that the two approaches are usually similar in results but that in an initial foray a cross-sectional study is less difficult and less expensive to execute with care.[3]

Results of factor analysis and cluster analysis have transcended mere bivariate correlations and rendered the findings far more coherent. We have also discovered that interpretations based on factor analysis are somewhat one-sided until compared with a cluster analysis, and vice versa. As complementary multivariate techniques, factor analysis combined with cluster analysis has more completely identified variables appropriate for causal models. Solution of causal models, however, has been as dependent upon a priori models as upon hints from factor analysis and cluster analysis. Our failure to model systemic processes remains a puzzle.

It is noteworthy that conceptual rigor in delineating categories for collecting data yielded a much longer list of factors than in other analyses of international relations data. Conceptual frameworks, consistent with the problem of conceptual dualism noted in Section 2.4.2, seldom have been mirrored by corresponding empirical dimensions in the data. Some conceptual distinctions lead to a generation of variables which do hang together, but there are more failures than successes. As a result, one could move in three possible directions. One could scrap existing conceptual frameworks as figments of the imagination. Alternatively, one might affirm the existence of a fundamental and unbridgeable dualism between the empirical world and heuristically or logically sound analytic distinctions. Thirdly, one may lament the paucity of theoretically relevant data for analysis and admit that much more effort is needed to obtain meaningful data within international relations. The present effort relied largely on existing sources of data in order to ascertain whether new types of data are needed, and it has revealed a great need for new types of indicators of conceptual cells which are either barren or filled with judgmentally scaled codings.[4]

12.3 CONCLUSIONS FOR POLICYMAKERS

Given the above findings about international conflict, what can a policymaker do today in order to avoid unnecessary wars and miscalculations that

---

[3] Cf. Michael Haas, "Aggregate Analysis," *World Politics*, XIX (October 1966), 106–21.

[4] Cf. J. David Singer, "Data-Making in International Relations," *Behavioral Science*, X (January 1965), 68–80. In some of Singer's work cited in Part IV of this volume, we find that he assembles new data on alliances but duplicates previous efforts to collect war data paralleling Quincy Wright's data in his *A Study of War*, 2d ed. (Chicago: University of Chicago Press, 1965). A major issue in data collection is whether one should collect many variables for few cases, or few variables for many cases. In this volume an optimizing strategy has been followed in the view that one needs to pursue both approaches in tandem.

lead to international disequilibrium? In order to answer this question it is necessary to separate short-run from long-run steps and unchangeable from changeable conditions. There is, of course, some interaction between the two aspects of policy advice. Interpersonal factors in specific decisional cycles are more subject to change and intervention than are the broad historical sweeps of time featured at the systemic level of analysis. Societal factors are not immediately reversible; but with governmental and private planning geared toward a mitigation of conflict situations, it is conceivable that middle-run changes could render warfare less necessary and more avoidable. At each of the three levels of analysis—interpersonal, societal, and systemic—some factors are more amenable to tampering than others; so we now proceed to analyze conditions that are the most free to vary in order to help bring an end to the suffering and destruction that follows from international violence.

At the interpersonal level, it would be futile to insist that decision-makers should take personality tests or have a predefined set of social background characteristics before taking office. In seeking cohorts or advisory bodies for particular decisions, according to public opinion studies summarized previously, a central decisionmaker in the United States would be well advised to select college graduates, Jews, Afro-Americans, and suburbanites as well as those whose personality structure disposes them toward cautious, flexible, uncynical, and optimistic appraisals, and who are neither ethnocentric nor authoritarian. But for a decisionmaker to deal with such a crew of thoughtful individuals in the first place, he must be able to tolerate considerable ambiguity. Once an agent starts to consider a decision, we would prefer the content of information on critical issues during information-processing to be cognitively multifaceted, though neither too complex nor too overloading in volume. Accordingly, some filtering of information inputs is necessary; stereotypic decoding is to be avoided and accurate summaries prepared. What will ensure that an agent receives proper inputs? Persons engaged in filtering should be checked for personality characteristics and social background, too. Filterers should forward projections of long-term implications of various options and draw up alternative contingency plans for discussion. But a key to rational decisionmaking is the target of a decision. If a target or an agent are dissimilar in culture, there is little hope to bridge such dissimilarity that often has developed over decades to a point of no return. It would be useful to have a specialist in a decisionmaking body reveal the thinking process of a target so that high-fidelity communication can break through dissimilarities. Moreover, if a target encodes its messages in a hostile tone it is imperative for a response to be moderate so that an upward spiral in emotional preoccupations will not become self-feeding. A detente may be brought about by stressing that an agent is not considering moves that will increase its power or present unwanted actions to a target. Controlling frustration is essential in order to work toward an adjustive outcome when high-priority values are in jeopardy.

The contemporary crisis in authority in the United States has arisen out of an inability to bridge gaps in cultural perspective. Repression by the police and violence in the streets bear witness to the failure to apply principles of decisionmaking that would resolve conflicts. Part of the difficulty is that political elites are often content to handle each crisis in a pragmatic manner, rather than generalize from such situations to develop more appropriate strategies and procedures. The freedom of decisionmaking elites to select advice that may be faulty, however, is being challenged by groups that demand an institutionalized role for minority sentiments in decisionmaking. The success of our Cultural Exchange Model of decisionmaking in tracing causal linkages with violent decisions speaks directly to the issue: for the only way to ensure that a decisionmaking body will function in a fiduciary capacity with all possible groups is to insist upon cultural diversity among the decisionmakers. Once a group tolerates internal diversity and has broadly based participation of representatives from many groups, it will be far better equipped to cope adjustively with other groups on the latters' own terms. A mere plea that elites should respect the integrity of differing value systems is insufficient in American politics today, for the backlog of decisions where the interests of blacks, chicanos, and students were not considered fairly is interpreted as evidence of a tyrannical rule by minority groups. The principle of minority participation in decisionmaking, in short, is brushed aside by current administrators precisely because it argues for an entirely new form of decisionmaking in contrast to the conventional wisdom of the past. To demonstrate the nature of the difference between current practice and the findings of this volume on decisionmaking, it is necessary to reflect on the writings of Max Weber, whose administrative theories have been so influential that political decisionmakers find it more comfortable to think of themselves as administrators than as political leaders faced with the responsibility of moral choice. Political elites today often try to avoid politics and seek refuge in a badly understood conception of Weber's administrative theory.[5] According to Weber, a highly rational administrative system is organized into subdivisions, each of which performs a set of related tasks uniquely; there is little duplication of effort. Compartmentalization for the sake of efficiency is viewed as a major characteristic of legal-rational administrative organs. Contemporary theories about how to implement deci-

[5] Max Weber, *The Theory of Social and Economic Organization*, trans. Arthur M. Henderson and Talcott Parsons (New York: The Free Press, 1947); Weber, *From Max Weber*, trans. H. H. Gerth and C. Wright Mills (New York: Oxford University Press, 1958).

sions by means of a bureaucracy depart very little from Weber in normative matters.

Weber argued for much collegial freedom of choice on the part of a decisionmaker up to the point of a decision, but afterwards he viewed hierarchy as a necessary means for ensuring that a decision will be carried out in practice. Weber's theory becomes perverted in the attempt by some theorists to generalize his depoliticized model of bureaucracy to a blueprint for overall societal organization. In particular, structural-functionalists argue that for each function there should be one and only one structure within a system. A primitive system, according to Gabriel Almond, has one omni-functional structure. Meanwhile, in a modern policy most of the articulation is performed by interest groups, aggregation by political parties, lawmaking by legislatures, and so forth.[6] Structural-functionalists, in other words, advance a *doctrine of functional specificity,* which means that decisionmaking bodies should be staffed by specialists in decisionmaking; budding architects should take courses only in architecture; and the world should be divided neatly into watertight compartments of maximum consensus on goals and means. A consequence of this position is that a university's board of regents is a braintrust reserved only for members of the local governmental and business community, without adequate administrative, faculty, and student representation. The result is clear. We end up with decisionmaking bodies that are so homogeneous that they too quickly come to a decision that is incapable of being sold to those whom the decision will most directly affect. When Weber's principles of administrative rationality become a model for the staffing of a political decisionmaking body, as Lenin insisted, it is no wonder that decisions are made for violence and repression. When decision-making bodies contain some diversity in cultural perspectives, according to the results presented above, there is more chance that decisionmakers will be attuned to perspectives of those whom a decision will affect. An explosive outcome can thereby be avoided. Perhaps the classic example in modern times where a decisionmaker tolerated and encouraged disparate points of view during decisionmaking was President Kennedy's handling of the Cuban missiles crisis in 1962.

A view contrary to the doctrine of Functional Specificity may be called the *doctrine of pluralistic confrontation.* According to this theory, which is far less radical than the Leninist version of Weberian thought, it is essential to expose decisionmakers at all times to a wide range of alternatives.[7] Where

---

[6] See Gabriel A. Almond and James S. Coleman, eds., *The Politics of the Developing Areas* (Princeton: Princeton University Press, 1960), esp. the Introduction.

[7] See Abbie Hoffman, *Revolution for the Hell of It* (New York: Dial, 1968); Henry S. Kariel, *Open Systems* (Itasca, Ill.: Peacock, 1969).

necessary, Pluralistic Confrontation implies that a decisionmaking body should contain reserved seats for a minority. In Mexico the ruling party is so embarrassed by its overwhelming majority that 10 percent of the seats in its national legislature are set aside for opposition party spokesmen. India has reserved seats for linguistic minorities, and many countries have proportional representation in parliament. In France, however, minority representation encourages immobilist, do-nothing systems: too much heterogeneity within a decisionmaking body may render it incapable of making any decisions at all. The doctrine of Pluralistic Confrontation can be carried to an extreme, but in practice this need not be so.

To what can we attribute the current crisis in authority? Surely it is the nonsensical rejection of the tenets of participatory and consultative democracy, rather than the protests against usurpers of power who cling to an anachronistic doctrine of Functional Specificity. The use of force, even by those quelling dissent, indexes a lack of coherent political dialogue between groups interested in the outcomes of decisions. Similarly, decisions to go to war constitute declarations that one state refuses to treat differences in political opinion as matters for diplomacy, discussion, bargaining, and compromise.

The doctrine of Pluralistic Confrontation is new. Even Marx, who emphasized the dialectical process in history, saw progress as the triumph of one group over another. His position was a *doctrine of survival of the fittest,* and in the form of Social Darwinism his doctrine could be used by smug capitalist and Communist ruling elites to justify their own control over the centers of power. Thus, the doctrine of Pluralistic Confrontation assumes that participants will conduct political discussion intelligently, and it sees rationality as a consequence of ongoing debates between persons who are not originally or even ultimately of like minds; it sees virtue in nonconformity so long as conformists and nonconformists alike are in discussion with one another. Pluralistic confrontation exists when those "doing their thing" are in communication with one another, but it ceases to be present when "doing one's thing" means to escape into havens of homogeneity from the options present in an open society. Acts of desperation, such as bombings or teargassing, are futile one-way efforts to communicate.

What positive suggestions follow from this discussion? Certainly we can agree that decisionmaking bodies need to be restaffed fundamentally throughout all of human civilization so that diversity of interests and perceptions will build mechanisms for properly decoding communications in crisis as well as noncrisis situations. Police officers should ride with critics of police brutality on patrols.[8] The adversary system of Anglo–American trial courts

---

[8] Cf. Bryce Nelson, "Kansas: Police–Student Violence Imperils University," *Science,* CLXIX (August 7, 1970), 567–69.

certainly does not need to be scrapped, but more care should be taken to insist upon diversity among members of the jury. A fresh look at academic decisionmaking bodies is in order. Faculty and students should have representation in a university's board of regents or trustees; department meetings should encourage student participation; and faculty should be represented in student council proceedings. There should be no separation of researchers from teachers either, since a curriculum as well as a community of scholars requires everpresent alternatives if it is to encourage excellence. Professional societies and interest groups should make extra efforts to reserve seats for minorities on decisionmaking bodies. And these efforts should be realistically aimed at picking those who represent different generations, races, and sexes; mere tokenism is a corruption of the doctrine of Pluralistic Confrontation.[9]

Violence breeds violence. In order to break into this vicious circle without revolutionary outburst, decisionmaking bodies, rather than protestors, must ultimately take the initiative to implement the doctrine of Pluralistic Confrontation. Police who themselves practice the doctrine of Functional Specificity are hardly in a position to urge a stance that negates the basis for their own formation, so more intelligent protest may be needed in the future in order that dissent may be expressed and controlled by diverse and heterogeneous groups.[10] The more we see of those who dress, think, and act

[9] The reader may well consider whether a group like Afro–Americans will demand more than their fair share in demanding equal representation after being granted token representation. What if Italian–Americans, Flemish-Americans, Filipino–Americans, and American gypsies demanded as much representation as blacks? If the Scylla is tokenism, the Charybdis is corporate representation of every interest on an equal basis. Rather than specifying a magic ideological formula, the doctrine of Pluralistic Confrontation is consistent with open negotiations among groups who seek redress of grievances because their perspectives are understood poorly within decisionmaking circles. The formula appropriate for representation in a particular time and place will depend upon which groups are convinced that they are not being heard adequately, and it will be balanced by an anticipatory sense of legitimate grievances that have not yet achieved a coherent form of expression within the political arena. This dilemma provides all the more reason to stress political, rather than administrative, skills among members of existing decisionmaking bodies.

[10] For evidence that peace demonstrations are, in fact, the few incidents in which diverse elements of the peace movement come together, see Donald F. Keys, "The American Peace Movement," *The Nature of Human Conflict*, ed. Elton B. McNeil (Englewood Cliffs, N. J.: Prentice-Hall, 1965), pp. 295–306; Robin Jenkins, "Who Are These Marchers?" *Journal of Peace Research*, IV, No. 1 (1967), 46–60. Bloodshed in demonstrations, like the one at Kent State University, has occurred when communications between factions within the demonstrators were broken and police were left without adequate communication with public officials when they attempted to handle the situation as instructed, even though the situation changed and instructions were no longer relevant.

unlike ourselves, the more comfortable we will be in the company of those who differ from ourselves.[11] Whether our values become more syncretic or more permissive, we will be less prone to use violence. The survival of the human race depends on the development of decisionmaking processes that allow more participation by diverse groups at the highest levels of political and social institutions.

Nevertheless, one madman acting as a decisionmaker may upset the best laid plans of social scientists to control war. Kaiser Wilhelm doubtless would regard the recommendations given so far as mere poppycock, preferring justice and honor to reason.[12] A "better dead than Red" mentality belittles a need to mitigate processes leading to unnecessary and disastrous wars. Because so much depends upon whims of central decisionmakers, many scholars prefer to modify societies so that a population will refuse to go to battle at the behest of an intemperate leader who demands war. It may also be pointed out that the central decisionmakers in Japan during 1931 did not agree to the Manchurian invasion at all: the operation was carried out by military leaders in order to embarrass civilian leaders in a country where democracy was under attack.[13] We therefore must make recommendations to enlightened leaders who are interested in long-range societal planning so that their successors in office will encounter a public that is more likely to be satisfied with peace than with war.

Rousseau's vision of the pacific nature of small, homogeneous states concurs with findings presented in Part III of this book. But since Germany, Italy, China, and the United States have been unified out of previously autonomous realms, one cannot expect a return to oak-tree polities.

The results of our analysis of societal factors point toward military spending as the most crucial factor accounting for foreign violence. But many countries cannot easily alter their military postures so long as their international rivals are also prepared for the possibility of an eventual war. What is modifiable at the societal level is the nature of developmental processes. Each of the six basic societal attributes suggests alternative strategies and ideologies of development, some of which may render a country more or less likely to become involved in warfare. Resources are stressed by those who espouse a doctrine of modernization; demotypes, by the doctrine

[11] William J. McGuire, "A Vaccine for Brainwash," *Psychology Today,* III (February 1970), 36 ff.

[12] See Ole R. Holsti and Robert C. North, "The History of Human Conflict," *The Nature of Human Conflict,* ed. Elton B. McNeil (Englewood Cliffs, N. J.: Prentice-Hall, 1965), pp. 155–71.

[13] Lewis Hasluck, *Foreign Affairs, 1919–1937* (New York: Macmillan, 1938), pp. 247–56.

of human development; attitudes, by advocates of populist doctrine; mass behavior, by elitists; functions, by functionalists; and structures, by structuralists.

The *doctrine of functionalism* provides the clearest remedy for developmental processes that lead toward warfare. A Functionalist, such as Gabriel Almond, counsels governments to expand the number of governmental functions without overcommitting itself to the performance of any one function. The Developmental causal model that fits best with societal data has high military expenditures as a prerequisite for high frequency of participation in war. The concept of a military-industrial complex, with all parts of the political and social systems subordinated to military objectives, is not only evidence of a propensity to engage in foreign conflict but also is contrary to predilections of functionalists. For underdeveloped states where there is no industrial sector, the military state is often a result of having recently won a war of independence or a coup in which military figures are heroes throughout the political system. The most developed states are tempted to play the role of bloc leader, one of whose functions is that of international policeman, thereby increasing the chances for a military-industrial stranglehold on governmental operations by only one sector of a society. Depending upon the level of development attained by a country, there is a need to implement not only Functionalist doctrine but other doctrines as well, as we will see in the following paragraphs.

According to the *structuralist doctrine* advocated by Fred Riggs, governments can cope with increased demands during eras of developmental change only if greater numbers of political structures are established to handle new and specialized tasks.[14] In our most successful causal model we observe that countries which fail to engage in structural innovation are far more liable to engage in military operations unless military spending is already at a low level in the society. Since the least developed countries are unlikely to have a differentiated administrative system, the doctrine of Structuralism needs to be sown especially in the lands where the military is the only developing sector. Military influence on national policy will be less than its share of the total gross national product if there is a strict civilian control on the military. An increase in bureaucratic capabilities can provide an effective check on a tendency for military rule to emerge.

The *doctrine of modernization* encourages states to increase their total resources as rapidly as possible. As the case for modernization is presented

[14] Fred W. Riggs, *Administration in Developing Countries* (Boston: Houghton Mifflin, 1964); cf. Joseph La Palombara, ed., *Bureaucracy and Political Development* (Princeton: Princeton University Press, 1963).

by David Apter and others,[15] there is a bias against traditional values and institutions that are likely to oppose rapid change. Modernization is a doctrine that is especially appropriate for states at intermediate levels of development, for the power of traditional elites will have already declined, and the state will not be so powerful that it will attempt to use its weight in international relations. Nevertheless, a rapid increase in governmental expenditures will lead toward war if most of the expenditures are military, as we have found in testing our Developmental model. The application of the Modernization doctrine, in short, must be tempered by a simultaneous observance of the doctrine of Structuralism, or else modernization will result in garrison states and military rule in order to accelerate the growth in material resources. One aspect of the Modernization doctrine is especially appropriate for countries at advanced levels of development, however. Bloc leaders that have economic downswings or administrative inefficiencies, typified by a deviation of electricity consumption figures from production levels, are vulnerable to using warfare as a way out of such situations. Perfecting modernization processes would obviate the need to invoke foreign conflict situations as a means for overcoming temporary difficulties.

The *doctrine of nation-building* regards higher attainments in levels of education and other phenotypic characteristics as essential in preparing a population to play an optimal role in developing societies.[16] Human development is required if a country is to overcome its genotypic handicaps and pull its population together for the pursuit of peaceful and developmental goals. Unfortunately for proponents of this doctrine, there is no direct connection between phenotypic attributes and levels of foreign conflict. Instead, we find that the number of nationality groups can present a problem, for there is a tendency among countries that are mono-ethnic to stay out of war. Polyethnicity represents a condition in which the political system must cope with differing cultural perspectives. The doctrine of Pluralistic Confrontation is not accepted in today's world as a guide to decisionmaking, so it is no surprise that in states where its application is most necessary one encounters the most susceptibility to foreign violence. The linkage between rapid expansion in governmental resources and foreign conflict may be mitigated in a mono-ethnic society, but the need to ensure that every cultural

---

[15] David E. Apter, *The Politics of Modernization* (Chicago: University of Chicago Press, 1965); C. E. Black, *The Dynamics of Modernization* (New York: Harper, Row, 1966); W. W. Rostow, *The Stages of Economic Growth* (Cambridge, England: Cambridge University Press, 1960).

[16] Karl W. Deutsch and William J. Foltz, eds., *Nation–Building* (New York: Atherton, 1963); Reinhard Bendix, *Nation–Building and Citizenship* (New York: Wiley, 1964).

group derives the benefits of development is more acutely faced in poly-ethnic societies. Where there are disparities in human development, in other words, we might expect domestic unrest and foreign conflict.

Our scenario of the ideal peaceful state encourages bureaucratic de-velopment, in accordance with the doctrine of Structuralism and as a counterweight to the rise of a military sector in society. It is possible to propose bureaucratic innovations, but it may be difficult for a student of international conflict to persuade government leaders to reduce the level of investment in military activities when national defense is involved. Govern-ments that accept the challenges of Structuralism and Functionalism in order to lessen the importance of the military profession will be attracted to the doctrine of Modernization as well. Too rapid a growth in governmental budgets, moreover, will cause political elites to use their new resources for military purposes, while too little concern for modernization may result in the weakening of major powers who will thereby find war an escape from a crisis situation. There needs to be an optimum pursuit of modernization, rather than a maximization that has little appreciation for problems in human development. The peaceful state has few ethnic groups and thus ad-heres to Mazzini's principle of "one nation, one country."

Modernization theories are usually thought to be more relevant to underdeveloped countries, but the finding that a lag in technological growth can trigger highly industrialized countries to go to war suggests that resource development will never reach a stage of self-sustained growth, as W. W. Rostow has claimed.[17] The complex, technological sophistication of modern times has been described as the result of so many decisions that ours is an "accidental century" of "unprepared societies."[18] Business firms require ad-vance planning in order to survive in the contemporary private or state capitalist world. The same need for anticipation of the future applies to government if political leaders are ever to keep abreast of future trends. The new science of futuristics, hence, is an integral part of research on conflict and peace.[19] Without knowledge about the present and planning for the future, industrial states are destined to engage in war when technological growth lags. Business has much to fear from the rising power of military-industrial complexes in which contracts for the manufacture of nonproduc-tive weapons subsidize firms that cooperate with the military, with war as the

[17] Rostow, *The Stages of Economic Growth.*

[18] Michael Harrington, *The Accidental Century* (New York: Macmillan, 1965); Donald N. Michael, *The Unprepared Society* (New York: Basic Books, 1968).

[19] John McHale, *The Future of the Future* (New York: Braziller, 1969). For the link with peace research, Robert Jungk's "Mankind 2000" project is the most notable. Jungk and a collaborator, Hans Josef Mundt, are editing a 15-volume series, *Designs for a New World,* of which the first three volumes have appeared thus far in German.

by-product; funds for productive investment and intensive futuristic analysis are decreasingly available.[20] Military control of the civilian sector is a central feature of the garrison state. The military is able to justify its role in advanced industrial states so long as it deters war from potential aggressors, while government defense contracts provide payoffs for industrialists. A political system unable to stop the development of a military-industrial complex to a garrison state will be headed for a series of wars of doubtful justification. Standards of efficiency should be invoked in highly developed societies so that they may avoid the temptation to remain content with subsidies disguised as safely earned profits, and attack the cancerous control of defense industries in the economy. The advice is based on our understanding of processes that are likely to account for the causal model which fits best with the data in Chapter 8.[21]

At the systemic level of analysis our advice is less extensive in view of the ambiguity of findings and the difficulty of making any impact either upon long-term historical processes or upon policymakers in several countries at once. For example, an implication of findings on the societal level is that subsystems with either entirely undeveloped or exclusively advanced economic systems are preferable to subsystems in which states are differentially going through a process of development.[22] Having made this observation, there is nothing that can be done to bring about either state of affairs. Similarly, although we may prefer bipolar and unipolar to tripolar and multipolar systems of power stratification, China and Europe today are potential superpowers which might increase the total number of poles within existing Asian and North Atlantic subsystems; it would hardly be a workable suggestion to urge that China and Europe disarm in order to arrest this potential situation.

Feasible proposals can center on alliance policies, which are more subject to change within world politics. Accordingly, alliances should be viewed as devices for building international communities of like-minded, mutually responsive states. This is precisely the strategy that was followed in transforming NATO from an ostensively military alliance into one with primarily political purposes.[23] In constructing communities of this sort, statesmen should avoid exclusivistic membership criteria and have interests broader than a mere anti-ideology; and leaders of community-building efforts should be prepared to sacrifice economic self-interest in order to continue

---

[20] Bruce M. Russett, "Who Pays for Defense?" *American Political Science Review*, LXIII (June 1969), 412–26.

[21] We have no precise measure of the strength of a military-industrial complex but instead several indirect indicators.

[22] This accords with the theory expounded in A. F. K. Organski, *World Politics*, 2d ed. (New York: Knopf, 1968).

[23] Harlan Cleveland, *NATO* (New York: Harper, 1970).

as political mobilizers and mediators. Alignments alone do not guarantee peace, however. There must be a strong regulator institution alongside cohesive yet incorporative alliance frameworks. Nations thus organized should strengthen the United Nations and regional international organizations so that they will enjoy a wider legitimacy. In addition, an international organization with the major powers alone as members might provide the advantages of concert-type stability. Japanese leaders' current plans for an organization composed of the People's Republic of China, Europe, Japan, the Soviet Union, and the United States, therefore, are deserving of support in the interest of peace.

No one decision can work a miracle for alliances to become transformed into communities and international organizations to gain more power. Consultations between allies before, during, and after incremental agreements are necessary. A new breed of decisionmakers may be needed to conduct such negotiations, particularly as discussions widen and more and more states enter into peaceful communities. We have already specified some characteristics which are likely to be found among a corps of statesmen who would be suited for the task. Inasmuch as leaders of states often are more peaceable than ethnocentric members of the public at large,[24] societal problems and systemic factors need attention simultaneously. Policymakers live amid three distinct and separate realms of problems— interpersonal, societal, and systemic. Peace is achieved when efforts proceed along three parallel tracks; one cannot sacrifice one strategy for another without risking an eventual breakdown in the pursuit of peace. The path may seem long and the journey may prove tiring, but unless concerted steps are taken in the immediate future a bomb may explode and an Armageddon will have arrived through thermonuclear holocaust.

As H. G. Wells would no doubt encourage us, now is the time to dream of a future state of affairs in which international conflict will be resolved short of violent self-destruction. Nevertheless, much dreaming involves pure phantasy. The aim of this volume is to permit our dreams to have some substance and thereby to open our imagination to more rigorous, more abundant, and ever more fruitful explorations on the nature of man, states, and international systems. In evolutionary perspective, war is learned behavior which can be unlearned by a species with a will to achieve a brighter tomorrow.

[24] See findings presented in Chapter 3, especially the study by Jerome Laulicht, "An Analysis of Canadian Foreign Policy Attitudes," *Peace Research Society, Papers,* III (1965), 121–36.

Appendices

Appendices

appendix A
Definitions of Concepts

DEFINITIONS OF CONCEPTS

Note: At the end of some definitions there is a code referring to the section of the volume where the term is found (DM = decisionmaking; SO = societal; SY = systemic). If there is no code, then the word is found in general use across all levels.

abstract game. An experimental game lacking a concrete setting in the real world (DM).

acceleration. Speed of growth in scope and level of function performance by a system (SY).

action path. Actions taken toward objectives (DM).

activity. Overt behavior; anything requiring expenditure of energy.

actor. An entity that interacts with other entities in a system (SY).

adaptation. A class of activities through which a system adjusts to changes in its internal and external environment so that it can continue to function as a system (SY).

adequacy. A condition in which there is no discrepancy between aspiration and achievement levels; the supply of resources meets the demand for them (SO: entropic resource symmetry).

administrative stagnation. A condition in which the number of government ministries fails to increase or decrease (SO).

affective. A style of performing a function in which activities are viewed as ends in themselves and emotions and psychic tensions are involved.

agent. A body including advisers and decisionmakers that is responsible for making a decision (DM).

487

agglutination. Collection of resources into particular domains, such that some areas have more, some less of the resources (SO: spatial resource asymmetry).

aggregate statistic. A number corresponding to the total measure for an entity on a quantitative scale.

aggregation. Combining interests of separate actors, such that general policy alternatives are demanded of elites (SY).

alienation. A condition in which an individual or social class is estranged from its surroundings (SO: kinetic attitudinal asymmetry).

allocational. Distributions of values among strata of a population (SO).

allocational asymmetry. The extent to which attributes are unequally distributed to strata within a system (SO).

amalgamated integration. Merger of two or more previously independent states (SY).

anarchy. A condition in which parts of a system are uncoordinated politically and infrequently in contact with each other (SY).

antecedents. Independent variables.

approach. A way of looking at a multifaceted subject, using a distinctive analogy.

articulation. Demands by a single actor upon elites in a political system in order to bring about incremental changes (SY).

asymmetrical. A way of relating parts in a system such that the converse of their relationship is logically impossible.

attention focus. The object toward which thought or behavior is directed; the most vivid component of a complex experience, which may include · persons or norms.

attentive public. Those who follow events taking place within a political unit by paying attention to news disseminated by media of communication (DM).

attitudes. General, verbalizable statements and intellectual positions that guide an individual in making congruent responses to similar stimulus situations; an enduring, learned predisposition to behave in a consistent way toward a given class of objects (DM).

attribute. A basic characteristic or property of a system, common to all actors and units within systems.

Augustinian analysis. The view that human behavior is dominated by emotions, with human reason unable to overcome passions (DM).

avulsive decisionmaker. A decisionmaker who undertakes rationalistic comprehensive shifts in the direction of policy (DM).

balanced. Resources input to a system equal resources output by the system (SO: transactional resource symmetry).

balance of power. A condition in which two or more power blocs have sufficient resources to prevent any of the other blocs from assuming hegemony (SY).

behavior. Meaningful physical action on the part of a living organism—or a noticeable lack thereof; behavior is not observed directly but is abstracted from a sequence of observed movements in an organism (actions only become meaningful to the observer when we recognize that they correspond to an analytically established category or form of behavior).

bidirectional. A condition in which a system is the target of behavior as often as it is the initiator (SO: transactional behavioral symmetry).

binomial expansion. The algebraic approximation of the normal frequency curve.

bipolarity. A condition in which there are two power blocs within an international conflict subsystem (SY).

bivariate analysis. Determining relationships between pairs of variables.

bottlenecked. Blockage of activity of one structure by another (SO: kinetic structural asymmetry).

bourgeois capitalist model. The Marxist-Leninist theory that war results from capitalism via insufficient attention to the needs of workers, on the one hand, and desperate efforts to retain topdog status, on the other hand (SO).

broad-gauge theory. Sometimes called metatheory, consists of three elements—a paradigmatic frame of reference, a systematic body of knowledge, and a metaconceptual classificatory scheme.

Carroll's oblimin. A form of oblique rotation (when gamma = .5, the rotation is biquartimin; if gamma = 1.0, the solution is quartimin) used in factor analysis.

case analysis. Focus on details of a single subject to achieve an in-depth understanding of internal dynamics and tendencies.

causal analysis. A technique by means of which we postulate a system of interrelationships and ascertain whether relevant multiple and partial correlations between variables in fact fit the model.

central decisionmaker. The leader of an agent (DM).

centralized. Performance of functions only within a single geographic sector of a system (SO: spatial functional asymmetry).

choice. Selection of one out of several possible actions (DM).

clarificatory labelling. To start with a set of conventional terms that refer, albeit fuzzily, to certain kinds of concepts and then to sharpen definitions by referring them to conceptual common denominators.

cleavage. Disagreement on common norms and attitudes on the part of sizable strata within the population of a system (SO: allocational attitudinal asymmetry).

cluster. A homogeneous set of empirical entities or characteristics.

cluster analysis. A procedure for grouping a body of data into similar and dissimilar empirical groupings.

coalition. A group of countries fighting on the same side in wartime (SY).

coercive factors. Capabilities of governments to use military force (SY).

cognitive. Aspects of decisionmaking involving awareness of facts and intellectual tasks equipping an individual to appraise reality on its own terms (DM).

cognitive rationalism. A theory that assumes that decisions are made on the basis of cognitive information concerning how a decisionmaker can maximize his attainment of desired values.

cohesiveness. Well-coordinated behavior; forces attracting members to a group; ability of parts of a group to stick together (SO: kinetic behavioral symmetry).

collective security model. A conception of the avoidance of violence in international subsystems through a multilateral establishment of institutional channels for controlling outbreaks of war (SY).

combat. Conflict involving physically destructive activity.

commitment. Degree of affective attachment to a system (SY).

common variance. The total amount of variance accounted for in a factor analysis; sum of eigenvalues for all factors extracted, divided by the number of variables.

communality. The proportion of variance in a variable accounted for by all factors in a factor analysis.

communication factors. Variables denoting the extent of international flow of symbols, goods, and persons (SY).

communication theory. A theory that regards flows of goods, persons, and messages between individuals, groups, and states as predictors to future behavior patterns and attitudes.

community. A set of persons who share common values and identify their fate and purpose with the destiny of the system to which they belong (SY).

community approach. An examination of the extent to which units of international systems engage in harmonized goal-seeking and establish permanent structures for interaction between states (SY).

comparability. Criterion for assessing whether a measure has a similar functional meaning from case to case.

comparative analysis. An examination of several cases systematically along a specific number of characteristics or dimensions.

comparative decisionmaking case analysis. Analysis of attributes of two or more decisionmaking case studies (DM).

complex (n). A system whose entities are loosely related to each other (SY).

comprehensive. Wide-ranging in scope (SY).

concentrated. A condition in which governmental structures are located in a small geographic area within a larger system (SO: spatial structural asymmetry).

concept. A category used to characterize a phenomenon generically.

conceptual dualism. The chasm between conceptual frameworks and empirical structures built from analyses of data selected to represent the concepts; a dualist does not try to bridge the chasm, taking its existence for granted.

conceptual framework. A classificatory scheme; a set of mutually exclusive, exhaustive categories for subsuming concepts.

conceptual idealism. A view that concepts are more real than data extracted to measure these concepts.

conceptual monism. A view that either the empirical structure of data or a priori category schemes are basic, the other illusory.

conflict. Norm-oriented activity by one entity that seeks attainment of a goal at the expense of another entity; a behavioral opposition between forces (SO: entropic behavioral asymmetry).

conformity. Presence of identical behavior patterns within all strata of the population of a system; a motivated tendency to behave consistently with established normative patterns (SO: allocational behavior symmetry).

congruity. A condition when attitudes within a system toward other systems are also held within other systems in relation to the system (SO: transactional attitudinal symmetry).

consensus. Agreement on common norms and attitudes within the population of a system (SO: allocational attitudinal symmetry).

consequences. Dependent variables.

consonant. The extent to which attitudinal configurations are internally consistent and tend to absorb or incorporate each other, thereby synthesizing contrary views (SO: entropic attitudinal symmetry).

constancy. No change in the quantity of a resource over time (SO: temporal resource symmetry).

contending. The extent to which different value systems and ideologies are inconsistent (SO: entropic attitudinal asymmetry).

content analysis. A procedure in which titles, words, and themes are counted as indicators of such notions as cognitive foci of attention, perceptual images, and psychological moods.

contention. Verbal disagreement; asymmetry in the value constellations of two entities (SO: temporal functional symmetry).

continuity. A condition in which function performance occurs at a regular rate, even if to a minimal extent (SO: temporal functional symmetry).

continuum. A conceptual dimension, such that there are always two possible values for a variable (from low to high).

contract orientation. Performance of a function by one actor toward another in accordance with the terms of a mutually agreed upon set of principles (SY).

conventionalist labelling. A view that vocabulary in the social sciences must always be communicable to the intelligent layman.

cooperation. A situation in which the behavioral vectors of groups point in the same direction (SO: entropic behavioral symmetry).

coordination. A class of activities through which parts of a system are related to each other and thereby work together (SY).

core member. A member of a subsystem that possesses more claim to being a member on the basis of its pattern of interaction; a member of a subsystem at the hub of its communications (SY).

correlation. A numerical measure of association; a representation of the direction and strength in an interrelationship between at least two variables.

cosmopolitanizing. A condition in which the demotypic composition of a population becomes less inbred over time (SO: temporal demotypic asymmetry).

crisis model. A conception of violent decisions as the outcome of situations where there are elements of surprise, time pressure, and cruciality (DM).

cross-sectional analysis. Examination and comparison of several entities at one point in time.

cultural exchange model. A conception of violent decisions as the outcome of insufficient knowledge and interaction between parties to a dispute (DM).

curtaining. Demotypes entering a system equal those leaving a system (SO: transactional demotypic symmetry).

data. Factual information used as a basis for constructing indices.

decentralized. Constituent units within a system have autonomous powers of function performance (SO: spatial functional symmetry).

decision. A formal selection of one out of several possible policies with an intent to execute it (DM).

decisionmaker. An individual who is in a position to commit the resources of an entity of which he is a leader (DM).

decisionmaking body. A central decisionmaker plus advisers who take an active role in deliberating alternatives (DM).

decisionmaking cycle. A sequence of actions starting with a background condition, triggered by a stimulus, involving deliberations and information-processing, terminated by a decision, and followed by feedback of the outcome of a decision (DM).

decisionmaking phase. A stage in coming to a decision (e.g., prestimulus, stimulus, information processing, outcome) (DM).

decisionmaking theory. Human behavior is assumed to be the outcome of decisions in which the relevant concepts are spheres of competence, communication and information, and motivation.

decision node. A point at which alternative action paths become evident to a decisionmaker (DM).

decisiveness. Effectiveness with which goals are accomplished (SY).

deconcentrated. A condition in which governmental structures are located in several geographic locations besides the center (SO: spatial structural symmetry).

defensive pact. An alliance whose terms state conditions under which the signatories will go to war (SY).

definition. A set of verbal symbols that denote a phenomenon by stating the general category of which an entity or characteristic is a subtype and the criteria by which one phenomenon is distinguished from all other subtypes.

definition of the situation. The way in which a decisionmaking situation is characterized, e.g., structural, cognitive, affective, evaluative aspects (DM).

democracy. A political system in which officeholders are selected on the basis of a plurality or majority vote and, thus, in which the voters are sovereign (SO).

demotypes. A general category, of which genotypes and phenotypes are subtypes, referring respectively to constitutional features of human beings that either originate through heredity or are acquired within a lifetime of an individual.

dependent variable. A condition resulting from previous or concomitant conditions.

desegregation. A condition in which demotypes live amidst one another in the same proportions in each geographic area (SO: spatial demotypic symmetry).

deterrence ideology. A view that conflict is best managed by causing an adversary to fear the consequences of his possible violent moves.

developmental labelling. Incremental addition of new words to an existing vocabulary.

developmental model. A theory that factors precipitating war differ, depending upon the level of a country's economic and political development (SO).

deviance. Presence of different patterns of behavior among various strata of the population of a system; a motivated tendency to behave in contravention of established normative patterns; assaultive, escapist, or self-destructive acts (SO: allocational behavioral asymmetry).

differentiated. Presence of many structures, each performing specialized and relatively nonoverlapping functions (SO: allocational functional asymmetry).

diffraction. A condition in which each structure performs exactly one function in a system (SO: entropic functional asymmetry).

diffuse. A condition in which a structure performs several functions, or a function is performed by several structures (SY).

dimension. A conceptual rendering of an independent source of variation in a set of entities or variables; a conceptual locus for an attribute.

dimensional analysis. Delineation of basic empirical sources of variation in phenomena.

diplomatic conflict. The use of formal methods by means of which states traditionally dramatize differences of opinion nonviolently, such as lodging protests, declaring diplomatic officials to be personae non grata, and withdrawing of ambassadors or officials of lower rank.

direction. Detailed guidance by elites of the conduct of non-elites in a system (SY).

discontinuity. A condition in which functions cease to be performed on schedule (SO: temporal functional asymmetry).

discriminatory. A condition in which functions are performed in a manner different for one stratum than another (SO: allocational functional asymmetry).

disparity. A condition in which strata within a system contain an unequal amount of resources (SO: allocational resource asymmetry).

distribution crisis. A situation in which there are many demands to extend the resources of government to different segments of a society (SO).

diversity. Presence of several demotypic groups in a system (SO: entropic demotypic asymmetry).

domain. The motive for study, main variables, or level of analysis employed in a study.

dove. A person who is reluctant to use force in resolving disputes (DM).

dualism, conceptual. See "conceptual dualism."

dualistic (interpersonal) theory. The view that human behavior is determined partly by cognition, partly by emotion (DM).

dynamic. Condition of a system in which outputs functionally correspond with inputs (SO: kinetic functional symmetry).

eclectic model. A theory that similar factors operate to dispose countries at various levels of political and economic development to enter war (SO).

eigenvalue. The amount of variance extracted by one factor in a factor analysis.

electricity inefficiency. A condition in which electricity consumption is far less than total electric production (SO).

elite decisionmaking approach. The study of processes in the decisionmaking of elites that lead to peaceful or warlike outcomes (DM).

empirical approach. The use of data to specify the nature of a situation.

empirical generalization. The result of a test of a hypothesis, namely, a statement of a relationship between measures of two variables.

empirical taxonomy. The structure of data, as decomposed into empirically generated categories.

endogenous. A condition in which decisionmakers perform a function inside the geographic core of a system (SY).

enforcement. Exercise of coercion or violence to quell insubordinate behavior (SY).

entente. An alliance in which heads of state make an agreement between themselves (SY).

entertainment approach. An approach to a subject that seeks to divert or to shock an audience by representation in a stylized manner.

entropic asymmetry. Contradiction between organizational properties in a system, lowering system efficiency (SO).

entropy. The extent of disorganization or randomness within a system; departure from an organized, efficient arrangement of parts within a system (SO).

equalitarian. A condition in which resources in each geographic region are equal (SO: spatial resource symmetry).

equalitarian integration. Structural interconnection between systems in which no one system dominates others (SY).

equality. A condition in which strata within a system contain a similar amount of resources (SO: allocational resource symmetry).

equilibrium theory. A theory in which systemic balance is viewed as a function of systemic attributes.

evaluative. Aspects of decisionmaking involving volition and the establishment of priorities (DM).

evenness. The extent to which all units of a system share in the benefits accruing to the system (SY).

event. A part of reality that changes over space and time; a discrete behavioral form that must be inferred and coded from verbal statements or observed activities.

exogenous. A condition in which decisionmakers perform a function outside the geographic core of a system (SY).

external validity. A condition in which a variable is empirically related to the variable one seeks to express in terms of measurements.

factor. An independent source of variation within a group of variables.

factor analysis. A mathematical procedure for obtaining the smallest set of independent sources of variation in a body of data.

factor loading. A coefficient that represents the weight of a variable on a factor.

factor matrix. The matrix of factor loadings.

factor score. An index of a case weighted for a factor composed of variables (or of a variable for a factor composed of cases).

feedback. An outcome of a decision that has an impact on the way in which the agent making a decision newly perceives a situation (DM).

field. A bounded set of dimensions constituting a coordinate system within which one can map one's basic conceptual units.

field theory. A theory in which the behavior of any one entity is viewed as contingent upon the proximity of its attributes to several empirical dimensions.

flexibility. Adherence to a view in an undoctrinaire manner (DM).

fluctuation. Change in the quantity of a resource over time due to proliferation or depletion (SO: temporal resource asymmetry).

formal. The manner in which a state consciously performs a systemic function (SY).

fragmentation. A system in which structures are not interconnected (SO: entropic structural asymmetry).

frame of reference. A focus on a particular level of analysis and on a metaphor, model, or generic phenomenon serving as the basis for a paradigm.

function. A generic task, the performance of which is postulated to be one among a number or necessary steps for a complete cycle in the operation of a system.

functional approach. Diagnosis of objective social consequences of social phenomena; analysis of claims made by elites that a policy, such as war, will lead to the fulfillment of certain goals (SO).

functional specificity doctrine. A preference to have roles staffed only by specialists in the tasks to be performed (DM).

functionalism doctrine. A preference to have political structures specialize in performing a single function (SO).

fusion. A condition in which structures in a system perform several functions (SO: entropic functional symmetry).

gatekeeping. Deciding whether a demand on a system should be handled politically or administratively (SY).

general systems theory. A theory with concepts applying at all levels of analysis.

genetic theory. A theory that regards present conditions as biological outgrowths of past conditions.

goal. A value toward which behavior may be directed.

goal attainment. A class of activities through which a system achieves new levels of functioning (SY).

government expansion. Growth in government budgets and functions (SO).

hawk. A person who is not reluctant to use force in resolving disputes (DM).

hegemonization model. A conception of the avoidance of violence in international subsystems through one country's drive to control an entire region (SY).

heterogeneity. Presence of several demotypic strata within a system (SO: allocational demotypic asymmetry).

hierarchical. A condition in which function performance is specific to a member of a system because of the member's status position in the system (SY).

historical approach. An approach to a subject that seeks to capture reality in full accuracy and with considerable detail.

homogeneity. The extent to which there is one large demotypic strata within a system (SO: allocational demotypic symmetry).

homoscedasticity. The extent to which there is little dispersion in the values surrounding a mean regression line.

hyperactivity. A condition in which a systemic function is being overperformed by members of a system (SY).

hypoactivity. A condition in which a systemic function is being underperformed by members of a system (SY).

identification. A condition in which an individual or social class is strongly attached to its culture or surroundings (SO: kinetic attitudinal symmetry).

identitive factors. Variables present when the members of a system share similar values, preferences, and common attachments to symbols (SY).

identity crisis. A quest to achieve a sense of national identity on the part of peoples in a country (SO).

ideological politics. A mode of decisionmaking in which values are viewed as ultimate (SY).

ideology. A set of beliefs combined with a program for action.

imbalance. Resources input to a system are greater or less than resources output by the system (SO: transactional resource asymmetry).

immobile. Lack of movement of individuals in levels of social status (SO: kinetic demotypic symmetry).

immobilism. Inability of a system to convert inputs into outputs (SO: kinetic functional asymmetry).

implementation. Activities of elites and their agents in carrying out substantive plans (SY).

inbreeding. A condition in which the demotypic composition of a population does not change with time (SO: temporal demotypic symmetry).

incongruity. Attitudes of a system toward other systems are not the same as attitudes on the part of other systems toward the system (SO: transactional attitudinal asymmetry).

incremental decisionmaking. A decisionmaker who conceives of his role as tinkering modestly with existing policy guides.

independent variable. A condition which produces changes in subsequent or concomitant conditions.

index construction. Finding variables that can stand for concepts.

indicator. A variable that is used to measure a concept.

informal. A condition in which a state or other entity unconsciously performs a systemic function (SY).

information choice node. A point at which a single past action branches out into paths that lead toward more than one objective (DM).

information-processing. A stage in a decisionmaking cycle in which information is input and evaluated as relevant to a possible decision (DM).

innovative labelling. Invention of a new conceptual language for characterizing phenomena.

input. A class of functions which enter a system as stimuli (SY).

instability. Change in behavior over time on the part of individuals, groups, or governmental leaders (SO: temporal behavioral asymmetry).

instrumental. A style of performing a function in which activities are viewed as means toward ends (SY).

integration. Communication linkage between any two entities in a system (SO: entropic structural symmetry).

integration crisis. A quest to solve the problems of penetration and participation simultaneously—of having democratic yet effective government (SO).

intended. A condition in which states or other actors consciously perform a systemic function (SY).

internal validity. A condition in which a variable is logically related to a concept.

international. A level of analysis the basic actor units of which are relatively autonomous political units that control mutually separate territories and populations; relations between these units, usually called states.

international conflict subsystem. A set of actors who are rivals for power; a relatively self-contained set of countries that are in contention with one another over their relative distribution of power (SY).

international political subsystem. A set of actors that engage in goal attainment, adaptation, pattern maintenance, and coordination vis-à-vis one another, such that there are authoritative allocations of values (SY).

international subsystem. A set of politically autonomous or semiautonomous entities that are located in space, time, and by issue-area (SY).

international system. The set of all states or other political entities (SY).

international violence. The use of military force by one country against another (SO).

interpersonal level. The level of analysis referring to individuals and their interrelations.

irrationality model. A conception of violent decisions as the outcome of emotional preoccupation with the subhuman and frustrating character of an adversary (DM).

issue area. A subject matter that serves to structure interactions (SY).

Kaiser's varimax. A form of orthogonal rotation.

kinetic asymmetry. A condition in which potentialities in attributes are not actualized but instead lie dormant or are far from being exploited (SO).

latent. Performance of a function accidentally, that is, when activity to accomplish one goal also entails accomplishing another goal as a by-product (SY).

legitimacy crisis. An as yet unresolved quest to achieve a sense of agreement on the nature and source of authority in a political system (SO).

level of analysis. The degree of aggregation of an entity, and relations between such entities, varying from the atomic level to the international level.

linear. A straight-line, rather than curvilinear, type of relationship between variables.

longitudinal analysis. Examination and comparison of a case or cases over several time points.

looseness. A systemic condition in which there are numbers outside the control of the strongest poles of an international conflict subsystem (SY).

macrocentric. Performance of a function by a decisionmaker who takes the interest of all systems (other than his own) into account (SY).

major power. An elite member of a conflict subsystem whose behavior is capable of upsetting or jeopardizing an existing equilibrium in power distribution (SY).

manifest. Performance of a function in a self-conscious manner (SY).

Marxism. An ideology which holds that present conditions reflect a struggle between theses and antitheses involving the fate of social classes.

mass public. The total group of persons who are affected by events within a political unit; usually refers to those who are unaware of political events (DM).

measurement. Assigning numbers to variables after performing a counting operation.

members (of a system). An actor that engages in a high level of interaction relevant to the issue-area defining the nature of a system (SY).

metaconcept. A term that is used to subsume concepts; a conceptual framework which consists of primitive, undefined notions that are posited to be exhaustive of a class and mutually exclusive in a logical sense.

metatheory. A conceptual and high-level propositional map that organizes a large body of more specific indicators and hypotheses by containing paradigms and an integrated set of tested propositions.

microcentric. Performance of a function by a decisionmaker who takes only the interest of his own system into account (SY).

middle-gauge proposition. A posited relationship between two concepts.

middle power. A member of a conflict subsystem with the capacity to subdue a minor power in combat but no such capacity vis-à-vis a major power (SY).

migration. Demotypes entering a system exceed or are less than demotypes departing from the system (SO: transactional demotypic asymmetry).

military conflict. Overt steps from a decisionmaker's decision to go to war up to the actual outbreak of combat between armed forces.

military-industrial complex. A condition in which military contracts bolster the stability of corporations, in exchange for which industrial leaders provide political support to the military sector of society (SO).

military viability. A capacity for an actor to maintain itself militarily in an international conflict subsystem; possession of at least 500,000 inhabitants (SY).

minor power. A member of a conflict subsystem, with minimal military viability, that cannot hold its own in combat with a middle power (SY).

mobile. Movement of persons upward or downward in social status (SO: kinetic demotypic asymmetry).

mobilized. A condition in a system when all potential resources are being fully utilized (SO: kinetic resource symmetry).

modernization doctrine. A commitment to an increase in resources of states, indefinitely and rapidly (SO).

mono-elite integration. Structural interconnection between members of a system in which there is only one dominant elite unit fostering the integration (SY).

motivation. Propensity of an individual to direct his own behavior.

multilateralism. Performance of a function by several actors in a system together (SY).

multipolarity. A condition in which five to nine members of an international conflict subsystem have much more power than all other members yet do not pool their resources into blocs (SY).

multivariate analysis. Procedure for ascertaining relationships between three or more variables.

narrow-gauge hypothesis. A relationship posited between measures of two variables.

nation-building doctrine. A commitment to increase the phenotypic attainments of a population (SO).

national interest ideology. A view that a struggle for power is the essence of politics; maximization of power is the end and means of political struggle.

negative peace. The absence of war.

neutralism. Failure to support norms governing international behavior that are made by powerful states.

neutrality. Nonparticipation in war by a state; to this legal status accrue rights and obligations vis-à-vis belligerents.

neutralization. Demilitarization of a territory.

nonaggression pact. An alliance in which the signatories pledge not to engage in war against each other (SY).

nonconforming behavior. A class of behavior including two subclasses—deviant and conflictual—which fail to correspond to dominant patterns of activity in a system.

nondecision. The outcome of a bypassing of public, formal decisionmaking channels by elites (DM).

noninstitutionalized conflict. Nonviolent behavior that takes place outside ordinary channels for articulating demands and displeasures; examples include severances of diplomatic relations and impositions of sanctions.

nonpenetration. A condition of a system in which functions are performed entirely by inside actors (SO: transactional functional asymmetry).

nonpreferential. A condition in which functions are performed the same vis-à-vis any stratum in a population (SO: allocational functional symmetry).

nonreciprocated. A condition in which a system has dispatched or received more structures vis-à-vis another system (SO: transactional structural asymmetry).

nonspecialized. A condition in which there is no single institution whose task it is to perform a particular function (SY).

normal distribution. A bell-shaped frequency distribution of cases about the mean value for a distribution of a variable.

normalcy. Eras when underlying values and symbols are affirmed (SO: temporal attitudinal symmetry).

normative approach. An approach to a subject that seeks to highlight elements of virtue and wrongdoing.

objective. A goal that may be achieved by actions (DM).

objectivity. Measurement criterion referring to the extent to which the data collectors avoid introducing bias.

objects of a system. Actors, members, or structural parts of a system (SY).

oblique factor analysis. A form of factor rotation in which the resulting factors may be intercorrelated with each other.

operationism. A view that data are more real than the concepts which data are selected to represent.

operationalization. A derivation of specific hypotheses from propositions; breaking down concepts into measurable variables.

orthogonal rotation. A rotation of a factor matrix yielding uncorrelated factors.

outcome. The consequence of a decision (DM).

output. A class of functions which leave a system as products or outcomes of the functioning of the system (SY).

pacifism. An ideology which regards violence as undesirable and avoidable.

paradigm. An analytical frame of reference that provides a behavioral image of reality.

partial correlation. A measure of the exact amount of relationship between any two variables, when other variables are held constant.

participation crisis. Active dissension on whether to listen to views of members of the population (SO).

particularistic. Performance of a function differently in various parts of a system (SY).

passivity. Failure to act; state of rest or inactivity.

pattern. A mathematically expressible arrangement of units within a system; a quantitative representation comparing two or more elements in a system.

pattern maintenance. A class of activities through which a system preserves its identity and autonomy vis-à-vis other systems (SY).

peace research. Research on why loyalties and positive identifications of men tend to stop at the level of one's own group, why states do not cooperate equally with one another, why systemic characteristics dispose actors to engage in violence.

Pearsonian product-moment correlation. A bivariate correlation based on absolute positions of cases on variables.

penetration. A condition of a system in which some functions are performed by inside, some by outside forces (SO: transactional functional symmetry).

penetration crisis. A quest on the part of a government to achieve an impact on the people by establishing rapport between government and the people (SO).

perfectibility theory. The view that human reason is capable of overcoming emotions (DM).

persistence. Continued presence of a structure over time (SO: temporal structural symmetry).

personalist decisionmaker. A decisionmaker who looks upon policy choices as involving few restraints but instead as opportunities for the exercise of complete free will (DM).

personification fallacy. Referring to a state as a person in a literal sense.

plan. A set of goals aimed toward allocating values in a system (SY).

plan-making. Designing ways of allocating resources within systems (SY).

pluralistic confrontation doctrine. A preference to have decisionmakers exposed at all times to spokesmen for a wide range of alternatives (DM).

pluralistic integration. Establishment of intergovernmental arrangements through which the international postures of states will be rendered harmonious and peaceful among themselves (SY).

pole. A power bloc to which one or more members of an international conflict subsystem commit themselves militarily (SY).

policymaking. Determining administrative strategies and procedures for implementing decisions (DM).

polis model. Plato's theory that war is a function of too much wealth or too much poverty in a country (SO).

political elite. A group of persons who constitute the most influential persons in the making of political decisions (DM).

politics. The process of making authoritative and wide allocations of values to persons in a particular locale or group.

polyarchic. A condition in which no single member of a system exclusively performs a function (SY).

polypolarity. A condition in which each of ten or more members of an international conflict subsystem are equally strong yet do not pool their resources into blocs (SY).

positive peace. A condition in which conflict leads to constructive social change rather than destructive violence.

power theory. A view that the outcome of conflict is the resultant of a parallelogram of forces and pressures.

pragmatic politics. A mode of decisionmaking in which values are viewed as finite for attaining small-scale goals; avoidance of ideological considerations in making decisions (SY).

preoccupation. A condition in which a state identifies most of its vital interests with the attainment of a goal (SY).

prerequisites approach. A search for societal conditions disposing elites to perceive that aggression is necessary or legitimate; a focus on aggregate characteristics of countries that enter war which are absent among countries avoiding war (SO).

prestimulus phase. A stage in decisionmaking before an agent has been triggered to consider alternative decisions (DM).

principal component. An unrotated factor extracted in a factor analysis.

prismatic polity. A political system in which there are elements of both diffraction and fusion in the performance of political functions.

problem-solving. Deliberating over alternative choices (DM).

procedural. Pertaining to the method or manner in which substantive actions are to be conducted (SY).

proposition. A statement positing a relationship between at least two conceptual variables; subsumes specific hypotheses.

public opinion approach. The study of strata and categories of persons that are prone to favor peaceful resolutions of disputes (DM).

Q-analysis. The analysis of the empirical structure of cases, or entities, with time constant.

quiescent. A condition of a system in which there is a low level of concern over the way in which functions are performed (SY).

R-analysis. The analysis of the empirical structure of variables, or characteristics, with time constant.

reciprocated. Exchange of similar structures between two systems (SO: transactional structural symmetry).

recording unit. The unit of measurement selected for counting data.

recruitment. Selection processes for determining new elites, eliminating actor from elite status (SY).

relationships between attributes. Hypotheses (SY).

relationships between objects. Linkages between members of a system (SY).

reliability. Criterion referring to the extent to which a measure is collected systematically across each case, such that a similar operation could be reproduced by different data collectors.

resource. A nonhuman element or pool of manpower that can be energized to perform work on behalf of a system (SY).

rigidity. Adherence to a view in a dogmatic manner (DM).

rotation of factors. Geometric transformation of factors so that the empirical structure will become more interpretable.

routinization. A condition in which a state regards performance of a function as peripheral to its major interests (SY).

rule-adapting. Applying or revising rules as applied to particular cases (SY).

sample. Part of a total population of entities, operations, events, or values of a variable.

satellite. A minor power controlled by a major or middle power in an international conflict subsystem (SY).

scaled data. Data obtained by coding an entity into qualitatively defined categories; data created by means of category construction.

scientific law. A relationship holding between two or more concepts, supported by metatheory.

search. Information-seeking behavior; information-processing to construct new options during a decisionmaking cycle (DM).

second-order factor analysis. A factor analysis based on intercorrelations between factors of a first-order factor analysis.

sectionalism. A phenomenon in which a significant percentage of the population of a nation lives in a sizable geographic area and identifies self-consciously and distinctively with that area (SO: spatial attitudinal asymmetry).

segregation. A condition in which particular demotypes are clustered together instead of being scattered more randomly (SO: spatial demotypic asymmetry).

self-abnegation. Nonassertion of self-interest; renunciation of a desire by a person or state to preserve its integrity.

sensitivity. Criterion referring to the extent to which a measure is calibrated to detect small increments in magnitude.

significant interaction. A condition in which an actor within an international subsystem exchanges enough communications with other actors to qualify as a member; diplomatic recognition by Britain or France is considered significant interaction by members of European international conflict subsystems since 1814 (SY).

similarity. Presence of one and only one genetic and cultural background in the population of a system (SO: entropic demotypic symmetry).

simple structure. A factor matrix in which loadings are all 1.0 or 0.0, with no variable equal to 1.0 on more than one factor and every factor having at least one 1.0 loading.

simulation experiment. An experiment in which components of the real world comprise the setting in which behavior takes place (DM).

situationality. Appearance of a structure at one time, disappearance at another time (SO: temporal structural asymmetry).

skewed distribution. A frequency distribution in which most cases are on one side of the mean value.

slack. A condition in which resources in a political system remain untapped (SO: kinetic resource asymmetry).

smallest space analysis. A nonlinear procedure for determining the way in which data may be configured on the basis of similar sources of variation.

socialization. The process of learning roles and norms appropriate to social situations.

societal level. The level of analysis referring to societies and states and the interrelationships between groups that compose a society.

society. A loose association of persons who band themselves together in order to accomplish certain definite goals (SY).

sovereignty. A condition in which an entity enjoys a high degree of decision-making autonomy in world politics.

space. Geographic location of entities (SO).

spatial asymmetry. A condition in which attributes are not the same across geographic territories; inequality of systems located in different locations (SO).

Spearman rank-difference correlation. A bivariate correlation based on relative ranks of cases or variables.

specialized. A condition in which there is an institution that specifically performs a particular function (SY).

specificity. A condition in which one and only one structure performs a particular function (SY).

sphere of competence. The hierarchical level of a group or individual; the extent of formal and effective power that accrues to an occupant of a role.

stability. An absence of temporal change in behavior, that is, a continuation in patterns of human conduct from one day to the next (SO: temporal behavioral symmetry).

statistical significance. The probability that a score obtained in hypothesis testing deviates from what one might expect if chance factors were operating.

status orientation. Performance of a function by an actor in a different manner toward other actors, depending upon the status of the latter (SY).

status score. Weighted index of the number and rank of diplomatic officials exchanged by a country (SY).

stimulus. An event that stirs an entity to reconsider its position vis-à-vis the environment (DM).

strain. The extent to which resources are oversupplied or undersupplied to parts of a system, such that normal relations between parts are distorted (SO: entropic resource asymmetry).

strategy theory. A theory which regards individual choice in terms of alternative payoffs derived from calculated moves in a game.

stratification approach. An examination of power distribution among members of an international system (SY).

stratification model. A conception of the avoidance of violence in international subsystems through an establishment of a hierarchy and partitioning in power among members of the system (SY).

streamlined. A system arranged structurally to allow rapid passage through structural channels (SO: kinetic structural symmetry).

structural. The hierarchical level of an agent, stimulus, target; its sphere of competence (DM).

structure. A social phenomenon describable in terms of meetings, number of members, rules of procedure, and a defined sphere of competence; an observable uniformity of action or operation.

structural-functional theory. A theory that looks upon systems as arrangements for accomplishing various generic tasks.

structuralism doctrine. A preference to have a new structure to handle every new function performed by a polity (SO).

struggle for power model. A conception of the incidence of excessive violence in international subsystems through continual jockeying for power (SY).

substantive. Pertaining to concrete actions and their effect (SY).

subsystem. A portion of a system.

success in integration. Duration of integrative bonds between systems (SY).

supervision. Gathering of information on the part of a member of a system looking out for its own interests and wishing to maintain or improve its power position (SY).

support. Actions or orientations promoting a polity, the demands therein, and the decisions issued therefrom (SY).

survey data. Responses to projective or scaling exercises, and to interviews or questionnaires.

survival of the fittest doctrine. A preference to have elites rule until they are deposed by counterelites (DM).

symmetrical. Elements in a system that are related in such a way that the converse of their relationship is logically possible.

system. A set of objects together with relationships between the objects and between their attributes.

systematic body of knowledge. An organized set of empirical findings.

systemic decisionmaker. A decisionmaker who perceives himself as constrained by law, balance of power rules, and other objective conditions (DM).

systemization. The embracing of similar attitudes by all persons in all geographic regions of a societal system (SO: spatial attitudinal symmetry).

target. An object of a decision, external to the decisionmaker (DM).

temporal asymmetry. A condition in which attributes do not remain fixed over time; inequality in characteristics of a system over two or more units of time (SO).

theoretical approach. A characterization of a phenomenon in terms of a paradigm, with a conceptual language, which postulates relationships between conceptualized components.

theoretical significance. The salience of a research finding to the acceptance or rejection of a proposition.

tides. Eras in which public sentiment shifts (SO: temporal attitudinal asymmetry).

tight. A systemic condition in which there are no members outside the control of the strongest poles of the system (SY).

time. The period during which an action or process takes place (SO).

transactional. Exchanges between a system and other systems composing its environment (SO).

transactional asymmetry. A condition in which there is a difference between inputs to and outputs from a system (SO).

transformation. A change in the shape of a distribution by multiplying each value by the same mathematical function, aimed often at producing a normal distribution.

tripolarity. A condition in which there are three power blocs within an international conflict subsystem (SY).

turbulent. A condition in which there is a high degree of concern over how functions are performed within a system (SY).

uncohesiveness. Uncoordinated behavior; lack of forces attracting members to a group; inability of parts of a system to stick together (SO: kinetic behavioral asymmetry).

undifferentiated. Presence of few structures, each performing several overlapping functions (SO: allocational functional symmetry).

unidirectional. A condition in which a system is more often either the initiator or the target of behavior (SO: transactional behavioral asymmetry).

uniformity. Similar patterns of behavior across geographic areas (SO: spatial behavioral symmetry).

unilateralism. Performance of a function by one actor in a system without consultation with other actors (SY).

unintended. A condition in which decisionmakers unconsciously perform a systemic function (SY).

unipolarity. A condition in which an international conflict subsystem is dominated by one member (SY).

univariate analysis. Assembling trend information, sorting cases into yes-no and presence-absence categories, or citing an individual datum to prove a point.

universalistic. Performance of a function, taking elements and actors within the entire system into account (SY).

unrotated factor matrix. The factor matrix resulting from use of the principal component method of factor analysis, in which the factors are orthogonal and decreasingly account for variance in the variables.

utilitarian factors. Economic resources (SY).

utility. Criterion for assessing costs versus benefits of collecting a measure.

validity. A condition in which a variable in fact measures a concept.

variable. A measure of a phenomenon that one may observe in different states.

variance. Average of squared deviations of scores from the mean value for a variable.

variation. Dissimilar patterns of behavior across geographic areas (SO: spatial behavioral asymmetry).

withinput. A class of functions carried on within a system which make it possible for outputs to emerge in response to inputs (SY).

world pluralism. An ideology in which no one value crowds out another; each goal is achieved to the fullest degree for the largest number of human beings, such that every state can make its own internal decisions in any fashion it chooses, consistent with the absence of violence.

appendix B
Definitions of Variables

DEFINITIONS OF DECISIONMAKING VARIABLES

1. *Prior cohesion.* The sum of all forces operating to keep units in the agent performing their tasks for the attainment of organizational goals.
2. *Probability of office-holding.* Satisfaction with consumption standards and levels of domestic security on the part of individuals and groups who occupy positions of political influence outside the immediate purview of the agents, such that the central decisionmaker is retained in office; a high probability that the central decisionmaker will stay in office, as measured by the duration of the tenure of the decision-maker's effective power.
3. *Correct intelligence estimates.* The image possessed by the agent concerning the target does not need to be revised by new information during information-processing; no failure of predecision intelligence estimates in corresponding with estimates derived from information processing.
4. *Accurate decoding of warning signs.* Accurate interpretation of information by an agent concerning an impending event or situation with possible consequences to that agent; no failure to receive or understand signals of a forthcoming dramatic move.
5. *Prior concern.* Keen interest by the agent in the subject of a subsequent decision; absence of inattention to the subject or relegation of the matter to a low order of priority before the decisional stimulus.
6. *Precedent invoked.* Drawing upon a past situation or case as a source of principles that may be used to resolve a problem-solving task; no consideration of a decision de novo.

510

7. *Prior planning.* Contingency plans are developed to go into effect under certain prespecified conditions or circumstances; pledges and commitments are made preparatory to a foreseen state of affairs, before the stimulus situation.

8. *Alignment status.* Prior alignment or joint membership in an agreement or organization on the part of both target and agent; absence of an adversary relationship, such as when target and agent belong to mutually antagonistic groups; neutrality is the midpoint between these two extremes.

9. *Ongoing violence.* Agent makes a decision while also engaging in violent operations elsewhere.

10. *Foreign stimulus.* The source requiring a decision is external to the agent, rather than internal to the agent's home jurisdiction.

11. *Cultural similarity.* An agent's perception at the time of the decision stimulus that the target is of the same sociocultural background and can, hence, speak the same language.

12. *Power superiority.* An agent's perception that its coercive capabilities, together with the target's compliance habits, are sufficient to control the destiny of the target, as expressed at the time of the decisional stimulus.

13. *Multi-issue.* An agent's view that the stimulus to decisionmaking involves not just one problem but, instead, a wide range of substantive issues and cognitive tasks from military to political to economic.

14. *Noise level.* The ratio between attention focused by the agent on all subjects to the attention paid to the specific issue under consideration; an issue finding itself submerged by all other issues at the time when the stimulus triggers information-processing.

15. *Trust.* An agent's perception at the time of a decisional stimulus that the target is well intentioned in its disposition toward the agent and does not aim to prevaricate in communications with the agent.

16. *Control over events.* An agent's perception that the decisional stimulus evokes a situation that is definable and knowable, and that the decision taken will be adequate to handle the problem; no lack of understanding of the nature of the problem, no conception of being unable to cope with an unpredictable chain of events.

17. *Time pressure.* An agent's perception that the stimulus demands a quick response or else serious consequences will follow; an absence of nonchalance toward the proper time when a decisional task is to be terminated.

18. *Cruciality.* An agent's perception at the time of the decisional stimulus that the target threatens, involves, or challenges its vital interests and high priority values; linkage of a situation with self-preservation and survival, rather than such values as prestige and status.

19. *Level of a problem.* International issues are at higher levels than national; national issues are higher than local; multilateral problems are at higher levels than those involving only two countries directly.

20. *Threat of violence.* An agent's perception that the stimulus suggests that the target may soon undertake or escalate in violent actions against the agent.

21. *Size of the decisionmaking body.* The number of persons actively engaged in narrowing alternatives toward the decision chosen; central decisionmaker as well as advisers who are permitted to influence his decision.

22. *Decision latitude.* The extent to which decisionmakers perceive themselves as free to decide without jeopardizing the level of validator satisfaction, such that they believe themselves to be sutured off from the validators' preferences during information-processing.

23. *Officiality.* The extent to which the decisionmaking body is formally constituted, rather than assembled on an ad hoc or extraordinary basis; the decision is announced subsequently by such a formal body, rather than being made public by actions or words of a lower administrative agency or ad hoc coterie.

24. *Authority contracted.* Consideration of an issue at a higher level than normal; an upward shift in the locus of decisionmaking during information-processing; a decrement in the number of persons that the central decisionmaker permits to advise him, such as by refusing to hear a minority or by refusing to invite an early member of the decisionmaking body to attend later deliberations.

25. *Decision time.* The number of days elapsing between a perceived stimulus to decisionmaking and the termination of information-processing in the form of a decision.

26. *Cognitive complexity.* The presence of many intellectual facets and a complicated role structure for filtering communication; ambiguity rather than simplicity in information decoding and encoding; task specialization during information-processing; development of elaborate contingency plans.

27. *Input load.* The decoding by decisionmakers of more information than necessary for arriving at a decision, rather than receiving an inadequate amount of information necessary to handle the task at hand and make a decision.

28. *Input intensity.* Lack of redundancy in messages decoded by decisionmakers, rather than repetitive messages that fail to supply new and useful information.

29. *Input range.* Variety of communication channels used and sources consulted during information-processing, such as when both oral and written messages play important roles and when messages des-

tined for the decisionmakers emerge from several hierarchical levels in the target and agent, or even from informal sources.

30. *Input/output ratio.* A preponderance in inputs over outputs; an imbalance between information received by decisionmakers and that which they send outside the agent, such that they keep ahead of the flow of events and messages; decisionmakers less actively express their own preferences than they digest information relevant to the decisional problem and examine communication feedback.

31. *Metacommunication level.* The extent to which agent and target communicate effectively, without semantic incongruities and jamming, because they are able to understand the meaning of each other's linguistic symbols and expressions; being in a position to learn the content of a target's messages, without having to first determine stylistic codes, with a high degree of fidelity.

32. *Reduction in communications.* Decrease in the agent's inputs or outputs during information-processing in order to escape overload or jamming; perception of closure in needed information inputs, reached prematurely.

33. *Learning rate.* The level at which decisionmakers eventually ascertain the relevant aspects of the task to which they are assigned, such that their response can be condign for resolving the problem.

34. *Risk propensity.* Tendency for the decisionmakers to prefer alternatives that might lead to a highly favorable outcome, even though there is a chance that a highly unfavorable outcome could result instead; preference for a choice that would maximize chances for an increase in utilities.

35. *Tolerance of ambiguity.* Ability of an information-processer to discriminate between various levels of subjective probability in assessing options; absence of a need to oversimplify a situation into black-and-white images; ambiguous information leads to further search, rather than being filtered out of consideration or relegated to a lesser role in decisionmaking.

36. *Self-esteem.* The central decisionmaker's confidence that he is capable of handling the decisionmaking problem; optimism concerning the successfulness of the eventual decision in resolving the problem.

37. *Desires for achievement.* Expressions made by a decisionmaker indicating high aspirations to bring about a new state of affairs by restructuring a situation.

38. *Desires for power.* Expressions made by a decisionmaker indicating deep-seated aspirations to dominate a target, to control the outcome, or to increase the coercive capabilities of the agent vis-à-vis the target.

39. *Desires for affiliation.* Expressions made by a decisionmaker indicat-

ing preferences to have friends and allies in order to resolve the decisional problem; consultation with such sources during information-processing.

40. *Perceptions of frustration.* Expressions by a decisionmaker that the agent is unable to achieve desired goals, usually due to blockage on the part of the target; a lack of feeling of satisfaction in goal attainment.

41. *Perceptions of hostility.* Expressions by a decisionmaker of enmity toward a target; regard for the target as unfriendly or even subhuman.

42. *Stereotypic decoding.* Decoding of messages by information-processers in which messages are interpreted to conform to preconceived views despite the objective challenge to these views; contrary information is filtered out or avoided.

43. *Structuredness.* Lack of uncertainty in formulating alternatives and in establishing a meaningful image of the decisional situation and problem.

44. *Range of alternatives.* The number or variety of options considered as possible solutions to the decisional problem; number of alternative decisions debated in terms of pros and cons.

45. *Intraorganizational consonance.* The extent to which information-processers and their advisers agree at all stages on their evaluation of the relative merits of alternative decisions; lack of disagreement among decisionmakers on goals, values, and means; percentage of decisionmakers expressing minority views.

46. *Hierarchical resolution.* Imposition of values and preferences of the central decisionmaker upon other members of the decisionmaking body, which contradict pressures representing public opinion; chain-of-command roles are invoked to resolve a decisional problem, rather than bargaining or polyarchy, in which each group member negotiates to gain as many utilities as his relative strength permits or exercises veto power, respectively.

47. *Pragmatism.* Information-processing geared toward achieving concrete objectives, rather than homage toward ideological, utopian models.

48. *Violent alternative considered.* One or more among the various alternative decisions evaluated by the decisionmakers involves the use of coercion or violence toward the target; percentage of alternatives involving coercive means.

49. *Penetration.* A decision outcome that results in widespread rather than limited change of the target; change of both attitudes and behavior, and even in structures.

50. *Transience.* A decisional impact that applies to present more than future changes in the target; momentary and temporary change, rather than changes that remain in force for long time periods.

51. *Procedurality.* A decision that involves a change or reaffirmation in procedures and rules of conduct, rather than substantive and concrete changes vis-à-vis the target.

52. *Formality.* A decision whose content is recorded in writing, such as in a document located in an archive, rather than being released orally; recorded as a statute or executive order, rather than in a speech or conversation.

53. *Degree of guidance.* A decisional outcome involving the agent in guiding the target toward a goal; change in the target that is meted out by the agent after the decision has been made.

54. *Revocability.* The ability of a decisionmaker to retract his decision and return thereby to the previous state of affairs or decision node unimpaired; changes that can be undone by subsequent counteracts; the ability of a central decisionmaker to rescind his decision before an impact upon the target, or to rescind the impact itself.

55. *Turning point.* A decision that constitutes a convergence of events resulting in new circumstances that dramatically affect the future of both target and agent.

56. *Success.* A decisional outcome which leads to desired ends and is consistent with high priority goals; lack of miscalculation or backfire.

57. *Implementation speed.* The duration between a decision and its impact on the target; immediate and fast rather than slow rates of change produced in the target.

58. *Sociometric change.* A decision resulting in realignment, such that former allies are opposed or former adversaries are supported; revision in like-dislike perceptions; central rather than peripheral change in the target.

59. *Continuousness.* Changes on the target that unfold without interruption rather than being sporadic or intermittent in occurrence.

60. *Cumulativity.* Changes produced on the target that follow cumulatively from one another, rather than independently.

61. *Stabilizing.* A decisional impact in which the agent promotes the coherence and stability of a target, rather than producing changes that subvert the target.

62. *Goal-restructuring.* A decisional outcome in which a new ends-means hierarchy results on the part of the agent vis-à-vis the target; a "flip" in decisionmaking style.

63. *Promotive.* Positive as opposed to negative change resulting from a decision; changing the status quo rather than maintaining it or awaiting a new state of affairs in which present problems will no longer necessitate attention; a decision to proceed to take action, rather than a decision not to decide.

64. *Maximizing.* A decision that results in maintenance or improvement

in the agent's resources, usually vis-à-vis the target, instead of one in which decisionmakers desire only psychological satisfaction.

65. *Decision for violence*. A decision in which the agent embarks on actions that result in the physical destruction of a target's goods or persons, or an escalation in the level of coercive activities.

66. *Extent of documentation*. Number of footnotes used in descriptions of the decision.

67. *Academic source*. The author of the account of the decisionmaking process is either a political scientist or historian.

68. *Length of description*. The number of words used by the author of the account to reconstruct the decisionmaking process.

DEFINITIONS OF SOCIETAL VARIABLES

1. *Ratio between percentage increases in national income and population*. (a) *National income:* the sum of incomes accruing to the factors of production supplied by the normal residents of a country, before deducting direct taxes, and equals the sum of compensation of employees, income from unincorporated enterprises, rent, interest and dividends accruing to households, saving of corporations, direct taxes on corporations and general government income; (b) *population:* de jure residents of a country, that is, including jungle tribes, aborigines, nomadic peoples, displaced persons, refugees, persons in military or diplomatic service, but excluding alien armed forces, alien diplomatic personnel, and enemy prisoners of war stationed inside the country; (a) is divided by (b) to derive the ratio.

2. *Commercial energy consumption* (per capita annual change). Gross energy consumed from inanimate sources in millions of megawatt hours from solid fuels, liquid fuels, natural gas, and hydroelectric power, that is, excluding fuelwood and other vegetable fuels which are not ordinarily available for sale for mass distribution (see variable 1 for the definition of "population").

3. *Gross national product* (per capita annual change). Market value of goods and services produced by normal residents of a country before deducting for the consumption of fixed capital and factor incomes derived from abroad.

4. *Radios* (per capita annual change). The number of radio receivers in use or number of licenses granted.

5. *Telephones per capita* (coefficient of annual variation). The number of public and private telephones installed that can be connected to a central exchange.

6. *Railroad freight ton-kilometers* (coefficient of annual variation). Both fast and ordinary freight, excluding service traffic, mail, baggage, and nonrevenue government stores.

7. *Electricity production per capita* (coefficient of annual variation). Energy generated from coal and lignite, crude petroleum, natural gas, and hydro sources (see variable 1 for the definition of "population").

8. *Population increase* (annual rate). The difference between (live) birth rates and death rates as recorded by governmental authorities (see variables 21 and 22 for definitions of "birth rates" and "death rates").

9. *Caloric intake* (per capita difference between two years). The amount of energy contained in foodstuffs consumed by individuals, excluding alcoholic beverages (see variable 1 for definition of "population").

10. *Protein grammage intake* (per capita difference between two years). The amount of amino acids contained in foodstuffs consumed by individuals.

11. *Government budget* (per capita annual change). Budgeted current and capital outlays of the national government, including grants to foreign governments but excluding debt redemption and capital transfers.

12. *National income instability.* The log variance of national income figures computed on a year-to-year basis, that is, relative changes corrected for trend influences (see variable 1 for definition of "national income").

13. *Urbanites* (average annual increase). Percentage of persons in a country living in localities of 20,000 or more in population.

14. *Agricultural employment* (percent annual change). Farmers, fishermen, hunters, lumbermen, and related persons who are or who seek to be engaged in producing goods and services.

15. *Literacy* (percent annual change). The ability of persons aged 15 and over to read and/or write.

16. *Communist Party strength/population* (coefficient of annual variation). Members of the Communist Party and associated splinter groups (see variable 1 for definition of "population").

17. *Government instability.* The existence of a situation in which a constitution is suspended, an elected president is ousted forcibly from office, or there are frequent cabinet changes.

18. *System instability.* The existence of governmental instability (as defined in variable 17), domestic conflict (as defined in variables 106–112), and/or a rapid turnover in executive heads of state (as defined in variable 20).

19. *Age of the latest two governments* (mean). Average tenure of the present and former executive heads of state, excluding executives now in office but who have served for three or fewer years.

20. *Years independent per chief executives.* The number of years in which a political unit has had an internationally recognized border and some form of autonomous central administration (for definition of "chief executive" see variable 19).

21. *Birth rate per capita* (coefficient of annual variation). Live births, that is, the product of conception completely expelled or extracted from its mother and which shows evidence of life, such as breathing, heart beat, or pulsation of the umbilical cord (see variable 1 for definition of "population").

22. *Death rate per capita* (coefficient of annual variation). Deaths, excluding foetal deaths.

23. *Marriage rates per capita* (coefficient of annual variation). Legal unions of persons of opposite sex.

24. *Major government crises.* Any rapidy developing situations that threaten to bring the downfall of a present regime, excluding situations of revolt aimed at such an overthrow.

25. *Government illegitimacy.* The present executive head of a country came into power through revolution, rather than through legal means (see variable 108 for definition of "revolution").

26. *Legality of the latest two governmental changes.* Last and present government came into being through legal means, that is, through constitutional provisions for transferring power or (in the absence of a constitution) the traditional practice of a country, rather than through nonlegal means, such as illegal elections or revolutions.

27. *Defense expenditures per capita* (coefficient of annual variation). Total current and capital outlays listed under the "defense" classification in the national account tables, that is, budgets for fiscal years (see variable 1 for definition of "population").

28. *Education expenditures per capita* (coefficient of annual variation). Total current and capital outlays listed under the "education" classification in the national account tables, that is, budgets for fiscal years.

29. *Welfare expenditures per capita* (coefficient of annual variation). Total current and capital outlays listed under the "welfare" classification in the national account tables, that is, budgets for fiscal years.

30. *Government budget expenditures per capita* (coefficient of annual variation). Budgeted current and capital outlays of the national government, including grants to foreign governments, and excluding redemption of debts and capital transfers.

31. *Party system instability.* A condition in which all political parties are situational, personalistic, or ad hoc.

32. *Government ministries* (coefficient of annual variation). The number of independent departmental subdivisions within the executive branch of government.

33. *Political parties with seats in parliament* (coefficient of annual variation). Political parties that have at least one delegate elected to a national legislature.

34. *Land area under cultivation* (difference from 50 percent of total land). Land that is arable, that is, areas suited for agricultural subjugation: land planted to crop, temporarily fallow, meadow lands, garden lands, areas under fruit trees, vines, fruit-bearing shrubs, or rubber plantation.

35. *Agricultural employment* (difference from 50 percent of work force). See variable 14 for definition of "agricultural worker," which is percentaged from all persons who are economically active, that is, all persons who are or who seek to be engaged in producing goods and services.

36. *Agricultural population* (difference from 50 percent of total population). Persons who depend upon agriculture for a livelihood, that is, persons actively engaged in agriculture and their nonworking dependents.

37. *Population in cities* (difference from 50 percent of total population). See variable 13.

38. *Urban primacy.* Population of the largest city as a percentage of the population of the four largest urban or metropolitan areas in a country.

39. *Lack of sectionalism.* A condition in which there is no significant percentage of the population of a nation that lives in a sizable geographic area and identifies self-consciously and distinctively with that area to a degree that the cohesion of the polity as a whole is appreciably challenged or impaired.

40. *Potential sectional separatism.* A polity containing regional or ethnic groups, often but not necessarily linguistically or religiously distinct from the group or groups controlling the state, which are dissatisfied with the polity in which they are formally members.

41. *Sectional group discrimination.* Presence of one or more groups that are substantially, deliberately, and systematically excluded from valued economic, political, or social positions because of ethnic, religious, linguistic, or regional characteristics by a significant portion of those controlling access to such positions, with the exception of groups that are geographically remote.

42. *Vertical power centralization.* Absence of either formal or effective federalism, that is, of a division in powers between local and central governments.

43. *Unitary system.* Nonexistence of a constitutional division of powers between central and local governments.
44. *Political decentralization.* Extent to which the executive and council for individual municipalities and intermediate government structures are directly elected by the people.
45. *Colonial power.* Possession of at least one colony, that is, of non-self-governing territories, dependencies, condominiums, and trust territories.
46. *National area* (percentage of total size). Total area of a geographic unit, including inland water as well as such uninhabited or uninhabitable stretches of land as may lie within their mainland boundaries, percentaged from the total of national and colonial areas (see variable 45 for definition of "colony").
47. *National population* (percentage of total population). National population, as defined in variable 1, percentaged from the total national and colonial populations.
48. *Ratio of electricity potential to actual electrical energy generated.* Energy resources potentially rather than actually available (see variable 7 for definition of "electricity production").
49. *Waterpower potential* (percentage developed). Hydroelectric resources potentially rather than actually available.
50. *Ratio of energy generation to consumption.* Electricity produced as compared with energy; that is, the discrepancy due to loss in transmission is measured as the departure from 1.0.
51. *Ratio of motor vehicles to road length.* (a) *Motor vehicles* seating less than eight persons in use, including taxis, jeeps, and station wagons, but excluding two- or three-wheeled cycles and motorcycles, trains, trolley-busses, hearses, ambulances, and vehicles operated by the military police, or other governmental security and special service, vehicles; (b) *road length* in total kilometers, whether the roadway is paved or unimproved; (a) divided by (b) to derive the ratio.
52. *Ratio of rail freight to rail length.* Length of rail tracks in kilometers (see variable 6 for the definition of "rail freight").
53. *Ratio of road length to land area.* See variables 46 and 51.
54. *Ratio of rail length to land area.* See variables 46 and 52.
55. *Illiteracy* (percent). Inability of persons over 10 years of age to read and/or write (see variable 1 for definition of "population").
56. *Primary school enrollment* (percent). Children between the ages of 5 to 14 who have regularly enrolled in either public or private schools providing basic educational instruction.
57. *Primary and secondary school enrollment* (percent). Children between the ages of 5 to 19 who are regularly enrolled in either public

or private schools that provide basic to general or specialized instruction.

58. *Education expenditures* (per capita). See variables 1 and 28.

59. *Enrollment in secondary and higher education* (percent). Pupils enrolled in secondary, vocational, and technical training institutions, as well as teacher's colleges and universities, but excluding adult education and community development programs (see variable 1 for definition of "population").

60. *Low political enculturation.* The extent to which there is a relatively nonintegrated or restrictive polity, with a majority or near majority in extreme opposition, communalized, fractionalized, disfranchised, or politically nonassimilated.

61. *Lack of a developmental ideology.* Absence of a fervor within a country constituting a commitment to development as a national goal or a transcendent ideological commitment.

62. *Articulation by anomic interest groups.* The presence of more or less spontaneous breakthroughs into the political system from the society, such as variables 107 and 112, all distinguished by relative structural and functional lability.

63. *Voter turnout* (percent). Number of ballots cast or votes cast for candidates in national elections as a percentage of the voting-age population, including those not enfranchised and blank or invalid ballots.

64. *Nonagricultural workers in trade unions* (percent). Number of workers aware that they belong to an organization that bargains on behalf of their interests vis-à-vis employers; unionization (see variable 14 for definition of "agricultural workers").

65. *Concern about politics.* Percentage of persons expressing concern or interest in political matters.

66. *Fear of politics.* Percentage of persons interested in political matters who express fears about political outcomes.

67. *Military population* (percentage of population). Percentage of persons between the ages of 15 and 64 in the service of a country's armed services (see variable 1 for definition of "population").

68. *Military mobilizations.* Rapid increases in military strength through the calling up of reserves, activation of additional military units, or the de-mothballing of military equipment.

69. *Divorce rate* (percentage of population). Final legal dissolutions of marriages by a judicial decree that confers on the parties the right of civil and/or religious remarriage (see variable 1 for definition of "population").

70. *Marriage rate* (percentage of population). See variables 1 and 23.

71. *Ratio of divorces to marriages.* See variables 69 and 70.

72. *Religious adherents voting for religious political parties* (percent). Votes cast for religious party candidates in the two most recent elections as a percentage of persons who are affiliated with or have a belief in an ethical or philosophical or theological doctrine other than one of atheism or agnosticism.

73. *Communist votes in national elections as a percentage of Communist Party strength.* Votes cast for Communist Party candidates as a percentage of Communist Party strength (see variable 16 for definition of "Communist Party strength").

74. *Nonmobilizational system style.* A polity in which human resources are not politically mobilized to meet problems perceived to be of national urgency.

75. *Government expenditures* (percentage of national income). See variables 1 and 11.

76. *Public administration and defense expenditures* (percentage of GNP). Expenditures on administration, defense, justice, and police, but not public enterprises or other services as a percentage of gross domestic product at factor cost (see variable 3 for definition of "GNP").

77. *Defense expenditures* (percentage of national income). See variables 1 and 27.

78. *Education expenditures* (percentage of national income). See variables 1 and 28.

79. *Welfare expenditures* (percentage of national income). See variables 1 and 29.

80. *General government expenditures* (percentage of GNP). Total current and capital outlays, including social security and public enterprises, in central and local government budgets for fiscal years (see variable 3 for definition of "GNP").

81. *Central government expenditures* (percentage of GNP). Total current and capital outlays, including social security and capital outlays, including social security and public enterprises, in central but not local government budgets for fiscal years.

82. *Horizontal concentration of power.* Complete dominance of government by one branch or by an extragovernmental agency without an allocation of power to functionally autonomous legislative, executive, and judicial organs.

83. *Bicameral legislature.* A polity in which there are two chambers in the legislature.

84. *Ratio of government revenue to expenditures.* Revenue from income and wealth, mainly including general and special taxes on individuals and corporate income, excess profits taxes, stamp duties taxes, stamp duties on dividends, death and gift taxes as receipted in national account tables, excluding grants from foreign governments and proceeds

of loans and surpluses from previous years (see variable 11 for definition of "government expenditures").

85. *Press censorship.* The extent to which there is a strict direct or indirect censorship or control on newsgathering and newsprinting.

86. *Press censorship.* See variable 85 for definition, though data sources vary.

87. *Political opposition restricted.* A polity where autonomous groups are incapable of organizing in politics and unable to oppose governmental policies.

88. *Political opposition unrestricted.* Groups are free to organize for political action and may campaign for control of the government.

89. *Executive weakness.* A head of a government who is incapable of imposing his will throughout the executive, legislative, and judical branches of government.

90. *Legislative weakness.* A legislature that is restricted to a consultative or "rubber-stamp" function by the executive or dominant party organization.

91. *Minimum voting age.* The age at which a citizen becomes eligible to vote in elections.

92. *Unemployment* (percentage of labor force). Number of wage persons out of work but seeking employment, excluding self-employed persons.

93. *Ratio of primary school pupils to teachers.* (a) *Instructors* in public or private primary schools: (b) see variable 56 for definition of *primary school enrollment* figures; (b) is divided by (a) to derive the ratio.

94. *Ratio between population and physicians.* Number of medical doctors engaged in medical practice (see variable 1 for definition of "population").

95. *Ratio between hospital beds and physicians.* Number of beds in medical establishments (see variable 94 for definition of "physician").

96. *Nutritional adequacy.* Departure of caloric intake from medically established minimum daily requirements based on climate, work load, and average body build.

97. *Ethnic groups.* Number of ethnic or racial groups with more than 1 percent of the total population (see variable 1 for definition of "population").

98. *Language communities.* Number of languages spoken by an individual in his early childhood exceeding 1 percent of the population, defining "language" as all varieties that share a single superposed variety (such as a literary standard) having substantial similarity in phonology and grammar and therefore whose varieties are mutually intelligible or are connected by a series of mutually intelligible varieties.

99. *Nationality groups.* Number of national groups whose members were born in the same foreign country and exceed 1 percent of the population.

100. *Religious groups.* Number of major religious affiliations or beliefs reported by individuals that exceed 1 percent of the population (see variable 72 for definition of "religion").

101. *Racial groups.* Number of groups that are racially similar in physical appearance from one of the following categories: Negro, Mongolian, Caucasian, mulatto, zambo, mestizo, or Eurasian groups in excess of 1 percent of the population.

102. *Duration of strikes.* Working days lost due to industrial disputes.

103. *Strikers* (percentage of population). Persons out of work because of work stoppages, including lockouts but excluding small-scale or politically motivated strikes (see variable 1 for definition of "population").

104. *Strikers* (percentage of workforce). See variables 92 and 103.

105. *Strikers* (ratio to total unionized workforce). See variables 64 and 103.

106. *General strikes.* Strikes of 1,000 or more industrial or service workers that involve more than one employer and are aimed at national government policies or authority.

107. *Antigovernment demonstrations.* Peaceful public gatherings of 100 or more persons for the primary purpose of displaying or voicing opposition to government policies or authority, excluding those directed at governments located abroad.

108. *Revolutions.* Illegal or forced changes in the top governmental elite; attempts at such changes; successful or unsuccessful armed rebellions aimed at achieving independence from the central government.

109. *Guerrilla warfare.* Any armed activity, sabotage, or bombings carried on by independent bands of citizens or irregular forces and aimed at the overthrow of the present regime.

110. *Assassinations.* Politically motivated murders or attempted murders of high government officials or politicians.

111. *Purges.* Systematic eliminations, by jailing or execution, of political opposition within other ranks of the regime or counterregime groups.

112. *Riots.* Violent demonstrations or clashes of more than 100 citizens involving the use of physical force.

113. *Domestic violence deaths* (percentage of population). Deaths resulting directly from intergroup violence, excluding murders and executions.

114. *Diffracted articulation.* A condition in which interests are formulated and demanded by a single specialized structure—such as by associ-

ational groups, institutional groups, nonassociational groups, anomic groups, or by political parties—vis-à-vis the governmental elites.

115. *Diffracted aggregation.* A condition in which interests are combined together and then presented thereafter either by political parties, the legislature, or the executive.

116. *Fragmentation in functions of political parties.* A condition in which political parties have an active or significant role both in interest articulation and in interest aggregation (see variables 114 and 115 for definitions of "articulation" and "aggregation").

117. *Weakness of executive and legislature.* See variables 97 and 98.

118. *Military interventions into politics.* A condition in which the military establishment exercises or has recently exercised direct power or performs a parapolitical role in support of a traditionalist, authoritarian, totalitarian, or modernizing regime.

119. *Police interventions into politics.* A condition which the police force exercises important continuing or intermittent political functions in addition to law enforcement.

120. *Cinema attendance* (per capita). All paid admissions to performances of 16 or 35 mm. films, including films shown at locations that are not permanent establishments for the showing of films or which possess fixed film equipment (see variable 1 for definition of "population").

121. *Library book circulation* (per capita). Number of volumes and other items lent or re-lent to readers either for home use or for use in the libraries serving the general public, including libraries for children or members of the armed forces, and administered by either government or research agencies.

122. *Newspaper circulation* (per capita). Daily number of copies of publications containing general news and appearing at least four times weekly, including sales both inside and outside a country.

123. *Telephones* (per capita). See variable 5.

124. *Domestic pieces of mail* (per capita). The number of letters (air, ordinary, or registered mail), postcards, printed matter, business papers, small merchandise samples, small packets, and phonopost packets, including mail carried without charge but excluding ordinary packages and letters or packages with a declared value, mailed for distribution within the national territory (see variable 1 for definition of "population").

125. *Radio receivers* (per capita). See variable 4.

126. *Television sets* (per capita). Number of sets receiving audio-visual broadcasting transmitted to the general public (see variable 1 for definition of "population").

127. *Land ownership inequality* (Gini index). The difference between actual proportions of land held by owners and a condition of equality in which each owner would possess land of an equal size.

128. *Population owning half of the land* (percent). The smallest percentage of the population owning half of the lands in a country (see variable 1 for definition of "population").

129. *Slope of Lorenz curve at 95 percent of land ownership.* The steepness of the slope in number of owners at 95 percent of land ownership as the last 5 percent of the lands owned by the rest of the population are taken into account.

130. *Inequality in income before taxes* (Gini index). The difference between actual proportions of income possessed by income-receiving units (individuals or families) and a condition of equality in which each income earner would receive the same amount of income before taxes.

131. *Inequality in income after taxes* (Gini index). The difference between actual proportions of income possessed after taxes are assessed from income-receiving units (individuals or families) and a condition of equality in which income earners would receive the same amount of income after taxes.

132. *Farms on rented land* (percent). Farm households that rent all of their land, as a percentage of the total number of farms.

133. *Tax revenues accounted for by customs fees* (percent). Import and export duties classified as receipts in national account tables (see variable 84 for definition of "government revenue").

134. *Religious heterogeneity.* A condition in which the dominant religious group accounts for less than 90 percent of the total population and there are other significant groups (see variable 100 for definition of "religious group").

135. *Racial heterogeneity.* A condition in which the dominant race in a population accounts for less than 80 percent of a population and there are significant minority groups (see variable 101 for definition of "race").

136. *Linguistic heterogeneity.* A condition in which the dominant language community accounts for less than 85 percent of the adult population and there are significant minority groups (see variable 98 for definition of "language community").

137. *Religious, racial, and linguistic heterogeneity.* A composite of variables 134, 135, and 136.

138. *Largest religious group* (percent). The percentage of the total population belonging to the dominant religion (see variable 1 for definition of "population" and variable 100 for definition of "religious group").

139. *Largest ethnic group* (percent). The percentage of the total population belonging to the dominant ethnic group (see variable 97 for definition of "ethnic group").

140. *Largest language group* (percent). The percentage of the total population belonging to the dominant language group (see variable 98 for definition of "language group").

141. *Native born* (percent). The percentage of the total population born and living inside the same country (see variable 99 for definition of "nationality").

142. *Largest racial group* (percent). The percentage of the total population belonging to the dominant racial group (see variable 101 for definition of "racial group").

143. *Political parties.* Number of political parties with a membership over 1 percent of the population (see variable 33 for definition of "political party").

144. *Two- or multi-party systems.* The presence of two or more political parties in a polity with a reasonable expectation of party rotation or coalition, or minority party government if there are several parties with seats in parliament.

145. *Multiparty system.* The presence of several political parties, with or without limitations on activity of extremist parties.

146. *Political party types.* Number of the following three distinct types of political parties—Communist, religious, and non-Communist secular parties—with at least 1 percent of total votes cast in the two most recent elections.

147. *Homicide rate* (percentage of population). Deaths caused by deliberate actions of other persons, including operations of war.

148. *Motor-vehicle accident death rate* (percentage of population). Deaths caused accidentally by motor vehicles (see variable 1 for definition of "population").

149. *Liver cirrhosis death rate* (percentage of population). Deaths due to a hardening and contracting of the liver.

150. *Syphilis death rate* (percentage of population). Deaths due to a chronic, specific, contagious disease caused by spirochete.

151. *Illegitimacy ratio.* Births out of wedlock as a percentage of females aged 10 to 49.

152. *Suicide rate* (percentage of population). Deaths due to self-inflicted injuries or other premeditated causes (see variable 1 for definition of "population").

153. *Accident death rate* (percentage of population). Deaths due to automobile accidents and all other accidents.

154. *Ulcer death rate* (percentage of population). Deaths due to a sore on the surface of the stomach or duodenum.

155. *Constitutional regime.* A government conducted with reference to recognized limitations on government power and with reference to rights of individuals and groups outside government.

156. *Nonauthoritarian regime.* A polity other than one where there is no effective constitutional limitation on government or fairly regular recourse to extraconstitutional powers, and arbitrary exercise of power is confined to the political sector but does not extend to the social sphere; either a constitutional or a totalitarian regime.

157. *Nontotalitarian regime.* A polity other than one where there is no effective constitutional limitation on government and broad exercise of power by the regime in both political and social spheres; either a constitutional or an authoritarian regime.

158. *Nonpolyarchic representativeness.* A condition in a polity where the franchise is narrowly based, if present at all, with some groups exercising oligarchic or autocratic control while others are prohibited from voting.

159. *Non-elitist recruitment.* A condition of a polity in which political leaders are recruited on the basis of achievement criteria, rather than being confined to a particular racial, social, or ideological stratum.

160. *Lack of personalismo in political parties.* A condition in which there is no tendency for politically active sectors of a population to follow or to oppose a leader of a political idea, program, or party on the basis of the leader's personal, individual, or family characteristics.

161. *Group discrimination.* Number of regional groups discriminated against (see variable 41 for definition of "regional group discrimination").

162. *Political structures.* The presence of one or more of each of the following in a polity: elections, an opposition group, a political party, autonomous units of local government, an upper and a lower chamber of a legislature, and an executive head of state.

163. *Bureaucratic traditionalism.* The existence of a largely nonrationalized bureaucratic structure performing in the context of an ascriptive or deferential stratification system, rather than an effective and responsible civil service performing in a functionally specific, nonascriptive social context.

164. *Lack of trade dependence.* The percentage of exports that consist of manufactured goods rather than food, beverages, tobacco, inedible crude materials, mineral fuels, lubricants, animal oils and fats, and unprocessed chemicals.

165. *Export trade ratio* (departure from 50 percent). Commercial intercourse from one country to others as a proportion of commercial intercourse into the same country, excluding transfers of military equipment, but including insurance and nonmilitary gifts.

166. *Balance of investments.* Annual average absolute value of income from investments in other countries minus payments on foreign domestic investments.

167. *Balance of donations.* Absolute value of official aid sent or received in the form of grants and reparations from metropolitan areas to overseas territories, excluding gifts of military supplies and equipment.

168. *Immigrants/migrants* (departure from 50 percent). Newly arrived aliens to a country intending to remain for a period exceeding one year as a percentage of all of these persons plus nationals leaving their home country with the intention of staying abroad for a period exceeding one year.

169. *Stereotypy.* Percentage of respondents in a sample survey of a country designating one country as "least friendly" minus the percentage designating the same country as "most friendly," averaged across all such ratings for all other countries by the sample population within a country.

170. *Friendliness.* Percentage of respondents in a sample survey of a country designating one country as "most friendly" minus the percentage designating the same country as "least friendly," averaged across all such ratings for all other countries by the sample population within a country.

171. *Foreign mail sent* (departure from 50 percent of all foreign mail). Percentage of all foreign mail sent by members of a country abroad, where *foreign* is defined as mail originating in one country for distribution within another country (see variable 124 for definition of "mail").

172. *Bloc prominence.* The extent to which a nation is recognized as a spokesman for a bloc or a faction within a bloc, as demonstrated by organizing conferences within or between blocs or by independently tabling major proposals for the solution, resolution, or control of interbloc political problems or conflict.

173. *Communist and quasi-Communist states* (except the USSR). A country aligned with the Soviet Union that adopts many of the features of a Communist form of government, including the Castroite Cuban regime.

174. *Penetrated polities.* Countries in which an external power controls political behavior taking place in the state, through military or other means.

175. *Bloc membership.* Membership in either the Communist or Western blocs (membership in the neutral bloc is a residual category, for countries lacking military treaties or alliances with either the Communist or Western bloc leaders).

176. *Expulsions and recalls of diplomats.* Number of ambassadors and diplomatic officials of lesser rank declared personae non grata or recalled, excluding cases where severances of diplomatic relations or administrative reasons are involved.
177. *Severances of diplomatic relations.* Complete withdrawals from all official contact with a particular country.
178. *Ratio of embassies and legations abroad to total at home and abroad* (difference from 0.5). Number of diplomatic missions located abroad as a percentage of all such missions plus missions from other countries at home, including High Commissioners of British Commonwealth countries, Political Representatives of Austria in Communist countries, and officially maintained but temporarily vacant legations, but excluding embassies and legations of governments-in-exile.
179. *Ratio of international organizations headquartered at home to all international organizations joined* (difference from 0.5). Number of all intergovernmental and nongovernmental international organizations with main (not secondary) headquarters located within a country as a percentage of all such organizations joined by the country.
180. *Wars.* Military actions of one country vis-à-vis another in which troops constitute more than 0.2 percent of the country's population.
181. *Foreign military clashes.* Military actions of one country vis-à-vis another involving gunfire but less than .02 percent of the country's population are militarily engaged.
182. *Foreign killed.* Persons dying from direct violent interchange between countries ("violent interchange" includes "wars" and "foreign clashes" as defined in variables 180 and 181).
183. *Foreign killed* (percentage population). See variables 1 and 182.

DEFINITIONS OF SYSTEMIC VARIABLES

1. *Wars.* Number of fatal military quarrels involving the use of armed force between sovereign members in an international conflict subsystem involving more than 314 deaths (L. F. Richardson) or involving independent nation-states with declarations of war (Quincy Wright); an interconnected set of military confrontations with at least two belligerents (see variable 34 for definition of "member," variable 36 for definition of "sovereign").
2. *Subnational participants in war* (percent). The proportion of wars involving members below the level of a nation-state with sufficient military viability and autonomy to constitute distinct participants (see variable 1 for definition of "war").

3. *Members at war* (percent). International conflict subsystem members entering at least one war, percentaged across all members (see variable 34 for definition of "member").

4. *Extraregion wars* (percent). Wars taking place between members of subsystems and occurring outside the core geographic region of the subsystem, percentaged from the total number of wars inside and outside the subsystem.

5. *Extra-era wars* (percent). Wars in one era that either begin in an earlier era or end in a later era, percentaged from the total wars in that international conflict subsystem era.

6. *Poles.* The number of militarily separate and significant sources of power in an international conflict subsystem; the number of unaligned major powers, or number of rival alliances involving major powers, or number of blocs (see variable 89 for definition of "major power," variable 19 for definition of "alliance").

7. *War participants per members at war.* The number of belligerents participating on all sides of all wars in a subsystem, expressed as a ratio of all members involved in at least one war (see variable 1 for definition of "war").

8. *Dyads at war with similar languages* (percent). Two-member military confrontations in which the members speak languages of a similar linguistic origin, percentaged across all war dyads.

9. *Dyads at war with similar bodily characteristics* (percent). Two-member military confrontations in which the members are of a similar somatype, percentaged across all war dyads in a subsystem.

10. *Dyads at war with similar clothing* (percent). Two-member military confrontations in which the belligerents wear dress of a similar style, percentaged across all war dyads.

11. *Dyads at war with similar religions and philosophies* (percent). Two-member military confrontations in which the belligerents subscribe to similar ethical systems, percentaged across all war dyads.

12. *Dyads at war involving former enemies* (percent). Two-member military confrontations in which the belligerents have fought within the previous thirty years, percentaged across all war dyads.

13. *Wars per member.* The number of wars expressed as a ratio to the number of members of an international subsystem.

14. *Participants per war* (mean). The average number of parties in wars of an international conflict subsystem.

15. *Years per war* (mean). The average duration of wars, rounding a fraction of a year up to a full calendar year for each war.

16. *Years with new wars* (percent). The number of years in which at least one new war begins, percentaged across all years in an international subsystem era.

17. *Wars resulting in destabilization* (percent). Wars in which the outcome is favorable to an aggressor seeking to obtain a larger territorial domain or a stronger power position vis-à-vis the country being attacked, percentaged across all wars in the subsystem.

18. *Battle-related deaths per war* (mean). Average number of lives lost in all wars in an international conflict subsystem.

19. *Alliances.* The number of interstate accords in which two or more states agree to a specific foreign policy stance toward each other, especially one that avoids war between the two partners to the agreement, e.g., defensive pacts, nonaggression pacts, and ententes.

20. *Satellites.* Members of an international conflict subsystem that remain internally autonomous in form but have foreign policy decisions made by another country (see variable 34 for definition of "member").

21. *Pacts* (percent). Alliances in which the parties agree either to defend each other in case of an outside attack or not to make war on each other, percentaged across pacts and ententes, in which signatories informally pledge to consult with one another in a contingent eventuality (see variable 19 for definition of "alliance").

22. *Aligned members* (percent). Members of an international conflict subsystem that belong to at least one alliance, percentaged across all sovereign members of an international conflict subsystem (see variable 36 for definition of "sovereign").

23. *Extraregion alliances* (percent). Alliances between partners whose respective metropolitan areas are located in at least two different geographic regions, percentaged from all alliances involving members in an international conflict subsystem.

24. *Extra-era alliances* (percent). Alliances between members of an international conflict subsystem that either begin in an earlier era or end in a later era, percentaged across all alliances in that subsystem.

25. *New nongovernmental international organizations formed.* The number of private associations founded, members of which are located in more than three different countries of an international subsystem.

26. *Alliance partnerships/aligned members.* The number of partners in all alliances, expressed as a ratio to all members joining at least one alliance (see variable 19 for definition of "alliance").

27. *Nonaggression pacts* (percent). Neutrality alliances in which countries pledge to refrain from military intervention against any of the other signatories in the event they become engaged in war, percentaged across all alliances in the subsystem.

28. *Alliances/members.* The number of total alliances expressed as a ratio to all the sovereign members of an international conflict subsystem (see variable 36 for definition of "sovereign").

29. *Partners per alliance.* The number of parties in all alliances, expressed as a ratio to the total number of alliances in an international subsystem (see variable 19 for definition of "alliance").
30. *Alliance durations* (mean). The duration of alliances in calendar years (rounding up parts of a year to full years), expressed as a ratio to the total number of alliances.
31. *Years of alliance formation* (percent). The number of years in which at least one alliance is formed, percentaged from the total number of alliances in an international conflict subsystem.
32. *Defensive pacts* (percent). The number of alliances in which the partners agree to intervene with military force on behalf of the others in case of an attack on one of the partners, usually formed to inhibit or to deter aggression from other countries, percentaged across all alliances.
33. *Dyads at war involving former allies* (percent). Wars between countries that were alliance partners during the past 30 years, percentaged from all two-member military confrontations (see variable 7 for definition of "war").
34. *Members.* An actor that engages in a high level of interaction relevant to the issue-area defining the nature of the system—here, interaction related to international stratification and international conflict.
35. *Decision latitude.* The average amount of elite freedom to make foreign policy without consulting non-elites within an international subsystem (see decisionmaking variable 22).
36. *Sovereign members* (percent). Members that enjoy a high degree of decisionmaking autonomy in foreign affairs, excluding satellites and subnational members (see variable 2 for definition of "subnational entity," variable 34 for definition of "member").
37. *Members retaining sovereignty* (percent). Members sovereign throughout a subsystem era, percentaged across all members (see variable 36 for definition of "sovereign").
38. *Extraregion members* (percent). Members whose metropolitan areas lie outside the geographic region of an international conflict subsystem, percentaged across all members.
39. *Status scores for all members* (mean). Sum of all weighted indexes of the number and rank of diplomatic officials exchanged by all countries of an international conflict subsystem, divided by the total number of sovereign members (see variable 36 for definition of "sovereign").
40. *Total members/major and middle powers.* Ratio of total members to the number of countries capable of defeating any other power militarily except each other: (a) a *major power* can defeat a middle power; (b) a *middle power* can be defeated by only a major power and can defeat in turn only a minor power.

41. *Diversity in ways of life.* Absence of a common culture or we-feeling that unites members of an international subsystem together.

42. *Power orientation.* Absence of a legalistic orientation in which international law and custom are observed by members of an international subsystem; presence of a struggle for power in which few rules govern the interaction between states.

43. *Incompleteness of interaction.* Presence of broken links of communication among members of an international subsystem.

44. *Extent of rational calculation.* The extent to which rational, rather than emotional, considerations are invoked by the foreign affairs ethos pervading an international subsystem.

45. *Extent of internal preoccupation.* The extent to which areas outside the core region of an international subsystem are regarded as of routine and secondary importance, in comparison with the core region.

46. *Internal wars* (percent). The number of fatal quarrels involving only subnational entities in struggles against their own government, percentaged across all internal and other wars, as defined in variable 1 (variable 1 excludes "internal" types of wars).

47. *Interventions* (percent). Wars originally internal in form in which foreign powers enter to side for the government or for the domestic belligerent, percentaged across all wars (including internal wars).

48. *Foreign wars* (percent). The number of fatal quarrels initially involving no subnational entities, percentaged across all foreign wars, interventions, and internal wars.

49. *Deaths per internal war* (mean). The sum of persons losing their lives as a result of internal wars, expressed as a ratio to the number of internal wars (see variable 46 for definition of "internal war").

50. *Deaths per intervention* (mean). The sum of persons losing their lives as a result of interventions, expressed as a ratio to the number of interventions (see variable 47 for definition of "intervention").

51. *Insecure domestic elite tenure.* The average propensity of each member of an international subsystem to have the positions of their respective governmental leaders threatened by counterelites.

52. *Members initiating wars* (percent). Members waging wars aggressively vis-à-vis other members of an international conflict subsystem (see variable 1 for definition of "war").

53. *Minor powers allied with major powers.* The number of minor powers having at least one major power as an alliance partner (see variable 40 for definition of "minor power" and "major power").

54. *Minor powers in coalitions with major powers.* The number of minor powers fighting on the same side of at least one major power during a war.

55. *Pacts between major and minor powers* (percent). Pacts in which at

least one major and one minor power are partners, percentaged across all alliances with at least one major and one minor power (see variable 21 for definition of "pact").

56. *Coalitions including subnational partners* (percent). Number of sides in wars in which there is at least one nonsovereign partner, percentaged from the total number of sides in wars in which there is at least one minor power (see variable 2 for definition of "subnational").

57. *Minor powers in alliances with major powers* (percent). The number of minor powers belonging to at least one alliance with a major power, percentaged from the number of minor powers.

58. *Minor powers serving as coalition partners with major powers* (percent). The number of minor powers in at least one wartime coalition with a major power, percentaged from the number of minor powers.

59. *Extraregion alliances contracted by minor powers* (percent). The number of alliances in which there is at least one minor power and one extraregional partner, percentaged from the total number of alliances with at least one minor power as a partner.

60. *Extra-era coalitions between major and minor powers* (percent). Sides to wars in which there is at least one major power and one minor power and the war either starts in an earlier era or ends in a later era, percentaged across all coalitions in a subsystem era with at least one minor power partner.

61. *Extra-era alliances between major and minor powers* (percent). Alliances in which there is at least one major power and one minor power and the alliance either starts in an earlier era or ends in a later era, percentaged across all alliances in a subsystem era with at least one minor power partner.

62. *Minor power status scores* (mean). Status scores summed across all minor powers, expressed as a ratio to the total number of minor powers (see variable 39 for definition of "status score").

63. *Partnerships in major-minor alliances* (mean). The number of alliance partners in all alliances with at least one major and one minor power, expressed as a ratio to the total number of minor powers aligned with at least one major power.

64. *Partnerships in major-minor coalitions* (mean). The number of partners in all coalitions with at least one major and one minor power, expressed as a ratio to the total number of minor powers in at least one coalition with a major power.

65. *Nonaggression pacts between major and minor powers* (percent). Nonaggression pacts with at least one major and one minor power as partners, percentaged across all alliances between at least one major and one minor power.

66. *Alliances between major and minor powers per major and minor pow-*

ers. Alliances in which there is at least one major and one minor power as partners, expressed as a ratio to the total number of major and minor powers.

67. *Partnerships in alliances between major and minor powers.* Members of all alliances in which there is at least one major and one minor power as partners, expressed as a ratio to the number of alliances in which there is at least one major and one minor power.

68. *Durations of alliances between major and minor powers* (mean). Sum of all calendar years in each alliance involving at least one major and one minor power, expressed as a ratio to the number of alliances involving at least one major and one minor power.

69. *Durations of coalitions between major and minor powers* (mean). Sum of all calendar years in each wartime coalition involving at least one major and one minor power, expressed as a ratio to the number of coalitions involving at least one major and one minor power fighting on the same side in a war.

70. *Years in which major powers are newly aligned with minor powers* (percent). The number of years in which at least one minor or one major power enters into a new alliance arrangement with each other, percentaged across all years in the subsystem era.

71. *Years in which major powers are newly in coalitions with minor powers* (percent). The number of years in which at least one minor or one major power joins together in a coalition anew, percentaged across all years in the subsystem era.

72. *Wars started, per minor power, to destabilize.* Wars newly started by minor powers with an aim to destabilize an international conflict subsystem, expressed as a ratio to the total number of minor powers.

73. *Disturbance level.* The extent to which there are severe and repeated challenges to the regulator of an international conflict subsystem.

74. *Increase in disturbance.* The extent to which challenges to the regulator of an international conflict subsystem are of increasing intensity during a subsystem era.

75. *Defensive pacts between major and minor powers* (percentage of alliances). The number of defensive pacts in which at least one major and one minor power are partners, percentaged from the total number of alliances in which at least one major and one minor power are partners.

76. *Gatepassers.* Number of members of an international subsystem either beginning or terminating their membership.

77. *Sovereign gatepassers* (percent). Gatepassers that are sovereign during at least one year of an international conflict subsystem, percentaged from the total number of gatepassers.

78. *Gatepassers* (percent). See variables 34 and 76.

79. *Extraregion gatepassers* (percent). Number of gatepassers whose metropolitan areas lie outside the core geographic region of an international conflict subsystem, percentaged from the total number of gatepassers.

80. *Re-gatepassers* (percent). Gatepassers in a subsystem era that are also gatepassers in the following subsystem era of the same geographic region, percentaged from the total gatepassers in the first era.

81. *Gatepasser status scores* (mean). Status scores summed across all gatepassers, expressed as a ratio to the total number of gatepassers (see variable 39 for definition of "status score").

82. *Net gatepassers.* Number of new members of an international conflict subsystem minus the members departing from membership in an international conflict subsystem.

83. *Aligned gatepassers* (percent). Gatepassers that are partners in at least one alliance, percentaged from the total number of gatepassers.

84. *Alliances per gatepasser.* Number of alliances in which there is at least one gatepasser as a member, expressed as a ratio to the total number of gatepassers.

85. *Partnerships in alliance with gatepassers.* Number of partners of each alliance in which there is at least one gatepasser as a partner, expressed as a ratio to the total number of alliances with at least one gatepasser as a partner.

86. *Duration of postgatekeeping* (mean). Sum of years of membership for each gatepasser after the year of gatepassing up to either the time of re-gatepassing or to the last year of the international conflict subsystem, expressed as a ratio to the total number of gatepassers.

87. *Years of gatepassing* (percent). Number of years in which at least one member of an international subsystem engages in gatepassing, percentaged from the total number of years in the subsystem era.

88. *Violent gatepassers* (percent). Number of gatepassers whose gatepassing is due to war, percentaged from the total number of gatepassers.

89. *Major powers.* See variable 40.

90. *Exclusive major power pacts* (percent). Pacts in which only major powers are partners, percentaged from the total number of alliances with only major powers as partners.

91. *Major powers exclusively aligned with other major powers* (percent). The number of major powers that belong only to alliances with other major powers, percentaged from the total number of major powers.

92. *Major powers belonging to extraregion alliances* (percent). Number of major powers that belong to an alliance with at least one partner whose metropolitan area lies outside the core region of an interna-

tional conflict subsystem, percentaged from the total number of alliances with at least one major power partner.

93. *Extra-era major power alliances* (percent). Alliances with at least one major power partner that start in an earlier or end in a later subsystem era, percentaged from the total number of alliances with at least one major power partner.

94. *New intergovernmental international organizations formed.* The number of intergovernmental organizations to which at least three sovereign nation-states are members in which there are formal arrangements for institutional machinery that transcend the national level.

95. *Partners per alliances exclusively between major powers.* Partners in alliances with only major powers as members, expressed as a ratio to all major powers that are partners in at least one alliance.

96. *Nonaggression pacts exclusively between major powers* (percent). Nonaggression pacts with only major powers as partners, percentaged from the total number of alliances with major powers alone as partners.

97. *Alliances exclusively between major powers* (percent). Number of alliances in which major powers alone are partners, percentaged from the total number of alliances in which at least one major power is a partner.

98. *Partnerships in exclusive major power alliances* (mean). The number of partners in all alliances that contain only major powers as members, expressed as a ratio to all alliances that contain only major powers as partners.

99. *Durations of alliances exclusively between major powers* (mean). Sum of calendar years for each alliance with only major powers as partners, expressed as a ratio to the total number of alliances with only major powers as partners.

100. *Years with new alliances exclusively between major powers* (percent). The number of years in an international conflict subsystem era in which at least one alliance is begun to which only major powers are partners, percentaged from the number of years in the subsystem era.

101. *Defensive pacts exclusively between major powers* (percent). Number of defensive pacts in which major powers alone are partners, percentaged from the total number of alliances in which major powers alone are partners.

102. *Recruitees.* Powers crossing the threshold from or to middle power status (in either direction).

103. *Formal recruitees* (percent). Number of recruitees admitted, read-

mitted, or deleted from major or middle power status, percentaged from the total recruitees, including those promoted or demoted.

104. *Recruitees* (percent). See variables 34 and 102.

105. *Extraregion recruitees* (percent). Number of recruitees whose metropolitan area lies outside the geographic core of an international conflict subsystem, percentaged from the total number of recruitees.

106. *Status scores of recruitees* (mean). Sum of status scores of all recruitees, expressed as a ratio to the number of recruitees (see variable 39 for definition of "status score").

107. *Net major power recruitees* (percent). New major powers minus members of an international conflict subsystem that lose major power status, percentaged from the number of recruitees.

108. *Aligned recruitees* (percent). Recruitees in at least one alliance, percentaged from the total number of recruitees.

109. *Partnerships in alliance with recruitees* (mean). Number of partners in alliances with at least one recruitee, expressed as a ratio to all alliances in which at least one recruitee is a partner.

110. *Alliances per recruitee.* Alliances in which there is at least one recruitee as a member, expressed as a ratio to the total number of recruitees.

111. *Postrecruitment durations* (mean). Calendar years elapsing between the year in which a member of an international conflict subsystem becomes a recruitee and either the year it becomes a re-recruitee or the last year of the subsystem era (whichever comes first) expressed as a ratio to the number of recruitees.

112. *Years of recruitment* (percent). Number of calendar years in which at least one member of an international conflict subsystem becomes a recruitee, percentaged from the total years in the subsystem era.

113. *Violent recruitees* (percent). Number of members of an international conflict subsystem that become recruitees through war, percentaged from the total number of recruitees.

114. *Major and middle powers.* See variable 40.

115. *Extent of indirect supervision.* The extent to which major and minor powers collect information about power capabilities only as a by-product of their activities, rather than directly.

116. *Level of technology.* The extent of industrial and technological capabilities maintained throughout the members of an international conflict subsystem.

117. *Ratio of intraregion to extraregion supervision.* The extent to which supervision is aimed more vis-à-vis other countries in the geographic core of an international conflict subsystem, rather than toward countries outside the core.

118. *Status scores of major and middle powers* (mean). See variables 39 and 40.

119. *Ratio of major to middle powers.* Major powers, expressed as a ratio to middle powers (see variable 39 for definition of "major" and "middle" powers).

120. *Macrocentric supervision.* The extent to which information collected by major and middle powers is aimed at improving conditions within an international conflict subsystem as a whole, rather than used selfishly for the benefit of major or middle powers.

121. *Ratio between auditing and policing.* The extent to which major and middle powers collect information with an aim to monitor conditions, rather than to provide a basis for coercive relations with other members of the same international conflict subsystem.

122. *Extent of cooperation between major and middle powers.* The degree of mutual assistance and consultation on the part of major and minor powers.

123. *Ideological consonance.* Degree of agreement among major and middle powers on a single ethos guiding their respective foreign and domestic policies.

124. *Unavailability of resources.* The extent to which territory is completely appropriated, that is, claimed by existing members of an international conflict subsystem; absence of neutrals and new areas for colonization.

125. *Ease of legitimizing changes by major and middle powers.* The extent to which foreign policies pursued by major and middle powers are accepted as legitimate, rather than imposed by coercion.

126. *Postwar treaties.* The total number of treaties negotiated to terminate wars within an international conflict subsystem.

127. *Ratio between overt and covert rule-adapting.* The extent to which rules governing interstate interaction are changed by legal means, rather than by custom or by faits accomplis.

128. *Decrease in international law.* The extent to which international law is decreasingly developed and observed during an era of an international conflict subsystem.

129. *Extraregion postwar treaties* (percent). The number of treaties concluding wars in which there is at least one participant whose metropolitan era is outside the core region of an international conflict subsystem, percentaged from the total number of postwar treaties.

130. *Extra-era postwar treaties* (percent). The number of treaties concluding wars that started in an earlier subsystem era, percentaged from the number of all postwar treaties in that era.

131. *Lack of international tribunals.* Absence of regular international

tribunals to which members of an international conflict system could refer justiciable disputes.

132. *Looseness in polarity.* Presence of neutral powers mediating between, or nonaligned with, power blocs of countries.

133. *Ratio between realism and idealism.* The extent to which countries in an international conflict subsystem pursue their self-interest narrowly, rather than broadly.

134. *Extent of procedural rule-adapting.* The degree to which changes in rules governing interstate relations are procedural, rather than substantive, in nature.

135. *Lack of cooperation across poles.* The extent to which leaders and members of blocs of power stratification cooperate with each other.

136. *Ratio between instrumental and ideological rule-adapting.* The extent to which changes in rules governing interstate relations are in accordance with pragmatic versus absolute-value considerations.

137. *Years with wars concluded by treaties* (percent). The number of calendar years in which at least one treaty concludes a war, percentaged from the total number of years in the international conflict subsystem era.

138. *Wars not concluded by treaties* (percent). Wars not terminated by treaty, percentaged from the total number of wars.

139. *Wars with major powers.* The number of wars in which there is at least one major power as a participant.

140. *Wars involving major powers and subnational powers* (percentage of major power wars). The number of wars in which there is at least one major power and one nonsovereign participant, percentaged from the total number of wars involving at least one major power.

141. *War entries by major powers* (mean). The number of instances of participation by major powers, expressed as a ratio to the number of major powers.

142. *Imperial wars* (percent). The number of wars in which a recognized state seeks to expand at the expense of peoples not recognized as a state, percentaged from the total number of wars in an international conflict subsystem era.

143. *Extraregion wars with major powers* (percent). Wars taking place outside the core region of an international conflict subsystem with at least one major power as a participant, percentaged from the number of wars with at least one major power participant.

144. *Extra-era wars with major powers* (percent). Wars with at least one major power participant in which the war either begins in an earlier subsystem era or ends in a later era of an international conflict sub-

system, percentaged from the total number of wars with at least one major power participant.

145. *Presence of regulator institution.* The presence of an institutionalized mechanism for equilibrating power stratification in an international conflict subsystem.

146. *Wars with major powers on opposite sides* (percent). Number of wars in which at least one major power is on at least two sides of the war, percentaged from the number of wars in which at least one major power is a participant.

147. *Wars exclusively between major powers* (percent). Wars in which the only participants are major powers, percentaged from the total number of wars with at least one major power participant.

148. *Wars with major powers aiming to destabilize* (percent). Wars involving at least one major power that hopes to obtain a larger territorial domain at the expense of the country attacked, percentaged from the number of wars in which at least one major power is a participant.

149. *Wars per major power* (mean). Wars with at least one major power participant, expressed as a ratio to all major powers.

150. *Wars involving major powers ended by treaties* (percent). Wars with at least one major power participant that are concluded by treaties, percentaged from the total number of wars with at least one major power participant.

151. *Participants per wars involving major powers* (mean). Number of countries involved in wars where there is at least one major power participant, expressed as a ratio to the number of wars with at least one major power participant.

152. *Durations of wars with major powers* (mean). Sum of calendar years for each war in which there is at least one major power participant, expressed as a ratio to the number of wars with at least one major power participant.

153. *Years with new wars involving major powers* (percent). The number of years with at least one new war involving a major power, percentaged from the number of years in the international conflict subsystem era.

154. *Wars with major powers resulting in destabilization* (percent). Wars in which at least one major power succeeds in gaining territory at the expense of another country as the spoils of war, percentaged from the total wars in which there is at least one major power participant.

155. *Wars initiated by major powers.* Number of wars started by at least one major power.

156. *Wars initiated by major powers involving subnational participants* (percent). Wars started by at least one major power in which there

is at least one nonsovereign participant, percentaged from the number of wars started by at least one major power.

157. *War initiations per major power* (mean). Number of instances in which major powers start wars, expressed as a ratio to the number of major powers.

158. *Extraregion wars initiated by major powers* (percent). Number of wars started by major powers outside the main geographic region of the international conflict subsystem, percentaged from the total number of wars started by major powers.

159. *Extra-era wars initiated by major powers* (percent). Number of wars started by major powers in an earlier era or terminating in a later era, percentaged from the total number of wars started by major powers in the subsystem era.

160. *Strength of regulator.* Effectiveness of power wielded by a regulator of an international conflict subsystem in maintaining an equilibrium in power stratification.

161. *Wars initiated by major powers opposing other major powers* (percent). Wars started by at least one major power with at least one major power on the opposite side of the war, percentaged from the number of wars started by at least one major power.

162. *Wars initiated by major powers to destabilize* (percent). Wars started by at least one major power for the purpose of extending its domain at the expense of another country, percentaged from the total number of wars started by at least one major power.

163. *Wars initiated by major powers ending in treaties* (percent). Wars started by at least one major power that are concluded by treaties, percentaged from the number of wars started by at least one major power.

164. *Wars initiated per major power* (mean). Number of wars started by at least one major power, expressed as a ratio to the total number of major powers.

165. *Partners in coalitions initiated by major powers* (mean). Number of members of coalitions containing at least one major power that starts the war, expressed as a ratio to the total number of wars started by at least one major power.

166. *Durations of wars initiated by major powers* (mean). Sum of calendar years of all wars that are started by at least one major power, expressed as a ratio to the number of wars started by at least one major power.

167. *Years with wars initiated by majors* (percent). Number of years in which at least one major power starts a war, percentaged from the total number of years in an international conflict subsystem.

168. *Wars initiated by major powers resulting in destabilization* (per-

cent). Wars started by at least one major power that results in an expansion of territory at the expense of the defeated countries, percentaged from the number of wars started by at least one major power.

169. *Wars won by major powers.* The number of wars in which at least one major power is on the victorious side.

170. *Wars won by major powers involving subnational members* (percent). Wars in which at least one major power is on the victorious side and at least one nonsovereign member is involved, percentaged from the total number of wars won by major powers.

171. *Victories achieved per major power* (mean). Number of instances in which major powers are on the winning side of wars, expressed as a ratio to the total number of major powers.

172. *Extraregion wars won by major powers* (percent). Number of wars in which at least one major power is on the winning side of a war fought outside the main region of an international conflict subsystem, percentaged from the total number of wars in which at least one major power is on the winning side of a war.

173. *Extra-era wars won by major powers* (percent). Number of wars in which at least one major power is on the winning side of a war that either begins in an earlier or ends in a later international conflict subsystem era, percentaged from the total number of wars in which at least one major power is on the winning side.

174. *Increase in regulator capacity.* A condition in which the regulator equilibrating power stratification within an international subsystem gains increasing capability to equilibrate during the era.

175. *Wars won by major powers opposing other major powers* (percent). Wars in which at least one major power is both on a winning and on a defeated side of a war in an international conflict subsystem, percentaged from the number of wars in which at least one major power is on the winning side.

176. *Wars won by major powers aiming to destabilize* (percent). Wars in which at least one major power is on the same side of a war that both is victorious and seeks to gain territory at the expense of the defeated side, percentaged from the total number of wars in which at least one major power is on the winning side.

177. *Wars won by major powers* (mean). Number of wars in which at least one major power is on the winning side, expressed as a ratio to the total number of major powers.

178. *Partners in winning coalitions with major powers* (mean). The number of countries on the winning side of a war in which at least one major power is a coalition partner, expressed as a ratio to the total

number of wars in which at least one major power is on the winning side.

179. *Durations of wars won by major powers* (mean). Sum of calendar years for all wars in which at least one major power is on the winning side, expressed as a ratio to wars in which at least one major power is on the winning side.

180. *Years with wars won by major powers* (percent). The number of years in which there is at least one war won by a side that has at least one major power, percentaged from the total number of years in the international conflict subsystem.

181. *Wars won by major powers resulting in destabilization* (percent). Number of wars in which at least one major power is on the side that wins by gaining territory at the expense of the defeated side, percentaged from the number of wars in which at least one major power is on the winning side.

182. *International instability.* The propensity for an equilibrium in power stratification at the beginning of an international subsystem to be under continual challenge.

183. *Duration of subsystem.* Total years in an international conflict subsystem era.

appendix C
Definitions
of Factors and Clusters

DECISIONMAKING FACTORS AND CLUSTERS

Q-Factors (first-order)

    I.   *Demarche.* A course of action involving a dramatic shift in policy, involving risks.

    II. *Debacle.* A miscalculated decision resulting in the defeat of an agent.

    III. *Status Clarification.* A decision in which power relations between an agent and a target become defined less ambiguously through a pragmatic conception of the role of the target.

    IV. *Value Reaffirmation.* A decision in which basic principles underlying institutions are reasserted through a nonpragmatic conception of the role of the target.

    V. *Target-Stabilizing.* A decision in which the entity affected directly by the agent is solidified.

    VI. *Armistice.* A decision in which agent and target call off hostilities without achieving a permanent settlement of the conflict.

    VII. *Aggressive(ness).* A decision in which the agent initiates violent acts against the target.

    VIII. *Detente.* A decision in which an agent deescalates or relaxes relations formerly strained with the target.

    IX. *Overcautious.* A decision in which the agent prefers to take few risks but fails to undertake the expense of verifying the truth of its perceptions concerning the situation.

Q-Factors (second-order)

I. *Institutionalization.* A class of decisions pertaining to situations where habituation to the routine of a decisionmaking body is reaffirmed or increased.

II. *Strategic.* A class of decisions where the scope and implications are broad.

III. *Instability.* A class of decisions in which the integrity and viability of an agent or target is in jeopardy.

Q-Clusters (first-order)

I. *Demarche.* Same as first-order Q-Factor I.

II. *Deescalation.* A decision in which an agent and target reduce threats to each other.

III. *Destructive.* A decision in which the agent endangers the existence of the target but simultaneously overcommits resources to the struggle.

IV. *Conflict-Terminating.* A decision in which discrepancies in policies are settled.

Q-Clusters (second-order)

I. *Level of Conflict.* The extent to which a decision involves a widening in the scope and salience of a conflict situation.

Q-Clusters (third-order)

I. *Mode of Resolution.* The extent to which a decision includes violence as a salient element in terminating the conflict.

R-Factors (first-order)

I. *Crisis.* The extent to which a decision is perceived as cognitively and affectively important.

II. *Bottleneck(ed).* The extent to which a decision process flows through bureaucratic channels and is lengthened thereby.

III. *Clientele.* The extent to which the agent making a decision acts in a fiduciary role vis-à-vis the target.

IV. *Rationality.* The extent to which a maximum amount of relevant information is processed and succeeds in reducing stereotypy on the part of an agent.

V. *Collegial.* The extent to which a decision is made by a group of peers, rather than imposed hierarchically.

VI. *Watershed.* The extent to which values and preferences are reversed subsequent to a decision.

VII. *Implementation Complexity.* The extent to which a decision must be carried out with many, rather than few, operations.

VIII. *Successful.* The extent to which a decisional outcome leads to desired ends and is consistent with high priority goals.

IX. *Unexpected.* The extent to which the occasion for a decision is a surprise.

X. *History-Mindedness.* The extent to which precedent is irrevocably invoked as a basis for a decision.

XI. *Pragmatism.* The extent to which information relevant to a decision is processed with a view toward achieving concrete objectives.

XII. *Multi-Issue.* The extent to which a decision involves several substantive issues and cognitive tasks.

XIII. *Imperious.* The extent to which a decision is made with minimal consultation by the agent with the target.

XIV. *Ethnographic Extensiveness.* The extent to which there is an abundance of information about a decision.

XV. *Consensus.* The extent to which decisions are reached through thorough discussion and unanimous consent within the agent.

XVI. *Aggressiveness.* Same as first-order Q-Factor VII.

XVII. *Academic Source.* The extent to which material about a decision has been examined by an academician and social scientist.

R-Factors (second-order)

I. *Channelled.* The extent to which a decision is referred to legitimate institutional bodies.

II. *Disputatiousness.* The extent to which the participants in a decision process are in disagreement over goals and means.

III. *Tactical.* The extent to which the scope and implications of a decision are narrow and subsidiary to other decisions.

IV. *Polyarchic.* The extent to which a decision is made after a process of bargaining or consultation with all relevant interests.

V. *Adaptiveness.* The extent to which a decision constitutes an adjustive, information-seeking response to an unexpectedly new situation.

VI. *Coup.* The extent to which a decision, made by an agent sharing a wide consensus, in fact achieves an objective through coercive means.

R-Factors (third-order)

I. *Incremental.* A class of characteristics pervading a decision process that denotes attention to short-range rather than comprehensive means and goals.

II. *Resolvative.* A class of characteristics pervading a decision process that denotes a stress on terminating a conflict and reintegrating an agent with a target.

R-Clusters (first-order)

I. *Bottlenecked.* Same as first-order R-Factor II.

II. *Cognitive Differentiation.* The extent to which a decision is multifaceted—that is, involving several issues —and consideration by decisionmakers takes the complexity into account.

III. *Clientele.* Same as first-order R-Factor III.

IV. *Solidarity.* The extent to which a decision is made by a group of peers who are of like mind in appraising the situation.

V. *Precipitate.* The extent to which a decision is made in a hurry yet has a short-term impact on the target.

VI. *Assiduous.* The extent to which an agent considers many intellectual facets of a decision in order to maximize his values.

VII. *Time Concern.* The extent to which a decision is of historical importance, marking the boundary between periods of history.

VIII. *Implementation Complexity.* Same as first-order R-Factor VII.

IX. *Showdown.* The extent to which a decision constitutes a significant salvo in a struggle for power, in which risks are taken and violence is employed.

R-Clusters (second-order)

I. *Imperative.* The extent to which a stimulus to a decision is viewed as requiring an immediate response.

II. *Machiavellian.* The extent to which a decision involves manipulating a target and using any means needed to achieve supremacy.

R-Clusters (third-order)

I. *Ordinary.* A class of characteristics denoting components of routine decisionmaking processes.

II. *Extraordinary.* A class of characteristics denoting components of decisions where the situation has evoked a departure from routine processes.

SOCIETAL FACTORS AND CLUSTERS

Q-Factors (first-order)

I. *Centrifugal.* A characteristic of a country that has extreme difficulties in maintaining itself internally.

II. *Politicoeconomic Development.* A characteristic of a country that has the capability of accomplishing a wide range of political and economic tasks.

III. *Lack of Modernization.* A characteristic of a country that fails to keep pace technologically with other countries.

IV. *Latin American.* Countries with multiracial populations, high illegitimacy, high homicide rates, low divorce rates, low suicide rates.

V. *Neocolonial Dependency.* A characteristic of a country in which political and economic functions of a country are being performed by a foreign power.

VI. *Open Societies.* A characteristic of a country in which government is weak: opposition to the government is found alongside high rates of crime.

VII. *Lack of Intergroup Accommodation.* A characteristic of a country in which intercultural communication is infrequent, while minority groups pursue separatist goals.

VIII. *Societal Paralysis.* A characteristic of a country in which contending forces strive to achieve dominance through internal wars of attrition.

Q-Factors (second-order)

I. *Dionysian.* A stratum of countries in which immediate gratification and pleasure-seeking are basic characteristics.

II. *Apollonian.* A stratum of countries in which the virtue of long-range planning for the attainment of goals is stressed.

III. *Lack of Modernization.* Same as first-order Q-Factor III.

IV. *Lack of Intergroup Accommodation.* Same as first-order Q-Factor VII.

V. *Neocolonial Dependency.* Same as first-order Q-Factor V.

Q-Factors (third-order)

I. *Disunited.* A stratum of countries in which the failure in welding together a nationalist sentiment is associated with a failure to achieve modernization.

II. *Activism.* A stratum of countries in which apollonianism is strong and dionysianism is weak.

Q-Clusters (first-order)

I. *Non-Western Centrifugal.* Same as first-order Q-Factor I, applying only to non-Western countries.

II. *Latin American.* Same as first-order Q-Factor IV.

III. *Closed Polities.* A characteristic of a country in which civil liberties and constitutional guarantees for an opposition are not observed.

IV. *Neocolonial Dependency.* Same as first-order Q-Factor V.

V. *Modernized.* Reverse of first-order Q-Factor III.

VI. *Economic Underdevelopment.* A characteristic of a country in which the tempo of economic progress is slow.

VII. *Political Underdevelopment.* A characteristic of a country in which there is a slow tempo in a government's drive to acquire more capacity to bring about change.

Q-Clusters (second-order)

I. *Centrifugal.* Same as first-order Q-Factor I.

Q-Clusters (third-order)

I. *Pattern Maintenance.* A stratum of countries in which internal difficulties are perceived as posing threats to the stability of the regime.

Q-Clusters (fourth-order)

    I.   *System-Wide Planning*. A stratum of countries in which goals are set for the maintenance or modernization of the society.

    II. *Underdeveloped*. A stratum of countries in which neither the economic nor the political system has a capacity for accomplishing system-wide objectives.

R-Factors (first-order)

    I.   *Sparse Social Communication*. A condition in which communication media usage is low in density and frequency.

    II.   *Despotism*. A condition in which political decisions are made by a single ruler or clique without due regard for the sentiments of other groups or persons.

    III. *Nonconflictual Domestic Political Behavior*. A condition in which a country is free from antigovernment demonstrations, riots, assassinations, general strikes, government crises, and guerrilla warfare.

    IV. *Separatism*. A condition in which an ethnic group seeks self-rule, rather than remaining subject to the rule of a people with foreign ethnicity.

    V.   *Monoracial Unity*. A condition in which a country contains one main ethnic group and channels conflict through institutions that are regarded widely as legitimate.

    VI. *Centripetal*. A condition in which a country easily maintains itself internally while assuming a leadership role in foreign affairs.

    VII. *Takeoff Stage*. A condition in which a country has achieved political institutions, social arrangements, and technological capacity to launch a drive toward an economy with a self-sustained rate of growth.

    VIII. *Politicoeconomic Paralysis*. Reverse of first-order Q-Factor II.

    IX. *Equalitarian*. A condition in which economic resources are distributed almost equally to each person in a country.

    X.   *Permeability*. A condition in which the borders of a country are easily and frequently crossed, especially by migrants and trade.

    XI. *Nonextractive*. A condition in which a government is unable to obtain tax revenues sufficient to finance a high level of governmental expenditures.

XII.   *Absentee Landlordism.* A condition in which landowners are distant from their tenants.

XIII. *Rural Austerity.* A condition in which a high proportion of a population lives outside major cities, has insufficient food, and governmental expenditures are at a low level.

XIV.   *Political Competition.* A condition in which there are many political parties, downfalls of cabinets, and counterelites seek to overthrow the regime.

XV.   *Nonconflictual Foreign Behavior.* A condition in which a country abstains from foreign wars, clashes, military mobilizations, and military expenditures.

XVI.   *Unguided Development.* A condition in which economic development proceeds with neither a developmental ideology nor a mobilizational system style.

XVII. *Modernizing Oligarchy.* A condition in which development is spearheaded by initiatives on the part of government leaders in whom considerable power is centralized.

XVIII. *Societal Tension.* A condition in which the presence of heterogeneous social groups is associated with suicides, accident proneness, Communist voting, and sectional discrimination.

XIX.   *Discontentment With Laxity.* A condition in which economic and governmental inefficiency and stagnation is associated with instability in the position of chief executive.

XX.   *Reactionary Development.* A condition in which economic growth proceeds in the absence of educational development.

XXI.   *Elite Scapegoatism.* A condition in which economic stagnation is associated with militarization, purges, expulsions and recalls of diplomats.

XXII. *Developmental Slowdown.* A condition in which technological, economic, and educational development have stagnated while the country has enough automobiles to experience a high rate of deaths due to accidents involving motor vehicles.

XXIII. *Domestic Disengagement.* A condition in which new experiences—marriages, economic growth, moviegoing, and military expenditures—are avoided while government undergoes crises and reorganization.

XXIV. *Internationally Guided Development.* A condition in which a large input of foreign aid is associated with a large increase in agricultural employment, bringing the amount of arable land up to the amount of nonarable land.

XXV. *Patriarchical Rule.* A condition in which rulers enjoy a long tenure in office and stability characterizes the social and political systems.

XXVI. *Lack of Professional Expertise.* A condition in which physicians, investors, entrepreneurs, and political leaders are in short supply, leaving the door open to centralized military rule.

XXVII. *Unstructured.* A condition in which a country imposes so few constraints on itself that few persons develop ulcers and alcoholism problems, while illegitimacy rates are high and Communist adherents are free to vote for Communist candidates.

XXVIII. *Modernizing Welfare Statism.* A condition in which governmental expenditures are growing rapidly, especially in the fields of welfare and education.

XXIX. *Labor Unrest Amid Affluence.* A condition in which prosperity is increasing but there is much employment and strikes are widespread.

XXX. *Governmental Philistinism.* A condition in which government responds to prosperity only in the area of military preparations.

XXXI. *Solidarity.* A condition in which a country joins a military bloc and supplies many troops thereto, in which divorces are rare, and where the population is not divided into political factions.

XXXII. *Cathectic Involvement.* A condition in which emotional attachments form the basis for political party leadership, suicides are frequent, religious groups and strikes are numerous yet economic and political conditions are in actuality quiescent.

XXXIII. *Bourgeois Revolution.* A condition in which bloody civil warfare is associated with the absence of land reform programs and little economic development.

XXXIV. *Phenotypic Symmetry.* A condition in which there is homogeneity and similarity within the population regarding such acquired characteristics as language, nationality, and religious preference.

XXXV. *Developmental Junta.* A condition in which governmental and economic development are associated with an illegal coup by military authorities to wrest control

from a weak political system that frightens away potential foreign investors.

XXXVI. *Evenness in Development.* A condition in which economic development benefits no single main city.

XXXVII. *Reorganization-Mindedness.* A condition in which new
government ministries are created, revolutions are frequent, diets are improving in nutrition, and urbanization increases even though politicization is at a low
level.

XXXVIII. *Incorporative Articulation.* A condition in which a colonial power, which provides considerable foreign aid
and receives large numbers of immigrants, faces widespread strikes at home for which it obviously has resources to meet the demands of workers.

XXXIX. *Unenlightened Rebellion.* A condition in which a new
government has seized power, despite the existence of
many political parties, yet has a high minimum voting
age, library books are not in wide circulation, and literacy levels are not on the increase.

XL. *Sustained Industrialization.* A condition in which technological development increases while national income
is stable—that is, unchanged.

XLI. *Neocolonialism.* A condition in which there is a severe
imbalance between exports and imports in a country
lacking political and economic growth.

XLII. *Guided Democracy.* A condition in which political free-
doms are curtailed while economic development is
increasing.

XLIII. *Entrepreneurial Development.* A condition in which
economic development favors the middle class at the
expense of the lower classes, in which foreign investment is heavy but general strikes are common.

R-Factors (second-order)

I. *Political Asymmetry.* A condition in which political
conditions are unstable, in a state of paralysis, and only
a few persons have professional qualifications to operate an administrative system.

II. *Societal Expansiveness.* A condition in which a country has reached a stage of takeoff into rapid economic
growth, especially by stressing the role of education.

III. *Social Symmetry.* A condition in which a population
is homogeneous and similar in social composition,

while lacking unrest among minority groups or other strata.

IV. *Laissez-faire Development.* A condition in which developmental processes are present but neither political leadership nor social solidarity is present.

V. *Volatility.* A condition in which a country has a multinational ethnic base, has centrifugal tendencies, and cannot attract foreign assistance in sufficient quantities.

VI. *Directive Rule.* A condition in which despotic rulers are unresponsive to demands made by non-elites on the political system and insist upon implementing their own conceptions.

VII. *Dialectical Development.* A condition in a country with one main population center wherein there is intense political competition and entrepreneurial development despite a slow tempo in development.

VIII. *Political Incrementalism.* A country in which there is a low propensity for political reorganization despite a high level of political competition.

IX. *Neocolonialism.* See first-order R-Factor XLI.

X. *Nontraditional Rule.* A condition in which there are few absentee landlords, for there is an equalitarian distribution of land, and government emerges from a crisis situation in which progress in economic growth had declined.

XI. *Modernizing Clique Rule.* A condition in which technological development assumes a high priority while affairs of government are handled by a dedicated cadre of leaders.

XII. *Lack of a Redistribution Crisis.* A condition in which government leaders, accustomed to a limited role for the government during eras of an economic upswing, are faced with neither an economic downswing nor insistent demands for the redistribution of income to include a larger share for the working class.

XIII. *Autarkic Economy.* A condition in which a country is neither economically advanced nor exploited.

XIV. *Disunited Scarcity.* A condition in which a country with low economic development and cultural diversity faces difficulties of political unrest and disorganization.

XV. *Aggressiveness.* A condition in which a country is likely to enter foreign conflict or to have domestic unrest.

XVI. *Subjectivism.* A condition in which affective orientations permeate social and political activities.

R-Factors (third-order)

I. *Disintegrative.* A class of characteristics pertaining to political systems in turmoil, social systems that are divisive, and downswings in economic systems.

II. *Administrative Inactivity.* A class of characteristics pertaining to polities where demands upon the bureaucracy are far below capabilities.

III. *Elite Development.* A class of characteristics pertaining to political systems where rule is authoritarian, the economy is on the verge of takeoff, and where international influences are strong.

IV. *Ideologism.* A class of characteristics pertaining to countries where social preferences are strongly held, there is considerable tension between rightism and leftism on political matters, and where the fate of the economy is tied to external political commitments.

V. *Change Orientation.* A class of characteristics pertaining to a country that is tied to neocolonial domination despite aggressive and revolutionary moves in its recent political history.

VI. *Non-Harmonizing Rule.* A class of characteristics pertaining to a situation in which modernizing clique rule proceeds in a country without social unrest or cultural diversity.

R-Factors (fourth-order)

I. *Task Orientation.* A class of societal characteristics denoting the primacy of attaining concrete objectives over the long run.

II. *Social-Emotional Orientation.* A class of societal characteristics denoting the primacy of expressing or manifesting displeasure and attaining short-range gratification of desires.

R-Clusters (first-order)

I. *Urban Sophistication.* A condition in which most of the population lives in cities and has broken traditional ties.

II. *Politicization.* A condition in which the population is politically active and accustomed to a large role for government in society.

III. *Dense Social Communication.* Reverse of first-order R-Factor I.

IV.   *Resource Mobilization.* A condition in which resources of a country are intensively exploited.

V.   *Braintrust Development.* A condition in which developmental processes are proceeding but elite elements control power.

VI.   *Articulation.* A condition in which groups make demands upon the government.

VII. *Legalistic.* A condition in which law pervades a society, with orderly processes of change.

VIII. *Structured.* Reverse of first-order R-Factor XXVII.

IX.   *Cultural Unity.* A condition in which most persons belong to the dominant ethnic and linguistic groups and sectionalism in absent.

X.   *Multipartism.* A condition in which there are many political parties, each performing the function of aggregation.

XI.   *Constitutionalism.* Reverse of first-order R-Factor II.

XII. *Multiracial Disparity.* A condition in which there are many racial groups and inequalities in land ownership.

XIII. *Political Fragility.* A condition in which constitutional forms are unlikely to persist because of extraconstitutional inputs and political instability.

XIV. *Noncolonial Inequality.* A condition in which there is an unequal distribution of resources within a noncolonial country.

XV.   *Traditional Society.* A condition in which a traditional bureaucracy governs over a rural, illiterate, unskilled population, deriving its revenue from indirect taxes.

XVI. *Separatism.* Same as first-order R-Factor IV.

XVII. *Penetrable.* A condition in which a political system is operated partly by a foreign power, while roads are clogged with automobiles and political parties are not just aggregators of interests.

XVIII. *Despotism.* Same as first-order R-Factor II.

XIX. *Bourgeois Revolution.* Same as first-order R-Factor XXXIII.

XX.   *Disruptive Political Activism.* Reverse of first-order R-Factor III.

XXI. *Class Struggle.* A condition in which wage-earners are on strike, most farms are rented, and politics engenders images of fear and stereotypy.

XXII. *Garrison State Development.* A condition in which the military sector of a population is increased in number and through economic rewards.

XXIII. *Power Orientation.* A condition in which a country, by dint of its position as leader of a bloc, resorts to measures just short of war while stereotyping its international rival.

XXIV. *Ethnic-Religious Diversity.* A condition in which the population of a country contains several ethnic and religious groups.

XXV. *Foreign Conflict.* Reverse of first-order R-Factor XV.

XXVI. *Takeoff Stage.* Same as first-order R-Factor VII.

XXVII. *Oligarchic Development.* A condition in which there is rule by a patriarchical elite over a heterogeneous population, though education is stressed despite lack of financial resources.

XXVIII. *Monoculture Society.* A condition in which there is one main ethnic group and religion, as well as one geographic focus of power in the political system.

R-Clusters (second-order)

I. *Secularization.* A condition in which traditional and religious influences have been replaced by values of modernity and legitimate political activity.

II. *Technological Development.* A condition in which resources are being utilized to the fullest, including communication facilities.

III. *Formalism.* A condition in which procedures are maintained as a matter of conventional propriety.

IV. *Unified Society.* A condition in which there is one dominant culture to which nearly everyone belongs, with the result that there is widespread consensus on goals.

V. *Polyarchy.* A condition in which decisions emerging from a political system meet the approval of a large number of powerful groups, all within a constitutional framework.

VI. *Revolutionary.* A condition in which political instability is associated with social and economic inequality.

VII. *Multinational Discrimination.* A condition in which a traditionalist polity rules over a people seeking autonomy or separatist goals.

VIII. *Neoprotectorate.* A condition in which a despotic elite handles domestic affairs, inviting foreign intervention on its behalf in return for which defense against foreign invasion is guaranteed.

IX. *Domestic Turmoil.* A condition in which domestic conflict is disruptive, revolution by or against the bourgeoisie is likely, and a class struggle is being waged.

X. *Zerosum Politics.* A condition in which many groups confront one another, and the military is active internally and aggressive externally.

XI. *Elite Development.* A condition in which economic growth is spearheaded by an oligarchy within a society with few genotypic differences.

R-Clusters (third-order)

I. *Bureaucratized Productivity.* A class of characteristics identifying a country wherein technological change is associated with agreement among a culturally unified society on rule by law.

II. *Prenationalist Internal Turbulence.* A class of characteristics identifying a country in which nationalist sentiment is dormant but revolution is recurrent or incipient.

III. *Control Orientation.* A class of characteristics identifying a country in which the maintenance of domestic political order—or control of the political arena—is of paramount importance.

Q-Clusters (fourth-order)

I. *Liberal Democratic Sustained Modernization.* A stratum of characteristics identifying a country with economic growth, political democracy, social uniformity, rule of law, civil rights, and an urbanized population.

II. *Directive But Faltering Modernization.* A stratum of characteristics identifying a country with economic stagnation, political instability, intense class differences, extraconstitutional political acts by a dominant elite to suppress counterelites, and aggressive foreign involvements.

SYSTEMIC FACTORS AND CLUSTERS

Q-Factors (first-order Richardson)

I. *Premodern.* A class of international subsystems formed before the technological advances of the late nineteenth century.

II. *Modern.* A class of international subsystems formed after the technological advances of the late nineteenth century.

III. *Elite Stabilization.* A class of international subsystems in which the elites actively attempt to stabilize interstate relations.

Q-Factors (first-order Wright)

I. *Concert.* A class of international subsystems in which major powers agree to cooperate together.

II. *Early State System.* A class of international subsystems formed in Europe before the nineteenth century, in Asia before the twentieth century, when the concept of the nation-state was not accepted widely.

III. *Modern.* Same as first-order Richardson Q-Factor II.

IV. *Elite Stabilization.* Same as first-order Richardson Q-Factor III.

Q-Clusters (first-order Richardson)

I. *Stabilizing.* A class of international subsystems in which international violence is at a low level and the regulator is effective.

II. *Modern.* Same as first-order Richardson Q-Factor II.

III. *Early State System.* Same as first-order Wright Q-Factor II.

Q-Clusters (first-order Wright)

I. *Early State System.* Same as first-order Wright Q-Factor II.

II. *Concert.* Same as first-order Wright Q-Factor I.

III. *Modern.* Same as first-order Richardson Q-Factor II.

R-Factors (first-order Wright)

I. *Alliance Nonsaturation.* A condition in which few countries belong to alliances in an international subsystem.

II. *Lack of War Disturbance.* A condition in which few wars occur and there is little destabilization in an international subsystem.

III. *Bloc Rivalry.* A condition in which dyads inconclusively fight wars over and over, while alliances include countries of high as well as low status in an international subsystem.

IV. *Peaceful Gatekeeping.* A condition in which new members enter an international subsystem but not by violence.

V. *Lack of Concert Pacification.* A condition in which major powers tend not to be aligned with each other; though there are few wars, the wars destabilize the international subsystem.

VI. *Elite Membership Linkage.* A condition in which there are many diplomatic contacts, and alliance ties are especially dense among major powers in an international subsystem.

VII. *Fratricidal Conflict.* A condition in which there are many wars between countries sharing the same philosophical or religious outlooks, while there are alliances long in duration and exclusively involving the major powers of an international subsystem.

VIII. *Noncosmopolitan.* A condition in which there is little ideological agreement or exogenous alliance linkage, with resources available for expansion within the international subsystem.

IX. *Temporal Continuity.* A condition in which membership does not change and there are few wars that are legacies from previous eras or continue into succeeding eras of international subsystems.

X. *Aggressive Alliance.* A condition in which multilateral alliances fail to serve as deterrents to war, gatepassers not joining such alliances in an international subsystem.

XI. *Imbalance of Power.* A condition in which there is no institutional regulator but many wars in an international subsystem.

XII. *Short Subsystem Duration.* A condition in which the power constellation of an international subsystem is eroded quickly.

XIII. *Internal Discord.* A condition in which internal warfare is prevalent among members of an international subsystem.

XIV. *Pragmatism.* A condition in which realistic, rather than idealistic, definitions of national interest guide foreign policy; most countries retain sovereign status, and there is little disturbance during the international subsystem.

XV. *Successful Major Power Wars.* A condition in which there are many wars started and won by major powers in an international subsystem.

XVI. *Elite Expansion.* A condition in which recruitment activity is at a high point as well as behavior outside the geographic confines of an international subsystem.

XVII. *Multipolar Disequilibrium.* A condition in which there are many poles as well as wars between major powers in an international subsystem.

R-Factors (second-order Wright)

I. *Incorporativeness.* A class of variables characterizing international subsystems with cosmopolitan and pragmatic outlooks, wherein new members join through peaceful means.

II. *Protracted Violence.* A class of variables denoting that there is a long international subsystem containing many wars.

III. *Schismatism.* A class of characteristics denoting fratricidal domestic and internal conflicts with few alliances and linkages between elites of an international subsystem.

IV. *Hierarchy.* A class of characteristics denoting cross-bloc linkage and cooperation, but wars are handled separately by the major powers.

V. *Empire-Building.* A class of characteristics denoting expansion by elites, through successful wars and in the absence of regulatory institutions within an international subsystem.

VI. *Stabilization.* A class of variables denoting few instances of aggression and much continuity in an international subsystem.

VII. *Atomization.* A class of characteristics denoting a low level of alliances while several major powers engage in wars in an international subsystem.

R-Factors (third-order Wright)

I. *Imperial Expansion.* A stratum of characteristics describing an international subsystem where empires are growing without upsetting the overall power balance over a long period of time.

II. *Stable Stratification.* A stratum of characteristics describing an international subsystem where there is a definite hierarchy that persists intact throughout the era.

III. *Permeability.* A stratum of characteristics describing an international subsystem which gains new members peacefully while beset with internal conflicts.

IV. *Polarization.* A stratum of characteristics describing an international subsystem where much violence takes place between major powers, there are few alliances, and the era is of long duration.

R-Clusters (first-order Richardson)

I. *Enforcement.* A set of characteristics denoting wars started by major powers in an international subsystem.

II. *Major Power Victories.* A set of characteristics denoting wars won by major powers in an international subsystem.

III. *Multipolar Jockeying for Power.* A set of variables denoting wars concluded within a multipolar international subsystem without the advancement of international legal principles.

IV. *War Incidence.* A set of variables denoting frequent wars within an international subsystem.

V. *Concert Equilibration.* A set of variables denoting that major powers of an international subsystem are cooperating widely.

VI. *Violent Power Struggle.* A set of variables denoting that there is an increase in wars started and won by major powers in an international subsystem.

VII. *International Lawlessness.* A set of characteristics denoting a waning or absence in law as a component of an international subsystem.

VIII. *Elite Turbulence.* A set of characteristics denoting frequent warfare between major powers, even between former allies, within an international subsystem.

IX. *Destabilization.* A set of characteristics denoting wars planned for destabilizing an international subsystem.

X. *Extraregion Membership.* A set of characteristics denoting membership in an international subsystem by countries whose home is outside the perimeter of the subsystem region.

XI. *Recruitment.* A set of characteristics denoting the addition or subtraction of several middle or major powers within an international subsystem.

XII. *Scattered Attention Focus.* A set of characteristics denoting intensive internal wars, extraregional wars concluded by treaties, and pragmatic adaptation of rules within an international subsystem.

XIII. *Imperial Penetration.* A set of characteristics denoting entry of several new major powers into an international subsystem vis-à-vis a strong regulator.

XIV. *Supervision.* A set of characteristics denoting quiescent foreign and turbulent domestic supervision within an international subsystem.

XV. *Membership Linkage.* A set of characteristics denoting considerable diplomatic exchange and gatepassing within an international subsystem.

XVI. *Extraregion Major Power Wars.* A set of characteristics denoting frequent wars by members of an international subsystem outside the geographic perimeter of the region.

XVII. *Affiliative Gatepassing.* A set of characteristics denoting much gatepassing on the part of aligned members of an international subsystem.

XVIII. *War and Alliance Continuity.* A set of characteristics denoting that wars are of long duration and alliances last at least through two eras of international subsystems.

XIX. *Major Power Alliances.* A set of characteristics denoting considerable alliance activity by major powers, either with each other or with minor powers in an international subsystem.

XX. *Treaty-Making.* A set of characteristics denoting the extensive practice of concluding wars by treaties in an international subsystem.

XXI. *Temporal Exogenousness.* A set of variables denoting considerable carryover of activities in one international subsystem to other eras.

XXII. *Bloc Rivalry.* Same as first-order R-Factor III.

XXIII. *Fratricidal Conflict.* Same as first-order R-Factor VII.

XXIV. *Membership Size.* A set of characteristics denoting that there are many members, some entering into an international subsystem anew.

XXV. *Status Preoccupation.* A set of variables denoting many years of gatekeeping, recruitment, and cross-status coalitions, with a high number of alliances for purposes of military action in an international subsystem.

XXVI. *Interventions.* A set of variables denoting a high incidence of interventions within an international subsystem.

XXVII. *Concert Alliances.* A set of variables denoting a high incidence of alliances exclusively between major powers, which are recognized as legitimate elites with an international subsystem.

XXVIII. *World War.* A set of characteristics denoting widespread participation in lengthy wars of an international subsystem.

XXIX. *Formal Alliance Saturation.* A set of characteristics denoting a high incidence of alliances, with the exception of ententes, within an international subsystem.

XXX. *Alliance Size.* A set of characteristics denoting the widespread membership in and incidence of alliances in an international subsystem.

XXXI. *Multilateralism.* A set of characteristics denoting the formation of several new international organizations and widespread membership in cross-status alliances and coalitions within an international subsystem.

XXXII. *Elite Alliance Saturation.* A set of characteristics denoting a large number of alliances exclusively between the several major powers serving as elites of an international subsystem.

R-Clusters (second-order Richardson)

I. *Successful Elite Enforcement.* A class of characteristics denoting a high incidence of wars involving major powers as participants and as victors within an international subsystem.

II. *Entropy Reduction.* A class of characteristics denoting frequent wars involving several poles with the effect of bringing an international subsystem to an equilibrium.

III. *Power Struggle.* A class of characteristics denoting a lack of international law, combined with wars between major powers that threaten the stability of an international system.

IV. *Elite Disturbance.* A class of characteristics denoting much participation in wars with major powers succeeding in destabilizing the international subsystem.

V. *Incorporativeness.* Same as second-order R-Factor I.

VI. *Empire-Building.* Same as second-order R-Factor V.

VII. *Melon-Slicing.* A class of characteristics denoting forcible entry of several major powers into a new international subsystem in a foreign arena, while they join alliances in their home arena.

VIII. *Settlement Era.* A class of characteristics denoting lengthy and numerous wars and alliances, especially between major powers, wherein treaties conclude wars.

IX. *Protracted Conflict.* A class of characteristics denoting wars between major powers that last longer than two international subsystem eras.

X. *Gatekeeping Activity.* A class of characteristics denoting a large number of new members entering at various times in an international subsystem era.

XI. *Reactionary Concert.* A class of characteristics denoting the operation of a concert and intervention into domestic conflicts within an international subsystem.

XII. *Bloc Confrontation.* A class of characteristics denoting the presence of many participants and years per wars, despite a high incidence of defensive pacts and non-aggression pacts in an international subsystem.

XIII. *Alliance Size.* Same as first-order R-Cluster XXX.

XIV. *Alliance Saturation.* Reverse of first-order R-Factor I.

R-Clusters (third-order Richardson)

I. *Power-Vacuuming.* A class of characteristics denoting a takeover of an international subsystem by foreign elites through unequal treaties and spheres of influence.

II. *Cold War.* A class of characteristics denoting a long struggle between opposing blocs, while few members enter the international subsystem.

III. *Regulation.* A class of characteristics denoting a concert of major powers or set of opposing blocs that control the stability of an international subsystem.

IV. *Alignment.* A class of characteristics denoting the frequent and multilateral use of alliances in an international subsystem.

R-Clusters (fourth-order Richardson)

I. *Violent Outputs.* A stratum of characteristics denoting the extensive use of war within an international subsystem.

II. *Imperial Expansion.* Same as third-order R-Factor III.

III. *Stratification.* A stratum of characteristics denoting an explicit definition of power status for each member of an international subsystem.

IV. *Collective Security.* A stratum of characteristics denoting regulation of force by a multilateral agreement among several countries in an international subsystem.

appendix D
Tables Continued from Text

TABLE 5–4

Correlations Between 68 Decisionmaking Variables and 9 Q-Factors

Variables	Biquartimin Q–Factors[a]								
	I	II	III	IV	V	VI	VII	VIII	IX
1. Prior cohesion	.22	.07	−.20	−.12	.13	(−.79)	.10	.41	.06
2. Probability of office-holding	.39	−.00	−.17	−.20	−.06	−.27	.37	.13	.27
3. Correct intelligence	−.06	−.00	.50	−.04	−.31	.29	.36	−.15	−.15
4. Warning signs decoded	−.28	−.06	(.60)	.05	−.17	.19	.35	−.30	−.18
5. Prior concern	(.58)	.10	−.06	−.42	−.26	−.07	−.02	.26	−.27
6. Precedent invoked	.03	−.04	−.21	.25	.17	−.05	.31	−.17	−.33
7. Prior planning	.18	.05	.45	−.25	−.42	.23	.30	−.11	−.08
8. Alignment status	−.41	−.34	.35	(.56)	.05	.10	−.12	−.26	.46
9. Ongoing violence	.17	.06	−.26	−.10	−.10	(.64)	−.14	−.31	.12
10. Foreign stimulus	.22	.29	−.30	−.36	.39	−.28	.18	−.09	−.09
11. Cultural similarity	−.27	−.41	.27	(.55)	−.14	.10	.08	.01	.14
12. Power superiority	.07	−.02	−.04	(.57)	−.43	−.47	.27	−.22	.14
13. Multi-issue	.40	−.31	−.01	.02	.21	.03	−.43	−.31	.02
14. Noise level	(−.64)	.09	.38	.07	.26	−.19	.31	−.04	.21
15. Trust	(−.56)	−.26	.32	.37	.33	.05	−.10	−.12	.17
16. Control over events	−.18	−.19	.13	(.70)	−.40	.19	.19	−.38	.38
17. Time pressure	.41	.05	(−.51)	.04	−.20	−.14	.13	.25	−.18
18. Cruciality	(.60)	.20	−.33	−.40	−.24	−.23	.04	.31	−.41
19. Level of problem	.08	.00	.06	−.44	(.60)	.04	.06	−.13	−.34
20. Threat of violence	(.60)	.19	−.49	−.43	.09	−.19	−.16	−.03	.04
21. Size of decisionmaking body	.01	−.37	(.53)	−.19	.21	.08	−.19	−.04	−.03
22. Decision latitude	−.10	.37	−.34	−.21	.17	−.34	.32	.28	−.06
23. Officiality	−.01	−.35	.37	.04	.04	(.71)	−.37	(−.59)	.20
24. Authority contracted	.24	.38	−.24	−.14	−.37	−.08	.27	.03	−.17
25. Decision time	−.21	−.40	(.80)	−.07	.08	.26	.14	−.15	.01
26. Cognitive complexity	(.69)	−.36	.12	(−.53)	.22	−.04	−.01	−.10	.03
27. Input load	−.21	−.46	.30	.47	.01	.26	.13	−.04	−.09

TABLE 5-4—Cont.
Correlations Between 68 Decisionmaking Variables and 9 Q-Factors

Variables	I	II	III	IV	V	VI	VII	VIII	IX
					Biquartimin Q-Factors[a]				
28. Input intensity	.29	−.23	−.22	−.18	(.52)	−.33	−.22	.06	.31
29. Input range	.29	−.43	.20	−.14	.49	−.34	−.12	−.07	−.26
30. Input/output ratio	.06	(−.58)	.41	.24	.14	.34	−.13	−.48	−.04
31. Metacommunication level	−.13	−.41	.42	.39	−.24	.05	.14	.07	−.25
32. Reduction in communications	.13	(.62)	−.34	.15	(−.67)	−.20	.25	.01	−.01
33. Learning rate	−.08	(−.59)	.06	.22	.47	.04	.11	.08	.02
34. Risk propensity	(.56)	.21	−.26	−.40	−.12	−.25	.10	.02	−.19
35. Tolerance of ambiguity	.10	−.49	.11	−.19	(.62)	.06	−.30	.17	−.28
36. Self-esteem	−.01	−.11	−.25	(.69)	−.35	.18	.11	(−.53)	.36
37. Desires for achievement	(.82)	−.44	−.22	−.08	−.22	.04	−.10	−.10	.22
38. Desires for power	(.75)	.12	(−.54)	−.11	−.49	−.12	.02	−.07	.10
39. Desires for affiliation	.18	(−.64)	.04	.16	(.53)	−.10	−.25	−.09	−.17
40. Perceptions of frustration	(.61)	−.07	−.38	−.27	−.24	.37	−.15	.05	−.07
41. Perceptions of hostility	(.58)	.32	−.42	−.31	−.44	−.04	.04	−.02	−.20
42. Stereotypic decoding	.01	(.67)	.02	−.24	−.40	−.14	.20	−.17	−.10
43. Structuredness	−.20	−.02	.11	(.63)	(−.56)	.11	.19	−.12	.18
44. Range of alternatives	.38	−.43	.25	−.16	.08	.16	−.42	−.29	.39
45. Intraorganizational consonance	−.08	.07	−.22	.41	−.11	(−.54)	−.09	.29	.06
46. Hierarchical resolution	.00	(.56)	−.14	−.24	−.04	(−.55)	.33	.16	−.28
47. Pragmatism	−.21	−.11	(.89)	−.03	.24	−.09	.34	.41	.02
48. Violent option considered	(.53)	.30	−.20	−.35	−.25	−.38	.32	.14	−.24
49. Penetration	(.67)	−.47	−.29	.43	−.27	−.11	.04	−.39	.15
50. Transience	−.19	(.56)	−.17	−.04	−.09	−.12	−.08	.26	−.12
51. Procedurality	(−.56)	−.29	.41	.11	.33	.28	−.17	.25	−.07
52. Formality	.09	−.36	(.64)	−.23	.14	.06	.31	−.23	−.18
53. Guidance	(.56)	−.46	−.01	.07	−.05	.05	.14	−.46	.02
54. Revocability	−.41	.11	.25	−.27	.38	.02	−.28	.45	−.15

TABLE 5–4—Cont.

Correlations Between 68 Decisionmaking Variables and 9 Q–Factors

Variables	I	II	III	IV	V	VI	VII	VIII	IX
					Biquartimin Q–Factors[a]				
55. Turning point	(.77)	−.04	−.25	−.21	−.32	−.13	−.24	−.05	.10
56. Success	.29	(−.61)	−.18	.17	−.09	.15	.02	.19	.36
57. Implementation speed	−.01	(.51)	(−.64)	.08	−.22	−.20	−.14	.25	−.08
58. Sociometric change	.19	.01	−.18	.06	−.03	.09	.36	−.10	.27
59. Continuousness	.27	−.48	−.39	.47	−.05	.40	−.25	−.46	.32
60. Cumulativity	.30	.01	(−.61)	.12	−.10	.30	−.08	−.23	.12
61. Stabilizing	−.48	−.34	.39	.34	.40	.17	−.21	−.21	.08
62. Goal-restructuring	(.53)	−.10	−.15	.20	−.22	−.08	.08	−.50	.36
63. Promotive	.18	−.48	.43	.09	−.11	.32	−.02	−.37	.27
64. Maximizing	(.63)	−.27	−.08	−.08	−.30	−.11	.31	.03	.05
65. Decision for violence	(.56)	.24	−.46	−.38	−.04	−.18	.10	−.11	−.13
66. Extent of documentation	(.50)	−.34	−.17	.28	−.03	−.13	−.29	−.44	.11
67. Academic source	−.16	−.39	.33	.21	.11	.23	−.18	−.07	−.06
68. Length of description	.47	−.40	−.08	.36	−.05	−.32	−.43	−.31	.10

[a] Correlations > ± .50 are enclosed in parentheses.

TABLE 5-7
Correlations Between 32 Decisionmaking Cases and 17 R-Factors

Decisions	Varimax R-Factors[a]																
	I	II	III	IV	V	VI	VII	VIII	IX	X	XI	XII	XIII	XIV	XV	XVI	XVII
1. Bohlen	(−.62)	.25	(.54)	.18	.15	−.16	.19	−.06	−.15	.27	.09	−.08	−.13	−.08	.19	−.14	.14
2. Quarantine	(.56)	−.06	−.46	.31	−.16	−.06	−.20	.21	.48	.20	.17	.12	.12	.25	−.11	.16	−.44
3. Japan	(−.50)	.50	.30	.19	.39	.12	.03	−.03	−.28	−.12	−.03	.00	.01	.38	.31	−.41	.19
4. Draft	−.40	(.52)	.43	.12	.32	−.09	−.27	−.14	−.13	−.20	−.03	.06	−.30	−.05	.43	−.33	.08
5. Korea	.40	−.13	−.34	.14	−.09	−.18	.05	.24	(.54)	.35	−.04	.18	.06	(.57)	−.09	.25	−.28
6. Monroney	(−.52)	(.52)	−.04	.42	.18	−.08	−.35	−.21	.14	−.18	.10	−.11	.11	.00	(.56)	−.32	−.00
7. Employment	−.34	(.52)	.32	.12	.09	−.30	−.26	−.04	.28	−.38	−.02	.15	−.06	.10	.35	−.33	.06
8. Hiroshima	(.61)	−.04	.46	−.19	−.16	.07	.06	.13	−.02	−.18	.31	.00	.24	.21	−.27	.23	−.46
9. Suzuki	(−.50)	−.16	.48	−.02	.31	−.00	.30	−.04	−.16	.15	.07	−.04	−.24	.08	.45	−.32	.17
10. Pearl Harbor	.49	.07	−.28	−.34	−.06	.40	.08	.11	−.20	−.04	−.05	−.08	.15	.11	.03	.11	−.35
11. Norway	.04	−.02	.18	−.25	−.27	.41	.15	.26	−.28	.28	.10	−.41	.31	−.28	.09	.14	−.34
12. Vietminh	−.21	−.33	−.34	−.04	−.24	−.03	−.30	.02	.08	−.08	.29	.27	.12	−.34	.06	−.20	−.35
13. Aswan	−.13	−.40	.10	(−.54)	−.42	.40	−.13	−.14	.04	−.09	−.22	−.07	.14	−.03	−.32	−.23	−.28
14. Suez	.48	.01	−.19	−.09	−.13	.04	−.12	−.11	−.17	.40	.01	−.31	.08	.25	−.08	.13	−.28
15. Laos	−.16	.08	−.14	.27	−.00	.26	−.16	.21	.23	−.13	.23	.19	.15	.10	.19	−.32	−.03
16. Bay of Pigs	.24	−.18	.25	−.47	−.25	.08	−.25	−.03	−.05	−.00	.03	.06	.22	−.10	−.07	.14	.24
17. U–Boat	.21	−.07	.04	−.35	−.13	.27	.17	−.21	−.24	.08	.09	−.18	−.05	−.28	.00	−.02	−.17
18. Wilson	.25	.16	−.05	.35	.20	.30	.07	.31	.02	−.03	−.35	.39	−.16	.27	−.05	.08	−.07
19. Murmansk	−.31	.21	−.18	.46	.10	−.03	.01	−.17	.16	.14	.15	.36	−.05	−.08	.11	.00	−.09
20. Siberia	−.22	.26	−.25	(.56)	.15	−.14	−.04	−.20	.38	.02	.16	.41	.04	.27	.15	.01	.18
21. Poland	.21	−.19	.20	−.43	−.20	.42	.01	.25	−.12	.24	.01	.02	.31	.17	−.25	.30	−.25
22. Stalingrad	.16	−.48	−.22	−.44	−.45	−.19	.39	−.24	.10	−.25	−.17	−.25	.44	−.19	−.34	−.07	−.42
23. Panmunjom	−.17	.23	.20	.18	.37	.04	.36	.06	−.46	−.12	−.05	−.24	−.36	−.29	−.15	(−.59)	−.01
24. POW's	.06	(.59)	−.10	.15	.49	.29	−.03	−.16	−.46	.04	−.21	.07	−.43	.06	−.03	−.34	.07
25. Truckers	−.48	−.18	(.58)	−.08	−.25	−.27	−.39	−.05	−.11	.08	.28	−.20	.11	−.16	−.16	−.35	−.11
26. Steel	.15	−.38	.21	.17	.28	−.07	−.17	.24	.21	−.08	.32	.24	.24	−.19	.08	−.24	−.00

TABLE 5-7—Cont.
Correlations Between 32 Decisionmaking Cases and 17 R-Factors

Decisions	I	II	III	IV	V	VI	VII	VIII	IX	X	XI	XII	XIII	XIV	XV	XVI	XVII
								Varimax R–Factors[a]									
27. Potsdam	.15	−.24	−.44	.18	−.18	−.28	−.11	−.47	−.06	−.38	.12	.09	−.15	−.03	.12	−.18	−.13
28. MacArthur	−.12	−.15	(.61)	−.05	.23	.15	.08	.09	−.07	−.03	.15	−.17	.14	.18	−.04	−.21	−.18
29. Evacuation	−.26	.07	.16	−.31	.16	.17	−.02	.21	.08	−.28	.29	−.12	−.13	−.03	.00	.12	−.37
30. Haymarket	.29	(−.60)	.01	(−.68)	−.04	.15	−.03	.29	−.09	.17	−.31	−.20	.17	−.07	−.08	.20	−.35
31. Oglesby	−.32	−.07	.48	.15	−.04	.10	−.12	.12	.11	.20	.25	−.15	.00	.37	−.11	−.15	.05
32. Bolshevik	(.57)	.18	−.08	−.17	−.10	−.17	.29	.48	−.04	−.00	−.19	.11	−.04	.12	.09	.08	.14

[a] Correlations > ± .50 are enclosed in parentheses.

TABLE 8-1
Societal Asymmetry Variable List

Variable Number	Source[a]	Years	Description	Transformation[b]	Cases
1.	DON 31	1950–1955	National income (% increase)/population (% increase)	Log	40
2.	AED 37	1937–1954	Commercial energy consumption (per capita annual change)	Log (X + 1)	71
3.	WH 45	c.1950–1960	Gross national product (per capita annual change)	Log	57
4.	WH 36	c.1950–1960	Radios (per capita annual change)	None	69
5.	UNSY 148,1	1955–1960	Telephones per capita (coefficient of annual variation)	Arcsin	76
6.	UNSY 138	1955–1960	Railroad freight ton-kilometers (coefficient of annual variation)	Sqrt	69
7.	UNSY 122,1	1955–1960	Electricity production per capita (coefficient of annual variation)	Log	82
8.	WH 7	c.1955–1960	Population increase (annual rate)	None	79
9.	FAO 89	1955–1960	Per capita caloric intake c.1955/caloric intake c.1960 (difference of normalized ratio from 1.0)	None	44
10.	FAO 89	1955–1960	Per capita protein grammage intake c.1955/c.1960 (difference of normalized ratio from 1.0)	Group	44
11.	G 3	1951–1960	Government budget (per capita annual change)	Log	84
12.	C A-2	1951–1957	National income instability	Log	54
13.	WH 10	c.1940–1960	Persons in localities of 20,000 or more (average annual increase)	Log	39
14.	WH 51	c.1940–1960	Agricultural employment (% annual change)	None	43
15.	WH 65	c.1933–1955	Literates/population aged 15 and over (% annual change)	Log	33
16.	USDS	1955–1960	Communist Party strength/population (coefficient of annual variation)	Group	84
17.	CPS 27R	c.1960	Government instability	Trich	84
18.	CPS 63R	c.1950–1960	System instability	Dich	84
19c.	DON 74	up to 1955	Average age of latest 2 governments	Log	69
20c.	WH 30	1945–1961	Years independent/chief executives	Log	82
21.	UNDY 20	1955–1960	Live births/population (coefficient of annual variation)	Arcsin	71
22.	UNDY 23	1955–1960	Deaths/population (coefficient of annual variation)	Sqrt	76
23.	UNDY 29	1955–1960	Marriages/population (coefficient of annual variation)	Log	62
24.	RT	1955–1960	Major governmental crises	Group	85
25.	DON 73	1955	Illegitimacy of present government	None	77

576

TABLE 8-1—Cont.
Social Asymmetry Variable List

Variable Number	Source[a]	Years	Description	Transformation[b]	Cases
26c.	DON 72	up to 1955	Legality of latest 2 governmental changes	None	79
27.	UNSY 171,1	1955–1960	Defense expenditures/population (coefficient of annual variation)	Arcsin	68
28.	UNSY 171,1	1955–1960	Education expenditures/population (coefficient of annual variation)	Arcsin	62
29.	UNSY 171,1	1955–1960	Welfare expenditures/population (coefficient of annual variation)	Group	50
30.	UNSY 171,1	1955–1960	Total government expenditures/population (coefficient of annual variation)	Arcsin	69
31.	CPS 153	c.1960	Party system instability	Dich	68
32.	SYB	1955–1960	Government ministries (coefficient of annual variation)	Group	76
33.	PHW	1955–1960	Political parties in parliament (coefficient of annual variation)	Geom	82
34.	AED 19	1957	Cultivated land/total land (absolute difference from 50%)	Group	82
35.	DON 1	1955	Agricultural workers/labor force (absolute difference from 50%)	Group	74
36.	DON 3	c.1950	Agricultural population/total population (absolute difference from 50%)	Group	66
37.	DON 20	1955	Residents in localities over 20,000/population (absolute difference from 50%)	Group	77
38.	DON 21	1955	Population of largest city/population of 4 largest cities	None	79
39c.	CPS 114	c.1960	Lack of sectionalism	Dich	79
40.	G 5	c.1960	Potential sectional separatism	Geom	85
41.	G 5	c.1960	Sectional group discrimination	Geom	85
42.	CPS 166	c.1960	Vertical power centralization	Dich	84
43.	DON 68	1955	Unitary system	Dich	82
44c.	DON 67	1955	Political decentralization	Scaled	37
45.	DON 174	1955	Colonial power	Dich	85
46c.	DON 175	1955	National area/national + colonial land area	None	85
47c.	DON 176	1955	National population/national + colonial population	None	85
48.	DON 84,79	1950	Electricity potential/generated	Arcsin	71
49c.	AED 40	1957	Waterpower developed/potential waterpower	Group	76
50.	DON 82,84	1955	Energy generation/consumption	Sqrt	76
51c.	DON 108,41,115	c.1955	Motor vehicles/road length	Group	76
52c.	DON 112	1955	Rail freight/rail length	Log $(X + 1)$	64

TABLE 8–1—Cont.
Societal Asymmetry Variable List

Variable Number	Source[a]	Years	Description	Transformation[b]	Cases
53c.	DON 108	c.1955	Road length/land area	Log $(X + 1)$	79
54c.	DON 110	c.1955	Rail length/land area	Log $(X + 1)$	81
55.	DON 10	c.1950	Illiterates/population aged 10 or more	Arcsin	64
56c.	DON 39	1958	Primary school pupils/population ages 5–14	None	71
57c.	WH 63	c.1960	Primary and secondary school enrollment/population aged 5–19	None	79
58c.	UNSY	1955–1960	Education expenditures/population	Log	57
59c.	DON 40	c.1955	Students in secondary and higher education/population	Arcsin	82
60.	CPS 111	c.1960	Low political enculturation	Dich	67
61.	CPS 87	c.1960	Lack of developmental ideology	Dich	63
62.	CPS 36R	c.1960	Articulation by anomic interest groups	Trich	70
63c.	WH 24	c.1960	Voters/persons of voting age	None	69
64c.	G 6	c.1960	Trade unionists/nonagricultural workers	Sqrt	82
65c.	PHC 20	c.1960	Persons concerned with politics/total sample	None	11
66.	PHC 26, 27	c.1960	Persons fearful re politics/persons concerned with politics	Trich	11
67c.	WH 22	c.1960	Military personnel/population aged 15–64	Log	84
68c.	RT	1955–1960	Military mobilizations	Geom	85
69.	UNDY 30	1955–1960	Divorces/population	Group	60
70c.	UNDY 29	1955–1960	Marriages/population	Sqrt	61
71.	UNDY 30,29	1955–1960	Divorces/marriages	Group	58
72c.	WH 26; UNDY 8	c.1960	Religious parties' votes/religious adherents	Geom	64
73c.	WH 25; USSD	c.1960	Communist votes/Communist strength	Group	84
74.	CPS 93	c.1960	Nonmobilizational system style	Dich	79
75c.	UNSY 171,1	1955–1960	Governmental expenditures/national income	Arcsin	58
76c.	DON 26	1955	Public administration and defense expenditures/GNP	None	48
77c.	UNSY 171,1	1955–1960	Defense expenditures/national income	Sqrt	58
78c.	UNSY 171,1	1955–1960	Education expenditures/national income	Arcsin	55
79c.	UNSY 171,1	1955–1960	Welfare expenditures/national income	Log	46

TABLE 8-1—Cont.
Societal Asymmetry Variable List

Variable Number	Source[a]	Years	Description	Transformation[b]	Cases
80c.	WH 15	1959	General government expenditures/GNP	None	25
81c.	WH 17	1959	Central government expenditures/GNP	None	38
82c.	CPS 169	c.1960	Horizontal concentration of power	Dich	77
83.	CPS 178	c.1960	Bicameral legislature	Dich	74
84.	DON 77	1955	Government revenue/expenditure	Sq	73
85.	CPS 50	c.1960	Press censorship	Dich	78
86.	N 2	c.1960	Press censorship	Geom	77
87.	CPS 107	c.1960	Political opposition restricted	Dich	81
88c.	DON 65	1955	Political opposition unrestricted	None	80
89.	CPS 179	c.1960	Executive weakness	Dich	70
90.	CPS 50R	c.1960	Legislative weakness	Trich	71
91.	DON 128	1955–1960	Minimum voting age	None	65
92.	ILO 10	1955–1960	Unemployed/labor force	Group	47
93.	DON 38	c.1955	Pupils/teachers (primary schools)	Log	79
94.	DON 48	c.1953	Population/physicians	Log	79
95.	DON 52,48	c.1953	Hospital beds/physicians	Log	78
96c.	DON 50	1957	Excess of calories consumed over calories required/calories required	Sq	34
97.	DON 92	c.1953	Ethnic groups over 1% of population	Log	70
98.	DON 94	c.1953	Language communities over 1% of population	Log	67
99.	DON 97	c.1953	Nationality groups over 1% of population	Log	67
100.	DON 90	c.1953	Religious groups over 1% of population	None	68
101.	DON 99–101	c.1953	Racial groups over 1% of population	Geom	82
102.	ILO 35	1955–1960	Days lost due to strikes	Group	49
103.	ILO 35; UNSY 1	1955–1960	Strikers/population	Group	46
104.	ILO 36; DON 18,32	1955	Strikers/work force	Arcsin	41
105.	ILO 35; G 6	1960	Strikers/unionists	Arcsin	43
106.	RT	1955–1960	General strikes	Geom	85

TABLE 8–1—Cont.
Social Asymmetry Variable List

Variable Number	Source[a]	Years	Description	Transformation[b]	Cases
107.	RT	1955–1960	Antigovernment demonstrations	Geom	85
108.	RT	1955–1960	Revolutions	Geom	85
109.	RT	1955–1960	Guerrilla warfare	Geom	85
110.	RT	1955–1960	Assassinations	Geom	85
111.	RT	1955–1960	Purges	Geom	85
112.	RT	1955–1960	Riots	Geom	85
113.	WH 29	1950–1962	Deaths from domestic group violence/population	Log	74
114.	CPS 33–37R	c.1960	Diffracted articulation	Dich	84
115.	CPS 38–40R	c.1960	Diffracted aggregation	Dich	84
116.	CPS 37–38R	c.1960	Fragmentation in party functions	Dich	85
117.	CPS 50,52R	c.1960	Weakness of executive and legislature	Dich	85
118.	CPS 54R	c.1960	Military interventions into politics	Dich	79
119.	CPS 55R	c.1960	Police interventions into politics	Dich	77
120c.	DON 5	1955	Cinema attendance/population	Sqrt	76
121c.	DON 7	c.1955	Library book circulation/population	Log	38
122c.	DON 8	1955	Newspaper circulation/population	Sqrt	79
123c.	UNSY 148,1	1955–1960	Telephones/population	Group	76
124c.	DON 12	1955	Domestic mail pieces/population	$\text{Log}(X + 1)$	60
125c.	DON 13	1955	Radio receivers/population	Log	78
126c.	WH 37	c.1955	Television sets/population	Log	60
127.	DON 34	c.1950	Land ownership inequality (Gini index)	None	40
128c.	DON 35	c.1950	Population owning half of land/total population	Log	40
129.	DON 36	c.1950	Slope of Lorenz curve at 95% of land ownership	None	40
130.	WH 71	c.1950	Income inequality before taxes (Gini index)	None	18
131.	WH 72	c.1950	Income inequality after taxes (Gini index)	None	12
132.	WH 70	c.1950	Farms on rented land/total farms	Log	46
133c.	DON 70	1955	Customs taxes/total taxes	Sqrt	58

TABLE 8-1—Cont.
Societal Asymmetry Variable List

Variable Number	Source[a]	Description	Years	Transformation[b]	Cases
134.	CPS 66	Religious heterogeneity	c.1960	Dich	78
135.	CPS 67	Racial heterogeneity	c.1960	Dich	79
136.	CPS 68	Linguistic heterogeneity	c.1960	Dich	83
137.	CPS 70	Religious, racial, linguistic heterogeneity	c.1960	Dich	77
138c.	DON 91	Largest religious group/population	c.1953	Sq	60
139c.	DON 93	Largest ethnic group/population	c.1953	None	67
140c.	DON 95	Largest language group/population	c.1953	None	66
141c.	DON 98	Native born/population	c.1953	None	58
142c.	DON 99–101	Largest racial group/population	c.1953	Geom	78
143.	DON 78	Political parties with voters over 1% of population	1956	Sqrt	79
144.	CPS 41R	Two- or multi-party system	c.1960	Dich	62
145.	DON 66	Multiparty system	1956	Trich	80
146.	WH 25,26,28	Support for Communist, religious, or non-Communist secular parties (party types with over 1% of electorate)	c.1958	Dich	51
147.	UNDY 27	Homicides/population	1955–1960	Log	51
148.	UNDY 27	Motor vehicle accident deaths/population	1955–1960	Sqrt	51
149.	UNDY 27	Liver cirrhosis deaths/population	1955–1960	Log	54
150.	UNDY 27	Syphilis deaths/population	1955–1960	Group	54
151.	UNDY (1959) 11	Illegitimate births/total births	1955–1960	Group	51
152.	UNDY 27	Suicides/population	1955–1960	Group	51
153.	DON 58	Accidental deaths/population	1955	None	49
154.	UNDY 27	Ulcer deaths/population	1955–1960	None	55
155c.	CPS 94	Constitutional regime	c.1960	Dich	77
156c.	CPS 96	Nonauthoritarian regime	c.1960	Dich	75
157c.	CPS 95	Nontotalitarian regime	c.1960	Dich	80
158.	CPS 102	Nonpolyarchic representativeness	c.1960	Dich	78
159c.	CPS 161	Non-elitist political recruitment	c.1960	Dich	71

TABLE 8-1—Cont.
Societal Asymmetry Variable List

Variable Number	Source[a]	Years	Description	Trans-formation[b]	Cases
160c.	CPS 158	c.1960	Lack of personalismo in political parties	Dich	69
161.	G 5	1960	Group discrimination (number excluded)	Geom	84
162.	CPS 29,30,41,47,50–52	c.1960	Political structures	Group	74
163c.	CPS 180	c.1960	Bureaucratic traditionalism	Dich	79
164.	AED 47	1955	Lack of trade dependence	Group	72
165.	UNT	1955–1960	Exports/exports + imports (absolute difference from 0.5)	Arcsin	78
166.	DON 233	1955	Balance of investments (absolute value)	Log $(X + 1)$	60
167.	DON 163	1955	Balance of donations (absolute value)	Log $(X + 1)$	64
168.	DON 216	1955	Immigrants/migrants (absolute difference from 0.5)	Sqrt	39
169.	HNS 8	1948	Stereotypy score	Trich	9
170c.	HNS 8	1948	Friendliness score	None	9
171.	DON 180	1955	Foreign mail sent/sent + received (absolute difference from 0.5)	Sqrt	52
172.	DON 197	1955	Bloc prominence	Dich	85
173c.	CPS 57	c.1960	Communist and quasi-Communist polities (except USSR)	Dich	85
174.	H 1	c.1960	Penetrated polities	Dich	85
175c.	DON 200	1955	Bloc membership	Dich	85
176.	RT	1955–1960	Expulsions and recalls of diplomats	Geom	85
177.	RT	1955–1960	Severances of diplomatic relations	Geom	85
178.	DON 182–83	1955	Embassies and legations abroad/home + abroad (absolute difference from 0.5)	Group	60
179.	DON 185–87	1954	International organization headquarters at home/IGO + NGO member-ships (absolute difference from 0.5)	Group	85
180.	RT	1955–1960	Wars	Geom	85
181.	RT	1955–1960	Foreign military clashes	Geom	85
182.	RT	1955–1960	Deaths due to foreign conflict	Log $(X + 1)$	85
183.	RT; UNSY 1	1955–1960	Foreign killed/population	Geom	85

TABLE 8–1—Cont.
Social Asymmetry Variable List

[a] *Key:*

AED = Ginsburg, *Atlas of Economic Development* (1961).
C = Coppock, *International Economic Instability* (1962).
CPS = Banks and Textor, *A Cross-Polity Survey* (1963) (R = raw characteristic).
DON = Rummel, *Dimensions of Nations.*
FAO = Food and Agriculture Organization, *Production Yearbook.*
G = Gurr, *New Error-Compensated Measures for Comparing Nations* (1966).
HNS = Buchanan and Cantril, *How Nations See Each Other* (1952).
H 1 = Haas, this volume.
H 2 = Haas, *Some Societal Correlates of International Political Behavior* (1964).
ILO = International Labor Office, *Yearbook of Labor Statistics.*
N = Nixon, "Factors Related to Freedom in National Press System" (1960).
PHC = Cantril, *The Pattern of Human Concerns* (1963).
PHW = Council on Foreign Relations, *Political Handbook of the World.*
RT = Rummel, "Dimensions of Conflict Behavior Within and Between Nations" (1963).
Tanter, "Dimensions of Conflict Behavior Within and Between Nations, 1958–60" (1966).
SYB = *Statesman's Yearbook.*
UNDY = United Nations, *Demographic Yearbook.*
UNT = United Nations, *Statistical Papers,* Series T.
USDS = United States, Department of State, *World Strength of Communist Party Organizations.*
WH = Russett et al., *World Handbook of Political and Social Indicators* (1964).
Numbers following source codes refer to tables where the variables are found in each source; for UN data, see 1956 yearbooks unless otherwise noted.

[b] *Key:*

Arcsin = arcsine.
Dich = dichotomization.
Geom = geometric progression.
Group = grouping by standard scores.
Log = logarithmic.
Scaled = scale scores assigned.
Sq = square.
Sqrt = square root.
Trich = trichotomization.

[c] These variables index symmetry, so in reporting bivariate findings in Chapter 7 their signs are reversed.

583

TABLE 8–4
Correlations Between 8 Q–Factors and 183 Asymmetry Variables

| Variable[b] | Varimax Factors[a] | | | | | | | | Data Pattern[b] |
	I	II	III	IV	V	VI	VII	VIII	
1. Δ National income/pop.	-.17	.01	-.21	-.45	-.02	-.40	-.12	-.03	A
2. Δ Elec. consumption/pop.	.16	.29	-.02	.34	.10	-.26	-.27	.09	A
3. Δ GNP/pop.	-.06	.09	-.38	-.34	-.01	-.49	.10	-.30	A
4. Δ Radios/pop.	-.21	.08	-.41	-.07	-.12	-.25	.16	-.09	A
5. Δ Phones/pop.	-.08	.19	-.25	-.03	-.15	.12	-.04	.26	A
6. Δ RR ton-km.	-.08	.27	-.35	.05	.20	-.01	-.22	.16	A
7. Δ Elec. production/pop.	-.21	.07	-.36	.23	-.23	-.09	-.01	.20	A
8. Δ Population	-.16	-.21	.47	.28	.10	.41	-.01	.01	A
9. Δ Caloric intake	-.01	.12	-.13	.07	.06	-.21	.03	-.16	A
10. Δ Protein intake	.02	.13	-.18	.16	.17	-.12	-.02	-.37	A
11. Δ Government budget	-.10	-.22	.15	-.30	.09	-.11	.23	-.01	A
12. Δ National income	.11	-.04	.18	.16	-.07	.10	-.17	.10	A
13. Δ Urban population	-.04	-.09	.08	(.56)	.06	.01	-.09	-.35	A
14. Δ Agr. employment	-.22	-.06	-.12	-.22	.06	-.09	.20	-.11	A
15. Δ Literacy rate	.04	-.29	.24	-.13	-.16	-.16	-.18	-.41	A
16. Δ % Communist Party strength	-.07	.07	-.30	-.03	-.15	-.09	.08	.07	A
17. Government instability	.36	.09	.42	.32	.22	.35	-.05	.15	A
18. System instability	.47	.15	(.58)	.47	.20	.29	.13	.39	S
19. Government tenure	-.04	-.19	.14	-.20	-.18	-.23	.06	-.10	S
20. Elite tenure	-.13	-.13	-.01	-.29	.01	-.41	.09	-.25	A
21. Δ Birth rate	-.07	.21	-.39	.16	-.22	.15	.16	.08	A
22. Δ Death rate	-.21	.15	(-.71)	-.04	-.18	-.05	.24	-.26	A
23. Δ Marriage rate	-.07	.17	(-.54)	-.08	-.17	-.12	.16	-.38	A
24. Government crises	.13	.26	.14	.40	.10	.37	-.10	(.51)	A
25. Government illegitimacy	.18	.11	.21	.07	.00	-.22	-.13	-.01	A
26. Legal government change	-.27	-.02	-.36	-.11	-.04	.25	.12	.06	S
27. Δ Defense exp./pop.	.03	.14	-.39	-.30	-.12	-.20	.08	-.25	A

TABLE 8-4—Cont.
Correlations Between 8 Q-Factors and 183 Asymmetry Variables

Variable[b]	I	II	III	IV	V	VI	VII	VIII	Data Pattern[b]
				Varimax Factors[a]					
28. Δ Education exp./pop.	.20	.19	−.19	.13	.01	−.02	−.17	−.39	A
29. Δ Welfare exp./pop.	.10	.08	−.20	−.15	−.06	.00	−.16	−.24	A
30. Δ Government exp./pop.	−.07	−.16	−.11	−.01	−.11	−.03	−.10	−.30	A
31. Pol. party instability	.29	.03	.46	.48	.18	(.51)	−.08	.18	A
32. Δ Government ministries	−.02	.14	−.20	−.05	−.13	−.19	.00	−.07	A
33. Δ Parl. parties	−.07	.21	−.32	.28	−.05	.36	.03	−.11	A
34. Cultivated land ≠ noncultivated	.13	−.11	.21	.19	−.04	.48	−.28	−.06	A
35. Farm workers ≠ nonfarm	−.13	−.22	−.16	−.37	−.14	.31	−.19	.03	A
36. Rural pop. ≠ nonrural	−.22	−.27	−.17	(−.54)	−.31	.33	−.19	.14	A
37. Urban pop. ≠ nonurban	.25	−.36	(.71)	−.05	.04	.11	−.17	−.25	A
38. Urban primacy	.08	.04	.06	.23	.01	.11	−.23	−.06	A
39. Lack of sectionalism	−.13	.11	−.18	.21	.06	−.34	−.41	−.22	S
40. Sectional separatism	.16	−.31	.40	−.37	−.13	.25	(.51)	.34	A
41. Sectional discrimination	.35	−.25	.40	−.05	−.24	.39	.23	−.08	A
42. Vertical centralization	.03	−.11	.25	−.05	−.01	−.20	−.11	−.04	A
43. Unitary system	−.00	−.08	.14	−.10	.05	−.19	−.24	−.19	A
44. Decentralization	−.24	−.09	−.33	.01	−.21	.05	.08	−.14	A
45. Colonial power	−.28	.11	−.50	−.06	−.14	−.08	.13	.10	A
46. % National area	.18	−.17	.40	.03	.08	.11	−.16	−.13	A
47. % National pop.	.09	−.17	.29	.04	.02	.06	−.12	−.12	S
48. Pot./elec. produced	−.15	.23	−.35	−.02	.00	−.15	−.03	.03	A
49. % Waterpower exploited	−.17	.35	(−.54)	−.20	.14	−.34	−.05	−.09	S
50. Energy prod./consumed	.29	−.08	.44	.01	.01	−.00	.21	.17	A
51. Cars/road length	.25	−.25	.40	−.31	−.15	−.19	.13	−.15	S
52. RR freight/miles	−.07	.18	−.44	−.18	−.09	−.33	.33	.01	S
53. Road miles/area	−.18	.33	(−.69)	−.13	−.02	−.35	.26	.01	S
54. Rail miles/area	−.05	.48	(−.67)	.11	.10	−.37	.28	.11	S

TABLE 8-4—Cont.
Correlations Between 8 Q-Factors and 183 Asymmetry Variables

Variable[b]	Varimax Factors[a]								Data Pattern[b]
	I	II	III	IV	V	VI	VII	VIII	
55. Illiteracy rate	.26	-.37	(.85)	-.12	.16	.24	-.08	.03	A
56. % Primary pupils	-.38	.20	(.72)	-.04	-.15	-.35	.21	-.13	S
57. % Youth schooled	-.23	.31	(-.77)	.05	-.06	-.32	.23	-.17	S
58. Educ. exp./pop.	-.18	.07	(-.57)	-.20	-.29	-.04	-.03	-.08	S
59. % in higher educ.	-.26	.29	(-.74)	.08	-.06	-.10	.20	.07	A
60. Low. pol. enculturation	.09	-.16	(.52)	.10	.24	.17	-.16	.06	A
61. No development ideology	-.09	-.09	.20	-.25	-.05	-.03	.10	-.20	A
62. Anomic articulation	.26	-.27	(.70)	.05	.08	.14	.09	.30	A
63. % Voter turnout	-.01	.26	-.50	-.20	-.01	-.28	-.01	-.17	S
64. % Unionization	-.09	.25	-.41	-.12	-.01	(-.52)	-.05	-.03	S
65. % Concerned about Politics	.20	.14	.12	.20	-.11	-.40	(-.61)	-.16	A
66. % Fearful re politics	(.50)	.36	(.71)	.46	.04	.03	.26	.41	S
67. % Military pop.	-.06	-.03	-.07	-.26	.23	-.30	.11	-.18	S
68. Mobilizations	-.08	-.05	.04	.20	.00	-.06	-.01	.05	A
69. Divorce rate	-.15	-.06	-.32	(-.62)	-.01	-.35	.05	-.05	S
70. Marriage rate	.08	.18	-.21	-.09	-.05	-.14	.13	-.35	A
71. Divorces/marriages	-.11	-.13	-.23	(-.59)	-.02	-.21	.04	.06	S
72. % Religious voting	.03	.31	-.36	.04	.04	.32	.11	.22	S
73. % Communist vote mobilization	.06	.22	-.39	-.02	-.14	-.13	.16	-.16	A
74. Nonmobilizational	-.03	.21	-.29	.25	.07	.46	-.03	.08	S
75. Gov. exp./national income	-.04	.15	-.43	-.18	-.21	-.04	-.14	.07	S
76. Adm. + defense exp./GNP	.19	.15	-.13	-.16	.07	.04	.03	-.15	A
77. Defense exp./national income	.06	.01	-.19	-.18	-.05	.10	.03	.07	S
78. Educ. exp./national income	-.10	.07	-.36	-.18	-.18	.03	-.16	-.04	S
79. Welfare exp./national income	-.16	.14	(-.65)	-.30	-.38	-.03	-.24	-.14	S
80. Gen. gov. exp./national income	-.35	.07	-.47	-.17	-.01	.22	-.39	-.07	S
81. Cen. gov. exp./national income	-.17	.22	-.36	-.09	.32	-.04	.00	.16	S

TABLE 8-4—Cont.
Correlations Between 8 Q-Factors and 183 Asymmetry Variables

Variable[b]	I	II	III	IV	V	VI	VII	VIII	Data Pattern[b]
				Varimax Factors[a]					
82. Horizontal power conc.	.03	−.46	(.61)	−.41	.03	−.40	−.14	−.10	S
83. Bicameralism	−.04	.14	−.24	.09	.04	.42	.11	.21	A
84. Government rev./exp.	−.14	−.08	−.21	.00	−.24	−.21	−.06	−.26	A
85. Press censorship	.11	−.35	(.71)	−.18	.16	−.17	−.12	.14	A
86. Press censorship	.29	−.25	(.69)	−.11	.10	−.43	−.07	−.03	A
87. Restricted opposition	.02	−.47	(.68)	−.26	.10	−.31	−.13	.06	A
88. Unrestricted opposition	−.16	.29	−.44	.32	.26	(.65)	.14	.19	S
89. Weak executive	−.16	.36	(−.66)	.24	.01	.42	.06	−.05	A
90. Weak legislature	.20	−.42	(.74)	−.20	.07	−.38	−.13	−.14	A
91. Minimum voting age	−.16	.15	−.37	−.11	−.03	.30	.03	.07	A
92. % Unemployment	−.14	.20	−.43	.06	.20	.20	.04	−.19	A
93. Pupils/teachers	.09	−.01	.12	.08	.12	.06	.02	−.09	A
94. Persons/doctors	.27	−.31	(.66)	−.23	.10	.25	−.19	−.12	A
95. Hospital beds/doctors	−.03	.14	−.06	.23	.14	−.08	.19	.24	A
96. Nutritional adequacy	.41	−.12	−.47	(−.56)	−.40	−.25	−.15	−.08	S
97. Ethnic groups	.21	−.21	.30	.10	−.10	.13	.35	.02	A
98. Language communities	.19	−.21	.28	−.10	.04	.18	.23	.12	A
99. Nationalities	−.02	−.07	−.18	−.26	−.21	.06	.21	.02	A
100. Religions	.29	.14	.09	−.07	.01	.06	.14	.08	A
101. Racial groups	.10	.03	.17	(.60)	−.15	.19	−.03	.03	A
102. Strike days	.09	.39	−.31	.16	−.19	.35	.19	.21	A
103. Strikers/pop.	.15	.49	−.34	−.01	−.18	.06	.08	.14	A
104. Strikers/workers	−.02	.40	−.31	−.05	−.08	.00	−.01	.14	A
105. Strikers/unionists	.12	.39	−.01	.05	.16	.12	.18	.12	A
106. General strikes	.08	.33	−.01	.38	−.06	.00	.21	.46	A
107. Antigovernment demonstrations	.15	.28	.10	.42	.10	.19	.17	.47	A
108. Revolutions	.37	.00	(.63)	.35	−.17	.41	−.14	.41	A

587

TABLE 8-4—Cont.

Correlations Between 8 Q-Factors and 183 Asymmetry Variables

Variable[b]	Varimax Factors[a]								Data Pattern[b]
	I	II	III	IV	V	VI	VII	VIII	
109. Guerrilla warfare	.23	.16	.35	.41	−.04	.32	−.13	.46	A
110. Assassinations	.18	.36	.20	.34	.36	.23	−.05	.47	A
111. Purges	.29	.12	.34	.36	−.03	.09	.03	.29	A
112. Riots	.24	.37	.15	(.53)	.19	.25	.22	(.61)	A
113. Domestic violence death rate	.24	.26	.18	.24	−.03	−.15	−.14	.18	A
114. Diffracted articulation	−.04	.04	−.08	.02	−.08	−.28	−.03	−.09	A
115. Diffracted aggregation	−.07	.24	−.48	−.12	−.03	.11	.11	.01	A
116. Party function fragmentation	.28	−.05	.48	−.17	.10	−.26	−.12	.03	A
117. Weak executive and legislature	.16	−.31	(.58)	−.17	.00	−.25	−.14	−.10	A
118. Military interventions	.11	−.14	.41	.41	.05	.36	−.17	.15	A
119. Police interventions	.19	−.34	(.82)	.01	.13	−.15	−.17	.07	A
120. Moviegoers/pop.	−.25	.34	(−.67)	.10	−.06	−.23	.22	−.01	S
121. Library book circ./pop.	−.16	.04	(−.57)	−.24	−.38	−.32	.05	−.18	S
122. Newspapers/pop.	−.36	.26	(−.83)	.01	−.17	−.19	.14	−.06	S
123. Telephones/pop.	−.35	.20	(.76)	−.24	−.13	−.10	.08	−.07	S
124. Domestic mail/pop.	−.30	.34	(−.79)	.01	−.12	−.25	.10	.03	S
125. Radios/pop.	−.35	.29	(−.76)	.21	−.12	−.25	.12	.10	S
126. TV's/pop.	−.20	.16	(−.56)	−.23	−.16	.06	.12	.06	S
127. Land ownership inequality	.42	.19	.33	.29	.11	(.54)	−.15	.18	A
128. % Owning ½ land	−.49	−.19	−.39	−.28	−.14	−.41	.13	−.13	S
129. % Owning 5% land	−.09	.04	−.08	.05	−.07	−.04	−.12	.04	A
130. Income inequality	.18	.07	.19	.46	.16	−.06	.15	.08	A
131. Income inequality	.34	.18	.18	.44	.03	−.24	.09	−.18	A
132. % Rented farms	−.12	.00	.07	.03	−.19	−.21	.16	.36	A
133. % Customs-excise taxes	.27	−.14	.46	.07	.17	.12	.03	−.20	S
134. Religious heterogeneity	−.03	.00	−.06	−.17	.00	.11	−.09	−.07	A
135. Racial heterogeneity	.27	.12	.26	.48	−.07	.23	−.22	.12	A

TABLE 8–4—Cont.
Correlations Between 8 Q–Factors and 183 Asymmetry Variables

Variable[b]	Varimax Factors[a]								Data Pattern[b]
	I	II	III	IV	V	VI	VII	VIII	
136. Linguistic heterogeneity	.12	−.28	.32	−.23	−.07	.26	.30	.13	A
137. Heterogeneity	.17	−.10	.31	−.01	−.02	.26	.08	.14	A
138. % Largest religion	.00	.03	.11	.24	.06	.26	−.18	.08	S
139. % Largest ethnic group	−.22	.11	−.19	−.12	.15	.01	−.34	−.07	S
140. % Largest language	−.18	.07	−.28	−.04	−.12	−.40	−.14	−.23	S
141. % Native born	−.05	−.19	.37	.15	.21	−.27	−.21	−.19	S
142. % Largest race	−.17	−.04	−.21	(−.56)	.15	−.09	.09	−.07	S
143. Number of parties	.19	.41	−.22	.37	.21	−.26	.15	.20	A
144. Two- or multi-party system	−.03	.23	−.37	.36	−.04	.25	−.00	.12	A
145. Multiparty system	−.16	.28	(−.53)	.10	.27	(.63)	.28	.15	A
146. Political party types	.04	.29	−.19	.12	.11	(.51)	.21	.33	A
147. Homicide rate	.30	−.07	.47	(.50)	.03	.40	−.03	.10	A
148. Car death rate	−.23	.15	−.50	−.23	−.37	.14	.05	.18	A
149. Liver cirrhosis death rate	−.07	−.02	−.16	−.01	−.17	.16	.09	.05	A
150. Syphilis death rate	−.06	.09	−.14	.06	−.16	−.17	.02	.08	A
151. Illegitimacy rate	.33	.04	.42	(.65)	.01	−.25	−.17	.02	A
152. Suicide rate	−.09	.28	−.46	−.40	−.08	.28	.07	−.04	A
153. Accident death rate	−.05	.18	−.19	.05	−.09	−.20	.00	.21	A
154. Ulcer death rate	−.32	−.22	−.16	−.23	.03	.39	.04	−.00	A
155. Constitutional	−.12	.43	(−.64)	.32	−.10	−.07	.18	.11	S
156. Nonauthoritarian	−.13	.31	(−.57)	.14	−.21	.28	.24	−.06	S
157. Nontotalitarian	.01	.18	−.14	.25	.09	−.35	−.08	.23	S
158. Nonpolyarchic	.14	−.46	(.61)	−.32	−.05	(.73)	−.15	−.11	A
159. Non-elitist	−.06	.44	(−.56)	.02	−.16	−.29	−.00	.16	S
160. Lack of personalismo	−.32	−.15	−.29	−.31	−.19	.17	.13	.05	S
161. Group discrimination	.13	−.29	.37	−.39	−.06	−.44	(.52)	.21	A
162. Political structures	−.08	.39	(−.59)	.36	−.06	.19	.15	.25	A

TABLE 8-4—Cont.
Correlations Between 8 Q-Factors and 183 Asymmetry Variables

Variable[b]	I	II	III	IV	V	VI	VII	VIII	Data Pattern[b]
				Varimax Factors[a]					
163. Bureaucratic traditionalism	.14	-.38	.46	-.34	-.11	.50	-.14	.02	S
164. Lack of trade dependence	.31	-.08	(.52)	.24	.09	.36	-.27	.06	S
165. Exports ≠ imports	-.21	-.11	.20	-.02	.47	.34	.07	.05	A
166. Balance of investments	-.28	.05	-.36	.06	-.01	.18	.25	.21	A
167. Balance of donations	-.01	-.05	-.07	-.20	.05	.12	.33	.01	A
168. Immigrants ≠ emigrants	-.23	-.06	-.25	-.23	-.01	.01	.07	.10	A
169. Stereotypy	.06	.28	-.13	-.14	-.40	-.10	-.07	.20	A
170. Friendliness	-.05	.04	.09	.36	.28	-.19	-.02	.05	S
171. Foreign mail sent ≠ received	.24	-.00	.15	-.07	-.19	.17	-.14	-.05	A
172. Bloc prominence	.05	.02	.01	.06	-.07	.20	.31	.08	A
173. Communist countries	.35	.21	.33	.34	.10	-.10	.13	.46	S
174. Penetrated polity	.01	-.24	.21	-.23	-.06	.34	.07	-.41	A
175. Bloc membership	.10	.19	-.24	.32	-.04	-.50	.08	-.06	A
176. Diplomatic expulsions + recalls	-.06	.11	-.11	.20	.09	-.19	.20	.38	A
177. Severances	.28	.15	.15	.19	-.04	-.08	-.07	.13	A
178. Diplomats abroad ≠ at home	-.03	-.13	.02	-.18	-.06	.09	.04	-.22	A
179. I.O.'s HQ'd abroad ≠ at home	.21	-.16	(.51)	-.00	.12	-.04	-.24	-.13	A
180. Wars	-.04	-.03	-.00	-.13	.06	-.03	.15	-.08	A
181. Foreign military clashes	.05	-.06	.24	-.02	.04	-.14	.26	.12	A
182. Foreign killed	-.01	-.06	.14	-.03	.09	.01	.26	.13	A
183. For. viol. death rate	.00	.03	.14	.12	.08	.01	.08	.20	A

[a] Correlations > ± .50 are enclosed in parentheses.
[b] Key: A = asymmetry.
S = symmetry.
Δ = change in.

590

TABLE 8-7
R-Factor Analysis of Asymmetry Variables

Variables	h²	Varimax Factors[a]									
		I	II	III	IV	V	VI	VII	VIII	IX	X
1. Δ National income/pop.	.93	—44	24	—09	04	22	—03	15	—10	—07	—12
2. Δ Elec. consumption/pop.	1.19	—13	02	—08	—12	—18	—10	10	04	—17	01
3. Δ GNP/pop.	.95	—43	29	06	02	16	—04	(52)	—10	08	—22
4. Δ Radios/pop.	.57	(—54)	—01	08	02	—12	07	04	—19	—01	—18
5. Δ Phones/pop.	.33	—25	—24	—05	—00	09	00	—14	06	—05	—04
6. Δ RR ton-km.	.81	—21	—27	—03	—22	08	18	—07	27	—14	13
7. Δ Elec. production/pop.	.67	—39	—27	01	—08	—14	00	—24	15	—17	—02
8. Δ Population	1.00	(61)	—06	01	07	—25	—17	01	04	—12	—05
9. Δ Caloric intake	1.01	—06	—03	—06	—03	—02	—09	(92)	05	01	—01
10. Δ Protein intake	1.07	01	—14	10	—09	—08	—26	(88)	—01	13	09
11. Δ Government budget	.23	—06	26	—02	07	28	—07	—06	03	01	—05
12. Δ National income	.66	26	04	—12	—20	09	—23	—01	29	13	—39
13. Δ Urban population	.97	07	10	02	—10	(—58)	—31	36	17	28	—12
14. Δ Agr. employment	1.06	—10	01	09	—02	21	22	—05	—07	04	05
15. Δ Literacy rate	1.23	14	25	25	—06	07	—05	35	07	19	—10
16. Δ % Communist Party strength	.72	—31	—06	—00	03	13	08	07	—17	—35	—30
17. Government instability	.76	(50)	07	—32	06	—06	—25	08	10	—11	—02
18. System instability	1.00	41	15	(—65)	19	—14	—10	09	16	—02	—01
19. Government tenure	1.07	—03	24	07	06	—10	02	01	—09	—00	—03
20. Elite tenure	.81	07	24	28	00	07	17	13	06	16	10
21. Δ Birth rate	.74	—22	—45	03	05	—15	29	—08	13	—02	18
22. Δ Death rate	.72	(—56)	—41	15	—03	—04	11	—14	—08	—06	—03
23. Δ Marriage rate	.39	—30	—23	21	—09	06	17	01	01	05	—15
24. Government crises	.81	22	—15	—48	—08	06	09	01	31	—08	00
25. Government illegitimacy	.21	07	19	03	—08	—12	01	—11	06	—06	—05
26. Legal government change	.64	—15	—38	05	22	13	—03	09	—03	12	—16
27. Δ Defense exp./pop.	.87	—31	—02	11	—02	07	23	—00	(—74)	06	04

591

TABLE 8-7—Cont.
R-Factor Analysis of Asymmetry Variables

Variables	h²	I	II	III	IV	V	VI	VII	VIII	IX	X
						Varimax Factors[a]					
28. △ Education exp./pop.	.76	−02	−07	10	−25	−10	−03	02	−07	−03	−04
29. △ Welfare exp./pop.	1.03	−01	−11	10	−05	09	−06	09	−08	02	15
30. △ Govt. exp./pop.	.81	01	00	23	02	−17	02	−05	−42	−02	01
31. Pol. party instability	.89	(63)	−11	−24	06	−22	−07	−09	23	−13	02
32. △ Government ministries	.32	−15	−18	07	−07	08	04	24	−01	08	03
33. △ Parl. parties	.26	−01	−37	−03	−06	−04	04	13	08	04	−07
34. Cultivated land ≠ noncultivated	.86	33	−21	10	−00	−39	−32	−10	−02	−19	−00
35. Farm workers ≠ nonfarm	.96	−08	−02	07	08	13	13	−13	−05	−02	−05
36. Rural pop. ≠ nonrural	.93	−05	−09	12	08	26	12	−19	−16	−08	−05
37. Urban pop. ≠ nonurban	.80	(71)	32	08	07	−06	−07	−03	−10	11	15
38. Urban primacy	.19	14	00	−02	−17	−09	−05	05	−04	−04	−01
39. Lack of sectionalism	.79	−17	06	09	(−59)	−16	−23	20	03	−04	20
40. Sectional separatism	.86	16	20	−17	(78)	11	−01	−10	−15	02	02
41. Sectional discrimination	.74	31	10	02	47	−30	−12	−12	11	−15	17
42. Vertical centralization	.91	13	27	−09	02	02	09	14	−04	09	11
43. Unitary system	.94	17	14	12	−23	12	12	02	02	−00	−08
44. Decentralization	.92	−44	−12	−03	03	−04	−41	18	−30	31	−10
45. Colonial power	.74	−33	−24	09	−05	07	(60)	−12	−09	−00	−08
46. % National area	1.04	24	16	02	03	−13	(−85)	07	06	−11	−07
47. % National pop.	.79	19	08	10	02	−09	(−79)	13	−02	06	−09
48. Pot./elec. produced	.46	−26	−15	17	−20	21	14	00	−21	20	−02
49. Waterpower exploited	.75	(−52)	−09	−06	−24	38	08	02	−20	21	−12
50. Energy prod./consumed	1.00	23	29	−24	16	−03	02	−00	−04	04	02
51. Cars/road length	.65	21	41	14	20	17	−22	13	−02	41	13
52. RR freight/miles	.60	(−60)	06	−18	11	17	11	−03	−05	02	−04
53. Road miles/area	.96	(−69)	−16	−03	−06	34	26	06	−06	20	−05
54. Rail miles/area	1.00	(−76)	−12	−21	−07	25	17	09	−07	07	08

TABLE 8–7—Cont.
R-Factor Analysis of Asymmetry Variables

Variables	h²	Varimax Factors[a]									
		I	II	III	IV	V	VI	VII	VIII	IX	X
55. Illiteracy rate	1.16	(84)	35	−03	22	−11	−12	−05	07	−05	13
56. % Primary pupils	1.00	(−88)	−20	12	−12	12	01	−03	07	07	−14
57. % Youth schooled	.91	(−87)	−20	06	−08	13	08	06	−08	09	−04
58. Educ. exp./pop.	.99	−44	−40	27	−02	06	13	04	−12	−13	−03
59. % in higher educ.	.70	(−69)	−34	−06	−04	20	07	00	04	12	−11
60. Low pol. enculturation	.72	33	43	−18	00	−22	08	−16	19	−16	05
61. No development ideology	.99	−18	03	03	14	27	05	−21	−12	12	−02
62. Anomic articulation	.88	49	48	−32	17	−01	−19	−01	02	−04	−11
63. % Voter turnout	.85	(−52)	−01	06	01	16	−01	36	−05	16	01
64. % Unionization	.79	(−64)	16	05	−14	08	−05	37	−10	−06	04
65. % Concerned re politics[b]											
66. % Fearful re politics[b]											
67. % Military pop.	.70	−18	26	11	00	31	06	35	04	02	09
68. Mobilizations	.66	−01	16	−03	−04	−18	17	−13	12	18	−17
69. Divorce rate	.93	−48	24	16	05	36	−14	06	−22	12	−15
70. Marriage rate	.22	−19	−01	18	−03	11	−04	01	−09	−04	12
71. Divorces/marriages	.76	−33	18	11	12	38	−14	05	−22	06	−14
72. % Religious voting	1.41	−04	−47	−15	04	04	18	01	15	−10	−10
73. % Communist vote mobilization	.70	−32	−09	04	−08	04	10	13	01	44	−18
74. Nonmobilizational	.95	15	(−61)	−07	−06	−02	18	−37	02	07	−03
75. Government exp./national income	1.13	−26	−19	01	−10	12	02	−02	−01	16	−03
76. Adm. + defense exp./GNP	.78	05	03	07	−00	20	−15	16	−19	−07	−10
77. Defense exp./national income	.77	−05	−07	08	13	15	17	−19	−19	09	−10
78. Educ. exp./national income	1.02	−10	−28	16	−09	17	06	01	12	10	09
79. Welfare exp./national income	1.11	−41	−41	34	−17	−03	07	05	−15	−03	−04
80. Gen. govt. exp./national income	1.24	−44	−45	04	−15	12	−19	15	11	−05	−00
81. Cen. govt. exp./national income	.97	−34	−13	−18	−11	18	03	08	06	−15	03

TABLE 8-7—Cont.

R–Factor Analysis of Asymmetry Variables

Variables	h²	I	II	III	IV	V	VI	VII	VIII	IX	X
						Varimax Factors[a]					
82. Horizontal power conc.	1.14	20	(92)	09	03	19	00	−04	−01	08	−05
83. Bicameralism	.90	13	−47	−13	23	−02	21	10	05	05	−09
84. Government rev./exp.	.70	−29	04	26	−02	−15	02	−01	02	00	−04
85. Press censorship	.98	32	(75)	−10	05	06	−06	−05	23	−01	−01
86. Press censorship	.75	24	(73)	−04	07	−04	−16	04	18	02	−00
87. Restricted opposition	.92	28	(86)	−03	04	05	−07	−12	−04	02	00
88. Unrestricted opposition	.94	03	(−78)	−17	−01	01	−05	−03	04	09	−02
89. Weak executive	.92	−25	(−87)	17	−06	−06	−01	04	−03	−12	−03
90. Weak legislature	1.00	33	(88)	05	10	−01	−06	04	08	00	05
91. Minimum voting age	.69	−02	(−53)	10	16	25	23	−19	09	15	−08
92. % Unemployment	.35	−05	−45	12	−07	08	05	07	−12	15	07
93. Pupils/teachers	.71	28	−01	−05	02	05	−06	13	−01	16	01
94. Persons/doctors	.88	(85)	23	07	08	02	−04	−05	−08	09	−04
95. Hospital beds/doctors	.31	−13	−04	−22	02	02	−05	19	−00	−08	06
96. Nutritional adequacy	2.02	(−64)	−04	31	08	25	24	−09	08	−21	12
97. Ethnic groups	1.62	11	18	04	(72)	−35	−13	11	18	01	08
98. Language communities	.38	22	08	02	36	07	−19	09	−02	08	05
99. Nationalities	.65	−31	−06	19	25	18	−08	−19	07	−29	−05
100. Religions	.68	−03	10	−22	17	14	−19	06	−14	−02	−05
101. Racial groups	.94	14	−17	−12	−00	(−88)	−06	06	02	−08	07
102. Strike days	.61	−02	−47	−41	03	−00	26	−14	−10	02	04
103. Strikers/pop.	.52	−30	−25	−22	−06	11	27	−08	06	−10	−17
104. Strikers/workers	.34	−22	−24	−08	−05	05	21	02	03	−15	−16
105. Strikers/unionists	.34	05	−19	−35	04	20	08	−06	−01	09	−07
106. General strikes	.87	−09	−15	(−55)	−01	−11	15	10	20	−05	−04
107. Antigovernment demonstrations	.94	−05	00	(−86)	01	−13	17	−04	−06	06	02
108. Revolutions	.66	48	05	−34	07	−30	−12	−21	01	−09	19

594

TABLE 8-7—Cont.
R-Factor Analysis of Asymmetry Variables

Variables	h²	Varimax Factors[a]									
		I	II	III	IV	V	VI	VII	VIII	IX	X
109. Guerrilla warfare	.43	30	−08	−41	06	−03	−00	−10	05	−03	07
110. Assassinations	.68	25	−14	(−66)	−05	02	−09	08	−01	12	01
111. Purges	.41	15	14	−35	−07	−04	−10	−13	−04	−14	07
112. Riots	.89	06	−18	(−78)	06	−23	08	−10	01	−11	−01
113. Domestic violence death rate	.32	−08	23	−17	−08	−13	−05	04	03	−07	03
114. Diffracted articulation	.46	−25	25	−04	−12	−20	09	04	−05	03	10
115. Diffracted aggregation	.74	−33	−42	12	−00	15	21	03	00	01	11
116. Party function fragmentation	.59	26	(51)	−24	−05	06	−01	09	11	−04	14
117. Weak executive and legislature	.83	27	(78)	06	08	09	−05	−04	06	−04	−09
118. Military interventions	.65	38	08	−21	−09	−24	−11	−38	02	02	09
119. Police interventions	.97	40	(73)	−11	06	−18	−16	−10	17	−16	15
120. Moviegoers/pop.	.87	(−78)	−27	03	03	−05	−00	−02	−03	−13	04
121. Library book circ./pop.	1.22	(−87)	−04	34	08	−05	−00	−22	−03	12	03
122. Newspapers/pop.	1.20	(−83)	−35	08	−11	04	13	−02	−08	08	−06
123. Telephones/pop.	.84	(−66)	−35	22	−07	24	24	−13	−04	02	03
124. Domestic mail/pop.	1.08	(−82)	−32	03	−07	12	12	−00	04	−04	10
125. Radios/pop.	1.05	(−89)	−28	01	−09	−14	04	−03	04	−00	−02
126. TV's/pop.	.78	(−52)	−27	08	09	01	14	−15	−36	−02	−08
127. Land ownership inequality	1.06	36	−21	−02	05	−35	−00	−18	13	(−75)	−01
128. % Owning ½ land	1.20	−43	08	06	−01	28	07	07	−00	(76)	01
129. % Owning 5% land	1.06	−09	−04	−02	−05	−05	−07	−12	06	16	04
130. Income inequality[b]											
131. Income inequality[b]											
132. % Rented farms	.77	−07	12	−18	15	11	(63)	08	05	−11	10
133. % Customs-excise taxes	.74	44	15	17	11	−10	−08	−09	−04	−05	31
134. Religious heterogeneity	.97	−15	01	01	05	−03	−05	−05	−05	−02	13
135. Racial heterogeneity	.84	26	−05	−14	−02	(−78)	−04	02	−05	−04	02

TABLE 8-7—Cont.
R-Factor Analysis of Asymmetry Variables

596

Variables	h²	Varimax Factors[a]									
		I	II	III	IV	V	VI	VII	VIII	IX	X
136. Linguistic heterogeneity	.64	22	11	02	(51)	08	-00	08	07	-07	-09
137. Heterogeneity	.75	15	09	-12	31	-31	-05	00	-02	-05	-11
138. % Largest religion	.82	23	-12	-02	-17	-17	-01	05	00	-18	03
139. % Largest ethnic group	.83	-29	20	-06	(-62)	22	-08	-06	-19	14	-26
140. % Largest language	.20	-26	06	10	-16	08	00	09	-00	02	04
141. % Native born	.87	41	16	-07	-15	-26	-01	35	-20	28	01
142. % Largest race	1.05	-21	15	09	-03	(84)	10	06	-03	07	-10
143. Number of parties	.93	-11	-29	-26	-14	02	-11	-06	02	-04	04
144. Two- or multi-party system	.94	01	(-77)	11	03	-14	02	-21	-01	-21	02
145. Multiparty system	.84	-13	(-73)	-12	09	17	01	04	01	06	-07
146. Political party types	.63	17	(-50)	-19	-03	-02	20	15	12	12	-20
147. Homicide rate	.83	45	24	-24	-01	(-51)	-23	10	03	-11	-10
148. Car death rate	1.00	(-51)	-31	01	10	-06	13	-10	08	-04	10
149. Liver cirrhosis death rate	.70	-06	14	01	-04	-10	13	22	08	00	-13
150. Syphilis death rate	.87	-12	15	-03	-03	-19	29	18	-06	-10	13
151. Illegitimacy rate	.90	43	-07	-16	-06	(-63)	36	-13	-13	-13	17
152. Suicide rate	.72	-50	-09	04	-16	18	-12	00	-04	05	-12
153. Accident death rate	1.01	-06	-36	-21	03	-13	13	-34	-00	02	-23
154. Ulcer death rate	.32	-11	-01	06	-06	26	07	05	03	09	00
155. Constitutional	1.20	-26	(-93)	-01	-02	-09	01	09	08	-04	05
156. Nonauthoritarian	.95	(-67)	-31	03	-01	-02	01	27	-01	-02	08
157. Nontotalitarian	1.03	39	(-78)	-10	-01	-06	-07	-20	09	-06	-07
158. Nonpolyarchic	1.91	23	(92)	08	09	04	02	-07	-11	06	-07
159. Non-elitist	.78	-27	(-63)	-02	-11	27	05	16	16	-01	14
160. Lack of personalismo	.75	(-57)	13	17	02	26	08	07	-22	02	04
161. Group discrimination	.86	16	18	-08	(80)	15	02	-07	-11	03	-08
162. Political structures	.99	-17	(-92)	-10	00	-09	03	-06	04	-03	-01

TABLE 8–7—Cont.
R–Factor Analysis of Asymmetry Variables

Variables	h²	I	II	III	IV	V	VI	VII	VIII	IX	X
						Varimax Factors[a]					
163. Bureaucratic traditionalism	.85	(61)	22	13	26	12	03	—03	—05	—02	—13
164. Lack of trade dependence	.75	(58)	01	02	—08	—21	—15	—05	25	—22	—16
165. Exports ≠ imports	.26	23	—05	—07	—01	19	—07	20	03	—03	07
166. Balance of investments	.57	—39	—23	—12	14	—20	06	07	—13	—03	—17
167. Balance of donations	.58	—01	—02	—05	16	21	—00	04	03	15	—12
168. Immigrants ≠ emigrants	1.06	—29	—03	07	—01	26	—15	—08	02	—03	(—85)
169. Stereotypy[b]											
170. Friendliness[b]											
171. Foreign mail sent ≠ received	.50	22	01	06	12	11	—03	—21	02	—18	—07
172. Bloc prominence	.80	—14	07	—27	11	—07	20	—13	—11	32	—07
173. Communist countries	.99	22	—04	(—64)	18	—07	—08	—07	16	—08	03
174. Penetrated polity	.91	—21	(63)	18	01	—08	—15	36	—01	02	16
175. Bloc membership	.44	—26	04	—13	—14	—22	17	—00	—10	—06	—00
176. Diplomatic expulsions + recalls	.57	—31	01	—33	11	—01	04	03	—02	10	05
177. Severances	1.10	20	04	—15	—01	—14	—12	—11	07	—11	04
178. Diplomats abroad ≠ at home	.90	08	01	19	—10	20	—10	12	05	—06	—03
179. I. O.'s HQ'd abroad ≠ at home	.82	38	27	08	—08	—04	(—64)	11	21	—05	08
180. Wars	.96	—07	11	07	—08	06	13	12	09	—01	—12
181. Foreign military clashes	.81	08	15	—08	05	13	03	—26	10	—01	—02
182. Foreign killed	.97	—00	10	—16	14	14	03	04	01	01	12
183. For. viol. death rate	.75	05	02	—20	—04	03	—05	13	—09	—17	14

[a] Factor loadings are multiplied by 100; loadings > ± .50 are enclosed in parentheses.
[b] Deleted from the factor analysis.
Note: Eigenvalues for each of the 43 R–Factors appear at the bottom of Table 8–8.

TABLE 8-8
Correlations Between 43 R-Factors and 85 Countries[a]

| Country | Varimax Factors | | | | | | | | | | | |
	I	II	III	IV	V	VI	VII	VIII	IX	X	XI	XII
1. Afghanistan	.01	.06	.19	−.11	.02	−.06	.15	−.00	.07	.05	−.00	.04
2. Albania	−.08	.09	.21	−.10	.10	−.02	.33	.00	.20	.03	−.05	.02
3. Argentina	−.08	−.01	.13	−.06	−.02	.07	.01	.01	−.25	.07	.02	−.02
4. Australia	−.14	−.05	.16	−.01	.02	.05	−.01	−.09	−.17	.02	−.07	.03
5. Austria	−.08	−.04	.10	−.09	−.01	−.02	.09	−.02	−.15	.00	−.11	−.01
6. Belgium	−.15	−.05	.11	−.01	.05	.14	.02	−.05	−.21	.04	−.08	−.02
7. Bolivia	.03	.01	.03	−.09	−.11	−.02	.06	.05	−.27	.03	.04	−.05
8. Brazil	−.01	−.05	.10	−.07	−.08	−.04	.01	.03	−.30	.00	.01	.01
9. Bulgaria	−.11	.05	.14	−.09	.06	−.05	.28	−.03	.13	−.01	−.06	.00
10. Burma	−.09	−.02	.12	−.13	.04	−.09	.23	.02	.02	.04	−.22	−.05
11. Cambodia	.04	.03	.08	−.13	−.02	−.11	.10	−.02	−.01	−.02	.04	.05
12. Canada	−.18	−.05	.14	.00	.05	.06	−.00	−.17	−.01	.00	−.12	.03
13. Ceylon	−.04	.03	.11	−.10	−.01	−.08	.14	−.03	.09	.00	−.04	.00
14. Chile	.03	.00	.10	−.07	−.10	−.03	.04	.05	−.24	.02	.09	−.02
15. China	−.01	.04	.12	−.17	−.01	−.19	.12	−.07	.01	−.12	.02	.06
16. Taiwan	−.00	.15	.17	−.04	.08	.08	.16	.06	.08	.12	.08	.03
17. Colombia	−.01	−.00	.09	−.05	−.09	−.02	−.00	.05	−.32	.02	.08	−.02
18. Costa Rica	.03	−.01	.08	−.07	−.09	−.06	.07	.02	−.22	.01	.06	.01
19. Cuba	−.04	.05	.02	−.06	−.06	.03	.05	−.05	−.14	.05	.02	−.07
20. Czechoslovakia	−.15	.00	.14	−.05	.06	.00	.18	−.15	.11	−.01	−.20	.03
21. Denmark	−.16	−.05	.14	−.03	.04	.06	.01	−.13	−.10	.01	−.10	.04
22. Dominican Rep.	.03	.03	.11	−.07	−.07	−.01	.14	.04	−.17	.04	.07	.00
23. Ecuador	.06	−.01	.07	−.06	−.12	−.03	.02	.05	−.31	.01	.10	.01
24. Egypt	.04	−.02	.06	−.08	−.08	−.02	−.02	.06	−.33	.01	.03	.01
25. El Salvador	.06	−.00	.07	−.08	−.12	−.05	.03	.03	−.26	.00	.09	.01
26. Ethiopia	.01	.06	.17	−.05	.01	.03	.11	.03	.10	.08	.04	.03
27. Finland	−.14	−.04	.16	−.07	.03	−.00	.06	−.01	−.17	.02	−.15	.01

TABLE 8–8—Cont.
Correlations Between 43 R–Factors and 85 Countries[a]

Country	I	II	III	IV	V	VI	VII	VIII	IX	X	XI	XII
						Varimax Factors						
28. France	−.16	−.04	.13	−.07	.06	.07	.07	−.02	−.17	.05	−.15	.01
29. E. Germany	−.11	−.01	.16	−.05	−.01	.02	.12	−.18	−.04	−.02	−.13	.04
30. W. Germany	−.10	−.02	.15	−.05	.00	.02	.07	−.07	−.06	.01	−.09	.02
31. Greece	−.16	.01	.17	−.10	.11	.02	.14	.01	−.03	.06	−.14	−.01
32. Guatemala	.07	−.01	.06	−.07	−.12	.03	.03	.03	−.27	.01	.09	.02
33. Haiti	−.06	.02	.09	−.13	.03	−.08	.24	−.05	.10	−.01	−.12	−.00
34. Honduras	.06	.01	.08	−.07	−.12	−.05	.07	.05	−.24	.02	.09	.01
35. Hungary	−.07	.05	.04	−.11	−.02	−.06	.15	−.08	.03	−.00	−.08	−.08
36. India	−.03	.06	.12	−.04	.05	.08	.13	.03	.10	.09	−.02	−.04
37. Indonesia	−.06	.06	.04	−.08	−.01	−.09	.20	−.01	.05	.02	−.04	−.08
38. Iran	.06	.04	.09	−.12	−.03	−.11	.16	−.03	−.01	.01	.04	.04
39. Iraq	.07	−.02	.03	−.09	−.12	−.07	.01	.06	−.35	.01	.05	.01
40. Ireland	−.07	−.04	.10	−.12	−.02	−.07	.11	−.00	−.12	.00	−.10	−.02
41. Israel	−.04	.01	.09	−.07	.00	−.03	.13	.03	−.19	.02	−.03	.01
42. Italy	−.15	−.05	.13	−.04	.04	.06	.05	−.01	−.22	.04	−.10	−.01
43. Japan	−.14	−.07	.10	−.08	.02	−.03	.07	−.12	−.08	−.04	−.16	.00
44. Jordan	−.05	.03	.05	−.12	.10	−.07	.13	.02	−.08	.02	−.11	−.00
45. N. Korea	−.02	.08	.13	−.13	.11	−.09	.29	−.05	.05	.02	.09	.07
46. S. Korea	−.04	.10	.14	−.13	.09	−.07	.30	−.02	.14	.05	.05	.01
47. Lebanon	−.05	.00	.08	−.09	−.00	−.10	.18	−.04	.06	−.01	−.05	.01
48. Liberia	−.07	.06	.20	−.03	.06	.05	.21	.01	.17	.10	−.08	−.00
49. Libya	.04	.03	.12	−.12	−.03	−.07	.07	−.05	−.01	.03	.03	.02
50. Mexico	−.04	.04	.14	−.11	−.00	−.05	.14	−.07	.08	.02	−.01	.05
51. Nepal	.06	.03	.10	−.16	−.05	−.11	.13	−.08	.03	−.01	.03	.06
52. Netherlands	−.16	−.04	.14	−.02	.06	.12	.06	−.04	−.15	.06	−.11	−.02
53. New Zealand	−.13	−.03	.15	−.06	.04	.04	.07	.07	−.20	.07	−.08	−.03
54. Nicaragua	.00	−.00	.11	−.09	−.07	−.06	.15	.01	−.14	.00	−.03	.01

TABLE 8–8—Cont.
Correlations Between 43 R–Factors and 85 Countries[a]

Country	I	II	III	IV	V	VI	VII	VIII	IX	X	XI	XII
						Varimax Factors						
55. Norway	−.13	−.03	.17	−.07	.04	.02	.07	.02	−.17	.06	−.08	−.00
56. Mongolia	.03	.06	.16	−.14	−.02	−.06	.15	−.05	.11	.02	.05	.04
57. Pakistan	−.02	.01	.13	−.11	.01	−.04	.08	.04	−.07	.08	−.04	−.03
58. Panama	−.00	−.02	.08	−.07	−.10	−.05	.08	−.01	−.19	−.02	−.04	.01
59. Paraguay	−.01	.04	.11	−.14	−.03	−.08	.10	−.06	.07	.01	−.03	.03
60. Peru	.04	−.01	.08	−.07	−.10	−.06	.00	.03	−.28	.00	.05	.02
61. Philippines	.01	.03	.06	−.08	−.06	−.00	.10	.03	−.15	.02	.05	−.04
62. Poland	−.07	.03	.16	−.07	.00	−.02	.20	−.02	.00	.01	−.02	.02
63. Portugal	−.03	.05	.14	−.07	.05	.09	.10	.03	.09	.07	−.01	−.01
64. Rumania	−.09	.04	.14	−.11	.06	−.05	.27	−.04	.13	−.02	−.14	.01
65. Saudi Arabia	.05	.06	.21	−.12	−.02	−.05	.20	−.01	.09	.08	.05	.03
66. Spain	.02	.04	.13	−.02	−.02	.10	.06	.06	−.10	.07	.06	.01
67. Sweden	−.18	−.04	.15	−.04	.08	.07	.04	−.13	−.00	.03	−.15	.01
68. Switzerland	−.14	.03	.20	−.04	.08	.10	.04	−.02	−.01	.07	−.02	.02
69. Syria	−.05	.03	.12	−.09	.01	−.15	.16	.00	.04	.00	.00	.01
70. Thailand	.03	.02	.11	−.13	.00	−.04	.11	−.00	.01	.00	.03	.00
71. Turkey	−.13	.02	.16	−.06	.10	.01	.14	.03	−.01	.09	−.06	.01
72. South Africa	−.13	−.02	.15	−.08	.06	−.01	.05	.07	−.08	.07	−.10	−.01
73. USSR	−.18	.03	.20	−.03	.11	.02	.20	−.02	.02	.06	−.05	.02
74. UK	−.15	−.06	.12	−.01	.04	.11	−.02	−.13	−.13	.02	−.11	.02
75. USA	−.15	−.05	.11	.01	.02	.08	−.04	−.18	−.10	−.02	−.08	.04
76. Uruguay	−.07	−.02	.16	−.06	−.01	.07	.00	−.01	−.26	.05	−.01	−.00
77. Venezuela	−.04	−.01	.07	−.05	.07	−.02	.08	−.01	−.21	.00	−.02	.01
78. Yemen	−.01	.08	.27	−.06	.03	.01	.16	.01	.15	.10	.05	.03
79. Yugoslavia	−.08	.05	.22	−.03	.06	.07	.12	.03	−.01	.10	−.02	.02
80. Laos	.03	.11	.16	−.08	.12	−.26	.29	.02	.06	.00	.15	.03
81. N. Vietnam	.03	.06	.13	−.11	.04	−.16	.21	−.03	−.01	−.00	.06	.04

600

TABLE 8-8—Cont.
Correlations Between 43 R-Factors and 85 Countries[a]

Country	Varimax Factors											
	I	II	III	IV	V	VI	VII	VIII	IX	X	XI	XII
82. S. Vietnam	.03	.07	.14	-.10	.02	.00	.17	-.00	.07	.05	.06	.01
83. Morocco	.01	.07	.18	-.00	.04	-.17	.12	.04	.10	.03	.10	-.00
84. Sudan	.07	.09	.20	.01	-.01	-.31	.16	.05	.11	.01	.12	-.00
85. Tunisia	-.15	.05	.18	-.03	.11	-.10	.32	-.02	.24	.02	-.08	-.03
Eigenvalues[b]	34.8	17.5	10.0	8.7	8.1	7.1	6.7	5.4	5.1	4.6	4.4	4.2
Percent total variance[b]	19.6	9.9	5.6	4.9	4.6	4.0	3.8	3.1	2.9	2.6	2.5	2.4
Percent common variance[b]	19.0	9.6	5.5	4.8	4.4	3.8	3.6	3.0	2.8	2.5	2.4	2.3

Country	Varimax Factors													
	XIII	XIV	XV	XVI	XVII	XVIII	XIX	XX	XXI	XXII	XXIII	XXIV	XXV	XXVI
1	.13	-.17	.07	-.07	-.03	.01	-.23	-.01	.03	-.14	-.02	.09	.25	.01
2	-.07	-.12	.05	-.10	.00	.04	-.16	-.17	.02	-.27	.01	.02	.18	-.10
3	-.18	-.07	.03	-.07	.01	-.01	-.08	.06	-.01	-.11	-.05	-.01	.07	-.03
4	-.23	-.09	.01	-.02	-.05	.09	-.10	.08	-.01	-.08	-.04	-.05	.12	-.11
5	-.16	-.04	.01	-.01	.02	.02	-.09	.03	-.03	-.14	-.02	-.01	.13	-.10
6	-.27	-.07	-.02	-.07	.02	.06	-.05	.07	-.03	-.12	-.03	-.02	.12	-.08
7	-.03	-.03	.04	.04	.00	-.05	-.05	.00	.01	-.12	-.03	.03	-.00	-.02
8	-.14	-.04	.03	-.01	.02	-.02	-.09	.03	.03	-.14	-.06	-.08	.03	-.04
9	-.14	-.04	.02	-.10	.02	-.02	-.10	-.08	-.04	-.11	-.02	-.00	.10	-.12
10	-.14	-.08	.04	-.05	.11	-.01	-.14	.04	-.10	-.12	-.04	-.01	.07	-.11
11	.04	-.04	.02	-.06	.09	-.08	-.13	.01	.02	-.02	.01	.04	-.06	-.00
12	-.21	-.11	-.00	-.03	-.07	.12	-.06	.10	-.02	.01	.02	-.03	.17	-.14
13	-.05	-.04	.06	-.08	.05	-.02	-.11	-.06	-.05	-.11	-.01	.06	.05	-.08

TABLE 8–8—Cont.
Correlations Between 43 R–Factors and 85 Countries[a]

Country	XIII	XIV	XV	XVI	XVII	XVIII	XIX	XX	XXI	XXII	XXIII	XXIV	XXV	XXVI
							Varimax Factors							
14	−.06	−.03	.05	−.03	.03	−.06	−.10	−.02	−.04	−.14	−.03	−.02	.04	.00
15	.05	−.05	.04	−.06	.08	−.00	−.15	−.05	−.03	−.01	−.07	.01	−.06	−.01
16	.08	−.16	−.00	−.12	−.02	.05	−.20	−.07	.12	−.10	.08	.11	.33	.08
17	−.10	−.05	.05	.00	−.04	−.02	−.08	.01	.01	−.13	−.05	−.09	.04	−.03
18	−.05	−.01	.05	.00	.00	−.04	−.08	−.05	.02	−.14	−.06	.02	.02	−.03
19	−.02	−.08	.04	.08	−.08	.02	−.02	.08	−.03	−.02	−.01	.06	.02	−.07
20	−.15	−.07	.02	−.05	−.06	.06	−.07	−.02	−.02	−.04	.01	.07	.15	−.16
21	−.25	−.07	−.01	−.03	−.02	.07	−.07	.11	−.03	−.04	−.01	−.04	.07	−.13
22	−.02	−.06	.06	−.03	.01	−.03	−.11	−.07	.05	−.19	−.02	−.04	.15	−.03
23	−.01	−.02	.05	−.01	.01	−.06	−.08	−.03	.06	−.15	−.03	.03	.03	.02
24	−.08	−.04	−.02	−.01	.08	−.06	−.10	.06	.03	−.13	−.06	−.11	−.02	.04
25	−.01	−.02	.05	−.00	.01	−.03	−.09	−.04	.05	−.15	−.03	−.02	.02	−.00
26	.21	−.18	.08	−.06	−.10	.04	−.23	−.01	.05	−.15	.00	.10	.31	.03
27	−.30	−.06	−.01	−.05	.08	.02	−.10	.08	−.06	−.12	−.06	−.14	.03	−.10
28	−.31	−.06	−.04	−.07	.08	.04	−.08	.08	−.05	−.10	−.04	−.07	.06	−.10
29	−.12	−.08	.05	−.03	−.11	.06	−.09	−.01	.00	−.07	−.02	.09	.20	−.14
30	−.10	−.10	.02	−.01	−.07	.09	−.12	.02	.01	−.10	−.00	.01	.28	−.10
31	−.29	−.08	−.01	.12	.14	−.01	−.09	.05	−.10	−.11	−.06	−.07	.04	−.08
32	.00	−.02	.05	−.01	.02	−.06	−.08	−.01	.05	−.13	−.01	.01	.01	.00
33	−.11	−.02	.06	−.08	.05	−.04	−.09	−.06	−.08	−.09	−.07	−.08	.03	−.11
34	.00	−.04	.06	−.00	.01	−.05	−.10	−.04	.04	−.15	−.01	.06	.06	−.01
35	−.07	−.04	.02	.03	−.00	−.00	−.02	.02	−.08	−.03	−.00	.02	−.00	−.13
36	.05	−.15	.05	−.12	−.03	.03	−.16	−.04	.02	−.13	.00	.11	.33	−.00
37	−.13	−.02	.05	.02	−.02	−.03	−.02	−.02	−.09	−.06	−.03	.06	.01	−.12
38	.05	−.07	.03	−.08	.11	−.09	−.12	.03	.03	−.09	.05	.04	−.03	−.01
39	−.00	−.02	−.01	.07	.06	−.06	−.08	.04	−.06	−.12	−.03	−.06	−.05	.04
40	−.15	−.03	.01	−.01	.07	−.03	−.09	.01	.03	−.14	−.03	−.04	.07	−.10

TABLE 8–8—Cont.
Correlations Between 43 R–Factors and 85 Countries^a

Country	Varimax Factors													
	XIII	XIV	XV	XVI	XVII	XVIII	XIX	XX	XXI	XXII	XXIII	XXIV	XXV	XXVI
41	−.15	.01	−.04	−.02	.04	−.05	−.07	−.03	.03	−.14	−.05	−.00	.06	−.03
42	−.31	−.05	−.02	−.05	.04	.04	−.07	.07	−.05	−.12	−.06	−.09	.09	−.10
43	−.21	−.05	−.01	.01	.02	.06	−.06	.06	−.04	−.06	−.01	−.04	.08	−.15
44	−.10	−.04	−.13	−.04	.17	−.10	−.08	.05	.03	−.05	.01	−.06	.04	.02
45	−.11	−.07	−.08	−.09	.13	−.08	−.16	−.03	.10	−.05	.09	.01	.00	.01
46	−.06	−.09	−.01	−.13	.06	−.04	−.15	−.08	.03	−.11	.04	.07	.16	−.02
47	−.08	−.01	.04	−.06	.04	−.01	−.09	−.05	−.07	−.08	−.02	.07	.01	−.08
48	.05	−.16	.09	−.13	−.11	.04	−.22	−.05	.01	−.13	−.04	.12	.45	−.04
49	.11	−.09	.07	−.11	.05	−.09	−.14	.02	.03	−.07	.04	.08	.06	.00
50	−.03	−.11	.04	−.07	.03	−.03	−.16	−.02	.01	−.09	.02	.01	.11	−.07
51	.06	−.07	.06	−.09	.10	−.05	−.17	.04	−.00	−.10	.02	.07	−.02	−.01
52	−.29	−.09	−.01	−.08	.02	.08	−.07	.07	−.03	−.10	−.03	−.03	.15	−.01
53	−.28	−.08	.00	−.07	.08	.03	−.13	.05	−.07	−.17	−.09	−.09	.12	−.09
54	−.08	−.02	.06	−.04	.00	−.05	−.08	−.06	−.00	−.15	−.05	−.01	.07	−.05
55	−.27	−.08	.00	−.06	.06	.02	−.13	.07	−.05	−.14	−.06	−.09	.10	−.06
56	.17	−.14	.09	−.06	.01	−.02	−.28	−.00	.01	−.13	−.01	.09	.24	−.00
57	−.08	−.13	.04	−.16	.16	−.03	−.16	.08	−.02	−.10	.01	−.01	.14	.02
58	−.09	−.03	.07	−.02	.00	−.02	−.04	−.06	.01	−.18	−.03	.00	.03	−.06
59	.02	−.07	.06	−.10	.08	−.03	−.17	−.03	−.03	−.11	.00	.07	.04	−.06
60	−.03	−.01	.04	.01	.01	−.06	−.08	−.01	.03	−.13	−.04	.02	.01	−.01
61	−.04	−.05	.05	−.03	.04	−.04	−.07	−.07	.01	−.15	−.01	.01	.07	−.03
62	−.07	−.08	.05	−.06	−.06	.01	−.12	−.07	.02	−.15	−.03	.03	.21	−.08
63	.09	−.16	.04	−.07	−.02	.02	−.20	−.01	.02	−.11	.02	.06	.36	.01
64	−.13	−.04	.05	−.10	.01	−.00	−.10	−.11	−.05	−.11	−.03	.06	.08	−.12
65	.20	−.20	.11	−.09	−.03	−.05	−.25	.01	.05	−.18	.05	.11	.26	.03
66	.11	−.15	.04	−.05	−.05	.02	−.18	−.02	.09	−.14	.01	.08	.29	.06
67	−.21	−.12	−.01	−.04	−.02	.10	−.10	.10	−.03	−.04	.01	−.03	.18	−.13

TABLE 8–8—Cont.
Correlations Between 43 R–Factors and 85 Countries[a]

							Varimax Factors							
Country	XIII	XIV	XV	XVI	XVII	XVIII	XIX	XX	XXI	XXII	XXIII	XXIV	XXV	XXVI
68	−.14	−.17	.04	−.11	−.02	.07	−.18	.07	−.05	−.09	−.05	−.03	.22	−.02
69	−.10	−.03	.02	−.09	.04	−.00	−.14	−.08	.02	−.14	.02	.04	.02	−.06
70	.03	−.06	.03	−.06	.12	−.07	−.10	−.04	−.01	−.08	.05	.00	.02	.01
71	−.27	−.07	−.01	−.13	.10	−.03	−.11	.02	−.08	−.13	−.06	−.08	.06	−.06
72	−.22	−.13	−.00	−.08	.11	.04	−.17	.13	−.10	−.12	−.06	−.23	.11	−.05
73	−.31	−.09	.01	−.12	−.01	.09	−.13	−.00	−.07	−.11	−.10	−.09	.12	−.11
74	−.22	−.09	−.02	−.02	−.03	.11	−.05	.10	−.01	−.03	.01	−.01	.12	−.11
75	−.18	−.09	−.01	−.01	−.09	.11	−.03	.10	.02	.01	.02	−.01	.10	−.12
76	−.19	−.09	.04	−.08	.02	−.01	−.08	.05	−.02	−.12	−.09	.00	.06	−.03
77	−.14	−.06	.02	−.01	−.01	−.01	−.04	−.03	.00	−.15	−.06	−.05	.05	−.07
78	.25	−.24	.13	−.14	−.12	.00	−.37	−.00	.06	−.19	.01	.11	.37	.05
79	−.08	−.13	.04	−.10	−.04	.04	−.18	−.01	.00	−.15	−.06	−.01	.33	−.02
80	−.04	−.07	−.07	−.08	.00	−.02	−.16	−.11	.16	−.01	.05	−.05	.21	.08
81	−.05	−.05	−.03	−.08	.10	−.06	−.14	−.01	.07	−.00	.07	.02	−.04	−.00
82	.16	−.16	.03	−.09	−.01	−.01	−.19	−.01	.06	−.07	.04	.12	.26	.03
83	.18	−.19	.06	−.08	−.18	.06	−.27	−.09	.09	−.11	.04	.01	.47	.04
84	.21	−.18	.10	−.02	−.22	.08	−.24	−.14	.10	−.12	−.05	.04	.47	.09
85	−.12	−.07	.05	−.08	−.12	.04	−.12	−.18	−.05	−.14	−.11	.12	.34	−.15
Eigenvalues	3.9	3.8	3.6	3.4	3.1	3.0	2.8	2.7	2.7	2.6	2.5	2.4	2.2	2.2
Percent total variance	2.2	2.2	2.1	1.9	1.8	1.7	1.6	1.5	1.5	1.5	1.4	1.4	1.3	1.2
Percent common variance	2.2	2.1	2.0	1.8	1.7	1.7	1.5	1.5	1.5	1.4	1.4	1.4	1.2	1.2

TABLE 8-8—Cont.
Correlations Between 43 R–Factors and 85 Countries[a]

Varimax Factors

Country	XXVII	XXVIII	XXIX	XXX	XXXI	XXXII	XXXIII	XXXIV	XXXV	XXXVI	XXXVII	XXXVIII	XXXIX	XL	XLI	XLII	XLIII
1	-.08	.04	.01	.03	-.04	.10	-.03	-.02	-.15	-.28	-.05	-.14	-.05	-.08	.07	-.00	.01
2	-.06	-.12	-.10	.03	.05	.15	-.03	.02	-.01	-.19	-.01	-.04	-.13	-.05	.09	.08	-.07
3	.04	-.08	-.07	.06	.03	.14	.16	.03	.01	-.27	-.02	-.05	-.04	.07	.05	.09	.02
4	-.03	-.06	-.01	.04	.02	.17	.03	.06	.01	-.08	.03	-.01	-.05	.08	.05	.05	-.01
5	.01	-.04	-.07	-.02	.00	.12	.06	.07	.06	-.29	-.09	-.04	-.03	-.03	-.02	.00	-.06
6	.02	-.06	-.01	.04	.02	.18	.12	.06	.04	-.13	-.00	-.02	-.04	.08	.01	.06	-.04
7	.08	-.10	-.15	-.00	.03	.09	.32	-.00	.04	-.32	-.10	-.02	.06	.00	-.03	.02	.00
8	.05	-.06	-.12	-.00	.04	.13	.06	.07	.05	-.24	-.07	-.02	-.01	.04	.01	.03	.01
9	-.01	-.11	-.04	.02	.07	.10	.03	.04	.02	-.33	-.05	-.02	-.10	-.06	.03	.05	-.06
10	-.04	.02	.10	-.04	-.07	.06	.10	.11	.11	-.43	-.14	-.12	-.10	-.12	-.05	-.03	-.09
11	-.09	-.03	-.01	.05	.03	.04	.06	.06	-.03	(-.55)	-.11	-.15	-.08	-.02	-.02	-.10	.05
12	-.07	-.05	.12	.06	.01	.19	.02	.06	-.03	-.01	.05	-.03	-.05	.08	.04	-.01	-.02
13	-.02	-.03	-.05	.02	.02	.05	.08	.01	.02	-.46	-.05	-.07	-.08	-.05	-.01	-.01	.02
14	.04	-.08	-.10	.03	.06	.10	.08	.02	-.00	-.33	-.07	-.04	-.01	.02	.02	.03	.04
15	-.08	.04	-.05	.03	.02	.01	.06	.10	-.04	(-.57)	-.08	-.15	-.08	-.05	-.05	-.11	.08
16	-.08	-.07	.03	-.02	.06	.21	-.03	-.07	-.18	.07	-.02	-.07	-.02	-.01	.11	.04	-.03
17	.04	-.10	-.10	.05	.05	.12	.20	.03	.01	-.25	-.04	-.02	.03	.04	.02	.09	.02
18	.05	-.07	-.11	.02	.06	.09	.09	.01	.03	-.39	-.07	-.03	-.01	.00	-.01	.02	.04
19	.01	-.11	-.04	.01	.01	.11	(.52)	.01	.00	-.22	-.08	-.05	.11	-.00	-.03	-.00	-.02
20	-.04	-.09	.04	.03	.06	.18	.04	.03	-.03	-.22	.00	.02	-.07	-.02	.04	-.00	-.04
21	-.05	-.06	.05	.06	.02	.17	.04	.09	.01	-.16	.02	-.03	-.08	.08	.05	.01	-.02
22	.05	-.09	-.11	.04	.06	.12	.08	-.01	-.00	-.31	-.05	-.02	-.01	-.02	.01	.06	.02
23	.06	-.08	-.13	.01	.06	.12	.09	-.00	.01	-.29	-.08	.00	.03	.01	-.01	.03	.04
24	.08	-.02	-.09	.02	-.00	.09	.04	.06	.00	-.26	-.11	-.08	-.01	.09	.05	-.00	.01
25	.06	-.06	-.12	.03	.06	.08	.10	.02	.01	-.36	-.07	-.04	-.01	.02	-.02	.01	.05
26	-.07	.02	.02	.02	-.06	.10	-.06	-.09	-.17	-.10	-.00	-.08	-.01	-.08	.06	.05	.02
27	-.00	-.05	-.04	.04	-.00	.15	.03	.11	.08	-.22	-.03	-.06	-.10	.07	.05	.06	-.05

TABLE 8–8—Cont.
Correlations Between 43 R–Factors and 85 Countries[a]

Varimax Factors

Country	XXVII	XXVIII	XXIX	XXX	XXXI	XXXII	XXXIII	XXXIV	XXXV	XXXVI	XXXVII	XXXVIII	XXXIX	XL	XLI	XLII	XLIII
28	.01	-.05	-.03	.03	.03	.06	.06	.11	.08	-.22	-.04	-.05	.11	.07	.03	.04	-.06
29	-.01	-.12	.03	.03	.04	.18	.03	.02	-.04	-.19	.00	.01	-.02	-.01	.04	.03	-.01
30	-.02	-.04	.00	-.01	.01	.18	.01	.03	-.04	-.08	-.02	-.02	-.01	-.01	.04	.01	-.04
31	-.03	-.02	-.04	.05	-.02	.10	.04	.11	.08	-.29	-.03	-.09	-.16	.04	.05	.08	-.07
32	.05	-.07	-.10	.03	.06	.09	.11	-.01	.00	-.40	-.08	-.04	.02	.01	-.01	-.01	.06
33	-.00	-.06	-.06	.05	-.00	.05	.08	.05	.05	(-.51)	-.07	-.05	-.10	-.08	-.04	.01	-.01
34	.06	-.07	-.11	.04	.05	.09	.14	-.06	-.01	-.35	-.08	-.05	.05	-.01	-.02	.03	.05
35	-.02	-.08	-.02	.01	.03	.06	.42	.03	.03	-.36	-.08	-.07	.02	-.04	-.01	-.02	-.04
36	-.02	.01	-.04	.00	-.05	.12	.05	-.07	-.07	-.08	-.01	-.05	.00	-.08	.01	.09	-.01
37	.00	-.10	-.08	.01	-.00	.04	.40	-.01	.05	-.32	-.08	-.05	.00	-.08	-.02	.03	-.06
38	-.05	-.05	.05	.04	.02	.10	.04	.01	-.06	-.47	-.12	-.16	-.07	-.01	.01	-.10	.02
39	.10	-.08	-.13	-.05	.05	.08	.18	.07	-.01	-.24	-.15	-.06	.04	.04	.04	-.06	-.01
40	.00	-.03	-.07	-.03	.02	.12	.05	.09	.07	-.35	-.09	-.06	-.06	-.02	.01	-.02	-.05
41	.09	-.10	-.10	-.03	.08	.14	.04	.03	.02	-.22	-.11	-.01	-.05	-.00	.06	.03	-.07
42	.02	-.06	-.05	.03	.01	.15	.06	.09	.08	-.12	-.02	-.02	-.07	.06	.04	.10	-.06
43	-.07	-.03	-.01	-.02	.01	.15	.04	.12	.06	-.20	-.05	-.03	-.05	.01	.00	-.06	-.06
44	.04	-.03	-.02	-.06	.04	.14	-.03	.13	-.05	-.15	-.18	-.13	-.11	.04	.10	-.12	-.14
45	-.05	-.19	.04	-.00	.15	.22	-.03	.11	-.07	-.11	-.17	-.11	-.08	.04	.16	-.09	-.09
46	-.09	-.10	.01	.00	.08	.17	.02	.06	-.08	-.22	-.07	-.08	-.09	-.02	.09	-.02	-.07
47	-.03	-.04	-.04	.04	.03	.04	.10	.02	.03	(-.54)	-.06	-.09	-.10	-.05	-.04	-.03	.01
48	-.02	-.04	-.03	.01	-.06	.13	-.07	-.07	-.11	.07	.02	-.00	-.01	-.13	.06	.14	-.05
49	-.07	.01	.02	.05	-.01	.08	.06	-.02	-.09	(-.52)	-.11	-.16	-.06	-.08	.00	-.05	.05
50	-.06	-.05	.02	.04	.03	.12	.02	.03	-.05	-.34	-.04	-.09	-.06	-.02	.04	-.03	.02
51	-.07	.02	.06	.06	-.00	.06	.03	.02	-.06	(-.58)	-.12	-.20	-.08	-.04	-.04	-.17	.08
52	.00	-.05	-.01	.03	.01	.17	.09	.08	.04	-.09	-.00	-.03	-.06	.07	.02	.06	-.05
53	.02	-.03	-.11	.02	-.02	.13	.05	.09	.09	-.15	-.03	-.05	-.09	.05	.04	.11	-.06
54	.08	-.09	-.11	.01	.04	.10	.07	-.01	.04	-.35	-.05	.02	-.02	-.05	.02	.06	-.01

TABLE 8–8—Cont.
Correlations Between 43 R–Factors and 85 Countries[a]

Varimax Factors

Country	XXVII	XXVIII	XXIX	XXX	XXXI	XXXII	XXXIII	XXXIV	XXXV	XXXVI	XXXVII	XXXVIII	XXXIX	XL	XLI	XLII	XLIII
55	.01	−.05	−.06	.03	−.01	.14	.03	.09	.06	−.19	−.03	−.06	−.09	.05	.06	.09	−.05
56	−.09	.06	.02	.05	−.05	.11	−.01	−.07	−.12	−.37	−.07	−.15	−.03	−.06	.03	−.02	.05
57	−.10	.03	−.06	.02	−.08	.09	.07	.08	.01	−.36	−.10	−.18	−.10	−.01	−.03	−.03	−.00
58	.04	−.07	−.08	.03	.07	.11	.10	.03	.03	−.38	−.04	−.01	−.02	.01	−.01	−.01	.04
59	−.04	.00	−.02	.03	.03	.06	.09	.02	−.00	(−.51)	−.06	−.12	−.09	−.03	−.02	−.05	.04
60	.05	−.07	−.12	.01	.06	.08	.07	.02	.01	−.40	−.09	−.02	.00	−.00	.00	−.01	.03
61	.01	−.05	−.10	.03	.04	.08	.23	−.03	.02	−.40	−.06	−.06	.00	−.01	−.02	.02	.02
62	.02	−.08	−.04	−.00	.04	.14	.01	−.01	−.05	−.15	−.01	.02	−.03	−.05	.06	.08	−.04
63	−.07	.01	−.00	−.00	−.05	.13	−.03	−.02	−.11	−.06	−.02	−.07	−.01	−.05	.06	.04	−.01
64	−.01	−.10	−.06	.03	.04	.09	.04	.03	.03	−.40	−.04	−.03	−.11	−.08	.02	.04	−.04
65	.11	−.01	.05	.04	−.07	.14	−.08	−.00	−.19	−.15	−.06	−.14	−.01	−.11	.12	.03	.01
66	−.01	−.03	−.04	−.01	−.01	.16	−.00	−.09	−.12	.01	−.02	−.03	.05	−.02	.06	.06	.00
67	−.08	−.03	.06	.04	−.02	.19	.02	.07	−.01	−.06	.03	−.05	−.07	.05	.05	.01	−.04
68	−.07	−.01	.02	.08	−.05	.14	−.00	.03	−.08	−.06	.05	−.08	−.08	.07	.08	.11	.00
69	.00	−.12	−.04	.02	.10	.08	.12	.03	.02	−.43	−.09	−.13	−.11	−.01	−.04	−.03	−.02
70	−.24	−.01	−.02	.04	.02	.05	.06	.04	−.02	−.45	−.08	−.14	−.08	−.00	−.00	−.08	.02
71	−.01	−.07	−.04	.06	.01	.10	.00	.08	.03	−.20	−.02	−.08	−.15	.05	.09	.11	−.07
72	−.06	.06	−.02	.04	−.09	.09	−.01	.09	.04	−.13	−.03	−.15	−.12	.07	.05	.07	−.06
73	−.03	−.10	−.02	.10	.03	.17	.01	.04	.01	−.19	.02	−.06	−.16	.03	.09	.12	−.05
74	−.06	−.05	.05	.04	.03	.19	.07	.07	.00	−.07	.03	−.02	−.04	.08	.02	−.01	−.02
75	−.05	−.07	.12	.05	.04	.19	.11	.05	−.05	−.01	.04	−.01	−.01	.10	.03	−.02	.00
76	.04	−.06	−.02	.10	.03	.14	.13	.03	.01	−.36	−.00	−.05	−.07	.06	.03	.09	.04
77	.09	−.07	−.08	−.01	.06	.12	.13	.05	.04	−.26	−.05	−.02	−.01	.01	.02	.02	−.02
78	−.14	−.00	.04	−.02	−.11	.17	−.13	−.03	−.24	.26	.02	−.08	.02	−.12	.18	.11	−.02
79	−.01	−.05	−.02	.04	−.00	.14	−.04	−.03	−.07	−.03	.02	−.02	−.06	−.01	.10	.15	−.00
80	−.04	−.17	−.01	−.04	.11	.21	−.08	.01	−.12	.24	−.07	−.08	−.08	.04	.16	.02	−.04
81	−.04	−.09	.02	.04	.11	.14	.03	.02	−.07	−.45	−.19	−.16	−.12	−.01	.06	−.13	−.01

TABLE 8-8—Cont.
Correlations Between 43 R-Factors and 85 Countries[a]

Country								Varimax Factors									
	XXVII	XXVIII	XXIX	XXX	XXXI	XXXII	XXXIII	XXXIV	XXXV	XXXVI	XXXVII	XXXVIII	XXXIX	XL	XLI	XLII	XLIII
82	−.10	−.00	.03	.04	−.00	.12	.04	−.09	−.16	−.33	−.07	−.11	−.03	−.03	.03	−.02	.03
83	−.04	−.04	.03	.04	−.05	.14	−.06	−.19	−.21	.21	−.03	−.11	.04	.03	.06	.12	−.02
84	−.05	−.01	.03	.01	−.07	.13	−.07	−.17	−.21	.21	−.02	−.16	.03	−.01	.07	.10	−.01
85	.04	−.09	−.06	.02	−.01	.11	.01	−.09	−.01	−.06	−.03	−.01	−.06	−.09	.04	.16	−.12
Eigenvalues[c]	2.1	2.0	1.9	1.8	1.7	1.7	1.6	1.5	1.5	1.4	1.3	1.3	1.2	1.2	1.1	1.1	1.0
Percent total variance	1.2	1.1	1.1	1.0	1.0	0.9	0.9	0.8	0.8	0.8	0.7	0.7	0.7	0.7	0.6	0.6	0.6
Percent common variance	1.2	1.1	1.0	1.0	0.9	0.9	0.9	0.8	0.8	0.8	0.7	0.7	0.7	0.7	0.6	0.6	0.6

[a] Correlations > ±.50 are enclosed in parentheses.
[b] Based on principal axis factors.
[c] Based on 29 factors.

TABLE 8–9
Factor XI: Nonextractive Polity

Variable	Loading	Description
75	—90	Few government expenditures/national income
78	—78	Few education expenditures/national income
79	—65	Few welfare expenditures/national income
77	—64	Few military expenditures/national income
81	—58	Few government expenditures/national income
58	—57	Few per capita education expenditures
80	—49	Few government expenditures/national income
36	—36	Agricultural = nonagricultural population
63	—28	Low voter turnout
1	—28	Unchanged income per capita

TABLE 8–10
Factor XII: Absentee Landlordism

Variable	Loading	Description
129	—94	Few own 95 % of land, many own the rest
171	—39	Foreign mail sent = received
83	—38	Not a bicameral legislature
7	—37	Unchanged per capita electricity production
58	33	High per capita education expenditures
128	—28	Few own half of land
28	26	Much change in per capita education expenditures
84	26	Government revenue ≠ expenditures
9	26	Change in caloric intake per capita
72	—25	Few religious persons vote for nonsecular parties

TABLE 8–11
Factor XIII: Rural Austerity

Variable	Loading	Description
35	—90	Agricultural = nonagricultural employment
96	—53	Caloric inadequacy
80	—45	Few government expenditures/national income
36	—45	Agricultural = nonagricultural population
150	41	High syphilis death rate
63	—40	Low voter turnout
44	—31	Political centralization
163	—26	Not a traditional bureaucracy
156	26	Nonauthoritarian regime
153	—25	Low accident death rate

TABLE 8–12
Factor XIV: Political Competition

Variable	Loading	Description
143	78	Many political parties
24	41	Many government crises
17	38	Government instability
144	34	Two- or multi-party system
31	33	Party system instability
16	29	Change in per capita Communist Party strength
76	27	High army, administrative expenditures/GNP
73	27	Many Communists vote Communist
133	26	High customs taxes/total taxes
108	25	Many revolutions

TABLE 8–13
Factor XV: Nonconflictual Foreign Behavior

Variable	Loading	Description
182	—90	Few deaths due to foreign conflict
180	—83	Few wars
181	—79	Few foreign military clashes
183	—72	Low foreign conflict death rate
68	—51	No military mobilizations
172	—49	Bloc follower
76	—47	Few army, administrative expenditures/GNP
167	—43	Little foreign aid sent or received
81	—36	Few central government expenditures/national income
67	—35	Few soldiers/persons aged 15–64

TABLE 8–14
Factor XVI: Unguided Development

Variable	Loading	Description
61	—75	Developmental ideology
100	33	Many religious groups
74	—31	Mobilizational system style
6	30	Change in rail freight
115	29	Diffuse aggregation
159	27	Non-elitist political recruitment
21	—27	Unchanged birth rate
174	—26	Nonpenetrated polity
12	—23	National income stability
22	—22	Unchanged death rate

TABLE 8–15
Factor XVII: Modernizing Oligarchy

Variable	Loading	Description
42	83	Vertical power centralization
43	84	Unitary system
148	—50	Low automobile accident death rate
153	—50	Low death rate due to accidents
141	49	Many percent native born
149	—44	Low liver cirrhosis death rate
83	—38	Not a bicameral legislature
81	34	High central government expenditures/national income
80	32	High general government expenditures/national income
138	30	Large main religious group

TABLE 8–16
Factor XVIII: Societal Tension

Variable	Loading	Description
134	89	Religious heterogeneity
138	—66	Small main religious group
137	45	Heterogeneity
36	42	Agricultural $\neq$ nonagricultural population
84	40	Government revenue $\neq$ expenditure
152	29	High suicide rate
41	26	Sectional discrimination
148	24	High automobile accident death rate
73	22	Many Communists voting Communist
126	22	Many television sets per capita

TABLE 8–17
Factor XIX: Discontentment with Laxity

Variable	Loading	Description
50	77	Energy generation = consumption
84	—39	Government revenue < expenditure
30	—33	Unchanged per capita government budget
149	—31	Low liver cirrhosis death rate
150	—27	Low syphilis death rate
20	—26	Few years of tenure per chief executive
93	—21	Few pupils per teacher
171	21	Foreign mail sent $\neq$ received
163	21	Traditional bureaucracy
49	—20	Much unexploited waterpower

TABLE 8–18
Factor XX: Reactionary Development

Variable	Loading	Description
178	—81	Foreign missions abroad = at home
15	—66	Unchanged literacy rate
93	—60	Few pupils per teacher
100	—39	Few religious groups
6	37	Change in railroad freight
99	—36	Few nationality groups
26	36	Legal government changes
74	27	Nonmobilizational system style
137	—25	Demotypic homogeneity
152	25	High suicide rate

TABLE 8–19
Factor XXI: Elite Scapegoatism

Variable	Loading	Description
177	89	Severances in diplomatic relations
76	47	Many army, administrative expenditures/GNP
1	—44	Unchanged per capita national income
8	26	Change in total population
111	23	Many purges
3	—22	Unchanged per capita GNP
176	22	Many expulsions, recalls of diplomats
44	22	Political decentralization
67	22	Many soldiers/persons aged 15–64
83	21	Bicameral legislature

TABLE 8–20
Factor XXII: Developmental Slowdown

Variable	Loading	Description
2	—96	Unchanged per capita electricity consumption
15	—43	Unchanged literacy rate
176	—33	No expulsions, recalls of diplomats
152	30	High suicide rate
141	—28	Few percent native born
86	—26	Press freedom
52	—24	Low railroad freight density
48	22	Much unexploited energy
148	21	High automobile accident death rate
145	21	Multiparty system

TABLE 8–21
Factor XXIII: Domestic Disengagement

Variable	Loading	Description
70	—95	Low marriage rate
3	—37	Unchanged GNP per capita
120	—34	Few moviegoers per capita
76	—27	Low army, administrative expenditures/GNP
1	—22	Unchanged per capita national income
24	22	Many government crises
137	21	Heterogeneity
93	21	Many pupils per teacher
30	21	Change in government expenditures per capita
32	20	Change in number of ministries

TABLE 8–22
Factor XXIV: Internationally Guided Development

Variable	Loading	Description
14	95	Change in agricultural employment
34	—35	Arable land = nonarable
167	34	Much foreign aid sent or received
109	—32	No guerrilla warfare
132	25	High percent farms rented
15	—24	Unchanged literacy rate
150	—24	Low syphilis death rate
144	—20	Fewer than two political parties
95	18	Many hospital beds per physician
96	—18	Caloric inadequacy

TABLE 8–23
Factor XXV: Patriarchical Rule

Variable	Loading	Description
19	91	Long tenure of governments
20	53	Long tenure of chief executives
71	—32	Few divorces per marriage
77	—32	Few military expenditures/national income
132	32	High percent farms rented
173	—31	Not a Communist satellite
18	—30	System stability
31	—27	Party system stability
160	26	Lack of personalismo in political parties
153	—25	Low accident death rate

TABLE 8–24
Factor XXVI: Lack of Professional Expertise

Variable	Loading	Description
95	85	Many hospital beds per physician
118	44	Military interventions into politics
94	—36	Few inhabitants per physician
166	—34	Low net amount of foreign investments
44	—33	Political decentralization
172	—24	Bloc follower
173	—23	Not a Communist satellite
1	—23	Unchanged per capita national income
63	—21	Low voter turnout
80	—21	Few general government expenditures/national income

TABLE 8–25
Factor XXVII: Unstructured

Variable	Loading	Description
154	—96	Low ulcer death rate
163	—37	Not a traditional bureaucracy
16	—33	Unchanged percent Communist strength
149	—32	Low liver cirrhosis death rate
171	—28	Foreign mail sent = received
151	26	High illegitimacy ratio
124	—24	Little domestic mail per capita
73	21	Many Communists vote Communist
83	—20	Not a bicameral legislature
39	18	Lack of sectionalism

TABLE 8–26
Factor XXVIII: Modernizing Welfare Statism

Variable	Loading	Description
29	92	Change in welfare expenditures per capita
28	63	Change in education expenditures per capita
30	47	Change in government expenditures per capita
149	—37	Low liver cirrhosis death rate
21	28	Change in birth rate
146	—27	Few types of political parties
67	—27	Few soldiers/persons aged 15–64
152	—24	Low suicide rate
171	—23	Foreign mail sent = received
151	—23	Low illegitimacy ratio

TABLE 8–27
Factor XXIX: Labor Unrest amid Affluence

Variable	Loading	Description
92	87	High unemployment in labor force
4	52	Change in radios per capita
167	37	Much foreign aid sent or received
30	34	Change in government expenditures per capita
102	32	Many days lost due to strikes
84	—31	Government revenue = expenditures
152	—28	Low suicide rate
133	—27	Few customs taxes/total taxes
146	—25	Few types of political parties
59	24	High percent secondary, higher education students

TABLE 8–28
Factor XXX: Governmental Philistinism

Variable	Loading	Description
11	—85	Unchanged government expenditures per capita
171	43	Foreign mail sent ≠ received
93	29	Many pupils per teacher
6	25	Change in railroad freight
77	24	Many military expenditures/national income
146	—24	Few types of political parties
52	23	High railroad freight density
13	—21	Low urbanization rate
64	—20	Low unionization
73	—20	Few Communists vote Communist

TABLE 8–29
Factor XXXI: Solidarity

Variable	Loading	Description
175	81	Bloc member
69	—36	Low divorce rate
115	—33	Diffuse aggregation
67	29	Many soldiers/persons aged 15–64
71	—28	Few divorces per marriage
8	27	Change in population
72	—27	Few religious persons vote for nonsecular parties
163	—26	Not a traditional bureaucracy
146	—26	Few types of political parties
159	—25	Elitist political recruitment

TABLE 8–30
Factor XXXII: Cathective Involvement

Variable	Loading	Description
171	40	Foreign mail sent ≠ received
160	—37	Personalismo in political parties
152	35	High suicide rate
1	—31	Unchanged per capita national income
176	—30	Few expulsions, recalls of diplomats
60	23	Low political enculturation
100	23	Many religious groups
67	23	Many soldiers/persons 15–64
103	21	Many strikers/population
174	21	Penetrated polity

TABLE 8–31
Factor XXXIII: Bourgeois Revolution

Variable	Loading	Description
113	83	High domestic violence death rate
109	55	Many guerrilla wars
132	44	High percent rented farms
111	36	Many purges
48	30	Much unexploited energy
108	26	Many revolutions
164	25	Lack of trade dependence
73	—25	Few Communists vote Communist
100	24	Many religious groups
149	—24	Low liver cirrhosis death rate

TABLE 8–32
Factor XXXIV: Phenotypic Symmetry

Variable	Loading	Description
140	91	Large main language group
98	—81	Few language communities
136	—61	Linguistic homogeneity
99	—35	Few nationality groups
178	—32	Foreign missions abroad = at home
81	28	High central government expenditures/national income
100	—27	Few religious groups
137	—27	Homogeneity
49	25	Much exploited waterpower
93	25	Many pupils per teacher

TABLE 8–33
Factor XXXV: Developmental Junta

Variable	Loading	Description
68	49	Many military mobilizations
91	—40	Low minimum voting age
80	29	High general government expenditures/national income
26	—25	Illegal government change
1	24	Change in per capita national income
166	—22	Low net foreign investment balance
114	—20	Diffuse articulation
99	—20	Few nationality groups
145	20	Multiparty system
20	—19	Short tenure per chief executive

TABLE 8–34
Factor XXXVI: Evenness in Development

Variable	Loading	Description
38	—84	No urban primacy
166	33	High net foreign investment balance
67	29	Many soldiers/persons aged 15–64
171	—28	Foreign mail sent = received
52	27	High railroad freight density
160	24	Lack of personalismo in political parties
63	—22	Low voter turnout
72	22	Many religious persons vote for nonsecular parties
30	—21	Unchanged government expenditures per capita
151	—21	Low illegitimacy ratio

TABLE 8–35
Factor XXXVII: Reorganization-Mindedness

Variable	Loading	Description
32	75	Change in number of ministries
76	—36	Few army, administrative expenditures/GNP
51	29	High automobile density
48	—29	High exploitation of energy
108	25	Many revolutions
81	—23	Low central government expenditures/national income
9	22	Change in caloric intake per capita
13	21	Change in urbanization
146	—21	Few types of political parties
176	—20	Few expulsions, recalls of diplomats

TABLE 8–36
Factor XXXVIII: Incorporative Articulation

Variable	Loading	Description
104	89	Much of work force on strike
105	83	Many strikers/union members
114	67	Diffracted articulation
103	66	Many strikers/population
44	35	Political decentralization
102	34	Many days lost due to strikes
21	30	Change in birth rate
45	26	Colonial power
167	25	Much foreign aid sent or received
168	24	Immigrants $\neq$ emigrants

TABLE 8–37
Factor XXXIX: Unenlightened Rebellion

Variable	Loading	Description
25	88	Illegitimate government
146	35	Many types of political parties
153	29	High accident death rate
133	—29	Few customs taxes/total taxes
91	28	High minimum voting age
121	—24	Few library books circulated per capita
15	—23	Unchanged literacy rate
26	—23	Illegal government change
74	—21	Mobilizational system style
164	—20	High trade dependence

TABLE 8–38
Factor XL: Sustained Industrialization

Variable	Loading	Description
23	—76	Unchanged marriage rate
7	53	Change in per capita electricity production
28	—37	Unchanged education expenditures per capita
3	—35	Unchanged GNP per capita
22	—27	Unchanged death rate
110	23	Many assassinations
12	—22	National income stability
21	21	Change in birth rate
151	—21	Low illegitimacy ratio
96	20	Caloric adequacy

TABLE 8–39
Factor XLI: Neocolonialism

Variable	Loading	Description
165	88	Exports ≠ imports
52	—39	Low railroad freight density
60	33	Low political enculturation
23	—28	Change in marriage rate
84	—27	Government revenue = expenditure
13	26	Change in urbanization rate
171	—25	Foreign mail sent = received
124	—25	Low domestic mail per capita
7	—23	Unchanged electricity production per capita
152	—23	Low suicide rate

TABLE 8–40
Factor XLII: Guided Democracy

Variable	Loading	Description
33	—76	No change in number of parliamentary parties
116	46	Fragmented functions of political parties
86	27	Press censorship
13	—26	Unchanged urbanization rate
96	23	Caloric adequacy
119	18	Police interventions into politics
138	18	Large main religious group
166	—18	Low net foreign investment balance
1	17	Change in per capita national income
79	17	High welfare expenditures/national income

TABLE 8–41
Factor XLIII: Entrepreneurial Development

Variable	Loading	Description
5	71	Change in telephones per capita
72	—41	Few religious persons vote for nonsecular parties
12	—32	National income stability
167	—32	Little foreign aid sent or received
111	30	Many purges
1	—29	Unchanged per capita national income
81	—27	Few central government expenditures/national income
166	26	High net foreign investment balance
106	26	Many general strikes
51	—23	Low automobile density

TABLE 11-1
International Subsystems Variable List

Variable Number[a]	Source[b]	Description	Cases
1a.	RFB	Number of wars	17
1b.	W	Number of wars	16
2.	RFB	Wars with subnational entities/wars	17
3a.	RFB	Members at war/members	16
3b.	W	Members at war/members	16
4a.	RFB	Extraregion wars/wars	14
4b.	W	Extraregion wars/wars	21
5a.	RFB	Extra-era wars/wars in era	18
5b.	W	Extra-era wars/wars in era	16
6.	H	Poles	21
6a.	H	Unipolarity	21
6b.	H	Bipolarity	21
6c.	H	Tripolarity	21
6d.	H	Multipolarity	21
7a.	RFB	War participants/members at war	16
7b.	W	War participants/members at war	16
8.	R	Similar language war dyads/war dyads	8
9.	R	Similar bodily characteristics war dyads/war dyads	8
10.	R	Similar clothing war dyads/war dyads	8
11.	R	Similar religion and philosophy war dyads/war dyads	8
12.	R	Former enemies in war dyads/war dyads	8
13a.	RFB	Wars/members	16
13b.	W	Wars/national members	16
14a.	RFB	War participants/wars	17
14b.	W	War participants/wars	16
15a.	RFB	Durations of wars/wars	16
15b.	W	Durations of wars/wars	16
16a.	RFB	Years with new wars/years in era	18
16b.	W	Years with new wars/years in era	16
17.	RFB	Destabilizing wars/wars	16
18.	RB	War deaths/wars	11
19.	SSF	Number of alliances	15
20.	H	Number of satellites	21
21.	SSF	Pacts/alliances	15
22.	SSF	Aligned members/national members	15
23.	SSF	Extraregion alliances/alliances	15
24.	SSF	Extra-era alliances/alliances in era	15
25.	Sp	New nongovernmental organizations formed	21
26.	SSF	Alliance partnerships/aligned members	15
27.	SSF	Nonaggression pacts/alliances	15
28.	SSF	Alliances/national members	14

TABLE 11-1—Cont.
International Subsystems Variable List

Variable Number[a]	Source[b]	Description	Cases
29.	SSF	Alliance partnerships/alliances	15
30.	SSF	Durations of alliances/alliances	15
31.	SSF	Years with new alliances/years in era	15
32.	SSF	Defensive pacts/alliances	15
33.	R	Former allies in war dyads/war dyads	10
34.	H	Number of members	21
35.	Ro	Decision latitude (dynastic = 1; nationalist = 0)	11
36.	H	Sovereign members/members	21
37.	H	Members retaining sovereignty through era/members	21
38.	H	Extraregion members/members	21
39.	SS	Total "status scores"/members	9
40.	H	Members/middle and major powers	21
41.	H	Diversity in ways of life	21
42.	H	Extent of (nonlegalistic) power orientation	21
43.	H	Incompleteness of external interaction	21
44.	H	Extent of rational calculation	21
45.	H	Extent of internal preoccupation (= lack of external interaction)	21
46a.	RFB	Internal wars/total wars	15
46b.	W	Internal wars/total wars	16
47a.	RFB	Interventions/total wars	17
47b.	W	Interventions/total wars	16
48.	RFB	Foreign wars/total wars	16
49.	RB	Internal war deaths/internal wars	11
50.	RB	Intervention war deaths/interventions	15
51.	Ro	Insecurity of domestic elite tenure	11
52a.	RFB	Members initiating wars/members	17
52b.	W	Members initiating wars/national members	16
53.	SSF	Number of minor powers allied with major powers	14
54.	RFB	Number of minor powers in coalitions with major powers	17
55.	SSF	Pacts between major and minor powers/alliances between major and minor powers	15
56.	RFB	Subnational partners in coalitions with major powers/minor powers in coalitions with major powers	18
57.	SSF	Minor powers allied with major powers/minor powers	15
58.	RFB	Minor powers in coalitions with major powers/minor powers	17
59.	SSF	Extraregion alliances with minor powers/total alliances with minor powers	15
60.	RFB	Extra-era coalitions between minor and major powers/coalitions with minor power partners in era	18
61.	SSF	Extra-era alliances between major and minor powers/alliances with minor power partners in era	15
62.	SS	Minor power "status scores"/minor powers	10

TABLE 11-1—Cont.
International Subsystems Variable List

Variable Number[a]	Source[b]	Description	Cases
63.	SSF	Partnerships in alliances with minor powers/minor powers aligned with major powers	15
64.	RFB	Partnerships in coalitions with major and minor powers/minor powers in coalitions with major powers	17
65.	SSF	Nonaggression pacts between major and minor powers/alliances between major and minor powers	15
66.	SSF	Alliances between minor and major powers/minor and major powers	15
67.	SSF	Partnerships in alliances with major and minor powers/all such alliances	15
68.	SSF	Durations of alliances between major and minor powers/all such alliances	15
69.	RFB	Durations of coalitions between major and minor powers/all such coalitions	17
70.	SSF	Years with new alliances between major and minor powers/years in era	15
71.	RFB	Years with new coalitions between major and minor powers/years in era	17
72a.	RFB	Minor powers initiating wars/minor powers	18
72b.	W	Minor powers initiating wars/minor powers	16
73.	Ro	Level of disturbance	12
74.	Ro	Increase in disturbance	9
75.	SSF	Defensive pacts between major and minor powers/alliances between major and minor powers	15
76.	H	Number of gatepassers	20
77.	H	Sovereign gatepassers/gatepassers	20
78.	H	Gatepassers/members	20
79.	H	Extraregion gatepassers/gatepassers	20
80.	H	Gatepassers gatepassing in following era/gatepassers	18
81.	SS	Gatepasser "status scores"/gatepassers	9
82.	H	Net gatepassers/gatepassers	20
83.	SSF	Aligned gatepassers/gatepassers	15
84.	SSF	Alliances with gatepassers/gatepassers	15
85.	SSF	Partnerships in alliances with gatepassers/all such alliances	15
86.	H	Durations of new status of members after gatepassing/years in era	20
87.	H	Years of gatepassing/years	20
88.	H	Violent gatepassers/gatepassers	20
89.	H	Number of major powers	21
90.	SSF	Pacts exclusively between major powers/alliances exclusively between major powers	16

TABLE 11–1—Cont.
International Subsystems Variable List

Variable Number[a]	Source[b]	Description	Cases
91.	SSF	Major powers exclusively allied with other major powers/ major powers	15
92.	SSF.	Extraregion major power alliances/major power alliances	15
93.	SSF	Extra-era major powers alliances/major power alliances	15
94.	Sp	New intergovernmental organizations formed	21
95.	SSF	Partnerships in alliances exclusively between major powers/ aligned major powers	15
96.	SSF	Nonaggression pacts between major powers exclusively/ exclusive major power alliances	15
97.	SSF	Exclusive major power alliances/alliances with major powers	15
98.	SSF	Partnerships in exclusive major power alliances/exclusive major power alliances	15
99.	SSF	Durations of exclusive major power alliances/all such alliances	15
100.	SSF	Years with new exclusive major power alliances/years in era	15
101.	SSF	Defensive pacts exclusively between major powers/alliances exclusively between major powers	15
102.	H	Number of recruitees	20
103.	H	Recruitees admitted, readmitted, or deleted/recruitees	20
104.	H	Recruitees/members	20
105.	H	Extraregion recruitees/recruitees	20
106.	SS	Recruitee "status scores"/recruitees	9
107.	H	Net recruitees/recruitees	20
108.	SSF	Aligned recruitees/recruitees	15
109.	SSF	Partnerships in alliances with recruitees/all such alliances	15
110.	SSF	Alliances with recruitees/recruitees	15
111.	H	Durations of new recruitment status/years in era	20
112.	H	Years of recruitment/years in era	20
113.	H	Violent recruitees/recruitees	20
114.	H	Major and middle powers	21
115.	H	Extent of indirect supervision	21
116.	Ro	Level of technology	11
117.	H	Intraregional/extraregional supervision	21
118.	SS	Major and middle power "status scores"	10
119.	H	Major powers/middle powers	21
120.	H	Macrocentric supervision	21
121.	H	Ratio between auditing and policing	21
122.	H	Extent of cooperation among major and middle powers	21
123.	Ro	Ideological consonance	11
124.	Ro	Unavailability of resources	21
125.	H	Ease of legitimizing changes of major and middle powers	21
126.	W	Number of postwar treaties	20

TABLE 11-1—Cont.
International Subsystems Variable List

Variable Number[a]	Source[b]	Description	Cases
127.	H	Overt/covert rule-adapting	21
128.	H	Decrease in international law	21
129.	WF	Extraregion postwar treaties/postwar treaties	20
130.	WF	Postwar treaties for wars starting in earlier eras/ postwar treaties in era	20
131.	H	Lack of international tribunals	21
132.	H	Looseness in polarity	21
133.	H	Extent of realism/idealism	21
134.	H	Extent of procedural rule-adapting	21
135.	H	Cooperation across poles	21
136.	H	Instrumental/ideological rule-adapting	21
137.	WF	Years with postwar treaties/years	21
138.	WF	Wars not concluded by treaties/wars	21
139a.	RFB	Number of wars with major powers	16
139b.	W	Number of wars with major powers	16
140.	RFB	Wars with major and subnational powers/ wars with major powers	18
141a.	RFB	Participation in war by major powers/major powers	16
141b.	W	Participation in war by major powers/major powers	16
142.	W	Imperial wars/wars	19
143a.	RFB	Extraregion wars with major powers/wars with major powers	16
143b.	W	Extraregion wars with major powers/wars with major powers	21
144a.	RFB	Extra-era wars with major powers/wars with major powers in era	17
144b.	W	Extra-era wars with major powers/wars with major powers in era	16
145.	Ro	Presence of regulator institution	13
146.	RFB	Wars with major powers on opposite sides/wars with major powers	17
147.	W	Wars exclusively between major powers/wars with major powers	16
148.	RFB	Wars fought by major powers aiming to destabilize/ wars with major powers	17
149a.	RFB	Wars fought by major powers/major powers	16
149b.	W	Wars fought by major powers/major powers	16
150.	WF	Wars with major powers concluded by treaties/wars with major powers	19
151a.	RFB	Participants in wars with major powers/all such wars	17
151b.	W	Participants in wars with major powers/all such wars	16
152a.	RFB	Durations of wars with major powers/all such wars	16
152b.	W	Durations of wars with major powers/all such wars	16
153a.	RFB	Years with new wars involving major powers/years in era	18

TABLE 11–1—Cont.
International Subsystems Variable List

Variable Number[a]	Source[b]	Description	Cases
153b.	W	Years with new wars involving major powers/years in era	16
154.	RFB	Wars with major powers resulting in destabilization/ wars with major powers	17
155a.	RFB	Number of wars initiated by major powers	16
155b.	W	Number of wars initiated by major powers	16
156.	RFB	Wars initiated by major powers including subnationals/ wars initiated by major powers	16
157a.	RFB	War initiations by major powers/major powers	16
157b.	W	War initiations by major powers/major powers	16
158a.	RFB	Extraregion wars initiated by major powers/total wars initiated by major powers	18
158b.	W	Extraregion wars initiated by major powers/total wars initiated by major powers	17
159a.	RFB	Extra-era wars initiated by major powers/wars initiated by major powers in era	18
159b.	W	Extra-era wars initiated by major powers/wars initiated by major powers in era	16
160.	Ro	Strength of regulator	12
161a.	RFB	Wars initiated by major powers opposing major powers/ wars initiated by major powers	17
161b.	W	Wars initiated by two or more major powers/ wars initiated by major powers	16
162.	RFB	Wars initiated by major powers aiming to destabilize/ wars initiated by major powers	16
163.	WF	Wars initiated by major powers concluded by treaties/ wars initiated by major powers	21
164a.	RFB	Wars initiated by major powers/major powers	17
164b.	W	Wars initiated by major powers/major powers	16
165a.	RFB	Partners in coalitions with major powers initiating wars/ wars initiated by major powers	17
165b.	W	Partners in coalitions with major powers initiating wars/ wars initiated by major powers	16
166a.	RFB	Durations of wars initiated by major powers/all such wars	16
166b.	W	Durations of wars initiated by major powers/all such wars	16
167a.	RFB	Years with new wars initiated by major powers/years in era	17
167b.	W	Years with new wars initiated by major powers/years in era	16
168.	RFB	Wars initiated by major powers resulting in destabilization/ wars initiated by major powers	18
169.	RFB	Number of wars won by major powers	17
170.	RFB	Wars won by major powers involving subnationals/ wars won by major powers	17
171.	RFB	Victories achieved by major powers/major powers	16

TABLE 11–1—Cont.
International Subsystems Variable List

Variable Number[a]	Source[b]	Description	Cases
172.	RFB	Extraregion wars won by major powers/total wars won by major powers	17
173.	RFB	Extra-era wars won by major powers/wars won by major powers in era	17
174.	Ro	Increase in regulator capacity	10
175.	RFB	Wars with major powers opposing other major powers/wars won by major powers	17
176.	RFB	Wars won by major powers aiming to destabilize/wars won by major powers	18
177.	RFB	Wars won by major powers/major powers	16
178.	RFB	Partners in winning coalitions with major powers/all such wars	16
179.	RFB	Durations of wars won by major powers/all such wars	16
180.	RFB	Years with wars won by major powers/years in era	17
181.	RFB	Wars won by major powers resulting in destabilization/all such wars	18
182.	Ro	International instability	10
183.	H	Duration of subsystem	21

[a] Letters appearing after variable numbers indicate when the same variable has been operationalized using (a) Richardson's data, (b) Wright's data, or, in the case of variable 6, by selecting different cutting points.

[b] Key to Sources:
  B = Bendix System Division, ONR study of low-intensity warfare.
  F = Fornander, *An Account of the Polynesian Race* (1880).
  H = Haas, this volume.
  R = Richardson, *Statistics of Deadly Quarrels* (1960).
  Ro = Rosecrance, *Action and Reaction in World Politics* (1963).
  Sp = Speeckaert, *The 1,978 International Associations Founded Since the Congress of Vienna* (1957).
  SS = Singer and Small, "Alliance Aggregation and the Onset of War" (1968).
  W = Wright, *A Study of War* (1965).

TABLE 11-5

Correlations Between 183 Subsystem Variables and Q-Factors[a]

Variable	Richardson Sample				Wright Sample		
	I	II	III	I	II	III	IV
1. Wars	−29	26	04	33	25	01	−17
2. % Wars with subnationals	−39	−01	31	−04	−33	−18	19
3. War participants/members	−05	43	−38	−26	27	43	−20
4. % Extraregion wars	−35	−17	49	−35	−05	−16	35
5. % Extra-era wars	−17	(67)	−20	29	−27	43	−11
6. Poles	06	09	−12	41	15	02	−05
7. War participants/members at war	09	13	−33	24	(58)	−27	−38
8. % Dyads with same language	(62)	−43	(−62)	00	(71)	−43	(−74)
9. % Dyads with same body type	−30	27	−18	−13	−06	27	01
10. % Dyads with same clothing	33	00	(−67)	−12	(69)	00	(−64)
11. % Dyads with same philosophy	31	−14	−19	14	05	−14	−19
12. % Former enemy dyads	−30	−18	(79)	30	(−60)	−18	(66)
13. Wars per member	17	12	−48	−09	(75)	−18	−48
14. Participants per war	(−61)	(65)	36	−13	−23	30	20
15. Years per war	−10	40	−14	00	31	12	−10
16. % Years with new wars	−11	36	−13	(52)	−25	37	−14
17. % Destabilizing wars	−10	34	−03	17	(66)	−01	(−66)
18. Deaths per war	(−60)	(90)	−08	−35	−42	(91)	13
19. Alliances	(−90)	(52)	(80)	−05	(−73)	42	(94)
20. Satellites	−47	22	39	17	−35	08	12
21. % Pacts	−30	35	16	42	−44	32	12
22. % Aligned	−39	−12	(51)	−01	−10	−07	49
23. % Extraregion alliances	10	02	−15	(−67)	(64)	20	−33
24. % Extra-era alliances	−44	28	(50)	12	21	−41	−42
25. New NGO's	(−62)	26	(79)	−19	−50	09	(80)
26. Partners per alliance	(−85)	(51)	(68)	(−56)	−39	35	(64)
27. % Nonaggression pacts	−35	46	42	−13	−43	(72)	(72)

627

TABLE 11-5—Cont.
Correlations Between 183 Subsystem Variables and Q–Factors[a]

	Richardson Sample			Wright Sample			
Variable	I	II	III	I	II	III	IV
28. Alliances per member	(−82)	41	(61)	(−67)	−28	38	(55)
29. Partners per alliance	−36	−11	(60)	45	07	(−66)	−36
30. Years per alliance	08	−38	02	−15	−05	−14	−07
31. % Years with new alliances	(−90)	(66)	(78)	11	(−84)	(62)	(90)
32. % Defensive alliances	−30	41	11	47	22	−19	(−52)
33. % Dyads former allies	(−52)	(83)	−36	−27	−27	(72)	45
34. Members	(−73)	39	(64)	28	(−54)	06	46
35. High decision latitude	(67)	19	29	41	(81)	−03	−15
36. % Sovereign members	03	28	22	22	22	−08	−01
37. % Retaining sovereignty	−11	−20	50	26	16	−32	−11
38. % Extraregion members	10	14	−24	(−56)	00	37	09
39. Mean status score	−45	(57)	−10	(−53)	−08	(60)	33
40. Members/major and middle powers	−08	−01	32	27	−47	−04	41
41. Diverse ways of life	−26	20	01	−30	05	06	02
42. Nonlegalist power orientation	17	50	(−54)	03	12	36	−38
43. Incomplete external interaction	09	−30	19	02	36	−47	04
44. Rational calculation	10	−46	39	02	19	−48	08
45. Internal preoccupation	(79)	−44	(−77)	21	(80)	−38	(−64)
46. % Internal wars	49	−13	−33	26	(60)	−14	−35
47. % Interventions	−40	−05	43	11	−26	−27	18
48. % Foreign wars	−11	30	−10	08	16	14	−35
49. Deaths per internal war	(61)	−07	(−81)	17	(78)	−07	(−79)
50. Deaths per intervention	(−67)	33	47	27	(−56)	29	(56)
51. Insecure domestic elites	−04	−27	(51)	07	09	−20	09
52. % Starting wars	−19	46	−21	(−56)	33	−00	−02
53. Minors allied with majors	(−61)	38	(76)	36	(−66)	−15	(50)
54. Minors in coalition with majors	(−62)	(64)	35	20	(−59)	49	45

628

TABLE 11-5—Cont.
Correlations Between 183 Subsystem Variables and Q-Factors[a]

Variable	Richardson Sample			Wright Sample			
	I	II	III	I	II	III	IV
55. % Formal major-minor alliances	-21	37	(55)	(67)	(-55)	00	33
56. % Subnational entities aligned with majors	24	-02	-22	00	29	15	13
57. % Minors allied with majors	(-60)	38	(79)	(60)	(-69)	-03	(64)
58. % Minors in coalitions with majors	-30	(64)	-13	08	(-50)	(81)	22
59. % Extraregion minors' alliances	26	37	33	-08	33	25	14
60. % Extra-era major-minor coalitions	19	34	-02	29	-18	41	46
61. % Extra-era major-minor alliances	-20	06	49	29	-10	-38	-15
62. Minor power status scores	(-85)	(62)	(68)	-17	(-65)	(58)	(85)
63. Partners per major-minor alliances	(-67)	36	(64)	-26	(-65)	18	(72)
64. Partners per major-minor coalition	17	-03	-05	35	09	-22	26
65. % Major-minor nonaggression pacts	-31	(64)	(71)	-07	-48	(60)	(83)
66. Major-minor alliances/majors and minors	(-64)	42	(72)	06	(-74)	18	(87)
67. Members per major-minor alliance	-43	13	(55)	45	-29	-39	-09
68. Years per major-minor alliance	-33	31	32	-10	-28	12	22
69. Years per major-minor coalition	-39	(55)	05	38	-04	39	-13
70. % Years with new major-minor alliances	(-53)	47	(78)	33	(-82)	16	(69)
71. % Years with new major-minor coalitions	-46	36	39	48	-49	09	38
72. % Minors starting wars	-24	42	01	-46	-26	17	27
73. Disturbance level	05	(65)	-25	-17	-05	(56)	21
74. Increase in disturbance	(56)	(56)	-44	31	46	(54)	01
75. % Defensive major-minor alliances	-11	11	27	(52)	05	-35	-18
76. Gatepassers	(-62)	38	33	21	-46	16	12
77. % Sovereign gatepassers	07	-08	-09	-04	04	-12	-12
78. % Gatepassers	16	13	-46	-05	-21	37	-15
79. % Extraregion gatepassers	18	29	-34	-49	38	39	-17
80. % Re-gatepassers in next era	-20	40	-30	-21	22	21	-01
81. Gatepasser status scores	-43	33	24	-23	-15	42	45

TABLE 11-5—Cont.
Correlations Between 183 Subsystem Variables and Q–Factors[a]

Variable	Richardson Sample			Wright Sample			
	I	II	III	I	II	III	IV
82. % Net gatepassers	−21	(53)	−10	06	−07	25	−30
83. % Aligned gatepassers	−32	−06	45	13	07	−39	−02
84. Alliances per gatepasser	(−51)	−01	(56)	−10	09	−33	26
85. Members per gatepasser alliance	−27	−18	41	14	28	(−79)	(−53)
86. % Years past gate	(−59)	19	43	16	−41	−08	−09
87. % Years of gatepassing	−45	(59)	28	45	−44	46	−09
88. % Violent gatepassing	−11	15	−19	−31	30	05	−04
89. Major powers	−42	15	(59)	20	−21	05	20
90. % Major-only pacts	−46	17	(73)	(52)	(−67)	05	31
91. % Majors allied only with each other	−26	−02	(57)	(67)	−21	−26	−06
92. % Extraregion majors' alliances	−29	41	07	−40	28	30	02
93. % Extra-era major-only alliances	−24	00	49	36	18	−41	19
94. New IGO's	(−79)	39	(72)	−23	(−81)	32	(71)
95. Partners per major-only alliance	(−65)	47	(73)	−02	(−54)	42	(66)
96. % Major-only nonaggression pacts	−19	30	(57)	−03	−45	(58)	(82)
97. % Major alliances only with each other	−29	00	(51)	18	−21	−06	26
98. Partners per major-only alliance	−39	05	(70)	(69)	(−61)	−16	23
99. Years per major-only alliance	−27	−10	40	−01	−11	−27	02
100. % Years with new major-only alliances	(−69)	48	(75)	−07	(−78)	(52)	(69)
101. % Defensive major-only alliances	−44	21	(62)	(58)	−16	−30	−16
102. Recruitees	−31	33	−04	−30	16	29	−19
103. % Formal recruitees	−26	−05	18	−15	−23	−15	25
104. % Recruitees	11	09	−40	−47	(55)	12	−45
105. % Extraregion recruitees	−12	29	−01	−33	42	13	−32
106. Status score per recruitee	(−71)	(90)	−24	(−65)	−20	(83)	37
107. % Net major power recruitees	07	−22	16	−02	17	−34	−14
108. % Aligned recruitees	(−86)	(64)	(72)	−45	−19	29	(51)

TABLE 11-5—Cont.
Correlations Between 183 Subsystem Variables and Q-Factors[a]

Variable	Richardson Sample				Wright Sample		
	I	II	III	I	II	III	IV
109. Members per recruitee alliance	-48	14	48	-09	37	-40	04
110. Alliances per recruitee	(-80)	(67)	(68)	-33	-48	(53)	(75)
111. Net recruitment duration	-36	17	19	08	37	-06	-49
112. % Years with recruitment	-33	(59)	06	40	-42	44	-09
113. % Violent recruitees	18	28	-06	13	(52)	-02	-06
114. Major and middle powers	(-74)	34	(78)	19	-22	07	21
115. Extent of indirect supervision	34	10	(-59)	03	47	03	-22
116. Level of technology	(-79)	16	16	(-54)	(-86)	36	(69)
117. % Intraregion supervision	39	-09	-36	10	41	-24	-49
118. Status score per elite	(-77)	(83)	-07	-31	-36	(77)	(55)
119. Major powers/middle powers	45	-13	-17	16	-17	02	27
120. Macrocentric supervision	10	-29	21	11	-48	08	-00
121. Auditing/policing	17	(-56)	27	19	10	-45	01
122. Elite cooperativeness	(56)	03	(-70)	-31	(73)	-12	-34
123. Ideological agreement	10	10	00	08	-03	28	18
124. Unavailable resources	06	-02	14	-14	-04	19	25
125. Elite legitimacy	-09	07	41	39	17	-11	-06
126. Postwar treaties	-31	32	49	18	40	-15	-13
127. Overt rule-adapting	-07	-07	17	-17	(-58)	15	21
128. Decrease in international law	(69)	-14	(-59)	21	(53)	-11	-22
129. % Extraregion postwar treaties	(52)	-26	(-55)	-40	22	-11	26
130. % Extra-era postwar treaties	04	(52)	(54)	29	-04	30	04
131. No international tribunals	(86)	-44	(-62)	25	(75)	-50	(-64)
132. Looseness in polarity	-11	-11	48	02	50	-33	10
133. Realism/idealism	-02	16	-35	-34	(51)	-26	-03
134. Procedural rule-adapting	25	14	-47	32	(56)	-10	(-54)
135. Cross-pole cooperation	13	19	(-51)	-41	27	-04	04

TABLE 11-5—Cont.
Correlations Between 183 Subsystem Variables and Q-Factors[a]

Variable	Richardson Sample			Wright Sample			
	I	II	III	I	II	III	IV
136. Instrumental rule-adapting	43	−32	−36	−21	(59)	−38	−14
137. % Years with postwar treaties	−32	36	(55)	45	17	−07	−13
138. % Wars not ending with treaties	02	−00	−22	09	−37	05	11
139. Major power wars	−13	18	−07	17	44	−26	−21
140. % Majors' wars with subnationals	−36	−07	44	06	−43	−16	42
141. War participation per major power	−06	38	−25	07	(58)	−23	−32
142. % Imperial wars	04	−29	19	−02	(−62)	21	(61)
143. % Extraregion majors' wars	−48	15	(56)	−03	−44	−12	(56)
144. % Extra-era majors' wars	−08	(60)	04	31	−20	29	04
145. Institutional regulator	50	50	50	20	−30	(52)	(63)
146. % Wars between major powers	09	14	04	10	(68)	−25	−34
147. % Wars only between major powers	−03	36	−16	01	01	30	20
148. % Majors' wars to destabilize	−05	13	−31	03	(69)	−33	−38
149. Wars per major power	−21	23	43	17	(62)	−31	−28
150. % Majors' wars ended by treaty	(−62)	(77)	21	−02	−24	48	15
151. Participants per majors' wars	−36	39	11	02	40	19	−23
152. Years per majors' wars	−11	24	−12	(55)	17	01	−27
153. % Years with new majors' wars	−02	19	08	01	38	−04	−10
154. % Majors' wars that destabilize	04	14	−15	16	38	−20	−14
155. Major-started wars	02	15	10	−26	14	10	05
156. % Major-started wars with subnational entities	−11	14	−29	04	39	−14	−05
157. Wars started per major power	−30	−25	(64)	22	−42	−05	(51)
158. % Major-started extraregion wars	22	43	07	09	04	34	21
159. % Extra-era major-started wars	00	−08	25	21	−23	06	11
160. Strong regulator	21	24	−13	14	15	13	07
161. % Major-started wars vs. majors	(53)	−28	26	40	28	−24	09
162. % Major-started wars aiming to destabilize	07	42	−06	−13	−13	(51)	38

TABLE 11-5—Cont.
Correlations Between 183 Subsystem Variables and Q-Factors[a]

Variable	Richardson Sample			Wright Sample			
	I	II	III	I	II	III	IV
163. % Major-started wars ended by treaty	−24	31	50	45	21	−02	−05
164. Wars started per major power	16	13	−32	07	41	−19	−14
165. Mean major-started coalition partners	−09	25	05	−04	−08	−06	35
166. Years per major-started war	−11	31	−07	−05	30	−04	03
167. % Years when majors start new wars	20	10	−29	25	20	−14	−19
168. % Major-started wars ending in destabilization	28	06	−15	35	(53)	−02	02
169. Wars won by major powers	01	−09	02	36	01	−32	02
170. % Major victories with subnational entities	−07	−33	41	17	−16	(−51)	32
171. Victories per major power	06	04	−18	21	39	−23	30
172. % Extraregion majors' victories	−36	−14	(63)	−15	−19	−25	(58)
173. % Extra-era majors' victories	05	43	11	22	−26	39	45
174. Increase in regulator capacity	38	38	−13	21	26	32	05
175. % Majors' victories over majors	26	01	−29	−09	06	10	12
176. % Majors' victories aiming to destabilize	17	33	−07	26	18	38	40
177. Wars won per major power	13	−04	−24	33	(60)	−39	−21
178. Partners per winning majors' coalition	(−60)	45	48	−25	−30	39	42
179. Years per war won by majors	−36	41	16	06	25	12	−05
180. % Years with majors' victories	11	−03	−02	(69)	31	44	−09
181. % Majors' victories that destabilize	13	03	07	36	37	−09	16
182. International instability	−07	(79)	−50	−35	−09	(65)	31
183. Subsystem duration	05	−20	−06	−41	(62)	−27	−11

[a] Correlations multiplied by 100; figures > ±.50 enclosed in parentheses.

TABLE 11–6
First–Order R–Factor Analysis of International Subsystem Performance Data: Wright Sample[a]

Variable	h²	I	II	III	IV	Varimax Factors V	VI
1. Wars	1.23	−16	(−82)	14	−40	08	−01
2. % Wars with subnationals	1.24	−37	16	14	−18	−32	(−71)
3. % Members at war	1.08	−01	−43	(−69)	−04	11	49
4. % Extraregion wars	1.27	−06	41	−06	(54)	15	−17
5. % Extra-era wars	1.04	−09	−07	18	−50	−17	−16
6. Poles	1.12	27	−40	−09	−48	−13	−20
8. % Dyads with similar language	1.59	(54)	−44	−45	−11	21	(−77)
10. % Dyads with similar clothing	1.46	45	−17	(−94)	−10	−03	08
11. % Dyads with similar philosophy	1.59	25	−37	18	−34	11	08
12. % Former enemy dyads	1.42	−35	04	(101)	04	14	13
13. Wars per member	1.30	11	(−75)	−44	27	29	05
14. Participants per war	1.18	−24	(−56)	−24	−26	−05	26
16. % Years with new wars	1.13	05	−14	18	(−82)	−15	17
18. Deaths per war	1.27	−26	−02	−31	−20	20	(56)
19. Alliances	1.27	(−95)	−25	17	−40	11	25
20. Satellites	1.06	08	−09	−03	(−91)	05	−17
21. % Pacts	1.27	27	−09	33	−43	−02	07
22. % Aligned	1.23	(−74)	−04	−29	04	−39	10
25. New NGO's	1.15	(−68)	−19	40	−07	24	−01
26. Partners per alliance	1.19	(−98)	05	−28	07	06	21
27. % Nonaggression pacts	1.13	(−57)	−13	−05	−16	22	17
29. Partners per alliance	1.23	38	01	(69)	−00	−18	−38
30. Years per alliance	1.13	−38	−15	−19	00	−34	(−53)
32. % Defensive alliances	1.24	(85)	−22	26	−31	01	05
33. % Dyads former allies	1.29	−38	−43	−45	−47	32	19
34. Members	1.01	−31	−32	42	(−62)	06	−25
35. High decision latitude	1.68	05	(−80)	05	16	−35	−07
36. % Sovereign members	1.08	03	−06	(62)	43	11	37
37. % Retain sovereignty	1.06	05	15	(55)	41	−44	−09
38. % Extraregion members	1.16	01	33	(−86)	21	16	20
40. Members/major+middle powers	1.01	−29	−16	(52)	(−67)	17	−15
41. Diverse ways of life	1.28	15	39	(−70)	−11	35	02
42. Nonlegalist power orientation	1.30	(68)	13	−24	−06	13	44
43. Incomplete external interaction	1.03	18	10	−07	21	25	−04
44. Rational calculation	1.15	07	03	(57)	47	−07	−19
45. Internal preoccupation	1.11	41	−15	(−60)	30	−05	−07
46. % Internal wars	1.11	11	−17	−03	(71)	41	−02
47. % Interventions	1.17	10	−18	11	−36	−16	(−85)
48. % Foreign wars	1.39	−24	−19	−34	−19	03	11
49. Deaths per internal war	1.40	(52)	10	(−59)	25	−09	−07
50. Deaths per intervention	1.10	−31	02	17	−47	−10	08
51. Insecure domestic elites	1.45	18	18	31	43	(−50)	−38
52. % Starting wars	1.10	02	−23	−37	37	(58)	09
54. Minors in coalition with majors	1.17	−35	−37	12	(−75)	23	08
55. % Formal major-minor alliances	1.21	−09	−09	(87)	−25	−39	−09
57. % Minors allied with majors	1.28	−49	−26	(53)	(−61)	−37	−01

VII	VIII	IX	X	XI	XII	XIII	XIV	XV	XVI	XVII
07	−04	−11	04	42	−27	03	−05	12	−03	26
−05	−30	−23	39	−06	−02	20	10	−14	08	−17
14	−04	−07	10	03	−12	−28	−15	−03	−06	12
17	−42	22	11	(−59)	−01	17	−12	03	13	−30
06	−11	(−80)	10	−00	−06	−13	−06	05	01	10
03	09	−18	−01	−04	−01	06	30	09	−01	(67)
−04	−22	21	−12	−05	−22	29	−06	09	05	05
−06	04	34	−23	−12	−02	17	13	01	00	30
(105)	−05	−09	11	−19	−00	04	05	−03	12	22
08	17	−22	−21	−23	01	17	−13	−07	07	12
21	05	−02	−10	37	−30	13	−08	−06	−06	22
−17	11	19	26	−22	−02	(−58)	−21	08	−10	18
28	−00	−38	10	11	07	18	−20	−13	−02	14
−27	02	(−54)	26	−11	−06	−48	−11	−09	−10	07
09	05	09	09	−06	02	01	−08	−04	03	07
−13	−24	15	−16	−11	06	−12	−14	−11	09	−10
(−79)	22	−15	04	−19	09	−20	−02	−02	−07	35
04	−22	43	−27	−00	02	33	01	04	00	−12
−24	−02	18	18	−39	−08	−28	13	07	07	20
14	−14	−10	−07	−04	−11	−10	−02	−07	00	−14
(−72)	−07	−19	08	−24	−12	−09	−05	−08	06	18
12	−22	−26	(−52)	−12	−05	−03	−08	07	08	−05
(58)	−15	−36	18	−00	−03	03	−04	−02	01	−12
22	05	−14	02	−26	07	−07	07	−02	04	39
07	−03	−02	(55)	−14	−04	−15	03	−06	03	21
−06	−06	−03	19	−16	−05	−23	−00	21	01	13
−09	(−69)	−19	−01	06	−37	20	−09	13	22	34
15	09	−22	−14	−07	−13	18	20	05	06	41
−04	−24	−26	−10	12	−09	08	42	−08	−02	10
−01	−18	−05	08	−40	05	−01	−07	−00	−03	−03
−08	−24	−09	−04	02	−08	−08	10	08	05	−07
34	−31	−00	−05	−31	01	32	05	−03	10	−25
06	−11	−38	08	−38	10	−06	−44	−13	−01	−13
(66)	−26	09	−11	−18	−10	30	42	18	08	10
−21	−28	15	−44	−18	−12	−22	20	25	08	10
04	−34	−06	−36	32	−17	02	28	−09	−03	−05
−16	−08	−23	−18	04	−28	39	−20	−05	09	04
−11	−09	−00	14	−27	02	−26	08	21	−02	12
39	33	−15	(−78)	08	−10	29	−34	03	−01	16
−11	−06	−16	−06	−06	01	(79)	02	−06	−06	13
(−76)	−22	22	11	−07	−01	19	12	02	−02	07
(−56)	−32	−07	−04	−27	01	−04	32	08	08	30
32	13	−13	−01	−22	−18	−21	11	06	03	40
−19	11	−32	26	−00	−08	−04	−05	10	−08	19
−17	−04	−30	04	−20	08	02	−07	03	05	21
−10	−09	20	−27	−01	11	−02	−14	15	05	05

TABLE 11–6—Cont.
First–Order R–Factor Analysis of International Subsystem Performance Data: Wright Sample[a]

Variable	h²	I	II	III	IV	Varimax Factors V	VI
58. % Minors in coalitions with majors	1.26	—41	—24	—16	(—54)	13	36
59. % Extraregion minors' alliances	1.38	—20	—04	—44	02	—21	42
60. % Extra-era major-minor coalitions	1.17	—42	—27	10	—40	04	—01
61. % Extra-era major-minor alliances	1.11	—06	03	37	19	—43	(—63)
62. Minor power status scores	1.28	(—70)	10	08	—15	06	(74)
63. Partners per major-minor alliances	1.24	(—104)	—14	—02	—17	00	—19
64. Partners per major-minor coalition	1.38	—01	(—63)	—09	—10	(—64)	—16
66. Major-minor alliances/ majors+minors	1.21	(—95)	—10	24	—28	—14	18
67. Partners per major-minor alliance	1.24	—06	—24	39	—33	—43	(—72)
69. Years per major-minor coalition	1.20	10	—14	—18	—36	—13	—26
70. % Years with new major-minor alliances	1.20	(—56)	—11	(57)	—47	—09	05
71. % Years with new major-minor coalitions	1.26	—09	—16	25	(—101)	01	—04
72. % Minors starting wars	1.06	—05	20	17	—05	(73)	23
73. Disturbance level	1.36	—31	—33	(—54)	—32	44	34
74. Increased disturbance	1.67	—16	(—81)	—40	—32	26	18
75. % Defensive major-minor alliances	1.19	—03	—11	04	—07	(—86)	—39
76. Gatepassers	1.01	—09	—22	—03	(—88)	11	—16
77. % Sovereign gatepassers	1.01	—28	—04	—05	32	(—59)	12
78. % Gatepassers	1.04	09	04	(—57)	(—62)	16	—11
79. % Extraregion gatepassers	1.09	09	00	(—73)	31	37	30
80. % Re-gatepassers in next era	1.18	—16	(—59)	41	—08	10	—14
81. Gatepasser status scores	1.27	—41	20	—35	10	—09	(77)
82. % Net gatepassers	1.19	20	35	08	03	00	—30
83. % Aligned gatepassers	1.25	14	18	23	02	08	44
84. Alliances per gatepasser	1.24	—29	00	—03	02	26	19
85. Members per gatepasser alliance	1.28	27	08	01	01	—22	—41
86. % Years postgatekeeping	1.22	03	20	—17	(—81)	—28	(—55)
87. % Years of gatepassing	1.18	—01	15	—15	(—92)	—39	10
88. % Violent gatepassing	1.15	—18	(—54)	(—68)	—02	—02	23
90. % Major-only pacts	1.32	—33	13	39	—31	(—81)	07
91. % Majors allied only with each other	1.30	—02	10	31	—04	(—102)	—20
92. % Extraregion majors' alliances	1.19	—33	—19	(—94)	04	—09	—19
93. % Extra-era major-only alliances	1.30	—27	—25	06	05	—32	—08
94. New IGO's	1.14	(—56)	27	18	—40	26	02
95. Partners per major-only alliance	1.19	(—86)	—05	—11	—17	—48	20
96. % Major-only nonaggression pacts	1.16	(—77)	—05	19	—03	01	18

VII	VIII	IX	X	XI	XII	XIII	XIV	XV	XVI	XVII
—41	26	—44	20	—01	—02	—00	—19	02	—16	21
04	(—64)	—09	(—52)	—35	—16	—19	10	10	20	07
07	(—51)	(—53)	22	—16	—22	12	13	13	18	06
—02	17	—43	—01	—12	02	31	—09	—05	—02	13
—28	—17	10	—13	—14	00	—20	—01	—07	01	—01
04	15	—14	—06	02	—02	05	—12	—07	—03	—03
17	—08	(51)	16	—26	—03	—11	—00	22	—03	25
—09	13	11	—19	—02	08	11	—06	—05	—02	08
26	08	—29	—06	—01	06	06	—16	10	02	08
(—68)	—26	—27	41	01	—04	38	—07	07	—04	01
—32	18	—13	—29	—09	06	—16	—11	02	01	15
—06	—12	05	06	05	04	16	24	08	05	17
02	09	—14	—20	—46	—04	—25	—03	—08	15	18
06	—04	10	—06	—34	—14	09	(—52)	10	14	—01
21	—42	—10	03	—13	—36	18	—26	24	26	16
38	—07	—08	—01	—07	14	29	00	08	03	12
02	19	—14	—07	—09	06	—20	—12	11	—03	06
—35	—03	—22	—24	24	—04	—26	10	—24	—19	05
—20	20	—16	—22	—18	09	02	—14	17	—04	17
03	—23	—27	—00	—19	—17	—05	09	03	05	14
08	—25	—10	(66)	15	—18	00	—11	—14	—05	00
—33	—01	34	—18	—17	06	06	13	—11	—05	13
07	—07	(—92)	16	—11	—04	15	03	05	03	02
—17	—05	24	(—91)	—14	—03	—01	04	01	03	12
—23	—23	42	(—85)	—05	—14	14	—02	05	06	—08
12	01	—09	(—98)	—01	—03	—05	—04	08	02	01
02	—01	—08	—26	—03	15	—02	01	—00	02	—09
—11	—10	—17	—06	—01	17	10	—14	05	—01	—07
04	—12	16	13	20	—15	—33	15	—11	—14	17
—29	11	—16	—23	—04	22	—19	—01	04	—07	14
—03	—04	—09	—07	—08	19	19	—03	06	—04	10
—01	—08	00	16	—13	—08	21	01	—07	01	13
(52)	—04	39	—06	—13	06	(75)	02	01	08	18
—28	18	—02	02	(—54)	12	—22	01	—05	06	19
12	—23	—03	22	—05	06	—05	—02	—01	—01	—11
—42	—12	—37	—08	—30	—12	—02	—03	—07	14	18

TABLE 11-6—Cont.
First–Order R–Factor Analysis of International Subsystem Performance Data: Wright Sample[a]

					Varimax Factors		
Variable	h²	I	II	III	IV	V	VI
97. % Major alliances only with each other	1.25	—49	03	26	30	(—55)	38
98. Partners per major-only alliance	1.29	—12	—21	(69)	(—54)	(—50)	—29
99. Years per major-only alliance	1.12	—38	—16	—10	—04	—29	—34
100. % Years with new major-only alliances	1.24	(—84)	08	23	—05	—37	16
101. % Defensive major-only alliances	1.27	06	—14	04	—43	(—87)	—20
102. Recruitees	.76	—23	—44	(—53)	—02	12	—08
103. % Formal recruitees	.70	—17	43	13	—05	01	19
104. % Recruitees	.76	02	—16	(—66)	33	19	01
106. Recruitee status scores	1.06	—24	—12	—42	—08	41	(56)
108. % Aligned recruitees	.83	—33	18	14	22	24	(65)
109. Partners per recruitee alliance	1.09	—06	—21	13	08	24	—26
110. % Alliances per recruitee	.90	—48	—07	—11	—18	06	(54)
111. Net recruitment duration/years	.84	03	—33	—42	—07	—24	—20
112. % Years with recruitment	.77	05	03	—06	(—70)	—13	25
113. % Violent recruitees	.99	—01	—47	—07	13	—02	25
114. Major and middle powers	1.17	—20	—36	20	—07	—46	05
115. No direct supervision	.54	23	—13	—18	05	41	25
117. % Intraregion supervision	.93	32	—36	19	04	18	04
119. Major powers/middle powers	.68	—48	—41	38	13	—13	—00
120. Macrocentric supervision	.88	—12	09	02	—21	(—51)	—01
121. Auditing/policing	.94	—19	—17	32	27	—29	(—52)
122. Elite cooperativeness	1.11	26	—16	—40	43	19	00
123. Ideological consonance	1.00	—13	—08	—25	—32	03	—11
124. Unavailable resources	.75	12	33	22	11	26	16
125. Elite legitimacy	.82	—11	—16	34	—12	09	36
126. Postwar treaties	.95	—41	(—71)	03	10	—00	03
127. Overt rule-adapting	.75	—32	12	33	—30	—03	10
128. Decrease in international law	.67	44	—14	14	20	—02	—04
129. % Extraregion postwar treaties	.85	12	10	—17	(53)	31	—10
130. % Extra-era postwar treaties	.95	—07	—45	24	—22	—25	—18
131. Lack of international tribunals	.69	42	—12	19	28	—09	—18
132. Looseness in polarity	.72	—02	—35	16	31	02	26
133. Realism/idealism	.73	13	—08	—25	30	30	04
134. Procedural rule-adapting	.69	(62)	—05	—05	—09	23	14
135. Cross-pole cooperation	.87	12	02	—30	09	(69)	09
136. Instrumental rule-adapting	.77	22	—13	—19	(62)	05	04
137. % Years with postwar treaties	1.06	—07	(—85)	22	—12	—21	16
138. % Wars not ending with treaties	.58	29	02	07	—39	12	—28
139. Major power wars	1.04	—02	(—89)	03	—08	10	—14
140. % Majors' war with subnationals	.94	—14	—33	49	03	—26	—30
142. % Imperial wars	.83	—41	22	03	02	—12	—13
143. % Extraregion majors' wars	.61	—47	—20	06	22	—28	—12
144. % Extra-era majors' wars	.98	—23	—40	16	—36	—12	02
145. Institutional regulator	1.75	—28	—37	—13	—22	—22	—09

VII	VIII	IX	X	XI	XII	XIII	XIV	XV	XVI	XVII
00	−18	−22	32	−11	00	42	−09	−04	−02	−10
−00	00	−17	−13	−04	14	−13	−10	13	03	15
(67)	30	−17	08	−04	08	34	−02	−08	−01	18
−05	−04	−38	32	−10	05	−13	−08	−11	−05	−04
34	14	−05	−11	−03	−27	−03	11	−10	12	06
−13	18	−19	−05	−07	29	04	−08	−00	19	−01
−17	−22	01	−42	14	−37	05	13	−05	−09	06
01	03	−12	−23	05	04	−08	−13	14	19	02
−25	02	−07	20	−12	22	−09	06	14	−33	−08
−01	−13	−06	−11	−01	−02	−05	−13	29	03	05
37	−32	02	−09	−02	−31	23	−06	04	(67)	−23
06	05	−04	−00	−15	−15	−14	10	31	27	−26
−30	09	−06	−21	26	−04	−03	01	03	48	−02
−09	19	−03	−05	−12	−31	06	−09	11	10	−08
33	−13	−05	05	−12	03	−15	15	16	(67)	14
03	36	−28	15	−40	−15	−26	28	07	42	−03
18	−18	−12	07	02	−02	21	11	25	01	−02
−15	02	−16	−17	21	20	−37	−13	17	47	24
02	07	−23	09	−15	02	05	02	−03	07	−05
−33	35	09	−22	−20	−08	−13	−20	−06	38	−16
−03	06	−07	−18	11	−19	20	21	−09	29	27
18	(−52)	−09	07	16	29	−02	13	15	32	27
−14	(−84)	−02	−11	−08	11	08	−04	−11	01	−13
−03	(−56)	−20	19	08	−08	−11	08	17	04	15
−02	−29	−07	−37	36	−06	−02	−07	34	14	10
24	−03	−09	−05	16	28	07	06	05	23	19
−13	18	−31	−11	07	−03	−24	15	−08	42	01
−07	−32	21	05	−14	−15	09	−16	−39	−04	−14
−01	−13	06	06	−15	04	17	−26	19	49	−04
−05	−00	(−53)	04	−37	−08	−11	31	−06	−04	−07
19	−16	−13	−27	−10	−32	14	−06	04	−20	−06
07	−09	32	−23	−29	−26	01	29	01	−09	−04
08	−02	−10	04	−07	−05	06	(64)	12	05	05
02	−08	−01	−12	−13	−18	13	−01	−02	37	−06
09	−26	02	−08	03	16	12	22	−13	03	30
−07	18	08	−19	−19	05	06	20	29	17	01
07	−11	−02	−15	00	31	−04	−09	−12	24	05
12	05	−01	04	−05	01	05	09	22	34	23
03	−19	04	01	09	34	07	00	−13	14	03
−18	−10	−27	25	−12	27	−04	03	−33	19	00
01	−21	−01	14	−21	36	23	−05	−20	48	−12
06	−05	04	10	−12	26	16	16	03	16	−17
01	−20	(−65)	02	05	20	−03	10	−08	22	−07
02	−11	−35	−31	(−106)	06	21	04	−00	01	15

TABLE 11–6—Cont.
First–Order R–Factor Analysis of International Subsystem Performance Data: Wright Sample[a]

Variable	h²	I	II	III	IV	*Varimax Factors* V	VI
146. % Wars between major powers	.80	33	—40	—38	11	—02	—09
147. % Wars only between major powers	1.28	—04	(—79)	—11	—24	34	10
148. % Majors' wars to destabilize	.96	35	(—77)	—06	07	10	—01
149. Wars per major power	.94	—09	(—52)	04	(53)	—32	26
151. Participants per majors' wars	.96	—04	(—67)	—31	02	17	—16
152. Years per majors' wars	1.03	30	(—74)	11	—37	—30	04
155. Major-started wars	.99	—18	(—64)	—27	11	10	—39
156. % Major-started wars with subnational entities	.97	01	(—87)	—05	—04	00	—13
158. % Extraregion major-started wars	.85	—44	—37	15	—15	—20	—06
160. Strong regulator	.93	—32	—47	—13	05	—39	—01
161. % Wars started by majors against other major powers	.93	—19	(—75)	07	—16	—13	—23
162. % Majors' aims to destabilize	1.14	—19	(—68)	—16	—27	42	22
163. % Major-started wars ended by treaty	1.00	—38	—46	10	21	(—53)	25
165. Coalition partners per major-started war	.82	—47	(—62)	11	11	04	—17
166. Years per major-started war	.78	04	(—65)	—12	—03	—16	—10
167. % Years when majors start new wars	.66	08	(—68)	06	—08	—16	—03
168. % Major-started wars ending in destabilization	.94	—02	(—60)	—30	18	01	—11
169. Wars won by major powers	.61	—05	—20	10	—29	—08	—29
170. % Major victories with subnational entities	.74	—03	03	(50)	12	—21	—36
172. % Extraregion majors' victories	.62	(—54)	—06	05	04	10	01
175. % Majors' victories over majors	.74	—37	—09	—30	—09	—10	—14
176. % Wars won by major powers aiming to destabilize	.72	—14	—15	—20	—37	16	06
178. Partners per winning majors' coalition	.62	—33	—03	—02	12	03	25
179. Years per war won by majors	.66	24	—10	05	19	08	—03
180. % Years with majors' victories	1.57	26	—36	15	—23	—28	—01
181. % Majors' victories that destabilize	.89	—27	—17	—08	30	—33	—01
183. Subsystem duration	1.13	—00	—22	—24	29	23	00
Eigenvalues[b]		31.6	26.4	21.3	17.0	13.8	11.6
Percent total variance[b]		20.6	17.3	13.9	11.1	9.0	7.6
Percent common variance[b]		17.6	14.7	11.9	9.5	7.7	6.7

[a] Factor loadings are multiplied by 100; loadings > ±.50 are enclosed in parentheses.
[b] Based on principal axis factors.

VII	VIII	IX	X	XI	XII	XIII	XIV	XV	XVI	XVII
16	−14	−04	−06	10	−19	26	23	03	36	−16
−12	23	−31	18	−15	09	−14	14	45	−04	−03
−05	00	21	−17	03	−20	−20	04	−16	01	−22
03	−01	02	−37	01	02	05	07	11	07	−21
−26	−05	−11	26	20	00	31	15	17	05	−16
15	21	−06	06	12	06	−14	06	−10	04	13
−04	−17	−25	−06	−10	−12	−11	−12	25	−02	−29
01	19	21	21	−06	−17	07	07	−10	06	11
−05	−20	−26	00	−17	−45	−13	−23	−08	−01	11
45	−04	−11	19	−15	−16	−04	−18	31	−08	−00
13	05	−07	−19	−20	−16	15	09	24	−04	−17
−19	02	−28	−13	−27	05	−26	01	15	14	05
−03	−06	−10	02	−08	08	08	−03	35	−29	−09
10	−15	−03	19	−12	−00	−06	−02	19	−19	−03
−07	−02	16	22	−02	−48	03	06	−04	01	01
−03	15	13	03	−11	−15	−05	−16	07	−12	15
09	−38	14	07	01	10	13	05	47	−08	02
04	−14	35	04	05	13	00	−16	14	−04	41
−29	−18	04	−22	−10	05	−17	05	29	−02	04
09	−02	36	−32	03	−24	−04	−03	09	06	08
40	01	−08	18	12	−29	−09	−23	17	−04	30
−25	−16	07	−15	−18	−26	−02	−07	−01	−04	(51)
−32	−11	−11	29	−00	−22	−39	−06	−03	04	10
−24	−08	−21	(52)	−01	−29	−07	−16	20	02	11
08	−06	14	−17	06	−24	−01	07	(103)	18	06
−04	−22	29	11	11	33	25	−32	−13	24	28
05	04	−00	−05	08	(−91)	−04	12	12	15	00
10.0	9.2	7.4	6.4	5.8	4.9	4.6	3.4	3.0	1.8	1.0
6.6	6.0	4.8	4.2	3.8	3.2	3.0	2.2	2.0	1.2	0.7
5.6	5.1	4.1	3.6	3.2	2.7	2.6	1.9	1.7	1.0	0.6

Index

Note: Entries in italics refer to variables, factor labels, and cluster labels used in the volume. Page numbers in italics indicate definitions appearing in the Appendices.

Abbott, W., 111n
Abel, E., 92n
Abel, T., 72n, 87, 88
Aberle, D. F., 359n
Absentee Landlordism, 225, 268, 271, 272, 277, 464, 553, 609
abstract game. *See* experimental research
Academic Source, 142, 146, 147, 148, 150, 153, *516*, *548*, 573
acceleration, 316, *487*
accident death rate, 229, 230, 279, *527*, 581, 589, 596, 609, 611, 613, 618
accidental century, 481
accurate decoding of warning signs, 124, 128, 134, 140, 150, 458, *510*
accusations, 8, 9, 10
achievement, need for, 85, 116, 119, 128, 133, 141, 151, 457, *513*, 572
Achinese, 349, 350
Ackoff, R. L., 84, 85, 86
action, 100
action path, 100, *487*
Activism, 255, 256, 259, 260, 461, *551*
actor. *See* international systems and subsystems
adaptation, 329, 330, 363–365, 439, 469, *487*
Adaptiveness, 148, 149, 153, 459, *548–549*
Adelman, I., 176n
Adelson, M., 176n, 178n
adequacy, 215–216, 253, *487*
Administrative Inactivity, 276, 277, 463, *557*

administrative stagnation, 291, 295, 466, 479, 480, *487*
Adorno, T. W., 74n
Adrian, C. R., 173n, 205n
affective, 50, 89, 105, 106, 109, 111–112, 113, 115–116, 119, 121, 123, 126, 130, 143, 152, 154, 368–369, 372–373, 380–381, 451, *487*. *See also* instrumental
affiliation, need for, 85, 116, 119, 128, 141, *513–514*, 572
Affiliative Gatepassing, 442, 444, 445, 447, 448, 470, *565*
Afghanistan, 248, 249, 257, 347, 352, 598
Africa, 200, 279, 286, 304, 324, 329, 356
age, 20, 84, 457. *See also* minimum voting age
age of latest two governments, 193, 194, 284, *518*, 576, 584, 591, 613
agent, 101, 103n, 104, 108, 109, 115, *487*
agglutination, 197, 199, 241, 242, *488*
aggregate statistical data, 33, 34, 37, *488*. *See also* data
aggregation, 329, 365–366, 373, 377–381, 382, 389, 401, 420, 428, *488*. *See also* diffraction, diffracted aggregation
Aggressive, 15, 16, 76n, 135, 136, 138, 139, 146, 147, 148, 153, 154, 271, 275, 277, 290, 464, *546*, *548*, *556*
Aggressive Alliance, 432, 433, 434, 437, 438, 442, 447, 469, *562*

643